WELCOME TO SCOTLAND

Scotland packs spectacular landscapes, as well as rich history and tradition, into a small country. From the Lowlands to the Highlands, its lush woodlands, windswept moors, and deep lochs may take your breath away. Impressive castles, whisky distilleries, and golf courses entice, and cities such as Edinburgh and Glasgow tweak tradition with cutting-edge festivals and vibrant cultural scenes. Scotland's iconic products and customs—from tartans to bagpipes—may travel the globe, but there's nothing like experiencing them firsthand.

TOP REASONS TO GO

★ **Castles:** Stirling, Glamis, Floors, and others tell tales of a complex, turbulent past.

★ **Cool Cities:** Edinburgh's International Festival and Fringe; Glasgow's nightlife.

★ **Islands:** Skye's misty mountains, Islay's seabirds, Orkney's prehistoric remains.

★ **Whisky:** Distillery tours and tastings refine an appreciation for the national drink.

★ **Landscapes:** Crystal-clear lochs and rivers, wooded hills, wide-open moors.

★ **Golf:** The great names here include St. Andrews, Gleneagles, and Western Gailes.

13

TOP EXPERIENCES

Scotland offers terrific experiences that should be on every traveler's list. Here are Fodor's top picks for a memorable trip.

1 Prehistoric Monuments

Around Scotland, haunting structures like the Calanais Standing Stones (pictured) on the Isle of Lewis provide an intriguing glimpse into the past. Sights are scattered across the landscape, but Orkney claims a large concentration. *(Ch. 8, 10, 11)*

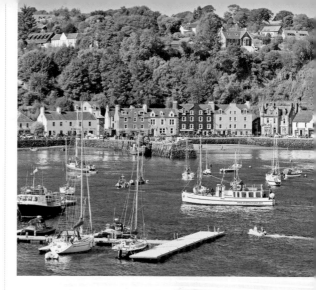

2 Seaside Towns

The country's jagged coastline and many islands create scenic settings for towns such as Tobermory on the Isle of Mull, with its colorfully painted houses. *(Ch. 8)*

3 Isle of Skye

With the misty Cuillin Mountains and rocky shores, Skye has few rivals among the country's islands for sheer loveliness. Links to Bonnie Prince Charlie add further allure. *(Ch. 10)*

4 Glencoe

The wild beauty of Glencoe's craggy peaks and deep valley provided the background for a tragic massacre in 1692. Today the area is popular for outdoor activities. *(Ch. 9)*

5 Whisky Tours

From Speyside to Islay (pictured), whisky distilleries offer tours and tastings of Scotland's signature drink. Their often-spectacular settings are an added bonus. *(Ch. 4, 6–11)*

6 Loch Lomond and the Trossachs

Its clear water, plus access to Edinburgh and Glasgow, make Loch Lomond a coveted retreat. The Trossachs' lakes and hills are the essence of the Highlands. *(Ch. 6)*

7 Glasgow

An urban renaissance has brought great shopping and nightlife to complement the city's rich architectural heritage and museums like the Kelvingrove (pictured). *(Ch. 3)*

8 Edinburgh

Scotland's capital charms with its Royal Mile and Old Town, and events such as the Edinburgh International Festival and the Fringe keep areas like the Grassmarket lively. *(Ch. 2)*

9 Castles

Whether in ruins or full of treasure, castles dating from the medieval period to Victorian times are among Scotland's glories. Dunnottar (pictured) overlooks the North Sea. *(Ch. 2–11)*

10 Seafood

From salmon to oysters, the superb fish and seafood from rivers, lakes, and the sea are treats to savor. Delicately smoked fish is a specialty, served hot or cold. *(Ch. 2–11)*

11 Border Abbeys

The towering ruins of the region's great medieval abbeys, such as red-sandstone Melrose (pictured), retain echoes of their past grandeur and recall Scottish history. *(Ch. 4)*

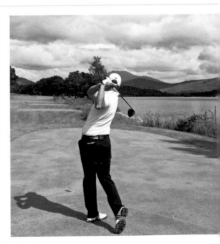

12 Jacobite Steam Train

The famous trip from Fort William to the coast at Mallaig offers spectacular views of mountains and lochs as well as a ride over the 21 arches of the Glenfinnan Viaduct. *(Ch. 9)*

13 Golf

The home of golf, Scotland claims some of the world's most challenging holes but has courses for all levels, many in beautiful settings by lakes, hills, or the ocean. *(Ch. 2–10)*

CONTENTS

ABOUT THIS GUIDE

Fodor's Recommendations

Everything in this guide is worth doing—we don't cover what isn't—but exceptional sights, hotels, and restaurants are recognized with additional accolades. **Fodor's Choice★** indicates our top recommendations; and **Best Bets** call attention to notable hotels and restaurants in various categories. Care to nominate a new place? Visit Fodors.com/contact-us.

Trip Costs

We list prices wherever possible to help you budget well. Hotel and restaurant price categories from **$** to **$$$$** are noted alongside each recommendation. For hotels, we include the lowest cost of a standard double room in high season. For restaurants, we cite the average price of a main course at dinner or, if dinner isn't served, at lunch. For attractions, we always list adult admission fees; discounts are usually available for children, students, and senior citizens.

Hotels

Our local writers vet every hotel to recommend the best overnights in each price category, from budget to expensive. Unless otherwise specified, you can expect private bath, phone, and TV in your room. For expanded hotel reviews, facilities, and deals visit Fodors.com.

Restaurants

Unless we state otherwise, restaurants are open for lunch and dinner daily. We mention dress code only when there's a specific requirement and reservations only when they're essential or not accepted. To make restaurant reservations, visit Fodors.com.

Credit Cards

The hotels and restaurants in this guide typically accept credit cards. If not, we'll say so.

Top Picks	Hotels &
★ Fodor's Choice	Restaurants
	☒ Hotel
Listings	⬱ Number of rooms
✉ Address	
✉ Branch address	⦿⊙⦿ Meal plans
☎ Telephone	✕ Restaurant
🖶 Fax	⬠ Reservations
⊕ Website	🏛 Dress code
✉ E-mail	▭ No credit cards
🎫 Admission fee	$ Price
⊙ Open/closed times	**Other**
Ⓜ Subway	⇨ See also
⬦ Directions or Map coordinates	☞ Take note
	🏌 Golf facilities

EXPERIENCE
SCOTLAND

SCOTLAND TODAY

Travelers arriving in Scotland were once welcomed to the "best small country in the world." It may have just 5.3 million people, but today Scotland has some big ideas about where it's headed socially, culturally, and economically. International sporting events being hosted here will be transmitted all over the world. And in 2014 the people will vote on whether to become an independent nation.

Travel in the 21st Century

The experience of traveling in Scotland has changed for the better from the days of the esteemed 18th-century London diarist Dr. Samuel Johnson, who wrote of Scottish hospitality, "*Of the provisions the negative catalogue was very copious. Here was no meat, no milk, no bread, no eggs, no wine. We did not express much satisfaction.*" Even 20 years ago some visitors may have echoed Dr. Johnson at times, thanks to poor food and dreary B&Bs.

Scotland has always had stirring landscapes, interesting cities, and rich historic sites. But in the last two decades the country has caught on to other things visitors want and need, and delivered superbly. Stylish modern hotels and renovated older ones satisfy the most discerning customers with the latest amenities. Around the country a culinary revolution is well under way: restaurants serve excellent food by internationally trained chefs who take advantage of Scotland's superb produce.

Today hotels and restaurants charge prices similar to those in the rest of the United Kingdom. On the other hand, most of Scotland's biggest and best museums and galleries are free. Walks through well-tended gardens, along bustling waterfronts, and in beautifully renovated neighborhoods mean that a good day out can show you everything but cost nothing at all.

In 2014 Scotland will present its second year of Homecoming, following the first successful event in 2009. A year of celebrations throughout the country will focus on themes including food and drink, natural beauty and outdoor adventure, creativity, and ancestry—all strong suits. All in all, it's an exciting time to travel here.

The Issue of Independence

Dominating Scotland's public life at the moment is the looming referendum on independence, slated for September 18, 2014. Through devolution, Scotland elected its first parliament in 300 years in 1999. The country already has the power to make its own laws regarding health care, education, and the legal system, but some Scots want to split completely from the United Kingdom. At the time of this writing, polls indicate that the canny Scots may vote "No." But unhappiness with the U.K. government could make a swing to "Yes" a possibility.

Why are many Scots dissatisfied with the U.K. government? In a time of budget woes, the government has been slashing public services. Many of these cuts deeply offend the Scots who are committed to free education and free health care from the publicly owned National Health Service. The question everyone asks is, can Scotland afford to mind its own affairs? And can Scotland fund the kind of independent nation some Scots want?

Culture

The arts continue to thrive, a sign of Scotland's creative energy. Edinburgh's arts festivals grow bigger and bigger every year, attracting visitors from around the globe. The National Theatre of Scotland has been such a resounding success that productions have made their way to Broadway. Glasgow is renowned for contemporary arts: a Glasgow artist often seems to win the Turner Prize, Britain's most prestigious art honor.

In a sign of vitality, culture is not confined only to the large cities. Far to the north, Shetland (already drawing audiences with its folk festivals) has built Mareel, a remarkable live music venue and cinema. Dundee will be the location of the first outpost of London's Victoria and Albert Museum.

In 2013 a new mural was unveiled in Glasgow's subway system that employs the words of Scottish novelist Alastair Grey: "Work as if you live in the early days of a better nation." Undoubtedly the artists of Scotland have taken him to heart.

Land

It's a disturbing fact that just 500 people own half the land in Scotland, many of them wealthy foreigners who have become absentee landlords. Experts say that giving residents a say on what happens to the land they live on is crucial if communities are going to thrive. New models of community ownership and management are being hard won, particularly in the Western Isles. There have been some community buyouts in which farming communities get the government's help to purchase the land where they live and work.

Still, the depopulation of rural Scotland continues. The popularity of holiday homes has meant that some villages are fully inhabited for only a few weeks each summer. Those who want to live here permanently find that low wages, a high cost of living, and a lack of affordable housing mean that they are priced out of a home surrounded by such beauty.

Wind Power

Urged by the government to help the country meet its ambitious targets for renewable energy, Scottish landowners have begun leasing land to the corporations behind wind farms. At the time of this writing there were eight huge commercial wind farms—including Europe's largest—and hundreds of smaller ones scattered across Scotland. This has sparked vociferous debate. The pro-wind lobby argues in favor of emission-free energy that's better for the environment than coal or nuclear plants, while the anti-wind camp decries the environmental damage to ancient peat bogs and bird populations.

Turbines are now being built offshore, which is another cause for dispute. Developer Donald Trump, who ignored environmental activists while building his sprawling golf estate, has had a very public fallout with government officials over the "ugly" planned offshore turbine plant that will be seen from his golf course.

Scotland, Finally Winning

When it comes to sports, the Scots have reveled in their traditional role as the underdog. But Olympic gold medal-winning cyclist Chris Hoy and tennis Grand Slam winner Andy Murray have shown that this narrative needs rewriting.

Whatever the medal count at the Commonwealth Games, which will be held in Glasgow in 2014, or the fortunes of the Scottish golfers in the Ryder Cup at Gleneagles in 2014, that Scotland is staging such major sporting events means it's a nation that competes on an international stage. It's a time of feeling proud to be Scottish.

WHAT'S WHERE

Numbers refer to chapters.

2 Edinburgh and the Lothians. Scotland's captivating capital is the country's most popular city, famous for its high-perched castle, Old Town and 18th-century New Town, ultramodern Parliament building, and Georgian and Victorian architecture. Among the city's highlights are superb museums, including the newly refurbished National Museum of Scotland, and the most celebrated arts festival in the world, the International Festival. If Edinburgh's crowds are too much, escape to the Lothians and visit coastal towns, beaches, ancient chapels, and castles.

3 Glasgow. The country's largest city has evolved from prosperous Victorian hub to depressed urban center to thriving modern city with a strong artistic, architectural, and culinary reputation. Museums and galleries such as the Kelvingrove and Burrell are here, along with the Arts and Crafts architecture of Charles Rennie Mackintosh and iconic institutions such as Glasgow University. Glasgow is also the place to shop in Scotland.

4 The Borders and the Southwest. Scotland's southern gateway from England, the Borders, with its moors and gentle hills and river valleys, is rustic but historically rich. It's known for being the home of Sir Walter Scott, and has impressive stately homes such as Floors Castle and ruined abbeys including Melrose. The Southwest, or Dumfries and Galloway region, is perfect for scenic drives, castles, and hiking.

5 Fife and Angus. The "kingdom" of Fife is considered the sunniest and driest part of Scotland, with sandy beaches, fishing villages, and stone cottages. St. Andrews has its world-famous golf courses, but this university town is worth a stop even for nongolfers. To the north in Angus are Glamis Castle, the legendary setting of Shakespeare's *Macbeth*, as well as the reviving city of Dundee.

6 The Central Highlands. Convenient to both Edinburgh and Glasgow, this area encompasses some of Scotland's most beautiful terrain, with rugged, dark landscapes broken up by lochs and fields. Not to be missed are Loch Lomond and the Trossachs, Scotland's first national park. Perth and Stirling are the main metropolitan hubs and worth a stop; Stirling Castle has epic views that stretch from coast to coast.

WHAT'S WHERE

7 Aberdeen and the Northeast. Malt-whisky buffs can use the prosperous port city of Aberdeen, known for its silvery granite buildings, as a base for exploring the region's distilleries, including those on the Malt Whisky Trail. Aberdeen also makes a good starting point for touring Royal Deeside, with its purple moors and piney hills as well as the notably rich selection of castles built over many centuries, including Balmoral.

8 Argyll and the Isles. Remote and picturesque, this less visited region of the southwestern coastline has excellent gardens, religious sites, and distilleries. To experience the region in full, catch a ferry from adorable Oban to Mull and the southern isles. If you like whisky, a trip to Islay is a must; if it's mountains you're after, try Jura; if a Christian site strikes a chord, head to Iona. The Isle of Arran is the place to see Scotland's diversity shrunk down to more intimate size.

9 Around the Great Glen. An awe-inspiring valley laced with rivers and streams defines this part of the country. A top spot for hikers, this Highland glen is ringed by tall mountains, including Ben Nevis, Britain's tallest mountain. Rugged Cairngorms National Park lies to the east

of this area. Glencoe and Culloden are historic sites not to miss; those who believe in Nessie, Scotland's famous monster, can follow the throngs to Loch Ness. Inverness, the capital of the Highlands, is useful as a base for exploring.

10 The Northern Highlands and the Western Isles. This rugged land is home to the lore of clans, big moody skies, and wild rolling moors. It's also the place to see one of Scotland's most picturesque castles, Eilean Donan, which you pass on the way to the beautiful, popular Isle of Skye. The stark, remote Outer Hebrides, or Western Isles, offer ruined forts and chapels. This is where you go for real peace and quiet.

11 Orkney and Shetland Islands. Remote and austere, these isles at the northern tip of Scotland require tenacity to reach but have an abundance of intriguing prehistoric sites including standing circles, *brochs* (circular towers), and tombs, as well as wild, open landscapes. A Scandinavian heritage gives them a unique flavor. The Shetland Isles, with their barren moors and vertical cliffs, are well-known for bird-watching and diving opportunities.

SCOTLAND PLANNER

When to Go

Peak tourist season runs from mid-May through mid-September. City museums stay open year-round, but some tourist sites such as castles and historic houses close from November to Easter. You can get some excellent deals in spring and fall; weather can be pleasant and crowds are not as intense.

The Scottish climate is extreme; there is often a combination of all four seasons in a 24-hour period. Winter nights are very long, as are summer days. Summer temperatures can linger in the 60s, sometimes the 70s or 80s, with dry spells lasting a week or two. Winter sees lots of rain, snow depending on latitude, and icy, sharp winds. Spring and fall are on the cool side; again, expect rain. *Below are average daily maximum and minimum temperatures.*

Getting Here and Around

You can arrive in Scotland by plane, train, or boat, and there are many places to disembark. Most international flights arrive at Glasgow International Airport (GLA). Edinburgh (EDI), and Prestwick (PIK) airports are much smaller and handle mainly regional flights.

Scotland is not a large country: the entire United Kingdom (including England, Scotland, Wales, and Northern Ireland) is about the size of Oregon, so you're less likely to fly. The country's train and bus systems are extensive and relatively well maintained; for major towns and cities, there is generally no need to rent a car. To see castles and historic houses—which may be far from towns—you may have to rent a car or join a tour. Driving is on the left, and gas (petrol) is expensive at $9–$10 a U.S. gallon. *For more details, see Getting Here and Around in Travel Smart Scotland.*

Distances and Travel Times

Edinburgh to Glasgow	51 miles; 1 hr by car, 1 hr by train
Edinburgh to Stirling	36 miles; 1 hr by car; 50 mins by train
Edinburgh to Aberdeen	127 miles; 2 hrs by car; 2½ hrs by train
Edinburgh to Inverness	158 miles; 3¼ hrs by car; 3½ hrs by train
Edinburgh to Dumfries	73 miles; 2 hrs by car; ¾ hr by train
Glasgow to Stirling	27 miles; 45 mins by car; 40 mins by train
Glasgow to Aberdeen	145 miles; 3¼ hrs by car; 2¾ hrs by train
Glasgow to Inverness	170 miles; 3½ hrs by car; 3¼ hrs by train
Glasgow to Dumfries	77 miles; 1½ hrs by car; 2 hrs by train
Aberdeen to Dumfries	215 miles; 4¼ hrs by car; 5¼ hrs by train

Restaurants: The Basics

Scotland has a great variety of restaurants, both casual and formal, in both urban and country areas. Overall, food has improved substantially over the past decade, and the country has become a good destination for foodies interested in fresh seasonal and local fare. All major cities have more than a handful of good Scottish and international restaurants to choose from, but some rural pubs are also known for serving fresh hearty meals and scrumptious baked goods. Sandwich shops, tearooms, cafés, and places serving familiar fast foods round out the options.

Along the coasts, and up north in Inverness and Aberdeen, fish and seafood dominate the menus: salmon, shellfish, and white fish like haddock are among the favorites. Stirling, Edinburgh, and Glasgow are well known for their love of beef, lamb, and venison; Indian and French restaurants are popular in these regions as well. In Orkney and Shetland and in the Borders and southwest, lamb and seafood are staples. *For details, see Eating Out in Travel Smart Scotland.*

Lodging: The Basics

Edinburgh and Glasgow have hotels that run the gamut from luxurious grandes dames to basic chain establishments, as well as inns and bed-and-breakfasts. Prices fluctuate greatly depending on the time of year, as well as when concerts, sporting events, and festivals come to town. It's a good idea to book online and well in advance to get the best rates and secure your room. Off-season deals can also be promising.

In the smaller cities and towns you have more options than in rural areas, where hotels are harder to find. In all these places, you may want to stay in a small bed-and-breakfast in a family's home. B&Bs are popular with British travelers and can be a great way to meet locals. Prices can be half of what an inn or hotel might charge, and some B&Bs give discounts for extended stays.

Other options include old country inns with a traditional Scottish pub underneath bedrooms. There are modern inns, too, and although they don't have the same character, amenities can be better. Some older inns can be old-fashioned, but they're usually less pricey. House and apartment rentals can be an excellent option, too. *For details, see Accommodations in Travel Smart Scotland.*

Visitor Information

Both VisitScotland (⊕ *www.visitscotland.com*) and VisitBritain (⊕ *www.visitbritain.com*) have websites useful for basic planning. Both have information about events such as the 2014 Homecoming and Glasgow's Commonwealth Games. Travelers will want to plan ahead for special events.

Saving Money

■ Take advantage of free breakfasts if your hotel, inn, or B&B offers them.

■ Many pubs serve lunches for less than £10; most restaurants offer cheap lunch or pretheater deals.

■ Make one meal a prepared sandwich from a bakery or sandwich shop.

■ Carry your own tap water.

■ In the larger cities, consider staying in a house or apartment.

■ Outside the cities, stay in a B&B or small guesthouse.

■ Check the websites of major chains for deals.

■ Ask about family tickets at major sights.

■ Spend time in the free national museums.

■ Check out sightseeing passes such as the Explorer Pass from Historic Scotland.

■ Use the exceptional public transportation system.

QUINTESSENTIAL SCOTLAND

Time for Tea

Scots are always eager to stop for a cup of tea and catch up with the local gossip. Tea is still the most popular refreshment, but the spread of café culture has introduced a new generation of coffeehouses—and not just in the cities but in the countryside. The Willow Tearooms in Glasgow and the Balmoral Hotel in Edinburgh are perhaps the most gentrified places to enjoy an afternoon pot of tea, tiny sandwiches with the crusts removed, and a slice of cake; they are well worth the stop. City coffeehouses are becomingly increasingly popular; they offer a different but equally worthwhile atmosphere. But if you're looking to taste a little of what life has to offer in smaller towns and villages, there is always some local haven that can offer you tea and delicious scones, probably with homemade jam.

Pubs

Going to the pub is a pastime enjoyed by men and women of all ages and backgrounds; you can find out why when you explore a few. The no-smoking laws mean that the pub environment is fresher now. In the cities you can take your pick of every kind of pub; traditional favorites are now joined by Australian, Cuban, and chic cocktail bars. In more rural areas options may be fewer, but the quality of the experience, which may include pub quizzes or local folk bands, may be better. There isn't a pub in Scotland that doesn't sell whisky, but if you seek to sample a wee dram of the more obscure malts, ask someone to point you in the right direction. Fans of whisky will want to go beyond the pubs and head for a distillery or two for a tour and a tasting—you will find these in many areas of the country.

If you want to get a sense of contemporary Scottish culture, and indulge in some of its pleasures, start by familiarizing yourself with the rituals of daily life. These are a few highlights—things you can take part in with relative ease.

Football

Listening to Scots talk about football—please don't call it soccer—gives a fine insight into the national temperament. "Win, lose, or draw, you go home to your bed just the same," sang Scottish singer Michael Marra, and the Scots will try to make you believe it's only a game. But go to a match or be in a pub when a game is on the TV, and you can see plenty of grown men (and women) having a vigorous emotional workout. Since the Rangers were relegated to the third division, the main league, the Scottish Premiership, has opened up a little, although Celtic still dominate. The state of the national team is debated everywhere, but although Scotland loses out in collecting trophies, the Tartan Army is consistently applauded as the most agreeable and entertaining traveling fans.

Baked Goods

Although the treats may not perhaps be as elegant as those produced in an Italian *panificio* or a French patisserie, Scots love their bakeries. Go beyond shortbread and oatcakes and sample local favorites during your travels. From the Aberdeen buttery (a melting, salty *bap,* or roll) to the Selkirk bannock (a sweet, raisin-strewn scone, perfect when buttered and served with tea) to *Forfar bridies* (an Angus specialty, similar to a meat pasty), regional specialties are abundant. Most areas have their own interpretations of the popular Scotch pie (with beef mince, mutton, bean, and macaroni among the varieties available). There's even a Scotch Pie Championship each year. The rise of large supermarkets is putting many establishments out of business, but it's worth seeking out an independent bakery and trying the delicacies.

IF YOU LIKE

Castles

Whether a jumble of stones or a fully intact fortress, whether in private ownership or under the care of a preservation group—such as Historic Scotland (a government agency) or the National Trust for Scotland (a private, charitable organization)—Scotland's castles powerfully demonstrate the country's lavish past and its once-uneasy relationship with its southern neighbor.

Caerlaverock. This triangular 13th-century fortress with red sandstone walls was a last bastion in the 17th-century struggle for religious reform.

Castle Trail. Along Royal Deeside, west of Aberdeen, the Castle Trail has an eclectic group of castles all within a 100-mile radius. There's stirring Drum; stately Crathes; baronial Balmoral; memorabilia-packed Braemar; Corgarff; Kildrummy; and windswept Dunnottar.

Edinburgh Castle. This royal palace dominates the capital's history and skyline.

Eilean Donan. A ruin on the edge of several lochs, this is the most photogenic of Scottish castles and inspiration for the castle in the animated movie *Brave*.

Floors Castle. On the Duke of Roxburghe's estate, this castle has grand turrets, pinnacles, and cupolas.

Glamis Castle. Northeast of Dundee, Glamis Castle connects Britain's royalty from Macbeth to the late Queen Mother.

Hermitage Castle. This dark and foreboding place is where Mary, Queen of Scots traveled to visit her lover, the earl of Bothwell.

Stirling Castle. Beautifully restored Stirling Castle is the childhood home of Mary, Queen of Scots and one of finest Renaissance palaces in the United Kingdom.

Mountains and Lochs

For the snowcapped mountains and glassy lochs (lakes) for which Scotland is famous, you have to leave the south and the cities behind you—though some Lowland lakes are beautiful. Wherever you go in Scotland, nature is at your fingertips.

Ben Nevis. Looming over Fort William is dramatic Ben Nevis. No matter when you visit, you'll probably see snow on the summit.

Cairngorms National Park. The Great Glen is home to half of Scotland's highest peaks, many of them in Cairngorms National Park. This is an excellent place for hiking, skiing, and reindeer sightings.

Glen Torridon. East of Shieldaig in the Northern Highlands, Glen Torridon has the country's finest mountain scenery.

Loch Achray. This pretty loch is where you set out for the climb to Ben An, a sheer-faced mountain with fabulous views of the Trossachs.

Loch Katrine. In the heart of the Trossachs, this lake in the Central Highlands was the setting of Walter Scott's narrative poem *The Lady of the Lake*. In summer you can take the steamer SS *Sir Walter Scott*.

Loch Leven. Located in Fife, this loch is famed for its birdlife. It was also where Mary, Queen of Scots signed the deed of abdication in her island prison.

Loch Lomond. Among Scotland's most famous lakes, Loch Lomond's shimmering shores, beautiful vistas, and plethora of water-sport options are 20 minutes from Glasgow.

Loch Maree. One of Scotland's most scenic lakes, Loch Maree is framed by Scots pines and Slioch Mountain.

Fabulous Festivals

With a culture that dates back hundreds of years, there's always something to celebrate in Scotland. No matter where you are, you can probably find a festival to suit you.

Celtic Connections. During the last two weeks of January, musicians from all over the world gather in Glasgow to play Celtic-inspired music.

Edinburgh Fringe. Running at the same time as the Edinburgh International Festival, this is a less formal, rowdier celebration.

Edinburgh International Book Festival. Some of the world's most famous authors head to this annual festival, along with an audience that knows and loves literature.

Edinburgh International Festival. The most spectacular and famous event on Scotland's cultural calendar, August's festival has everything from traditional music to modern dance to cutting-edge theater.

Edinburgh Military Tattoo. Three weeks every August you can listen to the sound of pipe and drum while fireworks explode overhead.

Glasgay. During October and November, Glasgow hosts a massive celebration of gay and lesbian culture.

Hogmanay. The world's biggest New Year's celebration takes place over several days in Edinburgh.

St. Magnus Festival. Held in Orkney in June, this classical festival draws musicians from all over the world.

Up Helly Aa. This festival comes to a spectacular end with the torching of a replica of a Viking ship. It takes place in Lerwick, Shetland, on the last Tuesday of January.

Whisky Tours

Even for non-connoisseurs, whisky tours are a great way to appreciate the many varied flavors of Scotland's signature drink. Many distilleries are in lovely settings, and tours give you a sense of the craft that transforms malted barley, water, and yeast. In-depth tours and special tastings are available at some places, but it's always best to check ahead and reserve if needed. Here's a sampling of distilleries from around the country.

Bladnoch. Scotland's southernmost whisky producer, in Galloway, offers tours and tastings of its single malt.

Edradour. This small distillery near Pitlochry makes a fine single malt and offers an informative and fun tour.

Glenfiddich. An entertaining visitor center enhances the tour of this Dufftown distillery; it also has an art gallery.

Glenlivet. Tours at the first licensed distillery in the Highlands include not only whisky making but also the fascinating story of the founder.

Highland Park. If you make it north to Orkney, visit Scotland's northernmost distillery and try its smoky but sweet malt.

Lagavulin. Among Islay's whiskies, this one has the strongest iodine scent; the distillery offers a number of special tours .

Laphroaig. Its distinctively peaty, iodine-and-seaweed flavor has earned this Islay whisky many devoted followers.

Macallan. There's a choice of two tours at this distillery that matures its whisky in sherry and bourbon casks.

Talisker. The single malt from the Isle of Skye's only distillery has a peaty aroma but is less intense than other island whiskies; tours are popular.

Island Havens

A remote, windswept world of white-sand beaches, forgotten castles, and crisp, clear rivers awaits you in the Scottish isles. Out of the hundreds of isles (islands), only a handful are actually inhabited, and here ancient culture and tradition remain alive and well. Each island has its own distinct fingerprint; getting to some might be awkward and costly, but the time and expense are worth your while.

Arran. With activities ranging from golf to hiking, this island has everything you'll find on the mainland but on a smaller, more intimate scale.

Bute. One of the more affordable and accessible islands, Bute draws celebrities to its estates for lavish weddings and Glaswegians to its rocky shores for summer holidays.

Iona. This spiritual and spectacular island was the burial place of Scottish kings until the 11th century.

Islay. Near the Kintyre Peninsula, this island is where you go to watch rare birds, purchase woolen goods, and sample the smoothest malt whiskies.

Northern Isles. Orkney and Shetland, two remote island groups collectively known as the Northern Isles, have a colorful Scandinavian heritage. Both have notable prehistoric artifacts and rollicking festivals. The green pastures of Orkney are an hour from the mainland, and wind-flattened Shetland will suit those who want a more remote feel.

Skye. With hazy mountains, hidden beaches, and shady glens, the Isle of Skye is unsurpassed for sheer beauty. It also has good selection of hotels, B&Bs, and restaurants.

Hiking

People who have hiked in Scotland often return to explore the country's memorable rural landscapes of loch-dotted glens and forested hills. From Edinburgh's Arthur's Seat to Ben Nevis, Britain's tallest peak, the country holds unsurpassed hiking possibilities, no matter what your ambitions. Keep in mind that weather conditions can and do change rapidly in the Scottish hills, even at low altitude. The best time for hiking is from May to September.

Fife Coastal Path. This seaside trail is 116 miles long, but can be done in chunks. It skirts along golden beaches, rocky inlets, and picturesque fishing villages.

Glen Nevis. Home of the magnificent peak of Ben Nevis, Glen Nevis has a number of moderate hikes with footpaths leading past waterfalls, ruined crofts, and forested gorges. There are also some more challenging climbs.

The Grampians. In the northeastern part of the country, this mountain range offers walks through some of the country's most varied terrain. The 8-mile route around Loch Muick, which passes Glas-allt Shiel, Queen Victoria's holiday home, is beautiful in any weather.

Southern Upland Way. The famous 212-mile coast-to-coast journey from Portpatrick to Cockburnspath is an undertaking, but it can be tackled in sections.

Trossachs National Park. In the Central Highlands, this vast area includes everything from quiet country strolls to ambitious climbs up craggy cliffs.

West Highland Way. From Milngavie to Fort William, this well-marked and well-trodden 95-mile trek follows a series of old coaching roads.

Megalithic Monuments

Scattered throughout the Scottish landscape are prehistoric standing stones, stone circles, tombs, and even stone houses that provide a tantalizing glimpse into the country's remarkable past and people. If you're interested in ancient remains, leave the mainland and head for the isles, where many of the most impressive and important sites are found.

Calanais Standing Stones. On the Isle of Lewis in the Outer Hebrides, this ancient site is reminiscent of Stonehenge. The impressive stones are believed to have been used for astronomical observations.

Jarlshof. A Bronze Age settlement dating from 2500 BC, Jarlshof has been called the most remarkable archaeological site in the British Isles.

Machrie Moor Stone Circles. On the Isle of Arran these granite boulders and reddish sandstone circles have a startling setting in the middle of an isolated moor.

Maes Howe. An enormous burial mound on Orkney, Maes Howe is renowned for its imposing burial chamber.

Mousa Broch. Accessible by boat, this beautifully preserved fortified Iron Age stone tower is now a bird sanctuary. Each summer bird-watchers gather here at dusk to watch up to 40,000 storm petrels return from sea.

Ring of Brodgar. Between Loch Harray and Loch Stennes sits this magnificent circle made up of 36 Neolithic stones.

Skara Brae. Orkney's Neolithic village, first occupied around 3000 BC, was buried beneath the sand until its discovery in 1850. The houses are joined by covered passages, and with stone beds, fireplaces, and cupboards are intriguing remnants from the distant past.

Retail Therapy

No longer is Scotland simply the land of whisky and wool. International names from Louis Vuitton to Vivienne Westwood have all set up shop here, and top British department stores like John Lewis, Harvey Nichols, and Debenhams, as well as stylish boutiques, pepper the major cities. Rich chocolates (often with whisky fillings), marmalades, heather honeys, and the traditional petticoat-tail shortbread are easily portable gifts. So, too, are the boiled sweets (hard candies).

Aberdeen. If trying and buying malt whisky is on your itinerary, you won't find a much better spot than Aberdeen.

Central Highlands. Bristling with old bothies (farm buildings) that have been turned into small craft workshops, the villages in this region sell handmade crafts.

Dundee. Topped with a rich fruit mixture and almonds, Dundee cake is among the other prize edibles on sale in the city they're named after.

Edinburgh. Jenner's, Scotland's most prestigious department store, is a must-see in Edinburgh. Head toward the New Town for clusters of antiques shops.

Glasgow. Scotland's biggest city claims the best shopping in Britain, outside of London's Oxford Street. Start at Buchanan Street with Princes Gardens and Buchanan Galleries before heading to the West End for clothing boutiques and antiques shops.

Perth. A shopper's paradise, Scotland's former capital city offers a wide array of crafts, including fine china, exquisite jewelry, and freshwater pearls.

Shetland. Traditional crafts such as tartan blankets, Celtic silver, and pebble jewelry are among the big draws.

FLAVORS OF SCOTLAND

Locally Sourced, Seasonally Inspired

A new focus of culinary interest, in Scotland as elsewhere, is on local and seasonal foods. Whether restaurants are riding the green wave or just following good food sense, they are trying their best to buy from local suppliers; many proudly advertise their support. Farmers' markets, too, seem to be popping up on every other street corner.

From meats and fish to fruits and vegetables, most urban and many country restaurants are now designing their menus around seasonal foods. In winter, look for Angus beef, venison, rabbit, and pigeon on menus; in spring, summer, and fall, langoustines (small lobsters with slender claws), crab, halibut, and trout appear. The rotating array of (often organic) blackberries, brambles, raspberries, strawberries, apples, and rhubarb offers choices so fat and flavorful that the fruits themselves could make any meal memorable. When in season, asparagus and green beans are tender, but fresh enough that you can actually taste their snap. Scottish pies, puddings, and jams are also inspired by the land and time of year.

Superb Fish and Seafood

Some of the most coveted fish and seafood in the world lives in the rivers and lakes, as well as off the coasts, of Scotland. Fortunately, restaurants and markets all around the country showcase this local bounty. Treats not to miss include wild salmon, trout, haddock, mackerel, herring (often served as cold-smoked kippers), langoustines, scallops, mussels, oysters, and crabs.

Fish is prepared in a tantalizing variety of ways in Scotland, but smoked fish is the national specialty—so much so that the process of both hot and cold smoking has developed to a fine art. Scots eat smoked fish for breakfast and lunch, and as an appetizer with their evening meal. The fish is often brushed with cracked pepper and a squeeze of lemon, and accompanied by thin slices of hearty bread or oat crackers. Places like Arbroath as well as the isles of North Uist and Skye have won international praise for locally smoked haddock, salmon, and trout, which are synonymous with delicacy.

Other seafood to try includes the traditional fish-and-chips, *the* Scottish favorite not to be overlooked. The fish is either cod or haddock, battered and deep-fried until it's crispy and golden. Another classic preparation is Cullen skink, a creamy fish stew thick with smoked haddock, potatoes, and onions. It's perfect on cold winter nights as a tasty hot appetizer. For a special treat, grilled, sautéed, or baked langoustines offer the ultimate seafood indulgence, succulent and tasty.

Tempting Baked Goods

The Scots love their cakes, biscuits, breads, and pies. There's always something sweet and most likely crumbly to indulge in, whether after a meal or with a nice cup of tea. Bakeries are the perfect places to sample fresh goodies.

Some of the local favorites range from conventional butter-based shortbreads, empire biscuits (two shortbread cookies with jam in between, glazed in white icing and topped with a bright red cherry), whisky cake, mince pies (small pies filled with brandy, stewed dried fruits, and nuts), and scones. Treacle tarts, gingerbread, butterscotch apple pie, and oatcakes (more a savory cracker than a sweet cake) with local cheese are also popular as late-morning or early-afternoon temptations.

Not to be missed are the many treats named after their place of origin: Balmoral tartlets (filled with cake crumbs, butter, cherries, and citrus peel), Abernethy biscuits (cookies with extra sugar and caraway seeds), Islay loaves (sweet bread with raisins, walnuts, and brown sugar), and Dundee cake (full of cherries, raisins, sherry, and spices). Home bakers are much celebrated, and the catering tents at Highland Games are worth seeking out to sample a community's finest.

Traditional Scottish Fare

Food in Scotland is steeped in history, and a rich story lies behind many traditional dishes. Once the food of peasants, haggis—a mixture of sheep's heart, lungs, and liver cooked with onions, oats, and spices, and then boiled in a sheep's stomach—has made a big comeback in more formal Scottish restaurants. If the dish's ingredients turn you off, there's often an equally flavorful vegetarian option. You'll find "neeps and tatties" alongside haggis; the three are inseparable. Neeps are yellow turnips, potatoes are the tatties, and both are boiled and then mashed.

Black pudding is another present-day delicacy (and former peasant food) that you can find just about everywhere, from breakfast table to local fish-and-chip shop to formal dining establishment. It's made from cooked sheep's- or goat's blood that congeals and is mixed with such ingredients as oats, barley, potato, bread, and meat. Black pudding can be grilled, boiled, or deep-fried. The Scottish prefer it for breakfast with fried eggs, bacon, beans, square sausages, toast, and potato scones. These fried, triangular-shape scones have the consistency of a dense pancake and are an intimate part of the Scottish breakfast, aptly called a fry-up because—apart from the beans and toast—everything else on the plate is fried. Another popular breakfast dish is porridge with salt instead of sugar, cinnamon, or honey. Sweet porridge doesn't go down well in Scotland.

Whiskies and Real Ales

"Uisge beatha," translated from Scottish Gaelic, means "water of life," and in Scotland it most certainly is. Whisky helps weave together the country's essence, capturing the aromas of earth, water, and air in a single sip.

Whiskies differ greatly between single malts and blends. This has to do with the ingredients, specialized distillation processes, and type of oak cask. Whisky is made predominantly from malted barley that, in the case of blended whiskies, can be combined with grains and cereals like wheat or corn. Malts or single malts can come only from malted barley.

The five main whisky regions in Scotland produce distinctive tastes, though there are variations even within a region: the Lowlands (lighter in taste), Speyside (sweet, with flower scents), the Highlands (fragrant, smooth, and smoky), Campbeltown (full-bodied and slightly salty), and Islay (strong peat flavor). Do sample these unique flavors; distillery tours are a good place to begin.

Real ales—naturally matured, cask-conditioned beer made from traditional ingredients—have arrived in the United Kingdom. These ales are not, at present, as popular as whisky, but are quickly making their mark on the Scottish beverage scene. Good brews to try include Arran Blonde (Arran Brewery), Dark Island (Orkney Brewery), White Wife (Shetland), Duechars (Caledonian Brewery), and Red Cuillin (Skye Brewery).

PLAYING GOLF IN SCOTLAND

There are some 550 golf courses in Scotland and only 5.3 million residents, so the country has probably the highest ratio of courses to people anywhere in the world. If you're visiting Scotland, you'll probably want to play the "famous names" sometime in your career.

So by all means play the championship courses such as the Old Course at St. Andrews, but remember they *are* championship courses. You may enjoy the game itself much more at a less challenging course. Remember, too, that everyone else wants to play the big names, so booking can be a problem at peak times in summer. Reserving three to four months ahead is not too far for the famous courses, although it's possible to get a time up to a month (or even a week) in advance if you are relaxed about your timing. If you're staying in a hotel attached to a course, get the concierge to book a tee time for you.

Happily, golf has always had a peculiar classlessness in Scotland. It's a game for everyone, and for centuries Scottish towns and cities have maintained courses for the enjoyment of their citizens. Admittedly, a few clubs have always been noted for their exclusive air, and some newer golf courses are losing touch with the game's inclusive origins, but these are exceptions to the tradition of recreation for all. Golf here is usually a democratic game, played by ordinary folk as well as the wealthy.

Tips About Playing

Golf courses are everywhere in Scotland. Most courses welcome visitors with a minimum of formalities, and some at a surprisingly low cost. Other courses are very expensive, but a lot of great golf can be played for between about £30 to £100 a round. Online booking at many courses has made arranging a golf tour easier, too.

Be aware of the topography of a course. Scotland is where the distinction between "links" and "parkland" courses was first made. Links courses are by the sea and are subject to the attendant sea breezes—some quite bracing—and mists, which can make them trickier to play. The natural topography of sand dunes and long, coarse grasses can add to the challenge. A parkland course is in a wooded area and its terrain is more obviously landscaped. A "moorland" course is found in an upland area.

Here are three pieces of advice, particularly for North Americans: (1) in Scotland the game is usually played fairly quickly, so don't dawdle if others are waiting; (2) caddy carts are hand-pulled carts for your clubs and driven golf carts are rarely available; and (3) when they say "rough," they really mean "rough."

Unless specified otherwise, hours are generally sunrise to sundown, which in June can be as late as 10 pm. Note that some courses advertise the SSS, "standard scratch score," instead of par (which may be different). This is the score a scratch golfer could achieve under perfect conditions. Rental clubs, balls, and other gear are generally available from clubhouses, except at the most basic municipal courses. Don't get caught by the dress codes enforced at many establishments: in general, untailored shorts, round-neck shirts, jeans, and sneakers are frowned upon.

The prestigious courses may ask for evidence of your golf skills by way of a handicap certificate; check in advance and carry this with you.

Costs and Courses

Many courses lower their rates before and after peak season—at the end of September, for example. It's worth asking about this. ■ TIP→ **Some areas offer regional golf passes that save you money. Check with the local tourist board.**

For a complete list of courses, contact local tourist offices or VisitScotland's official and comprehensive golf website, ⊕ *golf. visitscotland.com.* It has information about the country's golf courses, special golf trails, regional passes, special events, and tour operators, as well as on conveniently located accommodations. U.K. Golf Guide (⊕ *www.uk-golfguide.com*) has reviews by recent players. *For information about regional courses, also see individual chapters; see Tours in Travel Smart Scotland for some golf tour operators.*

Best Bets Around Scotland

If your idea of heaven is teeing off on a windswept links, then Scotland is for you. Dramatic courses, many of them set on sandy dunes alongside the ocean, are just one of the types you'll encounter. Highland courses that take you through the heather and moorland courses surrounded by craggy mountains have their own challenges.

Boat of Garten Golf Club, Inverness-shire. With the Cairngorm Mountain as a backdrop, this beautiful course has rugged terrain that requires even seasoned players to bring their A game. As an added bonus, a steam railway runs alongside the course.

Carnoustie Golf Links, Angus. Challenging golfers for nearly 500 years, Carnoustie is on many golfers' must-do list. The iconic Championship Course has tested many of the world's top players, while the Burnside and Buddon courses attract budding Players and Watsons.

Castle Stuart Golf Links, Inverness-shire. A more recent addition to Scotland's world-class courses offers cliff-top hazards, sprawling bunkers, and rolling fairways overlooking the Moray Firth.

Cruden Bay Golf Club, Aberdeenshire. This challenging and enjoyable links course was built by the Great North of Scotland Railway Company in 1894. Its remote location beside a set of towering dunes makes it irresistible.

Gleneagles, Perthshire. Home of the 2014 Ryder Cup championship, Gleneagles has three 18-hole courses that challenge the pros and a nine-hole course that provides a more laid-back game. It's also home to the PGA National Golf Academy.

Machrihanish Golf Club, Argyll. A dramatic location on the Mull of Kintyre and some exciting match play makes these links well worth a journey.

Royal Dornoch Golf Club, Sutherland. Extending across a coastal shelf, Royal Dornoch has fast greens, pristine beaches, and mountain views. In spring yellow gorse sets the green hills ablaze.

St. Andrews Links, Fife. To approach the iconic 18th hole in the place where the game was invented remains the holy grail of golfers worldwide.

Turnberry, Ayrshire. Along the windswept Ayrshire coast, Turnberry's famous Ailsa Course pits golfers against the elements and, on one hole, a stretch of ocean.

Western Gailes Golf Club, near Glasgow. This splendid links course is a final qualifying course for the British Open. Sculpted by Mother Nature, it's the country's finest natural links course.

GREAT ITINERARIES

HIGHLIGHTS OF SCOTLAND: CASTLES, LOCHS, GOLF, AND WHISKY IN 10 DAYS

Edinburgh

Days 1 and 2. The capital of Scotland is loaded with iconic sights in its Old Town and New Town. Visit Edinburgh Castle and the National Gallery of Scotland, and take tours of the National Museum of Scotland and the modern Scottish Parliament building. Walk along Old Town's Royal Mile and New Town's George Street for some fresh air and retail therapy. When the sun goes down, feast on the food of your choice and seek out a traditional pub with live music that will keep your toes tapping.

Logistics: Fly into Edinburgh Airport if you're flying via London and take a taxi or bus to the city center. If you're flying directly into Glasgow from overseas, make your way from Glasgow Airport to Queen Street Station via taxi or bus. It takes an hour to travel from Glasgow to Edinburgh by car or bus, about 45 minutes to an hour by train. Once in the city, explore on foot or by public transportation or taxi. There's no need to rent a car.

Stirling to St. Andrews

Day 3. Rent a car in Edinburgh and drive to the historic city of Stirling. Spend the day visiting Stirling Castle and the National Wallace Monument. If you're eager to tour a distillery, make time for a stop at the Famous Grouse Experience in Crieff. Then drive to the legendary seaside town of St. Andrews, famous for golf. Have dinner at the city's exceptional seafood restaurant.

Logistics: Leave Edinburgh after 9 am to miss the worst of the rush-hour traffic. It's 35 miles or a one-hour drive to Stirling from Edinburgh, and 50 miles and 90 minutes from Stirling to St. Andrews. You can easily take a train or bus to these destinations.

St. Andrews to Inverness

Day 4. Spend the morning exploring St. Andrews, known for its castle and the country's oldest university as well as its famous golf courses. The British Golf Museum is here, too. If you've booked well in advance (the time varies by season), play a round of golf. After lunch, drive to Inverness. Along the way, stretch your legs at one of Scotland's notable sights, Blair Castle (just off the A9 and 10 miles north of Pitlochry), a turreted white treasure with a war-torn past. Head to Inverness in the Highlands for the night.

Logistics: It's 150 miles from St. Andrews to Inverness via the A9, a drive that will take 3½ hours. This is a scenic journey, so do stop along the way. You can also take a train or bus.

Around Inverness and Castle Country

Day 5. Use Inverness as a base for exploring the Northeast, a region known for tempting castles and whisky distilleries. Don't visit too many sights or your day may become a forced march; two to three castles or distilleries is a good number. Some of the region's most interesting castles are Kildrummy, a 13th-century architectural masterpiece, and Balmoral, popular because of its royal connection to Queen Elizabeth. Castle Fraser has beautiful gardens. Keep Inverness as your base because of the number of restaurants and entertainment venues.

Portree
Isle of Skye
Broadford
Kyle of Lochalsh
Eilean Donan Castle
Glen Brittle
Inverness
Culloden Moor
Glen Grant Distillery and Garden
Balvenie
Huntly
Glenlivet
Castle Fraser
Loch Ness
HIGHLANDS
Aviemore
Kildrummy Castle
Aberdeen
Invergarry
Balmoral Castle
GRAMPIAN MOUNTAINS
Banchory
Fort William
Glen Nevis
Blair Castle
Duror
Ben Nevis
Pitlochry
Oban
Crieff
Perth
St. Andrews
Tarbet
National Wallace Monument
North Sea
Loch Lomond
Stirling
Balloch
EDINBURGH
GLASGOW

Alternatives: Prefer whisky to castles? Explore distilleries both on and off the Malt Whisky Trail in Speyside, near Inverness. Balvenie, Glenlivet, and Glen Grant are good choices; check hours and tour times, and note that some distilleries require prebooking. Another option for the day is to visit Loch Ness, though it's not one of Scotland's prettiest lochs; still, perhaps you'll spot Nessie. It's a 20-minute drive from Inverness. Just east of Inverness is Culloden Moor, where Bonnie Prince Charlie's forces were destroyed by the Duke of Cumberland's army.

Logistics: A car is best for this part of your journey. Rent one in Inverness or sign up for an organized tour; public transportation is not a viable option. Castles are often closed in winter; check in advance. It's about two hours from Inverness to Kildrummy. Some sample distances are 30 miles (one hour) from Balmoral Castle to Kildrummy Castle; 20 miles (30 minutes) from Kildrummy Castle to Castle Fraser; and Castle Fraser to Balmoral, 40 miles (90 minutes). The distilleries are about 90 minutes from Inverness. Some distances between distilleries are 18 miles (50 minutes) from Balvenie to Glenlivet; 17 miles (30 minutes) from Glenlivet to

Glen Grant; and 13 miles (30 minutes) from Glen Grant to Glenfiddich.

The Isle of Skye

Day 6. Leave Inverness early and head south to Skye. The drive to the island is peaceful, full of raw landscapes and big, open horizons. Stop at Eilean Donan Castle on the way. Set on an island among three lochs, the castle is the stuff postcards are made of. Explore Skye; Glen Brittle is the perfect place to enjoy mountain scenery; and Armadale is a good place to go crafts shopping. End up in Portree for dinner and the night.

Logistics: It's 80 miles (a two-hour drive) from Inverness to Skye. Public transportation is possible but connections can take time, so it's best to have the freedom of a car.

Oban via Ben Nevis

Day 7. Leave Skye no later than 9 am and head for Fort William. The town isn't worth stopping for, but the view of Britain's highest mountain, the 4,406-foot Ben Nevis, is. If time permits, take a hike in Glen Nevis. Continue on to Oban, a traditional Scottish resort town on the water. Outside Oban, stop by the Scottish Sealife Sanctuary. At night, feast on fish-and-chips in a local pub.

TIPS

■ You can begin this itinerary in Glasgow and finish in Edinburgh, or adjust the timing to your interests. For example, if you enjoy castles, you might stay in Inverness longer; if you like golf, St. Andrews may deserve more time.

■ August is festival season in Edinburgh; make reservations there well in advance during that month.

■ Remember to drive on the left side of the road and keep alert, especially on small, narrow country roads. Travel will take longer on smaller roads.

■ Weather is unpredictable; always dress in layers. Hikers should bring a map and compass for anything other than a ramble and always tell someone where they're going. Golfers and everyone else should carry rain gear.

■ Pack bug repellent for the midges (small, biting insects that travel in swarms). These insects breed in stagnant water, but they are *everywhere* from May through September.

■ Check distillery tour times and book arrangements in advance. When visiting distilleries, choose a designated driver or take a bus tour. Drunken drivers aren't tolerated.

Logistics: It's nearly 100 miles from Skye to Oban; the drive is 3½ hours without stopping. Public transportation is an option but a challenging one.

Loch Lomond to Glasgow

Days 8 and 9. Enjoy a leisurely morning in Oban and take a waterfront stroll. Mid-morning, set off for Glasgow via Loch Lomond. Stop in Balloch on the loch for fresh oysters and a walk along the bonnie banks. Arrive in Glasgow in time for dinner; take in a play or concert. Spend the next day and night visiting the sights: Kelvingrove Art Gallery and Museum, Charles Rennie Mackintosh's Glasgow School of Art, and the new Riverside Museum are a few highlights.

Logistics: It's 127 miles (a three-hour drive) from Oban to Glasgow via Balloch. Traveling by train is a possibility, but you won't be able to go via Balloch. Return your rental car in Glasgow; it's easy to travel around the city on foot or by subway or train.

Glasgow and Home

Day 10. On your final day, stow your suitcases at your hotel and hit Buchanan and Sauchiehall Streets for some of Britain's best shopping. Clothes, whisky, and tartan items are good things to look for.

Logistics: It's less than 10 miles (15 minutes) by taxi to Glasgow's international airport in Paisley but more than 30 miles (40 minutes) to the international airport in Prestwick. Be sure you have the correct airport information.

EDINBURGH AND THE LOTHIANS

Updated by
Nick Bruno

Edinburgh is to London as poetry is to prose, as Charlotte Brontë once wrote. One of the world's stateliest cities and proudest capitals, it's built—like Rome—on seven hills, making it a striking backdrop for the ancient pageant of history. In a skyline of sheer drama, Edinburgh Castle watches over the capital city, frowning down on Princes Street's glamour and glitz. But despite its rich past, the city's famous festivals, excellent museums and galleries, as well as the modern Scottish Parliament, are reminders that Edinburgh has its feet firmly in the 21st century.

Nearly everywhere in Edinburgh (the *burgh* is always pronounced *burra* in Scotland) there are spectacular buildings, whose Doric, Ionic, and Corinthian pillars add touches of neoclassical grandeur to the largely Presbyterian backdrop. Large gardens are a strong feature of central Edinburgh, where the city council is one of the most stridently conservationist in Europe. Arthur's Seat, a mountain of bright green and yellow furze, rears up behind the spires of the Old Town. This child-size mountain jutting 822 feet above its surroundings has steep slopes and little crags, like a miniature Highlands set down in the middle of the busy city. Appropriately, these theatrical elements match Edinburgh's character—after all, the city has been a stage that has seen its fair share of romance, violence, tragedy, and triumph.

Modern Edinburgh has become a cultural capital, staging the Edinburgh International Festival and the Fringe Festival in every possible venue each August. The stunning Museum of Scotland complements the city's wealth of galleries and artsy hangouts. Add Edinburgh's growing reputation for food and nightlife and you have one of the world's most beguiling cities.

Today the city is the second most important financial center in the United Kingdom, and the fifth most important in Europe. The city regularly is ranked near the top in quality-of-life surveys. Accordingly, New Town apartments on fashionable streets sell for considerable sums. In some senses the city is showy and materialistic, but Edinburgh still supports learned societies, some of which have their roots in the Scottish Enlightenment. The Royal Society of Edinburgh, for example, established in 1783 "for the advancement of learning and useful knowledge," remains an important forum for interdisciplinary activities.

Even as Edinburgh moves through the 21st century, its tall guardian castle remains the focal point of the city and its venerable history. Take time to explore the streets—peopled by the spirits of Mary, Queen of Scots; Sir Walter Scott; and Robert Louis Stevenson—and pay your respects to the world's best-loved terrier, Greyfriars Bobby. In the evenings you

TOP REASONS TO GO

Kaleidoscope of culture: Edinburgh covers it all, from floor-stomping *ceilidhs* to avant-garde modern dance, from traditional painting and sculpture to cutting-edge installations, from folksy fiddlers to the latest rock bands. The city's calendar of cultural festivals, including the famous Edinburgh International Festival, is outstanding.

The Royal Mile: History plays out before your eyes in this centuries-old capital along the Royal Mile. Edinburgh Castle and the Palace of Holyroodhouse were the locations for some of the most important struggles between Scotland and England.

Awe-inspiring architecture: From the Old Town's labyrinthine medieval streets to the neoclassical orderliness of the New Town to imaginative modern developments like the Scottish Parliament, the architecture of Auld Reekie spans the ages.

Food, glorious food: Edinburgh has a burgeoning restaurant scene that attracts celebrity chefs serving up dishes from around the world. Perhaps the most exotic, however, is genuine Scottish cuisine, with its classic dishes like Cullen skink and haggis with neeps and tatties.

Handcrafted treasures: Scotland has a strong tradition of distinctive furniture makers, silversmiths, and artists. Look to the "villages" of Edinburgh—such as Stockbridge—for exclusive designer clothing, edgy knitwear, and other high-end items.

can enjoy candlelit restaurants or a folk *ceilidh* (pronounced *kay-lee,* a traditional Scottish dance with music), though you should remember that you haven't earned your porridge until you've climbed Arthur's Seat. Should you wander around a corner, say, on George Street, you might see not an endless cityscape, but blue sea and a patchwork of fields. This is the county of Fife, beyond the inlet of the North Sea called the Firth of Forth—a reminder, like the mountains to the northwest that can be glimpsed from Edinburgh's highest points, that the rest of Scotland lies within easy reach.

ORIENTATION AND PLANNING

GETTING ORIENTED

For all its steep roads and hidden alleyways, Edinburgh is not a difficult place to navigate. Most newcomers gravitate to two areas, the Old Town and the New Town. The former funnels down from the castle on either side of the High Street, better known as the Royal Mile. Princes Street Gardens and Waverly Station separate the oldest part of the city from the stately New Town, known for its neoclassical architecture and verdant gardens. To the north, the city sweeps down to the Firth of Forth. It is here you will find the port of Leith with its trendy pubs and fine restaurants. The southern and western neighborhoods are mainly residential, but are home to such attractions as the Edinburgh Zoo.

Old Town. The focal point of Edinburgh for centuries, the Old Town is picturesque jumble of medieval tenements. Here are prime attractions such as Edinburgh Castle and the newer symbol of power, the Scottish Parliament. Amid the historic buildings you will find everything from buzzing nightclubs and bars to ghostly alleyways where the spirits of the past often make their presence felt.

New Town. Built in the 18th and 19th century to prevent the residents of overcrowded Old Town from decamping to London, the neoclassical sweep of the New Town is a masterpiece of city planning. Significant sights include the National Gallery of Scotland and Calton Hill, which offers some of the best views of the city from its summit. The city's main shopping thoroughfares, Princes Street and George Street, are also found here.

Leith. On the southern shore of the Firth of Forth, Edinburgh's port of Leith is where you'll find the former royal yacht *Britannia*. These days it's also filled with smart bars and restaurants.

Side Trips from Edinburgh. The historic houses, castles, towns, and museums in the green countryside outside Edinburgh—Midlothian, West Lothian, and East Lothian, collectively called the Lothians—can be reached quickly by bus or car, welcome day-trip escapes from the festival crush at the height of summer.

PLANNING

WHEN TO GO

Scotland's reliably inclement weather means that you could visit at the height of summer and be forced to wear a scarf. Conversely, conditions can be balmy in early spring and late autumn. You may want to avoid the crowds during July and August, but you'd also miss the famed Edinburgh International Festival and other summer celebrations. May, June, and September are probably the most hassle-free months in which to visit. Short days and grim conditions make winter less appealing, but Edinburgh's New Year celebrations are justly renowned.

PLANNING YOUR TIME

One of Edinburgh's greatest virtues is its compact size, which means that it is possible to pack a fair bit into even the briefest of visits. The two main areas of interest are the Old Town and the New Town, where you'll find Edinburgh Castle, the Scottish Parliament, Princes Street Gardens, and the National Gallery of Scotland. You can cover all four attractions in one day, but two days is more realistic. You can also choose between the Palace of Holyroodhouse and the important museums of Edinburgh, as well as entertaining sights such as the Real Mary King's Close, or explore the Royal Botanic Gardens and Holyrood Park. Head down to leafy, villagelike Stockbridge, then immerse yourself in the greenery along the Water of Leith, visiting the Gallery of Modern Art along the way.

Getting out of town is also an option for stays of more than a few days, depending on your interests: hop on a bus out to Midlothian to see the magnificent Rosslyn Chapel at Roslin (it's of interest to more than *Da Vinci Code* fans), and visit Crichton Castle, parts of which date back to the 14th century. Consider spending another half day traveling out to South Queensferry to admire the Forth rail and road bridges; then visit palatial Hopetoun House, with its wealth of portraits and fine furniture.

GETTING HERE AND AROUND

AIR TRAVEL

Airlines serving Edinburgh include Aer Arann, Aer Lingus, British Airways, British Midland, United, easyJet, flybe, KLM, Lufthansa, Ryanair, Air France, and Jet2.

A few transatlantic flights come through Edinburgh (United has service from Newark Liberty, near New York City). Except for these flights, you'll probably have to fly into Glasgow, 50 miles away. Ryanair and easyJet have sparked a major price war on the Anglo-Scottish routes. They offer unbeatable, no-frills airfares on routes connecting Edinburgh Airport, Glasgow International, Prestwick Airport (30 miles south of Glasgow), and London's major airports.

AIRPORTS   Edinburgh Airport, 7 miles west of the city center, offers only a few transatlantic flights, including seasonal service to and from Chicago by United Airlines. It does, however, have air connections throughout the United Kingdom—London (Heathrow, Gatwick, Stansted, Luton, and City), Birmingham, Bristol, East Midlands, Humberside, Jersey, Kirkwall (Orkney), Inverness, Leeds–Bradford, Manchester, Norwich, Sumburgh (Shetlands), Southampton, Wick, and Belfast (in Northern Ireland)—as well as with a number of European cities, including Amsterdam, Brussels, Copenhagen, Cork, Dublin, Frankfurt, Paris, Rome, Stockholm, and Zurich. Flights bound for Edinburgh depart virtually every hour from London's Gatwick and Heathrow airports.

Glasgow Airport, 50 miles west of Edinburgh, serves as the major point of entry into Scotland for transatlantic flights. Prestwick Airport, 30 miles southwest of Glasgow, after some years of eclipse by Glasgow Airport, has grown in importance, not least because of the activities of Ryanair.

Airport Information Edinburgh Airport ✉ *Glasgow Rd., Ingliston* ☎ *0844/481–8989* ⊕ *www.edinburghairport.com.* **Glasgow Airport** ✉ *Caledonia Way, Paisley* ☎ *0844/481–5555* ⊕ *www.glasgowairport.com.* **Prestwick Airport** ✉ *A79, Prestwick* ☎ *0871/223–0700* ⊕ *www.gpia.co.uk.*

TRANSFERS   There are no rail links to the city center, even though the airport sits
FROM   between two main lines. By bus or car you can usually make it to Edin-
EDINBURGH   burgh in a half hour, unless you hit the morning (7:30 to 9) or evening
AIRPORT   (4 to 6) rush hours. Lothian Buses runs between Edinburgh Airport and the city center every 15 minutes daily from 9 to 5 and roughly every hour during off-peak hours. The trip takes about 40 minutes, or up to an hour during peak traffic times. A single-fare ticket costs £1.50. Lothian Buses runs an Airlink express service to Waverley Station via Haymarket that takes 25 minutes. Buses run every 10 minutes, and single-fare tickets cost £3.50. A new tram service to the airport, slated to debut in 2014, costs £4.50.

You can arrange for a chauffeur-driven limousine to meet your flight at Edinburgh Airport through Transvercia Chaffeur Drive, Little's Chauffeur Drive, or WL Sleigh Ltd., for about £50.

Taxis are readily available outside the terminal. The trip takes 20 to 30 minutes to the city center, 15 minutes longer during rush hour. The fare is roughly £22. Note that airport taxis picking up fares from the terminal are any color, not the typical black cabs.

Airport Transfer Contacts Little's Chauffeur Drive ⌧ *1282 Paisley Rd. W, Paisley* ☏ *0141/883–2111* ⊕ *www.littles.co.uk.* **Transvercia Chaffeur Drive** ⌧ *6/19 Pilrig Heights, Leith* ☏ *0131/555–0459* ⊕ *www.transvercia.co.uk.* **W L Sleigh Ltd.** ⌧ *11A W. Craigs Ave., off Turnhouse Rd.* ☏ *0131/339–9607* ⊕ *www.sleigh.co.uk.*

TRANSFERS
FROM
GLASGOW
AIRPORT

Scottish Citylink buses leave Glasgow Airport and travel to Glasgow's Buchanan Street (journey time is 25 minutes), where you can transfer to an Edinburgh bus (leaving every 20 minutes). The trip to Edinburgh takes around two hours and costs £13.20 one-way. ■ TIP➔ **A far more pleasant option is to take a 20-minute cab ride from Glasgow Airport to Glasgow's Queen Street train station (about £20) and then take the train to Waverley Station in Edinburgh.** Trains depart about every 30 minutes; the trip takes 50 minutes and costs £13 to £20. Another, less expensive alternative—best for those with little luggage—is to take the bus from Glasgow Airport to Glasgow's Buchanan bus station, walk five minutes to the Queen Street train station, and catch the train to Edinburgh. Taxis from Glasgow Airport to downtown Edinburgh take about 70 minutes and cost around £100.

Glasgow Transfer Contact Scottish Citylink ☏ *0871/2663333* ⊕ *www.citylink.co.uk.*

BUS TRAVEL

National Express provides bus service to and from London and other major towns and cities. The main terminal, St. Andrew Square bus station, is a short walk north of Waverley Station, immediately east of St. Andrew Square. Long-distance coaches must be booked in advance online, by phone, or at the terminal. Edinburgh is approximately eight hours by bus from London.

Lothian Buses provides much of the service between Edinburgh and the Lothians and conducts day tours around and beyond the city. First runs buses out of Edinburgh into the surrounding area. Megabus offers dirt-cheap fares to selected cities if you book in advance.

Bus Contacts First ☏ *0871/2002233* ⊕ *www.firstgroup.com.* **Lothian Buses** ☏ *0131/555–6363* ⊕ *www.lothianbuses.com.* **Megabus** ☏ *0900/160–0900* ⊕ *www.megabus.com.* **National Express** ☏ *08717/818178* ⊕ *www.nationalexpress.co.uk.*

TRAVEL
WITHIN
EDINBURGH

Lothian Buses is the main operator within Edinburgh. You can buy tickets on the bus. The Day Ticket (£3.50), allowing unlimited one-day travel on the city's buses, can be purchased in advance or from the driver on any Lothian bus (exact fare is required when purchasing on a bus). The Ridacard (for which you'll need a photo) is valid on all buses for seven days (Sunday through Saturday night) and costs £17;

PARLIAMENT AND POWER

Three centuries after the Union of Parliaments with England in 1707, Edinburgh is once again the seat of a Scottish parliament. A new parliament building, designed by the late Spanish architect Enric Miralles, stands adjacent to the Palace of Holyroodhouse, at the foot of the Royal Mile.

The first-time visitor to Scotland may be surprised that the country still has a capital city at all, perhaps believing the seat of government was drained of its resources and power after the union with England—but far from it. The Union of Parliaments brought with it a set of political partnerships—such as separate legal, ecclesiastical, and educational systems—that Edinburgh assimilated and integrated with its own surviving institutions.

Scotland now has significantly more control over its own affairs than at any time since 1707, and the 129 Members of the Scottish Parliament (MSPs), of whom 40% are women, have extensive powers in Scotland over education, health, housing, transportation, training, economic development, the environment, and agriculture. Foreign policy, defense, and economic policy remain under the jurisdiction of the U.K. government in London. A referendum, set for September 2014, will let voters decide whether Scotland should remain in the United Kingdom or go it alone as an independent state.

the four-week Rider costs £51. ■ TIP➜ Buses are great for cheap daytime travel, but in the evening you'll probably want to take a taxi.

Information Lothian Buses ✉ *Waverley Bridge, Old Town* ☎ *0131/555–6363* ⊕ *www.lothianbuses.com.*

CAR TRAVEL
Driving in Edinburgh has its quirks and pitfalls, but don't be intimidated. Metered parking in the city center is scarce and expensive, and the local traffic wardens are a feisty, alert bunch. Note that illegally parked cars are routinely towed away, and getting your car back will be expensive. After 6 pm the parking situation improves considerably, and you may manage to find a space quite near your hotel, even downtown. If you park on a yellow line or in a resident's parking bay, be prepared to move your car by 8 the following morning, when the rush hour gets under way. Parking lots are clearly signposted; overnight parking is expensive and not always permitted.

TAXI TRAVEL
Taxi stands can be found throughout the downtown area. The following are the most convenient: the west end of Princes Street; South St. David Street and North St. Andrew Street (both just off St. Andrew Square); Princes Mall; Waterloo Place; and Lauriston Place. Alternatively, hail any taxi displaying an illuminated "for hire" sign.

TRAIN TRAVEL

Edinburgh's main train hub, Waverley Station, is downtown, below Waverley Bridge and around the corner from the unmistakable spire of the Scott Monument. Travel time from Edinburgh to London by train is as little as 4½ hours for the fastest service.

Edinburgh's other main station is Haymarket, about four minutes (by rail) west of Waverley. Most Glasgow and other western and northern services stop here.

Train Contacts National Rail Enquiries ☎ *08457/484950* ⊕ *www.nationalrail. co.uk.* **ScotRail** ☎ *0845/601–5929* ⊕ *www.scotrail.co.uk.*

TRAM TRAVEL

Absent since 1956, trams return to the streets of Edinburgh in mid-2014. After much delay, disruption, and controversy a 14-km (8.5-mile) stretch of track is being completed from Edinburgh Airport in the west to York Place in the east. Useful stops for travelers will include Haymarket, Princes Street, and St Andrew Square (near Waverley Station). Tickets are £1.50 for a single journey and £3.50 for a day ticket, which includes buses as well. The airport service will be a little more expensive than the Airlink bus (£4.50 one-way).

Tram Contact Edinburgh Trams ☎ *0800/328–3934* ⊕ *www.edinburghtrams.co.uk.*

TOURS
ORIENTATION TOURS

The best way to get oriented in Edinburgh is to take a bus tour, most of which are operated by Lothian Buses. Its "City Sightseeing" open-top bus tours include multilingual commentary; its "MacTours" are conducted in vintage open-top vehicles. All tours take you to the main attractions, including Edinburgh Castle, the Royal Mile, Palace of Holyroodhouse, and museums and galleries. Buses depart from Waverley Bridge, and are hop-on/hop-off services, with tickets lasting 24 hours. Lothian Buses' 60-minute Majestic Tour operates with a professional guide and takes you from Waverly Bridge to the New Town, past Charlotte Square, the Royal Botanic Garden, and Newhaven Heritage Museum until it reaches the royal yacht *Britannia* moored at Leith. Tickets cost £13 and are available from ticket sellers on Waverley Bridge or on the buses themselves.

If you want to get to know the area around Edinburgh, Rabbie's Trail Burners leads small groups on several different excursions, including a one-day trip to Rosslyn Chapel.

Orientation Tours Contacts Edinburgh Bus Tours ☎ *0131/220–0770* ⊕ *www.edinburghtour.com.* **Rabbie's Trail Burners** ✉ *207 High St.* ☎ *0131/226–3133* ⊕ *www.rabbies.com.*

PERSONAL GUIDES

Scottish Tourist Guides can supply guides (in 19 languages) who are fully qualified and will meet clients at any point of entry into the United Kingdom or Scotland. They can also tailor tours to your interests.

Personal Guide Contact Scottish Tourist Guides ☎ *01786/451953* ⊕ *www.stga.co.uk.*

WALKING TOURS

Cadies and Witchery Tours, a member of the Scottish Tourist Guides Association, has built a reputation for combining entertainment and historical accuracy in its lively and enthusiastic Ghosts & Gore Tour and Murder & Mystery Tour (£8.50), which take you through the narrow Old Town alleyways and closes. Costumed guides and other theatrical characters show up en route. The Scottish Literary Tour Company takes you around Edinburgh's Old Town or New Town (£12), with guides invoking Scottish literary characters.

Walking Tour Contacts Cadies and Witchery Tours. Spooky tours tracing the steps of Edinburgh's ghouls, gore, and mysteries commence outside the Witchery Restaurant at 352 Castlehill. ☎ *0131/225–6745* ⊕ *www.witcherytours.com.* **Scottish Literary Tour Trust** ⊠ *18–20 Grassmarket* ☎ *0800/169–7410* ⊕ *www.edinburghliterarypubtour.co.uk.*

VISITOR INFORMATION

The Edinburgh and Scotland Information Centre, next to Waverley Station (follow the "tic" signs in the station and throughout the city), offers an accommodations-booking service in addition to the more typical services. Complete information is also available at the information desk at the Edinburgh Airport. Information centers also sell the Edinburgh Pass, which offers free admission to more than 30 attractions, rides on Airlink express buses, and lots of discounts. Prices start at £30 for a one-day pass.

Visitor Information Edinburgh and Scotland Information Centre
⊠ *3 Princes St., East End* ☎ *0131/473–3868* ⊕ *www.edinburgh.org.*

EXPLORING EDINBURGH

Edinburgh's Old Town, which bears a great measure of symbolic weight as the "heart of Scotland's capital," is a boon for lovers of atmosphere and history. In contrast, if you appreciate the unique architectural heritage of the city's Enlightenment, then the New Town's for you. If you belong to both categories, don't worry—the Old and New towns are only yards apart. Princes Street runs east–west along the north edge of the Princes Street Gardens. Explore the main thoroughfares but don't forget to get lost among the tiny *wynds* and *closes*: old medieval alleys that connect the winding streets.

Like most cities, Edinburgh incorporates small communities within its boundaries, and many of these are as rewarding to explore as Old Town and New Town. Dean Village, for instance, even though it's close to the New Town, has a character all of its own. Duddingston, just southeast of Arthur's Seat, has all the feel of a country village. Then there's Corstorphine, to the west of the city center, famous for being the site of Murrayfield, Scotland's international rugby stadium. Edinburgh's port, Leith, sits on the shore of the Firth of Forth, and throbs with smart bars and restaurants.

OLD TOWN

East of Edinburgh Castle, the historic castle esplanade becomes the street known as the Royal Mile, leading from the castle down through Old Town to the Palace of Holyroodhouse. The Mile, as it's called, is actually made up of one thoroughfare that bears, in consecutive sequence, different names—Castlehill, Lawnmarket, Parliament Square, High Street, and Canongate. The streets and passages winding into their tenements, or "lands," and crammed onto the ridge in back of the Mile really *were* Edinburgh until the 18th century saw expansions to the south and north. Everybody lived here, the richer folk on the lower floors of houses, with less well-to-do families on the middle floors—the higher up, the poorer.

Time and progress (of a sort) have swept away some of the narrow closes and tall tenements of the Old Town, but enough survive for you to be able to imagine the original profile of Scotland's capital. There are many guided tours of the area, or you can walk around on your own. The latter is often a better choice in summer when tourists pack the area and large guided groups have trouble making their way through the crowds.

PLANNING
YOUR TIME
An exploration of the Old Town could be accomplished in a day, but to give the major sights—Edinburgh Castle, the Palace of Holyroodhouse, and the National Museum of Scotland—their due, you should allow more time. ■TIP→ Don't forget that some attractions have special hours during the Edinburgh International Festival. If you want to see something special, check the hours ahead of time.

TOP ATTRACTIONS

FAMILY
Fodor'sChoice
★
Edinburgh Castle. The crowning glory of the Scottish capital, Edinburgh Castle is popular not only because it's the symbolic heart of Scotland but also because of the views from its battlements: on a clear day the vistas—stretching to the "kingdom" of Fife—are breathtaking. ■TIP→ There's so much to see that you need at least three hours to do the site justice, especially if you're interested in military sites.

You enter across the **Esplanade,** the huge forecourt built in the 18th century as a parade ground. The area comes alive with color and music each August when it's used for the Military Tattoo, a festival of magnificently outfitted marching bands and regiments. Heading over the drawbridge and through the gatehouse, past the guards, you can find the rough stone walls of the **Half-Moon Battery,** where the one-o'clock gun is fired every day in an impressively anachronistic ceremony; these curving ramparts give Edinburgh Castle its distinctive appearance from miles away. Climb up through a second gateway and you come to the oldest surviving building in the complex, the tiny 11th-century **St. Margaret's Chapel,** named in honor of Saxon queen Margaret (1046–93), who had persuaded her husband, King Malcolm III (circa 1031–93), to move his court from Dunfermline to Edinburgh. Edinburgh's environs—the Lothians—were occupied by Anglian settlers with whom the queen felt more at home, or so the story goes (Dunfermline was surrounded by Celts). The **Crown Room,** a must-see, contains the "Honours of Scotland"—the crown, scepter, and sword that once graced the Scottish monarch. Upon the **Stone of Scone,** also in the Crown Room, Scottish monarchs once sat to be crowned. In the section now called

Queen Mary's Apartments, Mary, Queen of Scots, gave birth to James VI of Scotland. The **Great Hall** displays arms and armor under an impressive vaulted, beamed ceiling. Scottish parliament meetings were conducted here until 1840.

Military features of interest include the **Scottish National War Memorial,** the **Scottish United Services Museum,** and the famous 15th-century Belgian-made cannon *Mons Meg.* This enormous piece of artillery has been silent since 1682, when it exploded while fir-

> **SAVE ON SIGHTS**
>
> **Edinburgh Pass.** The Edinburgh Pass includes city bus transport (including a return ticket on the airport bus), access to more than 30 attractions, and other money-savers. Passes cost £30 for one day, £40 for two, and £50 for three. Passes are available from tourist information centers, at the airport, or online. ☎ 0845/225–5121 ⊕ www.edinburghpass.org.

ing a salute for the duke of York; it now stands in an ancient hall behind the Half-Moon Battery. Contrary to what you may hear from locals, it's not *Mons Meg* but the battery's gun that goes off with a bang every weekday at 1 pm, frightening visitors and reminding Edinburghers to check their watches. ✉ *Castle Esplanade and Castlehill, Old Town* ☎ *0131/225–9846 Edinburgh Castle, 0131/226–7393 War Memorial* ⊕ *www.edinburghcastle.gov.uk* 🎫 *£14* ⏱ *Apr.–Sept., daily 9:30–6; Oct.–Mar., daily 9:30–5; last entry 1 hr. before closing.*

NEED A BREAK?

Red Coat Café. You can have lunch or afternoon tea with panoramic views of the city at the Red Coat Café. Cakes, sandwiches, soups, and drinks are all available at reasonable prices. ✉ *Edinburgh Castle, Castlehill, Old Town* ☎ *0131/225–9746.*

High Kirk of St. Giles. Sometimes called St. Giles's Cathedral, this is one of the city's principal churches. However, anyone expecting a rival to Paris's Notre Dame or London's Westminster Abbey will be disappointed: St. Giles is more like a large parish church than a great European cathedral. There has been a church here since AD 854, although most of the present structure dates from either 1120 or 1829, when the church was restored.

The tower, with its stone crown towering 161 feet above the ground, was completed between 1495 and 1500. The most elaborate feature is the **Chapel of the Order of the Thistle,** built onto the southeast corner of the church in 1911 for the exclusive use of Scotland's only chivalric order, the Most Ancient and Noble Order of the Thistle. It bears the belligerent national motto "nemo me impune lacessit" ("No one provokes me with impunity"). Inside the church stands a life-size statue of the Scot whose spirit still dominates the place—the great religious reformer and preacher John Knox, before whose zeal all of Scotland once trembled. The church lies about one-third of the way along the Royal Mile from Edinburgh Castle. ✉ *High St., Old Town* ☎ *0131/225–9442* ⊕ *www.stgilescathedral.org.uk* 🎫 *£3 suggested donation* ⏱ *May–Sept., weekdays 9–7, Sat. 9–5, Sun. 1–5; Oct.–Apr., Mon.–Sat. 9–5, Sun. 1–5.*

High Street. Some of Old Town's most impressive buildings and sights are on High Street, one of the five streets making up the Royal Mile. Also here are other, less obvious historic relics. Near Parliament Square, look on the west side for a **heart** set in cobbles. This marks the site of the vanished Tolbooth, the center of city life from the 15th century until the building's demolition in 1817. The ancient civic edifice housed the Scottish parliament and was used as a prison—it also inspired Sir Walter Scott's novel *The Heart of Midlothian*.

Just outside Parliament House is the **Mercat Cross** (*mercat* means "market"), a great landmark of Old Town life. It was an old mercantile center, where in the early days executions were held, and where royal proclamations were—and are still—read. Most of the present cross is comparatively modern, dating from the time of William Ewart Gladstone (1809–98), the great Victorian prime minister and rival of Benjamin Disraeli (1804–81). Across High Street from the High Kirk of St. Giles stands the **City Chambers,** now the seat of local government. Built by John Fergus, who adapted a design of John Adam in 1753, the chambers were originally known as the Royal Exchange and intended to be where merchants and lawyers could conduct business. Note how the building drops 11 stories to Cockburn Street on its north side.

A *tron* is a weigh beam used in public weigh houses, and the **Tron Kirk** was named after a salt tron that used to stand nearby. The kirk itself was built after 1633, when St. Giles's became an Episcopal cathedral for a brief time. In this church in 1693, a minister offered an often-quoted prayer for the local government: "Lord, hae mercy on a' [all] fools and idiots, and particularly on the Magistrates of Edinburgh." ✉ *Between Lawnmarket and Canongate, Old Town.*

John Knox House. It's not certain that Scotland's severe religious reformer John Knox ever lived here, but there's evidence that he died here in 1572. Mementos of his life are on view inside, and the distinctive dwelling gives you a glimpse of what Old Town life was like in the 16th century. The projecting upper stories were once commonplace along the Royal Mile, darkening and further closing in the already narrow passage. Look for the initials of former owner James Mossman and his wife, carved into the stonework on the marriage lintel. Mossman was goldsmith to Mary, Queen of Scots, and was hanged in 1573 for his allegiance to her. ✉ *45 High St., Old Town* ☎ *0131/556–9579* ⊕ *www.scottishstorytellingcentre. co.uk* 🖸 *£5* ⊙ *Sept.–June, Mon.–Sat. 10–6; July and Aug., Mon.–Sat. 10–6, Sun. 10–6; last admission ½ hr before closing.*

Kirk of the Greyfriars. Greyfriars Church, built circa 1620 on the site of a medieval monastery, was where the National Covenant, declaring that the Presbyterian Church in Scotland was independent of the monarch and not Episcopalian in government, was signed in 1638. The covenant plunged Scotland into decades of civil war. Informative panels tell the story. Be sure to search out the graveyard—one of the most evocative in Europe. Its old, tottering, elaborate tombstones mark the graves of some of Scotland's most respected heroes and despised villains. Nearby, at the corner of George IV Bridge and Candlemaker Row, stands one of the most photographed sites in Scotland, the Greyfriars Bobby statue.

Edinburgh's Castle Fit for a King

Archaeological investigations have established that the rock on which Edinburgh Castle stands was inhabited as far back as 1000 BC, in the latter part of the Bronze Age. There have been fortifications here since the mysterious people called the Picts first used it as a stronghold in the 3rd and 4th centuries AD. Anglian invaders from northern England dislodged the Picts in AD 452, and for the next 1,300 years the site saw countless battles and skirmishes.

In the castle you'll hear the story of how Randolph, Earl of Moray and nephew of freedom fighter Robert the Bruce, scaled the heights one dark night in 1313, surprised the English guard, and recaptured the castle for the Scots. During this battle he destroyed every one of the castle's buildings except for St. Margaret's Chapel, dating from around 1076, so that successive Stewart kings had to rebuild the castle bit by bit.

The castle has been held over time by Scots and Englishmen, Catholics and Protestants, soldiers and royalty. In the 16th century Mary, Queen of Scots, gave birth here to the future James VI of Scotland (1566–1625), who was also to rule England as James I. In 1573 it was the last fortress to support Mary's claim as the rightful Catholic queen of Britain, causing the castle to be virtually destroyed by English artillery fire.

✉ *Greyfriars Pl., Old Town* ☎ *0131/225–1900* ⊕ *www.greyfriarskirk. com* 🖾 *Free* ☉ *Easter–Oct., weekdays 10:30–4:30, Sat. 11–2; Nov.– Easter, Thurs. 1:30–3:30.*

FAMILY

Fodor's Choice

★

National Museum of Scotland. This museum traces the country's fascinating story from the oldest fossils to the most recent popular culture, making it a must-see for first-time visitors to Scotland or anyone interested in history. One of the most famous treasures is the Lewis Chessmen, 11 intricately carved ivory chess pieces found in the 19th century on one of Scotland's Western Isles. An extensive renovation of the basement has created a dramatic, cryptlike entrance. Visitors now rise to the light-filled, birdcage wonders of the Victorian grand hall and the upper galleries in glass elevators. Highlights include the hanging hippo and sea creatures of the Wildlife Panorama, a life-size skeleton cast of a Tyrannosaurus rex, Viking brooches, Pictish stones, Jacobite relics, the Stevenson family's inventions, including lighthouse optics, and Queen Mary's *clarsach* (harp). ✉ *Chambers St., Old Town* ☎ *0300/123–6789* ⊕ *www.nms.ac.uk* 🖾 *Free* ☉ *Daily 10–5.*

FAMILY

Our Dynamic Earth. Using state-of-the-art technology, the 11 theme galleries at this interactive science gallery educate and entertain as they explore the wonders of the planet, from polar regions to tropical rain forests. Geological history, from the big bang to the unknown future, is also examined. ✉ *Holyrood Rd., Old Town* ☎ *0131/550–7800* ⊕ *www. dynamicearth.co.uk* 🖾 *£11.50* ☉ *Apr.–June, Sept., and Oct., daily 10–5:30; July and Aug., daily 10–6; Nov.–Mar., Wed.–Sun. 10–5:30; last admission 90 mins before closing.*

NEW TOWN

TO ROYAL BOTANIC GARDEN EDINBURGH

Water of Leith

Howe St.

India St.

Gloucester La.

Heriot Row

Moray Place

41

QUEEN ST. GARDENS

Queen St.

Dundas St.

St. Andrew St.

34

St. David St.

St. Andrew's

Bus Station

George St.

Ainslie Place

Thistle St.

38

St. Andrew Square

Randolph Crescent

39

Charlotte

George St.

Assembly Rooms

Hanover St.

Frederick St.

Castle St.

Waverley Market

32

31 Princes St.

N Charlotte St.

Rose St.

S Charlotte St.

40

Square

Hope St.

Princes St.

30

The Mound

33

Queensferry St.

29

WEST END

West Maitland

WEST PRINCES STREET GARDENS

Market St.

OLD TOWN

Bank St.

Ramsay Ln.

St Giles St.

TO SCOTTISH NATIONAL GALLERY OF MODERN ART

King's Stables Rd.

Edinburgh Castle

1

Cannonball House

2

Lawnmarket

5

3 **6** **7**

Esplanade

4

Tolbooth Kirk

George IV Bridge

TO EDINBURGH ZOO

Lothian Rd.

Johnston Ter.

Upper Bow

Victoria St.

8

W. Bow

Grindlay St.

Grassmarket

9

Cowgate

Candlemaker Row

Bread St.

West Port Ter.

The Vennel

Flodden Wall

11

Morrison St.

Fountainbridge

HAYMARKET

Earl Gray St.

Lauriston Pl.

Lauriston Pl.

Home St.

TOLLCROSS

Chalmers St.

Middle Meadow Walk

KEY

𝑖 Tourist information

├─┼─┤ Rail Lines

Old Town ▼		
Brass Rubbing Centre **18**	Edinburgh Castle **1**	John Knox House **19**
Camera Obscura **3**	Fruitmarket Gallery **21**	Kirk of the Greyfriars **11**
Canongate **25**	George IV Bridge **8**	Lawnmarket **7**
Canongate Kirk **24**	Gladstone's Land **5**	Museum of Childhood **17**
Canongate Tolbooth **22**	Grassmarket **9**	Museum of Edinburgh **23**
Castlehill **2**	High Kirk of St. Giles **15**	National Library of Scotland **10**
	High Street (Royal Mile) .. **13**	National Museum

of Scotland **12**

Our Dynamic Earth **27**

Palace of Holyroodhouse **28**

Parliament House **14**

Real Mary King's Close ... **16**

Scotch Whisky Experience **4**

Edinburgh

- St. James Centre
- Royal Bank of Scotland **36**
- Regent Arch
- West Register St.
- Waterloo Pl. **35**
- Temporary Bus Station (Local Service)
- Calton Burial Ground
- North Bridge
- Edinburgh Waverley Station
- Calton Hill **37**
- National Monument
- Nelson Monument
- Regent Rd.
- Calton Rd.
- Calton New Burial Ground
- Burns Monument
- Canongate Graveyard
- Tolbooth Wynd
- Abbey Hill
- Abbey Strand
- Palace of Holyroodhouse **28**
- **26**
- E. Market St.
- Jeffrey St.
- Cockburn St.
- City Chambers
- Royal Mile
- St. Mary's St.
- Canongate
- Bull's Close
- **CANONGATE**
- **22** **24**
- **23**
- **25**
- **21** **18** **19** **20**
- **16** **17**
- High St. Tron Kirk
- **13** Mercat Cross
- **15** Old Fishmarket Close
- **14**
- Blackfriars St.
- **10** Parliament Square
- **27**
- Holyrood Rd.
- Cowgate
- Chambers St.
- South Bridge
- Drummond St.
- Pleasance
- **HOLYROOD PARK**
- Salisbury Crags
- Queen's Dr.
- **12**
- Greyfriars Pl.
- George Square
- Buccleuch St.
- Nicolson St.
- TO ARTHUR'S SEAT →
- TO DUDDINGSTON →
- 0 — 1/8 mi
- 0 — 1/5 km
- **42**

Fodor'sChoice
★
Palace of Holyroodhouse. Once the haunt of Mary, Queen of Scots, and the setting for high drama—including at least one notorious murder, several major fires, and centuries of the colorful lifestyles of larger-than-life, power-hungry personalities—this is now Queen Elizabeth's official residence in Scotland. A doughty and impressive palace standing at the foot of the Royal Mile in a hilly public park, it's built

> **WORD OF MOUTH**
>
> "When you walk down the Royal Mile during the day, pop down some of the closes that project off it left and right. There are some interesting architectural features and it gives some indication of living conditions in days past."
> —TheInTeam

around a graceful, lawned central court at the end of Canongate. When the queen or royal family is not in residence you can take a tour. The free audio guide is excellent.

Many monarchs, including Charles II, Queen Victoria, and George V, have left their mark on its rooms, but it's Mary, Queen of Scots whose spirit looms largest. For some visitors, the most memorable room here is the little chamber in which David Rizzio (1533–66), secretary to Mary, Queen of Scots, met an unhappy end in 1566. In part because Rizzio was hated at court for his social-climbing ways, Mary's second husband, Lord Darnley (Henry Stewart, 1545–65), burst into the queen's rooms with his henchmen, dragged Rizzio into an antechamber, and stabbed him more than 50 times; a bronze plaque marks the spot. Darnley himself was murdered the next year, which made way for the queen's marriage to her lover, the Earl of Bothwell.

■ TIP→ **There's plenty to see here, so make sure you have at least two hours to tour the palace, gardens, and the ruins of the 12th-century abbey.** The **King James Tower** is the oldest surviving section, containing the rooms of Mary, Queen of Scots on the second floor, and Lord Darnley's rooms below. Though much has been altered, there are fine fireplaces, paneling, plasterwork, tapestries, and 18th- and 19th-century furnishings throughout. At the south end of the palace front you can find the **Royal Dining Room,** and along the south side are the **Throne Room** and other drawing rooms now used for social and ceremonial occasions.

At the back of the palace is the **King's Bedchamber.** The 150-foot-long **Great Picture Gallery,** on the north side, displays the portraits of 110 Scottish monarchs. These were commissioned by Charles II, who was eager to demonstrate his Scottish ancestry—some of the royal figures here are fictional and the likenesses of others imaginary. All the portraits were painted by a Dutch artist, Jacob de Witt, who signed a contract in 1684 with the queen's cash keeper, Hugh Wallace. The contract bound him to deliver 110 pictures within two years, for which he received an annual stipend of £120. The **Queen's Gallery,** in a former church and school at the entrance to the palace, holds rotating exhibits from the Royal Collection. There is a separate admission charge.

Holyroodhouse has its origins in an Augustinian monastery founded by David I (1084–1153) in 1128. In the 15th and 16th centuries Scottish royalty, preferring the comforts of the abbey to the drafty rooms of

THE BUILDING OF EDINBURGH

Towering over the city, Edinburgh Castle was actually built over the plug of an ancient volcano. Many thousands of years ago, an eastward-grinding glacier encountered the tough basalt core of the volcano and swept around it, scouring steep cliffs and leaving a trail of matter. This material formed a ramp gently leading down from the rocky summit. On this *crag* and *tail* would grow the city of Edinburgh and its castle.

CASTLE, WALLED TOWN, AND HOLYROODHOUSE

By the 12th century Edinburgh had become a walled town, still perched on the hill. Its shape was becoming clearer: like a fish with its head at the castle, its backbone running down the ridge, and its ribs leading briefly off on either side. The backbone gradually became the continuous thoroughfare now known as the Royal Mile, and the ribs became the closes (alleyways), some still surviving, that were the scene of many historic incidents.

By the early 15th century Edinburgh had become the undisputed capital of Scotland. The bitter defeat of Scotland at Flodden in 1513, when Scotland aligned itself with France against England, caused a new defensive city wall to be built. Though the castle escaped destruction, the city was burned by the English earl of Hertford under orders from King Henry VIII (1491–1547) of England. This was during a time known as the "Rough Wooing," when Henry was trying to coerce the Scots into allowing the young Mary, Queen of Scots (1542–87) to marry his son Edward. The plan failed and Mary married Francis, the Dauphin of France.

By 1561, when Mary returned from France already widowed, the guesthouse of the Abbey of Holyrood had grown to become the Palace of Holyroodhouse, replacing Edinburgh Castle as the main royal residence. Mary's legacy to the city included the destruction of most of the earliest buildings of Edinburgh Castle; she was eventually executed by Elizabeth I.

ENLIGHTENMENT AND THE CITY

In the trying decades after the union with England in 1707, many influential Scots, both in Edinburgh and elsewhere, went through an identity crisis. Out of the 18th-century difficulties, however, grew the Scottish Enlightenment, during which educated Scots made great strides in medicine, economics, and science.

Changes came to the cityscape, too. By the mid-18th century it had become the custom for wealthy Scottish landowners to spend the winter in the Old Town of Edinburgh, in town houses huddled between the high Castle Rock and the Royal Palace below. Cross-fertilized in coffeehouses and taverns, intellectual notions flourished among a people determined to remain Scottish despite their parliament's having voted to dissolve itself. One result was a campaign to expand and beautify the city, to give it a look worthy of its future nickname, the Athens of the North. Thus was the New Town of Edinburgh built, with broad streets and gracious buildings creating a harmony that even today's throbbing traffic cannot obscure.

2

Edinburgh Castle, settled into Holyroodhouse, expanding and altering the buildings until the palace eventually eclipsed the monastery. You can still walk around some ruins though.

After the Union of the Crowns in 1603, when the Scottish royal court packed its bags and decamped for England, the building fell into decline. It was Charles II (1630–85) who rebuilt Holyrood in the architectural style of Louis XIV (1638–1715), and this is the style you see today.

In 1688 an anti-Catholic faction ran riot within the palace, and in 1745, during the last Jacobite campaign, Charles Edward Stuart occupied the palace, followed a short while later by the duke of Cumberland, who defeated Charles at Culloden. After the 1822 visit of King George IV (1762–1830), at a more peaceable time, the palace sank into decline once again. But Queen Victoria (1819–1901) and her grandson King George V (1865–1936) renewed interest in the palace: the buildings were once more refurbished and made suitable for royal residence. Behind the palace lie the open grounds and looming crags of Holyrood Park, the hunting ground of early Scottish kings. From the top of Edinburgh's mini mountain, **Arthur's Seat** (822 feet), views are breathtaking. ⊠ *Abbey Strand, Old Town* ☎ *0131/556–5100* ⊕ *www.royalcollection. org.uk* ≤ *£11, £15.50 includes the Queen's Gallery* ⊙ *Apr.–Oct., daily 9:30–6; Nov.–Mar., daily 9:30–4:30; last admission 1 hr before closing. Closed during royal visits.*

FAMILY

Fodor's Choice

★

Real Mary King's Close. Hidden beneath the City Chambers, this narrow, cobbled *close*, or lane, named after a former landowner, is said to be one of Edinburgh's most haunted sites. The close was sealed off in 1645 to quarantine residents who became sick when the bubonic plague swept through the city, and many victims were herded there to die. After the plague passed, the bodies were removed and buried, and the street was reopened. A few people returned, but they soon reported ghostly goings-on and departed, leaving the close empty for decades. In 1753 city authorities built the Royal Exchange (later the City Chambers) directly over the close, sealing it off and, unwittingly, ensuring it remained intact, except for the buildings' upper stories, which were destroyed. Today you can walk among the remains of the shops and houses. People still report ghostly visions and eerie sounds, such as the crying of a young girl. Over the years visitors have left small offerings for her, such as dolls, pieces of ribbon, or candy. ■ TIP→ Although kids like the spookiness of this attraction, it's not for the youngest ones. In fact, children under age five are not admitted. ⊠ *Writers' Court, Old Town* ☎ *0845/070–6244* ⊕ *www.realmarykingsclose. com* ≤ *£12.95* ⊙ *Apr.–Oct., daily 10–9; Nov.–Mar., weekdays 10–5, weekends 10–9.*

Scottish Parliament. Scotland's somewhat controversial Parliament building is dramatically modern, with irregular curves and angles that mirror the twisting shapes of the surrounding landscape. The structure's artistry is most apparent when you step inside, where the gentle slopes, forest's worth of oak, polished concrete and granite, and walls of glass create an understated magnificence. It's worth taking a free tour to see the main hall and debating chamber, a committee room, and other

A GOOD WALK IN THE OLD TOWN

A perfect place to start your stroll through the Old Town is Edinburgh Castle. After exploring its extensive complex of buildings and admiring the view from the battlements, set off down the first part of the Royal Mile. The Camera Obscura's Outlook Tower affords more splendid views of the city. The six-story tenement known as Gladstone's Land, a survivor of 16th-century domestic life, is on the left as you head east. Near Gladstone's Land, down another close, stands the Writers' Museum, in a fine example of 17th-century urban architecture called Lady Stair's House. Farther down on the right are the Tolbooth Kirk (a *tolbooth* was a town hall or prison, and *kirk* means "church") and Upper Bow.

Turn right down George IV Bridge to reach the historic Grassmarket, where parts of the old city walls still stand. Turn left up Candlemaker Row and you can see the Kirk of the Greyfriars, and the little statue of faithful Greyfriars Bobby. On Chambers Street, at the foot of George IV Bridge, are the impressive galleries of the National Museum of Scotland.

Returning to the junction of George IV Bridge with the Royal Mile, turn right (east) down High Street to visit the old Parliament House; the High Kirk of St. Giles; the Mercat Cross; and the elegant City Chambers, bringing a flavor of the New Town's neoclassicism to the Old Town's severity. Beneath the chambers is the eerie Real Mary King's Close, a lane that was closed off in the 17th century when the bubonic plague struck the city.

A short distance down Canongate on the left is Canongate Tolbooth. The Museum of Edinburgh stands opposite, and the Canongate Kirk and Acheson House are nearby. This walk draws to a close, as it started, on a high note, at the Palace of Holyroodhouse, full of historic and architectural interest and some fine paintings, tapestries, and furnishings to admire, in Holyrood Park.

TIMING

This walk can expand greatly in length depending on how often you stop to explore different sights, so plan accordingly. You can walk the Royal Mile in an hour, take a day to stop and visit points of interest, or even spend a couple of days exploring the area.

areas. ■TIP→ **Call well in advance to get a free ticket to view Parliament in action.** Originally conceived by the late Catalan architect Enric Miralles, who often said the building was "growing out of the ground," the design was completed by his widow, Benedetta Tagliabue, in August 2004. ⊠ *Horse Wynd, Old Town* ☎ *0131/348–5200* ⊕ *www.scottish. parliament.uk* ⊠ *Free* ⊙ *Mon.–Sat. 10–5:30.*

Fodor's Choice ★ **Scottish Storytelling Centre.** This arts center is housed in a modern building that manages to blend seamlessly with the historic structures on either side. It hosts a year-round program of storytelling, theater, and literary events. A café serves lunch, tea, and homebaked cakes. ⊠ *43 High St., Old Town* ☎ *0131/556–9579* ⊕ *www.scottishstorytellingcentre.co.uk* ⊠ *Free* ⊙ *Sept.–June, Mon.–Sat. 10–6; July and Aug., Mon.–Sat. 10–6, Sun. noon–6.*

WORTH NOTING

FAMILY **Brass Rubbing Centre.** No experience is necessary for you to make your own souvenirs at this center. You can explore the past by creating do-it-yourself replicas (£2 to £6) from original Pictish stones and markers, rare Scottish brasses, and medieval church brasses, or you can buy ready-made versions in the shop. All the materials are here, and children find the pastime quite absorbing. The center occupies the surviving piece of a Gothic church down a close opposite the Museum of Childhood. ⊠ *Trinity Apse, Chalmers Close, Old Town* ☎ *0131/556–4364* ⊕ *www. cac.org.uk* ⊒ *Free* ⊙ *Apr.–Sept., Mon.–Sat. 10–5.*

FAMILY **Camera Obscura and World of Illusions.** Want to view Edinburgh as Victorian travelers once did? Then head for the 17th-century Outlook Tower's camera obscura, where an optical instrument—a sort of projecting periscope—affords bird's-eye views of the whole city (on a clear day, that is) illuminated onto a concave table. The tower was significantly altered in the 1850s with the installation of the telescopic "magic lantern." Other attractions include a Magic Gallery with optical illusions, holograms, pin-hole photography, and rooftop views. ⊠ *Castlehill, Old Town* ☎ *0131/226–3709* ⊕ *www.camera-obscura. co.uk* ⊒ *£11.95* ⊙ *Apr.–June, Sept., and Oct., daily 9:30–7; July–Aug., daily 9:30–9; Nov.–Mar., daily 10–6.*

Canongate. This section of the Royal Mile takes its name from the canons who once ran the abbey at Holyrood. Canongate—in Scots, *gate* means "street"—was originally an independent town, or *burgh,* another Scottish term used to refer to a community with trading rights granted by the monarch. Here you'll find **Canongate Kirk** and its graveyard, **Canongate Tolbooth,** and the **Museum of Edinburgh.** ⊠ *Royal Mile, between High St. and Abbey Strand, Old Town.*

Canongate Kirk. This unadorned building, built in 1688, is run by the Church of Scotland and has an interesting graveyard. This is the final resting place of some notable Scots, including economist Adam Smith (1723–90), author of *The Wealth of Nations* (1776), who once lived in the nearby 17th-century Panmure House. Also buried here are Dugald Stewart (1753–1828), the leading European philosopher of his time, and the undervalued Scots poet Robert Fergusson (1750–74). That Fergusson's grave is even marked is the result of efforts by the much more famous Robert Burns (1759–96), who commissioned an architect—by the name of Robert Burn—to design one. Burn also designed the Nelson Monument, the tall column on Calton Hill to the north, which you can see from the graveyard.

Against the eastern wall of the graveyard is a bronze sculpture of the head of Mrs. Agnes McLehose, the "Clarinda" of the copious correspondence in which Robert Burns engaged while confined to his lodgings with an injured leg in 1788. Burns and McLehose—a high-born, talented woman who had been abandoned by her husband—exchanged passionate letters for some six weeks that year. The missives were dispatched across town by a postal service that delivered them within the hour for one penny. The curiously literary affair ended when Burns left Edinburgh in 1788 to take up a farm tenancy and to marry Jean Armour. ✉ *153 Canongate, Old Town* ☎ *0131/556–3515* ⊕ *canongatekirk.org.uk* 🎟 *Free* ⊙ *May–Sept. daily 10–4.*

Canongate Tolbooth. Nearly every city and town in Scotland once had a tolbooth. Originally a customhouse where tolls were gathered, a tolbooth came to mean town hall and later prison because detention cells were in the basement. The building where Canongate's town council once met now has a museum, the **People's Story Museum,** which focuses on the lives of "ordinary" people from the 18th century to today. Exhibits describe how Canongate once bustled with the activities of the tradespeople needed to supply life's essentials in the days before superstores. Special displays include a reconstruction of a cooper's workshop and a 1940s kitchen. ✉ *163 Canongate, Old Town* ☎ *0131/529–4057* ⊕ *www.edinburghmuseums.org.uk* 🎟 *Free* ⊙ *Mon.–Sat. 10–5.*

QUICK BITES

Clarinda's. You can get a good cup of tea and a scone, a quintessentially Scottish indulgence, at Clarinda's homey tearoom. ✉ *69 Canongate, Old Town* ☎ *0131/557–1888.*

The Hub. For soups, sandwiches, and vegetarian-friendly options head to this spot, housed in the grand Tolbooth Kirk. Its comfy seats, stained-glass windows, and inviting terrace create a relaxing atmosphere to refuel and hear the latest cultural chatter. ✉ *Castlehill, Old Town* ☎ *0131/473–2067* ⊕ *www.thehub-edinburgh.com/cafe.*

Castlehill. In the late 16th century alleged witches were brought to what is now a street in the Royal Mile to be burned at the stake, as a bronze plaque here recalls. The cannonball embedded in the west gable of Castlehill's **Cannonball House** was, according to legend, fired from the castle during the Jacobite Rebellion of 1745, led by Charles Edward Stuart (also known as Bonnie Prince Charlie, 1720–88), the most romantic of the Stuart pretenders to the British throne. Most authorities agree on a more prosaic explanation, however; they say it was a height marker for Edinburgh's first piped water-supply system, installed in 1681. Atop the Gothic **Tolbooth Kirk,** built in 1844 for the General Assembly of the Church of Scotland, stands the tallest spire in the city, at 240 feet. The church now houses the cheery Edinburgh Festival offices and a café known as **The Hub.**

The **Upper Bow,** running from Lawnmarket to Victoria Street, was once the main route westward from the town and castle. Before Victoria Street was built in the late 19th century, the Upper Bow led down into a narrow dark thoroughfare coursing between a canyon of tenements. All traffic struggled up and down this steep slope from the Grassmarket, which joins the now-truncated West Bow at its lower end. ✉ *East of Esplanade and west of Lawnmarket, Old Town.*

OFF THE BEATEN PATH

Duddingston. Tucked behind Arthur's Seat, and about an hour's walk from Princes Street via Holyrood Park, this little community, formerly of brewers and weavers, still seems like a country village. The Duddingston Kirk has a Norman doorway and a watchtower that was built to keep body snatchers out of the graveyard. The church and adjoining garden overlook Duddingston Loch, popular with bird-watchers.

Pathways meander down to lochside Thomson's Tower, an octagonal tower built by William Playfair in 1825 as a curling clubhouse. Recently restored, it's home to a small museum. Moments away is Edinburgh's oldest hostelry, the Sheep Heid Inn, which serves a wide selection of beers and hearty food. For £13 you can have a go on the oldest skittle (bowling alley) in Scotland. To get here, take Lothian Bus 42. ✉ *Duddingston Low Rd., Duddingston Village* ⊕ *www.drneilsgarden.co.uk.*

Fruitmarket Gallery. This contemporary art gallery behind Waverley Station showcases world-renowned artists like Louise Bourgeois and Turner Prize–winning artist Martin Creed. Don't miss Creed's colorful yet subtle marbled transformation of the once-delapidated Scotman Steps nearby. ✉ *45 Market St., Old Town* 🕾 *0131/225–2383* ⊕ *www.fruitmarket.co.uk* 🎫 *Free* ☉ *Mon.– Sat. 11–6, Sun. noon–5.*

> ## GRASSMARKET GALLOWS
>
> Grassmarket's history is long and gory. The **cobbled cross** at the east end marks the site of the town gallows. Among those hanged here were many 17th-century Covenanters, members of the Church of Scotland who rose up against Charles I's efforts to enforce Anglican or "English" ideologies on the Scottish people. Judges were known to issue the death sentence for these religious reformers with the words, "Let them glorify God in the Grassmarket."

George IV Bridge. It's not immediately obvious that this is in fact a bridge, as buildings are closely packed most of the way along both sides. At the corner of the bridge stands one of the most photographed sculptures in Scotland, *Greyfriars Bobby.* This statue pays tribute to the legendary Skye terrier who kept vigil beside his master John Gray's grave in the Greyfriar's churchyard for 14 years after Gray died in 1858. The 1961 Walt Disney film *Greyfriars Bobby* tells a version of the heartrending tale that some claim to be a shaggy-dog story. ✉ *Bank St. and Lawnmarket, Old Town.*

Gladstone's Land. This narrow, six-story tenement, next to the Assembly Hall, is a survivor from the 17th century. Typical Scottish architectural features are evident on two floors, including an arcaded ground floor (even in the city center, livestock sometimes inhabited the ground floor). The house has magnificent painted ceilings and is furnished in the style of a 17th-century merchant's home. ✉ *477B Lawnmarket, Old Town* 🕾 *0844/493–120* ⊕ *www.nts.org.uk/property/gladstones-land* 🎫 *£6.50* ☉ *Apr.–Oct., daily 10–5; July and Aug., daily 10–6:30; last admission 30 mins before closing.*

Grassmarket. For centuries an agricultural marketplace, Grassmarket now is the site of numerous shops, bars, and restaurants, making it a hive of activity at night. Sections of the Old Town wall can be traced on the north side by a series of steps that ascend from Grassmarket to Johnston Terrace. The best-preserved section of the wall can be found by crossing to the south side and climbing the steps of the lane called the Vennel. Here the 16th-century **Flodden Wall** comes in from the east and turns south at Telfer's Wall, a 17th-century extension.

From the northeast corner of the Grassmarket, **Victoria Street**, a 19th-century addition to the Old Town, leads to the George IV Bridge. Shops here sell antiques and designer clothing. ⊠ *Grassmarket.*

Lawnmarket. A corruption of "land market," Lawnmarket is the second of the streets that make up the Royal Mile. It was formerly the site of the produce market for the city, with a once-a-week special sale of wool and linen. Now it's home to **Gladstone's Land** and the **Writers' Museum.** At different times the Lawnmarket Courts housed James Boswell, David Hume, and Robert Burns. In nearby Brodie's Close in the 1770s lived the infamous Deacon Brodie, pillar of society by day and a murdering gang leader by night. Robert Louis Stevenson (1850–94) may well have used Brodie as the inspiration for his *Strange Case of Dr. Jekyll and Mr. Hyde.* ⊠ *Between Castlehill and High St., Old Town.*

NEED A BREAK?

Jolly Judge. Several atmospheric pubs and restaurants bustle on this section of the Royal Mile. Try the friendly Jolly Judge, where firelight brightens the dark-wood beams and a mixed crowd of university professors and students sip ale and eat light lunches of soup, pasta, or baked potatoes. ⊠ *7 James Ct., Old Town* ☎ *0131/225–2669.*

FAMILY **Museum of Childhood.** Even adults tend to enjoy this cheerfully noisy museum—a cacophony of childhood memorabilia, vintage toys, antique dolls, and fairground games such as "Sweeney Todd." There are also a reconstructed schoolroom, street scene, a fancy-dress party, and a nursery. The museum claims to have been the first in the world devoted solely to the history of childhood. It's two blocks past the North Bridge–South Bridge junction on High Street. ⊠ *42 High St., Old Town* ☎ *0131/529–4142* ⊕ *www.edinburghmuseums.org.uk* 🔖 *Free* ⊙ *Sept.–July, Mon.–Sat. 10–5, Sun. noon–5.*

Museum of Edinburgh. A must-see if you're interested in the details of Old Town life, this house dating from 1570 is home to a fascinating museum of local history, displaying Scottish pottery and Edinburgh silver and glassware. One of the museum's most impressive documents is the National Covenant, signed by Scotland's Presbyterian leadership in 1639. This "profession of faith" begins with not one, but three verses from the Bible. ⊠ *142 Canongate, Old Town* ☎ *0131/529–4143* ⊕ *www.edinburghmuseums.org.uk* 🔖 *Free* ⊙ *Sept.–July, Mon.–Sat. 10–5; Aug., Mon.–Sat. 10–5, Sun. noon–5.*

National Library of Scotland. Founded in 1689, the library has a superb collection of books and manuscripts on the history and culture of Scotland, and also mounts regular exhibitions. Genealogists investigating family trees come here, and amateur family sleuths will find the staff helpful in their research. ⊠ *George IV Bridge, Old Town* ☎ *0131/623–3700* ⊕ *www.nls.uk* 🔖 *Free* ⊙ *Mon., Tues., Thurs., and Fri. 9:30–8:30, Wed. 10–8:30, Sat. 9:30–1. Exhibitions weekdays 10–8, Sat. 10–5, Sun. 2–5.*

Parliament House. This was the seat of Scottish government until 1707, when the governments of Scotland and England were united, 104 years after the union of the two crowns. Partially hidden by the bulk of the High Kirk of St. Giles, it now houses the Supreme Law Courts of Scotland. Interesting exhibits are displayed under the hammer-beam roof of cavernous Parliament Hall. ✉ *11 Parliament Sq., Old Town* ☎ *0131/225–2595* ⊕ *www.scotcourts.gov.uk* ✉ *Free* ⊙ *Weekdays 10–4.*

Scotch Whisky Experience. Transforming malted barley and spring water into one of Scotland's most important exports is the subject of this popular museum. Although the process is not packed with drama, the center manages an imaginative presentation that you take in while riding in low-speed barrel cars. Explore Scotland's diverse whisky regions and the flavors they impart. Sniff the various aromas and decide whether you like fruity, sweet, or smoky, and afterward experts will help you select your perfect dram. Your guide will then allow you access to a vault containing the Diageo Claive Vidiz Scotch Whisky Collection, the world's largest collection of Scotch whiskies. ✉ *354 Castlehill, Old Town* ☎ *0131/220–0441* ⊕ *www.whisky-heritage.co.uk* ✉ *£12.75* ⊙ *Tours daily 10:20–5.*

Writers' Museum. Down a close off Lawnmarket is the 1662 Lady Stair's House, a fine example of 17th-century urban architecture. Inside, the Writer's Museum evokes Scotland's literary past with such exhibits as the letters, possessions, and original manuscripts of Sir Walter Scott, Robert Louis Stevenson, and Robert Burns. The Stevenson collection is particularly compelling. ✉ *Lady Stair's Close, Old Town* ☎ *0131/529–4901* ⊕ *www.edinburghmuseums.org.uk* ✉ *Free* ⊙ *Sept.–July, Mon.–Sat. 10–5; Aug., Mon.–Sat. 10–5, Sun. noon–5.*

NEW TOWN

It was not until the Scottish Enlightenment, a civilizing time of expansion in the 1700s, that the city fathers decided to break away from the Royal Mile's rocky slope and create a new Edinburgh below the castle. This was to become the New Town, with elegant squares, classical facades, wide streets, and harmonious proportions. Clearly, change had to come. At the dawn of the 18th century Edinburgh's unsanitary conditions—primarily a result of overcrowded living quarters—were becoming notorious. The well-known Scots fiddle tune "The Flooers (flowers) of Edinburgh" was only one of many ironic references to the capital's unpleasant environment, which greatly embarrassed the Scot James Boswell (1740–95), biographer and companion of the English lexicographer Dr. Samuel Johnson (1709–84). In his *Journal of a Tour of the Hebrides,* Boswell recalled that on retrieving Johnson from his grubby inn in the Canongate, "I could not prevent his being assailed by the evening effluvia of Edinburgh. . . . Walking the streets at night was pretty perilous and a good deal odoriferous."

To help remedy this sorry state of affairs, in 1767 James Drummond, the city's lord provost (the Scots term for mayor), urged the town council to hold a competition to design a new district for Edinburgh. The winner was an unknown young architect named James Craig (1744–95). His plan called for a grid of three main east–west streets, balanced at either end by two grand squares. These streets survive today, though some of the buildings that line them have been altered

2

A GOOD WALK IN THE NEW TOWN

Start your walk on the Mound, the sloping street that joins the Old and New towns. Two museums immediately east of this great linking ramp, the National Gallery of Scotland and the Royal Scottish Academy, are the work of William Playfair (1789–1857), an architect whose neoclassical buildings contributed greatly to Edinburgh's title: the Athens of the North.

At the foot of the Mound is the city's most famous thoroughfare, Princes Street, the humming center of modern-day Edinburgh. Residents lament the disappearance of the dignified old shops that once lined this street; now a long sequence of chain stores has replaced them, although there is still a grand vista of the castle to the south. A block north is George Street, another row of shops, then one block farther lies Queen Street and the grand National Portrait Gallery.

The essence of the New Town spirit survives in Charlotte Square, at the west end of George Street, and especially in the beautiful Georgian House and West Register House. To explore further, choose your own route northward, down to the wide and elegant streets centering on Moray Place, a fine example of an 1820s development.

by later development. Princes Street is the southernmost, with Queen Street to the north and George Street as the axis, punctuated by St. Andrew and Charlotte squares. A look at the map will reveal a geometric symmetry unusual in Britain. Even the Princes Street Gardens are balanced by the Queen Street Gardens, to the north. Princes Street was conceived as an exclusive residential address, with an open vista facing the castle. It has since been altered by the demands of business and shopping, but the vista remains.

The New Town was expanded several times after Craig's death and now covers an area about three times larger than Craig envisioned. Indeed, some of the most elegant facades came later and can be found by strolling north of the Queen Street Gardens.

PLANNING YOUR TIME   If you want to get the most out of the museums of the New Town, take a whole day and allow at least an hour for each one.

TOP ATTRACTIONS

Georgian House. The National Trust for Scotland has furnished this house in period style to show the elegant domestic arrangements of an affluent family of the late 18th century. The hallway was designed to accommodate sedan chairs, in which 18th-century grandees were carried through the streets. ⊠ *7 Charlotte Sq., New Town* ☏ *0844/493–2117* ⊕ *www.nts.org.uk/visits* ⊡ *£6.50* ☉ *Mar., daily 11–4; Apr.–June, Sept., and Oct., daily 10–5; July and Aug., daily 10–6; Nov., daily 11–3; last admission ½ hr before closing.*

Fodor's Choice
★   **National Gallery of Scotland.** Opened to the public in 1859, the National Gallery presents a wide selection of paintings from the Renaissance to the postimpressionist period within a grand neoclassical building. Most famous are the old-master paintings bequeathed by the Duke of Sutherland, including Titian's *Three Ages of Man*. Many masters are

here; works by Velázquez, El Greco, Rembrandt, Goya, Poussin, Turner, Degas, Monet, and Van Gogh, among others, complement a fine collection of Scottish art, including Sir Henry Raeburn's *Reverend Robert Walker Skating on Duddingston Loch* and other works by Ramsay, Raeburn, and Wilkie. The Weston Link connects the National Gallery of Scotland to the Royal Scottish Academy and includes a restaurant, bar, café, shop, and information center. ⊠ *The Mound, New Town* ☎ *0131/624–6336* ⊕ *www.nationalgalleries.org* ⊠ *Free* ☉ *Fri.–Wed. 10–5, Thurs. 10–7.*

OFF THE
BEATEN
PATH

FAMILY
Fodor's Choice
★

Royal Botanic Garden Edinburgh. Britain's largest rhododendron and azalea gardens are part of this 70-acre garden just north of the city center. An impressive Chinese garden has the largest collection of wild-origin Chinese plants outside China. There's a cafeteria, a visitor center with exhibits exploring biodiversity, and a fabulous gift shop selling plants, books, and gifts. Handsome 18th-century Inverleith House hosts art exhibitions. ■ TIP➔ **Don't miss the soaring palms in the glass-domed Temperate House and the steamy Tropical Palm House.** The hilly rock garden and stream are magical on a sunny day. Guided tours are available. Take a taxi to the garden, or ride Bus 27 from Princes Street or Bus 23 from Hanover Street. To make the 20-minute walk from the New Town, take Dundas Street (the continuation of Hanover Street) and turn left at the clock tower onto Inverleith Row. ⊠ *23 Inverleith Row, Inverleith* ☎ *0131/552–7171* ⊕ *www.rbge.org. uk* ⊠ *Free; greenhouses £4.50* ☉ *Nov.–Jan., daily 10–4; Feb. and Oct. 10–5; Mar.–Sept., daily 10–6.*

Scott Monument. What appears to be a Gothic cathedral spire chopped off and planted in the east end of the Princes Street Gardens is the nation's tribute to Sir Walter—a 200-foot-high monument looming over Princes Street. Built in 1844 in honor of Scotland's most famous author, Sir Walter Scott, the author of *Ivanhoe, Waverley,* and many other novels and poems, it's centered on a marble statue of Scott and his favorite dog, Maida. It's worth taking the time to explore the immediate area, including Princes Street Gardens, one of the prettiest city parks in Britain. In the open-air theater, amid the park's trim flower beds, stately trees, and carefully tended lawns, brass bands occasionally play. Here, too, is the famous **monument to David Livingstone,** whose African meeting with H. M. Stanley is part of Scots-American history. ⊠ *Princes St., New Town* ☎ *0131/529–4068* ⊕ *www.edinburghmuseums.org.uk* ⊠ *£4* ☉ *Apr.–Sept., Mon.–Sat. 10–7, Sun. 10–6; Oct.–Mar., Mon.–Sat 9–4, Sun. 10–6.*

OFF THE
BEATEN
PATH

Scottish National Gallery of Modern Art. This handsome former school building, close to the New Town, displays paintings and sculptures by Pablo Picasso, Georges Braque, Henri Matisse, and André Derain, among others. The gallery houses an excellent restaurant in the basement and lavender-filled garden. Across the street in a former orphanage is the **Gallery of Modern Art Two** (formerly the Dean Gallery), which has Scots-Italian Sir Eduardo Paolozzi's intriguing re-created studio and towering sculpture *Vulcan.* ⊠ *Belford Rd., Dean Village* ☎ *0131/624–6200* ⊕ *www.nationalgalleries.org* ⊠ *Free* ☉ *Daily 10–5.*

Scottish National Portrait Gallery. A magnificent red-sandstone Gothic building dating from 1889 houses this must-see institution. Conceived as a gift to the people of Scotland, the gallery is organized under five broad themes: Reformation, Enlightenment, Empire, Modernity, and Contemporary. The refurbished complex features a photography gallery, a gallery for contemporary art, and a fancy glass elevator. New spaces hold exhibits on various aspects of Scots history and life, including "The Visual Culture of the Jacobite Cause" and "Playing for Scotland: The Making of Modern Sport," plus excellent temporary exhibitions. ⊠ *1 Queen St., New Town* ☎ *0131/624–6200* ⊕ *www.nationalgalleries.org* ⊠ *Free* ☉ *Fri.–Wed. 10–5, Thurs. 10–7.*

WORTH NOTING

Calton Hill. Robert Louis Stevenson's favorite view of his beloved city was from the top of this hill. The architectural styles represented by the extraordinary collection of monuments here include mock Gothic—the Old Observatory, for example—and neoclassical. Under the latter category falls the monument by William Playfair (1789–1857) designed to honor his talented uncle, the geologist and mathematician John Playfair (1748–1819), as well as his cruciform **New Observatory.** The piece that commands the most attention, however, is the so-called **National Monument,** often referred to as "Scotland's Disgrace." Intended to mimic Athens's Parthenon, this monument to the dead of the Napoleonic Wars was started in 1822 to the specifications of a design by Playfair. But in 1830, only 12 columns later, money ran out, and the facade became a monument to high aspirations and poor fundraising. The tallest monument on Calton Hill is the 100-foot-high **Nelson Monument,** completed in 1815 in honor of Britain's naval hero Horatio Nelson (1758–1805); you can climb its 143 steps for sweeping city views. The **Burns Monument** is the circular Corinthian temple below Regent Road. Devotees of Robert Burns may want to visit one other grave—that of Mrs. Agnes McLehose, or "Clarinda," in the Canongate Graveyard. ⊠ *Bounded by Leith St. to the west and Regent Rd. to the south, New Town* ☎ *0131/556–2716* ⊕ *www.edinburghmuseums.org. uk* ⊠ *Nelson Monument £4* ☉ *Nelson Monument Oct.–Mar., Mon.– Sat. 10–3; Apr.–Sept., daily 10–7.*

Charlotte Square. At the west end of George Street is the New Town's centerpiece—an 18th-century square with one of the proudest achievements of Robert Adam, Scotland's noted neoclassical architect. On the north side, Adam designed a palatial facade to unite three separate town houses of such sublime simplicity and perfect proportions that architects come from all over the world to study it. Happily, the Age of Enlightenment grace notes continue within, as the center town house is now occupied by the **Georgian House** museum. ⊠ *West end of George St., New Town.*

OFF THE BEATEN PATH

Edinburgh Zoo. Children love to visit the some 1,000 animals that live in Edinburgh Zoo, especially the two giant pandas—Tian Tian and Yang Gaung—that were flown in from China. Free 20-minute viewing sessions must be booked in advance. The ever-popular Penguin Parade begins at 2:15 (but since penguin participation is totally voluntary, the event is unpredictable). You can even handle some of the animals from

April to September. The zoo spreads over an 80-acre site on the slopes of Corstorphine Hill. Take buses 12, 26, or 31. ⊠ *Corstorphine Rd., 3 miles west of city center, Corstorphine* ☎ *0131/334–9171* ⊕ *www. edinburghzoo.org.uk* 🖭 *£16* ⊘ *Apr.–Sept., daily 9–6; Oct. and Mar., daily 9–5; Nov.–Feb., daily 9–4:30.*

George Street. With its upscale shops and handsome Georgian frontages, this is a more pleasant, less crowded street for wandering than Princes Street. The **statue of King George IV,** at the intersection of George and Hanover streets, recalls the visit of George IV to Scotland in 1822. He was the first British monarch to do so since King Charles II, in the 17th century. By the 19th century enough time had passed since the Jacobite Uprising of 1745 for Scotland to be perceived at Westminster as being safe enough for a monarch to visit.

The ubiquitous Sir Walter Scott turns up farther down the street. It was at a grand dinner in the **Assembly Rooms,** between Hanover and Frederick streets, that Scott acknowledged having written the Waverley novels (the name of the author had hitherto been a secret, albeit a badly kept one). You can meet Scott once again, in the form of a plaque just downhill, at 39 Castle Street, his Edinburgh address before he moved to Abbotsford, in the Borders region, where he died in 1832. ⊠ *Between Charlotte and St. Andrew Squares, New Town.*

Moray Place. With its "pendants" of Ainslie Place and Randolph Crescent, Moray Place was laid out in 1822 by the Earl of Moray. From the start the homes were planned to be of particularly high quality, with lovely curving facades, imposing porticos, and a central secluded garden reserved for residents. ⊠ *Between Charlotte Sq. and Water of Leith, New Town.*

The Mound. This rising street originated from the need for a dry-shod crossing of the muddy quagmire left behind when Nor' Loch, the body of water below the castle, was drained (the railway now cuts through this area). Work is said to have been started by a local tailor, George Boyd, who tired of struggling through the mud en route to his Old Town shop. The building of a ramp was under way by 1781, and by the time of its completion, in 1830, "Geordie Boyd's mud brig," as it was first known, had been built up with an estimated 2 million cartloads of earth dug from the foundations of the New Town. ⊠ *From Princes St. to George IV Bridge, New Town.*

Princes Street. The south side of this well-planned street is occupied by the well-kept Princes Street Gardens, which act as a wide green moat to the castle on its rock. The north side is now one long sequence of chain stores with unappealing modern fronts apart from the handsome Victorian facade of Jenners department store. ⊠ *Waterloo Pl. to Lothian Rd., New Town.*

Register House. Scotland's first custom-built archives depository, Register House, designed by the great Robert Adam, was partly funded by the sale of estates forfeited by Jacobite landowners after their last rebellion in Britain (1745–46). Work on the Regency-style building, which marks the end of Princes Street, started in 1774. The statue in front is of the first duke of Wellington (1769–1852). The recently installed

Ancestor Hunting

Are you a Cameron or a Campbell, Mackenzie or Macdonald? If so, you may be one of the more than 25 million people of Scottish descent around the world. It was the Highland clearances of the 18th and 19th century, in which tenant farmers were driven from their homes and replaced with sheep, that started the mass emigration to North America and Australia. Before or during a trip, you can do a little genealogical research or pursue your family tree more seriously.

VisitScotland (⊕ *www. ancestralscotland.com*) has information about clans and surnames, books, and family-history societies. At the Register House, the new ScotlandsPeople Centre (⊕ *www.scotlandspeople.gov.uk*) is the place to dip into the past or conduct in-depth genealogical research.

Willing to pay for help? Companies such as Scottish Ancestral Trail (⊕ *www.scottish-ancestral-trail. co.uk*) do the research and plan a trip around your family history. Throughout Scotland, you can check bookstores for information and visit clan museums and societies.

ScotlandsPeople Centre lets you conduct genealogical research. Free weekday research sessions, from 10 to 2 and 2 and 4, meet growing interest in Scots family history. Access to public records and the library is £15 per day. ⊠ *2 Princes St., New Town* ☎ *0131/314–4300* ⊕ *www. scotlandspeoplehub.gov.uk* ⊞ *Free* ⊙ *Weekdays 9–4:30.*

QUICK BITES
Café Royal. This café serves good Scottish lagers and ales, and simple lunch items and, of course, oysters. The 18th-century building has bags of character, with ornate tiles, stained-glass windows and—allegedly—its own ghost. ⊠ *19 W. Register St., New Town* ☎ *0131/556–1884* ⊕ *www.caferoyaledinburgh.co.uk.*

Royal Scottish Academy. Worth visiting for a look at the imposing, neo-classic architecture, this William Playfair–designed structure hosts temporary art exhibitions. The underground Weston Link connects the museum to the National Gallery of Scotland. ⊠ *The Mound, New Town* ☎ *0131/225–6671* ⊕ *www.royalscottishacademy.org* ⊞ *Free* ⊙ *Mon.– Sat. 10–5, Sun. noon–5.*

Waterloo Place. The fine neoclassical architecture on this street was designed as a piece by Archibald Elliot (d. 1823) in 1815. Waterloo Place extends over Regent Bridge, bounded by the 1815 **Regent Arch,** a simple, triumphal Corinthian-column war memorial at the center of Ionic screens bordering the bridge. ⊠ *Eastern extension of Princes St., New Town.*

Leith, Edinburgh's Seaport

On the south shore of the Firth of Forth, Leith was a separate town until it merged with the city in 1920. After World War II and up until the 1980s, the declining seaport had a reputation for poverty and crime. In recent years, however, it has been revitalized with the restoration of commercial buildings as well as the construction of new luxury housing, bringing a buzz of trendiness. All the docks have been redeveloped; the Old East and West docks are now the administrative headquarters of the Scottish Executive. Plans are afoot to make the docks a hub of renewable energy industries.

In earlier times, Leith was the stage for many historic happenings. In 1560 Mary of Guise, the mother of Mary, Queen of Scots, ruled Scotland from Leith; her daughter landed in Leith the following year to embark on her infamous reign. A century later, Cromwell led his troops to Leith to root out Scots royalists. An arch of the Leith Citadel reminds all of the Scots' victory. Leith also prides itself on being a "home of golf," because official rules to the game were devised in 1744, in what is today Links Park. The rolling green mounds here hide the former field and cannon sites of past battles.

LEITH

Just north of the city is Edinburgh's port, a place brimming with seafaring history and undergoing a slow revival after years of postwar neglect. It may not be as pristine as much of modern-day Edinburgh, but there are plenty of cobbled streets, dockside buildings, and bobbing boats to capture your imagination. Here along the lowest reaches of the Water of Leith (the river that flows through town), you'll find plenty of shops, pubs, and restaurants. Leith's major attraction is the former royal yacht *Britannia,* moored outside the huge Ocean Terminal shopping mall. Reach Leith by walking down Leith Street and Leith Walk, from the east end of Princes Street (20 to 30 minutes), or take Lothian Bus 22 (Britannia Ocean Drive, Leith).

WORTH NOTING

Britannia. Moored on the waterfront at Leith, Edinburgh's port north of the city center, is the former Royal Yacht *Britannia*, launched in Scotland in 1953 and now retired to her home country. The Royal Apartments and the more functional engine room, bridge, galleys, and captain's cabin are all open to view. The land-based visitor center within the huge Ocean Terminal shopping mall has exhibits and photographs about the yacht's history. ⊠ *Ocean Terminal, Leith* ☎ *0131/555–5566* ⊕ *www.royalyachtbritannia.co.uk* ⊠ *£12* ⊙ *Mar.–Oct., daily 9:30–4; Nov.–Feb., daily 10–3:30.*

HAYMARKET

West of the Old Town and south of the West End is Haymarket, a district with its own down-to-earth character and well-worn charm. It offers varied shopping and dining options that become more upmarket as you head toward the West End and Leith.

2

WEST END

Handsome Georgian town houses give this neighborhood a dignified feel. People head here for the small boutiques and cafés, as well as the wide range of cultural venues.

SOUTH SIDE

This residential district offers a peek at the comings and goings of regular Edinburghers. Here you'll find lots of affordable restaurants and B&Bs for cost-conscious visitors.

WHERE TO EAT

Edinburgh's eclectic restaurant scene has attracted a brigade of well-known chefs, including the award-winning trio of Martin Wishart, Tom Kitchin, and Paul Kitching. They and dozens of others have abandoned the tried-and-true recipes for more adventurous cuisine. Of course, you can always find traditional fare, which usually mean the Scottish-French style that harks back to the historical "Auld Alliance" of the 13th century. The Scots element is the preference for fresh and local foodstuffs; the French supply the sauces. In Edinburgh you can sample anything from Malaysian *rendang* (a thick, coconut-milk stew) to Kurdish kebabs, while the long-established French, Italian, Chinese, Pakistani, and Indian communities ensure that the majority of the globe's most treasured cuisines are well represented.

PRICES AND HOURS

It's possible to eat well in Edinburgh without spending a fortune. Multicourse prix-fixe options are common, and almost always less expensive than ordering à la carte. Even at restaurants in the highest price category, you can easily spend less than £30 per person. People tend to eat later in Scotland than in England—around 8 pm on average—or rather they finish eating and then drink on in leisurely Scottish fashion. *Prices in the reviews are the average cost of a main course at dinner or, if dinner is not served, at lunch.*

OLD TOWN

Use the coordinate (✥ B2) at the end of each listing to locate a site on the corresponding map.

The most historic part of the city houses the grander restaurants that many people associate with this city. It is also home to some of Edinburgh's oldest pubs, which serve informal meals.

$$
MODERN BRITISH ✕**Angels with Bagpipes.** The name may amuse or bemuse you, but there's no doubt this relaxed spot with windows overlooking the Royal Mile provides good-value, refined dining. Within the 16th-century building the understated decor includes a sculptural centerpiece of an angel with bagpipes copied from a carving in nearby St. Giles Cathedral. Menus are straightforward and not overlong, the service is slick, and the atmosphere is warm. Seafood and game dominate, with dishes such as hake

with chorizo and venison with red cabbage. For the best value, opt for the table d'hôte menu, available between noon and 6, with two courses for £13.95 and three for £17.95. $ *Average main: £18* ✉ *343 High St., Old Town* ☎ *0131/220–1111* ⊕ *www.angelswithbagpipes.co.uk* ✚ *G4.*

$

MODERN BRITISH

✕ **David Bann.** In the heart of the Old Town, this ultrahip eatery serving vegetarian and vegan favorites attracts young locals with its light, airy, modern dining room. Drinking water comes with mint and strawberries; the sizable and creative dishes include mushroom risotto and Jerusalem artichoke in puff pastry. The food is so flavorful that carnivores may forget they're eating vegetarian, especially with dishes like mushroom strudel with celeriac sauce. $ *Average main: £12* ✉ *56–58 St. Mary's St., Old Town* ☎ *0131/556–5888* ⊕ *www.davidbann.com* ✚ *H4.*

$

BRITISH

✕ **Doric Tavern.** Edinburgh's original gastropub offers a languid bistro environment and serves reliable Scots favorites. The menu has such daily-changing items as honey-baked salmon with oatcakes, and specialties include haggis, neeps and tatties, and grilled steaks. Try the creamy Cullen skink soup for a filling, good-value lunchtime choice. The stripped-wood interiors upstairs have been spruced up. The Doric is handy for rail travelers, as it's near Waverley Station. Sunday lunch includes a tradtional roast of Border beef with all the trimmings. $ *Average main: £13* ✉ *15/16 Market St., Old Town* ☎ *0131/225–1084* ⊕ *www.the-doric.com* ⌁ *Reservations essential* ✚ *G3.*

$

MIDDLE EASTERN

✕ **Hanam's.** A stone's throw from the castle, this enticing place transports you to the Middle East. Kurdish cuisine may not be as exalted as others in that region, but the *bayengaan surocrau* (marinated eggplant) and the lamb *tashreeb* (a kind of casserole) will convince you that it's among the best. There's also a great range of kebabs and more familiar Lebanese options. The deep-red interiors have a relaxed Middle Eastern vibe. It's possible to smoke a hookah pipe on the heated terrace, and you can bring your own alcohol. $ *Average main: £12* ✉ *3 Johnston Terr., Old Town* ☎ *0131/225–1329* ⊕ *www.hanams.com* ✚ *F4.*

$$

BRITISH

✕ **Howie's.** This chain of stylish neighborhood bistros serves contemporary Scottish fare—think lots of fresh local produce, fish, and game. The steaks are tender Aberdeen beef, and the Loch Fyne herring is sweet-cured to Howie's own recipe. The decor includes modern wood furnishings and warm colors—it's smart and understated. Try the fixed-price two-course lunch, a bargain at £9.95. There's another location at 29 Waterloo Place in the East End. $ *Average main: £16* ✉ *10–14 Victoria St., Old Town* ☎ *0131/225–1721* ⊕ *www.howies.uk.com* ✚ *F4.*

$$

FRENCH

✕ **La Garrigue.** Edinburgh is blessed with several affordable French bistros, and this is one of the best. Although the modern decor evokes Paris, the food has the rustic flavor of the Languedoc region. Regional favorites include a starter of croquette of slow-cooked pig's head and such main dishes as braised lamb shank and a casserole of shin of beef in a red wine sauce. Desserts such as a lavender crème brûlée offer a light finale to a heady dining experience. Ask about the lunch and dinner specials, which include a glass of house wine and coffee. $ *Average main: £16* ✉ *31 Jeffrey St., Old Town* ☎ *0131/557–3032* ⊕ *www.lagarrigue.co.uk* ✚ *H3.*

2

$

MODERN BRITISH

× **Michael Neave.** Young chef Michael Neave delivers fine food at reasonable prices in his restaurant just off the Royal Mile. Down an old close is this modern edifice with tranquil terrace. The downstairs dining area lacks much warmth, but the whisky bar upstairs sparkles. Quality Scots produce stars in dishes influenced by Asian and European cuisines: the west coast scallops with celeriac puree, black pudding, and caviar butter makes a wonderful starter. Meaty mains match Aberdeen Angus steaks, Perthshire venison, and roasted duck breast with imaginative sauces and beautifully cooked vegetables. Seafood lovers will enjoy the sea bass with crab and crayfish. Desserts inlcude a delicious pear tarte tatin with whisky marmalade ice cream. ■TIP→ **Two-course express lunches are a bargain at £7.95** ⑤ *Average main: £15* ⊠ *21 Old Fishmarket Close, Old Town* ☎ *0131/226–4747* ⊕ *www.michaelneave.co.uk* ⊗ *Closed Sun. and Mon.* ✛ *G4.*

$

INDIAN

× **Mother India Cafe.** Despite its popularity, good Indian food is hard to find in Scotland. Not so at this humble eatery, where the emphasis is on home-style cooking. A good selection of small dishes means you can sample the myriad flavors. The lamb *karahi* (a Pakistani curry made in a woklike pot) is particularly recommended, as are any of the fish dishes. The split-level dining area is smart and contemporary. ⑤ *Average main: £12* ⊠ *3–5 Infirmary St., Old Town* ☎ *0131/524–9801* ⊕ *www.motherindiaglasgow.co.uk* ✛ *H4.*

$$$

SEAFOOD

× **Ondine.** This fabulous seafood restaurant off the Royal Mile is making waves with its expertly prepared dishes from sustainable fishing sources. A wall of windows shines bountiful amounts of sunlight on an attractive monochromatic dining room and an art deco oyster bar. Standout starters include smoked salmon with horseradish cream and squid tempura with a tasty Vietnamese dipping sauce. Other briny delights include the juicy Shetland mussel marinière, Isle of Skye lobster thermidor, and wild Cornish sea bass. Traditional puddings include a treacle tart with clotted cream. The wine list is strong on old-world whites. ⑤ *Average main: £20* ⊠ *2 George IV Bridge, Old Town* ☎ *0131/226 1888* ⊕ *www.ondinerestaurant.co.uk* ⊛ *Reservations essential* ⊗ *Closed Sun.* ✛ *G4.*

$$

FRENCH

× **Petit Paris.** Even in typical Scottish weather it's possible to get a taste of warmer climes at this little bistro on the cobbled Grassmarket, cheerfully decorated with checked tablecloths, copper pots, and bunches of garlic. The staff is predominantly French, and the emphasis is on casual dining, local produce, and home cooking. Try the traditional French blood sausage and slow-baked rabbit with Dijon-mustard sauce. The £12.90 lunch/pretheater meal is a bargain. ⑤ *Average main: £16* ⊠ *38/40 Grassmarket, Old Town* ☎ *0131/226–2442* ⊕ *www.petitparis-restaurant.co.uk* ✛ *E5.*

$

THAI

× **Thai Orchid.** A golden Buddha, beautiful flowers, a traditionally dressed staff, and spicy cuisine transport you to Thailand, if only for a few hours. To start, try the *todd mun kao pode* (deep-fried corn cakes with a sweet-and-sour peanut-and-coriander dip). Tasty main courses include *pla priew wan* (monkfish poached with coconut milk) or *pedt Orchid,* duck stir-fried with mango, chili, garlic, and red peppers. The sticky rice with coconut milk and mango is a dessert not to

BEST BETS FOR EDINBURGH DINING

Where can you find the best food Edinburgh has to offer? Fodor's writers and editors have selected their favorite restaurants by price, cuisine, and experience in the lists below. In the first column, the Fodor's Choice properties represent the "best of the best" across price categories. You can also search by neighborhood for excellent eating experiences—just peruse our complete reviews on the following pages.

Fodor'sChoice★

Galvin Brasserie de Luxe $$, p. 72

Kalpna $, p. 75

Mark Greenaway, $$$, p. 73

Martin Wishart, $$$$, p. 77

Number One, $$$$, p. 73

Wedgwood, $$, p. 69

By Price

$

Chop Chop, p. 74

David Bann, p. 66

Kalpna, p. 75

$$

Galvin Brasserie De Luxe, p. 72

Wedgwood, p. 69

$$$

Mark Greenaway, p. 73

$$$$

Martin Wishart, p. 77

Number One, p. 73

By Cuisine

CHINESE

Chop Chop, $, p. 74

Jasmine, $, p. 75

FRENCH

Kitchin, $$$$, p. 76

La Garrigue, $$, p. 66

L'escargot Bleu, $$, p. 73

Martin Wishart, $$$$, p. 77

Pompadour, $$$$, p. 73

INDIAN

Kalpna, $, p. 75

Mother India Cafe, $, p. 67

MODERN BRITISH

21212, $$$$, p. 69

Mark Greenaway, $$$, p. 73

Howie's, $$, p. 66

Wedgwood, $$, p. 69

SEAFOOD

The King's Wark, $, p. 76

Ondine, $$$, p. 67

SPANISH

Rafael's, $$, p. 74

VEGETARIAN

David Bann, $, p. 66

Henderson's, $, p. 72

By Experience

BEST PRETHEATER EATS

Howie's, $$, p. 66

La Garrigue, $$, p. 66

BEST VIEW

Angels with Bagpipes, $$, p. 65

Forth Floor, $$$, p. 72

Ondine, $$$, p. 67

HOT SPOTS

Forth Floor, $$$, p. 72

L'escargot Bleu, $$, p. 73

MOST KID-FRIENDLY

Galvin Brasserie de Luxe, $$, p. 72

Howie's, $$, p. 66

MOST ROMANTIC

Le Café St. Honore, $$$, p. 72

The Witchery, $$$$, p. 69

be missed. The decor is contemporary, with banquette seating and lots of natural wood. $ *Average main: £12* ⊠ *5A Johnston Terr., Old Town* ☎ *0131/225–6633* ⊕ *www.thaiorchid.uk.com* ✢ *F4.*

$$ ✗ **Wedgwood.** Rejecting the idea that fine dining should be a stuffy affair, owners Paul Wedgwood and Lisa Channon opened this Royal Mile gem. The dining space is smart but informal, and the professional staff has mastered the tricky task of giving guests space to relax while remaining attentive. But Wedgwood's food is the standout. Flavorful local produce and some unusual foraged fronds enliven the taste buds. Asian, European, and traditional Scottish influences are apparent in dishes such as monkfish tail with shellfish paella and ham, and braised beef and mushroom ballotine. Save space for seasonal sweets like rhubarb-and-blackcurrant fool and sticky toffee pudding. Consider the great two- and three-course lunch deals (£12 and £16). $ *Average main: £18* ⊠ *267 Canongate, Old Town* ☎ *0131/558–8737* ⊕ *www. wedgwoodtherestaurant.co.uk* ⋒ *Reservations essential* ✢ *H3.*

MODERN BRITISH

Fodor'sChoice

★

$$ MODERN BRITISH

$$$$ ✗ **The Witchery.** The hundreds of "witches" who were executed on Castlehill, just yards from where you'll be seated, are the inspiration for this outstanding and atmospheric restaurant. The cavernous interior, complete with flickering candlelight, is festooned with cabalistic insignia and tarot-card characters. Gilded and painted ceilings reflect the close links between France and Scotland, as does the menu, which includes steak tartare, roasted quail with braised endive, shellfish bisque, and herb-baked scallops. Two-course pre- and posttheater (5:30–6:30 and 10:30–11:30) specials let you sample the exceptional cuisine for just £15.95. $ *Average main: £27* ⊠ *Castlehill, Old Town* ☎ *0131/225–5613* ⊕ *www.thewitchery.com* ⋒ *Reservations essential* ✢ *F4.*

MODERN BRITISH

NEW TOWN

Use the coordinate (✢ B2) at the end of each listing to locate a site on the corresponding map.

The New Town, with its striking street plan, ambitious architecture, and professional crowd, has restaurants where you can get everything from a quick snack to a more formal dinner.

$$$$ ✗ **21212.** Paul Kitching is one of Britain's most innovative chefs, and the theatrical dining experience at 21212 delivers surprises galore. In a grand Georgian house, the restaurant is sumptuously appointed. Belle époque decor and quirky cultlery make this a perfect destination for couples, who should ask for a romantic alcove window table. On display behind a large glass screen is a small army of chefs assembling the intricate dishes—perhaps a touch over-reverential, but thankfully the knowledgable and enthusiastic staff creates a relaxed atmosphere in the dining room. On the fixed-price menus you can expect creative takes on old classics, such as deconstructed fish-and-chips and intriguing desserts such as a layered banana trifle with apricot compote. $ *Average main: £67* ⊠ *3 Royal Terr., New Town* ☎ *0131/523–1030* ⊕ *www.21212restaurant.co.uk* ⋒ *Reservations essential* ✢ *H1.*

MODERN BRITISH

Where to Eat and Stay in Edinburgh

A   **B**   **C**   **D**

1

South Learmonth Gardens

Channings

Inverleith Hotel

Rafael's

Moray Place

Gloucester La.

India St.

Heriot Row

Howe St.

2

Water of Leith

Dean Bridge

QUEEN ST. GARDEN

Queen St.

Ainslie Place

Mark Greenaway

Le Café St. Honoré

Thistle St.

N Charlotte St.

Castle St.

George St.

Charlotte

Tigerlilly

Rose St.

3

Belford Rd.

Queensferry St.

S Charlotte St.

Princes S

B&B Edinburgh

The Bonham

Drums-heugh Gardens

Square

Rothesay Pl.

Howie's

Hope St.

WEST PRINCES STREET GARDENS

WEST END

Melville St.

Alva St.

Rutland Hotel

Pompadour

Caledonian

4

Chester St.

Manor Pl.

William St.

Melville St.

Galvin Brasserie de Luxe

Victorian Town House

Palmerston Pl.

West Maitland

King's Stables Rd.

Lothian Rd.

Grindlay St.

5

Grosvenor St.

First Coast

Chop Chop

Kew House and Apartments

Jasmine

Morrison St.

Bread St.

HAYMARKET STATION

HAYMARKET

Fountainbridge

Knight Residence

Dalry

Earl Gray St.

Lauriston P

6

Home St.

TOLLCROS

KEY

- ■ *Restaurants*
- □ *Hotels*
- ▬ *Pedestrian Zone*
- ├──┤ *Rail Lines*
- 🛈 *Tourist Information*
- ✦ *following dining and lodging reviews indicates a map-grid coordinate*

A   **B**   **C**   **D**

E   **F**   **G**   **H**

Dundas St.

↑ □ Ardenlee Guesthouse
  □ The Howard
  □ Walton Hotel

The Conifers □
L'escargot Bleu ■

21212 ■
Al Dente ■
Fishers Bistro ■
The King's Wark ■
Los Cardos ■
Martin Wishart ■
The Kitchin ■

1

Gerald's Place □

NEW
OWN

21212 □
Ardmor House □
Fraoch House □
The Glasshouse □
Malmaison □

St. Andrew St.

ST. JAMES
CENTRE

Leith St.

Calton Hill

Henderson's ■

Fishers in the City ■

St. David St.

St. Andrew Square

Forth Floor ■

Valvona
& Crolla
VinCaffe ■

West Register St.

Howie's ■

*Calton
Burial
Ground*

NELSON
MONUMENT ◆

Regent Rd.

2

George St.   Hanover St.

Waterloo Pl.

Number One ■
Balmoral Hotel ■

EDINBURGH
WAVERLEY
STATION

Calton Rd.

erick St.

The Mound

ℹ

North Bridge

E. Market St.

3

NATIONAL
GALLERY OF
SCOTLAND

Ramsay Ln.   Bank St.

The Scotsman □

Doric
Tavern ■

Jeffrey St.
La Garrigue ■

Wedgwood ■

Canongate

OLD
TOWN

Market St.

Cockburn St.

Royal Mile

St. Mary's St.

DINBURGH
CASTLE

Angels with
Bagpipes ■

CITY
CHAMBERS

High St.

Upper Bow

The Witchery
Witchery ■

Lawnmarket

Hotel
Missoni □ Ondine ■

ST. GILES
CATHEDRAL

Radisson Blu
Edinburgh ■

Michael
Neave ■

Old Fishmarket Close

Blackfriars St.

David Bann ■

4

Esplanade

Hanam's ■

Howie's ■

Victoria St.

PARLIAMENT
SQUARE

Cowgate

Mother India Cafe ■

Johnston Ter.

W. Bow   Thai Orchid ■

Cowgate

George IV Bridge

Chambers St.

South Bridge

Drummond St.

Petit Paris ■

GRASSMARKET

Candlemaker Row

ROYAL MUSEUM
AND MUSEUM
OF SCOTLAND

est Port Ter.

The Vennel

FLODDEN
WALL

Greyfriars
Pl.

Hotel du Vin □

Ten Hill Place □

5

Bonsai ■

Lauriston Pl.

Middle Meadow Walk

Buccleuch St.

Nicolson St.

Chalmers St.

⊕

0   1/8 mi
0   1/5 km

*George
Square*

Howie's ■
94DR □
AmarAgua □
Ashdene House □
Glenalmond House □
Teviotdale House □
23 Mayfield □

Kalpna ■
Prestonfield □

6

E   **F**   **G**   **H**

$$$
MODERN BRITISH

✕ **Forth Floor.** Harvey Nichols has become synonymous with chic shopping, so it stands to reason that the department store's restaurant is no slouch when it comes to style. The decor pulls off the trick of being minimalist without being too severe. Factor in a glorious view over Princes Street Gardens and Edinburgh Castle and it's a winner from the moment you walk in the door. The imaginative menu devised by chef Stuart Muir lives up to the lofty location. Scallops served with spring cabbage and pea mousse, and clam-and-cider chowder make for healthy starters, while the roast saddle of Highland venison and North Atlantic halibut with langoustines are memorable mains. ■TIP→ **Ask for a window or terrace table—weather permitting, of course.** ⑤ *Average main: £23* ✉ *Harvey Nichols, 30–34 St. Andrew Sq., New Town* ☎ *0131/524–8350* ⊕ *www.harveynichols.com* ⚞ *Reservations essential* ⊘ *No dinner Sun. and Mon.* ✚ *G2.*

$$
BRASSERIE
FAMILY
Fodor's Choice
★

✕ **Galvin Brasserie de Luxe.** This Parisian-style brasserie combines handsome surroundings with first-class cuisine from London brothers Chris and Jeff Galvin. Dapper waiters glide around the cavernous dining area with a central bar and blue banquette seating. The menu stars such classic French dishes as steak tartare, duck confit, and pork cassoulet alongside Scots staples like Loch Creran oysters, smoked salmon, and haggis. On Sunday, expect hearty, traditional options like slow roast beef brisket with trimmings for £15. Desserts include the melt-in-the-mouth meringue *oeuf a la neige* (eggs in snow). The wine list is extensive, and the staff knowledgable. ■TIP→ **A decent children's menu makes this a popular spot for families.** ⑤ *Average main: £18* ✉ *The Caledonian, Princes St., New Town* ☎ *0131/222 8988* ⊕ *www.galvinrestaurants.com* ✚ *C4.*

$
VEGETARIAN

✕ **Henderson's.** Edinburgh's pioneering canteen-style vegetarian restaurant opened in 1962, long before it was fashionable to serve healthy, meatless creations. The salad bar has more than a dozen different offerings each day, and a massive plateful costs £8. Tasty hot options include Moroccan stew with couscous and moussaka. Live mellow music plays six nights a week, and there's an art gallery as well. Around the corner on Thistle Street is the Bistro, from the same proprietors; it serves snacks, meals, and decadent desserts such as chocolate fondue. ■TIP→ **Drop by the fabulous deli for picnic supplies, including wonderful organic bread and pastries.** ⑤ *Average main: £8* ✉ *94 Hanover St., New Town* ☎ *0131/225–2605* ⊕ *www.hendersonsofedinburgh.co.uk* ⊘ *Closed Sun* ✚ *E2.*

$$$
FRENCH

✕ **Le Café St Honoré.** Chef Neil Forbes' quintessentially Parisian-style café champions sustainable local produce. From the moment you enter the beautifully lighted room you're transported into the decadently stylish belle époque. A concise menu that changes daily leaves more time for chatting. You might start off with a warm salad of scallops, monkfish, chorizo, and pine nuts, followed by Perthshire venison, North Sea hake, or Scotch shepherd's pie. ⑤ *Average main: £20* ✉ *34 N.W. Thistle Street La., New Town* ☎ *0131/226–2211* ⊕ *www.cafesthonore.com* ✚ *D2.*

2

$$ **✕ L'escargot Bleu.** Anyone still laboring under the misconception that
FRENCH French cuisine is pretentious should pay a visit to this gem. In one of
the city's trendiest quarters, this venture from the former co-owner of
Petit Paris would make anyone from France feel at home. The wel-
come is warm, the stripped wooden floors and period French posters
add to a convivial atmosphere that is loud and proud, and the food is
as authentic as gendarme whistling "La Marseillaise." Classic dishes
like snails in parsley butter and beef bourguignon certainly fly the tri-
color. ■ TIP→ Follow your nose to the French deli in the basement. $ *Av-
erage main: £18* ✉ *56A Broughton St., New Town* ☎ *0131/557–1600*
⊕ *www.lescargotbleu.co.uk* ⚐ *Reservations essential* ☾ *Sun.* ✛ *G1.*

$$$ **✕ Mark Greenaway.** Run by the talented star of the BBC's *Great British*
MODERN BRITISH *Menu*, this restaurant offers wonderful seasonal dishes and indulgent
Fodor'sChoice desserts. Greenaway's culinary style is perfectly reflected by the ele-
★ gant Georgian dining room's fireplace and gleaming brass chandeliers.
For an affordable introduction to his cooking, try the market menu
(£16.50 and £20 for two or three courses); main dishes might include
slow-roast pork or pan-seared cod fillet. Go à la carte for dishes like
pan-roasted hake fillet with lobster tortellini. The signature desserts
include his famed knot chocolate tart with popping candy. ■ TIP→ Ask
the sommelier for a tour of the wine cellar, in an old bank vault. $ *Average
main: £23* ✉ *69 N. Castle St., New Town* ☎ *0131/226–1155* ⊕ *www.
markgreenaway.com* ⚐ *Reservations essential* ✛ *D2.*

$$$$ **✕ Number One.** Clublike but unstuffy, this basement restaurant with a
BRITISH thoughtful layout perfect for intimate dining serves the best of Scot-
Fodor'sChoice tish seafood and meat within the Edwardian splendor of the Balmoral
★ Hotel. The regular three-course prix-fixe is £68; for special occasions, choose the chef's six-course tasting menu with amuse-bouche
delights, gourmet breads, and exquisite creations highlighting west
coast scallops, halibut, monkfish, beef, and lamb for £75. Desserts
include a rich, bitter chocolate and orange soufflé and the lighter,
candy-store-inspired hibiscus panna cotta. Service is impeccable and
friendly. $ *Average main: £68* ✉ *Balmoral Hotel, Princes St., New
Town* ☎ *0131/557–6727* ⊕ *www.restaurantnumberone.com* ⚐ *Reservations essential* ☾ *No lunch* ✛ *G2.*

$$$$ **✕ Pompadour.** Sophisticated surroundings and sumptuous cuisine make
FRENCH FUSION this restaurant dating from 1925 one of Edinburgh's best spots for
special occasions. London chef–restaurateur brothers Jeff and Chris
Galvin impart their expertise and high standards in the classic French
food and impressive wine list. Expect exquisite dishes that let quality
produce shine: Tamworth pork, rabbit, Isle of Skye crab, and Keltic
scallops, for example. Desserts include apple tarte tartin and lemon
thyme soufflé. The seasonal menu offers the best value, going for
£30 for three courses. For a splurge, go for the three-course gour-
mand menu and the sommelier's wine pairings. $ *Average main: £58*
✉ *The Caladonian, Princes St., New Town* ☎ *0131/222–8888* ⊕ *www.
thecaledonianedinburgh.com* ⚐ *Reservations essential* ☾ *Closed Sun.
and Mon. No lunch* ✛ *C4.*

$$ ✕**Rafael's.** In a pink-hued basement room replete with eccentric trinkets,
SPANISH the quaint restaurant is clearly not in thrall to prevailing trends, and is
all the better for it. Not only does chef/proprietor/all-around-good guy
Rafael Torrubia create affordably priced masterpieces with an Iberian
twist, he's also likely to deliver dishes such as a sea bass and salmon
duo with pesto or a wonderfully authentic tortilla with chorizo to your
table himself. Despite his Spanish background, Torrubia's use of ingre-
dients such as curry in his sauces shows that as well as being a man of
the people, he is also a man of the world. $ *Average main: £16* ⊠ *2
Deanhaugh St., New Town* ☎ *0131/332–1469* ⊕ *www.rafaels-bistro.
wikidot.com* ⊘ *Closed Sun. and Mon. No lunch* ✛ *D1.*

$$ ✕**Valvona & Crolla VinCaffe.** Every Scot with a passion for food knows
ITALIAN Valvona & Crolla, the country's first Italian delicatessen and wine mer-
chant. This eatery of the same name may lack the old-world feel of the
original on Elm Row, but the menu created by food writer and cook
Mary Contini is as wonderful as you would expect. The fare is relatively simple, but the quality of the ingredients ensures that treats such
as the pizza capricciosa, fried calamari, and linguine with crab meat do
nothing to tarnish the brand's reputation. $ *Average main: £15* ⊠ *11
Multrees Walk, New Town* ☎ *0131/557–0088* ⊕ *www.valvonacrolla.
co.uk* ⊘ *No dinner Sun.* ✛ *G2.*

HAYMARKET

*Use the coordinate (✛ B2) at the end of each listing to locate a site on
the corresponding map.*

This area has many restaurants that tend to be more affordable than
those in the center of town.

$ ✕**Chop Chop.** Authentic Chinese cuisine created by skilled chefs and
CHINESE served in a friendly dining room make this place especially popular.
Since arriving in Edinburgh from northern China, Jian Wang has won
many awards. Expect flavorful, robust creations like the trademark
dumplings with spiced minced meat or vegetables, spicy squid with
garlic, and lamb with cumin. The large eatery has splashes of Chinese
red and is suitably relaxed. $ *Average main: £11* ⊠ *248 Morrison St.,
Haymarket* ☎ *0131/221–1155* ⊕ *www.chop-chop.co.uk* ✛ *A5.*

$ ✕**First Coast.** This laid-back bistro, just a few minutes from Haymar-
BRITISH ket Station, has won a loyal following. Hardwood floors, stone walls,
soft blue hues, and seaside paintings add to the coastal theme. Savory
temptations include roasted butternut squash with chestnut-and-apple
salad; panfried sea bass with fennel, mustard, and ginger; and Aberdeen Angus sirloin with tomato-and-red-onion salad. The international wine list is as varied as the daily specials. $ *Average main:
£13* ⊠ *99–101 Dalry Rd., Haymarket* ☎ *0131/313–4404* ⊕ *www.first-
coast.co.uk* ⊘ *Closed Sun.* ✛ *A5.*

WEST END AND POINTS WEST

Use the coordinate (✣ B2) at the end of each listing to locate a site on the corresponding map.

Even after business hours, the city's commercial center is the place to find a variety of international restaurants.

$ ✕ **Jasmine.** Seafood matched with just the right spices is the main attrac-
CHINESE tion of this small, friendly Cantonese restaurant. Standout dishes at the long-established place include steamed sea bass with ginger and spring onions, and chicken with peanut sauce. Flickering candles add a relaxing feel to the interior, although the tables are quite closely spaced and the decor is looking a little dated. Prix-fixe lunches, starting at £9.50 for three courses, are a good value. A take-out menu is available. ⑤ *Average main: £13* ⊠ *32 Grindlay St., West End* ☎ *0131/229–5757* ⊕ *www.jasminechinese.co.uk* ✣ *D5.*

SOUTH SIDE

Use the coordinate (✣ B2) at the end of each listing to locate a site on the corresponding map.

The presence of university professors and students means eateries that are both affordable and interesting.

$ ✕ **Bonsai.** The owners of Bonsai regularly visit Tokyo to research the
JAPANESE casual dining scene, and their expertise is setting a high standard for Japanese cuisine in Edinburgh. The succulent *gyoza* (steamed dumplings) are pliant and tasty, while the wide variety of noodle and teriyaki dishes and the classy sushi balance sweet and sour deliciously. Try the raw prawns and scallops served with radish noodles and wasabi for refreshing, briny mouthfuls with a kick. The dining area has a bright informality, but the tiny tables may be a tad cramped for some, and the service can be patchy. ⑤ *Average main: £13* ⊠ *46 West Richmond St., South Side* ☎ *0131/668–3847* ⊕ *www.bonsaibarbistro.co.uk* ✣ *H5.*

$ ✕ **Kalpna.** Amid an ordinary row of shops, the facade of this vegetarian
INDIAN Indian restaurant may be unremarkable, but the food is exceptional and
Fodor's Choice a superb value. Try the *dam aloo kashmiri,* a medium-spicy potato dish
★ with a sauce made from honey, pistachios, and almonds. *Bangan mirch masala* has more of a kick, with eggplant and red chili peppers. Thaali, a variety of dishes served in bowls on a tray, is particularly appetizing, and a bargain at £13.95. The interior is enlivened by exotic Indian mosaics. Check out the lunchtime buffet for £8. With lots of meatless options on the menu, veggies and vegans flock here. ⑤ *Average main: £9* ⊠ *2–3 St. Patrick Sq., South Side* ☎ *0131/667–9890* ⊕ *www.kalpnarestaurant.com* ⊘ *Closed Sun. Jan.–Mar.* ✣ *H6.*

LEITH

Use the coordinate (✛ B2) at the end of each listing to locate a site on the corresponding map.

Seafood lovers are drawn to the old port of Leith to sample the freshest seafood and to admire the authentic seafaring feel of the docklands.

$ ╳ **Al Dente.** This friendly neighborhood favorite serves authentic Italian
ITALIAN cuisine in homey surroundings. Chef Graziano Spano, from Puglia, is attuned to the freshness and flavors that typify food from the Bel Paese. Fresh pasta and local produce feature prominently. Try the Puglian favorite, pasta orecchiette (little-eared pasta), served with lamb ragu, or sample classic dishes from the regions of Sardinia, Liguria, Lazio, Emilia-Romagna, and Tuscany. ⑤ *Average main: £14* ✉ *139 Easter Rd., Leith* ☏ *0131/652–1932* ⊕ *www.al-dente-restaurant.co.uk* ⌂ *Reservations essential* ⊘ *Closed Sun. No lunch Mon.* ✛ *H1.*

$$ ╳ **Fishers Bistro.** Locals and visitors flock to this laid-back pub-cum-
SEAFOOD bistro down on the waterfront, and to its sister restaurant, **Fishers in the City**, at 58 Thistle Street in the New Town. The menu is the same, but Fishers Leith has the better reputation and vibe. Bar meals are served, although for more comfort and elegance sit in the cozy, blue-walled dining room. Seafood is the specialty—the Loch Fyne oysters and queenie scallops from Tarbert are wonderful. Watch for the daily specials: perhaps a seafood or vegetarian soup followed by huge North African prawns. It's wise to reserve ahead. ⑤ *Average main: £16* ✉ *1 The Shore, Leith* ☏ *0131/554–5666* ⊕ *www.fishersbistros.co.uk* ✛ *H1.*

$ ╳ **The King's Wark.** Along the shoreline at Leith is a gastropub with
BRITISH a pleasant atmosphere and quality food that continues to win plaudits. At lunchtime the dark-wood bar does a roaring trade in simple fare such as gourmet burgers and fish cakes, but in the evening the kitchen ups the ante with such dishes as sea trout stuffed with smoked mackerel risotto. Old stone walls attest to the building's 15th-century origins. ■TIP➔ **Book early to sample the legendary breakfast menu.** ⑤ *Average main: £13* ✉ *36 The Shore, Leith* ☏ *0131/554–9260* ⊕ *www. thekingswark.com* ✛ *H1.*

$$$$ ╳ **The Kitchin.** One of the Edinburgh's most popular eateries, Tom
FRENCH Kitchin's award-winning venture packs in the crowds. It's not difficult to see why. Kitchin, who trained in France, runs a tight ship, and his passion for using seasonal and locally sourced produce to his own creative ends shows no sign of waning. Unfashionable ingredients such as ox tongue, tripe, and pig's head emerge heroic after Kitchin's alchemy, and he works his magic equally dexterously on more familiar elements such as seafood and venison. To sample this verified culinary world affordably, try the three-course lunch for £26.50. ⑤ *Average main: £35* ✉ *78 Commercial Quay, Leith* ☏ *0131/555–1755* ⊕ *www.thekitchin.com* ⌂ *Reservations essential* ⊘ *Closed Sun. and Mon.* ✛ *H1.*

$ ╳ **Los Cardos.** Offering tasty Mexican fare, Los Cardos is a superb value
MEXICAN for those on the move in Leith. There are only a couple of tables, so takeaway is a likely option. First decide whether you want a burrito, quesadilla, or soft tacos, then opt for one of many fillings: marinated

steak or chicken, perhaps, or slow-cooked pork. Toppings range from mild pico de gallo to creamy homemade guacamole with optional grilled peppers and onions. Many locals— including *Trainspotting* writer Irvine Welsh—have confessed their addiction to the haggis burrito. Ⓢ*Average main: £7* ✉*281 Leith Walk, Leith* ☎*0131/555–6619* ⊕*www.loscardos.co.uk* ✛*H1.*

$$$$

FRENCH

Fodor'sChoice

★

✕**Martin Wishart.** Slightly out of town but worth every penny of the taxi fare, this restaurant's well-known chef woos diners with an impeccable and varied menu of beautifully presented, French-influenced dishes. Shoulder fillet of beef wth Devonshire snails, chevril root, and parsely typify the cuisine, which costs £75 for three courses. For the very sweet of tooth there's a dessert tasting menu combing all three daily choices for an extra £7.50. On weekdays the three-course lunch is £28. Reservations are essential on Friday and Saturday night. Ⓢ*Average main: £65* ✉*54 The Shore, Leith* ☎*0131/553–3557* ⊕*www.martin-wishart. co.uk* ☉*Closed Sun. and Mon.* ✛*H1.*

WHERE TO STAY

From stylish boutique hotels to homey B&Bs, Edinburgh has a world-class array of accommodations to suit every taste. Its status as one of Britain's most attractive and fascinating cities ensures a steady influx of visitors, but the wealth of overnight options means there's no need to compromise on where you stay. Grand old hotels are rightly renowned for their regal bearing and old-world charm. If your tastes are a little more contemporary, the city's burgeoning contingent of chic design hotels offers an equally alluring alternative. For those on a tighter budget, the town's B&Bs are the most likely choice. If you feel B&Bs can be restrictive, keep in mind that Scots are trusting people—many proprietors provide front-door keys and few impose curfews.

Rooms are harder to find in August and September, when the Edinburgh International Festival and the Fringe Festival take place, so reserve at least three months in advance. Bed-and-breakfast accommodations may be harder to find in December, January, and February, when some proprietors close for a few weeks.

PRICES

Weekend rates in the larger hotels are always much cheaper than midweek rates, so if you want to stay in a plush hotel, come on the weekend. To save money and see how local residents live, stay in a B&B in one of the areas away from the city center, such as Pilrig to the north, Murrayfield to the west, or Sciennes to the south. Public buses can whisk you to the city center in 10 to 15 minutes. *Prices in the reviews are the lowest cost of a standard double room in high season, including 20% V.A.T.*

BEST BETS FOR EDINBURGH LODGING

Fodor's Choice★	**$$$**	**BEST HISTORIC HOTELS**
21212, $$$, p. 79	21212, p. 79	Balmoral Hotel, $$$$, p. 80
Balmoral Hotel, $$$$, p. 80	The Bonham, p. 82	Prestonfield, $$$$, p. 83
The Bonham, $$$, p. 82	Hotel Missoni, p. 78	
Hotel Missoni, $$$, p. 78	The Howard, p. 80	**BEST SPAS**
The Howard, $$$, p. 80		Balmoral Hotel, $$$$, p. 80
Rutland Hotel, $$, p. 82	**$$$$**	The Scotsman, $$$$, p. 79
The Scotsman, $$$$, p. 79	Balmoral Hotel, p. 80	
	Prestonfield, p. 83	**MOST KID-FRIENDLY**
By Price	The Scotsman, p. 79	The Caledonian, $$, p. 80
		Knight Residence, $$, p. 79
$	**By Experience**	
Ardenlee Guest House, p. 80		**MOST ROMANTIC**
	BEST CONCIERGE	Prestonfield, $$$$, p. 83
$$	Balmoral Hotel, $$$$, p. 80	The Witchery, $$$$, p. 79
Gerald's Place, p. 80	The Howard, $$$, p. 80	
Hotel Du Vin, p. 78		
Rutland Hotel, p. 82		

OLD TOWN

Use the coordinate (✛ B2) at the end of each listing to locate a site on the corresponding map.

The narrow *pends* (alleys), cobbled streets, and steep hills of the Old Town remind you that this is a city with many layers of history. Medieval to modern, these hotels all are within a stone's throw of the action.

$$
HOTEL
Fodor's Choice
★

Hotel du Vin. Leave it to one of the U.K.'s most forward-thinking chains to convert a Victorian-era asylum into this understated luxury property that feels steeped in history and lore despite its contemporary decor and trappings, like the hip bar and restaurant. **Pros:** very unique and historical building; trendy design; youthful feel; lively on-site dining and drinking. **Cons:** some rooms are better than others; in a noisy neighborhood. ⑤ *Rooms from: £160* ⊠ *11 Bristo Pl., Old Town* ☎ *0131/247–4900* ⊕ *www.hotelduvin.com* ➳ *37 rooms, 10 suites* ❙◎❙ *Breakfast* ✛ *G5.*

$$$
HOTEL
Fodor's Choice
★

Hotel Missoni. Glasgow is regarded as Scotland's most stylish city, but the capital has beaten its rival by becoming the site of Italian fashion house Missoni's first boutique hotel. **Pros:** perfect location; in the thick of the action; as far from staid as you can get. **Cons:** it's a little Austin Powers in places; some find it hard to relax in such chichi surrounds. ⑤ *Rooms from: £210* ✉ *1 George IV Bridge, Old Town* ☎ *0131/220–6666* ⊕ *www.hotelmissoni.com* ⇨ *129 rooms, 7 suites* ⦿ *Multiple meal plans* ✛ *F4.*

$$$
RENTAL
FAMILY
☷ **Knight Residence.** About 10 minutes from the Grassmarket, the Knight is made up of 19 different apartments that offer good value and convenient locations. **Pros:** comfortable apartments; secure location; good for families needing space and privacy. **Cons:** lack of staff won't suit everyone; better for stays of two or more nights. ⑤ *Rooms from: £168* ✉ *12 Lauriston St., Old Town* ☎ *0131/622–8120* ⊕ *www.theknightresidence. co.uk* ⇨ *19 apartments* ⦿ *No meals* ✛ *D5.*

$$$
HOTEL
☷ **Radisson Blu Hotel, Edinburgh.** Built in the late 1980s, this city-center hotel was designed to blend in among the 16th-, 17th-, and 18th-century buildings on the Royal Mile. **Pros:** central location; can-do staff. **Cons:** expensive breakfast; difficult to reach by car. ⑤ *Rooms from: £180* ✉ *80 High St., Royal Mile, Old Town* ☎ *0131/557–9797* ⊕ *www.radissonblu.co.uk/hotel-edinburgh* ⇨ *238 rooms, 10 suites* ⦿ *Multiple meal plans* ✛ *G4.*

$$$$
HOTEL
Fodor's Choice
★
☷ **The Scotsman.** A magnificent turn-of-the-20th-century building, with a marble staircase and a fascinating history—it was once the headquarters of the *Scotsman* newspaper—now houses this modern, luxurious hotel. **Pros:** gorgeous surroundings; personalized service. **Cons:** no air-conditioning; spa can be noisy. ⑤ *Rooms from: £270* ✉ *20 N. Bridge, Old Town* ☎ *0131/556–5565* ⊕ *www.thescotsmanhotel.co.uk* ⇨ *56 rooms, 13 suites* ⦿ *Multiple meal plans* ✛ *G3.*

$$
HOTEL
☷ **Ten Hill Place.** This stylish hotel on a quiet backstreet near the Festival Theatre is a dependable Old Town choice. **Pros:** well kept; close to everything but not in the midst of the brouhaha. **Cons:** rooms can be too dark; peekaboo glass doors on the bathrooms. ⑤ *Rooms from: £150* ✉ *10 Hill Pl., Old Town* ☎ *0131/662–2080* ⊕ *www.tenhillplace. com* ⇨ *78 rooms* ⦿ *Multiple meal plans* ✛ *H5.*

$$$$
HOTEL
☷ **The Witchery.** This lavishly theatrical lodging promises a night to remember. **Pros:** the Gothic drama and intriguing antiques; sumptuous dining. **Cons:** can be noisy at night; rooms may feel too cluttered for some. ⑤ *Rooms from: £325* ✉ *Castlehill, Royal Mile, Old Town* ☎ *0131/225–5613* ⊕ *www.thewitchery.com* ⇨ *9 suites* ⦿ *Breakfast* ✛ *F4.*

NEW TOWN

Use the coordinate (✛ B2) at the end of each listing to locate a site on the corresponding map.

Calton Hill, which offers some of the best views of the city from its summit, is just one of the reasons to base yourself in the New Town, filled with gorgeous 18th and 19th century architecture.

$$$
HOTEL
Fodor's Choice
★
☷ **21212.** In this handsome Royal Terrace town house, the spacious rooms are beautifully designed with an eye for detail: an enormous bed sits on a raised platform facing a stylish seating area with a flat-screen TV. **Pros:** stylish decor and service worthy of a special getaway; above a fab restaurant; huge beds. **Cons:** pricey add-ons. ⑤ *Rooms from: £200* ✉ *3 Royal Terr., New Town* ☎ *0131/523 1030* ⊕ *www.21212restaurant. co.uk* ⇨ *4 rooms* ⦿ *No meals* ✛ *G1.*

$
B&B/INN

🖼 **Ardenlee Guest House.** An exquisite Victorian-tile floor is one of many original features at this dependable guesthouse tucked away from the hustle and bustle of the city center. **Pros:** family-run establishment; good value, especially for long-term stays. **Cons:** few amenities; uphill walk to the city center. Ⓢ *Rooms from: £95 ⊠ 9 Eyre Pl., New Town* ☎ *0131/556–2838* ⊕ *www.ardenlee.co.uk* ⤴ *9 rooms, 7 with bath* ❏ *Breakfast* ✛ *E1.*

$$$$
HOTEL
Fodor'sChoice
★

🖼 **Balmoral Hotel.** The attention to detail in the elegant rooms—colors were picked to echo the country's heathers and moors—and the sheer élan that has re-created the Edwardian splendor of this grand, former railroad hotel make staying at the Balmoral a special introduction to Edinburgh. **Pros:** big and beautiful building; top-hatted doorman; quality bathroom goodies. **Cons:** small pool; spa books up fast; restaurants can be very busy. Ⓢ *Rooms from: £380 ⊠ 1 Princes St., New Town* ☎ *0131/556–2414* ⊕ *www.thebalmoralhotel.com* ⤴ *168 rooms, 20 suites* ❏ *Breakfast* ✛ *G2.*

$$$$
HOTEL

🖼 **The Caledonian, a Waldorf Astoria Hotel.** An imposing block of red sandstone beyond the west end of West Princes Street Gardens, "The Caley" has imposing Victorian decor and beautifully restored interiors. **Pros:** service with a smile; good breakfast choice. **Cons:** Internet access is extra; may lack the "wow factor" for some. Ⓢ *Rooms from: £240 ⊠ Princes St., New Town* ☎ *0131/222–8888* ⊕ *www.thecaledonian.waldorfastoria.com* ⤴ *241 rooms, 20 suites* ❏ *Breakfast* ✛ *C4.*

$$
B&B/INN

🖼 **Gerald's Place.** Although he is not a native of the city, Gerald Della-Porta is one of those B&B owners to whom Edinburgh owes so much. **Pros:** the advice and thoughtfulness of the owner; spacious rooms. **Cons:** stairs are difficult to manage; an uphill walk to the city center; no credit cards. Ⓢ *Rooms from: £150 ⊠ 21B Abercromby Pl.* ☎ *0131/558–7017* ⊕ *www.geraldsplace.com* ⤴ *2 rooms* ▭ *No credit cards* ❏ *Breakfast* ✛ *E1.*

$$$$
HOTEL

🖼 **The Glasshouse.** Glass walls extend from the 19th-century facade of a former church, foreshadowing the daring interior of one of the city's original boutique hotels. **Pros:** near all the attractions; very modern and stylish. **Cons:** perhaps a little sterile for some; noise from the street is sometimes a problem. Ⓢ *Rooms from: £330 ⊠ 2 Greenside Pl., New Town* ☎ *0131/525–8200* ⊕ *www.theglasshousehotel.co.uk* ⤴ *65 rooms, 18 suites* ❏ *Breakfast* ✛ *G1.*

$$$
HOTEL

🖼 **The Howard.** This hotel is in a classic New Town building, elegant proportioned and superbly outfitted. **Pros:** small but grand building; staff has a great attitude; special afternoon tea. **Cons:** decor is a little

---

LODGING ALTERNATIVE

InnerCity Lets. Affordable short-term rental in the Old Town, New Town, Stockbridge, and across the city range from small lofts to large apartments. Expect nicely maintained and fully equipped contemporary city pads with kitchens, online access, and even cots for families. You might choose a one-bedroom apartment off the Grassmarket or a three-bedroom loft with outdoor seating in the handsome New Town. ⊠ *9 High St., Old Town* ☎ *0131/208–1005* ⊕ *www.innercitylets.com* ⤴ *N/A.*

2

tired; noisy neighborhood. $\boxed{\$}$ *Rooms from: £190* ⊠ *34 Great King St., New Town* ☎ *0131/557–3500* ⊕ *www.thehoward.com* ➟ *18 rooms, 5 suites* ⦿ *Multiple meal plans* ✢ *E1.*

$ | **Inverleith Hotel.** Across from the Royal Botanical Gardens, this reno-
B&B/INN | vated Victorian town house has cozy, well-lighted rooms with velour bedspreads, dark-wood furniture, and pale-gold curtains. **Pros:** quiet surroundings; knowledgeable staff. **Cons:** some rooms are small; nar-row passageways; uphill walk to the city center. $\boxed{\$}$ *Rooms from: £99* ⊠ *5 Inverleith Terr., New Town* ☎ *0131/556–2745* ⊕ *www.inverleithhotel. co.uk* ➟ *12 rooms, 2 apartments* ⦿ *Breakfast* ✢ *C1.*

$$$$ | **Tigerlilly.** On hip George Street, this boutique hotel has everything
HOTEL | a girl could imagine—bowls of fresh fruit, designer candles, hair straighteners—for a night away from home. **Pros:** chic yet not intimi-dating; laid-back but efficient staff. **Cons:** no views; can be noisy and very busy. $\boxed{\$}$ *Rooms from: £294* ⊠ *125 George St., New Town* ☎ *0131/225–5005* ⊕ *www.tigerlilyedinburgh.co.uk* ➟ *33 rooms* ⦿ *Breakfast* ✢ *C3.*

$$ | **Walton Hotel.** A 10-minute walk from the city center, this B&B in
HOTEL | a Georgian town house is handy for when you want to investigate the quiet charms of leafy Stockbridge. **Pros:** top-class staff; bounti-ful breakfasts; unfussy style. **Cons:** limited parking; some rooms are below street level. $\boxed{\$}$ *Rooms from: £140* ⊠ *79 Dundas St., New Town* ☎ *0131/556–1137* ⊕ *www.waltonhotel.com* ➟ *10 rooms* ⦿ *Break-fast* ✢ *E1.*

HAYMARKET

Use the coordinate (✢ B2) at the end of each listing to locate a site on the corresponding map.

Close to one of the main train stations, Haymarket can make a good base for exploring the city if you're staying in one of the hotels beyond the west end of Princes Street.

$$$ | **Kew House and Apartments.** With such sumptuous rooms, you might
B&B/INN | think that Kew House was a full-service hotel. **Pros:** clean as a whistle; thoughtful touches throughout; close to Water of Leith walk. **Cons:** longish walk to the city center; traffic noise on street side. $\boxed{\$}$ *Rooms from: £185* ⊠ *1 Kew Terr., Haymarket* ☎ *0131/313–0700* ⊕ *www. kewhouse.com* ➟ *6 rooms, 1 apartment* ⦿ *Breakfast* ✢ *A5.*

$$ | **Victorian Town House.** In a leafy crescent, this handsome house once
B&B/INN | belonged to a cousin of Robert Louis Stevenson, and the celebrated writer would doubtless be happy to lay his head in this good-value B&B. **Pros:** serene surroundings near Water of Leith; gracious staff. **Cons:** no parking nearby; distance from Old Town. $\boxed{\$}$ *Rooms from: £110* ⊠ *14 Eglinton Terr., Haymarket* ☎ *0131/337–7088* ⊕ *www. thevictoriantownhouse.co.uk* ➟ *3 rooms* ⦿ *Breakfast* ✢ *A4.*

WEST END

Use the coordinate (✛ B2) at the end of each listing to locate a site on the corresponding map.

With easy access to some of the city's trendiest shops and cafés, the West End has lodgings that take advantage of the neighborhood's handsome Georgian-style town houses.

$$ | 🖼 **B + B Edinburgh.** Standing out along an elegant and tranquil West End
B&B/INN | terrace, this imposing Victorian mansion combines grand public spaces with affordable modern accommodation. **Pros:** fascinating building in tranquil area; superb views; handy for river walks and central attractions. **Cons:** no night porter; hint of previous institutional use; small bathrooms. **$** *Rooms from: £130* ⊠ *3 Rothesay Terr., West End* ☎ *0131/225 5084* ⊕ *www.bb-edinburgh.com* ➲ *27* ⍥ *Breakfast* ✛ *A3.*

$$$ | 🖼 **The Bonham.** There's a clubby atmosphere throughout this hotel,
HOTEL | which carries on a successful, sophisticated flirtation with modernity.
Fodor's Choice | **Pros:** thorough yet unobtrusive service; excellent restaurant. **Cons:** few
★ | common areas; can feel like a business hotel. **$** *Rooms from: £165* ⊠ *35 Drumsheugh Gardens, West End* ☎ *0131/226–6050* ⊕ *www.thebonham.com* ➲ *42 rooms, 6 suites* ⍥ *Multiple meal plans* ✛ *A3.*

$$ | 🖼 **Channings.** Five Edwardian terraced town houses make up this inti-
HOTEL | mate, elegant hotel in an upscale West End neighborhood just minutes from Princes Street. **Pros:** near Stockbridge shops and eateries; inventive color schemes. **Cons:** not all rooms are equal; breakfasts are not bountiful. **$** *Rooms from: £140* ⊠ *12–16 S. Learmonth Gardens, West End* ☎ *0131/315–2226* ⊕ *www.channings.co.uk* ➲ *36 rooms, 5 suites* ⍥ *Breakfast* ✛ *A1.*

$$ | 🖼 **Rutland Hotel.** The building may have once been the residence of
HOTEL | Sir Joseph Lister—known as the "father of antiseptic surgery"—but
Fodor's Choice | there's nothing clinical about this acclaimed boutique hotel at the
★ | west end of Princes Street. **Pros:** friendly staff; not pretentious; great bar and restaurant. **Cons:** decor may be too loud for some. **$** *Rooms from: £150* ⊠ *1–3 Rutland St., West End* ☎ *0131/229–3402* ⊕ *www.therutlandhotel.com* ➲ *12 rooms, 1 apartment* ⍥ *Breakfast* ✛ *C4.*

SOUTH SIDE

Use the coordinate (✛ B2) at the end of each listing to locate a site on the corresponding map.

The B&Bs and restaurants in this residential area offer good value.

$$ | 🖼 **23 Mayfield.** A self-styled "boutique guesthouse," 23 Mayfield is a cut
B&B/INN | above your average B&B: the Victorian villa features many original elements expertly complemented by dark-wood furniture, lovely artwork, and antiquarian books to create a sumptuous atmosphere. **Pros:** relaxing atmosphere; helpful yet unobtrusive service; gourmet breakfast featuring famed porridge. **Cons:** need to book well in advance. **$** *Rooms from: £150* ⊠ *23 Mayfield Gardens, South Side* ☎ *0131/667–5806* ⊕ *www.23mayfield.co.uk* ➲ *9 rooms* ⍥ *Breakfast* ✛ *H6.*

$$ | 🖼 **94DR.** Like owners Paul Lightfoot and John MacEwan—a self-
B&B/INN | described "high-octane" couple—94DR reaches for the stars with its

stylish decor and contemporary trappings. **Pros:** warm welcome; gay-friendly vibe; smashing breakfast. **Cons:** modern design may not please everyone; a long walk to the city center. ⑤ *Rooms from: £120* ✉ *94 Dalkeith Rd., South Side* ☎ *0131/662–9265* ⊕ *www.94dr.com* ⇆ *7 rooms* ¶⊙¶ *Breakfast* ✛ *H6.*

$ | ⛶ **AmarAgua.** Four-poster beds, a tranquil location, and bountiful
B&B/INN | breakfasts set this Victorian town house B&B apart. **Pros:** quiet setting; snug rooms; wonderful breakfasts. **Cons:** far from the city center; minimum two-night stay. ⑤ *Rooms from: £94* ✉ *10 Kilmaurs Terr., Newington* ☎ *0131/667–6775* ⊕ *www.amaragua.co.uk* ⇆ *5 rooms, 4 with bath* ☾ *Closed Jan.* ¶⊙¶ *Breakfast* ✛ *H6.*

$$ | ⛶ **Ashdene House.** On a quiet residential street sits this Edwardian house,
B&B/INN | one of the city's best-value B&Bs. **Pros:** homemade breads at breakfast; spacious rooms. **Cons:** not within walking distance of the center. ⑤ *Rooms from: £115* ✉ *23 Fountainhall Rd., The Grange* ☎ *0131/667–6026* ⊕ *www.ashdenehouse.com* ⇆ *5 rooms* ¶⊙¶ *Breakfast* ✛ *H6.*

$ | ⛶ **Glenalmond House.** Longtime hoteliers Jimmy and Fiona Mackie are
B&B/INN | well schooled in delighting guests, which makes elegant Glenalmond House a reliable choice. **Pros:** knowledgeable owners; nice furnishings; superb breakfasts. **Cons:** smallish bathrooms; a bit of a walk to the New Town. ⑤ *Rooms from: £92* ✉ *25 Mayfield Gardens, South Side* ☎ *0131/668–2392* ⊕ *www.glenalmondhouse.com* ⇆ *9 rooms* ¶⊙¶ *Breakfast* ✛ *H6.*

$$$$ | ⛶ **Prestonfield.** The cattle grazing on the hotel's 20-acre grounds let
HOTEL | you know that you've entered a different world, even though you're five minutes by car from the Royal Mile. **Pros:** eccentric grandeur; comfortable beds. **Cons:** slightly haphazard service; brooding decor can look gloomy. ⑤ *Rooms from: £250* ✉ *Priestfield Rd., Prestonfield* ☎ *0131/225–7800* ⊕ *www.prestonfield.com* ⇆ *18 rooms, 5 suites* ¶⊙¶ *Multiple meal plans* ✛ *H6.*

$ | ⛶ **Teviotdale House.** The interior of this 1848 town house—includ-
B&B/INN | ing canopy beds and miles of festive fabrics—makes it a special B&B option. **Pros:** owners take pride in their hospitality; wide range of breakfast items. **Cons:** a long walk from the city center; not all bathrooms have tubs. ⑤ *Rooms from: £94* ✉ *53 Grange Loan, The Grange* ☎ *0131/667–4376* ⊕ *www.teviotdalehouse.com* ⇆ *7 rooms* ¶⊙¶ *Breakfast* ✛ *H6.*

LEITH

Use the coordinate (✛ B2) at the end of each listing to locate a site on the corresponding map.

Staying here means you'll be away from the Old Town and New Town sights, but you can find some values—and good restaurants.

$$ | ⛶ **Ardmor House.** This excellent guesthouse combines the original fea-
B&B/INN | tures of a Victorian home with stylish contemporary furnishings. **Pros:** warm and friendly owner; decorated with great style; gay-friendly environment. **Cons:** a bit out of the way; double room on the ground floor is tiny. ⑤ *Rooms from: £140* ✉ *74 Pilrig St., Leith* ☎☎ *0131/554–4944* ⊕ *www.ardmorhouse.com* ⇆ *5 rooms* ¶⊙¶ *Breakfast* ✛ *G1.*

$$
B&B/INN

The Conifers. This small B&B in a red-sandstone town house north of the New Town offers simple, traditionally decorated rooms and warm hospitality. **Pros:** nice mix of old and new; many original fittings; hearty breakfasts. **Cons:** a long walk to the city center; not all rooms have en-suite bathrooms. $ *Rooms from: £120* ⊠ *56 Pilrig St., Leith* ☏ *0131/554–5162* ⊕ *www.conifersguesthouse.com* ⥲ *4 rooms, 3 with bath* ⊟ *No credit cards* �‖ *Breakfast* ⊹ *G1.*

$
B&B/INN

Fraoch House. This popular option manages to combine a homey feel and stylish decor without leaning too far in either direction. **Pros:** a warm welcome; great DVD library; free Wi-Fi. **Cons:** uphill walk to the city center. $ *Rooms from: £95* ⊠ *66 Pilrig St., Leith* ☏ *0131/554–1353* ⊕ *www.fraochhouse.com* ⥲ *9 rooms* �‖ *Breakfast* ⊹ *G1.*

$$$
HOTEL

Malmaison. Once a seamen's hostel, Edinburgh's link in the pioneering boutique hotel chain draws a refined clientele. **Pros:** impressive building; elegant feel; great location. **Cons:** not as immaculate as it was; bar can be rowdy at night; a long way from the center of town. $ *Rooms from: £175* ⊠ *1 Tower Pl., Leith* ☏ *0131/468–5000* ⊕ *www.malmaison-edinburgh.com* ⥲ *100 rooms, 9 suites* �‖ *Breakfast* ⊹ *G1.*

NIGHTLIFE AND THE ARTS

THE ARTS

Those who think Edinburgh's arts scene consists of just the elegiac wail of a bagpipe and the twang of a fiddle or two will be proved wrong by the hundreds of performing-arts options. The jewel in the crown, of course, is the famed Edinburgh International Festival, which now attracts the best in music, dance, theater, painting, and sculpture from all over the globe during three weeks from mid-August to early September. The *Scotsman* and *Herald,* Scotland's leading daily newspapers, carry listings and reviews in their arts pages every day, with special editions during the festival. Tickets are generally sold in advance; in some cases they're also available from certain designated travel agents or at the door, although concerts by national orchestras often sell out long before the day of the performance.

DANCE

Festival Theatre. Scottish Ballet productions and other dance acts appear at the Festival Theatre. ⊠ *13–29 Nicolson St., Old Town* ☏ *0131/529–6000* ⊕ *www.edtheatres.com.*

Royal Lyceum. Visiting contemporary dance companies perform in the Royal Lyceum. ⊠ *Grindlay St., West End* ☏ *0131/248–4848* ⊕ *www.lyceum.org.uk.*

FESTIVALS

Fodor'sChoice
★

Edinburgh Festival Fringe. While the world's largest fringe festival is going on, most of the city center becomes one huge performance area, with fire eaters, sword swallowers, unicyclists, jugglers, string quartets, jazz groups, stand-up comics, and magicians all thronging into High Street and Princes Street. Every available performance space—church halls, community centers, parks, sports fields, putting greens, and

Festivals in Edinburgh

Walking around Edinburgh in late July, you'll likely feel the first vibrations of the earthquake that is festival time, which shakes the city throughout August and into September. You may hear reference to an "Edinburgh Festival," but this is really an umbrella term for five separate festivals all taking place around the same time. For an overview, check out ⊕ *www.edinburghfestivals.co.uk.*

The best-known and oldest of the city's festivals is the **Edinburgh International Festival,** founded in 1947 when Europe was recovering from World War II. In recent years the festival has drawn as many as 400,000 people to Edinburgh, with more than 100 acts by world-renowned music, opera, theater, and dance performers filling all the major venues in the city.

If the Edinburgh International Festival is the parent of British festivals, then the **Edinburgh Festival Fringe** is its unruly child. The Festival Fringe started in 1947 at the same time as the International Festival, when eight companies that were not invited to perform in the latter decided to attend anyway. It's now the largest festival of its kind in the world. Its events range from the brilliant to the impossibly mundane, badly performed, and downright tacky.

Edinburgh festival time can fill almost any artistic need. Besides the International Festival and Festival Fringe, look for the **Edinburgh Jazz and Blues Festival,** the **International Book Festival,** and the **Military Tattoo.** The Edinburgh International Film Festival takes place in June.

2

---

nightclubs—is utilized for every kind of event, with something for all tastes. Many events are free, while others cost £2 to £15. During festival time—roughly the same as the Edinburgh International Festival—it's possible to arrange your own entertainment program from morning to midnight. ⊠ *Edinburgh Festival Fringe Office, 180 High St., Old Town* ☎ *0131/226–0026* ⊕ *www.edfringe.com.*

FAMILY **Edinburgh International Book Festival.** This two-week-long event in August pulls together a heady mix of the biggest-selling and the most challenging authors from around the world and gets them talking about their work in a magnificent tent village. Workshops for would-be writers and children are hugely popular. ⊠ *Charlotte Sq. Gardens, New Town* ☎ *0131/718–5666* ⊕ *www.edbookfest.co.uk.*

Fodor's Choice **Edinburgh International Festival.** Running from early August through
★ early September, the flagship arts event of the year attracts international performers to a celebration of music, dance, theater, and art. Programs, tickets, and reservations are available from the Hub, within the impressive Victorian-Gothic Tolbooth Kirk. Tickets for the festival go on sale in April, and many sell out within the month. However, you may still be able to purchase tickets, which range from £4 to £60, during the festival. ⊠ *Edinburgh Festival Centre, Castlehill, Old Town* ☎ *0131/473–2000* ⊕ *www.eif.co.uk.*

Edinburgh International Film Festival. One of Europe's foremost film festivals, the Edinburgh International Film Festival is held in late June. ✉ *Edinburgh Film Festival Office, 88 Lothian Rd., West End* ☎ *0131/228–2688* ⊕ *www.edfilmfest.org.uk.*

FAMILY **Edinburgh International Science Festival.** Held around Easter each year, the Edinburgh International Science Festival aims to make science accessible, interesting, and fun. Children's events turn science into entertainment and are especially popular. ✉ *The Hub, Castlehill* ☎ *0131/553–0320* ⊕ *www.sciencefestival.co.uk.*

Edinburgh Jazz and Blues Festival. Held in late July, the Edinburgh Jazz and Blues Festival attracts international top performers and brings local enthusiasts out of their living rooms and into the pubs and clubs to listen and play. ✉ *89 Giles St., Leith* ☎ *0131/467–5200* ⊕ *www. edinburghjazzfestival.co.uk.*

Edinburgh Military Tattoo. The Edinburgh Military Tattoo may not be art, but it is certainly Scottish culture. It's sometimes confused with the Edinburgh International Festival, partly because both events take place in August (though the Tattoo starts and finishes a week earlier). This celebration of martial music features bands, gymnastics, and stunt motorcycle teams on the castle esplanade. Dress warmly for late-evening performances. Even if it rains, the show most definitely goes on. ✉ *Edinburgh Military Tattoo Office, 32 Market St., Old Town* ☎ *0131/225–1188* ⊕ *www.edintattoo.co.uk.*

Hogmanay. Other places in Scotland have raucous New Year's celebrations, but Edinburgh's multiday Hogmanay is famous throughout Europe and beyond, with something for everyone. Yes, it's still winter and cold, but joining the festivities with up to 80,000 other people can be memorable. ✉ *Princes St., Old Town* ⊕ *www. edinburghshogmanay.com* 🎟 *£20.*

FILM

Cameo. The Cameo has one large and two small auditoriums, both of which are extremely comfortable, plus a bar with late-night specials. ✉ *38 Home St., Tollcross* ☎ *0871/902–5723* ⊕ *www.picturehouses.co.uk.*

Fodor's Choice **Filmhouse.** The excellent three-screen Filmhouse is the best venue for ★ modern, foreign-language, offbeat, or simply less commercial films. The café and bar are open late on the weekend. ✉ *88 Lothian Rd., West End* ☎ *0131/228–2688* ⊕ *www.filmhousecinema.com.*

MUSIC

Festival Theatre. The Festival Theatre hosts performances by the Scottish Ballet and the Scottish Opera. ✉ *13–29 Nicolson St., Old Town* ☎ *0131/529–6000* ⊕ *www.edtheatres.com.*

Playhouse. The Playhouse leans toward popular artists, comedy acts, and musicals. ✉ *Greenside Pl., East End* ☎ *0131/524–3333* ⊕ *www. edinburghplayhouse.org.uk.*

Queen's Hall. The intimate Queen's Hall hosts small musical recitals. ✉ *Clerk St., Old Town* ☎ *0131/668–2019* ⊕ *www.thequeenshall.net.*

Hogmanay: Hello, New Year

In Scotland, New Year's Eve is called Hogmanay. Around Scotland celebrations continue the next day with customs such as "first-footing"—visiting your neighbors with gifts that include whisky, all with the purpose of bringing good fortune. It's so important that January 2 as well as January 1 is a holiday in Scotland; the rest of the United Kingdom settles for recuperating on January 1.

WHAT TO EXPECT
Edinburgh's Hogmanay extends over several days with spectacles and performances (music, dance, and more); the yearly changing lineup includes many free events. Festivities featuring fire add a dramatic motif; buildings may open for rare night tours; a ceilidh offers dancing outdoors to traditional music; and family concerts and serious discussions during the

day round out the agenda. At the heart of Hogmanay, though, is the evening street party on New Year's Eve, with different music stages, food and drink (and people do drink), and the heart-lifting—despite the cold— sight of glowing fireworks over Edinburgh Castle and the singing of "Auld Lang Syne," written by Scotland's own Robert Burns.

PLANNING BASICS
Besides the £20 you'll pay to get into the Princes Street celebration, expect to shell out extra for related events. For example, the big-name concert in the Princes Street Gardens will run you £30 or more. Book rooms as far ahead as possible. Obvious but essential is warmth: crazy hats and the bundled-up look are de rigueur. Check out ⊕ *www. edinburghshogmanay.com* for full details, and have a happy Hogmanay!

Usher Hall. Edinburgh's grandest venue, Usher Hall hosts national and international performers and groups, including the Royal Scottish National Orchestra. ⊠ *Lothian Rd., West End* ☎ *0131/228–1155* ⊕ *www.usherhall.co.uk.*

THEATER

MODERN **Traverse Theatre.** With its specially designed space, the Traverse Theatre has developed a solid reputation for new, stimulating Scottish plays and dance performances. ⊠ *10 Cambridge St., West End* ☎ *0131/228–1404* ⊕ *www.traverse.co.uk.*

TRADITIONAL Edinburgh has three main theaters—the Festival Theatre, King's, and the Royal Lyceum—as well as others.

Brunton Theatre. On the eastern outskirts of Edinburgh, the Brunton Theatre presents a regular program of repertory, touring, and amateur performances. ⊠ *Ladywell Way, Musselburgh* ☎ *0131/665–2240* ⊕ *www.bruntontheatre.co.uk.*

Church Hill Theatre. The Church Hill Theatre hosts high-quality productions by local dramatic societies. ⊠ *Morningside Rd., Morningside* ☎ *0131/220–4348* ⊕ *www.assemblyroomsedinburgh.co.uk.*

Festival Theatre. This popular venue presents opera and ballet, as well as the occasional excellent touring play. ⊠ *13–29 Nicolson St., Old Town* ☎ *0131/529–6000* ⊕ *www.edtheatres.com.*

King's. The King's has a program of contemporary and traditional dramatic works. Its opulence has been augmented with vibrant murals by artist John Byrne. ⊠ *2 Leven St., Tollcross* ☎ *0131/529–6000* ⊕ *www.edtheatres.com.*

Playhouse. Popular concerts and musicals, along with the occasional ballet and opera production, are staged at the Playhouse. ⊠ *Greenside Pl., East End* ☎ *0844/871–3014* ⊕ *www.edinburghplayhouse.org.uk.*

Royal Lyceum. The Royal Lyceum presents traditional plays and contemporary works, often transferred from or prior to their London West End showings. ⊠ *Grindlay St., West End* ☎ *0131/248–4848* ⊕ *www.lyceum.org.uk.*

NIGHTLIFE

The nightlife scene in Edinburgh is vibrant—whatever you're looking for, you'll most certainly find it here, and you won't have to go far. Expect old-style pubs as well as cutting-edge bars and clubs. Live music pours out of many watering holes on weekends, particularly folk, blues, and jazz. Well-known artists perform at some of the larger venues.

Edinburgh's 400-odd pubs are a study in themselves. In the eastern and northern districts of the city you can find some grim, inhospitable-looking places that proclaim that drinking is no laughing matter. But throughout Edinburgh many pubs have deliberately traded in their old spit-and-sawdust images for atmospheric revivals of the warm, oak-paneled, leather-chaired howffs of a more leisurely age. Most pubs and bars are open weekdays and Saturday from 11 am to midnight, and from 12:30 to midnight on Sunday.

The List and *The Skinny* carry the most up-to-date details about cultural events. *The List* is available at newsstands throughout the city, while *The Skinny* is free and can be picked up at a number of pubs, clubs, and shops around town. The *Herald* and *Scotsman* newspapers are good for reviews and notices of upcoming events throughout Scotland.

OLD TOWN

BARS AND **Black Bo's.** One of the coziest places in town, Black Bo's has a decent selec-
PUBS tion of beers from around the world, vegetarian nibbles, and an eclectic soundtrack. ⊠ *57–61 Blackfriars St., Old Town* ☎ *0131/557–6136.*

Canons' Gait. The Canons' Gait has a fine selection of local real ales and malts. It stages live jazz and blues performances, as well as edgy comedy shows in the cellar bar. ⊠ *232 Canongate, Old Town* ☎ *0131/556–4481.*

The Last Drop. There's plenty of atmosphere amid the nooks and crannies at the Last Drop, which takes its name from a nearby site of public hangings. ⊠ *74–78 Grassmarket, Old Town* ☎ *0131/225–4851* ⊕ *www.nicholsonspubs.co.uk.*

Whiski. With 300-plus malts, this cheerful place is known for its haggis burger. Foot-stomping fiddle, bluegrass, and country music plays most nights. ⊠ *119 High St., Old Town* ☎ *0131/556–3095* ⊕ *www.whiskibar.co.uk.*

2

FOLK CLUBS You can usually find folk musicians performing in pubs throughout Edinburgh, although there's been a decline in the live-music scene because of dwindling profits and the predominance of popular theme bars.

Royal Oak. With a piano in the corner, this cozy bar presents live blues and folk music most nights. ⊠ *1 Infirmary St., Old Town* ☎ *0131/557–2976* ⊕ *www.royal-oak-folk.com.*

Whistle Binkies Pub. This friendly basement bar presents rock, blues and folk music every night of the week. ⊠ *4–6 South Bridge, Old Town* ☎ *0131/557–5114* ⊕ *www.whistlebinkies.com.*

NIGHTCLUBS **Bongo Club.** The bohemian Bongo Club stagess indie, rockabilly, dub, and techno gigs, as well as various club and comedy nights. ⊠ *66 Cowgate, Old Town* ☎ *0131/558–7604* ⊕ *www.thebongoclub.co.uk.*

Cabaret Voltaire. This vaulted ceilings of this subterranean club reverberates with music most nights. You'll find everything from cheesy raves to cutting-edge indie bands to trendy DJs. ⊠ *36–38 Blair St., Old Town* ☎ *0131/247–4704* ⊕ *www.thecabaretvoltaire.com.*

NEW TOWN

BARS AND **Abbotsford.** A handsome Victorian-era island bar serves an ever-changing
PUBS selection of real ales at the Abbotsford. ⊠ *3 Rose St., New Town* ☎ *0131/225–5276* ⊕ *www.theabbotsford.com.*

The Basement. A longtime favorite with the younger crowd, the Basement is a good stopover before heading out to the clubs. The Hawaiian-shirted bar staff adds to the general amiability. ⊠ *10A–12A Broughton St., New Town* ☎ *0131/557–0097.*

Blue Blazer. This cozy, dark-wood bar has a top-notch selection of real ales, 50 malt whiskies, and 75 rums, all of which are enjoyed by a friendly, diverse crowd. ⊠ *2 Spittal St., West End* ☎ *0131/229–5030.*

Bramble. You could easily miss this basement bar on Queen Street—look for a spray-painted sign below a clothing alteration shop. Friendly barmen, superb cocktails, eclectic music (DJs spin most nights), and lots of nooks and crannies in the whitewashed space make for late-night shenanigans that attract a young crowd. ⊠ *16A Queen St., New Town* ☎ *0131/226–6343* ⊕ *www.bramblebar.co.uk.*

Fodor's Choice **Café Royal Circle Bar.** Famed for its atmospheric Victorian interiors—
★ think ornate stucco, etched mirrors, tiled murals, stained glass, and leather booths—the Café Royal Circle Bar draws a cast of Edinburgh characters for its drinks (seven real ales and more than 30 whiskies) and tasty seafood platters. ⊠ *19 W. Regent St., New Town* ☎ *0131/556–1884* ⊕ *www.caferoyaledinburgh.co.uk.*

Cask and Barrel. A spacious, busy pub, the Cask and Barrel lets you sample hand-pulled ales at the horseshoe-shaped bar ringed by a collection of brewery mirrors. ⊠ *115 Broughton St., New Town* ☎ *0131/556–3132.*

Cumberland Bar. Fine ales on tap, classic pub mirrors, handsome wood trim, and a beer garden are the draws at the Cumberland Bar. ⊠ *1–3 Cumberland St., New Town* ☎ *0131/558–3134.*

Guildford Arms. This place is worth a visit just for its interior: ornate plasterwork, elaborate cornices, and wood paneling. The bartender serves some excellent draft ales, including Orkney Dark Island. ✉ *1 W. Register St., east end of Princes St., New Town* ☎ *0131/556–4312.*

FAMILY

Fodor's Choice

★

Joseph Pearce's. One of four Swedish-owned pubs in Edinburgh, Joseph Pearce's has a continental feel, thanks to the cosmopolitan staff. Scandinavian-themed cocktails are popular, as are meatballs and other Swedish dishes. There's a children's corner with toys to keep the small fry occupied. ✉ *23 Elm Row, New Town* ☎ *0131/556–4140.*

Kay's Bar. Housed in a former Georgian coach house, this friendly spot serves 50 single-malt whiskies, seven guest ales, and decent bottled beers. ✉ *39 Jamaica St., New Town* ☎ *0131/225–1858* ⊕ *kaysbar.co.uk.*

Milne's Bar. This spot is known as the poets' pub because of its popularity with Edinburgh's literati. Pies and baked potatoes go well with seven real ales and various guest beers (meaning anything besides the house brew). Victorian advertisements and photos of old Edinburgh give the place an old-time feel. ✉ *35 Hanover St., New Town* ☎ *0131/225–6738.*

Star Bar. Well worth seeking out, the tucked-away Star Bar has a beer garden, table soccer, and—a rarity—a good jukebox. ✉ *1 Northumberland Pl., New Town* ☎ *0131/539–8070* ⊕ *www.starbar.org.uk.*

Teuchters. With more than 80 whiskies, a cozy fire, and comfy sofas, Teuchters is a fine place to relax with a dram. ✉ *26 William St., West End* ☎ *0131/226–1036* ⊕ *www.aroomin.co.uk.*

Tonic. This stylish basement bar has bouncy stools, comfy sofas, and a long list of cocktails. There's relaxing music Monday to Wednesday, live bands Thursday, and resident DJs on the weekend. ✉ *34A Castle St., New Town* ☎ *0131/225–6431* ⊕ *www.bar-tonic.co.uk.*

CEILIDHS AND SCOTTISH EVENINGS

Thistle King James Hotel. For those who feel a trip to Scotland is not complete without hearing the "Braes of Yarrow" or "Auld Robin Gray," several hotels present traditional Scottish-music evenings in the summer season. Head for the Thistle King James Hotel to see *Jamie's Scottish Evening,* an extravaganza of Scottish song, tartan, plaid, and bagpipes that takes place nightly from April to October. The cost is £60, including a four-course dinner. ✉ *Thistle King James Hotel, 107 Leith St., New Town* ☎ *0131/200–7758* ⊕ *www.thistle.com.*

GAY AND LESBIAN

There's a burgeoning gay and lesbian scene in Edinburgh, and the city has many predominantly gay clubs, bars, and cafés. However, don't expect the scene to be as open as in London, New York, or even Glasgow. *The List* and *The Skinny* have sections that focus on gay and lesbian venues.

CC Blooms. Modern and colorful, CC Blooms plays a mix of musical styles. Open nightly, it's been a mainstay on the gay scene since the early '90s. ✉ *23–24 Greenside Pl., New Town* ☎ *0131/556–9331* ⊕ *ccbloomsedinburgh.com.*

GHQ. This stylish gay spot has glam contemporary decor and state-of-the-art sound and lighting. The DJ nights are very popular. ✉ *4 Picardy Pl., New Town* ☎ *0845/166–6024.*

Regent. The Regent has a homey vibe—dogs are welcome—and is renowned for its real ales. ✉ *2 Montrose Terr., Abbeyhill* ☎ *0131/661–8198* ⊕ *www.theregentbar.co.uk.*

NIGHTCLUBS **Liquid Room.** Top indie bands and an eclectic mix of club nights (techno, hip-hop, and alternative, to name a few) make the Liquid Room a superb venue. ✉ *9C Victoria St., New Town* ☎ *0131/225–2564* ⊕ *www.liquidroom.com.*

Opal Lounge. The Opal Lounge is a casual but stylish nightspot with a glam VIP lounge that was favored by Prince William while he attended university. ✉ *51A George St., New Town* ☎ *0131/226–2275* ⊕ *www.opallounge.co.uk.*

SOUTH SIDE

BARS AND PUBS **Cloisters.** The Cloisters prides itself on the absence of music, gaming machines, and all other modern pub gimmicks. Instead, it specializes in real ales, malt whiskies, and good food, all at reasonable prices. ✉ *26 Brougham St., Tollcross* ☎ *0131/221–9997.*

Leslie's Bar. Retaining its original mahogany island bar, the Victorian-era Leslie's is renowned for its range of traditional Scottish ales and malt whiskies. ✉ *45 Ratcliffe Terr., South Side* ☎ *0131/667–7205* ⊕ *www.realalepubedinburgh.co.uk.*

Under the Stairs. As you might guess from the name, Under the Stairs is below street level. This cozy, low-ceilinged place with quirky furniture and art exhibits serves specialty cocktails and decent bar food. ✉ *3A Merchant St., Old Town* ☎ *0131/466–8550* ⊕ *www.underthestairs.org.*

LEITH

BARS AND PUBS **Bond No 9.** This stylish bar with hidden corners specializes in cool cocktails and exotic liquors, including absinthe. There's also excellent bistro food. ✉ *84 Commercial St., Leith* ☎ *0131/555–5578* ⊕ *www.bondno9.co.uk.*

Fodor'sChoice ★ **The King's Wark.** A 15th-century building houses the popular King's Wark, renowned for its excellent food and good ales. Breakfasts are legendary, and are worth booking in advance. In warm weather you can snag a table on the sidewalk. ✉ *36 The Shore, Leith* ☎ *0131/554–9260* ⊕ *www.thekingswark.com.*

Malt and Hops. Having opened its doors in 1749, Malt and Hops has a resident ghost. With a fine spot on the waterfront, the place serves microbrewery cask ales. ✉ *45 The Shore, Leith* ☎ *0131/555–0083* ⊕ *www.barcalisa.com.*

Robbie's. This classic pub with friendly regulars is a great place for catching big sporting events while enjoying local ales. ✉ *367 Leith Walk, Leith* ☎ *0131/554–6850.*

EAST END

COMEDY CLUBS **Stand.** Throughout the year you can laugh until your sides split at the Stand, which hosts both famous names and up-and-coming acts. ✉ *5 York Pl., East End* ☎ *0131/558–7272* ⊕ *www.thestand.co.uk.*

SHOPPING

Despite its renown as a shopping street, **Princes Street** in the New Town may disappoint some visitors with its dull modern architecture, average chain stores, and fast-food outlets. One block north of Princes Street, **Rose Street** has many smaller specialty shops; part of the street is a pedestrian zone, so it's a pleasant place to browse. The shops on **George Street** in New Town tend to be fairly upscale. London names, such as Laura Ashley and Penhaligons, are prominent, though some of the older independent stores continue to do good business.

The streets crossing George Street—Hanover, Frederick, and Castle—are also worth exploring. **Dundas Street,** the northern extension of Hanover Street, beyond Queen Street Gardens, has several antiques shops. **Thistle Street,** originally George Street's "back lane," or service area, has several boutiques and more antiques shops.

As may be expected, many shops along the **Royal Mile** in Old Town sell what may be politely or euphemistically described as tourist-ware—whiskies, tartans, and tweeds. Careful exploration, however, will reveal some worthwhile establishments. Shops here also cater to highly specialized interests and hobbies. Close to the castle end of the Royal Mile, just off George IV Bridge, is **Victoria Street,** with specialty shops grouped in a small area. Follow the tiny West Bow to **Grassmarket** for more specialty stores.

Stafford and William streets form a small, upscale shopping area in a Georgian setting. Walk to the west end of Princes Street and then along its continuation, Shandwick Place, then turn right onto Stafford Street. William Street crosses Stafford halfway down.

North of Princes Street, on the way to the Royal Botanic Garden Edinburgh, is **Stockbridge,** an oddball shopping area of some charm, particularly on St. Stephen Street. To get here, walk north down Frederick Street and Howe Street, away from Princes Street, then turn left onto North West Circus Place.

OLD TOWN

SPECIALTY SHOPS

Fodor'sChoice
★

BOOKS,
PAPER, MAPS,
AND GAMES

Analogue Books. This bookshop and gallery has a wonderful and ever-changing selection of stimulating reads—books and magazines covering lots of genres—mostly from small publishers. There are also eye-catching prints to adorn your walls. ⊠ *39 Candlemaker Row, Old Town* ☎ *0131/220–0601* ⊕ *www.analoguebooks.co.uk.*

Armchair Books. Near the Grassmarket, Armchair Books is a chaotic secondhand bookshop heaving with tomes from your youth. ⊠ *72–74 W. Port, Old Town* ☎ *0131/229–5927.*

Carson Clark Gallery. This gallery specializes in antique maps, sea charts, and prints. ⊠ *181–183 Canongate, Old Town* ☎ *0131/556–4710.*

Main Point Books. This bibliophile's haven is stacked high with obscure first editions and bargain tomes. ⊠ *77 Bread St., Old Town* ☎ *0131/228–4837.*

2

CLOTHING
BOUTIQUES

Bill Baber. One of the most imaginative of the many Scottish knitwear designers, Bill Baber is a long way from the conservative pastel woolies sold at some of the large mill shops. ⊠ *66 Grassmarket, Old Town* ☎ *0131/225–3249.*

Ragamuffin. Hailing from the Isle of Skye, Ragamuffin sells the funkiest and brightest knits produced in Scotland. ⊠ *278 Canongate, Old Town* ☎ *0131/557–6007.*

JEWELRY

Clarksons. A family firm, Clarksons handcrafts a unique collection of jewelry, including Celtic styles. The pieces here are made with silver, gold, platinum, and precious gems, with a particular emphasis on diamonds. ⊠ *87 W. Bow, Old Town* ☎ *0131/225–8141.*

Fodor's Choice
★

SCOTTISH
SPECIALTIES

Cranachan & Crowdie. On Edinburgh's Royal Mile, this gourmet shop is brimming with the finest Scottish food and drink. There's even a chocolate counter for those with a sweet tooth, as well as shortbread and oatcakes. The staff is happy to put together hampers of food for any occasion—including an impromptu picnic back in your room. ⊠ *263 Canongate, Old Town* ☎ *0131/556–7194* ⊕ *www.cranachanandcrowdie.com.*

Edinburgh Old Town Weaving Company. At the Edinburgh Old Town Weaving Company, you can chat with the cloth and tapestry weavers as they work, then buy the products. The company can also provide information on clan histories and which tartan to wear. ⊠ *555 Castlehill, Old Town* ☎ *0131/226–1555.*

Geoffrey (Tailor) Highland Crafts. This shop can clothe you in full Highland dress, with kilts made in its own workshops. ⊠ *57–59 High St., Old Town* ☎ *0131/557–0256* ⊕ *www.geoffreykilts.co.uk.*

NEW TOWN

ARCADES AND SHOPPING CENTERS

St. James Centre. The St. James Centre has John Lewis, River Island, Thorntons, Wallis, and other chain stores. ⊠ *Leith St., New Town.*

DEPARTMENT STORES

Harvey Nichols. Affectionately known as Harvey Nicks, this high-style British chain has opened a Scots outpost. ⊠ *30–34 St. Andrew Sq., New Town* ☎ *0131/524–8388* ⊕ *www.harveynichols.com.*

Fodor's Choice
★

Jenners. Traditional china and glassware are a specialty here, as are Scottish tweeds and tartans. Its famous food hall, run by Valvona & Crolla, stocks Scots staples like shortbread, marmalade, and honey, alongside quality continental groceries. ⊠ *48 Princes St., New Town* ☎ *0844/800–3725.*

John Lewis. Part of a U.K.–wide chain, John Lewis specializes in furnishings and household goods, but also stocks designer clothes. ⊠ *69 St. James Centre, New Town* ☎ *0131/556–9121* ⊕ *www.johnlewis.com.*

Marks & Spencer. Fairly priced, stylish clothes and accessories are on offer at Marks & Spencer. You can also buy quality food and household goods. ⊠ *54 Princes St., New Town* ☎ *0131/225–2301* ⊕ *www.marksandspencer.com.*

SPECIALTY SHOPS

ANTIQUES **Elaine's Vintage Clothing.** This wee boutique on beguiling St. Stephen Street is crammed full of vintage threads for women and men. The finds span the 20th century, but most are from the '40s to the '70s. The friendly owner shares her knowledge of the many elegant and quirky outfits on her rails. ⊠ *55 St. Stephen, New Town* ☎ *0131/225–5783.*

Fodor's Choice **Unicorn Antiques.** This basement is crammed with fascinating antiques, ★ including artworks, ornaments, and drawerfuls of aged cutlery. ⊠ *65 Dundas St., New Town* ☎ *0131/556–7176.*

JEWELRY **Hamilton and Inches.** Established in 1866, this jeweler is worth visiting not only for its gold and silver pieces, but also for its late-Georgian interior. Designed by David Bryce in 1834, it's all columns and elaborate plasterwork. ⊠ *87 George St., New Town* ☎ *0131/225–4898* ⊕ *www. hamiltonandinches.com.*

Joseph Bonnar. Tucked behind George Street, Joseph Bonnar stocks Scotland's largest collection of antique jewelry, including 19th-century agate jewels. ⊠ *72 Thistle St., New Town* ☎ *0131/226–2811* ⊕ *www. josephbonnar.com.*

HOME **Hannah Zakari.** Quirky handmade pieces, including embroidered cush-
FURNISHINGS ions, are a specialty at Hannah Zakari. Also look for unusual jewelry, artwork, and accessories. ⊠ *43 Candlemaker Row, New Town* ☎ *0131/516–3264* ⊕ *www.hannahzakari.co.uk.*

In House. This shop sells designer furnishings and collectibles at the forefront of modern design. ⊠ *28 Howe St., New Town* ☎ *0131/225–2888* ⊕ *www.inhouse-uk.com.*

Studio One. This basement shop has a well-established and comprehensive inventory of jewelry, accessories, housewares, and more. ⊠ *10–16 Stafford St., New Town* ☎ *0131/226–5812* ⊕ *www.studio-one.co.uk.*

OUTDOOR **Tiso.** This shop stocks outdoor clothing, boots, and jackets ideal for
SPORTS GEAR hiking or camping in the Highlands. There's another branch at 41 Commercial Street. ⊠ *123–125 Rose St., New Town* ☎ *0131/225–9486* ⊕ *www.tiso.com.*

WEST END

SPECIALTY SHOPS

CLOTHING **Arkangel & Felon.** This small boutique sells interesting designer clothes,
BOUTIQUES jewelry, handbags, and accessories. ⊠ *4 William St., West End* ☎ *0131/226–4466* ⊕ *www.arkangelandfelon.com.*

Concrete Wardrobe. For an eclectic mix of quirky knitwear and accessories, dive into Concrete Wardrobe. You can also find vintage furnishings. ⊠ *50a Broughton St., West End* ☎ *0131/558–7130* ⊕ *www. concretewardrobe.com.*

Extra Inch. This shop stocks a full selection of clothing in larger sizes. ⊠ *12 William St., West End* ☎ *0131/226–3303* ⊕ *www.extrainch.co.uk.*

Herman Brown's. This secondhand clothing store is where cashmere twinsets and classic luxe labels are sought and found. ⊠ *151 W. Port, West End* ☎ *0131/228–2589* ⊕ *www.hermanbrown.co.uk.*

SOUTH SIDE

SPECIALTY SHOPS

ANTIQUES **Courtyard Antiques.** This lovely shop stocks a mixture of high-quality antiques, toys, and militaria. ⊠ *108A Causewayside, Sciennes* ☏ *0131/ 662–9008* ⊕ *www.edinburghcourtyardantiques.co.uk.*

LEITH

ARCADES AND SHOPPING CENTERS

Ocean Terminal. The Ocean Terminal houses a large collection of shops, as well as bars and eateries. Here you can also visit the former royal yacht *Britannia.* ⊠ *Ocean Dr., Leith.*

SPECIALTY SHOPS

SCOTTISH **Clan Tartan Centre.** For the tartan and clan curious, there's database con-
SPECIALTIES taining details of all known designs, plus information on clan histories. ⊠ *70–74 Bangor Rd., Leith* ☏ *0131/553–5161.*

SPORTS AND THE OUTDOORS

BICYCLING

Edinburgh is not the friendliest city for bikes; there's a lot of traffic, even on weekends. The tourist information center can point you toward some quieter routes just beyond the city center. Rentals cost £75 per week for a 21-speed or mountain bike. Daily rates (24 hours) are about £16, with half days costing £12.

Bike Trax. A wide range of bikes is available at Bike Trax, which also sells clothing and accessories. ⊠ *11–13 Lochrin Pl., Tollcross* ☏ *0131/228– 6633* ⊕ *www.biketrax.co.uk.*

CRICKET

Surprising even to many Scots, the game of bat and ball has a long history and healthy club scene in Scotland.

Grange Cricket Club. Between April and September, the beautiful Grange Cricket Club, established in 1832, stages county games and hosts various league matches. Local club games are free to watch and make for a civilized introduction to the game. ⊠ *Portgower Pl., Stockbridge* ☏ *0131/332–2148* ⊕ *www.grangecricket.org.*

GOLF

In Scotland, SSS indicates the "standard scratch score," the score a scratch golfer could achieve in ideal conditions.

Braid Hills. Known to locals and many others as Braids (no connection with golfer James Braid), this course is beautifully laid out over a rugged range of small hills in the southern suburbs of Edinburgh. The views to the south and the Pentland Hills and north over the city skyline toward the Firth of Forth are worth a visit in themselves. The city built this course at the turn of the 20th century after urban development forced golfers out of the city center. The 9-hole Princes Course was completed in 2003. Reservations are recommended for weekend play. ⊠ *27 Braids Hill Approach* ☏ *0131/447–6666 for Braids, 0131/666–2210* for *Princes* ⊕ *www.edinburghleisuregolf.co.uk* ✉ *Green fee: Braids weekdays £22, weekends £24.75; Princes weekdays £12.50, weekends £14* 🏌. *Braids: 18 holes, 5865 yds, par 71; Princes: 9 holes* ⊙ *Daily.*

Bruntsfield Links. The British Seniors and several other championship tournaments are held at this Willie Park–designed course, 3 miles west of Edinburgh. The course meanders among 155 acres of mature parkland and has fine views over the Firth of Forth. Bruntsfield takes its name from one of the oldest (1761) golf links in Scotland, in the center of Edinburgh—now just a 9-hole pitch-and-putt course—where the club used to play. A strict dress code applies. ✉ *32 Barnton Ave., Davidson's Mains* ☎ *0131/336–1479* ⊕ *www.sol.co.uk/b/bruntsfieldlinks* ✉ *Green fee: weekdays £65; weekends £70* ⚏ *Reservations essential* 🏌. *18 holes, 6446 yds, par 71* ⊙ *Daily.*

Duddingston. Founded in 1895, this public parkland course is 2 miles east of the city. The Braid Burn runs through the course, creating a perilous hazard on many holes. ✉ *Duddingston Rd. W, Duddingston* ☎ *0131/661–7688* ⊕ *www.duddingstongolfclub.co.uk* ✉ *Green fee: £44–£50* 🏌. *18 holes, 6525 yds, par 72.*

Liberton. Built in 1920, this rolling public parkland course has tight fairways and smallish greens. ✉ *Kingston Grange, 297 Gilmerton Rd., Liberton* ☎ *0131/664–3009* ⊕ *www.libertongc.co.uk* ✉ *Green fee: £31* 🏌. *18 holes, 5344 yds, par 67.*

Lothianburn. There are fine views of the countryside from this hillside course, which dates from 1893. It's 6 miles south of the city. ✉ *Biggar Rd., Fairmilehead* ☎ *0131/445–2288* ⊕ *www.lothianburngc.co.uk* ✉ *Green fee: £35* 🏌. *18 holes, 5692 yds, par 71.*

Murrayfield. Only five minutes from the city center, this heathland-style course is kept in fine condition and commands outstanding views over Edinburgh. ✉ *43 Murrayfield Rd., Murrayfield* ☎ *0131/337–3478* ⊕ *www.murrayfieldgolfclub.co.uk* ✉ *Green fee: £40* 🏌. *18 holes, 5781 yds, par 70.*

Royal Burgess Golfing Society. Dating to 1735, this is one of the world's oldest golf clubs. Its members originally played on Bruntsfield Links; now they and their guests play on elegantly manicured parkland in the city's northwestern suburbs. It's a challenging course with fine greens. ✉ *181 Whitehouse Rd., Barnton* ☎ *0131/339–2075* ⊕ *www.royalburgess.co.uk* ✉ *Green fee: weekdays £65; weekends £85* ⚏ *Reservations essential* 🏌. *18 holes, 6511 yds, par 71* ⊙ *Daily.*

RUGBY

Murrayfield Stadium. At Murrayfield Stadium, home of the Scottish Rugby Union, matches are played in early spring and fall. Crowds of good-humored rugby fans from all over the world add greatly to the sense of excitement in the streets of Edinburgh. ✉ *Roseburn Terr., Murrayfield* ☎ *0131/346–5000* ⊕ *www.scottishrugby.org.*

SOCCER

Like Glasgow, Edinburgh is soccer-mad, and there's an intense rivalry between the city's two professional teams. Remember, the game is called football in Britain.

Heart of Midlothian Football Club. The Heart of Midlothian Football Club, better known as the Hearts, plays in maroon and white and is based at Tynecastle. ⊠ *Tynecastle Stadium, McLeod St.* ☎ *0871/663–1874* ⊕ *www.heartsfc.co.uk.*

Hibernian Club. Known as the Hibs, the green-bedecked Hibernian Club plays its home matches at Easter Road Stadium. ⊠ *Easter Road Stadium, 12 Albion Pl.* ☎ *0131/661–2159* ⊕ *www.hibernianfc.co.uk.*

SIDE TRIPS FROM EDINBURGH

If you stand on an Edinburgh eminence—the castle ramparts, Arthur's Seat, Corstorphine Hill—you can plan a few Lothian excursions without even the aid of a map. The Lothians is the collective name given to the swath of countryside south of the Firth of Forth and surrounding Edinburgh. Many courtly and aristocratic families lived here, and the region still has the castles and mansions to prove it. The rich arrived and with them came deer parks, gardens in the French style, and Lothian's fame as a seed plot for Lowland gentility.

Although the region has always provided rich pickings for historians, it also used to offer even richer pickings for coal miners—for a century after the start of the industrial revolution, gentle streams steamed and stank with pollution. Although some black spots still remain, most of the rural countryside is once again a lovely setting for excursions.

You can explore a number of historic houses and castles of West Lothian and the Forth Valley, and territory north of the River Forth, in a day or two, or you can just pick one excursion. Stretching east to the sea and south to the Lowlands from Edinburgh, Midlothian and East Lothian are no more than one hour from Edinburgh. The inland river valleys, hills, and castles of Midlothian and East Lothian's delightful waterfronts, dunes, and golf links offer a taste of Scotland close to the capital.

WEST LOTHIAN AND THE FORTH VALLEY

West Lothian comprises a good bit of Scotland's central belt. The River Forth snakes across a widening floodplain on its descent from the Highlands, and by the time it reaches the western extremities of Edinburgh, it has already passed below the mighty Forth bridges and become a broad estuary. Castles and stately homes sprout thickly on both sides of the Forth.

GETTING HERE AND AROUND

BUS TRAVEL   First Bus and Lothian Buses services link most of this area, but working out a detailed itinerary by bus isn't always easy.

CAR TRAVEL   The Queensferry Road, also known as the A90, is the main thoroughfare running through this region. North of the Forth Bridge, the A985 goes to Culross, the M9 and A823 head to Dunfermiline, and the A91 passes Ochil Hills and Castle Campbell.

TRAIN TRAVEL   Dalmeny, Linlithgow, and Dunfermline all have rail stations and can be reached from Edinburgh stations.

West Lothian and the Forth Valley

2

VISITOR INFORMATION

VisitScotland has an information center about West Lothian in the town of Bo'ness, close to Blackness Castle and the House of Binns. It's open April to October. Visit West Lothian runs an information center at Burgh Halls in Linlithgow.

ESSENTIALS

Visitor Information **VisitScotland** ⊠ *Bo'ness Station, Union St., Bo'ness* ☎ *0845/225–5121* ⊕ *www.visitscotland.com/en-us/destinations-maps/ edinburgh-lothians.* **Visit West Lothian** ⊠ *Burgh Halls, The Cross, Linlithgow* ☎ *01506/282720* ⊕ *www.visitwestlothian.co.uk.*

SOUTH QUEENSFERRY

7 miles west of Edinburgh.

This pleasant little waterside community, a former ferry port, is completely dominated by the Forth Bridges, dramatic structures of contrasting architecture that span the Firth of Forth at this historic crossing point. It's near a number of historic and other sights.

GETTING HERE AND AROUND

The Queensferry Road, also known as the A90, is the main artery north toward the Forth Bridge heading to Hopetoun House, the House of the Binns, and Blackness Castle.

EXPLORING

Blackness Castle. Standing like a grounded ship on the very edge of the Forth, this curious 15th-century structure has had a varied career as a strategic fortress, state prison, powder magazine, and youth hostel. The countryside is gently green and cultivated, and open views extend across the blue Forth to the distant ramparts of the Ochil Hills. ⊠ *B903, 4 miles northeast of Linlithgow, Linlithgow* ☎ *01506/834807* ⊕ *www. historic-scotland.gov.uk/places* ☒ *£5.50* ☉ *Apr.–Sept., daily 9:30–5:30; Oct., daily 9:30–4:30; Nov.–Mar., Sat.–Wed. 9:30–4:30.*

Dalmeny House. The first of the stately houses clustered on the western edge of Edinburgh, Dalmeny House is the home of the earl and countess of Rosebery. This 1815 Tudor Gothic mansion displays among its sumptuous contents the best of the family's famous collection of 18th-century French furniture. Highlights include the library, the Napoléon Room, the Vincennes and Sevres porcelain collections, and the drawing room, with its tapestries and intricately wrought French furniture. Admission is only by guided tour. ⊠ *B924* ☎ *0131/331–1888* ⊕ *www.dalmeny.co.uk* ☒ *£8.50* ☉ *Tours June– July, Sun.–Wed. 2:15 and 3:30.*

FAMILY **Deep Sea World.** The former ferry port in North Queensferry dropped almost into oblivion after the Forth Road Bridge opened, but was dragged abruptly back into the limelight by the hugely popular Deep Sea World. This sophisticated aquarium on the Firth of Forth offers a fascinating view of underwater life. Go down a clear acrylic tunnel for a diver's-eye look at more than 5,000 fish, including 250 sharks (some over 9 feet long); and visit the exhibition hall, which has an Amazon-jungle display and an audiovisual presentation on local marine life. Ichthyophobes will feel more at ease in the adjacent café and gift shop. ✉ *Forthside Terr., North Queensferry* ☎ *01383/411880* ⊕ *www. deepseaworld.com* 🖅 *£13* ⊙ *Weekdays 10–5, weekends 10–6; last admission 1 hr before closing.*

Forth Rail Bridge. The Forth Rail Bridge was opened in 1890 and at the time hailed as the eighth wonder of the world, at 2,765 yards long; on a hot summer's day it expands by about another yard. Its neighbor is the 1,993-yard-long Forth Road Bridge, in operation since 1964. ✉ *Edinburgh Rd.*

Hopetoun House. The palatial premises of Hopetoun House, probably Scotland's grandest courtly seat and home of the Marquesses of Linlithgow, are considered to be among the Adam family's finest designs. The enormous house was started in 1699 to the original plans of Sir William Bruce (1630–1710), then enlarged between 1721 and 1754 by William Adam (1689–1748) and his sons Robert and John. There's a notable painting collection, and the house has decorative work of the highest order, plus all the trappings to keep you entertained: a nature trail, a restaurant in the former stables, farm shop, and a museum. Much of the wealth that created this sumptuous building came from the family's mining interests in the surrounding regions. ✉ *Off A904, 6 miles west of South Queensferry* ☎ *0131/331–2451* ⊕ *www.hopetoun. co.uk* 🖅 *£9.20; Grounds only £4.25* ⊙ *Apr.–Sept., daily 10:30–5, last admission at 4.*

House of the Binns. The 17th-century general "Bloody Tam" Dalyell (circa 1599–1685) transformed a fortified stronghold into a gracious mansion, the House of the Binns (the name derives from *bynn*, the old Scottish word for hill). The present exterior dates from around 1810 and shows a remodeling into a kind of mock fort with crenellated battlements and turrets. Inside, magnificent plaster ceilings are done in the Elizabethan style. ✉ *Off A904, 4 miles east of Linlithgow, Linlithgow* ☎ *0844/493–2127* ⊕ *www.nts.org.uk/visits* 🖅 *£10* ⊙ *June–Sept., Sat.–Wed. 2–5.*

WHERE TO EAT

$$
MODERN BRITISH
✕ **The Boat House.** Scotland's natural larder is on display at this romantic restaurant on the banks of the Forth. Seafood is the star of the show, and chef Paul Steward is the man behind the imaginative yet unfussy recipes. Standouts include halibut with an orange, ginger, and peppercorn reduction, panfried Oban scallops, and choice of cuts of steak. If you want a less formal affair, the bistro and cocktail bar next door has a friendly buzz. ⑤ *Average main: £18* ✉ *22 High St.* ☎ *0131/331–5429* ⊕ *www.theboathouse-sq.co.uk.*

JUPITER ARTLAND
10 miles west of Edinburgh.

For anyone drawn to interesting art and beautiful open spaces, a visit to this open-air collection of sculptures by world-renowned artists is a must.

GETTING HERE AND AROUND
To reach Jupiter Artland from Edinburgh, take the A71 toward Kilmarnock. Just after Wilkieston, turn right onto the B7015.

EXPLORING

Fodor's Choice **Jupiter Artland.** The beautiful grounds of a Jacobean manor house have
★ been transformed by an art-loving couple, Robert and Nicky Wilson,
into a sculpture park. With the aid of a map you can explore the magi-
cal landscapes and encounter artworks by Andy Goldsworthy, Anya
Gallaccio, Jim Lambie, Nathan Coley, Iam Hamilton Finlay, and Anish
Kapoor, among many others. A highlight is walking around Charles
Jencks' *Cells of Life,* a series of shapely, grass-covered mounds. Run by
First Bus, the 27 and X27 direct buses depart from Regent Road and
Dalry Road in Haymarket. ⊠ *Bonnington House Steadings, off B7015,
Wilkieston, Edinburgh* ☎ *01506/889900* ⊕ *www.jupiterartland.org*
🎫 *£8.50* ⊘ *Mid-May–Sept., Thurs.–Sun. 10–5.*

LINLITHGOW PALACE
12 miles west of Edinburgh.

These loch-side ruins retain impressive remnants of what was once the
seat of the Stewart kings.

GETTING HERE AND AROUND

From Edinburgh, take the M9 westward to Linlithgow Palace. You can
also board a train to Linlithgow Station, a short walk from the palace.

EXPLORING

Linlithgow Palace. On the edge of Linlithgow Loch stands the splendid
ruin of Linlithgow Palace, the birthplace of Mary, Queen of Scots in
1542. Burned, perhaps accidentally, by Hanoverian troops during the
last Jacobite rebellion in 1746, this impressive shell stands on a site
of great antiquity, though it's not certain anything survived an earlier
fire in 1424. The palace gatehouse was built in the early 16th century, and the central courtyard's elaborate fountain dates from around
1535. The halls and great rooms are cold, echoing stone husks now
in Historic Scotland's care. ⊠ *A706, south shore of Linlithgow Loch*
☎ *01506/842896* ⊕ *www.historic-scotland.gov.uk/places* 🎫 *£5.50*
⊘ *Apr.–Sept., daily 9:30–5:30; Oct.–Mar., daily 9:30–4:30.*

OCHIL HILLS
24 miles northwest of Edinburgh.

The scarp face of the Ochil Hills looms unmistakably. It's an old fault line
that yields up hard volcanic rocks and contrasts with the quantities of
softer coal immediately around the River Forth. The steep Ochils provided
grazing land and water power for Scotland's second-largest textile area.

GETTING HERE AND AROUND

There are two ways to get here by car: take the A90 north of the
Forth Bridge, or go via Stirling on the M9. The A91 passes Alva and
the Ochil Hills.

EXPLORING

Alva Glen. There's a breathtaking gorge at Alva Glen, and walking paths
(some are steep, so be prepared) that follow the gushing Alva Burn and
pass many abandoned woolen mills. ⊠ *A91, Alva* ⊕ *www.alvaglen.org.uk.*

Castle Campbell. With green woods below, bracken hills above, and a
view that on a clear day stretches right across the Forth Valley to the
tip of Tinto Hill near Lanark, Castle Campbell is certainly the most

atmospheric fortress within easy reach of Edinburgh. Formerly known as Castle Gloom, Castle Campbell stands out among Scottish castles for the sheer drama of its setting. The sturdy square of the tower house survives from the 15th century, when the site was fortified by the first Earl of Argyll. Other buildings and enclosures were subsequently added, but the sheer lack of space on this rocky eminence ensured that there would never be any drastic changes. John Knox, the fiery religious reformer, once preached here. In 1654 the castle was captured by Oliver Cromwell and garrisoned with English troops. It's now cared for by Historic Scotland and is part of the Clackmannanshire Tower Trail. To get here, follow a road off the A91 that angles sharply up the east side of the wooded defile. ⊠ *Off A91, Dollar Glen* ☎ *01259/742408* ⊕ *www.historic-scotland.gov. uk/places* ⊡ *£5.50* ⊙ *Apr.–Sept., daily 9:30–5:30; Oct., daily 9:30–4:30, Nov.–Mar., Mon.–Wed. and weekends 9:30–4:30.*

Mill Glen. Behind Tillicoultry (pronounced tilly-*coot*-ree), Mill Glen has a giant quarry, fine waterfalls, and interesting plants, making it a good hiking option for energetic explorers. ⊠ *A91, Tillicoultry.*

Ochil Hills Woodland Park. East of Alva is the Ochil Hills Woodland Park, which provides access to lovely Silver Glen, so called because the precious metal was mined here in the 18th century. ⊠ *A91, Alva* ☎ *01259/450000* ⊕ *www.ochils.org.uk/ochils-woodland-park.*

CULROSS

17 miles northwest of Edinburgh.

The town is a fascinating open-air museum that gives you a feel for life in the 17th and 18th centuries.

GETTING HERE AND AROUND
To get here by car, head north of the Forth Bridge on the A90, then westward on the A985.

EXPLORING
Fodor's Choice
★ **Culross.** With its Mercat Cross, cobbled streets, tolbooth, and narrow wynds (alleys), Culross, on the muddy shores of the Forth, is now a living museum of a 17th-century town and one of the most remarkable little towns in Scotland. It once had a thriving industry and export trade in coal and salt (the coal was used in the salt-panning process). It also had, curiously, a trade monopoly in the manufacture of baking *girdles* (griddles). As local coal became exhausted, the impetus of the industrial revolution passed Culross by, and other parts of the Forth Valley prospered. Culross became a backwater town, and the merchants' houses of the 17th and 18th centuries were never replaced by Victorian developments or modern architecture. In the 1930s the National Trust for Scotland started to buy up the decaying properties. With the help of other agencies, these buildings were brought to life. Today ordinary citizens live in many of the National Trust properties. A few—the Palace, Study, and Town House—are open to the public. ⊠ *Off A985, 8 miles south of Dollar* ☎ *0844/493–2189* ⊕ *www.nts.org.uk/visits* ⊡ *£10* ⊙ *June– Aug., daily noon–5; Apr., May and Sept., Thurs.–Mon. noon–5; Oct., Fri.–Mon. noon–4; last admission 1 hr before closing.*

2

DUNFERMLINE

16 miles northwest of Edinburgh.

Oft-overlooked Dunfermline was once the world center for the production of damask linen, but the town is better known today as the birthplace of millionaire industrialist and philanthropist Andrew Carnegie (1835–1919). Undoubtedly, Dunfermline's most famous son, Carnegie endowed the town with a park, library, fitness center, and, naturally, a Carnegie Hall, still the focus of culture and entertainment.

GETTING HERE AND AROUND

When you're driving, head north of the Forth Bridge on the A90, then the M90.

EXPLORING

Andrew Carnegie Birthplace Museum. The 18th-century weaver's cottage where Carnegie was born in 1835 is now the Andrew Carnegie Birthplace Museum. Don't be misled by the cottage's simple exterior—inside it opens into a larger hall, where documents, photographs, and artifacts relate Carnegie's fascinating life story. You can learn such obscure details as the claim that Carnegie was one of only three men in the United States then able to translate Morse code by ear as it came down the wire. ⊠ *Moodie St.* ☎ *01383/724302* ⊕ *www.carnegiebirthplace. com* ☞ *Free* ☉ *Mar.–Nov., Mon.–Sat. 10–5, Sun. 2–5.*

Dunfermline Abbey and Palace. The Dunfermline Abbey and Palace complex was founded in the 11th century by Queen Margaret, the English wife of the Scots king Malcolm III. Some Norman work can be seen in the present church, where Robert the Bruce (12744–1329) lies buried. The palace grew from the abbey guesthouse and was the birthplace of Charles I (1600–49). Dunfermline was the seat of the royal court of Scotland until the end of the 11th century, and its central role in Scottish affairs is explored by means of display panels dotted around the drafty but hallowed buildings. ⊠ *Monastery St.* ☎ *01383/739026* ⊕ *www.historic-scotland.gov.uk/places* ☞ *£4.50* ☉ *Apr.–Sept., daily 9:30–5:30; Oct.–Mar., daily 9:30–4:30; Nov.–Mar., Mon.–Wed. and weekends 9:30–4:30; last admission ½ hr before closing.*

Pittencrieff House Museum. Housed in a 17th-century laird's mansion surrounded by beautiful parkland with picnic areas and resident peacocks, Pittencrieff House Museum explores the town's history. The Magic of the Glen section features a family-friendly natural-history exhibit that includes dinosaurs, fossils, and wildlife. ⊠ *Pittencrieff Park* ☎ *01383/722935* ⊕ *www.scottishmuseums.org.uk* ☞ *Free* ☉ *Apr.– Sept., daily 11–5; Oct.–Mar., daily 11–4.*

MIDLOTHIAN AND EAST LOTHIAN

In spite of the finest stone carving in Scotland at Rosslyn Chapel, associations with Sir Walter Scott, outstanding castles, and miles of rolling countryside, Midlothian, the area immediately south of Edinburgh, for years remained off the beaten path. Perhaps a little in awe of sophisticated Edinburgh to the north and the well-manicured charm of the stockbroker belt of nearby upmarket East Lothian, Midlothian was quietly preoccupied with its own workaday little towns and dormitory suburbs.

As for East Lothian, it started with the advantage of golf courses of world rank, most notably Muirfield, plus a scattering of stately homes and interesting hotels. It's an area of glowing grain fields in summer and quite a few discreetly polite "strictly private" signs at the end of driveways. Still, it has plenty of interest, including photogenic villages, active fishing harbors, and vistas of pastoral Lowland Scotland, seemingly a world away (but much less than an hour by car) from bustling Edinburgh.

GETTING HERE AND AROUND

BUS TRAVEL   City buses travel as far as Swanston and the Pentland Hills. First buses serve towns and villages throughout Midlothian and East Lothian. For details of all services, inquire at the St. Andrew Square bus station in Edinburgh.

CAR TRAVEL   A quick route to Rosslyn Chapel follows the A701, while the A7 heads toward Gorebridge and the Scottish Mining Museum. The A1 passes Newhailes, Haddington, and Dunbar. Take the A198 to North Berwick, Dirleton Castle, and Tantallon Castle.

TRAIN TRAVEL   There is no train service in Midlothian. In East Lothian the towns of North Berwick, Drem, and Dunbar have train stations with regular service from Edinburgh.

NEWHAILES

5 miles east of Edinburgh.

With sumptuous interiors and relaxing grounds, this neo-Palladian villa a few miles east of Edinburgh hosted many luminaries of the Scottish Enlightenment.

GETTING HERE AND AROUND

To get here from Edinburgh take the A1 east, then transfer to the A6095. You can also get here by Lothian bus 30 or by train to Newcraighall Station, a 20-minute walk from the villa.

EXPLORING

Newhailes. This fine late-17th-century house (with 18th-century additions), owned and run by the National Trust for Scotland, was designed by Scottish architect James Smith (circa 1645–1731) in 1686 as his own home. He later sold it to Lord Bellendon, and in 1707 it was bought by Sir David Dalrymple (c. 1665–1721), first baronet of Hailes, who improved and extended the house, adding one of the finest rococo interiors in Scotland. The library played host to many famous figures from the Scottish Enlightenment, including inveterate Scot-basher Dr. Samuel Johnson, who dubbed the library "the most learned room in Europe." Most of the original interiors and furnishings remain intact, creating great authenticity. ✉ *Newhailes Rd.* ☎ *0844/493–2125* ⊕ *www.nts.org. uk/visits* 🎫 *£12* ⏲ *Apr.–Sept., Thurs.–Mon. noon–5.*

ROSLIN

7 miles south of Edinburgh.

Although the town is overshadowed by its chapel, Roslin is a pleasant place to while away some time. There are some nice walks by the North River Esk.

GETTING HERE AND AROUND

By car take the A701 south. Lothian buses service also shuttle passengers from Edinburgh.

EXPLORING

Fodor's Choice ★ **Rosslyn Chapel.** Rosslyn Chapel has always beckoned curious visitors intrigued by the various legends surrounding its magnificent carvings, but today it pulses with tourists as never before. Dan Brown's bestselling novel *The Da Vinci Code* has made visiting this Episcopal chapel (services continue to be held here) an imperative stop for many of its enthusiasts. Whether you're a fan of the book or not—and of the book's theory that the chapel has a secret sign that can lead you to the Holy Grail—this is a site of immense interest. Originally conceived by Sir William Sinclair (circa 1404–80) and dedicated to St. Matthew in 1446, the chapel is outstanding for the quality and variety of the carving inside. Covering almost every square inch of stonework are human figures, animals, and plants. The meaning of these remains subject to many theories; some depict symbols from the medieval order of the Knights Templar and from Freemasonry. The chapel's design called for a cruciform structure, but only the choir and parts of the east transept walls were completed. ⊠ *Chapel Loan* ☎ *0131/440–2159* ⊕ *www.rosslynchapel.com* ⊠ *£9* ☉ *Mon.– Sat. 9:30–5:30, Sun. noon–4:45.*

SCOTTISH MINING MUSEUM

9 miles southeast of Edinburgh.

The museum provides a sobering look into the lives of coal miners and conditions they endured down Scotland's mines.

GETTING HERE AND AROUND

To get here by car, head south on the A7 to Newtongrange. You can also take Lothian buses 33 or 29 or First buses 95 or X95.

EXPLORING

The Scottish Mining Museum. In the former mining community of Newtongrange, the Scottish Mining Museum provides a good introduction to the history of Scotland's mining industry. With the help of videos you can experience life deep below the ground. There are also interactive displays and "magic helmets" that bring the tour to life and relate the power that the mining company had over the lives of the individual workers here, in Scotland's largest planned mining village. This frighteningly autocratic system survived well into the 1930s—the company owned the houses, shops, and even the pub. The scenery is no more attractive than you would expect, with the green Pentland Hills hovering in the distance. ⊠ *A7* ☎ *0131/663–7519* ⊕ *www. scottishminingmuseum.com* ⊠ *£7.50* ☉ *Apr.–Sept., daily 10–5; Oct.– Mar., daily 10–4; last admission 1½ hrs before closing. Guided tours daily at 11:30, 1:30, and 3.*

BORTHWICK CASTLE

12 miles southeast of Edinburgh.

This hulking 15th-century fortress is famous for a visit from Mary, Queen of Scots.

GETTING HERE AND AROUND

The A7 is the best way to get here from Edinburgh.

EXPLORING

Borthwick Castle. Set in green countryside with scattered woods and lush hedgerows, the village of Borthwick is dominated by Borthwick Castle, which dates from the 15th century and is still occupied. Mary, Queen of Scots came to this stark, tall, twin-towered fortress on a kind of honeymoon with her ill-starred third husband, the Earl of Bothwell. Their already-dubious bliss was interrupted by Mary's political opponents, often referred to as the Lords of the Congregation, a confederacy of powerful nobles who favored the crowning of her young son, James. Rather insensitively, they laid siege to the castle while the newlyweds were there. Mary subsequently escaped disguised as a man. She was not free for long, however. It was only a short time before she was defeated in battle and imprisoned. She languished in prison for 21 years before Queen Elizabeth I of England (1558–1603) signed her death warrant in 1587. Bothwell's fate was equally gloomy: he died insane in a Danish prison. The castle now functions as a hotel, but it's well worth a look around. ⊠ *Off A7, North Middleton* ✛ *1 mile south of Gorebridge* ☎ *01875/820514* ⊕ *www.borthwickcastlehotel.com* 🎫 *Free* ☉ *Tour hrs vary.*

CRICHTON CASTLE

11 miles southeast of Edinburgh.

Sitting on a terrace above the River Tyne, this 14th-century structure with a diamond-faceted façade was home to the Crichtons and later to the Earls of Bothwell.

GETTING HERE AND AROUND

Heading south on the A68, take the turnoff at Pathhead.

EXPLORING

Crichton Castle. Crichton Castle stands amid rolling hills that are interrupted here and there by patches of woodland. Crichton was a Bothwell family castle; Mary, Queen of Scots attended the wedding here of Bothwell's sister, Lady Janet Hepburn, to Mary's brother, Lord John Stewart. The curious arcaded range reveals diamond-faceted stonework; this particular geometric pattern is unique in Scotland and is thought to have been inspired by Renaissance styles on the continent, particularly Italy. The oldest part of the work is the 14th-century keep (square tower). Do note that there are no toilets at the castle. ⊠ *B6367, 7 miles southeast of Dalkeith, Pathhead* ☎ *01875/320017* ⊕ *www.historic-scotland.gov. uk/places* 🎫 *£4.50* ☉ *Apr.–Sept., daily 9:30–5:30.*

DUNBAR

25 miles east of Edinburgh.

In the days before tour companies started offering package deals to the Mediterranean, Dunbar was a popular holiday beach resort. Now a bit faded, the town is still lovely for its spacious Georgian-style properties, characterized by the astragals, or fan-shape windows, above the doors; the symmetry of the house fronts; and the parapeted rooflines. Though not the popular seaside playground it once was, Dunbar has an attractive beach and a picturesque harbor.

GETTING HERE AND AROUND
Head east on the A1 to get to Dunbar. You can also take the train from Waverley.

EXPLORING
John Muir Country Park. Taking in the estuary of the River Tyne winding down from the Moorfoot Hills, the John Muir Country Park encompasses varied coastal scenery: rocky shoreline, golden sands, and the mixed woodlands of Tyninghame, teeming with wildlife. Dunbar-born conservationist John Muir (1838–1914), whose family moved to the United States when he was a child, helped found Yosemite and Sequoia national parks in California. ✉ *A1087, 2 miles west of Dunbar.*

GOLF
Dunbar Golf Club. There's a lighthouse at the 9th hole of this seaside course, founded in 1794. It's a good choice for experiencing a typical east-coast links. Within easy reach of Edinburgh, it has stunning views of the Firth of Forth and May Island. ✉ *East Links, off A1087* ☎ *01368/862086* ⊕ *www.dunbar-golfclub.co.uk* ✉ *Green fee: weekdays £65; weekends £85* ⚲ *Reservations essential* ⚑ *18 holes, 6597 yds, par 71* ⊙ *Fri.–Wed.*

NORTH BERWICK
20 miles northeast of Edinburgh.

The pleasant little seaside resort of North Berwick manages to retain a small-town personality even when it's thronged with city visitors on warm summer Sunday afternoons. Eating ice cream, the city folk stroll on the beach and in the narrow streets or gaze at the sailing craft in the small harbor. The town is near a number of castles and other sights.

GETTING HERE AND AROUND
Travel east on the A1 and A198, or take the train from Waverley.

EXPLORING
Dirleton Castle. In the center of tiny Dirleton sits the 12th-century Dirleton Castle, surrounded by a high outer wall. Within the wall you can find a 17th-century bowling green, set in the shade of yew trees and surrounded by a herbaceous flower border that blazes with color in high summer. The castle, now in Historic Scotland's care, was occupied in 1298 by King Edward I of England as part of his campaign for the continued subjugation of the unruly Scots. ✉ *A198, 2 miles west of North Berwick* ☎ *01620/850330* ⊕ *www.historic-scotland.gov.uk/ places* ✉ *£5.50* ⊙ *Apr.–Sept., daily 9:30–5:30; Oct.–Mar., daily 9:30– 4:30; last admission ½ hr before closing.*

FAMILY **Scottish Seabird Centre.** An observation deck, exhibits, and films at the Scottish Seabird Centre provide a captivating introduction to the world of the gannets and puffins that nest on nearby Bass Rock. Live interactive cameras let you take an even closer look at the bird colonies and marine mammals at Craigleith and the Isle of May. There are plenty of family-friendly activities, nature walks, and photography shows. ⊠ *The Harbour* ☎ *01620/890202* ⊕ *www.seabird.org* ☒ *£8.95* ⊙ *Apr.–Aug., daily 10–6; Feb., Mar., Sept. and Oct., weekdays 10–5, weekends 10–5:30; Nov.–Jan., weekdays 10–4, weekends 10–5; last admission 45 mins before closing.*

St. Mary's Parish Church. The unmistakable red-sandstone St. Mary's Parish Church, with its Norman tower, stands in the village of Whitekirk on a site occupied since the 6th century. It was a place of pilgrimage in medieval times because of its healing well. Behind the kirk, in a field, stands a tithe barn. Tithe barns originated with the practice of giving to the church a portion of local produce, which then required storage space. In the 15th century, the church was visited by a young Italian nobleman, Aeneas Sylvius Piccolomini, after he was shipwrecked off the East Lothian coast. Two decades later, Piccolomini became Pope Pius II. At one end of the barn stands a 16th-century tower house, which at one point in its history accommodated visiting pilgrims. The large three-story barn was added to the tower house in the 17th century. ⊠ *A198, 6 miles south of North Berwick, Whitekirk* ☒ *Free* ⊙ *Daily 9 am–sunset.*

Tantallon Castle. Rising on a cliff beyond the flat fields east of North Berwick, Tantallon Castle is a substantial ruin defending a headland with the sea on three sides. The red sandstone is pitted and eaten by time and sea spray, with the earliest surviving stonework dating from the late 14th century. The fortress was besieged in 1529 by the cannons of King James V (1512–42). Rather inconveniently, the besieging forces ran out of gunpowder. Cannons were used again, to deadlier effect, in a later siege during the Civil War in 1651. Twelve days of battering with the heavy guns of Cromwell's General Monk greatly damaged the flanking towers. Fortunately much of the curtain wall of this former Douglas stronghold, now cared for by Historic Scotland, survives. ⊠ *A198* ☎ *01620/892727* ⊕ *www.historic-scotland.gov.uk/places* ☒ *£5.50* ⊙ *Apr.–Sept., daily 9:30–5:30; Oct.–Mar., daily 9:30–4:30; last admission ½ hr before closing.*

WHERE TO STAY

$$
B&B/INN
Glebe House. This dignified 18th-century manse sits amid its own secluded grounds, yet it's in the heart of town, a 10-minute walk east of the station. **Pros:** peaceful atmosphere; interesting antiques; sociable breakfast around a mahogany table. **Cons:** books up well in advance; too precious for some. ⑤ *Rooms from: £130* ⊠ *Law Rd.* ☎ *01620/892608* ⊕ *www.glebehouse-nb.co.uk* ⟿ *4 rooms* ☰ *No credit cards* ❑ *Breakfast.*

GULLANE
15 miles northeast of Edinburgh.

Noticeable along this coastline are the golf courses of East Lothian, laid out wherever there is available links space. Gullane is surrounded by them, and its inhabitants are typically clad in expensive golfing sweaters. Apart from golf, you can enjoy restful summer evening strolls at Gullane's beach, well within driving distance of the village.

GETTING HERE AND AROUND

From Edinburgh, drive east on the A1, then head north on the A198.

GOLF

Gullane Golf Club. Often overshadowed by Muirfield, Gullane provides an equally authentic links experience and a far more effusive welcome than its slightly snooty neighbor just along the road. The three courses here crisscross Gullane Hill and all command outstanding views of the Firth of Forth. No. 1 is the toughest, but No. 2 and No. 3 offer up equally compelling sport. ⊠ *West Links Rd.* ☎ *01620/842123* ⊕ *www. gullanegolfclub.com* ✉ *Green fee: No. 1. Course £96. No. 2. Course £48. No. 3. Course £33* ⚐ *Reservations essential* ⅃. *No. 1. Course: 18 holes, 6583 yds, par 71; No. 2. Course: 18 holes, 6385 yds, par 71; No. 3. Course: 18 holes, 5259 yds, par 68* ☉ *Daily.*

Muirfield. Home of the Honourable Company of Edinburgh Golfers, the world's oldest golfing club, Muirfield has a pedigree that few other courses can match. Although this course overlooking the Firth of Forth is considered one of the world's most challenging, players also talk about it being "fair," meaning it has no hidden bunkers or sand traps. The club has a well-deserved reputation for being stuffy (pop star Justin Timberlake wasn't allowed in the restaurant because he wasn't wearing a jacket and tie), and women are not allowed to be members (although they can play as guests). Visitors are allowed only on Tuesday and Thursday, and you must apply for a tee time well in advance. ⊠ *Duncur Rd.* ☎ *01620/842123* ⊕ *www.muirfield.org.uk* ✉ *Green fee: £200* ⅃. *18 holes, 6601 yds, par 70.*

HADDINGTON

15 miles east of Edinburgh.

One of the best-preserved medieval street plans in the country can be explored in Haddington. Among the many buildings of architectural or historical interest is the Town House, designed by William Adam in 1748 and enlarged in 1830. A wall plaque at the Sidegate recalls the great heights of floods from the River Tyne. Beyond is the medieval Nungate footbridge, with the Church of St. Mary a little way upstream.

GETTING HERE AND AROUND

Head east on the A1, or take First buses X6, X8, or 106.

EXPLORING

Lennoxlove House. Just to the south of Haddington stands Lennoxlove House, the grand ancestral home of the very grand dukes of Hamilton since 1947 and the Baird family before them. A turreted country house, part of it dating from the 15th century, Lennoxlove is a cheerful mix of family life and Scottish history. The beautifully decorated rooms house portraits, furniture, porcelain, and items associated with Mary, Queen of Scots, including her supposed death mask. Sporting activities from falconry to fishing take place on the stunning grounds. ⊠ *B6369* ☎ *01620/828619* ⊕ *www.lennoxlove.com* ✉ *£5* ☉ *Tours Apr.–Sept., Wed., Thurs., and Sun. 1:30–3:30.*

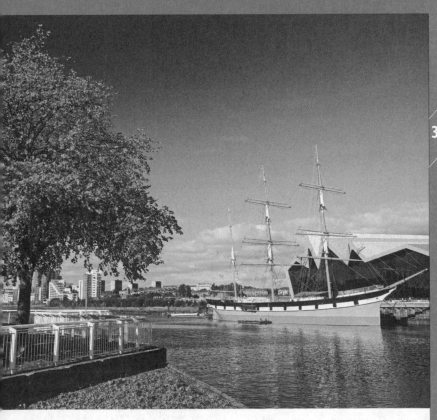

GLASGOW

Updated
by Mike
Gonzalez

Trendy stores, a booming cultural life, fascinating architecture, and stylish restaurants reinforce Glasgow's claim
to being Scotland's most exciting city. After decades of
decline, it has experienced an urban renaissance uniquely
its own. The city's grand architecture reflects a prosperous
past built on trade and shipbuilding. Today buildings by
Charles Rennie Mackintosh hold pride of place along with
the Zaha Hadid–designed Riverside Museum.

Glasgow (the "dear green place," as it was known) was founded some
1,500 years ago. Legend has it that the king of Strathclyde, irate about
his wife's infidelity, had a ring he had given her thrown into the river
Clyde. (Apparently she had passed it on to an admirer.) When the king
demanded to know where the ring had gone, the distraught queen
asked the advice of her confessor, St. Mungo. He suggested fishing
for it—and the first salmon to emerge had the ring in its mouth. The
moment is commemorated on the city's coat of arms.

The medieval city expanded when it was given a royal license to trade;
the current High Street was the main thoroughfare at the time. The
vast profits from American cotton and tobacco built the grand mansions of the Merchant City in the 18th century. In the 19th century
the river Clyde became the center of a vibrant shipbuilding industry,
fed by the city's iron and steel works. The city grew again, but its
internal divisions grew at the same time. The West End harbored the
elegant homes of the newly rich shipyard owners. Down by the river,
areas like the infamous Gorbals, with its crowded slums, sheltered the
laborers who built the ships. They came from the Highlands, expelled
to make way for sheep, or from Ireland, where the potato famines
drove thousands from their homes.

During the 19th century the population grew from 80,000 to more
than a million. And the new prosperity gave Glasgow its grand neoclassical buildings, such as those built by Alexander "Greek" Thomson, as
well as the adventurous visionary buildings designed by Charles Rennie Mackintosh and others who produced Glasgow's Arts and Crafts
movement. The City Chambers, built in 1888, are a proud statement in
marble and gold sandstone, a clear symbol of the wealthy and powerful
Victorian industrialists' hopes for the future.

The decline of shipbuilding and the closure of the factories led to much
speculation as to what direction the city would take now. The curious thing is that, at least in part, the past gave the city a new lease of
life. It was as if people looked at their city and saw Glasgow's beauty
for the first time: its extraordinarily rich architectural heritage, its
leafy parks, its artistic heritage, and its complex social history. Today
Glasgow is a vibrant cultural center and a commercial hub, as well as

a launching pad from which to explore the rest of Scotland, which, as it turns out, is not so far away. In fact, it takes only 40 minutes to reach Loch Lomond, where the other Scotland begins.

ORIENTATION AND PLANNING

GETTING ORIENTED

Glasgow's layout is hard to read in a single glance. The city center is roughly defined by the M8 motorway to the north and west, the River Clyde to the south, and High Street to the east. Glaswegians tend to walk a good deal, and the relatively flat and compact city center, most of which follows a grid pattern, is perfect for pedestrians. The West End has Glasgow University and lovely Kelvingrove Park. The River Clyde, around which Glasgow grew up as a trading city, runs through the center of the city—literally cutting it in two.

City Center. If you're interested in how the city blossomed in the 19th century, this is where to start. Look up to see wonderful Victorian buildings expressing the confidence of a burgeoning industrial capital. George Square's City Chambers are well worth a visit before you trawl the shops along Buchanan Street, duck into one of the trendy eateries, or explore the wide variety of bars and music venues on offer.

Merchant City. In the Middle Ages, the city grew up around Glasgow Cathedral. The oldest house, Provand's Lordship, was originally the home of a bishop. As the city expanded along with the growing transatlantic trade, wealthy traders built their palatial houses here. They were laid to rest in the glorious tombs of the Necropolis, which overlooks the city. Today the area is busy with restaurants, clubs, and shops.

West End. In this quieter, slightly hillier western part of the city is Glasgow University and the more bohemian side of Glasgow. The West End's treasures include the Botanic Gardens, Kelvingrove Park, and the Kelvingrove Art Gallery and Museum. There are also plenty of well-priced restaurants and lively bars. Byres Road is at its heart, especially when it fills with weekend revelers at its bars and clubs.

The Clyde. Once a hard-working river lined with shipyards, the Clyde has been reborn as a relaxing destination that entrances visitors and locals alike. The Glasgow Science Centre and the Museum of Transport face each other across the water. While the Scottish Exhibition Centre and the new SSE Hydro are major venues for all sorts of events.

East End. What was once a neglected corner of Glasgow is being treated to a major face-lift. Glasgow Green's wonderful People's Palace draws visitors throughout the year, and on weekends the nearby Barras market is a reminder of the area's past.

South Side. Often overlooked, this less visited side of the city has two world-class museums in beautiful Pollok Park: the handsome Burrell Collection and Pollok House, with its art collection and its elegant gardens. Its main thoroughfare, Pollokshaws Road, boasts several well-regarded cafés and restaurants.

TOP REASONS TO GO

Design and architecture: The Victorians left a legacy of striking architecture, and Glasgow's buildings manifest the city's love of grand artistic statements—just remember to look up. The Arts and Crafts buildings by Charles Rennie Mackintosh are reason alone to visit.

Art museums: Some of Britain's best museums and art galleries are in Glasgow. The Burrell Collection and the eclectic Kelvingrove Art Gallery and Museum are definitely worth a visit, even on a sunny day.

Gorgeous parks and gardens: From Kelvingrove Park to the Botanic Gardens, Glasgow has more parks per square mile than any other city in Europe. Stop by the Botanic Gardens for outdoor theatrical productions in summer, or Bellahouston Park for the annual piping festival.

Pints and great grub: Whether you fancy a Guinness in a traditional old-man's pub like the Scotia or one of the converted churches like Òran Mór, there's a pub to fit all thirsts. Locals love their cafés and tearooms; stop by the Willow Tearoom or Where the Monkey Sleeps for cake and a rest from sightseeing.

Retail therapy: The city has become known for cutting-edge design. Look for everything from Scottish specialties to stylish fashions on the city center's hottest shopping streets, Ingram or Buchanan, or at the elegant Princes Square.

Burns country: Scotland's national poet lived, wrote, and drank in Ayrshire, a great place to appreciate his work. The excellent Robert Burns Birthplace Museum in Alloway is fitting tribute to his life and work.

PLANNING

WHEN TO GO

The best times to visit Glasgow are spring and summer. Although you may encounter crowds, the weather is more likely to be warm and dry. In summer the days are long and pleasant—that is, if the rain holds off—and festivals and outdoor events are abundant. Fall can be nice, although cold weather begins to set in after mid-September and the days grow shorter. From November to February it is cold, wet, and dark. Although thousands of people flock to Glasgow for New Year's celebrations, the winter months are relatively quiet in terms of crowds.

PLANNING YOUR TIME

You could quite easily spend five comfortable days here, although in a pinch, two would do and three would be pleasant. The best strategy for seeing the city is to start in the Merchant City and work your way west. On the first day explore the city's medieval heritage, taking in Glasgow Cathedral, the Museum of Religious Life, and Provand's Lordship, as well as the Necropolis with its fascinating crumbling monuments. It is a gentle walk from here to the Merchant City and George Square, around which spread the active and crowded shopping areas. The Mackintosh Trail will take you to the many buildings designed by this outstanding Glasgow designer and architect. Another day could be well spent between the Kelvingrove Art Gallery (you can lunch here and listen to the daily concert on its magnificent organ) and the nearby Hunterian Museum and Gallery. From here it's only minutes to lively Byres Road and its shops, pubs, and cafés. Another option is to go to the South Side, make a beeline to the Burrell Collection and the House for an Art Lover.

If you have a few extra days, head out to Burns country and the extraordinary Burns Birthplace Museum in Ayrshire. It's a scenic 45-minute drive from Glasgow. Most destinations on the Clyde Coast are easily accessible from Glasgow. Direct trains from Central Station take you to Paisley, Irvine, Largs, Troon, Kilmarnock, and Lanark in less than an hour. These small towns need no more than a day to explore. To get a flavor of island life, take the hour-long train ride to Wemyss Bay and then the ferry to the Isle of Bute.

GETTING HERE AND AROUND
AIR TRAVEL

Airlines flying from Glasgow Airport to the rest of the United Kingdom and to Europe include Aer Lingus, Air Malta, British Airways, easyJet, Icelandair, and KLM. Several carriers fly from North America, including Air Canada, American Airlines, United, and Icelandair (service via Reykjavík).

Ryanair offers rock-bottom airfares between Prestwick and London's Stansted Airport. Budget-minded easyJet has similar services from Glasgow to London's Stansted and Luton airports. Loganair flies to the islands.

Air Contacts Aer Lingus ☎ *0871/718–2020* ⊕ *www.aerlingus.com.* **Air Canada** ☎ *0871/220–1111* ⊕ *www.aircanada.com.* **Air Malta** ☎ *00356/607–3710* ⊕ *www.airmalta.com.* **American Airlines** ☎ *0844/499–7300* ⊕ *www.americanairlines.co.uk.* **BMI Regional** ☎ *0844/848–4888* ⊕ *www.bmiregional.com.* **British Airways** ☎ *0844/493–0787* ⊕ *www.britishairways.com.* **easyJet** ☎ *0871/244–2366* ⊕ *www.easyjet.com.* **Icelandair** ☎ *0844/811–1190* ⊕ *www.icelandair.com.* **KLM** ☎ *0871/231–0000* ⊕ *www.klm.com.* **Loganair** ☎ *0871/848–7594* ⊕ *www.loganair.co.uk.* **Ryanair** ☎ *0871/246–0000* ⊕ *www.ryanair.com.* **United** ☎ *0845/844–4777* ⊕ *www.united.com.*

AIRPORTS Glasgow Airport is about 7 miles west of the city center on the M8 to Greenock. The airport serves international and domestic flights, and most major European carriers have frequent and convenient connections (some via airports in England) to many cities on the continent. There's a frequent shuttle service from London, as well as regular flights from Birmingham, Bristol, East Midlands, Leeds/Bradford, Manchester, Southampton, Isle of Man, and Jersey. There are also flights from Wales (Cardiff) and Ireland (Belfast, Dublin, and Londonderry). Local Scottish connections can be made to Aberdeen, Barra, Benbecula, Campbeltown, Inverness, Islay, Kirkwall, Shetland (Sumburgh), Stornoway, and Tiree.

Prestwick Airport sits on the Ayrshire coast about 30 miles southwest of Glasgow. Eclipsed for some years by Glasgow Airport, Prestwick has grown in importance, not least because of lower airfares from Ryanair.

Airport Contacts Glasgow Airport ✉ *Caledonia Way, Paisley* ☎ *0844/481–5555* ⊕ *www.glasgowairport.com.* **Prestwick Airport** ✉ *A79, Prestwick* ☎ *0871/223–0700* ⊕ *www.gpia.co.uk.*

Although there's a railway station about 2 miles from Glasgow Airport (Paisley Gilmour Street), most people travel to the city center by bus or taxi. It takes about 20 minutes, slightly longer at rush hour. Metered taxis are available outside domestic arrivals, and cost around £22.

Express buses run from Glasgow Airport (outside departures lobby) to Central and Queen Street stations and to the Buchanan Street bus station. They depart every 15 minutes throughout the day. The fare is £6.

The drive from Glasgow Airport into the city center is normally quite easy, even if you're used to driving on the right. The M8 motorway runs beside the airport (Junction 29) and takes you straight into the Glasgow city center. Thereafter Glasgow's streets follow a grid pattern, at least in the city center. A map is useful—get one from the car-rental company.

Most companies that provide chauffeur-driven cars and tours will also do limousine airport transfers. A company that is currently a member of the Greater Glasgow and Clyde Valley Tourist Board is Charlton.

An hourly coach service makes trips to Glasgow from Prestwick Airport, but takes much longer than the train. There's a rapid half-hourly train service (hourly on Sunday) direct from the terminal to Glasgow Central. Strathclyde Passenger Transport and ScotRail offer a discount ticket that allows you to travel for half the standard fare; just show a valid airline ticket for a flight to or from Prestwick Airport.

By car, the city center is reached via the fast M77 in about 40 minutes (longer in rush hour). Metered taxis are available at the airport. The fare to Glasgow is about £40.

Airport Transfer Contacts Charlton ☎ 0870/058–9500
⊕ www.charltonlimo.com.

BUS TRAVEL

The main intercity operators are National Express and Scottish Citylink, which serve numerous towns and cities in Scotland, Wales, and England, including London and Edinburgh. Glasgow's bus station is on Buchanan Street, not far from Queen Street Station.

When traveling from the city center to either the West End or the South Side, it's easy to use the city's integrated network of buses, subways, and trains. Service is reliable and connections are convenient from buses to trains and the subway. Many buses require exact fare, which is usually around £1.75.

Traveline Scotland provides information on schedules and fares, as does the Strathclyde Passenger Transport Travel Centre, which has an information center.

Bus Contacts Buchanan Street Bus Station ⊠ Killermont St., City Center ☎ 0141/333–3708 ⊕ www.spt.co.uk. **National Express** ☎ 0871/781–8181 ⊕ www.nationalexpressgroup.com. **Scottish Citylink** ☎ 0871/266–3333 ⊕ www.citylink.co.uk. **Strathclyde Passenger Transport Travel Centre** ⊠ 12 W. George St., City Center ☎ 0141/332–6811 ⊕ www.spt.co.uk ⊙ Mon.–Thurs. 8:30–4:45, Fri. 8:30–4. **Traveline Scotland** ☎ 0871/200–2233 ⊕ www.travelinescotland.com.

CAR TRAVEL

If you're driving to Glasgow from England and the south of Scotland, you'll probably approach the city via the M6, M74, and A74. The city center is clearly marked from these roads. From Edinburgh, the M8 leads to the city center. From the north, the A82 from Fort William and the A82/M80 from Stirling join the M8 in the city center.

You don't need a car in Glasgow, and you're probably better off without one. Although most modern hotels have their own lots, parking can be trying. In the city center meters are expensive, running about £2.40 per hour during the day. In the West End they cost 40 pence per hour, but you often have to feed the meter until 10 pm. Don't even consider parking illegally, as fines are upward of £30. Multistory garages are open 24 hours a day at the following locations: Anderston Centre, George Street, Waterloo Place, Mitchell Street, Cambridge Street, and Concert Square. Rates run between £1 and £2 per hour. More convenient are the park-and-ride operations at some subway stations (Kelvinbridge, Bridge Street, and Shields Road). You'll be downtown in no time.

SUBWAY TRAVEL

Glasgow's small subway system—it has 15 stations—is useful for reaching all the city center and West End attractions. Stations are marked by a prominent letter "S." You can choose between flat fares (£1.40) and a one-day pass (£2.60). Trains run regularly from Monday through Saturday, with more limited Sunday service. The distance between many central stops is no more than a 10-minute walk. More information is available from Strathclyde Passenger Transport Travel Centre.

TAXI TRAVEL

Taxis are a fast and cost-effective way to get around. You'll find metered taxis (usually black and of the London sedan type) at stands all over the city center. Most have radio dispatch. Some have also been adapted to take wheelchairs. You can hail a cab on the street if its "for hire" sign is illuminated. A typical ride from the city center to the West End or the South Side costs around £6.

Taxi Contact Glasgow Taxis ☎ *0141/429–7070* ⊕ *www.glasgowtaxisltd.co.uk.*

TRAIN TRAVEL

Glasgow has two main rail stations: Central and Queen Street. Central serves trains from London's Euston station (five hours), which come via Crewe and Carlisle in England. East Coast trains run from London's Kings Cross to Glasgow's Queen Street Station. Central also serves other cities in the northwest of England and towns in the southwest of Scotland: Kilmarnock, Dumfries, Ardrossan (for the island of Arran), Gourock (for Dunoon), Wemyss Bay (for the Isle of Bute), and Stranraer (for Ireland). Trains also run from here to Prestwick Airport.

Queen Street Station has frequent connections to Edinburgh (50 minutes), from where you can head south to Newcastle, York, and King's Cross. Other trains from Queen Street head north to Stirling, Perth, Dundee, Aberdeen, Inverness, Kyle of Lochalsh, Wick, and Thurso, and on the scenic West Highland line to Oban, Fort William, and Mallaig. For details contact National Rail.

A regular bus service links the Queen Street and Central stations (although you can easily walk if you aren't too encumbered). Queen Street is near the Buchanan Street subway station, and Central is close to St. Enoch. Taxis are available at both stations.

The Glasgow area has an extensive network of suburban railway services. Locals still call them the Blue Trains, even though most are now painted maroon and cream. For more information and a free map, contact the Strathclyde Passenger Transport Travel Centre or National.

Train Contacts National Rail ☎ *08457/484950* ⊕ *www.nationalrail.co.uk.*

> **WORD OF MOUTH**
>
> "I like Glasgow a lot. There is a great deal of art, architecture, and engineering to view, and the people are very upfront and witty, sort of like people in Brooklyn were thought to be before Brooklyn became trendy."
>
> —Ackislander

TOURS

You can sign on for a sightseeing tour to get a different perspective on the city and the surrounding area.

BOAT TOURS

Cruises are available on Loch Lomond and to the islands in the Firth of Clyde; contact the Greater Glasgow and Clyde Valley Tourist Board for details. Contact the *Waverley* paddle steamer from June through August.

Contacts Waverley Excursions ✉ *36 Lancefield Quay* ☎ *0845/221–8152* ⊕ *www.waverleyexcursions.co.uk.*

BUS TOURS

The popular City Sightseeing bus tours leave daily from the west side of George Square. The Greater Glasgow and Clyde Valley Tourist Board can give information about city tours and about longer tours northward to the Highlands and Islands.

Day trips in minivans (16 people maximum) to the surrounding areas, including Loch Lomond and Oban, are available from Rabbie's Trail Burners.

Contacts City Sightseeing ✉ *153 Queen St.* ☎ *0141/204–0444* ⊕ *www.citysightseeingglasgow.co.uk* 🎫 *£12.* **Rabbie's Trail Burners** ☎ *0845/643–2248* ⊕ *www.rabbies.com.*

PRIVATE GUIDES

Little's Chauffeur Drive arranges personally tailored car-and-driver tours, both locally and throughout Scotland. The Scottish Tourist Guides Association also provides a private-guide service.

Glasgow Taxis offers city tours. If you allow the driver to follow a set route, the cost is £38 for up to five people and lasts around an hour. A two-hour tour costs £59. You can book tours in advance and be picked up and dropped off wherever you like.

Contacts Glasgow Taxis ☎ *0141/429–7070* ⊕ *www.glasgowtaxisltd.co.uk* 🚕 *A city tour costs £38 per taxi (1hr 20mins).* **Little's Chauffeur Drive** ☎ *0141/883–2111* ⊕ *www.littles.co.uk.* **Scottish Tourist Guides Association** ☎ *01786/447784* ⊕ *www.stga.co.uk.*

WALKING TOURS

The Greater Glasgow and Clyde Valley Tourist Board can provide information on special walks on a given day. Glasgow Walking Tours organizes specialized tours of the city's architectural treasures.

Contacts Glasgow Walking Tours ☎ *07751/978935* ⊕ *www.greetinglasgow.com.*

VISITOR INFORMATION

The Greater Glasgow and Clyde Valley Tourist Board provides information about different types of tours and has an accommodations-booking service, a currency-exchange office, and a money-transfer service. Books, maps, and souvenirs are also available. The tourist board has a branch at Glasgow Airport, too.

Contact Greater Glasgow and Clyde Valley Tourist Board ✉ *11 George Sq., City Center* ☎ *0845/204–4400* ⊕ *www.visitscotland.com/glasgow* ⊗ *Weekdays 9–5.*

EXPLORING GLASGOW

As cities go, Glasgow is contained and compact. It's set up on a grid system, so it's easy to navigate and explore, and the best way to tackle it is on foot. In the eastern part of the city, start by exploring Glasgow Cathedral and other highlights of the oldest section of the city, then wander through the rest of the Merchant City. From there you can just continue into the City Center with its designer shops, art galleries, and eateries. From here you can either walk (it takes a good 45 minutes) or take the subway to the West End. If you walk, head up Sauchiehall Street and visit Mackintosh's Glasgow School of Art. Once in the West End, visit the Botanic Gardens, Glasgow University, and the Kelvingrove Art Gallery and Museum. Then take a taxi to the South Side to experience the Burrell Collection and Pollok House. For Glasgow's East End, walk down High Street from the Cathedral to the Tron Cross; from there you can walk to the Barras and Glasgow Green.

If you break your sightseeing up into neighborhoods, it's completely manageable to explore a variety of places in three days. Glasgow's pubs and clubs serve up entertainment until late in the evening; there's something for everyone.

CITY CENTER

Many of the city's most important historical buildings are found here. Along the streets of the city center are some of the best examples of the architectural confidence and exuberance that so characterized the burgeoning Glasgow of the turn of the 20th century. There are also plenty of shops, trendy eateries, and pubs.

GETTING HERE Every form of public transportation can bring you here, from bus to train to subway. Head to George Square and walk from there.

TOP ATTRACTIONS

City Chambers. Dominating the east side of George Square, this exuberant expression of Victorian confidence, built by William Young in Italian Renaissance style, was opened by Queen Victoria in 1888. Among the interior's outstanding features are the entrance hall's vaulted ceiling, sustained by granite columns topped with marble, the marble-and-alabaster staircases, and Venetian mosaics. The enormous banqueting hall has murals illustrating Glasgow's history. Free guided tours lasting about an hour depart weekdays at 10:30 and 2:30. ■ TIP→ **The building is closed to visitors during civic functions.** ⊠ *80 George Sq., City Center* ☎ *0141/287–4020* ⊕ *www.glasgow.gov.uk* ⊠ *Free* ⊙ *Weekdays 9–5* Ⓜ *Buchanan St.*

George Square. The focal point of Glasgow is lined with an impressive collection of statues of worthies: Queen Victoria; Scotland's national poet, Robert Burns (1759–96); the inventor and developer of the steam engine, James Watt (1736–1819); Prime Minister William Gladstone (1809–98); and towering above them all, Scotland's great historical novelist, Sir Walter Scott (1771–1832). The column was intended for George III (1738–1820), after whom the square is named, but when he was found to be insane toward the end of his reign, his statue was never erected. On the square's east side stands the magnificent Italian Renaissance–style **City Chambers**; the handsome **Merchants' House** fills the corner of West George Street, crowned by a globe and a sailing ship. The fine old Post Office building, now converted into flats, occupies the northern side. There are plenty of benches in the center of the square where you can pause and contemplate. ⊠ *Between St. Vincent and Argyle Sts., City Center* Ⓜ *Buchanan St.*

QUICK BITE **Peckham's.** Whether you're looking for coffee and a splendid slice of cake, a burger, or a plate of pasta, Peckham's fits the bill. An informal eatery in one of the Merchant City's grand buildings, there's an attached deli and wine shop. ⊠ *61–65 Glassford St., City Center* ☎ *0141/553–0666* ⊕ *www.peckhams.co.uk.*

Fodor'sChoice ★ **Glasgow School of Art.** This is the most stunning example of the genius of architect Charles Rennie Mackintosh, who was only 28 when he won the commission. He worked on every detail—down to the interior design, furnishings, and lighting—to make this iconic art nouveau building, built between 1897 and 1909, a unified whole. Even the drainpipes are an integral part of the design. The building still functions as an art school, so book ahead for the daily guided tours. Otherwise, you can visit four galleries that host frequently changing exhibitions. A visitor center has a small exhibit on the designer and sells a good selection of prints, postcards, and books. The School of Art also organizes walking tours of Mackintosh's Glasgow that cost £19.50. Opposite the school is the modern Reid Building, opening in 2014, part of ongoing campus redevelopment. ⊠ *11 Dalhousie St., City Center* ☎ *0141/353–4526* ⊕ *www.gsa.ac.uk/tours* ⊠ *Tours £9.75* ⊙ *Building daily 10:30–5. Exhibitions Mon.–Sat. 10:30–4:30, Sat. 10–2. Tours are frequent and available all yr, times vary.* Ⓜ *Cowcaddens.*

Glasgow Gallery of Modern Art. One of Glasgow's boldest, most innovative galleries occupies the neoclassical former Royal Exchange building. The modern art, craft, and design collections include works by Scottish conceptual artists such as David Mach, and also paintings and sculptures from around the world, including Papua New Guinea, Ethiopia, and Mexico. Each floor of the gallery reflects one of the elements—air, fire, earth, and water—which creates some unexpected juxtapositions and also allows for various interactive exhibits. In the basement are a café and an extensive library. The exchange building, designed by David Hamilton (1768–1843) and finished in 1829, was a meeting place for merchants and traders; later it became Stirling's Library. It incorporates the mansion built in 1780 by William Cunninghame, one of the wealthiest tobacco lords. ⊠ *Queen St., City Center* ☎ *0141/229–1996* ⊕ *www. glasgowmuseums.com* ⊠ *Free* ☻ *Mon.–Wed. 10–5, Thurs. 10–8, Fri.– Sun. 11–5* Ⓜ *Buchanan St.*

> **MACKINTOSH TRAIL**
>
> **Mackintosh Trail Ticket.** If you're interested in architect Charles Rennie Mackintosh, this is an excellent and economical way of seeing his work. Tickets cost £16 and include admission to all Mackintosh sites across Glasgow, as well as transportation on subways or buses. Tickets can be purchased online or at the individual sites. ☎ *0141/946–6600* ⊕ *www.crmsociety.com.*

The Lighthouse. Charles Rennie Mackintosh designed these former offices of the *Glasgow Herald* newspaper in 1893, with its emblematic Mackintosh Tower. Today it serves as Scotland's **Centre for Architecture, Design and the City,** which celebrates all facets of the architectural field. Regular and changing exhibitions on its second floor address issues of urban design and sustainability. On the third floor the **Mackintosh Interpretation Centre** is a great starting point for discovering more about this groundbreaking architect's work, illustrated in a glass wall with alcoves containing models of his buildings. From here you can climb the more than 130 steps up the tower and, once you have caught your breath, look out over Glasgow. The fifth-floor Doocot Cafe is a great place to take a break from sightseeing. Building tour cost £5. ⊠ *11 Mitchell La., City Center* ☎ *0141/271–5365* ⊕ *www. thelighthouse.co.uk* ⊠ *Free* ☻ *Mon–Sat. 10:30–5* Ⓜ *St. Enoch.*

WORTH NOTING

Centre for Contemporary Arts (CCA). Housed in a modern building constructed around the facade of the older center, this arts center hosts a wide range of activities, including cutting-edge art exhibitions, film screenings, and educational activities for community groups. There's a small theater on the first floor and a bookshop specializing in art books. The Café Saramago sits between old and new, under a glass roof that feels a little like an open courtyard. It has very good lunch and pretheater menus. ⊠ *350 Sauchiehall St., City Center* ☎ *0141/352– 4900* ⊕ *www.cca-glasgow.com* ⊠ *Free* ☻ *Tues.–Fri. 11–6, Sat. 10–6* Ⓜ *Cowcaddens.*

Glasgow

TO QUEEN'S CROSS CHURCH

Kelvinbridge

Great George St.

Belmont St.

River Kelvin

Garscu...

North Woodside Rd.

Maryhill Rd.

U Kelvin Bridge

Park Rd.

Bank St.

Great Western Road

U Hillhead

Byres Rd.

University Ave.

WEST END

Woodlands Road

St. George's Cross

U St. George's Cross

St. George's Rd.

Kelvin Way

River Kelvin

Kelvingrove Park

U Kelvinhall

Dunbarton Rd.

Argyle St.

Sauchiehall St.

Berkeley St.

Eldeslie St.

North St.

Newton St.

Buccleuch

Garnet St.

Renfrew St.

Scott St.

W. Regent

Holland St.

Pitt St.

W. George St.

Embank...

Argyle St.

St. Vincent St.

Street

Mitchell St.

Douglas St.

Blyths...

Waterloo St.

Scottish Exhibition Centre

Clydeside Expressway

Argyle St.

James Watt St.

M8

Bellahouston Park

Dumbreck Rd.

Mosspark Blvd.

M77

Haggs Castle

Dumbreck Rd.

Pollok Country Park

Guidmans Rd.

Pollok Ave.

Lancefield St.

Finnieston St.

Lancefield

Quay

River Clyde

Mavisbank Quay

Paisley Rd.

Nelso...

Wallace...

SOUTH SIDE

28 - 30 see detail map

TO SCOTLAND STREET SCHOOL

Cook St.

KEY

	Pedestrian Zone
+–+–+	Rail Lines
U	Underground Stop
i	Tourist Information

Cowcaddens

Theatre Royal

Glasgow Film Theatre

Royal Concert Hall

Buchanan St. Bus Station

Queen St. Station

Nelson Mandela Pl.

Buchanan St.

CITY CENTRE

Central Station

St. Enoch

St. Enoch Shopping Centre

Trades House

Argyll Arcade

Princes Sq.

Strathclyde University

Glasgow Cathedral

Cathedral Square

MERCHANT CITY

Trongate 103

Tron Steeple

Tolbooth Steeple

St. Andrew's Church

Glasgow Green

EAST END

Possil Rd.
Saracen St.
Keppochhill Rd.
Galscube Rd.
Craighall Rd.
Dobbie's Loan
M8
Cowcaddens Rd.
Dobbie's Loan
Springburn Rd.
Atexandra Parade
M8
Sauchiehall St.
Bath St.
Hope St.
Renfield St.
St. James Rd.
Castle St.
Taylor St.
John Knox St.
Wishart St.
Firpark St.
Rotten Row East
W. George St.
St. Vincent Pl.
George St.
Cathedral St.
Vincent St.
thwell St.
Gordon St.
Ingram St.
Wilson St.
Duke St.
Union St.
W. Nile St.
Buchanan St.
Queen St.
Miller St.
Virginia St.
Glassford St.
Hutcheson St.
Candleriggs
Bell St.
High St.
Albion St.
Osborne St.
Jamaica St.
Oswald St.
royal hange uare
Clyde St.
R. Clyde
Norfolk St.
Corbals
Bridgegate
Saltmarket
Trongate
Gallowgate
London Rd.
Greendyke St.
Lanark St.
Charlotte St.
Monteith Row
The Green
Green St.
Abercromby St.
London Rd.
Millroad St.
Bellgrove St.

1/4 mi
1/4 km

3
6 4 5
12 1 2
11 13
7
8
9 10
31

UNION AND GROWTH

Glasgow flourished quietly during the Middle Ages. Its cathedral was the center of religious life, its university a center of serious academia. Although the city was made a burgh (meaning that it was granted trading rights) in 1175 by King William the Lion, its population never numbered more than a few thousand people.

What changed Glasgow irrevocably was the 1707 Treaty of Union between Scotland and England, which allowed Scotland to trade with the essentially English colonies in America. Glasgow, with its advantageous position on Scotland's west coast, prospered. In came cotton, tobacco, and rum; out went various Scottish manufactured goods and clothing. The key to it all was tobacco. The prosperous merchants known as tobacco lords ran the city, and their wealth laid the foundation for the manufacturing industries of the 19th century. You can still see some of the buildings they created in the renovated neighborhood called the Merchant City.

Central Station. The railway bridge supporting the tracks going into the station is known as the Highlandman's Umbrella because it was the traditional gathering place for immigrant Highlanders looking for work in Glasgow in the early 20th century. There are several interesting shops in the station, which serves as the departure point for trains to England and the Ayrshire coast, including Prestwick Airport. The Champagne Bar in the Central Hotel is a good vantage point for watching the station concourse and its comings and goings. ⊠ *Gordon St., bounded by Gordon, Union, Argyle, Jamaica, Clyde, Oswald, and Hope Sts., City Center* ⊕ *www.glasgowcentralstation.com* ☞ *St. Enoch.*

Merchants' House. A golden sailing ship, a reminder of the importance of sea trade to Glasgow's prosperity, tops this handsome 1874 Victorian building, home to Glasgow's chamber of commerce. The interior isn't open to the public, but the exterior is impressive. ⊠ *West side of George Sq., City Center* Ⓜ *Buchanan St.*

Regimental Museum of the Royal Highland Fusiliers. Exhibits of medals, badges, and uniforms relate the history of a famous, much-honored regiment and the men who served in it. ⊠ *518 Sauchiehall St., City Center* ☎ *0141/332–0961* ⊕ *www.rhf.org.uk* ☜ *Free* ☉ *Weekday 8:30–4* Ⓜ *Cowcaddens.*

St. Vincent's Street Church. This 1859 church, the work of Alexander Thomson, exemplifies his Greek Revival style, replete with Ionic columns, sphinxlike heads, and rich interior color. You can see the interior only by attending a service Sunday at 11 am or 6:30 pm. ⊠ *Pitt and St. Vincent Sts., City Center* ⊕ *www.greekthomsonchurch.com* Ⓜ *Buchanan St.*

Tenement House. This ordinary first-floor apartment is anything but ordinary inside: it was occupied from 1937 to 1982 by Agnes Toward (and before that by her mother), who seems never to have thrown anything away. Her legacy is this fascinating time capsule, painstakingly preserved with her everyday furniture and belongings. The red-sandstone building dates from 1892 and can be found in the Garnethill area north of Charing Cross station. A small museum explores the life and times of its careful occupant. ⊠ *145 Buccleuch St., City Center* ☎ *0844/493– 2197* ⊕ *www.nts.org.uk* ⊠ *£6.50* ⊗ *Mar.–Oct., daily 1–5; last admission at 4:30* Ⓜ *Cowcaddens.*

MERCHANT CITY

Near the remnants of medieval Glasgow is the Merchant City, with some of the city's most important Georgian and Victorian buildings, many of them built by prosperous tobacco merchants. Today the area is noted for its trendy eateries and for the designer stores that line Ingram Street and others. Many of Glasgow's young and upwardly mobile make their home here, in converted buildings ranging from warehouses to the old Sheriff's Court. Shopping here is expensive, but the area is worth visiting if you're seeking the youthful Glasgow style. Stick to well-lit, well-traveled areas after sunset.

GETTING HERE   Buchanan Street is the handiest subway station when you want to explore the Merchant City, as it puts you directly on George Square. You can also easily walk from Central Station or the St. Enoch subway station.

TOP ATTRACTIONS

Fodor'sChoice ★   **Glasgow Cathedral.** The most complete of Scotland's cathedrals (it would have been more complete had 19th-century vandals not pulled down its two rugged towers), this is an unusual double church, one above the other, dedicated to Glasgow's patron saint, St. Mungo. Consecrated in 1136 and completed about 300 years later, it was spared the ravages of the Reformation—which destroyed so many of Scotland's medieval churches—mainly because Glasgow's trade guilds defended it. A late-medieval open-timber roof in the nave and lovely 20th-century stained glass are notable features.

In the lower church is the splendid crypt of St. Mungo, who was originally known as St. Kentigern (*kentigern* means "chief word"), but who was nicknamed St. Mungo (meaning "dear one") by his early followers. The site of the tomb has been revered since the 6th century, when St. Mungo founded a church here. Mungo features prominently in local legends; one such legend is about a pet bird that he nursed back to life, and another tells of a bush or tree, the branches of which he used to miraculously relight a fire. The bird, the tree, and the salmon with a ring in its mouth (from another story) are all found on the city's coat of arms, together with a bell that Mungo brought from Rome. ⊠ *Cathedral St., Merchant City* ☎ *0141/552–8198* ⊠ *Free* ⊗ *Apr.–Sept., Mon.–Sat. 9:30–5:30, Sun. 1–5; Oct.–Mar., Mon.–Sat. 9:30–4:30, Sun. 1–4:30* Ⓜ *Buchanan St.*

Fodor'sChoice ★   **Necropolis.** A burial ground since the beginning of recorded history, the large Necropolis, modeled on the famous Père-Lachaise Cemetery in Paris, contains some extraordinarily elaborate Victorian tombs. A great place to take it all in is from the monument of John Knox (1514–72), the leader of Scotland's Reformation, which stands at the top of the hill at the heart of the Necropolis. Around it are grand tombs that resemble Classical palaces, Egyptian tombs, or even the Chapel of the Templars in Jerusalem. You'll also find a smattering of urns and broken columns, a Roman symbol of a great life cut short. The Necropolis was designed as a place for meditation, which is why it is much more than just a graveyard. The main gates are behind the St. Mungo Museum of Religious Art and Life. Call ahead for free guided tours. ⊠ *70 Cathedral Sq., Merchant City* ☎ *0141/287–5064* ⊕ *www.glasgownecropolis.org* ▥ *Free* ☉ *Daily 7–dusk* Ⓜ *Buchanan St.*

Provand's Lordship. Glasgow's oldest house was built in 1471 by Bishop Andrew Muirhead. Before it was rescued by the Glasgow City Council, this building had been a pub, a sweetshop, and a soft drinks factory. It is now a museum that shows the house as it might have looked when it was occupied by officers of the church. The top floor is a gallery with prints and paintings depicting the characters who might have lived in the surrounding streets. The St Nicholas Garden behind the house is a medicinal herb garden, and the cloisters house rather disturbing carved stone heads. ⊠ *3 Castle St., Merchant City* ☎ *0141/552–8819* ⊕ *www. glasgowmuseums.com* ▥ *Free* ☉ *Tues.–Thurs. and Sat. 10–5, Fri. and Sun. 11–5* Ⓜ *Buchanan St.*

WORTH NOTING

St. Mungo Museum of Religious Life and Art. An outstanding collection of artifacts, including Celtic crosses and statuettes of Hindu gods, reflects the many religious groups that have settled throughout the centuries in Glasgow and the west of Scotland. A Zen Garden creates a peaceful setting for rest and contemplation, and elsewhere stained-glass windows include a depiction of St. Mungo himself. Pause to look at the beautiful Chilkat Blanketwofven, made from cedar bark and wool by the Tlingit people of North America. ⊠ *2 Castle St., City Center* ☎ *0141/276–1625* ⊕ *www.glasgowmuseums.com* ▥ *Free* ☉ *Tues.–Thurs. and Sat. 10–5, Fri. and Sun. 11–5* Ⓜ *Buchanan St.*

WEST END

Glasgow University dominates the West End, creating a vibrant neighborhood. Founded in 1451, the university is the third oldest in Scotland, after St. Andrews and Aberdeen. (It's at least 130 years ahead of the University of Edinburgh.) The industrialists and merchants who built their grand homes on Great Western Road and the adjacent streets endowed museums and art galleries and commissioned artists to decorate and design their homes, as a stroll around the area will quickly reveal. In summer the beautiful Botanical Gardens, with the iconic glasshouse that is the Kibble Palace, become a stage for new and unusual versions of Shakespeare's plays. A good way to save money is to picnic in the park (weather permitting, of course). You can buy sandwiches, salads, and other portable items at shops on Byres Road.

GETTING HERE   The best way to get to the West End from the city center is by subway; get off at the Hillhead station. A taxi is another option.

TOP ATTRACTIONS

FAMILY   **Botanic Gardens.** When the sun shines, the Botanics (as they're known to locals) quickly fill up with people enjoying the extensive lawns, beautiful flower displays, and herb garden. At the heart of the gardens is the

A GOOD WALK IN THE WEST END

This tranquil stroll, taking about an hour if you don't poke into the museums, showcases all of the beauty of the West End. Start in Kelvingrove Park, at the junction of Sauchiehall (pronounced *socky*-hall) and Argyle streets, where you'll find the city's main art museum, the Kelvingrove Art Gallery and Museum. The impressive red-sandstone building and its leafy surroundings are well worth a visit. From here stroll up tree-lined Kelvin Way; the skyline to your left is dominated dramatically by Glasgow University. Turn left onto University Avenue and walk past the Memorial Gates. On the south side of University Avenue is the Hunterian Museum, and across the street is the even more interesting Hunterian Art Gallery. From here make your way to the Botanic Gardens, where 12 Victorian conservatories and their fragrant collections await. To get there, continue west along University Avenue, turn right at Byres Road, and walk as far as Great Western Road. The 40 acres of gardens are across the busy intersection. Its peaceful garden makes you feel a million miles away from the city center.

spectacular circular glasshouse, the **Kibble Palace,** a favorite haunt of Glaswegian families. Originally built in 1873, it was the conservatory of a Victorian eccentric named John Kibble. Its domed, interlinked greenhouses contain tree ferns, palm trees, and the Tropicarium, where you can experience the lushness of a rain forest and briefly forget the weather outside. Another greenhouse holds a world-famous collection of orchids. In July the park becomes a stage for presentations of Shakespeare's plays. ☒ *730 Great Western Rd., West End* ☎ *0141/276–1614* ⊕ *www.glasgow.gov.uk* ✉ *Free* ☉ *Gardens daily 7–dusk; Kibble Palace Mar.–mid-Oct., daily 10–6; mid-Oct.–Feb., daily 10–4:15* Ⓜ *Hillhead.*

Glasgow University. Gorgeous grounds and great views of the city are among the many reasons to visit this university. The Gilbert Scott Building, the university's main edifice, was built more than a century ago and is a lovely example of the Gothic Revival style. **Glasgow University Visitor Centre,** near the main gate on University Avenue, has exhibits on the university, a small coffee bar, and a gift shop; it's the starting point for one-hour guided walking tours of the campus. A self-guided tour starts at the visitor center and takes in the east and west quadrangles, the cloisters, Professor's Square, Pearce Lodge, and the not-to-be-missed University Chapel. ☒ *University Ave., West End* ☎ *0141/330–5511* ⊕ *www.glasgow.ac.uk* ✉ *Tour £10* ☉ *Tours on Thurs., Fri., and weekends* Ⓜ *Hillhead.*

Hunterian Art Gallery. Opposite Glasgow University's main gate, this gallery houses William Hunter's (1718–83) collection of paintings. You'll also find prints, drawings, and sculptures by Tintoretto, Rembrandt, and Auguste Rodin, as well as a major collection of paintings by James McNeill Whistler, who had a great affection for the city that bought one of his earliest paintings. Also in the gallery is a replica of **Charles Rennie Mackintosh's town house,** which once stood nearby. The rooms contain Mackintosh's distinctive art nouveau chairs, tables, beds, and cupboards, and the walls are decorated in the equally distinctive style devised by him and his artist wife Margaret. ⊠ *Hillhead St., West End* ☏ *0141/330–5431* ⊕ *www.hunterian.gla.ac.uk* ☒ *Free* ☉ *Tues.–Sat. 10–5, Sun. 11–4* Ⓜ *Hillhead.*

Hunterian Museum. Set within Glasgow University, this museum dating from 1807 showcases part of the collections of William Hunter, an 18th-century Glasgow doctor who assembled a staggering quantity of valuable material. Look for Hunter's hoards of coins, manuscripts, scientific instruments, and archaeological artifacts in a striking Gothic building. A permanent exhibit chronicles the building of the Antonine Wall, the Romans' northernmost defense. ⊠ *University Ave., West End* ☏ *0141/330–4221* ⊕ *www.hunterian.gla.ac.uk* ☒ *Free* ☉ *Mon.–Sat. 9:30–5* Ⓜ *Hillhead.*

FAMILY

Fodor'sChoice

★

Kelvingrove Art Gallery and Museum. Worthy of its world-class reputation, the Kelvingrive Art Gallery and Museum attracts local families as well as international visitors. This combination of cathedral and castle was designed in the Renaissance style and built between 1891 and 1901. The stunning red-sandstone edifice is an appropriate home for works by Botticelli, Rembrandt, Monet, and others. The Glasgow Room houses extraordinary works by local artists. Whether the subject is Scottish culture, design, or storytelling, every wall and room begs you to look deeper; labels are thought-provoking and sometimes witty. You could spend a weekend here, but in a pinch three hours would do one level justice—there are three. Leave time to visit the gift shop and the attractive basement restaurant. Daily recitals on the massive organ (usually at 1) are well worth the trip. ⊠ *Argyle St., West End* ☏ *0141/276–9599* ⊕ *www.glasgowmuseums.com* ☒ *Free* ☉ *Mon.–Thurs. and Sat. 10–5, Fri. and Sun. 11–5* Ⓜ *Kelvinhall.*

FAMILY

Kelvingrove Park. A peaceful retreat, the park was purchased by the city in 1852 and takes its name from the River Kelvin, which flows through it. Among the numerous statues of prominent Glaswegians is one of Lord Kelvin (1824–1907), the Scottish mathematician and physicist who pioneered a great deal of work in electricity. The shady park has a massive fountain commemorating a lord provost of Glasgow from the 1850s, a duck pond, and playground, as well as an excellent eatery. ⊠ *Bounded by Sauchiehall St., Woodlands Rd., and Kelvin Way, West End* Ⓜ *Kelvinhall.*

Mitchell Library. The largest public reference library in Europe houses more than a million volumes, including what's claimed to be the world's largest collection about Robert Burns. A bust in the entrance hall commemorates the library's founder, Stephen Mitchell, who died in 1874. Minerva, goddess of wisdom, looks down from the library's dome, encouraging the library's users and frowning at the drivers thundering along the nearby motorway. The western facade, with its sculpted figures of Mozart, Beethoven, Michelangelo, and other artistic figures, is particularly beautiful. The on-site eatery is a good place to relax. The Aye Write Literature Festival takes place here every March, as do many other events celebrating Glasgow's history. ⊠ *North St., West End* ☏ *0141/287–2999* ⊕ *www.mitchelllibrary.org* ☒ *Free* ☉ *Mon.–Thurs. 9–8, Fri. and Sat. 9–5* Ⓜ *St. George's Cross.*

Charles Rennie Mackintosh

Not so long ago, the furniture of innovative Glasgow-born architect Charles Rennie Mackintosh (1868–1928) was broken up for firewood. Today art books are devoted to his distinctive, astonishingly elegant Arts and Crafts– and art nouveau–influenced interiors, and artisans around the world look to his theory that "decoration should not be constructed, rather construction should be decorated" as holy law. Mackintosh's stripped-down designs ushered in the modern age with their deceptively stark style.

AN ARCHITECT'S CAREER

Mackintosh trained in architecture at the Glasgow School of Art and was apprenticed to the Glasgow firm of John Hutchison at the age of 16. Early influences on his work included the Pre-Raphaelites, James McNeill Whistler (1834–1903), Aubrey Beardsley (1872–98), and Japanese art. But by the 1890s a distinct Glasgow style developed.

The building for the *Glasgow Herald* newspaper, which he designed in 1893, and which is now the Lighthouse Centre for Architecture, Design and the City, was soon followed by other major Glasgow buildings: Queen Margaret's Medical College; the Martyrs Public School; tearooms including the Willow Tearoom; the Hill House, in Helensburgh, now owned by the National Trust for Scotland; and Queen's Cross Church, completed in 1899 and now the headquarters of the Charles Rennie Mackintosh Society. In 1897 Mackintosh began work on a new home for the Glasgow School of Art, recognized as one of his major achievements.

Mackintosh married Margaret Macdonald in 1900, and in later years her decorative work enhanced the buildings' interiors. In 1904 he became a partner in Honeyman and Keppie and designed Scotland Street School, now the Scotland Street School Museum, in the same year. Until 1913, when he left Honeyman and Keppie and moved to England, Mackintosh's projects included buildings over much of Scotland. He preferred to include interiors as part of his overall design.

Commissions in England after 1913 included design challenges not confined to buildings, such as fabrics, furniture, and even bookbindings. Mackintosh died in London in 1928.

After 1904 architectural taste had turned against Mackintosh's style; his work was seen as strange. Mackintosh could not conform to the times; he lost commissions, drank heavily, and ended up poor and sick. His reputation revived only in the 1950s with the publication of his monographs, and has continued to grow over time.

HOW TO SEE HIS WORK

Glasgow is the best place in the world to admire Mackintosh's work: in addition to the buildings mentioned above, most of which can be visited, the Hunterian Art Gallery contains magnificent reconstructions of the principal rooms at 78 Southpark Avenue, Mackintosh's Glasgow home, and original drawings, documents, and records, plus the re-creation of a room at 78 Derngate, Northampton. The Kelvingrove Art Gallery and Museum also has displays of his creations in several galleries.

A Mackintosh Trail Ticket, purchased online or at various sites, is a good deal if you're visiting multiple sites: see www.crmsociety.com.

WORTH NOTING

Queen's Cross Church. The only church Mackintosh designed houses the Charles Rennie Mackintosh Society Headquarters. It is the ideal place to learn more about the famous Glasgow-born architect and designer. Although one of the leading lights in the art nouveau movement, Mackintosh died in relative obscurity in 1928. The church has beautiful stained-glass windows and a light-enhancing, carved-wood interior. The center's library and shop provide further insight into Glasgow's other Mackintosh-designed buildings, which include Scotland Street School, the Martyrs Public School, and the Glasgow School of Art. The church sits near the junction of Garscube Road and Maryhill Road. A taxi is probably the best way to get here, but you can also take a bus toward Queen's Cross from stops along Hope Street or walk up Maryhill Road from the St. George's Cross subway station. ✉ *870 Garscube Rd., West End* ☎ *0141/946–6600* ⊕ *www.crmsociety. com* ☞ *£4* ◷ *Apr.–Oct., Mon., Wed., and Fri. 10–5; Nov.–Mar., Mon., Wed., and Fri. 10–4* Ⓜ *St. George's Cross.*

> ### GLASGOW'S UNDERGROUND
>
> Glasgow is the only city in Scotland with a subway. The system was built at the end of the 19th century and takes the simple form of two circular routes, one going clockwise and the other counterclockwise. All trains eventually bring you back to where you started, and the complete circle takes 24 minutes. The tunnels are small, and so are the trains. This, together with the affection in which the system is held and the bright-orange paint of the trains, gave the system its nickname, the "Clockwork Orange." If you get off at Hillhead, stop to admire Alasdair Gray's wonderful mural.

THE CLYDE

The Clyde has long been the city's main artery, first as a trading route and later as the place where massive shipyards built everything from warships to ocean liners. The cranes can still be seen today, although the former industrial area has been transformed into a desirable destination for locals and visitors alike. The Riverside Museum commemorates the great days of shipbuilding, while the Scottish Exhibition Centre and the Glasgow Science Centre, facing one another across the river, proclaim new times.

GETTING HERE   From the Partick subway station it's a 10-minute walk to the Riverside Museum. From that museum it's a short stroll along the river to the Glasgow Science Centre.

TOP ATTRACTIONS

FAMILY   **Glasgow Science Centre.** Families with children love this museum, which has a fun-packed interactive Science Mall, an IMAX theater, and the futuristic Glasgow Tower. The 417-foot spire—with an aerodynamic profile that twists 360 degrees—is a marvel. In the three-level Science Mall, state-of-the-art displays educate kids and adults about exploration, discovery, and the environment. The ScottishPower Planetarium has a fantastic Zeiss Starmaster projector, which allows you to gaze at the glittering stars. Set aside half a day to see everything. The museum's setting, on the banks of the Clyde, sets it off beautifully. ✉ *50 Pacific Quay, Clyde* ☎ *0141/420–5000* ⊕ *www.glasgowsciencecentre. org* 🎫 *£9.95; planetarium £2.50* ⊙ *Apr.–Oct., daily 10–5; Nov.–Mar., Wed.–Sun. 10–5* Ⓜ *Cessnock.*

FAMILY

Fodor'sChoice

★

Riverside Museum: Scotland's Museum of Transport and Travel. Designed by Zaha Hadid to celebrate the area's industrial heritage, this huge metal structure with curving walls echoes the covered yards where ships were built on the Clyde. Glasgow's shipbuilding history is remembered with a world-famous collection of ship models. Locomotives built at the nearby St. Rollox yards are also on display, as are cars from every age and many countries. You can wander down Main Street, circa 1930, without leaving the building: the pawnbroker, funeral parlor, and Italian restaurant are all frozen in time. Relax with a coffee in the café, wander out onto the expansive riverside walk, or board the Tall Ship that is moored permanently behind the museum. Bus 100 from George Square brings you here, or you can walk from the Partick subway station in 10 minutes. ✉ *100 Poundhouse Pl., Clyde* ☎ *0141/287–2720* ⊕ *www.glasgowlife.org.uk/museums/riverside* 🎫 *Free* ⊙ *Mon.–Thurs. and Sat. 10–5, Fri. and Sun. 11–5* Ⓜ *Partick.*

WORTH NOTING

FAMILY

The Tall Ship at Riverside. Built in 1896, this fine tall sailing ship now sits on the river Clyde immediately behind the Riverside Museum. The *Glenlee* once belonged to the Spanish Navy (under a different name), but carried cargo all over the world in her day. She returned to Glasgow and the river Clyde in 1993, and now forms part of the museum. You can wander throughout this surprisingly large cargo ship with or without an audioguide, peer into cabins and holds, and stand on the forecastle as you gaze down the river. Bus 100 from George Square brings you here, or you can walk from the Partick subway station in 10 minutes. ✉ *150 Pointhouse Pl., Clyde* ☎ *0141/357–3699* ⊕ *www.thetallship.com* 🎫 *Free* ⊙ *Mar.–Oct., daily 10–5, last admission 4:15; Nov.–Feb., daily 10–4, last admission 3:15* Ⓜ *Partick.*

EAST END

Glasgow Green has always been the heart of Glasgow's East End, a formerly down-at-heel neighborhood that has seen many changes over the past several years. One of the top attractions is the People's Palace, which tells the story of daily life in the city. On Sunday head to the nearby Barras market to hunt for bargains.

GETTING HERE

To get to the East End, take the subway to the St. Enoch station and walk along Argyle Street to the Tron Cross. From there, London Road takes you to Glasgow Green.

TOP ATTRACTIONS

Barras. Scotland's largest indoor market—named for the barrows, or pushcarts, formerly used by the stallholders—is a must-see for anyone addicted to searching through piles of junk for bargains. The century-old institution, open weekends, consists of nine markets.

The atmosphere is always good-humored, and you can find just about anything here, in any condition, from dusty model railroads to antique jewelry. Haggling is compulsory. You can reach the Barras by walking along Argyle Street from the St. Enoch subway station. ✉ *Gallowgate, ¼ mile east of Glasgow Cross, East End* ☎ *0141/552–4601* ⊕ *www.glasgow-barrowland.com* ✉ *Free* ⊙ *Weekends 9:30–4:30* Ⓜ *St. Enoch.*

FAMILY **Glasgow Green.** Glasgow's oldest park, on the north side of the River Clyde, has a long history as a favorite spot for public recreation and political demonstrations. Note the Nelson Column, erected long before London's; the McLennan Arch, originally part of the facade of the old Assembly Halls in Ingram Street; and the Templeton Business Centre, a former carpet factory built in the late 19th century in the style of the Doge's Palace in Venice. Don't miss the **People's Palace** and the Doulton Fountain that faces it. ✉ *North side of River Clyde between Green St. and Saltmarket St., Trongate and East End* Ⓜ *St. Enoch.*

Hampden Park. Hampden Park is a mecca for football enthusasists, who come from far and near to tread the famous turf. The home field for the country's national soccer team, it was the largest stadium in the world when it was built in 1903. There are stadium tours on nonmatch days at 11, 12:30, 2, and 3. You can then visit the Scottish Football Museum, which traces the history of the game. ✉ *Letherby Dr., East End* ☎ *0141/620–4000* ⊕ *www.hampdenpark.co.uk* ✉ *£10.*

FAMILY **People's Palace.** An impressive Victorian red-sandstone building dating from 1894 houses an intriguing museum dedicated to the city's social history. Included among the exhibits is one devoted to the ordinary folk of Glasgow, called the "People's Story." Also on display are the writing desk of John McLean (1879–1923), the "Red Clydeside" political activist who came to Lenin's notice, and the famous banana boots worn on stage by Glasgow-born comedian Billy Connolly. On the top floor a sequence of fine murals by Glasgow artist Ken Currie tells the story of Glasgow's working-class citizens. Behind the museum are the restored Winter Gardens and a popular café. To get here from the St. Enoch subway station, walk along Argyle Street past Glasgow Cross. ✉ *Glasgow Green, Monteith Row, East End* ☎ *0141/276–0788* ⊕ *www.glasgowmuseums.com* ✉ *Free* ⊙ *Tues.–Thurs. and Sat. 10–5, Fri. and Sun. 11–5* Ⓜ *St. Enoch.*

WORTH NOTING

Glasgow Cross. This crossroads was the center of the medieval city. The Mercat Cross (*mercat* means "market"), topped by a unicorn, marks the spot where merchants met, where the market was held, and where criminals were executed. Here, too, was the *tron*, or weigh beam, installed in 1491 and used by merchants to check weights. The Tolbooth Steeple dates from 1626 and served as the civic center and the place where travelers paid tolls. ✉ *Intersection of Saltmarket, Trongate, Gallowgate, and London Rds., East End* Ⓜ *St. Enoch.*

GLASGOW EVENTS IN 2014

Glasgow is preparing for an extraordinary year. In 2014 the city will play host to 17 major sporting events at venues across the city when it hosts the Commonwealth Games between July 23 and August 3. The whole city is undergoing a small renaissance, especially the East End, which has seen the construction of several new sports venues and the renovation of others. There will also be cultural events throughout the year, including theater performances, music festivals, and community art projects on a scale that has seldom been seen in Glasgow.

All this coincides with the 2014 Homecoming Scotland, during which many Scots who left their native land are welcomed to return for a year of celebration; see www.visitscotland.com for information. The city is expecting even more visitors than during the last Homecoming Scotland back in 2009, so be sure to book your accommodations well in advance.

SOUTH SIDE

Just southwest of the city center in the South Side are two of Glasgow's dear green spaces—Bellahouston Park and Pollok Country Park—which have important art collections: Charles Rennie Mackintosh's House for an Art Lover in Bellahouston, and the Burrell Collection and Pollok House in Pollock Country Park. A respite from the buzz of the city can also be found in the parks, where you can have a picnic or ramble through greenery and gardens.

GETTING HERE Both parks are off Pollokshaws Road, about 3 miles southwest of the city center. You can take a taxi or car, city bus, or a train from Glasgow Central Station to Pollokshaws West Station or Dumbreck.

TOP ATTRACTIONS

Fodor's Choice **Burrell Collection.** An elegant, ultramodern building of pink sandstone ★ and stainless steel houses thousands of items of all descriptions, from ancient Egyptian, Greek, and Roman artifacts to Chinese ceramics, bronzes, and jade. You can also find medieval tapestries, stained-glass windows, Rodin sculptures, and exquisite French-impressionist paintings—Degas's *The Rehearsal* and Sir Henry Raeburn's *Miss Macartney*, to name two. Eccentric millionaire Sir William Burrell (1861–1958) donated this collection of some 8,000 pieces to the city in 1944. The 1983 building was designed with large glass walls so that the items on display could relate to their surroundings in Pollok Country Park: art and nature, supposedly in perfect harmony. You can get here via Buses 45, 48, and 57 from Union Street, or it's a leisurely 15-minute walk from the Pollokshaws West rail station. ⊠ *2060 Pollokshaws Rd., South Side* ☏ *0141/287–2550* ⊕ *www.glasgowmuseums.com* 🖾 *Free* ☉ *Mon.–Thurs. and Sat. 10–5, Fri. and Sun. 11–5.*

House for an Art Lover. Within Bellahouston Park is a "new" Mackintosh house, based on a competition entry Charles Rennie Mackintosh submitted to a German magazine in 1901. The house was never built in his lifetime, but took shape between 1989 and 1996. The building houses the Glasgow School of Art's postgraduate study center, and exhibits designs for the various rooms and decorative pieces by Mackintosh and his wife Margaret. The main lounge is spectacular. There's also a café and shop filled with art. Buses 9, 53, and 54 from Union Street will get you here. Call ahead, as opening times can vary. ⊠ *Bellahouston Park, 10 Dumbreck Rd., South Side* ☎ *0141/353–4770* ⊕ *www.houseforanartlover.co.uk* ✑ *£4.50* ⊙ *Apr.–Sept., Mon.–Wed. 10–4, Thurs.–Sun. 10–1; Oct.–Mar., weekends 10–1* Ⓜ *Ibrox*.

WORTH NOTING

OFF THE BEATEN PATH

Holmwood House. This large mansion was designed by Alexander "Greek" Thomson, Glasgow's second most famous and most active architect (after Mackintosh), for the wealthy owner of a paper mill. Its classical Greek architecture and stunningly ornamented wood and marble are among his finest, and have been lovingly restored by the National Trust for Scotland. You can witness the ongoing renovation process one or two days a week; call to check for times. The house is half hidden behind a residential street in the Cathcart area. ⊠ *61–63 Netherlee Rd., South Side* ☎ *0141/637–2129* ⊕ *www.nts.org.uk* ✑ *£6.50* ⊙ *Apr.–Oct., Thurs.–Mon. noon–5; last admission at 4:30.*

Pollok House. This classic Georgian house, dating from the mid-1700s, sits amid landscaped gardens and avenues of trees that are now part of Pollok Country Park. It still has the tranquil air of an expensive but unpretentious country house. The Stirling Maxwell Collection includes paintings by Blake and a strong grouping of Spanish works by El Greco, Murillo, and Goya. Lovely examples of 18th- and early-19th-century furniture, silver, glass, and porcelain are also on display. The house has beautiful gardens that overlook the White Cart River. The downstairs servants' quarters house the restaurant's kitchen, still hung with the cooking implements of its times. Eat in the small, pleasant garden if the weather allows. You can take Buses 45, 47, or 57 to the gate of Pollok Country Park. ⊠ *Pollok Country Park, 2060 Pollokshaws Rd., South Side* ☎ *0844/616–6410* ⊕ *www.nts.org.uk* ✑ *Apr.–Oct. £6.50, Nov.–Mar. free* ⊙ *Daily 10–5.*

OFF THE BEATEN PATH

Scotland Street School Museum. A former school designed by Charles Rennie Mackintosh, this building houses a fascinating museum of education. Classrooms re-create school life in Scotland during Victorian times and World War II, and a cookery room recounts a time when education for Scottish girls consisted of little more than learning how to become a housewife. There's also an exhibition space and a café. The building sits opposite Shields Road underground station. ⊠ *225 Scotland St., South Side* ☎ *0141/287–0500* ⊕ *www.glasgowlife.org.uk/museums/scotland-street* ✑ *Free* ⊙ *Tues.–Thurs. and Sat. 10–5, Fri. and Sun. 11–5* Ⓜ *Shields Rd.*

WHERE TO EAT

In the past few years, restaurants have been popping up all around Glasgow that emphasize the best that Scotland has to offer: grass-fed beef, free-range chicken, wild seafood, venison, duck, and goose—not to mention superb fruits and vegetables. The growing emphasis on organic food is reflected on menus that increasingly provide detailed information about the source of their ingredients. No wonder Glasgow is garnering a reputation among food lovers.

You can eat your way around the world in Glasgow. Chinese and Indian foods are longtime favorites, and Thai and Japanese restaurants have become popular. Spanish-style tapas are now quite common, and the "small plate" craze has extended to every kind of restaurant. Glasgow has a large Italian community, and its traditional cafés have been joined by a new generation of eateries serving updated versions of the classics. And seafood restaurants have moved well beyond the fish-and-chips wrapped in newspaper that were always a Glasgow staple.

Smoking isn't allowed in any enclosed space in Scotland, so many restaurants have placed tables outside under awnings during the warmer summer months. With this type of outdoor dining come more Mediterranean-style meals.

PRICES

Eating in Glasgow can be casual or lavish. For inexpensive dining, consider the benefit of lunch or pretheater set menus. Beer and spirits cost much the same as they would in a bar, but wine is relatively expensive in restaurants. Increasing numbers of pubs offer food, but their kitchens usually close early. ■TIP➔ **Some restaurants allow you to bring your own bottle of wine, charging just a small corkage fee. It's worth the effort.** *Prices in the reviews are the average cost of a main course at dinner or, if dinner is not served, at lunch.*

CITY CENTER

Use the coordinate (✛ B2) at the end of each listing to locate a site on the corresponding map.

The city center has restaurants catering to the 9-to-5 crowd, meaning there are a lot of fine-dining establishments as well as good restaurants catching people as they leave work, drawing them in with pretheater menus. The choice of eateries is extensive.

$$ ✕**Arta.** The narrow entrance doesn't prepare you for this huge spacious venue—restaurant, bar, dance club—nor for its extravagant decor. The interior is like an enormous hacienda somewhere in southern Spain, and the menu is made to match. There's an elaborate tapas menu, accentuated by resident musicians and salsa dancing. Paellas (with the usual meat and seafood though there's also a vegetarian version) are substantial and delicious. ⑤ *Average main: £16* ✉ *13–19 Wallis St., East End* ☎ *0845/166–6018* ⊗ *No lunch. Closed Sun.–Wed.* ✛ *H5.*

SPANISH

BEST BETS FOR GLASGOW DINING

Where can I find the best food Glasgow has to offer? Fodor's writers and editors have selected their favorite restaurants by price, cuisine, and experience in the lists below. In the first column, the Fodor's Choice properties represent the "best of the best" across price categories. You can also search by neighborhood for excellent eating experiences—just peruse our complete reviews on the following pages.

Fodor's Choice ★

Bistro du Vin, $$$, p. 143
The Corinthian Club, $$, p. 137
Crabshakk, $, p. 144
Mother India's Cafe, $, p. 146
Mussel Inn, $, p. 137
Number Sixteen, $$, p. 146
Opium, $$, p. 140
Rogano, $$$, p. 140
The Sisters, $$, p. 146
Stravaigin, $$, p. 146
Ubiquitous Chip, $$$, p. 147

By Price

$

Café Gandolfi, p. 141
Carluccio's, p. 137
Crabshakk, p. 144
Hanoi Bike Shop, p. 144
Kool Ba, p. 142
Mother India's Cafe, p. 146
Mussel Inn, p. 137
Where the Monkey Sleeps, p. 141

$$

Brasserie at Òran Mór, p. 143
City Merchant, p. 142
Cookies, p. 148
The Corinthian Club, p. 137
Loon Fung, p. 137
Number Sixteen, p. 146
Opium, p. 140
The Sisters, p. 146
Stravaigin, p. 146

$$$

Bistro du Vin, p. 143
Rogano, p. 140
Two Fat Ladies, p. 140
Ubiquitous Chip, p. 147

By Cuisine

ASIAN

Loon Fung, p. 137
Opium, $$, p. 140
Wudon, $, p. 147

FRENCH

Bistro du Vin, $$$, p. 143
La Vallée Blanche, $$, p. 145

INDIAN

Balbir's, $, p. 143
Kool Ba, $, p. 142
Mother India's Cafe, $, p. 146

ITALIAN

Battlefield Rest, $, p. 148
Carluccio's, $, p. 137
Cookies, $$, p. 148
La Parmigiana, $$, p. 145

La Vita Spuntini, $, p. 145
Little Italy, $, p. 145

MODERN BRITISH

Café Gandolfi, $, p. 141
City Merchant, $$, p. 142
Number Sixteen, $$, p. 146
Pelican Café Bistro, $$, p. 146
Rogano, $$$ p. 140
Stravaigin, $$, p. 146

SEAFOOD

Crabshakk, $, p. 144
Mussel Inn, $, p. 137
Rogano, $$$, p. 140
Two Fat Ladies, $$$, p. 140

SPANISH

Arta, $$, p. 135
Café Andaluz, $$, p. 144

By Experience

MOST KID-FRIENDLY

La Vita Spuntini, $, p. 145
Little Italy, $, p. 145
Pancho Villa's, $, p. 142

MOST ROMANTIC

Bistro du Vin, $$$, p. 143
Kool Ba, $, p. 142
La Vallée Blanche, $$, p. 145
Rogano, $$$, p. 140

3

$ ✕ **The Butterfly and the Pig.** Down an innocuous-looking flight of stairs,
BRITISH   this intimate restaurant is the type of place the locals love: flickering
candles, mix-and-match crockery, and food that is inventive, inexpensive,
and original. The menu reads like a comedic narrative, with descriptions
like "traditional fish and chips, battered to death" served with "beans
today, as the peas don't want to cook." Worth trying are dishes such as
hearty portobello-mushroom burgers with extra-thick potato chips or
black pudding with bacon, Parmesan cheese, and apples. The chef uses
only local ingredients, so the menu changes daily. A tea shop upstairs
serves wonderful cakes. ⑤ *Average main: £10* ✉ *153 Bath St., City Center*
☎ *0141/221–7711* ⊕ *www.thebutterflyandthepig.com* ✛ *E3.*

$ ✕ **Carluccio's.** Part of a well-established chain, Carluccio's has been an
ITALIAN   instant success. The menu is wide ranging and has an emphasis on
authenticity, which shows most clearly in the pasta dishes. No matter
what you order, from fish soup to beef stew, you can watch it being
prepared in the open kitchen. There's a well-stocked deli if you want
to take these flavors home with you. The restaurant is bright, busy,
and perhaps even a little crowded, and there is a healthy buzz of conversation partly absorbed by the high ceiling. The staff is efficient and
friendly. The fixed price menu (£10.95 for two courses, £14.45 for
three) is excellent value, and the Italian wine selection is reasonably
priced. ⑤ *Average main: £13* ✉ *West Nile St., City Center* ☎ *0141/248-*
1166 ⊕ *www.carluccios.com* ✛ *G4.*

$$ ✕ **The Corinthian Club.** Inside what was once the mansion of tobacco mer-
MODERN BRITISH   chant George Buchanan, the Corinthian has an ostentatiously elegant
Fodor'sChoice   restaurant where you can dine under a 26-foot-high glass dome as clas-
★   sical statues stare in your direction. The menu offers a good selection
of seafood and steaks from the standard to the enormous. The gloomy
basement, once a criminal court, now houses a beer and champagne
bar. Among the other on-site drinking establishments is the Prohibi-
tion Bar, which uses teacups rather than glasses. You can also enjoy
afternoon tea in an elegant dining room. ⑤ *Average main: £16* ✉ *191*
Ingram St., City Center ☎ *0141/552–1101* ⊕ *www.thecorinthianclub.*
co.uk ⚖ *Reservations essential* ✛ *G4.*

$$ ✕ **Loon Fung.** The pleasant, enthusiastic staff at this popular Cantonese
CANTONESE   eatery guides you to all the best dishes, including the famed dim sum,
barbecued duck, deep-fried wontons with prawns, and handmade rice
pasta, all specialties that have been served here over the past 40 years.
A newer emphasis on seafood has enlivened the expansive menu. This is
where you'll find the local Chinese population happily munching away.
It's not the place to come if you want intimacy—the restaurant is enormous—but it's perfect for good food in a lively atmosphere. ⑤ *Average*
main: £15 ✉ *417–419 Sauchiehall St., City Center* ☎ *0141/332–1240*
⊕ *www.loonfungglasgow.co.uk* ✛ *D3.*

$ ✕ **Mussel Inn.** West coast shellfish farmers own this restaurant and feed
SEAFOOD   their customers incredibly succulent oysters, scallops, and mussels. The
Fodor'sChoice   pots of mussels, steamed to order and served with any of a number of
★   sauces, are revelatory. The surroundings are simple but stylish, with cool
ceramic tiles, wood floors, and plenty of sleek wooden furniture. Another
plus is the staff, which is helpful yet unpretentious. This is where locals

Where to Eat and
Stay in Glasgow

E   F   G   H

1

M8

Dobbie's Loan

Dobbie's Loan

U Cowcaddens

Garscube St.

Buccleuch St.

2

Victorian
House

Scott St.

Cambridge St.

Dalhousie St.

Hope St.

Cowcaddens Rd.

BUCHANAN
BUS STATION

Port Dundas Pl.

North Hanover St.

0   1/8 mi

0   1/4 km

Sauchiehall St.

citizenM

Sauchiehall St.

Willow Tearooms

3

W. Regent St.

The Butterfly
and the Pig

Marks Hotel

Bath St.

Malmaison

Two Fat
Ladies

The
Arthouse

Buchanan
St.

STRATHCLYDE
UNIVERSITY

Cathedral St.

Blythswood
Square

Where the
Monkey Sleeps

W. George St.

Nelson
Mandela Pl.

QUEEN ST.
STATION

Frederick St.

Cathedral
House Hotel

Douglas St.

Blythswood St.

Mussel Inn

Opium

W. Nile St.

Renfield St.

Carlton
George

George St.

John St.

Rottenrow

4

Waterloo St.

Bothwell St.

Stereo

Carluccio's

St. Vincent Pl.

George
Square

Cochrane St.

Frederick St.

Premier Inn

Montrose St.

W. Campbell St.

Hotel
Indigo

Gordon St.

Rogano

ℹ

Wee Guy's Café

Hanover St.

Stewart's
Victorian
Tea Rooms

ANDERSTON
CROSS BUS
STATION

Grand Central

Grasshoppers

Buchanan St.

Union St.

The Corinthian
Club

Ingram St.

Kool Ba

James Watt St.

Radisson Blu

CENTRAL
STATION

Princes Sq.

Queen St.

TRADES
HOUSE

Brunswick

Miller St.

Virginia St.

Wilson St.

City Merchant

Café
Gandolfi

5

Oswald St.

Argyle St.

Argyll
Arcade

Glassford St.

Hutcheson St.

Pancho Villa's

Arta

Babbity
Bowster's

St. Enoch

Jamaica St.

Howard St.

ST. ENOCH
SHOPPING
CENTRE

Café-Gallery
Cossachok

TRON STEEPLE

Stockwell St.

Osborne St.

Trongate

Candleriggs

Albion St.

West

TOLBOOTH
STEEPLE

R. Clyde

Clyde St.

Bridgegate

London

6

☐ Number 10 Hotel
■ Glad Cafe
■ Cookie's
■ Battlefield Rest
■ Moyra Janes

ST. ANDREW'S
CHURCH

Greendyke St.

E   F   G   H

take their favorite out-of-towners. The £7.50 lunch menu includes a bowl of mussels and either salad or fries. A pretheater meal is £10.95 for two courses, £13.95 for three. ⑤ *Average main: £13* ⌧ *157 Hope St., City Center* ☎ *0141/572–1405* ⊕ *www.mussel-inn.com* ⊗ *No lunch Sun.* ✛ *F4.*

$$
ASIAN
Fodor's Choice
★

✕ **Opium.** This eatery has completely rethought Asian cuisine, taking Chinese, Malaysian, and Thai cooking in new directions. Sauces are fragrant and spicy, but never overpowering. The specialty of the house is dim sum, prepared by a chef who knows his dumplings. The wontons are fresh and crisp, with delicious combinations of crab, shrimp, and chicken peeking through the almost transparent pastry. But leave room for the main dishes, especially the tiger prawns and scallops in a sauce made from dried shrimp and fish. Familiar dishes like beef in black bean sauce are astonishingly delicate and aromatic. The vegetarian menu is adventurous, too. There are also capitivating cocktails. ⑤ *Average main: £15* ⌧ *191 Hope St., City Center* ☎ *0141/332–6668* ✛ *F4.*

$$$
MODERN BRITISH
Fodor's Choice
★

✕ **Rogano.** Modeled after the *Queen Mary,* this restaurant's spacious art deco interior—maple paneling, chrome trim, and dramatic ocean murals—is enough to recommend it. Portions are generous in the main dining area, where you'll find impeccably prepared seafood dishes like pan-seared scallops, as well as classics like roast rack of lamb. You can eat very well in the less expensive Cafe Rogano, where the brasserie-style food is more modern and imaginative. The gorgeous bar serves wonderful cocktails along with elegant sandwiches and a lovely fish soup. You can even sit on the terrace, obligingly warmed by open-air heaters throughout the winter. Few people know that between 3 and 6 you get a free starter or dessert with a main dish. ⑤ *Average main: £22* ⌧ *11 Exchange Pl., City Center* ☎ *0141/248–4055* ⊕ *www. roganoglasgow.com* ⌫ *Reservations essential* ✛ *G4.*

$
VEGETARIAN

✕ **Stereo.** Down a quiet lane near Central Station, this ultracool eatery dishes up a fantastic range of vegan food, from paella to gnocchi to a colorful platter with hummus, red-pepper pâté, and home-baked flatbread. Roasted sweet-potato chips are the perfect side dish. The decor is homey and relaxed, and there always seems to be someone nearby reading or writing. The walls are lined with paintings, posters, and announcements of upcoming concerts in the space downstairs. The music is excellent, but never so loud as to disturb the serious business of eating. The service is laid back but very friendly. ⑤ *Average main: £9* ⌧ *20–28 Renfield La., City Center* ☎ *0141/222–2254* ⊕ *www.stereocafebar.com* ⌫ *Reservations not accepted* ⊗ *Open noon–9 for food; bar open late* ✛ *F4.*

$$$
SEAFOOD

✕ **Two Fat Ladies.** It might have the same name as the owner's other restaurants at 88 Dumbarton Road and 652 Argyle Street, but this branch of Two Fat Ladies deserves a visit because it has more space, more light, and a better location. The menu is predominantly fish, from the delicate smoked salmon, crab, and asparagus salad to the whole sea bass stuffed with tomatoes, red onions, and thyme to the cod with a chorizo and bean cassoulet. But if fish doesn't rock your boat, then the Angus beef with wild mushrooms and spinach jus is also delicious. The berry crème brûlée is the perfect dessert. ⑤ *Average main: £20* ⌧ *118A Blythswood St., City Center* ☎ *0141/847–0088* ⊕ *www.twofatladiesrestaurant.com* ⊗ *No lunch Sun.* ✛ *E3.*

3

$ **✕ Where the Monkey Sleeps.** This
BRITISH quirky basement café serves huge
sandwiches with amusing names—
the "Wytchfinder" has chorizo sausage and cheese, while the "Serious
Operation" contains practically
everything on the menu. Enjoy your
choice with one of the wonderful
smoothies. The café consists of a
series of small rooms with brightly
colored sofas, and the music is
muted just enough to encourage
intimate conversation. The place is
just around the corner from Blythswood Square. ⑤ *Average main:
£5* ✉ *182 West Regent St., City
Center* ☎ *0141/226–3406* ⊕ *www.
monkeysleeps.com* ⊘ *Closed weekends. No dinner* ✛ *E3.*

> ### TAKE TIME FOR TEA
>
> In the Victorian tradition, while
> men went to pubs, Glasgow
> women's social interaction would
> take place in the city's many tea-
> rooms and cafés. Today *everyone*
> goes to the café. Glaswegians
> have succumbed to the worldwide
> love for Italian-style, espresso-
> based coffees, but they'll never
> give up the comfort of a nice cup
> of tea, so you'll find both at most
> tearooms, along with scones, Scot-
> tish pancakes, other pastries, and
> light lunch fare like sandwiches
> and soup.

$ **✕ Willow Tearooms.** Very Scottish breakfasts, tasty lunches, and an array
BRITISH of cakes and scones baked in-house are served in a tearoom that was
once part of a department store designed by Charles Rennie Mackintosh. At the back of a Mackintosh-theme jewelry and gift shop, it retains
the designer's trademark furnishings, including high-backed chairs with
elegant lines and subtle curves. Don't pass up the St. Andrew's Platter, an exquisite selection of trout, salmon, and prawns. ⑤ *Average
main: £8* ✉ *217 Sauchiehall St., City Center* ☎ *0141/332–0521* ⊕ *www.
willowtearooms.co.uk* ⊘ *No dinner* ✛ *F3.*

MERCHANT CITY

*Use the coordinate (✛ B2) at the end of each listing to locate a site on
the corresponding map.*

Despite covering a relatively small area, the Merchant City has a wide
variety of restaurants. The selection of cafés and restaurants includes
many budget-friendly options that cater to the working population.

$ **✕ Café-Gallery Cossachok.** At this spacious and quirky restaurant, the
EASTERN Russian owner pays homage to her homeland (and other Eastern
EUROPEAN European countries) in a menu that includes blintzes, beef Stroga-
noff, and a Moldavian vegetable stew called *gouvetch*. There is, of
course, a variety of chilled vodkas from which to choose. The colorful
shawls stretched across the ceiling, the hand-carved furniture, and the
jewelry on display add to the festive atmosphere. On Sunday night
there's live music, from tango to jazz. ⑤ *Average main: £12* ✉ *10
King St., Merchant City* ☎ *0141/553–0733* ⊕ *www.cossachok.com*
⊘ *Closed Mon.* ✛ *H5.*

$ **✕ Café Gandolfi.** Occupying what was once the tea market, this trendy
MODERN BRITISH café draws the style-conscious crowd. Wooden tables and chairs crafted
by Scottish artist Tim Stead are so fluidly shaped it's hard to believe
they're inanimate. The café opens early for breakfast, serving croissants,

eggs *en cocotte* (casserole-style), and strong espresso. Don't miss the smoked venison or the finnan haddie (smoked haddock). There are daily specials, too, like the John Dory fillets served with clams and garlic butter. The bar on the second floor is more intimate and much less busy—and lets you order from the same menu. $ *Average main: £14* ⊠ *64 Albion St., Merchant City* ☎ *0141/552–6813* ⊕ *www.cafegandolfi.com* ✚ *H5.*

$$ ✕ **City Merchant.** If you have a penchant for fresh and flavorful cuisine,
MODERN BRITISH head to this welcoming spot with simple but traditional furnishings, including white tablecloths, dark wood, soft lighting, and tartan carpets. The secret is the kitchen's use of only local ingredients. You can sample the tasty cuts of venison and beef (including a fillet with haggis mousse), but seafood remains the star attraction. The mussels and oysters from Loch Etive are wondrous, as is the sea bass. There's a relatively inexpensive selection of wines and a wonderful cheese board that's served, as the locals like it, with oatcakes, celery, and quince. A two-course lunch special is a bargain at £12.50. $ *Average main: £19* ⊠ *97–99 Candleriggs St., Merchant City* ☎ *0141/553–1577* ⊕ *www. citymerchant.co.uk* ⊗ *No lunch Sun.* ✚ *H5.*

$ ✕ **Kool Ba.** This atmospheric haven serves an intriguing mix of Indian
ECLECTIC and Persian fare. It's all about healthy, flavorful cooking: chicken tikka masala in a yogurt sauce or lamb korma with coconut cream and fruit are good picks. Accompany your meal with bowls of basmati saffron rice and fluffy naan bread. Thick wooden tables, Persian tapestries, and soft candlelight make you feel at home in the small, comfortable dining room. This popular place continues to win award after award; reserve ahead on Friday and Saturday. $ *Average main: £14* ⊠ *109– 113 Candleriggs, Merchant City* ☎ *0141/552–2777* ⊕ *www.koolba. com* ⚲ *Reservations essential* ✚ *H5.*

$ ✕ **Pancho Villa's.** Images of Pancho Villa and Emiliano Zapata are every-
MEXICAN where in this festive Mexican eatery, whose pink, yellow, and blue
FAMILY walls are decorated with authentic papier-mâché masks. Locals can't get enough of the cocktails or the food, which includes all the old favorites—enchiladas, burritos, tacos, and fajitas—as well as some new dishes. Try the flour tortillas filled with marinated lamb, or the chipotle chicken in a dark, spicy sauce. If what you crave is a margarita, look no further. $ *Average main: £12* ⊠ *26 Bell St., Merchant City* ☎ *0141/552–7737* ⊕ *www.panchovillas.co.uk* ✚ *H5.*

$ ✕ **Stewarts Victorian Tea Rooms.** Afternoon tea, complete with cakes and
CAFÉ tiny sandwiches served on a three-tier stand, has become popular in Glasgow. In this city-center tearoom, decorated with the obligatory large potted plants and floral teapots, you can enjoy afternoon tea, consisting of dainty sandwiches and cakes, or high tea, an old-time ritual that includes more substantial fare along with scones and tea. $ *Average main: £13* ⊠ *89 Glassford St., Merchant City* ☎ *0141/552–0646* ⊕ *www.stewartsvictoriantearooms.com* ⊗ *No dinner* ✚ *H4.*

$ ✕ **Wee Guy's Café.** Settle in at one of the tables at this airy café off
CAFÉ George Square for a quick, healthy, and well-priced breakfast or lunch.
FAMILY The food is simple, but hearty—the "full Scottish breakfast" is genuinely full. For lunch there are sandwiches with rich fillings, homemade soup, and tasty salads, as well as a small deli counter where you can

construct your own meal. ⑤ *Average main: £5* ⊠ *51 Cochrane St., Merchant City* ☎ *0141/552–5338* ⌂ *Reservations not accepted* ⊗ *Closed weekends. No dinner* ✛ *G4.*

WEST END

Use the coordinate (✛ B2) at the end of each listing to locate a site on the corresponding map.

Because of Glasgow University, the eateries in this area were once just the domain of students and professors. In recent years, this elegant residential area has also attracted fine restaurants that attract a wide range of visitors.

$ ✕ **Balbir's.** Don't let the tinted windows discourage you: this place is
INDIAN a temple for pure, healthy Indian food that's impressive in taste and presentation. Twinkling chandeliers, immaculate white tablecloths, and perfectly polished silverware set the stage. All food is prepared with cholesterol-free canola oil; no artificial colors or additives are used. Try the chicken *tikka chasni* (with mango chutney, lemon juice, and mint) or lamb *korma* (with coconut, cream, and mild spices). The tandoori salmon is also a good bet. The waitstaff tends to your every need. ⑤ *Average main: £12* ⊠ *7 Church St., West End* ☎ *0141/339–7711* ⊕ *www. balbirsrestaurants.co.uk* ⊗ *No lunch* ✛ *A6.*

$ ✕ **Bay Tree.** This small café in the university area serves wonderful Middle
MIDDLE EASTERN Eastern food—mostly vegetarian dishes, but there are a few lamb and chicken creations as well. Egyptian *phool* (broad beans dressed with spices and herbs), Turkish *mulukia* (fried eggplant with a tomato-and-herb sauce), and *kurma* (stew with spinach, herbs, and beans) are among its delights. Two-course lunch and pretheater menus are £7.95. ⑤ *Average main: £11* ⊠ *403 Great Western Rd., West End* ☎ *0141/334–5898* ✛ *C5.*

$$$ ✕ **Bistro du Vin.** A kilted doorman and stylish blue-and-green tartan car-
FRENCH pets beckon you into the city's most elegant eatery. The service is impec-
Fodor's Choice cable from beginning to end, and all the food is locally sourced from a
★ 35-mile radius. It's the perfect place for cold, wet days, as romantic fires flicker in the background, crystal chandeliers hang overhead, and stained-glass murals twist the natural light into colorful new shades. From the menu of French and Scottish fare, try the venison or the halibut with asparagus and herb gnocchi. The starters are seductive, and the coffee-and-chocolate soufflé with caramel ice cream is a tempting dessert. For serious indulence, there's a seven-course taster menu for £69. Ask for a tour of the superb wine cellar. Sunday brunch is popular. ⑤ *Average main: £24* ⊠ *Hotel du Vin, 1 Devonshire Gardens, West End* ☎ *0141/339–2001* ⊕ *www.hotelduvin.com* ⌂ *Reservations essential* ✛ *A4.*

$$ ✕ **Brasserie at Òran Mór.** This is the more formal eatery (the other being the
BRITISH bistro-style Conservatory) within this handsome former church. There's lots of elegantly curved wood and high-backed bench seating, as well as some Alasdair Gray murals to savor. The food is equally well crafted, and you can expect contemporary treats using Angus beef, Gressingham duck, and halibut. There's a busy bar just beyond the door. ⑤ *Average main: £16* ⊠ *731–735 Great Western Rd., West End* ☎ *0141/357–6226* ⊕ *www.oran-mor.co.uk* ⌂ *Reservations essential* ✛ *B5.*

$ CAFÉ ✕**Café Alba.** This small café is famous for its wonderful cakes and great coffee. The tasty lunch options—soups, sandwiches, and quiches—are all made on the premises. There's a comfortable upstairs dining room and free Wi-Fi connections, so feel free to linger. Ⓢ *Average main: £6* ✉ *481 Great Western Rd., West End* ☎ *0141/237-7902* ⊕ *www. albacafe.wordpress.com* ⊗ *Closed Sun. and Mon. No dinner* ✛ *C6.*

$$ TAPAS ✕**Cafe Andaluz.** With its Spanish flair, this beautifully designed basement eatery is always busy and lively. The first tapas place to make an impact in Glasgow, its has been followed by others (and has opened a second location of its own in the city center) but remains the most successful. This is an ideal way to dine with friends: sharing the dishes as they arrive and as you down some good Spanish wine. (Rioja is always a reliable choice.) Booking ahead is strongly advised. Ⓢ *Average main: £15* ✉ *2 Cresswell La., West End* ☎ *0141/339-1111* ⊕ *www. cafeandaluz.com* ⊗ *Mon–Thurs. noon–10, Fri. and Sat. noon–11, Sun. noon–10* Ⓜ *Hillhead* ✛ *B5.*

$$ BRITISH ✕**Cafezique.** Small but inviting, this West End magnet has a vibrant, changing breakfast, lunch, and dinner menu that is always fresh and exciting. The food is divided on the dinner menu into "wee things," "big things," and "sweet things." Try the roasted globe artichoke as your wee thing (if it's in season), the roast lamb with Mediterranean vegetables as your big thing, and fruit crumble with custard as your sweet thing. The curved wooden bar that snakes around the belly of the restaurant allows you to watch your food being prepared. The excellent breakfasts are popular on Sunday, so you'll have to battle for a table. Ⓢ *Average main: £15* ✉ *66 Hyndland St., West End* ☎ *0141/339-7180* ⊕ *www.delizique.com* ⌂ *Reservations essential* ✛ *A6.*

$$ MODERN BRITISH ✕**Cottier's.** A converted Victorian church decorated by Glasgow artist Daniel Cottier is the unusual setting for this bar and restaurant. Red walls and beamed ceilings warm up the downstairs bar, where the pub grub has a Tex-Mex flavor. The restaurant has a small but interesting menu, including Malaysian seafood curry and sea bream with wild garlic. Ⓢ *Average main: £15* ✉ *93 Hyndland St., West End* ☎ *0141/357-5825* ⊕ *www.cottiers.com* ✛ *A5.*

$ SEAFOOD Fodor'sChoice ★ ✕**Crabshakk.** This place is anything but a shack. The intimate dining room has heavy wooden tables and chairs and a bar so shiny and inviting that it seems to almost insist you have a drink. The lamps are like half-moons, and the ceiling is elegantly ornate. Mirrors make the place feel bigger, though it's fine the way it is. The food comes from the sea—oysters, lobster, and squid—and you can have your choice served iced, grilled, roasted, or battered. The fish sandwich and crab cakes (no fillers, just the real stuff) are favorites on the lunch menu. In the evening, mussels and scallops draw the eye. Only local and sustainably sourced Scottish seafood is featured. The buzz of conversation and the perfectly modulated music creates the right atmosphere. Ⓢ *Average main: £12* ✉ *1114 Argyle St., West End* ☎ *0141/334-6127* ⊕ *www.crabshakk. com* ⌂ *Reservations essential* ⊗ *Closed Mon.* ✛ *B3.*

$ VIETNAMESE ✕**Hanoi Bike Shop.** Glasgow's first Vietnamese canteen offers a different style of dining, which is apparent from the moment you walk through the door. There are no starters or mains as such—couples are advised to share three dishes. It could be roast pigeon with bok choy, hot-and-sour fish soup, or rice noodles in a savory broth. The setting is rustic, the tables are low, and the seating, mostly stools, takes a little getting used to, but it's also part of the experience. $ *Average main: £14* ✉ *8 Ruthven La., West End* ☎ *0141/334–7165* ⊕ *www.thehanoibikeshop.co.uk* ✛ *B5.*

$$ ✕ **La Parmigiana.** The refreshing elegance of the surroundings is mirrored by the consistently exquisite fare at this longtime favorite. The Giovanazzis pride themselves on using the freshest ingredients—this means you may be able to enjoy simply prepared sea bass or veal one day, guinea fowl or scallops the next. Expertise in the kitchen is reflected in the well-balanced wine list and the impeccable attentiveness of the black-jacketed waiters in this small restaurant. $ *Average main: £19* ✉ *447 Great Western Rd., West End* ☎ *0141/334–0686* ⊕ *www.laparmigiana. co.uk* ⚐ *Reservations essential* ⊘ *Closed Sun.* ✛ *C5.*

ITALIAN

$$ ✕ **La Vallée Blanche.** Above a record store, this fine-dining restaurant has an alpine atmosphere, with the dark wood eaves that you might find in a chalet. The theme is rustic, and the food is hearty and adventurous: veal osso buco comes with foie gras and a port veloute, while the sea bream is accompanied by razor clams and bok choy. Good lunch and pretheater menus are £12.95 for two courses. $ *Average main: £18* ✉ *360 Byres Rd., West End* ☎ *0141/334–3333* ⊕ *www.lavalleeblanche. com* ⊘ *Closed Mon.* ✛ *B5.*

FRENCH

$ ✕ **La Vita Spuntini.** Part of the burgeoning restaurant scene on Byres Road, Spuntini has tapped successfully into the small-plates market with its Italian-style tapas. It's furnished in dark wood, and the large booths at the back of the dining room are sought after. The restaurant is particularly popular with families because of its good-value children's menu. $ *Average main: £14* ✉ *199–201 Byres Rd., West End* ☎ *0141/339–4222* ✛ *B6.*

ITALIAN
FAMILY

$ ✕ **The Left Bank.** Close to Glasgow University, this popular hangout attracts a more mature student crowd. It's an airy spot with high ceilings, leather sofas, and wood floors, and the specialty is good, eclectic food at reasonable prices. Breakfast is your best bet, with thick-sliced French toast, or eggs served on an English muffin with spinach and smoked salmon. Tapas-style plates are an option at lunch: try roasted eggplant and wild-garlic hummus with whole grain flatbread, or sticky pork ribs cooked in maple syrup and sesame. Among the main dishes, the seafood curry stands out. This is also a nice place to relax with a a beer after walking around Kelvingrove Park. $ *Average main: £14* ✉ *33–35 Gibson St., West End* ☎ *0141/339–5969* ⊕ *www.theleftbank. co.uk* ✛ *C6.*

ECLECTIC

$ ✕ **Little Italy.** This busy, noisy, and extremely friendly Italian café sits in the heart of the West End. You can perch on a stool by the window with a cappuccino while watching the world go by, or grab a seat at one of the crowded tables and enjoy one of the pizzas, probably the best around. Create your own combination from the many topping options and wait while it's made, or skip the main dishes and move straight to the tiramisu. $ *Average main: £9* ✉ *205 Byres Rd., West End* ☎ *01451/339–6287* ⊕ *www.littleitalyglasgow.com* ✛ *B5.*

ITALIAN

$
INDIAN
Fodor's Choice
★

✕ Mother India's Cafe. Overlooking the Kelvingrove Art Gallery and Museum, this quaint, casual eatery has a spectacular view as well as an impressive menu. It's usually quite crowded, so don't expect much intimacy. The food is served tapas-style in small dishes—the idea is that you get to try lots of different flavors. Chili-flavored king prawns, chicken cooked with lime, and *aloo saag dosa* (potato and spinach stuffed in a rice-and-lentil pancake) are all rich in flavor and presentation. The popular café doesn't accept reservations, so be prepared for a (fast-moving) line. It's worth bringing your own wine; there's a small corkage charge. ⑤ *Average main: £14* ⊠ *1355 Argyle St., West End* ☎ *0141/339–9145* ⊕ *www.motherindiaglasgow. co.uk* ✛ *B6.*

$$
BRITISH
Fodor's Choice
★

✕ Number Sixteen. This tiny, intimate restaurant serves only the freshest ingredients, superbly prepared. Seared mullet is served with risotto, chorizo, broad beans, and artichokes—a typically unpredictable meeting of flavors. The pork belly with black pudding, white onion marmalade, and spiced apple sauce is tantalizing, and desserts are equally seductive. There's room for only 40 diners, and the result is cozy but never cramped. Book ahead, particularly on weekends. ⑤ *Average main: £17* ⊠ *16 Byres Rd., West End* ☎ *0141/339–2544* ⊕ *www.number16.co.uk* ⚐ *Reservations essential* ✛ *A6.*

$$
ECLECTIC

✕ Pelican Café Bistro. The hum of conversation and a glimpse of the busy kitchen through the open hatch give this restaurant a relaxed vibe. A horseshoe-shape bar in dark wood contrasts with the cream-color walls displaying local art. The food is adventurous and resolutely fresh, with the source of the ingredients carefully listed on the menu. The dishes vary with the seasons and the conditions on the high seas, but you might find delicious sea bream with saffron-herb mash, or monkfish tails with a delicate pea risotto. There are always unusual and exciting options for vegetarians and vegans. The owner has a passion for wine, which shows in the huge wine list. ⑤ *Average main: £15* ⊠ *1377 Argyle St., West End* ☎ *0844/573–0670* ⊕ *www.thepelicancafe.co.uk* ⚐ *Reservations essential* ✛ *B6.*

$$
BRITISH
Fodor's Choice
★

✕ The Sisters. Walk up the smooth sandstone steps to this restaurant, which aims to inspire both your palate and your heart. The menu is locally sourced and always changing: a typical dish is chicken with haggis in a whisky-mustard cream. No matter what you choose, it will be served in generous portions. The homegrown Arran gooseberry fool is the ultimate Scottish dessert. Douglas Gray tartan pads the pristine room, and polished floorboards reflect the natural light shining in from the long windows around the unusual oval-shape room. Wild seascape paintings are a nice touch in a space that feels both wide open and contained. ⑤ *Average main: £19* ⊠ *36 Kelvingrove St., West End* ☎ *0141/564–1157* ⊕ *www.thesisters.co.uk* ✛ *B3.*

$$
ECLECTIC
Fodor's Choice
★

✕ Stravaigin. A genuinely cosmopolitan menu that changes regularly, a wine list that is long but economical, and reasonably priced cocktails, all served in a warm and inviting interior buzzing with conversation, explain Stravaigin's continuing popularity. Wooden tables, booths, and assorted chairs in the bar create an informal atmosphere. Stravaigin takes pride in its well-traveled menu, with regular nights

3

featuring less familiar cuisines. Look for fine fish dishes like hake and mussels in a lemongrass broth. There's always a curry plate on the menu, as well as reliable Scottish favorites like haggis and neeps and beer-battered fish-and-chips. For dessert, the kitchen makes its own ice cream. If you prefer a quieter atmosphere, the downstairs restaurant serves the same menu. $ *Average main: £16* ⊠ *28 Gibson St., West End* ☎ *0141/334–2665* ⊕ *www.stravaigin.com* ⌖ *Reservations essential* ✥ *C6.*

$$$ ✕ **Ubiquitous Chip.** Occupying a converted stable behind the Hillhead
BRITISH subway station, this restaurant is an institution among members of
Fodor's Choice Glasgow's media and theater communities, who most days can be found
★ in the busy bar. The more informal upstairs brasserie serves haggis with neeps and tatties (turnips and potatoes, if you prefer) or slow-roasted pork shoulder. The ground-floor restaurant has a large cobbled courtyard with a glass roof. The more expensive menu offers fish and game dishes that vary from week to week. Try the roast saddle of rabbit or the monkfish with pork belly. There's an excellent lunch and pretheater menu for £15.95. $ *Average main: £24* ⊠ *12 Ashton La., West End* ☎ *0141/334–5007* ⊕ *www.ubiquitouschip.co.uk* ⌖ *Reservations essential* ✥ *B5.*

$ ✕ **Wudon.** This pleasant and relaxed Japanese restaurant offers beauti-
JAPANESE fully prepared food presented with great charm by the staff. Whether your taste is for hearty broths, just-made sushi, or savory rice and noodle dishes, the chef will combine the elements to your taste. Vegetarians are well served here. The lunchtime bento boxes (£6.50) are a particularly good value, with miso soup, rice, meat or fish, and a piece of fresh fruit. Asian beers and a range of drinks are available, too. $ *Average main: £9* ⊠ *535 Great Western Rd., West End* ☎ *0141/357–3039* ⊕ *www.wudon-noodlebar.co.uk* ✥ *B5.*

EAST END

Use the coordinate (✥ B2) at the end of each listing to locate a site on the corresponding map.

The East End is not well furnished with places to eat. An exception is West, housed in the Templeton's Carpet Factory opposite the People's Palace.

$ ✕ **West.** This microbrewery serves beer brewed "according to German
GERMAN purity laws of 1516"—in other words, no additives to muddy the flavor. The German theme is continued with the convivial dining space dotted with large wooden tables, and the food, which includes wursts, Wiener schnitzel, and goulash. West is in the famous Templeton Carpet Factory on Glasgow Green, built to resemble the Doge's Palace in Venice. $ *Average main: £12* ⊠ *Templeton Building, Templeton St., East End* ☎ *0141/550–0135* ⊕ *www.westbeer.com* ✥ *H5.*

SOUTH SIDE

Use the coordinate (✛ B2) at the end of each listing to locate a site on the corresponding map.

A number of places on the South Side are worth a stop if you're in the area.

$ **✕ Battlefield Rest.** Built in 1915, this former tram station has been lov-
ITALIAN ingly transformed into a popular Italian restaurant where the walls of windows are framed by heavy cream drapes. The food is authentic, well seasoned, and full of flavor—try the chicken stuffed with goat cheese and wrapped in Parma ham, or the panfried duck with figs. There are also plenty of pastas and pizzas. To get to this restaurant near Queen's Park, take Bus 66 from the St. Enoch underground station. ⑤ *Average main: £13* ✉ *55 Battlefield Rest, South Side* ☎ *0141/636–6955* ⊕ *www. battlefieldrest.co.uk* ⊗ *Closed Sun.* ✛ *E6.*

$$ **✕ Cookies.** One of the new breed of Italian eateries, with wooden tables
ITALIAN and assorted chairs, Cookies has a menu that changes daily according to what ingredients are available. Wild garlic, pea, and blue-cheese risotto might be prominently displayed on the blackboard the day you visit, or a perfectly made Arnold Bennett omelet (a local specialty made with haddock). They make their own bread, and their vegetables come from local farmers. ■ **TIP→ You get a discount if you have a ticket to the Citizens Theatre.** ⑤ *Average main: £15* ✉ *72 Nithsdale St., South Side* ☎ *0141/423–1411* ⊗ *Closed Mon.* ✛ *E6.*

$ **✕ Glad Cafe.** This excellent café serves delicious homemade cakes and
CAFÉ coffee, and the breakfast and lunch options are always worth a look. Homemade pâté is a possibilty, as are soups and pastas. It holds regular cultural events, too; the calendar includes music, film, and theater. The small entrance belies the spacious premises within. It sits opposite Langside Halls on Pollokshaws Road. ⑤ *Average main: £8* ✉ *1006A Pollokshaws Rd., South Side* ☎ *0141/636–6119* ⊕ *www.thegladcafe. co.uk* ⊗ *No dinner* ✛ *E6.*

$ **✕ Moyra Janes.** Pull up a chair to one of the marble-topped tables in
BRITISH this former bank building and soak up the genteel Scots charm. This South Side favorite serves a splendid tea with mouthwatering cakes. There's a healthy dash of cosmopolitan flair to boot: alongside the all-day breakfast menu are lamb tagine and chicken dopiazza. The £11.95 two-course dinner is a real bargain. ⑤ *Average main: £12* ✉ *20 Kildrostan St., Pollokshields* ☎ *0141/423–5628* ✛ *E6.*

WHERE TO STAY

Glasgow's city center never sleeps, so downtown hotels will be noisier than those in the leafy and genteel West End. Downtown hotels are within walking distance of all the main sights, while West End lodgings are more convenient for museums and art galleries. Over the past few years the hotel scene has become noticeably more stylish, with new hotels opening, including Blythswood Square and Grand Central.

Although big hotels are spread out all around the city, B&Bs are definitely a more popular, personal, and cheaper option. For country-house luxury you should look beyond the city—try Mar Hall, near Paisley.

Regardless of the neighborhood, hotels are about the same in price. Some B&Bs as well as the smaller properties may also offer discounts for longer stays. Make your reservations in advance, especially when there's a big concert, sporting event, or holiday (New Year's Eve is popular). In 2014 the Commonwealth Games will take place in Glasgow between July 23 and August 3, and city officials expect hotels to book up months in advance. Glasgow is busiest in summer, but it can fill up when something special is going on. If you arrive in town without a place to stay, contact the Glasgow Tourist Board.

3

PRICES AND MONEY-SAVING OPTIONS

It is always worthwhile to inquire about special deals or rate, especially if you book online and in advance. Another money-saving option is to rent an apartment. B&Bs are the best-priced short-term lodging option, and you're sure to get breakfast.

Most smaller hotels and all guesthouses include breakfast in the room rate. Larger hotels usually charge extra for breakfast. Also note that the most expensive hotels often exclude V.A.T. (Value Added Tax, the sales tax) in the initial price quote but budget places include it. *Prices in the reviews are the lowest cost of a standard double room in high season, including 20% V.A.T.*

CITY CENTER

Use the coordinate (✛ B2) at the end of each listing to locate a site on the corresponding map.

Here you'll be close to everything—the main sights, shops, theaters, restaurants, and bars—the pulse of the city. You don't have to worry about transportation in the center of town, but it can get noisy on weekend nights.

$$
HOTEL
🏨 **The Arthouse.** This stylish hotel was once the home of a prime minister, and it retains architectural features like the wrought-iron elevator and walls lined with 2,000 gold-leaf lions. **Pros:** stylish rooms; great location; nice mix of old and new in public areas. **Cons:** no dinner available; some front rooms can be noisy; parking is pricey. $ *Rooms from: £160* ⊠ *129 Bath St., City Center* ☎ *0141/221–6789* ⊕ *www.thearthouseglasgow.co.uk* ☞ *59 rooms, 1 suite* ❘⊘❘ *Breakfast* ✛ *F3.*

$$$
HOTEL
Fodor's Choice
★
🏨 **Blythswood Square.** History and luxury come together at this smart conversion of the former headquarters of the Royal Automobile Club of Scotland, which occupies a classical building on peaceful Blythswood Square. **Pros:** airy and luxurious; glorious bathrooms; lovely common areas that retain the original gold-topped columns. **Cons:** room lighting may be too dim for some; some street noise. $ *Rooms from: £200* ⊠ *11 Blythswood Sq., City Center* ☎ *0141/248–8888* ⊕ *www.blythswoodsquare.com* ☞ *100 rooms, 6 suites* ❘⊘❘ *Breakfast* ✛ *E3.*

$$
HOTEL
🏨 **Carlton George.** A narrow revolving doorway, a step back from busy West George Street, creates the illusion of a secret passageway leading into this lavish boutique hotel. **Pros:** near city-center attractions; discounted parking nearby. **Cons:** breakfast is extra during the week. $ *Rooms from: £154* ⊠ *44 W. George St., City Center* ☎ *0141/353–6373* ⊕ *www.carltonhotels.co.uk/george* ☞ *64 rooms* ❘⊘❘ *Multiple meal plans* ✛ *G4.*

BEST BETS FOR GLASGOW LODGING

$
HOTEL
Fodor's Choice
★
citizenM. There's no lobby at the futuristic citizenM—no reception area at all, because you can only book online—but there are chic "living rooms" with ultramodern furnishings where guests congregate. **Pros:** wonderful design; all the creature comforts; central location. **Cons:** not for the claustrophobic. *Rooms from: £90 ✉ 60 Renfrew St., corner of Hope St., City Center ☎ 01782/488–3490 ⊕ www.citizenm.com/glasgow ➶ 198 rooms ⧉ Some meals ✛ F3.*

$$$$
HOTEL
Fodor's Choice
★
Grand Central Hotel. This hotel certainly deserves its name, as everything about it, from the magnificent marble-floor champagne bar to the ballroom fully restored to its original glory, is grand. **Pros:** a real air of luxury; most rooms are quite spacious; champagne bar is a wonderful place to linger. **Cons:** some noise from street; parking is a couple of blocks away; some rooms are small. *Rooms from: £289 ✉ 99 Gordon St., City Center ☎ 0141/240–3700 ⊕ www.principal-hayley.com/grandcentralhotel ➶ 230 rooms, 3 suites ⧉ Multiple meal plans ✛ F4.*

$$
HOTEL
Grasshoppers. Not visible from the street, this hotel occupies the sixth floor above Central Station—just look for the door marked "Caledonian Chambers" on Union Street and take the elevator. **Pros:** bright and

clean; quiet atmosphere; central location. **Cons:** no lobby; rooms are quite small. $ *Rooms from: £105* ✉ *87 Union St., City Center* ☎ *0141/222–2666* ⊕ *www.grasshoppersglasgow.com* ⬠ *30 rooms* ⦿ *Breakfast* ✚ *F4.*

$$$$
HOTEL

⊞ **Hotel Indigo.** In the center of the city, the fashionable Indigo is awash with bold colors and modern designs that emphasize comfort and calm. **Pros:** well-designed rooms; subdued colors and lighting; no conference rooms. **Cons:** narrow corridors; only showers in the rooms. $ *Rooms from: £300* ✉ *75 Waterloo St., City Center* ☎ *0141/226 7700* ⊕ *www.hotelindigoglasgow.com* ⬠ *94 rooms* ⦿ *No meals* ✚ *E4.*

$$
HOTEL
Fodor's Choice
★

⊞ **Malmaison.** Housed in a converted church, this modern boutique hotel prides itself on personal service and outstanding amenities like plasma televisions and high-end stereo systems. **Pros:** stunning lobby; attention to detail; five-minute walk to Sauchiehall Street. **Cons:** bland views; dark hallways; no on-site parking. $ *Rooms from: £129* ✉ *278 W. George St., City Center* ☎ *0141/572–1000* ⊕ *www.malmaison.com* ⬠ *64 rooms, 8 suites* ⦿ *Breakfast* ✚ *E3.*

$$
HOTEL

⊞ **Marks Hotel.** This hotel's small reception area doesn't prepare you for its sheer size; the 108 rooms and suites are plain and fairly compact. **Pros:** good location; free Wi-Fi; great views from front rooms. **Cons:** parking garage is a five-minute walk away; restaurant is windowless; tired decor in some rooms. $ *Rooms from: £115* ✉ *110 Bath St., City Center* ☎ *0141/353–0800* ⊕ *www.markshotels.com* ⬠ *103 rooms, 5 suites* ⦿ *No meals* ✚ *F3.*

$$$
HOTEL

⊞ **Radisson Blu.** You can't miss this eye-catching edifice behind Central Station: its glass facade makes the interior, particularly the lounge, seem as though it were part of the street. **Pros:** kilted doorman; impeccable service; free Wi-Fi and other amenities. **Cons:** neighborhood can get noisy; most rooms have poor views; no on-site parking. $ *Rooms from: £205* ✉ *301 Argyle St., City Center* ☎ *0141/204–3333* ⊕ *www.radissonblu.co.uk/hotel-glasgow* ⬠ *247 rooms, 3 suites* ⦿ *No meals* ✚ *E5.*

$
B&B/INN

⊞ **Victorian House.** Compared with the bright-yellow entrance hall, the rooms in this hotel are rather plain. **Pros:** appealing location; great front patio; basement rooms very spacious. **Cons:** some rooms need freshening up; no elevator; on-street parking can be difficult to find. $ *Rooms from: £59* ✉ *212 Renfrew St., City Center* ☎ *0141/332–0129* ⊕ *www.thevictorian.co.uk* ⬠ *58 rooms* ⦿ *Breakfast* ✚ *E2.*

MERCHANT CITY

Use the coordinate (✚ B2) at the end of each listing to locate a site on the corresponding map.

The hotels in the Merchant City are best for those who plan to spend most of their time out and about. In general, this busy area is not the place to come if you want peace and quiet.

$
B&B/INN

⊞ **Babbity Bowster's.** Babbity Bowster's is a welcoming pub in an old merchant's house in the heart of the Merchant City. **Pros:** couldn't be more central; good food; great atmosphere. **Cons:** a bit noisy; finding parking can be difficult; no elevator. $ *Rooms from: £60* ✉ *16–18 Blackfriars St., Merchant City* ☎ *0141/552–5055* ⊕ *www.babbitybowster.com* ⬠ *6 rooms* ⦿ *Breakfast* ✚ *H5.*

$ **Brunswick.** This modest but comfortable six-story hotel sits at the
HOTEL   heart of Glasgow's nightlife. **Pros:** excellent value; lively downstairs
café; very central. **Cons:** area can be noisy on weekends; some rooms
are very small; rooms at the back have unappealing views over neighboring roofs. *$ Rooms from: £65 ⊠ 106–108 Brunswick St., Merchant
City ☎ 0141/552–0001 ⊕ www.brunswickhotel.co.uk ⌁ 18 rooms, 1
suite ❍| Breakfast ✚ H5.*

$ **Cathedral House Hotel.** Adjacent to Glasgow Cathedral, this Scottish
HOTEL   Baronial–style building dating back to 1867 once served as the church's
ecclesiastical headquarters—hence the name. **Pros:** historic atmosphere;
quiet location; good views. **Cons:** no elevator; a long 10-minute walk
to the center of town. *$ Rooms from: £90 ⊠ 28–32 Cathedral Sq.,
Merchant City ☎ 0141/552–3519 ⊕ www.cathedralhousehotel.co.uk
⌁ 7 rooms ❍| Breakfast ✚ H4.*

$ **Premier Inn.** It may be part of a chain, but this hotel's bright rooms
HOTEL   and reasonable prices appeal to savvy travelers. **Pros:** great location;
bargain rates; modern rooms. **Cons:** some front rooms are noisy; extra
charges for parking and Internet access. *$ Rooms from: £70 ⊠ 187
George St., Merchant City ☎ 0870/238–3320 ⊕ www.premierinn.com
⌁ 239 rooms ❍| No meals ✚ H4.*

WEST END

*Use the coordinate (✚ B2) at the end of each listing to locate a site on
the corresponding map.*

Many lodgings are on quieter Great Western Road, set apart from busy
Byres Road. There are a number of hotels on the other side of Kelvingrove Park in a lively area.

$ **Amadeus Guest House.** This adorable Victorian town house sits on
B&B/INN   a leafy residential street overlooking the river Kelvin. **Pros:** near West
End attractions; two-minute walk from subway; kids under six stay
free. **Cons:** some rooms are small; finding parking can be difficult.
*$ Rooms from: £60 ⊠ 411 N. Woodside Rd., West End ☎ 0141/339–
8257 ⊕ www.amadeusguesthouse.co.uk ⌁ 9 rooms ❍| Breakfast ✚ C5.*

$ **Ambassador Hotel.** Opposite the West End's peaceful Botanic Gar-
HOTEL   dens, the Ambassador is part of a string of elegant town houses on
the banks of the river Kelvin. **Pros:** views of Botanical Gardens; great
for families with kids; five-minute walk to public transportation and
West End amenities. **Cons:** no elevator; on-street parking can be difficult after 6 pm; staff a little frosty. *$ Rooms from: £75 ⊠ 7 Kelvin
Dr., West End ☎ 0141/946–1018 ⊕ www.ambassador-hotel.net ⌁ 26
rooms ❍| Breakfast ✚ B5.*

$ **Argyll Guest House.** In this budget-minded annex to the Argyll Hotel,
B&B/INN   across the road on Sauchiehall Street, the rooms are plainly furnished
but scrupulously clean. **Pros:** close to Kelvingrove Park; near public
transportation; bargain prices. **Cons:** front rooms noisy on weekends; decor is bland and uninspiring; no elevator. *$ Rooms from:
£60 ⊠ 966–970 Sauchiehall St., West End ☎ 0141/357–5155 ⊕ www.
argyllhotelglasgow.co.uk ⌁ 20 rooms ❍| Breakfast ✚ A2.*

3

$ 🏨**Argyll Hotel.** The tartan in the reception area reflects the clan theme
HOTEL   throughout the hotel. *⑤Rooms from: £80 ✉ 973, Sauchiehall St., West
End, Glasgow ☎0141/337-3313 ⊕ www.argyllhotelglasgow.co.uk
↘38 rooms ⦿Breakfast ✢A2.*

$ 🏨**Clifton Hotel.** Occupying two of the grand houses along a terrace
HOTEL   above Great Western Road, this popular hotel offers wallet-friendly
rates and simply furnished rooms done up in cheerful shades. **Pros:**
conveniently located; attentive staff. **Cons:** some rooms overlook the
parking lot; no elevator. *⑤Rooms from: £59 ✉ 26–27 Buckingham
Terr., West End ☎0141/334-8080 ⊕ www.cliftonhotelglasgow.co.uk
↘25 rooms ⦿Breakfast ✢B5.*

$$ 🏨**Hilton Glasgow Grosvenor.** Behind a row of grand terrace houses, this
HOTEL   modern hotel overlooks the Botanical Gardens. **Pros:** close to Byres
Road; some rooms have good views; tasty eatery. **Cons:** rooms at the
back overlook a parking lot; a rather institutional feel. *⑤Rooms from:
£109 ✉ 1–9 Grosvenor Terr., West End ☎0141/339-8811 ⊕ www.
hilton.com/glasgowgrosvenor ↘96 rooms ⦿Breakfast ✢B5.*

$$$ 🏨**Hotel du Vin Glasgow.** Once the legendary One Devonshire Gardens,
HOTEL   frequented by such celebrities as Luciano Pavarotti and Elizabeth Tay-
Fodor'sChoice   lor, the Hotel Du Vin Glasgow is still a destination for those in search
★   of luxury. **Pros:** stunning Scottish rooms; doting service; complimentary
whisky on arrival. **Cons:** no elevator; on-street parking can be difficult
after 6 pm. *⑤Rooms from: £180 ✉ 1 Devonshire Gardens, West End
☎084473/339-2001 ⊕ www.hotelduvin.com/glasgow ↘41 rooms, 8
suites ⦿Breakfast ✢A4.*

$ 🏨**Kirklee Hotel.** This West End B&B occupies a cozy Edwardian town
B&B/INN   house with dark paneling and tartan carpets in the public areas. **Pros:**
friendly service; quiet street; close to West End attractions. **Cons:** on-
street parking is challenging; city center is 2 miles away. *⑤Rooms
from: £80 ✉ 11 Kensington Gate, West End ☎0141/334-5555
⊕ kirkleehotel.co.uk ↘9 rooms ⦿Breakfast ✢A5.*

$ 🏨**Manor Park Guest House.** On a quiet street close to Victoria Park, one of
B&B/INN   Glasgow's nicest green spaces, this stately terraced town house is spacious
and has charm to spare. **Pros:** quiet residential area; helpful staff; delicious breakfast. **Cons:** 20-minute walk from the nearest subway station.
*⑤Rooms from: £65 ✉ 28 Balshagray Dr., West End ☎0141/339-2143
⊕ www.themanorpark.com ↘10 rooms ⦿Breakfast ✢A6.*

$ 🏨**The Sandyford.** The Victorian exterior of this hotel anticipates the
HOTEL   colorful decor you'll find inside, where the large windows in the reception area let in lots of light. **Pros:** on the doorstep of Kelvingrove Park;
minutes from several good eateries; newly refurbished rooms. **Cons:**
front rooms can get late-night noise; no elevator. *⑤Rooms from:
£65 ✉ 904 Sauchiehall St., West End ☎0141/334-0000 ⊕ www.
sandyfordhotelglasgow.com ↘55 rooms ⦿Breakfast ✢B3.*

$ 🏨**The White House Apartments.** On a tranquil crescent just west of the
RENTAL   Botanical Gardens, this well-managed cluster of Victorian town houses
FAMILY   has more than 30 individually furnished apartments. **Pros:** large rooms;
courtyard gardens; good for families. **Cons:** sometimes feels old-fashioned;
bathrooms are fairly basic. *⑤Rooms from: £79 ✉ 11–13 Cleveden Crescent, West End ☎0141/339-9375 ⊕ www.whitehouse-apartments.com
↘33 apartments, 2 suites ⦿No meals ✢A4.*

THE CLYDE

Use the coordinate (✛ B2) at the end of each listing to locate a site on the corresponding map.

Besides a handful of interesting museums and a cluster of busy bars and restaurants, this up-and-coming area also has a few well-regarded lodgings.

$$ 🏨 **Hilton Garden Inn Glasgow City Centre.** Overlooking the Clyde, this
HOTEL hotel is a short walk along the riverside to Riverside Museum and other popular destinations. **Pros:** relaxing lounge area; lovely terrace; some great views. **Cons:** isolated from the rest of the city. ⑤ *Rooms from: £119 ⊠ Finnieston Quay, Clyde ☎ 0141/240–1002 ⊕ hiltongardeninn3. hilton.com ⌂ 164 rooms* |◎| *Breakfast ✛ C5.*

SOUTH SIDE

Use the coordinate (✛ B2) at the end of each listing to locate a site on the corresponding map.

This residential area near the center of the city has some lovely parks; there's not much to do at night, though.

$$ 🏨 **Number 10 Hotel.** In one of the grand houses overlooking Queens
HOTEL Park, this elegant hotel's guest rooms are quite large and are decorated in pleasantly muted colors. **Pros:** nice setting; ample parking; pretty garden. **Cons:** can be crowded with wedding parties on weekends. ⑤ *Rooms from: £100 ⊠ 10–16 Queens Dr., South Side ☎ 0141/424–0160 ⊕ www.10hotel.co.uk ⌂ 26 rooms* |◎| *No meals ✛ E6.*

$$ 🏨 **Sherbrooke Castle Hotel.** Set high above the road, the Sherbrooke is
HOTEL one the grand homes built by the newly prosperous industrialists of the 19th century. **Pros:** relaxed atmosphere; top-notch service; large bathrooms. **Cons:** some rooms are small; weekend functions can get very loud; no elevator. ⑤ *Rooms from: £140 ⊠ 11 Sherbrooke Ave., South Side ☎ 0141/427–4227 ⊕ www.sherbrooke.co.uk ⌂ 14 rooms* |◎| *Breakfast ✛ D6.*

NIGHTLIFE AND THE ARTS

Glasgow's music scene is vibrant and creative, and many successful pop artists began their careers in its pubs and clubs. Celtic Connections is probably one of the world's most important festivals of its kind, and the city's summer Jazz Festival has attracted some of the world's finest players.

When it comes to nightlife, the city center and the West End are alive with pubs and clubs offering an eclectic mix of everything from bagpipes to salsa to punk. The biweekly magazine the *List,* available at newsstands and many cafés and arts centers, is an indispensable guide to Glasgow's bars and clubs.

THE ARTS

Because the Royal Scottish Conservatoire is in Glasgow, there is always a pool of impressive young talent that's pressing the city's artistic boundaries in theater, music, and film. The city has a well-deserved reputation for its theater, with everything from cutting-edge plays to over-the-top pantomimes. The Citizens Theatre is one of Europe's leading companies, and the Kings and the Theatre Royal play host to touring productions.

Scottish Music Centre. Besides having a library, the Scottish Music Centre serves as the main ticket office for all music events at venues like the Royal Concert Hall and for annual events like the the Glasgow Jazz Festival. ⊠ *Candleriggs, City Center* ☎ *0141/353–8000* ⊕ *www.glasgowconcerthalls.com.*

ARTS CENTERS

FAMILY **Tramway.** South of the city center, this innovative arts center is well worth seeking out. It hosts regular exhibitions in its two galleries, and plays—often of a very experimental nature—in its flexible theater space. It has a café and a more formal restaurant on the first floor. Don't miss the Hidden Garden, which has transformed a lot behind the building into a sculpture park. This is a great place to go with kids. ⊠ *25 Albert Dr., South Side* ☎ *0845/276–0950* ⊕ *www.tramway.org.*

Trongate 103. This vibrant contemporary arts center, housed in a converted Edwardian warehouse, is home base for diverse groups producing film, photography, paintings, and prints. It contains the Russian Cultural Centre and the Sharmanka Kinetic Theatre, as well as the Glasgow Print Studio, Street Level Photoworks, and the Transmission Gallery. Part of the complex, the well-established Street Level Photoworks aims at making photography more accessible. ⊠ *103 Trongate, Merchant City* ☎ *0141/276–8380* ⊕ *www.trongate103.com.*

CONCERTS

City Halls. One of the top music venues in the City Center, the stone-fronted City Halls hosts orchestral, jazz, and folk concerts. ⊠ *Candleriggs, City Center* ☎ *0141/353–8000* ⊕ *www.glasgowconcerthalls.com.*

Glasgow Royal Concert Hall. The 2,500-seat Glasgow Royal Concert Hall is the venue for a wide range of concerts, from classical to pop. It also hosts the very popular late-night club. ⊠ *2 Sauchiehall St., City Center* ☎ *0141/353–8000* ⊕ *www.glasgowconcerthalls.com.*

O2 ABC. One of the city's major music venues, O2 ABC is housed inside what was once a cinema. It's the city's main showcase for well-known pop and rock bands. ⊠ *300 Sauchihall St., City Center* ☎ *0141/332–2232* ⊕ *www.o2abcglasgow.co.uk.*

The Old Fruitmarket. A wonderful venue for almost every type of music, this was once the city's fruit and vegetable market. The first-floor balcony, with its intricate iron railings, still carries some of the original merchants' names. It's adjacent to City Halls. ⊠ *Candleriggs, Merchant City* ☎ *0141/353–8000* ⊕ *www.glasgowconcerthalls.com.*

Royal Scottish Conservatoire. An important venue for music and drama, the Royal Scottish Conservatoire hosts regular concerts by well-known performers, as well as by its own students. The lunchtime concert series is popular. ⊠ *100 Renfrew St., City Center* ☎ *0141/332–4101* ⊕ *www.rcs.ac.uk.*

Scottish Exhibition and Conference Centre. Known as the Armadillo for its distinctive design, the Scottish Exhibition and Conference Centre hosts large-scale pop concerts. ⊠ *Exhibition Way, The Clyde* ☎ *0141/248–3000* ⊕ *www.secc.co.uk.*

SSE Hydro. The newest addition to Glasgow's list of concert venues, the SSE Hydro can accommodate 12,000 people underneath its huge silver dome. ⊠ *SECC Exhibition Way, The Clyde* ☎ *0141/248–3000* ⊕ *www.thehydro.com.*

St. Andrew's in the Square. A beautifully restored 18th-century church close to Glasgow Cross, the glorious St. Andrew's in the Square is a popular arts venue. Drop by to see fiddle players on Monday evening or take traditional Scottish dance classes on Wednesday night. Concerts are held here from time to time. The downstairs café serves a good range of Scottish food for lunch or dinner. ⊠ *1 St. Andrew's in the Square, East End* ☎ *0141/559–5902* ⊕ *www.standrewsinthesquare.com.*

DANCE AND OPERA

Theatre Royal. Glasgow is home to the Scottish Opera and Scottish Ballet, both of which perform at the Theatre Royal. Visiting dance and theater companies from many countries appear here as well. ⊠ *282 Hope St., City Center* ☎ *0141/332–9000.*

FESTIVALS

Fodor's Choice
★

Celtic Connections. This ever-expanding music festival is held in the second half of January in a number of venues across the city. Musicians from Scotland, Ireland, and other countries celebrate Celtic music, both traditional and contemporary. There are a series of hands-on workshops and a popular late-night club at the Royal Concert Hall. ☎ *0141/353–8000* ⊕ *www.celticconnections.com.*

Glasgay. Held between November and December, Glasgay is the United Kingdom's largest arts festival focusing on LGBT culture. The international lineup is always impressive and draws a huge audience. ☎ *0141/552–7575* ⊕ *www.glasgay.co.uk.*

Glasgow Jazz Festival. In late June and early July, Glasgow hosts jazz musicians from around the world in venues throughout the city, though mainly in the City Center. ⊠ *81 High St., City Center* ☎ *0141/552–3552* ⊕ *www.jazzfest.co.uk.*

FILM

Center for Contemporary Arts. The Center for Contemporary Arts screens classic, independent, and children's films, mounts major art exhibitions and other arts events. It also has a restaurant and an upstairs bar and a very good small bookshop. ⊠ *350 Sauchiehall St., City Center* ☎ *0141/352–4900* ⊕ *www.cca-glasgow.com.*

Cineworld Glasgow. An 18-screen facility, this is Glasgow's busiest movie complex. A glass-walled elevator whisks you to the top of the 170-foot-tall building, which is also the world's tallest cinema. ✉ *7 Renfrew St., City Center* ☎ *0871/200–2000* ⊕ *www.cineworld. co.uk/cinemas/28.*

Glasgow Film Theatre. An independent operation, the three-screen Glasgow Film Theatre hosts the best new releases, documentaries, and classic films. It has several programs for young people and hosts the annual Glasgow Film Festival. ✉ *12 Rose St., City Center* ☎ *0141/332–6535* ⊕ *www.glasgowfilm.org.*

Grosvenor. This popular, compact cinema has two screens and extremely comfortable leather seats (some of them big enough for two). It's part of a small complex that includes two street-level bars and a spacious upstairs café and bar. ✉ *Ashton La., West End* ☎ *0845/339–8444* ⊕ *www.grosvenorcafe.co.uk.*

THEATER

Ticketmaster. Tickets for theatrical performances can be purchased at theater box offices or online through Ticketmaster. ⊕ *www. ticketmaster.co.uk.*

Fodor's Choice ★ **Arches.** The labyrinth of passageways under Central Station has become the Arches, a flexible space for theater and music. It hosts various festivals through the year, including October's Glasgay celebration of gay arts. There's also a basement café-bar that's open throughout the day and into the evening. ✉ *253 Argyle St., City Center* ☎ *0141/565–1000* ⊕ *www.thearches.co.uk.*

Fodor's Choice ★ **Citizens' Theatre.** Some of the most exciting theatrical performances take place at the internationally renowned Citizens' Theatre, where productions are often of hair-raising originality. Behind the theater's striking contemporary glass facade is a glorious red-and-gold Victorian-era auditorium. ✉ *119 Gorbals St., East End* ☎ *0141/429–0022* ⊕ *www. citz.co.uk.*

Cottier's Arts Theatre. Contemporary works are staged at Cottier's Arts Theatre, housed in a converted church. ✉ *93 Hyndland St., West End* ☎ *0141/357–5825* ⊕ *www.cottiers.com.*

King's Theatre. Dramas, variety shows, and musicals are staged at the King's Theatre. ✉ *297 Bath St., City Center* ☎ *0141/240–1111* ⊕ *www. uktw.co.uk.*

Fodor's Choice ★ **Òran Mór.** Head to Òran Mór at lunchtime for the hugely successful series called "A Play, Pie and Pint" (and you do get all three). The series, which showcases new writing from Scotland and elsewhere, has included more than 250 works. It sells out quickly, particularly late in the week, so book well in advance. ✉ *731 Great Western Rd., West End* ☎ *0141/357–6200* ⊕ *www.playpiepint.com.*

Pavilion Theatre. The Pavilion hosts family-friendly entertainment, along with some rock and pop concerts. ✉ *121 Renfield St., City Center* ☎ *0141/332–1846* ⊕ *www.paviliontheatre.co.uk.*

FAMILY
Fodor's Choice
★
Sharmanka Kinetic Theatre. A unique spectacle, Sharmanka Kinetic Theatre is the brainchild of Eduard Bersudsky, who came to Glasgow from Russia in 1989 to continue making the mechanical sculptures that are his stock in trade. They are witty and sometimes disturbing, perhaps because they are constructed from scrap materials. They move in a kind of ballet to haunting, specially composed music punctuated by a light show. Kids under 15 get in free when accompanied by an adult. ⊠ *103 Trongate, Merchant City* ☎ *0141/552–7080* ⊕ *www.sharmanka.com* ✉ *£5–£8* ⊙ *Wed. at 3, Thurs. and Fri. at 3 and 7, Sat. at 1 and 3, Sun. at 1, 3, and 7.*

Tron Theatre. Come here for contemporary theater from Scotland and around the world. ⊠ *63 Trongate, Merchant City* ☎ *0141/552–4267* ⊕ *www.tron.co.uk.*

NIGHTLIFE

Glasgow's busy nightlife scene is impressive and varied. Bars and pubs often close at midnight on weekends, but nightclubs often stay open until 3 or 4 am. Traditional *ceilidh* (a mix of country dancing, music, and song; pronounced *kay*-lee) is not as popular with locals as it used to be (except at weddings), but you can still find it at many more tourist-oriented establishments.

Glasgow's pubs were once hangouts for serious drinkers who demanded few comforts. Times have changed, and many of these gritty establishments have been transformed into trendy cocktail bars or cavernous spaces with multiple video monitors, though a few traditional bars do survive. Bars and pubs vary according to location; many of those in the city center cater to business types, although some still draw a more traditional clientele.

As elsewhere in Britain, electronic music—from house to techno to drum and bass—is par for the course in Glasgow's dance clubs. Much of the scene revolves around the city center, as a late-night walk down Sauchiehall Street on Friday or Saturday will reveal.

CITY CENTER
BARS AND PUBS
Baby Grand. One of Glasgow's best-kept secrets, this intimate piano bar is hidden behind the King's Theatre. It serves good food all day, and it somehow manages to be crowded but never overcrowded, even at the busiest times. The pretheater menu is a good value, and there are tapas available on weekends. ⊠ *3 Elmbank Gardens, City Center* ☎ *0141/248–4942* ⊕ *www.babygrandglasgow.com.*

Black Sparrow. A cool Charles Bukowski theme bar named after the American writer's publishing company, the Black Sparrow serves potent cocktails and sophisticated bar food. There's also a great outdoor beer garden. ⊠ *241 North St., City Center* ☎ *0141/221–5530* ⊕ *www. theblacksparrow.co.uk.*

Bloc. At Bloc you can step behind a curious version of the Iron Curtain where Tex-Mex diner food mixes with an eclectic musical mash of DJs and live rock and folk bands. ⊠ *117 Bath St., City Center* ☎ *0141/574–6066* ⊕ *www.bloc.ru/barbloc.html.*

King Tut's Wah Wah Hut. Hosting live music most nights, King Tut's Wah Wah Hut claims to have been the venue that discovered the U.K. pop band Oasis. It's a favorite with students, but the cozy and traditional pub setting draws people of all ages. ⊠ *227A St. Vincent St., City Center* ☎ *0141/221–5279* ⊕ *www.kingtuts.co.uk.*

Moskito. For a splash of Mediterranean style, head to Moskito. Amid the cool, aquatic hues you can watch people dancing to laid-back tunes Thursday to Sunday nights. ⊠ *200 Bath St., City Center* ☎ *0141/331–1777* ⊕ *www.moskitoglasgow.com.*

WHAT TO ORDER
First-timers to Glasgow should order a pint, meaning a pint of lager. Bottled beers are available, but draft beer is the most popular beverage for men; women tend to drink wine or cocktails (yes, this gender difference is extremely obvious).

3

Fodor's Choice ★ **Sloans.** One of Glasgow's oldest and most beautiful pubs, the wood-paneled Sloans is always lively and welcoming and serves traditional pub food like fish-and-chips throughout the day. The upstairs ballroom is a magnificent mirrored affair, and on the floor above that is a dance floor where there's traditional music every Friday night. There's a good selection of beers and spirits, and the outdoor area is always lively when the weather cooperates. ⊠ *108 Argyle St., City Center* ☎ *0141/221–8886* ⊕ *www.sloansglasgow.com.*

CLUBS

Arches. One of the city's largest arts venues, the Arches thumps with house and techno on Friday and Saturday nights. The club welcomes big music names like Colours and Inside Out at legendary parties. A few times a month it holds dressed-up gay nights. ⊠ *253 Argyle St., City Center* ☎ *0141/565–1000* ⊕ *www.thearches.co.uk.*

Stereo. The small downstairs music venue gets crowded quickly when bands play Sunday to Thursday night, but that only adds to the electric atmosphere at Stereo. There's also a hopping nightclub where DJs spin on Friday and Saturday nights until the wee hours of the morning. Upstairs, a café-bar serves tasty vegan food and organic drinks. ⊠ *20–28 Renfield La., City Center* ☎ *0141/222–2254* ⊕ *www.stereocafebar.com.*

Sub Club. This atmospheric underground venue has staged cutting-edge music events since its jazz club days in the '50s. Legendary favorites like Saturday's SubCulture (House) and Sunday's Optimo (a truly eclectic mix for musical hedonists) pack in friendly and sweaty crowds. ⊠ *22 Jamaica St., City Center* ☎ *0141/248–4600* ⊕ *www.subclub.co.uk.*

MERCHANT CITY
BARS AND PUBS

Babbity Bowster's. A busy, friendly spot, Babbity Bowster's serves real ales and excellent, mainly Scottish food, prepared for more than a decade now by a French chef who adds his own very special touch. The atmosphere is lively and very friendly; there is an outdoor terrace in summer and a fireplace in winter. If you like traditional music, make a point of coming on Saturday and Wednesday afternoon. ⊠ *16–18 Blackfriars St., Merchant City* ☎ *0141/552–5055* ⊕ *www.babbitybowster.com.*

Fodor's Choice
★

Scotia Bar. The Scotia Bar serves up a taste of an authentic, old-time Glasgow pub, with some traditional folk music occasionally thrown in. ⊠ *112 Stockwell St., Merchant City* ☎ *0141/552–8681* ⊕ *www. scotiabar.net.*

CLUBS

Polo Lounge. Oozing with Edwardian style, the Polo Lounge is Glasgow's largest gay club. Upstairs is a bar that resembles an old-fashioned gentlemen's club. On the two dance floors downstairs, the DJs spin something for everyone. ⊠ *84 Wilson St., Merchant City* ☎ *0141/553–1221* ⊕ *www.pologlasgow.co.uk.*

WEST END

BARS AND PUBS

78. The 78 has cozy sofas, a real coal fire, and tasty vegan food. There's live music every night, with jazz on Sunday. ⊠ *10–14 Kelvinhaugh St., West End* ☎ *0141/576–5018* ⊕ *www.the78cafebar.com.*

Ben Nevis. This eccentric pub is full of Highland artifacts. There are more than 180 whiskies from which to choose and traditional live music on Wednesday, Thursday, and Sunday. ⊠ *1147 Argyle St., West End* ☎ *0141/576–5204* ⊕ *thebennevis.co.uk.*

Cottiers. Despite its former austere incarnation as a church, the always-busy Cottiers is a famous haunt of the young, particularly in the summer months. The best seats are outside in the popular beer garden. ⊠ *93 Hyndland St., West End* ☎ *0141/357–5825* ⊕ *www.cottiers.com.*

Dram. With mismatched furnishings and the odd stag's head on the wall, Dram's four large rooms are decorated in a style that can only be described as "ultra eclectic." There's a wide range of beers, but the place takes special pride in the 75 whiskies. On Thursday and Sunday musicians gather in an informal jam session. Food is served every night until 9. ⊠ *232–246 Woodlands Rd., West End* ☎ *0141/332–1622* ⊕ *www.dramglasgow.co.uk.*

Halt. There's a wide selection of beers and whiskies at the Halt. Look for a good lineup of established and up-and-coming rock groups in the adjoining Halt 2, which attracts a diverse crowd of music lovers. ⊠ *160 Woodlands Rd., West End* ☎ *0141/564–1527.*

Òran Mór. At the top of Byres Road, Òran Mór is in a massive church that still has its beautiful stained-glass windows. The beer garden fills up quickly in good weather. The place caters to different crowds at different times, and is open until the wee hours. ⊠ *731 Great Western Rd., West End* ☎ *0141/357–6200* ⊕ *www.oran-mor.co.uk.*

Rio Cafe. With the feel of a 1950s diner, the laid-back Rio Cafe is all things to all people. Drop by in the evening to listen to musicians, DJs, and poets (or even play poker on some nights). During the day there are economical breakfasts and lunches. ⊠ *27 Hyndland St., West End* ☎ *0141/334–9909.*

Tennents. A spacious corner bar, Tennents prides itself on its comprehensive selection of beers. You can expect lively conversation, as there's a refreshing lack of loud music. ⊠ *191 Byres Rd., West End* ☎ *0141/341–1021.*

COMEDY CLUBS

Stand Comedy Club. With live shows every night of the week, the Stand Comedy Club is most popular on Thursday and Friday. Prices vary according to who is appearing, and the doors open at 7:30. ⊠ *333 Woodlands Rd., West End* ☎ *0844/335–8879* ⊕ *www.thestand.co.uk.*

SHOPPING

You'll find the mark of the fashion industry on the city center's hottest shopping streets. In the Merchant City Ingram Street is lined on either side by high-fashion and designer outlets like Cruise and Agent Provocateur. Buchanan Street, in the city center, is home to many chains geared toward younger people, including Diesel, Monsoon, and USC, and malls like the elegant Princes Square and Buchanan Galleries. The adjacent Argyle Street Arcade is filled with jewelry stores. Antiques tend be found on and around West Regent Street in the city center.

The West End has a number of small shops selling crafts, vintage clothing, and trendier fashions—punctuated by innumerable cafés and restaurants. The university dominates the area around West End, and many shops cater to students. The easiest way to get here is by taking the subway to Hillhead.

CITY CENTER

ARCADES AND SHOPPING CENTERS

Argyll Arcade. An interesting diversion off Argyle Street is the covered Argyll Arcade, the region's largest collection of jewelers under one roof. The L-shape edifice, built in 1904, houses several locally based jewelers and a few shops specializing in antique jewelry. ⊠ *Buchanan St., City Center* ⊕ *www.argyll-arcade.com.*

Barras. This indoor market, on London Road in the Glasgow Cross neighborhood east of the city center, prides itself on selling everything "from a needle to an anchor." Stalls hawk antique (and not-so-antique) furniture, bric-a-brac, good and not-so-good jewelry, and textiles—you name it, it's here. ⊠ *Gallowgate, East End.*

Buchanan Galleries. Next to the Glasgow Royal Concert Hall, Buchanan Galleries is packed with high-quality shops. Its top attraction is the John Lewis department store. ⊠ *220 Buchanan St., City Center* ☎ *0141/333–9898* ⊕ *www.buchanangalleries.co.uk.*

Fodor's Choice ★ **Princes Square.** The city's best shopping center is the art nouveau Princes Square, a lovely space filled with high-quality shops and pleasant cafés and restaurants. A stunning glass dome was fitted over the original building, which dates back to 1841. ⊠ *48 Buchanan St., City Center* ☎ *0141/221–0324* ⊕ *www.princessquare.co.uk.*

St. Enoch's Shopping Centre. St. Enoch's Shopping Centre is eye-catching if not especially pleasing—it's a modern glass building that resembles an overgrown greenhouse. It houses various stores, but most are also found elsewhere. ⊠ *55 St. Enoch Sq., City Center* ☎ *0141/204–3900* ⊕ *www.stenoch.co.uk.*

DEPARTMENT STORES

Debenham's. One of Glasgow's principal department stores, Debenham's has fine china and crystal as well as women's and men's clothing. ⊠ 97 *Argyle St., City Center* ☎ *0844/561–6161* ⊕ *www.debenhams.com.*

House of Fraser. A Glasgow institution, the House of Fraser stocks wares that reflect the city's material aspirations, including European designer clothing. There are also home-produced articles, such as tweeds, tartans, glass, and ceramics. The magnificent interior, set off by the grand staircase rising to various floors and balconies, is itself worth a visit. ⊠ *21–45 Buchanan St., City Center* ☎ *0141/221–3880* ⊕ *www. houseoffraser.co.uk.*

John Lewis. This shop is a favorite for its stylish mix of clothing, household items, electronics, and practically everything else. John Lewis claims to have "never been knowingly undersold" and prides itself on its customer service. It has a very elegant second-floor balcony café. ⊠ *Buchanan Galleries, 220 Buchanan St., City Center* ☎ *0141/353–6677* ⊕ *www.johnlewis.com/glasgow.*

Marks & Spencer. With sturdy, practical clothing and accessories at moderate prices, Marks & Spencer also offers gourmet foods and household goods. There's a second location at 172 Sauchiehall Street. ⊠ *2–12 Argyle St., City Center* ☎ *0141/552–4546* ⊕ *www.marksandpencer.com.*

SHOPPING DISTRICTS

Argyle Street. On the often-crowded pedestrian area of Argyle Street you'll find chain stores like Debenham's.

Buchanan Street. The usual suspects are clustered on this pedestian-only street: Monsoon, Topshop, Burberry, Jaeger, and other chain stores. There are usually plenty of street entertainers to accompany you from shop to shop.

West Regent Street. If you love art or antiques, a walk along West Regent Street is highly recommended. Look for vintage jewelry and other collectibles at Victorian Village.

SPECIALTY SHOPS

ANTIQUES AND FINE ART

Compass Gallery. The gallery is something of an institution, having opened in 1969 to provide space for young and unknown artists. It shares space with Cyril Gerber Fine Arts, which specializes in British paintings from 1880 to the present. ⊠ *178 W. Regent St., City Center* ☎ *0141/221–3095* ⊕ *www.compassgallery.co.uk.*

BOOKS, PAPER, AND MUSIC

Art Store. Selling cards, books, and games, the Art Store has a wonderful array of all things connected with art—paper, paints, pens—as well as craft items like beads for stringing. ⊠ *94 Queen St., City Center* ☎ *0141/221–1101* ⊕ *www.artstore.co.uk.*

Monorail Music. For the latest on the city's ever-thriving music scene try Monorail Music, inside a café-bar called Mono. The shop specializes in indie music and has a large collection of vinyl with everything from rock to jazz. ⊠ *12 Kings Ct., Merchant City* ☎ *0141/552–9458* ⊕ *www. monorailmusic.com.*

Waterstone's. In an age of online sales, bookstores seem to be becoming scarcer. Waterstone's remains, and it has an excellent selection on its four floors. There's also a good basement café. ⊠ *153-57 Sauchiehall St., City Center* ☎ *0141/248–4814* ⊕ *www.waterstones.com.*

CLOTHING

Cruise. Male and female fashionistas shouldn't miss Cruise, which caters to those at the high end of fashion. ⊠ *180 Ingram St., City Center* ☎ *0141/572–3200* ⊕ *www.cruisefashion.co.uk.*

Mr. Ben. A funky selection of vintage clothing is what you'll find at Mr. Ben. ⊠ *6 King's Ct., City Center* ☎ *0141/553–1936.*

HOME FURNISHINGS AND TEXTILES

Linens Fine. This shop carries wonderful embroidered and embellished bed linens and other textiles. ⊠ *Princes Sq., Unit 6, City Center* ☎ *0141/248–7082.*

SCOTTISH SPECIALTIES

Catherine Shaw. For high-quality gifts in Charles Rennie Mackintosh style, head to Catherine Shaw. ⊠ *32 Argyll Arcade, City Center* ☎ *0141/221–9038.*

Hector Russell Kiltmakers. This shop specializes in Highland outfits, wool and cashmere clothing, and women's fashions. ⊠ *110 Buchanan St., City Center* ☎ *0141/221–0217* ⊕ *www.hector-russell.com.*

MacDonald MacKay Ltd. The well-regarded MacDonald MacKay Ltd. makes, sells, and exports Highland dress and accessories. ⊠ *161 Hope St., City Center* ☎ *0141/204–3930.*

SPORTS GEAR

Tiso Glasgow Outdoor Experience. You'll find good-quality outerwear at Tiso Glasgow Outdoor Experience, handy if you're planning some Highland walks. There's a second location at 50 Couper Street in the West End. ⊠ *129 Buchanan St., City Center* ☎ *0141/248–4877* ⊕ *www.tiso.com.*

MERCHANT CITY

Many of Glasgow's young and upwardly mobile types make their home in Merchant City. Shopping here is expensive, but the area is worth visiting if you're seeking the youthful Glasgow style. You'll find Cruise, Jigsaw, and Agent Provocatur here, among many others.

SPECIALTY SHOPS

ANTIQUES AND FINE ART

Fodor's Choice ★ **Glasgow Print Studio.** Essentially an artists' cooperative, the Glasgow Print Studio's facilities launched a generation of outstanding painters, printers, and designers. The work of members past and present can be seen (and bought) at the Print Studio Gallery on King Street. ⊠ *103 Trongate, Merchant City* ☎ *0141/552–0704* ⊕ *www.gpsart.co.uk* ☉ *Tues.–Sat. 10–5:30.*

JEWELRY

Orro. The beautiful and contemporary jewelry here uses modern designs and new materials in unexpected ways. The shop has a gallery feel, and you can browse uninterrupted. ⊠ *12 Wilson St., Merchant City* ☎ *0141/552–7888* ⊕ *www.orro.co.uk.*

WEST END

SPECIALTY SHOPS

BOOKS, PAPER, AND MUSIC

Caledonia Books. This well-organized and well-stocked secondhand bookstore fills the gap left by the departure of other bookstores. The owners are knowledgeable and willing to search for even the most obscure volumes. ⊠ *483 Great Western Rd., West End* ☎ *0141/334–9663* ⊕ *www.caledoniabooks.co.uk.*

Fopp. This funky shop is an extravaganza of music, books, and DVDs. It's a small space, but the selection is huge. The prices are a lot more reasonable than those at most chain stores. ⊠ *358 Byres Rd., West End* ☎ *0141/222–2128* ⊕ *www.foppreturns.com* ☯ *Mon.–Sun. 9–6.*

Papyrus. Here you'll find designer cards as well as a selection of books and a trendy kitchen shop in the basement. There's a second location in the city center on Sauchiehall Street. ⊠ *374 Byres Rd., West End* ☎ *0141/334–6514* ⊕ *www.papyrusgifts.co.uk.*

CLOTHING BOUTIQUES

Pink Poodle. This stylish fashion boutique is mainly for younger dressers, and sells some lovely and often quirky accessories. ⊠ *181–183 Byres Rd., West End* ☎ *0141/357–3344* ⊕ *www.lovelaboutique.com.*

Strawberry Fields. Full of darling designs, Strawberry Fields sells colorful, high-end children's wear. ⊠ *517 Great Western Rd., West End* ☎ *0141/339–1121.*

FOOD

Demijohn. Specializing in infused wines, spirits, oils, and vinegars, Demijohn calls itself a "liquid deli." ⊠ *382 Byres Rd., West End* ☎ *0141/337–3600* ☯ *Mon.–Sat. 10–6, Sun. 11:30–5.*

Iain Mellis Cheesemonger. This shop has a superb, seemingly endless selection of fine Scottish cheeses, as well as others from England and across Europe. ⊠ *492 Great Western Rd., West End* ☎ *0141/339–8998* ⊕ *www.mellischeese.net.*

Peckham's Delicatessen. This deli is *the* place for continental sausages, cheeses, and anything else you'd need for a delicious picnic, including wine and beer. The sandwiches are also outstanding. ⊠ *61–65 Glassford St., West End* ☎ *0141/553–0666* ⊕ *www.peckhams.co.uk.*

HOME FURNISHINGS AND TEXTILES

Nancy Smillie. Local to the floorboards, Nancy Smillie is a one-of-a-kind boutique that sells unique glassware, jewelry, and furnishings. It also runs a jewelry boutique at 425 Great Western Road. ⊠ *53 Cresswell St., West End* ☎ *0141/334–0055* ⊕ *www.nancysmillieshop.com.*

SOUTH SIDE

ARCADES AND SHOPPING CENTERS

Silverburn. One of Europe's largest shopping malls, Silverburn is a good option on a rainy day. The interior feels like a village with streams, waterfalls, and restaurants galore, plus everything from small boutiques to retail giants like Marks & Spencer. Direct buses from Buchanan Street Station leave every 20 minutes. ⊠ *Barrhead Rd., South Side* ☎ *0141/880–3200.*

EAST END

ARCADES AND SHOPPING CENTERS

Barras. This indoor market, on London Road in the Glasgow Cross neighborhood east of the city center, prides itself on selling everything "from a needle to an anchor." Stalls hawk antique (and not-so-antique) furniture, bric-a-brac, good and not-so-good jewelry, and textiles—you name it, it's here. ⊠ *Gallowgate, East End.*

SPORTS AND THE OUTDOORS

You can't go far these days without seeing a runner or cyclist; because of the city's numerous parks, there is plenty of space. Rarely is the weather conducive to outdoor exercise; it rains a lot in Glasgow, but don't let that deter you. It doesn't deter the locals who play soccer, tennis, hike, bike, run, swim, and walk in the rain.

FOOTBALL

The city has been sports mad, especially for football (soccer), for more than 100 years. The historic rivalry between its two main football clubs, the Rangers and the Celtic, is legendary. Partick Thistle is a less contentious alternative for football fans. Matches are held usually on Saturday or Sunday in winter. Admission prices start at about £20. Don't go looking for a family-day-out atmosphere; football remains a fiercely contested game attended mainly by males, though the stadiums at Ibrox and Celtic Park are fast becoming family-friendly.

Celtic. This famous football club wears white-and-green stripes and plays in the east at Celtic Park. There are regular stadium tours, which must be booked ahead. The stadium is known locally as Parkhead, which refers to the area where it is located. ⊠ *Celtic Park, 18 Kerrydale St., East End* ☎ *0871/551–4308* ⊕ *www.celticfc.net* ☎ *Tours £8.50* ☉ *Tours daily at 11, noon, 1:45, and 2:30, except game days.*

Partick Thistle. Soccer in Glasgow isn't just blue or green, nor is it dominated by international players and big money. Partick Thistle Football Club, known as the Jags, wears red and yellow, and its home field is Firhill Park. ⊠ *80 Firhill Rd., West End* ☎ *0141/579–1971* ⊕ *www.ptfc.co.uk.*

Rangers. The Rangers wear blue and play at Ibrox, on the south side of the Clyde. Stadium tours on Friday, Saturday, and Sunday cost £8, and booking ahead is essential. ⊠ *Ibrox, 150 Edmiston Dr., South Side* ☎ *0871/702–1972* ⊕ *www.rangers.co.uk* ☎ *Tours £8.*

GOLF

Several municipal courses are operated within Glasgow proper by the local authorities. Bookings are relatively inexpensive and should be made directly to the course 24 hours in advance to ensure prime tee times (courses open at 7 am). A comprehensive list of contacts, facilities, and green fees of the 30 or so other courses near the city is available from the tourist board. The abbreviation SSS means standard scratch score, which is often used here instead of par.

Douglas Park Golf Club. Masses of rhododendrons bloom in early summer at Douglas Park, an attractive course set among birch and pine trees. The Campsie Fells form a pleasant backdrop. ✉ *Milngavie Rd., Hillfoot, Bearsden* ☎ *0141/942–0985* ⊕ *www.douglasparkgolfclub.co.uk* 🖂 *Green fee: £30 weekdays, £40 weekends* ⅄ *18 holes, 5962 yds, par 69.*

Gailes Links. The Glasgow Golf Club originally played on Glasgow Green in the heart of the city, but as the pressure for space grew, the club moved north to the leafy suburb of Bearsden, on the road to Loch Lomond. Killermont, the club's home course, is not open to visitors, but you can play the club's other course at Gailes, near Irvine on the Firth of Clyde. The Glasgow Club's Tennant Cup, in June, is the oldest open amateur tournament in the world. ✉ *Gailes Rd., Gailes* ☎ *0141/942– 2011* ⊕ *www.glasgowgailes-golf.com* 🖂 *Green fee: weekdays £95; weekends £100* ⅄ *18 holes, 6535 yds, SSS 72* ☉ *Daily.*

Lethamhill. The fairways of this city-owned parkland course overlook Hogganfield Loch. To get here, take the M8 north to Junction 12, and drive up the A80 about a quarter mile. ✉ *1240 Cumbernauld Rd., North City* ☎ *0141/276–0810* 🖂 *Green fee: winter £6.50, summer £7.85* ⅄ *18 holes, 5836 yds, par 70.*

Littlehill. Level fairways and greens make this municipal course not too difficult to play. It's about 4 miles north of the city center. ✉ *Auchinairn Rd., North City* ☎ *0141/276–0704* 🖂 *Green fee: £10 weekdays, £11.50 weekends* ⅄ *18 holes, 6240 yds, par 70.*

SIDE TRIPS: AYRSHIRE, CLYDE COAST, AND ROBERT BURNS COUNTRY

The jigsaw puzzle of firths and straits and interlocking islands that you see as you fly into Glasgow Airport harbors numerous tempting one-day excursion destinations. You can travel south to visit the fertile farmlands of Ayrshire—Robert Burns country—or west to the Firth of Clyde, or southeast to the Clyde Valley, all by car or by public transportation. Besides the Burns sites, key treasures in this area include the Marquess of Bute's Mount Stuart House on the Isle of Bute, and Culzean Castle, as famous for its Robert Adam (1728–92) design as it is for its spectacular seaside setting and grounds.

For many people a highlight of this region is Robert Burns country, a 40-minute drive from Glasgow. The poet was born in Alloway, beside Ayr, and the towns and villages where he lived and loved make for an interesting day out. English children learn that Burns (1759–96) is a good minor poet. But Scottish children know that he's Shakespeare, Dante, Rabelais, Mozart, and Karl Marx rolled into one. As time goes by, it seems that the Scots have it more nearly right. As poet and humanist, Burns increases in stature. When you plunge into Burns country, don't forget that he's held in extreme reverence by Scots of all backgrounds. They may argue about Sir Walter Scott and Bonnie Prince Charlie, but there's no disputing the merits of the author of "Bonnie Doon."

On your way here you travel beside the estuary and firth of the great River Clyde and will be able to look across to Dumbarton and its Rock, a nostalgic farewell point for emigrants leaving Glasgow. The river is surprisingly narrow here, considering that the *Queen Elizabeth II* and the other great ocean liners sailed these waters from the place of their birth.

GETTING HERE AND AROUND

From Glasgow you can take the bus to Ayr for the Burns Heritage Trail; and Troon, Prestwick, and Ayr to play golf. Bus companies also operate one-day guided excursions; for details, contact the tourist information center in Glasgow or the Strathclyde Passenger Transport Travel Centre. Traveline Scotland has a helpful information.

If you're driving from Glasgow, there are two main routes to Ayr. The quickest is to take the M77 to the A77, which takes you all the way to Ayr. Alloway is well signposted when you get to Ayr. The alternative and much slower route is the coast road; take the M8 to Greenock and continue down the coast on the A78 until you meet the A77 and continue on into Burns Country.

You can travel by train to Ayr for the Burns Heritage Trail; and Troon, Prestwick, and Ayr to play golf.

PAISLEY

7 miles south of Glasgow.

The industrial prosperity of Paisley came from textiles and, in particular, from the woolen paisley shawl. The internationally recognized paisley pattern is based on the shape of a palm shoot, an ancient Babylonian fertility symbol brought from Kashmir. Today you can explore this history at several attractions.

GETTING HERE AND AROUND

Paisley-bound buses depart from the Buchanan Street bus station in Glasgow. Trains to Paisley depart daily every 5 to 10 minutes from Glasgow Central Station. If you're driving, take the M8 westbound and turn off at Junction 27, which is clearly signposted to Paisley.

ESSENTIALS

Visitor Information Paisley Visitor Information Centre ✉ *9A Gilmour St.* ☎ *0141/889–0711* ⊕ *www.visitscotland.com/paisley.*

Ayrshire and
the Clyde Coast

EXPLORING

Abbey. Paisley's 12th-century Cluniac Abbey dominates the town center. Almost completely destroyed by the English in 1307, the abbey was not totally restored until the early 20th century. It's associated with Walter Fitzallan, the high steward of Scotland, who gave his name to the Stewart monarchs of Scotland (Stewart is a corruption of "steward"). Outstanding features include the vaulted stone roof and stained glass of the choir. ⊠ *13 High St.* ☎ *0141/889–7654* ⊕ *www.paisleyabbey.org. uk* ⊠ *Free* ⊘ *Mon.–Sat. 10–3:30, Sun. services at 11, 12:15, and 6:30.*

Paisley Museum. The full story of the pattern and of the innovative weaving techniques introduced in Paisley is told in the Paisley Museum, which has a world-famous shawl collection. ⊠ *High St.* ☎ *0141/887–1010* ⊕ *www. renfrewshire.gov.uk/museums* ⊠ *Free* ⊘ *Tues.–Sat. 10–5, Sun. 2–5.*

Sma' Shot Cottages. To get an idea of the life led by textile industry workers, visit the Sma' Shot Cottages. These re-creations of mill workers' houses contain displays of linen, lace, and paisley shawls. An 18th-century weaver's cottage is open to visitors. ⊠ *11–17 George Pl.* ☎ *0141/889–1708* ⊠ *Free* ⊘ *Apr.–Sept., Wed. and Sat. noon–4; Oct.–Mar. by appointment.*

WHERE TO STAY

$ HOTEL 🏨 **Glynhill Hotel.** This mansion combines old-fashioned living with modern convenience. **Pros:** elegant rooms; nice pool and sauna; close to transportation. **Cons:** airport noise; lacks atmosphere. ⑤ *Rooms from: £95* ⊠ *169 Paisley Rd., Renfrew* ☎ *0141/886–5555* ⊕ *www.glynhill. com* ⥅ *145 rooms* ⏹ *Breakfast.*

$$$$ HOTEL 🏨 **Mar Hall.** This imposing baronial house sits amid formal gardens and overlooks the river Clyde and verdant woodlands. **Pros:** spacious rooms; fantastic pool; wonderful setting. **Cons:** quite remote; an expensive treat. ⑤ *Rooms from: £245* ⊠ *Earl of Mar Estate, Mar Hall Dr., Bishopton* ☎ *0141/812–9999* ⊕ *www.marhall.com* ⥅ *53 rooms* ⏹ *Breakfast.*

ISLE OF BUTE

75 miles west of Glasgow.

The Isle of Bute affords a host of relaxing walks and scenic vistas. Mount Stuart, a stately home, is a popular attraction. Like the nearby Isle of Arran *(see Chapter 8)*, the Isle of Bute was a Victorian holiday favorite convenient for Glaswegians.

Rothesay, a faded but appealing resort, is the main town. Some of the ornate Victorian architecture is striking. In the old Victorian village of Wemyss Bay there's ferry service to the island. The many handsome buildings, especially the station, are a reminder of the grandeur and style of a century ago.

GETTING HERE AND AROUND

Take the train from Glasgow Central Station to Wemyss Bay, where you can hop aboard the ferry to Rothesay. If you're driving, take the A8/A78 coast road and park at the ferry terminal.

ESSENTIALS

Visitor Information Isle of Bute Discovery Centre ⊠ *The Winter Garden, Victoria St., Rothesay* ☎ *08452/255121* ⊕ *www.isle-of-bute.com.*

EXPLORING

Mount Stuart. Bute's biggest draw is spectacular Mount Stuart, ancestral home of the marquesses of Bute. The massive Victorian Gothic palace, built in red sandstone, has ornate interiors, including the Marble Hall, with a star-studded vault, stained glass, arcaded galleries, and magnificent tapestries woven in Edinburgh in the early 20th century. The paintings and furniture throughout the house are equally outstanding. You can also appreciate the lovely gardens and grounds. ⊠ *Off A844, Rothesay* ☎ *01700/503877* ⊕ *www.mountstuart.com* ✉ *Gardens £5; house and gardens £11* ⊙ *Gardens Apr.–Oct., daily 10–6; house Apr.– Oct., Sun.–Fri. 11–5, Sat. 10–2:30.*

Rothesay. A faded but appealing resort, Rothesay is the main town on the Isle of Bute. Some of the ornate Victorian architecture is striking.

WHERE TO STAY

$ 🖼 **Munro's Bed and Breakfast.** Surrounded by colorful gardens, this small
B&B/INN   B&B in a peaceful residential area has a home-away-from-home feel. **Pros:** beautiful location; nicely remodeled; environmentally aware. **Cons:** hilltop location is a steep climb; no restaurant; sea-view rooms cost extra. ⑤ *Rooms from: £85* ⊠ *Ardmory Rd., Ardbeg* ☎ *01700/502346* ⊕ *www.visitmunros.co.uk* ⮓ *6 rooms* ⏀ *Breakfast.*

IRVINE

24 miles south of Glasgow.

Beyond Irvine's cobbled streets and grand Victorian buildings, look for a peaceful crescent-shape harbor and fishermen's cottages huddled in solidarity against the Atlantic winds. The Scottish Maritime Museum pays homage to the town's seafaring past. Scotland's national poet, Robert Burns, lived here in 1781.

GETTING HERE AND AROUND

By car, take the M8 from Glasgow, then the A726 and the A736 to Irvine. By rail, it's a 40-minute journey from Glasgow Central Station.

ESSENTIALS

Visitor Information Irvine Tourist Information Centre ⊠ *New St.* ☎ *01294/313886.*

EXPLORING

Denny Tank. The size of a football field, this tank was where ship designs were tested. You can see how in demonstrations that are offered throughout the day—a must for anyone following the history of shipbuilding on the Clyde. Denny Tank is part of Irvine's Scottish Maritime Museum. ⊠ *Castle St., Dumbarton* ☎ *01294/278283* ⊕ *www. scottishmaritimemuseum.org* ✉ *£2* ⊙ *Mon.–Sat. 10–4.*

Scottish Maritime Museum. On the waterfront in the coastal town of Irvine, this museum brings together ships and boats—both models and the real thing—to tell the tale of Scotland's maritime history, as well as chronicle the lives of its boatbuilders, its fishermen, its sailors. The atmospheric Linthouse Engine Building, part of a former shipyard, hosts most of the displays. The museum also includes a shipyard worker's tenement home that you can explore. ⊠ *6 Gottries Rd.* ☎ *01294/278283* ⊕ *www. scottishmaritimemuseum.org* 🖾 *£7* ⊗ *Mar.–Oct., daily 10–5.*

Vennel Art Gallery. The Vennel Art Gallery occupies the 18th-century cottage where poet Robert Burns lived and the shed where he learned to heckle—or dress—flax (the raw material for linen). Both buildings have on display paintings, photographs, and sculpture by mainly Scottish artists. ⊠ *10 Glasgow Vennel* ☎ *01294/275059* 🖾 *Free* ⊗ *Thurs.– Sat. 10–1 and 2–5.*

GOLF

Fodor's Choice
★ **Western Gailes Golf Club.** Known as the finest natural links course in Scotland, Western Gailes is entirely nature-made, and the greens are kept in truly magnificent condition. This is the final qualifying course when the British Open is held at Royal Troon or Turnberry. Tom Watson lists the par-5 sixth hole as one of his favorites. ⊠ *Gailes Rd.* ☎ *01294/311649* ⊕ *www.westerngailes.com* 🖾 *Green fee: Apr.–Sept., Mon., Wed., and Fri. £130, Sat. £125, Sun. £130. Mar. and Oct. £85; Nov.–Feb. £60* ⚑ *18 holes, 6640 yds, par 71* ⊗ *Mon., Wed., Fri., and weekend afternoons.*

TROON

4 miles south of Irvine, 30 miles south of Glasgow, 6 miles north of Ayr.

The small coastal town of Troon is famous for its outstanding golf course, Royal Troon. You can easily see that golf is popular here and in this area: at times the whole 60-mile-long Ayrshire coast seems one endless course. The town's several miles of sandy beaches provide other diversions. It's easy to get to Troon by train or bus from both Glasgow and Ayr.

GETTING HERE AND AROUND

From Glasgow Central Station, board an Ayr-bound train and get off at Troon. By car, take the M77/A77 toward Prestwick Airport and follow the signs to Troon.

WHERE TO EAT AND STAY

$$
SEAFOOD
Fodor's Choice
★ ✕ **MacCallums Oyster Bar.** Located in Troon Harbor, this outstanding seafood restaurant's menu varies according to the day's catch, but you can usually count on lobster in garlic butter, seared scallops, or grilled langoustines that taste of the sea. The fish pie is justly famous, and excellent light white wines match the freshness of the food. Solid wooden tables and other simple furnishings add a rustic touch to the dining room. For a more modest price, or if you prefer to watch the fishing boats bob in the harbor, try the adjacent Wee Hurrie, possibly one of the best fish-and-chips shops in Scotland, serving monkfish and oysters with chips as well as the usual fare. Finding McCallums is a bit of an adventure, but it's well worth the trek. ⑤ *Average main: £17* ⊠ *Harbour Rd.* ☎ *01292/319339* ⊗ *Closed Mon. No dinner Sun.*

$$
HOTEL
🏨 **Piersland House Hotel.** A late-Victorian mansion on the southern edge of town, formerly the home of a whisky magnate, is now a country-house hotel. **Pros:** gorgeous gardens and grounds; close to golf courses; near Prestwick Airport. **Cons:** helps to have a car to get around; can get crowded with private functions. ⑤ *Rooms from: £136* ⊠ *15 Craigend Rd.* ☎ *01292/314747* ⊕ *www.piersland.co.uk* ➷ *37 rooms* ⦿ *Breakfast.*

GOLF

Royal Troon Golf Club. Of the two courses at Royal Troon, it's the Old Course—a traditional links course with superb sea views—that's frequently used for the British Open. Visitor season tee times are limited to certain days from spring through early fall, and change each year according to the tournament program. ■ TIP→ **Advance payment and a deposit are required, as is a handicap certificate.** ✉ *Craigend Rd.* ☎ *01292/311555* ⊕ *www.royaltroon.com* ✉ *Green fee: Old Course £180 (includes one round on Portland Course)* ⅃ *Old Course: 18 holes, 6641 yds, SSS 73; Portland Course: 18 holes, 6289 yds, SSS 71* ⊙ *Mid-Apr.–early Sept. and mid-Sept.–mid-Oct., Mon., Tues., and Thurs. for visitors.*

SHOPPING

Regalia Fashion Salon. Many Glaswegians frequent Regalia Fashion Salon for its unusual collection of designer clothing for women. ✉ *46-48 Church St.* ☎ *01292/312162.*

Tantalus Antiques. For a fascinating look at local antiquities, visit Tantalus Antiques. ✉ *79 Temple Hill* ☎ *01292/315999.*

AYR AND ALLOWAY

6 miles south of Troon, 34 miles south of Glasgow.

The commercial port of Ayr is Ayrshire's chief town, a peaceful and elegant place with an air of prosperity. Poet Robert Burns was baptized in the Auld Kirk (Old Church) here and wrote a humorous poem about the Twa Brigs (Two Bridges) that cross the river nearby. Burns described Ayr as a town unsurpassed "for honest men and bonny lasses." If he were to visit today, he might also mention the good shopping.

If you're on the Robert Burns trail, head for Alloway, on B7024 in Ayr's southern suburbs. A number of sights here are part of the **Burns National Heritage Park**, including the magnificent Robert Burns Birthplace Museum.

GETTING HERE AND AROUND

From Glasgow you can take the bus or train to Ayr; travel time is about an hour (a bit less by train). Drivers can use the A78 and A77 near the coast; a car would provide more flexibility to see the Burns sites around Alloway.

ESSENTIALS

Visitor Information Ayr Visitor Information Centre ✉ *22 Sandgate* ☎ *01292/288688* ⊕ *www.ayrshire-arran.com.*

EXPLORING

TOP ATTRACTIONS

Burns Cottage. In the delightful Burns Heritage Park, this thatched cottage is where Scotland's national poet lived for his first seven years. It has a living room, a kitchen, and a stable, one behind the other. The life and times of Burns, born in 1759, are beautifully and creatively illustrated, particularly in the videos of daily life in the 18th century. The garden is lush with the types of vegetables the poet's father might have grown. Take the Poet's Path through the village to the Robert Burns

Birthplace Museum, the spooky churchyard where Tam o 'Shanter faced fearsome ghosts, and the Brig o' Doon. ⊠ *Greenfield Ave., Alloway* ☎ *0844/493–2601* ⊕ *www.burnsmuseum.org.uk* 🎫 *£8, includes Burns Monument and Robert Burns Birthplace Museum* ⊘ *Apr.–Sept., daily 10–5:30; Oct.–Mar., daily 10–5.*

Fodor'sChoice **Robert Burns Birthplace Museum.** Besides being a poet of delicacy and
★ depth, Robert Burns was also a rebel, a thinker, a lover, a good companion, and a man of the countryside. This wonderful museum explains why the Scots so admire this complex "man o' pairts." The imaginative museum presents each of his poems in context, with commentaries sensitively written in a moderrn version of the Scots language in which he spoke and wrote. Headsets let you hear the poems sung or spoken. The exhibit is vibrant and interactive, with touch screens that allow you to debate his views on politics, love, taxation, revolution, and Scottishness. An elegant café offers a place to pause, while the kids can play in the adjoining garden. ⊠ *Murdoch's Lone, Alloway* ☎ *0844/493–2601* ⊕ *www.burnsmuseum.org.uk* 🎫 *£8, includes Burns Cottage and Burns Monument* ⊘ *Apr.–Sept., daily 10–5:30; Oct.–Mar., daily 10–5.*

WORTH NOTING

Auld Kirk Alloway. Auld Kirk Alloway is where Tam o' Shanter, in Robert Burns's great epic poem, unluckily passed a witches' revel—with Old Nick himself playing the bagpipes—on his way home from a night of drinking. Tam, in flight from the witches, managed to cross the medieval **Brig o' Doon** (*brig* is Scots for *bridge*; you can still see the bridge) just in time. His gray mare, Meg, lost her tail to the closest witch. (Any resident of Ayr will tell you that witches cannot cross running water.) The church is in ruins, but the graveyard includes the tomb of Burns's father, William. ⊠ *Murdoch's Lone, Alloway* ⊕ *www.burnsmuseum.org.uk.*

Bachelors' Club. About 8 miles northeast of Ayr is the Bachelors' Club, the 17th-century house where Robert Burns learned to dance, founded a debating and literary society, and became a Freemason. ⊠ *Sandgate St., Tarbolton* ☎ *0844/493–2146* ⊕ *www.nts.org.uk* 🎫 *£2.50* ⊘ *Apr.–late Sept., daily 1:30–5:30; Oct., weekends 1:30–5:30.*

Burns Monument. This neoclassical structure, built in 1823, overlooks the Brig o' Doon. ⊠ *Murdoch's Lone, Alloway* ⊕ *www.burnsmuseum.org. uk* 🎫 *£8, includes Burns Cottage and Robert Burns Birthplace Museum* ⊘ *Apr.–Sept., daily 9:30–5; Oct.–Mar., daily 10–4.*

Dumfries House. Built in the 1750s by the Adam brothers, Dumfries House has preserved unchanged the living conditions of the landed aristocracy of the time. The restored house contains a large collection of furniture by Chippendale that is original to the property, as well as pieces by other great designers of the period. Run by a charity headed by Prince Charles, the surrounding 2000-acre estate is projected as a site for a new eco village and centers practicing historic crafts. Entry is by guided tour only; booking is essential. The house is about 10 miles east of Ayr. ⊠ *Cumnock, Ayrshire* ☎ *01290/421742* ⊕ *www.dumfries-house.org.uk* 🎫 *Admission by guided tour only. £8.50 (1-hr tour), £12.50 (1½ hrs). Grounds are free to visitors* ⊘ *Mar., Sun.–Fri. tours at 12:15 and 1:45; Apr.–Oct., Sun.–Fri. 11–3.30 (tours throughout the day); Nov.–Feb., weekend tours at 12:15 and 1:45.*

WHERE TO EAT

$$
BRITISH

✕ **Brig o' Doon House.** Originally built in 1827, this attractive restaurant often has a piper by the door to greet hungry travelers. The setting is very Scottish, with tartan carpets, dark-wood paneling, and buck heads mounted on the walls. The bar is a shrine to Robert Burns, and the surrounding gardens overlook the Brig o' Doon as well as a small, rushing river. The food keeps to the Scottish theme: try panfried scallops with citrus butter to start, and venison casserole with juniper berries and creamed potatoes or the haggis with neeps and tatties (served with a dram) as a main course. There are several rooms for rent upstairs. ⑤ *Average main: £16* ✉ *High Maybole Rd., Alloway* ☎ *01292/442466.*

> ### REMEMBERING MR. BURNS
>
> Born in Ayrshire, Robert Burns (1759–96) is one of Scotland's treasures. The poet and balladeer had a style that was his and his alone. His most famous song, "Auld Lang Syne," is heard everywhere on New Year's Day. Burns's talent, charisma, and good looks made him an icon to both the upper and lower classes (and made him quite popular with the ladies). Today his birthday (January 25) is considered a national holiday; on "Burns Night" young and old alike get together for Burns Suppers and recite his work over neeps, tatties, and drams of the country's finest whisky.

$$
BRITISH

✕ **Fouter's Bistro.** In the center of Ayr, Fouter's is in a long and narrow cellar that was an 18th-century bank vault, yet its white walls and decorative stenciling create a sense of airiness. The cuisine is light and skillful—no heavy sauces here. Try the roast Ayrshire lamb with red wine and mint, or sample the Taste of Scotland appetizer—smoked salmon, trout, and other goodies. This is modern Scottish and French cooking at its best. ⑤ *Average main: £18* ✉ *2A Academy St.* ☎ *01292/261391* ⊙ *Closed Sun. and Mon.*

GOLF

Girvan. Opened in 1902, scenic Girvan plays along a narrow coastal strip and a lush inland section next to the Water of Girvan—a challenging hazard at the 15th hole unless you're a big hitter. Like its illustrious neighbor Turnberry, this course has fine views of Ailsa Craig and the Clyde Estuary. ✉ *40 Golf Course Rd., Girvan* ☎ *01465/714346* ⊕ *www.golfsouthayrshire.com* 🏌 *Green fee: £17.50* 🏌 *18 holes, 5064 yds, par 64* ⊙ *Daily.*

Prestwick Golf Club. Tom Morris helped to design this challenging Ayrshire coastal links course, which saw the birth of the British Open Championship in 1860. Prestwick has excellent, fast rail links with Glasgow. ■ **TIP→ There are a limited number of tee times on Saturday afternoon.** ✉ *2 Links Rd., Prestwick* ☎ *01292/477404* ⊕ *www.prestwickgc.co.uk* 🏌 *Green fee: weekdays £130; weekends £155* 🏌 *18 holes, 6544 yds, par 71* ⊙ *Daily.*

Fodor's Choice
★

Turnberry. One of the most famous links courses in Scotland, the Ailsa Course is open to the elements, and the 9th hole requires you to hit the ball over the open sea. The British Open was hosted here in 1977, 1986, 1994, and 2009. A second course, the Kintyre, is more compact, with tricky sloped greens. Five of the holes have sea views. ✉ *Turnberry Resort, Maidens Rd., off A719, Turnberry* ☎ *01655/331000* ⊕ *www. turnberryresort.co.uk* ⛳ *Green fee: Ailsa Course: £165 for hotel guests, £199 for nonguests; Kintyre Course: £105 for hotel guests, £135 for nonguests* 🏌 *Ailsa Course 18 holes, 7217 yds, par 70; Kintyre Course 18 holes, 6921 yds, par 72* ☉ *Daily.*

SHOPPING

Ayr has a good range of shops.

Begg & Co. Upscale Begg & Co. sells a good selection of scarves, stoles, plaids, and travel rugs handmade on the premises. ✉ *Viewfield Rd.* ☎ *01292/267615* ⊕ *www.beggscotland.com.*

Diamond Factory. You can watch craftspeople at work at this jewelry workshop. Particularly coveted are the handmade Celtic wedding bands. The store will happily ship your purchases. ✉ *26 Queen's Ct., Sandgate* ☎ *01292/280476.*

CULZEAN CASTLE AND COUNTRY PARK

12 miles south of Ayr, 50 miles south of Glasgow.

There's plenty to do at this popular spot between visiting the Adam-designed house and touring the extensive grounds.

GETTING HERE AND AROUND

Stagecoach buses run from Ayr to the park entrance; the nearest train station from Glasgow is at Maybole, 4 miles to the east, but there is Stagecoach bus service to the park entrance. Note that the park entrance is a mile walk from the castle visitor center.

EXPLORING

FAMILY
Fodor's Choice
★

Culzean Castle and Country Park. The dramatic cliff-top castle of Culzean (pronounced ku-*lain*) is the National Trust for Scotland's most popular property. Robert Adam designed the neoclassical mansion, complete with a walled garden, in 1777. The grounds are enormous, combining parkland, forests, and a beach looking out over the Atlantic Ocean; the surprisingly lush shrubberies reflect the warm currents that explain the mild climate. There are caves in the cliffs; tours are occasionally available. In the castle itself you can visit the armory, luxuriously appointed salons and bedchambers, and a nursery with its lovely cradle in a boat. Adams's grand double spiral staircase is the high point of its design. There's a free audio tour, and guided tours are available daily at 11 and 2:30. A short walk through the woods brings you to the visitor center with shops and a restaurant. ✉ *A719, Maybole* ☎ *0844/493–2149* ⊕ *www.culzeanexperience.org* ⛳ *Park £10, park and castle £15* ☉ *Park daily 9:30–sunset; Castle Apr.–Oct., daily 10:30–5; last admission at 4.*

WHERE TO STAY

$$$$
HOTEL

Eisenhower Hotel. It would be hard to imagine a more spectacular location than the upper floors of Culzean Castle, which looks out towards Arran and the Atlantic Ocean. **Pros:** beautiful setting; luxurious lodging; a strong sense of history. **Cons:** A little remote; rather formal; not for minimalists. ⑤ *Rooms from: £250* ✉ *Culzean Castle, A719, Maybole* ☎ *01655/884455* ⊕ *www.culzeanexperience.org* ⤳ *6 rooms* ⎟⊙⎟ *No meals.*

SIDE TRIPS: THE CLYDE VALLEY

The River Clyde is (or certainly was) famous for its shipbuilding, yet its upper reaches flow through some of Scotland's most fertile farmlands, rich with crops of tomatoes and fruit. It's an interesting area with some museums, most notably at New Lanark, that tell the story of the growth of manufacturing.

GETTING HERE AND AROUND

If you're driving from Glasgow, head south on the M74 and turn on to the A72. This is the main road through the Clyde Valley, ending at Lanark. The A702 is the turnoff to Biggar. Train service runs from Glasgow Central Station to Hamilton (near Blantyre) and Lanark; for details check National Rail. There are no trains to Biggar, but there's a connecting bus from Hamilton to Biggar.

BLANTYRE

8 miles southeast of Glasgow.

Blantyre, a suburb of Hamilton, is not a pretty town. The explorer David Livingstone was born here.

GETTING HERE AND AROUND

From Glasgow, drive along the M74, then transfer to the A725 at junction 5. The train from Glasgow Central takes just 20 minutes.

EXPLORING

David Livingstone Centre. Set among gardens above the river bank, the David Livingstone Centre is based partly in the tiny one-room tenement apartment where the explorer-missionary (1813–73) spent his first 23 years. The rest of the museum is devoted to his travels across Africa, depicted in small, framed tableaux that light up as you walk past them. His meeting with Henry Stanley, sent by the *New York Times* to find him and bring him back, is commemorated. On meeting him, Stanley famously said, "Dr Livingstone, I presume." Livingstone refused the invitation and died in Africa. Copies of Livingstone's letters are displayed, and there is plenty of opportunity for youngsters to interact with the exhibits. ⊠ *165 Station Rd.* ☎ *0844/493–2207* ⊕ *www.nts. org.uk* ☞ *£6.50* ☉ *Mar.–Oct., Mon.–Sat. 10–5:30, Sun. 12:30–5:30.*

FAMILY **Chatelherault Country Park.** The grand building at the heart of this 500-acre estate served only as hunting lodge and dog kennel for the immensely wealthy dukes of Hamilton, who lived in a palace that disappeared into the mine beneath (the source of the family's wealth). The park contains the ruins of Cadzow Castle and some beautiful walks, as well as a wonderfully designed children's park. There are guided tours around the lodge and the surrounding gardens, but it's just as satisfying to take in the fabulous view of Glasgow from the front of the house and then wander around independently. The visitor center has an eatery and wildlife displays for the kids. ⊠ *Carlisle Rd., Ferniegair* ☎ *01698/426213* ☞ *Free* ☉ *Mon.–Sat. 10–5, Sun. noon–5.*

NATIONAL MUSEUM OF RURAL LIFE

9 miles south of Glasgow.

The effect of farming on the land and on people's lives is the focus of this museum near Glasgow.

EXPLORING

FAMILY **National Museum of Rural Life.** This lovely museum, a 20-minute drive from Glasgow, is slightly off the beaten track but well worth the trip. Set in a rural area, it explores every aspect of the country's agricultural heritage. In a modern building resembling a huge barn you learn about how farming transformed the land, experience the life and hardships of those who worked it, and see displays of tools and machines from across the ages. Take a tractor ride to a fully functioning 1950s farmhouse. There are also some great exhibits geared toward children. ⊠ *Philipshill Rd., East Kilbride* ☎ *0300/123–6789* ⊕ *www.nms.ac.uk/ rural* 🏷 *£6.50* ⊗ *Daily 10–5.*

SUMMERLEE–MUSEUM OF SCOTTISH INDUSTRIAL LIFE

10 miles east of Glasgow.

A former ironworks is now a museum with a re-created mine and exhibits on both industry and the lives of workers.

EXPLORING

FAMILY **Summerlee–Museum of Scottish Industrial Life.** On the site of the old Summerlee Ironworks, this vast and exciting museum re-creates a mine and the miners' rows (the cottages where miners and their families lived). An electric tram transports you here from the huge hall where industrial machines vie with exhibits about ordinary life. Later you can stroll along the canal and take the kids to a fine playground. The drive from Glasgow takes less than 15 minutes. ⊠ *Heritage Way, Coatbridge* ☎ *01236/638460* ⊕ *www.visitlanarkshire.com/summerlee* ⚏ *Free.*

LANARK

19 miles east of Glasgow.

Set in pleasing, rolling countryside, Lanark is a typical old Scottish town. It's now most often associated with its unique neighbor New Lanark, a model workers' community about a mile to the south.

GETTING HERE AND AROUND

If you're driving, take the M74 to the A72. The train from Glasgow Central Station takes 50 minutes or so.

ESSENTIALS

Visitor Information Lanark Visitor Information Centre ⊠ *Horsemarket, Ladyacre Rd.* ☎ *01555/661661.*

EXPLORING

FAMILY **New Lanark.** Now a World Heritage Site, New Lanark was home to a
Fodor's Choice social experiment at the beginning of the Industrial Revolution. Rob-
★ ert Owen (1771–1858), together with his father-in-law David Dale (1739–1806), set out to create a model industrial community with well-designed worker homes, a school, and public buildings. Owen went on to establish other communities on similar principles, both in Britain and in the United States. Robert Owen's son, Robert Dale Owen (1801–77), helped found the Smithsonian Institution.

After many changes of fortune, the mills eventually closed. One of the buildings has been converted into a visitor center that tells the story of this brave social experiment. You can also explore Robert Owen's house, the school, and a mill worker's house, and enjoy the Annie McLeod Experience, a fairground ride that takes you through the story of one mill worker's life. Other restored structures hold various shops and eateries; one has a rooftop garden with impressive views of the entire site.

The river Clyde powers its way through a beautiful wooded gorge here, and its waters were once harnessed to drive textile-mill machinery. Upstream it flows through some of the finest river scenery anywhere in Lowland Scotland, with woods and spectacular waterfalls. ⊠ *New Lanark Rd., New Lanark* ☎ *01555/661345* ⊕ *www.newlanark.org* ⚏ *£8.50* ⊙ *Oct.–Mar., daily 11–5; Apr.–Sept., daily 10–5.*

WHERE TO STAY

$$
HOTEL

⛄ **New Lanark Mill Hotel.** Housed in a converted cotton mill in the 18th-century village of New Lanark, this hotel is decorated in a spare, understated style that allows the impressive architecture of barrel-vaulted ceilings and elegant Georgian windows to speak for itself. **Pros:** beautiful views of the river; large rooms; impressive spa. **Cons:** bland bar; some rooms can get cold; restaurant is the only one in the vicinity. $ *Rooms from: £119* ⊠ *New Lanark Rd., New Lanark* ☎ *01555/667200* ⊕ *www.newlanarkmillhotel.co.uk* ⇋ *38 rooms, 8 cottages* ⏃⏃ *Breakfast.*

SHOPPING

Lanark has an interesting selection of shops within walking distance of each other; there are also some shops such as the Edinburgh Woollen Mill at New Lanark.

McKellar's. This shop sells Charles Rennie Mackintosh–inspired designs in gold and silver. ⊠ *41 High St.* ☎ *01555/661312.*

Strands. The amusingly named Strands carries yarns and knitwear, including Arran designs and one-of-a-kind creations by Scottish designers. ⊠ *8 Bloomgate* ☎ *01555/665757.*

BIGGAR

34 miles southeast of Glasgow.

A pleasant town built of stone, Biggar is a rewarding place to spend an hour or two, out of all proportion to its size, thanks to an excellent collection of small, specialized museums. At Biggar you are near the headwaters of the Clyde, on the moors in the center of southern Scotland. The Clyde flows west toward Glasgow and the Atlantic Ocean, and the Tweed, only a few miles away, flows east toward the North Sea. There are fine views around Biggar to Culter Fell and to the Border Hills in the south.

GETTING HERE AND AROUND

From Glasgow, take the M74 and then the A72 to reach Biggar. On public transportation, your best option is a train to Lanark, where you can transfer to a bus bound for Biggar.

ESSENTIALS

Visitor Information Biggar Visitor Information Centre ⊠ *155 High St.* ☎ *01899/221066* ⊕ *www.visitscotland.com/biggar.*

EXPLORING

Biggar Gasworks. The Biggar Gasworks, built in 1839, is a fascinating reminder of the efforts once needed to produce gas for light and heat. ⊠ *Gasworks Rd.* ☎ *01899/221050* ⊕ *www.biggarmuseumtrust.co.uk* ⏃ *£1* ⏃ *June–Sept., daily 2–5.*

FAMILY **Biggar Puppet Theatre.** Purves Puppets, famous for its "black box" puppetry, regularly performs at the Biggar Puppet Theatre. Before and after performances, puppeteers lead hands-on tours (£3). One tour ducks backstage, while the other explores the puppet museum. These tours should be booked well in advance, as should tickets for very popular performances. ⊠ *8 Broughton Rd.* ☎ *01899/220631* ⊕ *www.purvespuppets.com* ⏃ *Tours £3; performances £8.*

Gladstone Court Museum. This museum paints a fascinating picture of life in the town in years past, with reconstructed Victorian-era shops, a bank, a phone exchange, and a school. ☒ *Northback Rd.* ☎ *01899/221050* ⊕ *www.biggarmuseumtrust.co.uk* 🎫 *£2.50* ☉ *Mar.–Sept., Mon., Tues., and Thurs.–Sat. 11–4:30, Sun. 2–4:30.*

Greenhill Covenanters' House. This farmhouse is filled with 17th-century furnishings, costume dolls, and rare farm breeds. The Covenanters were breakaway supporters of Presbyterianism in the 17th century. ☒ *Burn Braes, off Carwood Rd.* ☎ *01899/221050* ⊕ *www.biggarmuseumtrust. co.uk* 🎫 *£1.50* ☉ *May–Sept., 1st Sat. of each month by appointment 2–4:30.*

Moat Park Heritage Centre. For a look at Biggar's geology and prehistory, plus an interesting embroidery collection (including samplers and fine patchwork coverlets), visit the Moat Park Heritage Centre, housed in a former church. ☒ *Kirkstyle* ☎ *01899/221050* ⊕ *www. biggarmuseumtrust.co.uk* 🎫 *£2.50* ☉ *May–Sept., Mon. and Wed.–Sat. 11–4:30, Sun. 2–5.*

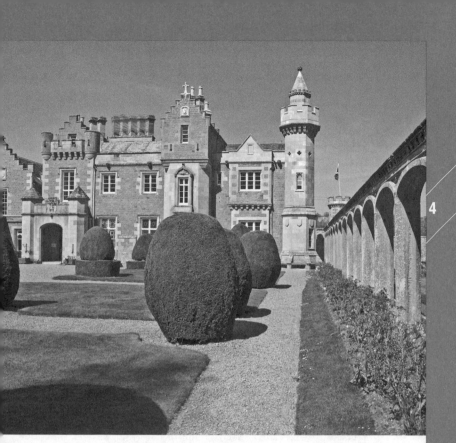

THE BORDERS AND
THE SOUTHWEST

Updated
by Mike
Gonzalez

In the Borders region, south of Edinburgh, are more stately homes, fortified castles, and medieval abbeys than in any other part of Scotland. This is also Sir Walter Scott territory, including his pseudo-baronial home at Abbotsford. The area embraces the whole 90-mile course of one of Scotland's greatest rivers, the Tweed. Passing woodlands luxuriant with game birds, the river flows in rushing torrents through this fertile land. To the west of the Borders is Dumfries and Galloway, a low-key area with gentle coastal and upland areas.

For centuries the Borders was a battlefield, where English and Scottish troops remained locked in a struggle for its possession. At different times, parts of the region have been in English hands, just as slices of northern England (Berwick-upon-Tweed, for example) have been in Scottish hands. The castles and fortified houses across the Borders are the surviving witnesses to those times. After the Union of 1707, fortified houses gradually gave way to the luxurious country mansions that pepper the area. And by the 19th century they had become grand country houses built by fashionable architects.

All the main routes between London and Edinburgh traverse the Borders, whose hinterland of undulating pastures, woods, and valleys is enclosed within three lonely groups of hills: the Cheviots, the Moorfoots, and the Lammermuirs. Hamlets and prosperous country towns dot the land, giving valley slopes a lived-in look, yet the total population is still sparse. The sheep that are the basis of the region's prosperous textile industry outnumber human beings by 14 to 1.

To the west is the region of Dumfries and Galloway, on the shores of the Solway Firth. It might appear to be an extension of the Borders, but the southwest has a history all its own. From these ports ships sailed to the Americas, carrying country dwellers driven from their land to make room for the sheep that still roam the hills across southern Scotland. Inland, the earth rises toward high hills, forest, and bleak but captivating moorland, whereas nearer the coast you can find pretty farmlands, small villages, and unassuming towns. The shoreline is washed by the North Atlantic Drift (Scotland's answer to the Gulf Stream), and first-time visitors are always surprised to see palm trees and exotic plants thriving in gardens and parks along the coast.

At the heart of the region is Dumfries, the "Queen o' the South." Once a major port and commercial center, its glamour is now slightly faded. But the memory of poet Robert Burns, who spent several years living and working here and who is buried in the town, burns as bright as ever.

TOP REASONS TO GO

Ancient abbeys: The great abbeys of the Border regions, and the Whithorn Priory and the wonderful Sweetheart Abbey in the Southwest, are in ruins, but they retain hints of their former grandeur.

Outdoor activities: You can walk, bicycle, or even ride horses across Galloway or through the Borders. Abandoned railway tracks make good paths, and there are forests and moorlands if you prefer wilder country. Most towns have bike-rental shops.

Stately homes and castles: The landed aristocracy still lives in these grand mansions, and most of the homes are open to visitors. Try Floors Castle or the wonderful

Traquair House in the east. Threave, Drumnlarig, and the magical Caerlaverock Castle near Dumfries evoke grander times.

Literary Scotland: The Borders region has enough monuments dedicated to Sir Walter Scott that you could make him a theme of your visit. Abbotsford House, which he built for himself, is unmissable. The poet Robert Burns spent much of his working life in Dumfries.

Shopping: The sheep you see everywhere explain why so many locals became involved in textile production. Mill shops are abundant, and are well worth a visit for their wonderful woolens.

4

ORIENTATION AND PLANNING

GETTING ORIENTED

Once a battleground region separating Scotland and England, today the Borders area is a gateway between the two countries. This is a place of upland moors and hills, fertile farmland, and forested river valleys. Yet it also embraces the rugged coastline between Edinburgh and Berwick. It's rustic and peaceful, with century-old textile mills, abbeys, castles, and gardens. The area is a big draw for hikers and walking enthusiasts, too. The Borders region is also steeped in history, with Mary, Queen of Scots a powerful presence despite the relatively short time she spent here.

The Borders. Borders towns cluster around and between two rivers—the Tweed and its tributary, the Teviot. These are mostly textile towns with plenty of personality, where residents take fierce pride in their local municipalities. The area's top attractions include Jedburgh Abbey, Floors Castle in Kelso, and Abbotsford House just outside Melrose.

Dumfries and Galloway. Easygoing and peaceful, towns in this southwestern region are usually very attractive, with wide streets and colorful buildings. The Solway Firth is a vast nature preserve, and the climate of the west sustains the surprising tropical plants at the Logan Botanic Gardens and the gardens at Threave Castle.

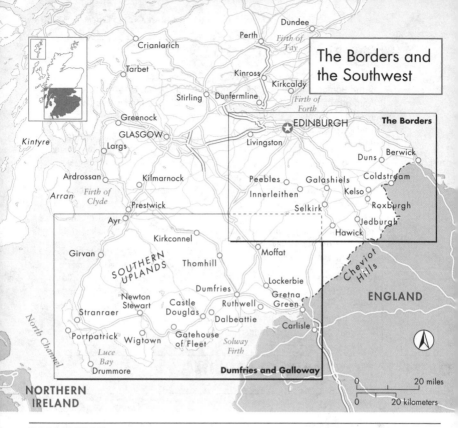

The Borders and
the Southwest

The Borders

Dumfries and Galloway

ENGLAND

NORTHERN
IRELAND

0   20 miles

0   20 kilometers

PLANNING

WHEN TO GO

Because many lodgings and some sights are privately owned and shut down from early autumn until early April, the area is less suited to off-season touring than some other parts of Scotland. The best time to visit is between Easter and late September. The region does look magnificent in autumn, especially along the wooded river valleys of the Borders. Late spring is the time to see the rhododendrons in the gardens of Dumfries and Galloway.

PLANNING YOUR TIME

Beginning in 2014 you'll be able travel by train to the Borders from Edinburgh. The new rail line from Edinburgh's Waverley Station to Tweedbank, in the heart of the Borders, will help to open up a fascinating region that until now has too often been seen as a corridor for travelers en route to the capital.

If you're driving north along the A1 toward Edinburgh, take a tour around the prosperous Borders towns. Turn onto the A698 at Berwick-upon-Tweed, which will take you along the Scottish–English border toward Coldstream, and from there to Kelso, Jedburgh, Dryburgh, and Melrose. It's 36 miles from Jedburgh to Peebles, a good place to stay overnight. Another day might begin with a visit to Walter Scott's lovely Abbotsford House, and then some shopping in any of these prosperous towns.

To the west, Dumfries and Galloway beckon. Travel east on the A708 to Moffat and across the A74 toward Dumfries. Two days would give you time to explore Burns sites and more in Dumfries. From Dumfries you can visit Sweetheart Abbey (8 miles away), Caerlaverock Castle (9 miles away), and Threave Gardens (20 miles away). Castle Douglas is a good place to stop for lunch. The A710 and A711 take you along the dramatic coastline of the Solway Firth. Farther west along the A75 are the towns of Newton Stewart, Portpatrick, and Glen Trool.

GETTING HERE AND AROUND
AIR TRAVEL
The nearest Scottish airports are at Edinburgh, Glasgow, and Prestwick (outside of Glasgow).

BOAT AND FERRY TRAVEL
P&O European Ferries and Stena Line operate from Larne, in Northern Ireland, to Cairnryan, near Stranraer, several times daily. The crossing takes one hour on the Superstar Express, two hours on other ferries.

Boat and Ferry Contacts P&O European Ferries ☎ 08716/642020 ⊕ www.poferries.com. **Stena Line** ☎ 08447/707070 ⊕ www.stenaline.co.uk.

BUS TRAVEL
If you're approaching from the south, check with Scottish Citylink, National Express, or First about buses from Edinburgh and Glasgow. In the Borders, Munro's of Jedburgh and Perryman's Buses offer service within the region. Stagecoach Western is the main bus company serving Dumfries and Galloway.

Bus Contacts First ☎ 08708/727271 ⊕ www.firstgroup.com.
Munro's of Jedburgh ☎ 01835/862253 ⊕ www.munrosofjedburgh.co.uk.
National Express ☎ 08717/818178 ⊕ www.nationalexpress.com.
Perryman's Buses ☎ 01289/308719 ⊕ www.perrymansbuses.co.uk.
Scottish Citylink ☎ 0871/266–3333 ⊕ www.citylink.co.uk. **Stagecoach Western** ☎ 01387/253496 in Dumfries, 01563/525192 in Kilmarnock, 01776/704484 in Stranraer ⊕ www.stagecoachbus.com.

CAR TRAVEL
Traveling by car is the best way to explore the area. The main route into both the Borders and Galloway from the south is the M6, which becomes the M74 at the border. You can also take the scenic and leisurely A7 northwestward through Hawick toward Edinburgh, or the A75 and other parallel routes westward into Dumfries, Galloway, and the ferry ports of Stranraer and Cairnryan.

There are several other possible routes: starting from the east, the A1 brings you from the English city of Newcastle to the border in about an hour. The A1 has the added attraction of Berwick-Upon-Tweed, on the English side of the border, but traffic on the route is heavy. Moving west, the A697, which leaves the A1 north of Morpeth (in England) and crosses the border at Coldstream, is a leisurely back-road option. The A68 is probably the most scenic route to Scotland: after climbing to

Carter Bar, it reveals a view of the Borders hills and windy skies before dropping into the ancient town of Jedburgh.

The best way to explore the region is to get off the main, and often crowded, arterial roads and onto the little back roads. You may occasionally be delayed by a herd of cows on their way to the milking parlor, or a pheasant fluttering across the road, but this is often far more pleasant than, for example, tussling on the A75 with heavy-goods vehicles rushing to make the Irish ferries.

TRAIN TRAVEL

Apart from the main London–Edinburgh line, there has been no train service in the Borders. In 2014 a new rail link from Edinburgh to Tweedbank, near Galashiels, will open up the region to visitors. In the southwest, trains headed from London's Euston to Glasgow stop at Carlisle, just south of the border, and some also stop at Lockerbie. Trains between Glasgow and Carlisle stop at Gretna Green, Annan, and Dumfries. From Glasgow there is service on the coastal route to Stranraer.

First Edinburgh has buses linking Hawick, Selkirk, and Galashiels with train service at Carlisle, Edinburgh, and Berwick.

Train Contacts First Edinburgh ☎ *0131/663–9233, 0871/200–2233* ⊕ *www.firstgroup.com.* **National Rail** ☎ *08457/484950* ⊕ *www.nationalrail. co.uk.* **ScotRail** ☎ *08457/550033* ⊕ *www.scotrail.co.uk.*

RESTAURANTS

Until recently, most good restaurants in the region were located in hotels, but today things are beginning to change. Good independent eateries are popping up in small (and sometime unlikely) towns and villages, and many of these new establishments specialize in fresh local ingredients. Seasonal menus are now popular in the area. *Prices in the reviews are the average cost of a main course at dinner or, if dinner is not served, at lunch.*

HOTELS

From top-quality, full-service hotels to quaint 18th-century drovers' inns to cozy bed-and-breakfasts, the Borders has all manner of lodging options. Choices in Dumfries and Galloway may be a little less expensive than in the Borders (with the same full range of services). These days many establishments have a shifting scale and are willing to lower their rates depending on availability. *Prices in the reviews are the lowest cost of a standard double room in high season, including 20% V.A.T.*

VISITOR INFORMATION

Visit Scottish Borders has offices in Jedburgh, Hawick, and Peebles. The Dumfries & Galloway Tourist Board can be found in Dumfries and Stranraer. Seasonal information centers are at Castle Douglas, Coldstream, Eyemouth, Galashiels, Gretna Green, Kelso, Kirkcudbright, Langholm, Melrose, Moffat, Newton Stewart, Sanquhar, and Selkirk.

THE BORDERS

Although the Borders has many attractions, it's most famous for being the home base for Sir Walter Scott (1771–1832), the early-19th-century poet, novelist, and creator of *Ivanhoe,* who single-handedly transformed Scotland's image from that of a land of brutal savages to one of romantic and stirring deeds and magnificent landscapes. The novels of Scott are not read much nowadays—frankly, some of them are difficult to wade through—but the mystique that he created, the aura of historical romance, has outlasted his books. The ruined abbeys, historical houses, and grand vistas of the Borders provide a perfect backdrop.

A visit to at least one of the region's four great ruined abbeys makes the quintessential Borders experience. The monks in these powerful, long-abandoned religious orders were the first to work the fleeces of their sheep flocks, thus laying the groundwork for what is still the area's main manufacturing industry.

Borders folk take great pride in the region's fame as Scotland's main woolen-goods manufacturing area. Its main towns—Jedburgh, Hawick, Selkirk, Peebles, Kelso, and Melrose—retain an air of prosperity and confidence with their solid stone houses and elegant town squares. Although many of the mills have closed in recent years, the pride in local identity is evident in the fiercely contested Melrose Sevens rugby competition in April and the annual Common Ridings—local events commemorating the time when towns needed to patrol their borders—throughout June and July.

JEDBURGH

50 miles south of Edinburgh, 95 miles southeast of Glasgow, 14 miles northeast of Hawick.

The town of Jedburgh (-*burgh* is always pronounced *burra* in Scots) was for centuries the first major Scottish target of invading English armies. In more peaceful times it developed textile mills, most of which have since languished. The large landscaped area around the town's tourist information center was once a mill but now provides an encampment for the armies of modern tourists. The past still clings to this little town, however. The ruined abbey dominates the skyline, a reminder of the formerly strong governing role of the Borders abbeys.

GETTING HERE AND AROUND

The best and easiest way to travel in this region is by car. From Edinburgh you can take the A68 (about 45 minutes) or the A7 (about an hour). From Glasgow take the M8, then the A68 direct to Jedburgh (about two hours).

There are fairly good bus connections from all major Scottish cities to Jedburgh. From Edinburgh, direct routes to Melrose take about two hours. From Glasgow it takes 3½ hours to reach Melrose. From Melrose it's just 20 minutes to Jedburgh.

The new rail link will run between Edinburgh and Tweedbank, about 15 miles northwest of Jedburgh.

ESSENTIALS

Visitor Information Jedburgh Visitor Centre ⊠ *Abbey Pl.* ☎ *01835/863170* ⊕ *www.visitscotland.com/jedburgh.*

EXPLORING

TOP ATTRACTIONS

FAMILY **Harestanes Countryside Visitor Centre.** Housed in a former farmhouse 3 miles north of Jedburgh, this visitor center portrays life in the Scottish Borders through art exhibitions and natural history displays. Crafts such as woodworking and tile-making are taught here, and finished projects are often on display. There's a gift shop and tearoom, and outside are meandering paths, quiet roads for bike rides, and the biggest children's play area in the Borders. It is also on one of the best-known walking routes in the Borders, the St. Cuthbert's Path. ⊠ *Junction of A68 and B6400, 4 miles north of Jedburgh, Ancrum* ☎ *01835/830306* ☞ *Free* ☉ *Apr.–Oct., daily 10–5.*

Fodor's Choice **Jedburgh Abbey.** The most impressive of the Borders abbeys towers above
★ Jedburgh. The abbey was nearly destroyed by the English earl of Hertford's forces in 1544–45, during the destructive time known as the Rough Wooing. This was English King Henry VIII's (1491–1547) armed attempt to persuade the Scots that it was a good idea to unite the kingdoms by the marriage of his young son to the infant Mary, Queen of Scots (1542–87); the Scots disagreed and sent Mary to France instead. The story is explained in vivid detail at the visitor center, which also has information about the ruins and an audio tour. Ground patterns and foundations are all that remain of the once-powerful religious complex. ⊠ *High St.* ☎ *01835/863925* ⊕ *www.historic-scotland.gov.uk/places* ☞ *£5.50* ☉ *Apr.–Sept., daily 9:30–5:30; Oct.–Mar., daily 9:30–4:30.*

Mary, Queen of Scots House. This *bastel* (from the French *bastille*) was the fortified town house in which, as the story goes, Mary stayed before embarking on her famous 20-mile ride to Hermitage Castle to visit her wounded lover, the Earl of Bothwell (circa 1535–78). Interesting displays relate the tale and illustrate other episodes in her life. Some of her possessions are on display, as are tapestries and furniture of the period. The ornamental garden surrounding the house has ranks of pear trees leading down to the river. ⊠ *Queen St.* ☎ *01835/863331* ☞ *Free* ☉ *Mar.–Nov., Mon.–Sat. 10–4:30, Sun. 11–4.*

WORTH NOTING

OFF THE **Hermitage Castle.** To appreciate the famous 20-mile ride of Mary,
BEATEN Queen of Scots—she rushed to the side of her wounded lover, the earl
PATH of Bothwell—travel southwest from Jedburgh to this, the most complete remaining example of the bare and grim medieval border castles. Restored in the early 19th century, it was built in the 14th century to guard what was at the time one of the important routes from England into Scotland. The original owner, Lord Soulis, notorious for diabolical excess, was captured by the local populace, which wrapped him in lead and boiled him in a cauldron—or so the tale goes. ⊠ *2 miles west of B6399, about 15 miles south of Hawick, Liddesdale* ☎ *01387/376222* ⊕ *www.historic-scotland.gov.uk/places* ☞ *£4.50* ☉ *Apr.–Sept., daily 9:30–5:30; last admission ½ hr before closing.*

Jedburgh Castle Jail. This was the site of the Howard Reform Prison, established in 1820. It sits behind the front of the castle that previously stood in the same spot. Today you can inspect prison cells, rooms arranged with period furnishings, and costumed figures. Audiovisual displays recount the history of the Royal Burgh of Jedburgh. It's reputedly one of the most haunted buildings in the area. ⊠ *Castlegate* ☎ *01835/864750* ✉ *Free* ⊗ *Mar.–Oct., Mon.–Sat. 10–4:30, Sun. 1–4; last admission ½ hr before closing.*

THE COMMON RIDINGS

Borders communities have reestablished their identities through the gatherings known as the Common Ridings. Long ago it was essential that each town be able to defend its area, and this need became formalized in mounted gatherings to "ride the marches," or patrol the boundaries. The Common Ridings, which celebrate this history, possess much more authenticity than the concocted Highland Games so often taken to be the essence of Scotland. You can watch the excitement of clattering hooves and banners proudly displayed, but this is essentially a time for native Borderers.

WHERE TO EAT

$$ SPANISH

✕ **Vino y Tapas.** Mediterranean colors are splashed across the interior of this Spanish-style eatery, where a modern tapas menu was inspired by the years that the Scottish owners spent in Spain. The simple and authentic dishes have an occasional dramatic touch, like the "carne de chocolate" (literally, chocolate meat), a beef stew with a touch of cocoa. Tapas are generous, and cost between £5 and £6. There's a good, if modest, wine list. ⑤ *Average main: £15* ⊠ *23 Castlegate* ☎ *01835/862380* ⊕ *www.theforrestersrestaurantsb.com* ⊗ *No lunch.*

WHERE TO STAY

$
B&B/INN
FAMILY

🏠 **Hundalee House.** This 18th-century manor house has richly decorated Victorian-style rooms with nice touches like four-poster beds and cozy fireplaces. **Pros:** fantastic views of apple orchards; hearty breakfasts; good children's facilities. **Cons:** farm aromas; far from shops and restaurants. ⑤ *Rooms from: £60* ⊠ *Off A68, 1 mile south of Jedburgh* ☎ *01835/863011* ⊕ *www.accommodation-scotland.org* ⇆ *5 rooms* ▭ *No credit cards* ⊗ *Closed Christmas, Jan.–Mar.* ❙◎❙ *Breakfast.*

$
B&B/INN

🏠 **Meadhon House.** On a row of medieval buildings, Meadhon House is a charming 17th-century house with a history to match. **Pros:** central; pleasant rooms; welcoming atmosphere. **Cons:** rooms on the small side. ⑤ *Rooms from: £65* ⊠ *48 Castlegate* ☎ *01835/862504* ⊕ *www.meadhon.co.uk* ⇆ *5 rooms* ❙◎❙ *Breakfast.*

SPORTS AND OUTDOORS

Christopher Rainbow Tandem & Bike Hire. This shop rents tandem bikes, mountain bikes, and touring bikes. The location, between Jedburgh and Ancrum, makes it ideal for exploring the four abbeys, as well as the Tweed Cycleway and Borderloop Cycleway. The company provides tour itineraries, as well as extra services such as luggage forwarding. ⊠ *8 Timpendean Cottages* ☎ *01835/830326* ⊕ *www.chrisrainbow.net.*

The Borders

North Sea

Berwick-upon-Tweed

Paxton House

Manderston House

Duns

Cockburnspath

ENGLAND

Coldstream

R. Tweed

B6437

A6112

B6461

Swinton

Blackadder

A6105

B6437

Eccles

A698

A697

Floors Castle

Kelso

Roxburgh

Morebattle

CHEVIOT HILLS

B6352

Kale Wr.

Smailholm Tower

Mellerstain House

B6397

B6360

Dryburgh Abbey

B6404

A699

A6089

B6356

A68

Jedburgh

Lanton

A698

A6088

Thirlestane Castle

Lauder

Melrose

Tweedbank

Scott's View

Ancrum

B6400

Harestanes Countryside Visitor Centre

Haddington

A68

Galashiels

Old Gala House

Abbotsford House

A707

A699

A7

Selkirk

Ashkirk

Teviot

Hawick

A698

TO HERMITAGE CASTLE

A7

Fala

A7

Heriot

B709

Three Brethren

Bowhill

Roberton

A6093

A68

Dalkeith

A72

Innerleithen

A708

EDINBURGH

Penicuik

S. Esk

A703

R. Tweed

Peebles

N. Esk

PENTLAND HILLS

A702

A721

Kirkliston

Livingston

M9

M8

A71

TO CRAIK FOREST

R. Tweed

10 miles

10 kilometers

KEY

✈ Airport

SHOPPING

Jedburgh Woollen Mill. This shop has shelves bursting with sweaters, kilts, tartan knitwear, and scarves. It's a good place to stock up on gifts. ⊠ *Bankend North, Edinburgh Rd.* ☎ *01835/863585* ⊕ *www.ewm.co.uk.*

Scottish Tradition. The knitwear and hats here are of the finest quality. Scottish Tradition also sells beautiful cashmere items, as well as Scottish tartan goods. ⊠ *New Bongate Mill* ☎ *01835/863306* ⊕ *www.cashmere-in-scotland.com.*

KELSO

12 miles northeast of Jedburgh.

One of the most charming Borders burghs, Kelso is often described as having a continental flavor—some people think its broad, paved square makes it resemble a Belgian market town. The community has some fine examples of Georgian and Victorian Scots town architecture.

GETTING HERE AND AROUND

There are direct bus routes from Jedburgh to Kelso. Edinburgh has direct buses to Jedburgh; buses from Glasgow aren't direct. Your best option is to travel by car. From Jedburgh to Kelso take the A698, which is 12 miles, or about 20 minutes. Alternatively, the A699 is a scenic half-hour drive.

ESSENTIALS

Visitor Information Kelso Tourist Information Centre ⊠ *The Square* ☎ *01835/863170* ⊕ *www.visitscotland.com.*

EXPLORING

Fodor's Choice ★ **Floors Castle.** The palatial Floors Castle, the largest inhabited castle in Scotland, is an architectural extravagance bristling with pepper-mill turrets. Not so much a castle as the ancestral seat of a wealthy and powerful landowning family, the Roxburghes, it stands on the "floors," or flat terrain, on the banks of the River Tweed. The enormous home was built in 1721 by William Adam (1689–1748) and modified by William Playfair (1789–1857), who added the turrets and towers in the 1840s. The interior rooms are crowded with valuable furniture, paintings, porcelain, and a strangely eerie circular room full of stuffed birds. Each room has a knowledgable guide at the ready. The surrounding 56,000-acre estate is home to more than 40 farms. ⊠ *A6089* ☎ *01573/223333* ⊕ *www.floorscastle.com* ☑ *Grounds £4,50, castle and grounds £8.50* ☉ *May.–Sept., daily 10:30–5; Oct. 10:30-3:30. Last admission ½ hr before closing.*

Kelso Abbey. The least intact ruin of the four great abbeys, Kelso Abbey is just a bleak fragment of what was once the largest of the group. It was here in 1460 that the nine-year-old James III was crowned king of Scotland. On a main invasion route, the abbey was burned three times in the 1540s alone, on the last occasion by the English Earl of Hertford's forces in 1545, when the 100 men and 12 monks of the garrison were butchered and the structure all but destroyed. ⊠ *Bridge St.* ☎ *0131/668–8800* ⊕ *www.kelso.bordernet.co.uk* ☑ *Free* ☉ *Apr.–Dec., daily 24 hrs.*

Mellerstain House. One fine example of the Borders area's ornate country homes is Mellerstain House. Begun in the 1720s, it was finished in the 1770s by Robert Adam (1728–92) and is considered one of his finest creations. Sumptuous plasterwork covers almost all interior surfaces, and there are outstanding examples of 18th-century furnishings, porcelain and china, and paintings and embroidery. The beautiful terraced gardens (open an hour before the house itself) are as renowned as the house. ⊠ *Off A6089, 7 miles northwest of Kelso, Gordon,* ☏ *01573/410225* ⊕ *www.mellerstain.com* ⊠ *Gardens £5, house and gardens £8.50* ⊙ *May–Sept., Fri.–Mon. 12:30–5; last admission ½ hr before closing.*

WORD OF MOUTH

"The Borders abbeys like Melrose will fulfill your dreams. Melrose Abbey was not my favorite because it is surrounded by a town, but Dryburgh Abbey was in the country on the River Tweed. Jedburgh Abbey, like Melrose, is in a town; these three abbeys in a small area are great."

—PalenQ

Fodor's Choice ★ **Smailholm Tower.** The characteristic Borders structure Smailholm Tower stands uncompromisingly on top of a barren, rocky ridge in the hills south of Mellerstain. The 16th-century peel was built solely for defense, and its unadorned stones contrast with the luxury of Mellerstain House. If you let your imagination wander in this windy spot, you can almost see the flapping pennants and rising dust of an advancing raiding party and hear the anxious securing of doors and bolts. Sir Walter Scott found this spot inspiring. His grandfather lived nearby, and the young Scott visited the tower often during his childhood. A museum displays costumed figures and tapestries relating to Scott's folk ballads. A free audio tour is available. ⊠ *Off B6404, 4½ miles south of Mellerstain House* ☏ *01573/460365* ⊕ *www.historic-scotland.gov.uk* ⊠ *£4.50* ⊙ *Apr.–Sept., daily 9:30–5:30; Oct.–Mar., weekends 9:30–4:30; last admission ½ hr before closing.*

WHERE TO EAT AND STAY

$$ **BRITISH** ✕ **Cobbles Inn.** A lively bar and restaurant off the town square, Cobbles is much favored by locals. The bar menu is an excellent value, and includes such dishes as breaded pork fillets with perfectly prepared root vegetables in a red wine sauce. The dinner menu features a savory cheesecake starter made with chestnuts and balsamic vinegar, and lamb cutlets with parsnips and artichokes. Vegetarian dishes are also on offer. Desserts are well made and come in generous portions. $ *Average main: £16* ⊠ *7 Bowmont St.* ☏ *01573/223548* ⊕ *www.thecobbleskelso.co.uk.*

$ **MEDITERRANEAN** ✕ **Oscar's Wine Bar and Restaurant.** Winner of numerous culinary and entrepreneurial awards, this establishment is a local favorite. The space is well lit, with bright yellow walls, contemporary furniture, and the work of local artists lining the walls. In season, try the medallions of venison with black pudding or char-grilled monkfish and salmon kebabs. The homemade banoffee pie (with banana, toffee, and cream) is to die for. The staff is attentive and well informed. $ *Average main: £14* ⊠ *35–37 Horsemarket* ☏ *01573/224008* ⊕ *www.oscars-kelso.com* ⊙ *Closed Tues. and Sun.*

$$ **⚏ Edenwater House.** This handsome stone house overlooks Edenwater,
B&B/INN   a trout stream that runs into the River Tweed. **Pros:** excellent food;
romantic atmosphere; peaceful surroundings. **Cons:** not good for families with small children; far from urban amenities. ⑤ *Rooms from: £110*
⊠ *Off B6461, Ednam* ☎ *01573/224070* ⊕ *www.edenwaterhouse.co.uk*
🛏 *4 rooms* ⊗ *Restaurant closed Sun.–Tues.* ❮❮❭ *Breakfast.*

$$ **⚏ Ednam House Hotel.** People return again and again to this large, stately
HOTEL   hotel on the banks of the River Tweed, close to Kelso's grand abbey and
Fodor'sChoice   sprawling market square. **Pros:** great outdoor activities; atmospheric lobby;
★   impressive restaurant. **Cons:** some rooms need a makeover. ⑤ *Rooms
from: £159* ⊠ *Bridge St.* ☎ *01573/224168* ⊕ *www.ednamhouse.com*
🛏 *32 rooms* ⊗ *Closed late Dec. to early Jan.* ❮❮❭ *Breakfast.*

SHOPPING

John Moody. This shop sells soft cashmere and lambs wool sweaters, along
with purses, scarves, and gloves. It's a real treat for knitwear fanatics, or
those simply looking for something Scottish to keep them warm. ⊠ *38
The Square* ☎ *01573/224400* ⊕ *www.johnmoodyknitwear.co.uk.*

COLDSTREAM

9 miles east of Kelso.

Three miles west of Coldstream, the England–Scotland border comes
down from the hills and runs beside the Tweed for the rest of its journey
to the sea. Coldstream itself is still a small town, with a mix of attractive
18th- and 19th-century buildings. Like Gretna Green, this was once a
place where runaway couples from the south could come to get married in
a time when the marriage laws of Scotland were more lenient than those
of England. A plaque on the former bridge tollhouse recalls this fact.

The town is also celebrated in military history: in 1659 General Monck
raised a regiment of foot guards here on behalf of his exiled monarch,
Charles II of England (1630–85). Known as the Coldstream Guards, the
successors to this regiment have become an elite corps in the British army.

GETTING HERE AND AROUND

There is no direct bus service from Jedburgh or Kelso. Your best bet is
to drive. From Jedburgh, take the A68/A698/A697 (30 minutes). From
Kelso, take the A698 (15 minutes).

ESSENTIALS

Visitor Information Coldstream Tourist Information Centre ⊠ *76 High St.*
☎ *08706/080404* ⊕ *www.visitscottishborders.com.*

EXPLORING

FAMILY   **Coldstream Museum.** In the former headquarters of the Coldstream
Guards, the Coldstream Museum examines the history of the regiment
and the community. You can see 18th-century marriage contracts, pieces
of masonry from the village's lost medieval convent, weapons, uniforms,
and photographs. A children's play area has toys and costumes, including a child-size guard uniform and a bearskin hat made by the regimental tailor. ⊠ *12 Market Sq.* ☎ *01890/882630* ⊕ *www.scotborders.gov.uk*
⚏ *Free* ⊗ *Mar.–Sept., Mon.–Sat. 10–4, Sun. 2–4; Oct., Mon.–Sat. 1–4.*

4

FAMILY   **Harestanes Countryside Visitor Centre.** This complex of farmyard buildings houses a museum and crafts center. With extensive grounds—superb rhododendrons bloom here in late spring—this is a favorite spot for walkers, cyclists, and bird-watchers. There's plenty for children, including a large play park and a fascinating puzzle gallery full of sturdy wooden games. There's also a café and exhibition space. ⊠ *A697* ☎ *01835/830306*   ⊕ *www.scotborders.gov.uk/harestanes*   ▨ *Free* ⊙ *Mar.–Oct., weekdays 10–5, weekends noon–5.*

OFF THE
BEATEN
PATH
Manderston House. Rebuilt by Sir James Miller, whose family made its fortune selling herring to Russia, Manderston is a masterful example of the no-expense-spared Edwardian country house. Designed by John Kinross, a young local architect, the original Georgian house from the 1790s was completely renovated between 1903 and 1905. The silver-plated staircase was modeled after the one in the Petit Trianon, at Versailles. Look for the collection of late-19th- and early-20th-century cookie tins. There's much to see downstairs in the kitchens, and outside, among a cluster of other buildings, is the octagonal, one-of-a-kind marble dairy where lunch, dinner, or afternoon tea can be arranged for groups. You can reach the house by traveling northeast from Coldstream along the A6112 to Duns, then taking the A6105 east. ⊠ *Off A6105, Duns* ☎ *01361/882636* ⊕ *www.manderston.co.uk* ▨ *Grounds £5, house and grounds £9* ⊙ *Mid-May–Sept., Thurs. and Sun. 1:30–5.*

OFF THE
BEATEN
PATH
Paxton House. Stately Paxton House is a comely Palladian mansion designed in 1758 by James and John Adam, with interiors by their brother Robert. There's Chippendale and Trotter furniture, and the splendid Regency picture gallery has a magnificent collection of paintings. The garden is delightful, with a squirrel hide and a restored boathouse containing a museum of salmon fishing. The adjacent crafts shop and tearoom are open April to October, daily 9 to 5. There's also croquet in the gardens. ⊠ *B6461, 15 miles northeast of Coldstream, Paxton* ☎ *01289/386291* ⊕ *www.paxtonhouse.co.uk* ▨ *Grounds £4, house and grounds £7.60* ⊙ *Mar.–Nov., daily 11–5. Guided tours at 11, 11:45, 12:30, 1:15, 2, and 3:30.*

WHERE TO EAT

$$
MODERN BRITISH
✕ **Wheatsheaf Hotel and Restaurant.** The Wheatsheaf is a dining establishment that also provides accommodations—an important distinction, according to the owner. You can enjoy an outstanding meal in the black-beamed bar, but the real treat is the formal restaurant. Focusing on beef, venison, and salmon, the excellent Scottish cuisine has won widespread praise, yet neither the food nor the small but carefully chosen wine list is overpriced. The lobster and vanilla pod risotto followed by wild boar with black pudding and juniper berries would grace any table. Extend your stay in the 10 country-style bedrooms; room prices include breakfast or dinner. The inn is in Swinton, 6 miles north of Coldstream. ⑤ *Average main: £17* ⊠ *Main St., Swinton* ☎ *01890/860257* ⊕ *www. wheatsheaf-swinton.co.uk* ⚠ *Reservations essential* ⊙ *Closed 1st 2 wks of Jan. No lunch.*

MELROSE

24 miles west of Coldstream, 4 miles southeast of Galashiels.

Though it's small, there is nevertheless a bustle about Melrose, the perfect example of a prosperous Scottish market town and one of the loveliest in the Borders. It's set round a square lined with 18th- and 19th-century buildings housing myriad small shops and cafés. Despite its proximity to the much larger Galashiels, Melrose has rejected industrialization. You'll likely hear local residents greet each other by first name in the square.

GETTING HERE AND AROUND

Buses do go to Melrose. However, driving is the easiest, fastest, and most efficient way to travel here. From Coldstream, take the A699 (40 minutes). From Galashiels, take the A6091 (10 minutes).

ESSENTIALS

Visitor Information Melrose Tourist Information Centre ⊠ *Abbey St.* ☎ *01896/822283* ⊕ *www.visitscottishborders.com.*

EXPLORING
TOP ATTRACTIONS

Fodor's Choice ★ **Abbotsford House.** In this great house overlooking the Tweed, Sir Walter Scott lived, worked, and received the great and the good in luxurious salons. In 1811 the writer bought a farm on this site named Cartleyhole, which was a euphemism for the real name, Clartyhole (*clarty* is Scots for "muddy" or "dirty"). The name was surely not romantic enough for Scott, who renamed the property after a ford in the nearby Tweed used by the abbot of Melrose. Scott eventually had the house entirely rebuilt in the Scots baronial style. It was, of course, an expensive project, and Scott wrote feverishly to keep his creditors at bay. John Ruskin, the art critic, disapproved, calling it an "incongruous pile," but most contemporary visitors find it fascinating, particularly because of its expansive views and delightful gardens.

The interior, reopened after extensive renovations in 2013, now includes new areas of the house. A free audio tour guides you around the salon, the wonderful circular study, and the library with its 9,000 leather-bound volumes. The newly built visitor center houses displays about Scott's life, a gift shop, and an upstairs restaurant serving lunch. To get here, take the A6091 from Melrose and follow the signs for Abbotsford. ⊠ *B6360, Galashiels* ☎ *01896/752043* ⊕ *www.scottsabbotsford.co.uk* ⌚ *House and gardens £8.75; gardens only £3.50* ⊙ *Apr.–Sept., daily 10–5; Oct.–Mar., daily 10–4.*

Fodor's Choice ★ **Melrose Abbey.** Just off Melrose's town square sit the ruins of Melrose Abbey, one of the four Borders abbeys. "If thou would'st view fair Melrose aright, go visit it in the pale moonlight," wrote Scott in *The Lay of the Last Minstrel,* and so many of his fans took the advice literally that a sleepless custodian begged him to rewrite the lines. Today the abbey is still impressive: a red-sandstone shell with slender windows, delicate tracery, and carved capitals, all carefully maintained. Among the carvings high on the roof is one of a bagpipe-playing pig. An audio tour is included in the admission price. The heart of Robert

the Bruce is rumored to be buried here. ⊠ *Abbey St.* ☎ *01896/822562*
⊕ *www.historic-scotland.gov.uk* ✉ *£5.50* ⊙ *Apr.–Sept., daily 9:30–*
5:30; Oct.–Mar., daily 9:30–4:30; last entry ½ hr before closing.

WORTH NOTING

Dryburgh Abbey. The final resting place of Sir Walter Scott and his
wife, and the most peaceful and secluded of the Borders abbeys, the
"gentle ruins" of Dryburgh Abbey sit on parkland in a loop of the
Tweed. The abbey, founded in 1150, suffered from English raids
until, like Melrose, it was abandoned in 1544. The style is transi-
tional, a mingling of rounded Romanesque and pointed early English.
The north transept, where the Haig and Scott families lie buried,
is lofty and pillared, and once formed part of the abbey church.
⊠ *B6404* ☎ *01835/822381* ⊕ *www.historic-scotland.gov.uk/places*
✉ *£5* ⊙ *Apr.–Sept., daily 9:30–5:30; Oct.–Mar., daily 9:30–4:30; last*
entry ½ hr before closing.

Priorwood Gardens. The National Trust for Scotland's Priorwood Gardens, next to Melrose Abbey, specializes in flowers for drying. Dried
flowers are on sale in the shop. Next to the gardens is an orchard with
some old apple varieties. The nearby walled Harmony Garden is also
included in the entry price. ⊠ *Abbey St.* ☎ *0844/4932257* ⊕ *www.nts.*
org.uk ✉ *£6.50* ⊙ *Mar.–Oct., Mon.–Sat. 10–5, Sun. 1–5; Nov. and*
Dec., Mon.–Sat. 10–4.

Scott's View. This is possibly the most photographed rural view in the
south of Scotland. (It's almost as iconic as Eilean Donan Castle, far to
the north.) The sinuous curve of the River Tweed and the gentle landscape unfolding to the triple peaks of the Eildons and then rolling out
into the shadows beyond are certainly worth seeking out. ⊠ *B6356, 3*
miles north of Dryburgh, Dryburgh.

Trimontium Roman Heritage Centre. Here you'll find such artifacts as tools,
weapons, and armor retrieved from the largest Roman settlement in
Scotland, which was at nearby Newstead. A blacksmith's shop, several
examples of pottery, and scale models of the fort are also on display.
A guided four-hour walk along the 5-mile trail to the site departs at
1:30 on Thursday (also on Tuesday in July and August). The cost is £3.
⊠ *The Ormiston, Market Sq.* ☎ *01896/822651* ⊕ *www.trimontium.org.*
uk/wb ✉ *£2* ⊙ *Apr.–Oct., daily 10:30–4:30.*

WHERE TO EAT AND STAY

$

ECLECTIC

✗ **Herge's at the Lock.** A wall of windows allows you to contemplate
swans floating serenely across this eatery's namesake lock, a man-made
pond in the village of Tweedbank. Don't worry: this light and airy place
has views of the lake from nearly every table, and if you want a closer
look at the birds you can dine on the terrace. The elegant but understated food, nicely presented and served in generous portions, includes
familiar dishes like steak pie and such European dishes as lamb rump
with balsamic onions and roasted beetroot. The restaurant is named
after the creator of Tintin, the beloved cartoon character. ⑤ *Average*
main: £12 ⊠ *Tweedbank Dr., Tweedbank* ☎ *01896/759909* ⊕ *www.*
hergesontheloch.com.

CLOSE UP

The World of Sir Walter Scott

Sir Walter Scott (1771–1832) was probably Scottish tourism's best propagandist. Thanks to his fervid "Romantik" imagination, his long narrative poems—such as "The Lady of the Lake"—and a long string of historical novels, including *Ivanhoe, Waverley, Rob Roy,* and *The Heart of Midlothian,* the world fell in love with the image of heroic Scotland. Scott wrote of Scotland as a place of Highland wilderness and clan romance, shaping outsiders' perceptions of Scotland in a way that to an extent survives even today.

Scott was born in College Wynd, Edinburgh. A lawyer by training, he was an assiduous collector of old ballads and tales. "The Lay of the Last Minstrel," a romantic poem published in 1805, brought him fame. In 1811 Scott bought the house that was to become Abbotsford, his Borders mansion near Melrose.

Scott started on his series of Waverley novels in 1814, at first anonymously, and by 1820 had produced *Waverley, Guy Mannering, The Antiquary, Tales of My Landlord,* and *Rob Roy.* Between 1820 and 1825 there followed an additional 11 titles,

including *Ivanhoe* and *The Pirate.* Many of his verse narratives and novels focused on real-life settings, in particular the Trossachs, northwest of Stirling, an area that rapidly became, and still remains, popular with visitors.

Apart from his writing, Scott is also remembered for rediscovering the Honours of Scotland—the crown, scepter, and sword of state of the Scottish monarchs—in 1819. These symbols had languished at the bottom of a chest in Edinburgh Castle since 1707, when Scotland lost its independence. Today they're on display in the castle.

SCOTT SIGHTS

Abbotsford, Scott's home near Melrose in the Borders, is well worth a visit. Other houses associated with Scott can be seen in Edinburgh: 25 George Square, which was his father's house, and 39 Castle Street, where he lived from 1801 to 1826. The site of his birthplace, in College Wynd, is marked with a plaque. The most obvious structure associated with Scott in Edinburgh is the Scott Monument on Princes Street, which looks like a Gothic rocket ship with a statue of Scott and his pet dog as passengers.

4

$$
BRITISH
Fodor's Choice
★

✕ **Hoebridge Inn.** Whitewashed walls, oak-beamed ceilings, and an open fire welcome you into this converted 19th-century bobbin mill. The cuisine is a blend of British and Mediterranean styles with occasional Asian influences. You might have lamb served with rosemary mashed potatoes and red-currant sauce or panfried tiger prawns with chili and lime syrup, accompanied by a salad of bean sprouts and *mangetout* (peas in their edible pods). Rabbit and guinea fowl also appear regularly on the menu. The inn lies in Gattonside, Melrose's across-the-river neighbor, but a 2-mile drive is required to cross to the other side; you can reach the inn more easily via a footbridge. ⑤ *Average main: £17* ⊠ *B6360, Gattonside* ☎ *01896/823082* ⚓ *Reservations essential* ☉ *Closed Sun. and Mon.*

$$ 　**⊡ Burts Hotel.** This charming whitewashed building dating from the 18th
HOTEL 　century sits in the center of Melrose. **Pros:** walking distance to restau-
rants and pubs; good menu in restaurant. **Cons:** some rooms are tiny;
bland room decor. ⑤ *Rooms from: £133 ⊠ Market Sq.* ☎ *01896/822285*
⊕ *www.burtshotel.co.uk* ⇄ *20 rooms* ⦿ *Breakfast.*

$$ 　**⊡ Dryburgh Abbey Hotel.** Mature woodlands and verdant lawns sur-
HOTEL 　round this imposing, 19th-century mansion, which is adjacent to the
abbey ruins on a sweeping bend of the River Tweed. **Pros:** beautiful
grounds; romantic setting. **Cons:** some rooms need to be freshened up;
service can be on the slow side. ⑤ *Rooms from: £140 ⊠ Off B6404,
St. Boswells* ☎ *01835/822261* ⊕ *www.dryburgh.co.uk* ⇄ *36 rooms,
2 suites* ⦿ *Breakfast.*

THE ARTS

Wynd Theatre. Concerts of folk, blues, jazz, or classical music are on the
roster at the Wynd Theatre, which also hosts theatical events and film
screenings. ⊠ *3 Buccleuch St.* ☎ *01896/820028.*

SHOPPING

Abbey Mill. Take a break from sightseeing at Abbey Mill, where you'll
find hand-woven knitwear as well as homemade jams and fudge. There's
also a wee tearoom. ⊠ *Annay Rd.* ☎ *01896/822138.*

GALASHIELS

5 miles northwest of Melrose.

A busy gray-stone Borders town, Galashiels is still active with textile
mills and knitwear factories.

GETTING HERE AND AROUND

There is regular bus service from Melrose to Galashiels (20 minutes).
You can also drive; from Melrose, take the B6374 or the A6091 (both
10 minutes).

EXPLORING

Old Gala House. Dating from 1583, Old Gala House is the former
home of the lairds (landed proprietors) of Galashiels. It now serves as
a museum with displays on the history of the building and the town, as
well as a contemporary art gallery. You can trace your family history
at a comprehensive genealogy facility. The house is a short walk from
the town center. ⊠ *Scott Crescent* ☎ *01896/75611* ⊕ *www.galashiels.
bordernet.co.uk/oldgalahouse* ⊡ *Free* ☉ *Apr.–Sept., Tues.–Sat. 10–4;
July and Aug., Mon.–Sat. 10–4, Sun. 2–4; Oct., Tues.–Sat. 1–4.*

SELKIRK

6 miles southwest of Galashiels, 11 miles north of Hawick.

Selkirk is a hilly outpost with a smattering of antiques shops and an
assortment of bakers selling Selkirk bannock (fruited sweet bread) and
other cakes. It is the site of one of Scotland's iconic battles, Flodden Field,
commemorated here with a statue in the town. Sir Walter Scott was sheriff (judge) of Selkirkshire from 1800 until his death in 1832, and his statue
stands in Market Place. The town is also near Bowhill, a stately home.

GETTING HERE AND AROUND

If you're driving, take the A7 south to Galashiels. The scenic journey is less than 7 miles and takes around 10 minutes. First Edinburgh Bus offers a regular service between Galashiels and Selkirk.

ESSENTIALS

Visitor Information Selkirk Visitor Information Centre ⊠ *Halliwell's House, Market Pl.* ☎ *08706/080404* ⊕ *www.visitscotland.com.*

SELKIRK'S PRIDE

The little town of Selkirk claims its Common Riding is the largest mounted gathering anywhere in Europe. More than 400 riders take part in the event. It's also the oldest Borders festival, dating back to the Battle of Flodden in 1513.

EXPLORING

TOP ATTRACTIONS

Bowhill. Home of the Duke of Buccleuch, Bowhill dates from the 19th century and houses an outstanding collection of works by Gainsborough, Van Dyck, Canaletto, Reynolds, and Raeburn, as well as porcelain and period furniture. Access is by guided tour on specific days in summer. There is an excellent adventure playground for the kids and a 57-mile country ride for those who prefer horseback riding. A local stable hires out horses. ⊠ *Off A708, 3 miles west of Selkirk* ☎ *01750/22204* ⊕ *www.bowhill.org* ⊠ *Grounds £3.50, house and grounds £8* ⊙ *Grounds Apr.–Sept, daily 10–5. House: July–Sept., by guided tour only.*

Sir Walter Scott's Courtroom. The historic courtroom, where Sir Walter Scott presided as sheriff from 1804 to 1832, contains a display examining his life, writings, and time on the bench. It includes an audiovisual presentation. His statue overlooks the comings and goings outside the court. ⊠ *Market Sq.* ☎ *01750/720096* ⊕ *www.scotborders.gov.uk* ⊠ *Free* ⊙ *Mar., Apr., and Sept., weekdays 10–4, Sat. 11–3; May–Aug., Mon.–Sun. 11–3; Oct., Mon.–Sat. noon–3.*

Waverly Mill. You can take an informative tour of this world-renowned mill and also purchase some of the best woolen goods on offer, from knitwear to tartans and tweeds. The shop also sells Scottish jewelry. ⊠ *Dinsdale Rd., Selkirk* ☎ *01750/726100.*

WORTH NOTING

Halliwell's House Museum. Tucked off the main square, Halliwell's House Museum was once an ironmonger's shop, which is now re-created downstairs. Upstairs, an exhibit tells the town's story, illustrates the working lives of its inhabitants, and provides useful background information on the Common Ridings. ⊠ *Market Pl.* ☎ *01750/20096* ⊕ *www.scotborders.gov.uk* ⊠ *Free* ⊙ *Apr.–Oct., Mon.–Sat. 10–5, Sun. noon–3.*

Lochcarron of Scotland Cashmere and Wool Centre. Love tartans and tweeds? The Lochcarron of Scotland Cashmere and Wool Centre houses a museum where you can tour a mill and learn about the manufacturing process. The shop also sells Scottish jewelry. ⊠ *Waverley Mill, Dinsdale Rd.* ☎ *01750/726000* ⊕ *www.lochcarron.com* ⊠ *Museum free, tour £2.50* ⊙ *Mon.–Sat. 9–5. Guided tours Mon.–Thurs. at 10:30, 11:30, 1:30, and 2:30.*

Philiphaugh Salmon Centre. The site of a famous battle in 1645 in which the Scottish Covenanters drove off the pro-English armies under the Earl of Montrose, the Philiphaugh Salmon Centre is now devoted to more peaceful pursuits. Its salmon-viewing platforms allow you to follow the life cycle of the salmon. There are also country walks and cycling routes to follow, and the Waterwheel Tea Room is open all year. ⊠ *A708* ☎ *01750/21766* ⊕ *www.salmonviewingcentre.com* ⊠ *Free* ⊙ *Daily 10–4.*

WHERE TO EAT AND STAY

$
CAFÉ

✕ **Court Coffee Shop.** This modest, old-fashioned café serves savory soups, tasty scones, and locally made cakes on floral crockery. It sits beside Selkirk's Old Court House. ⑤ *Average main: £8* ⊠ *28 Market St.* ☎ *01750/21766.*

$$
HOTEL

⌂ **Best Western Philipburn House Hotel.** West of Selkirk, this alpine-style hotel enjoys a lovely setting among the woods and hills. **Pros:** pleasant rural setting; bright rooms; on-site parking. **Cons:** no elevator; restaurant closes rather early. ⑤ *Rooms from: £135* ⊠ *Off A708* ☎ *01750/720747* ⊕ *www.bw-philipburnhousehotel.co.uk* ⊷ *12 rooms, 4 lodges* ⦿ *Breakfast.*

HAWICK

10 miles south of Selkirk, 14 miles southwest of Jedburgh.

Hawick (pronounced *hoyk*) is a busy town at the center of the region's textile industry, commemorated in the interesting Borders Textile Towerhouse. The Victorian buildings along its High Street recall the town's heyday. The largest community in the Borders, it's a good place to buy the delicate cashmere and wool goods that made the region famous. Hawick's Common Riding festival, held each June, draws onlookers from all over Scotland.

GETTING HERE AND AROUND

Driving here from Selkirk or Jedburgh is no trouble—it's a straight shot on major roads. There is also bus service from many of the other Borders towns.

ESSENTIALS

Visitor Information Hawick Visitor Centre ⊠ *Kirkstyle* ☎ *01450/373993* ⊕ *www.visitscotland.com.*

EXPLORING

FAMILY

Borders Textile Towerhouse. In the former Drumlanrig Tower, this museum includes a good exhibition about the textile industry, once the lifeblood of the Borders. Plenty of interactive elements make it interesting for children as well. One room commemorates the demonstrations by textile workers who were demanding the right to vote in the 1880s. On the upper floor are up-to-the-minute fabrics that define the 21st century. Check out the shop, too. ⊠ *1 Tower Knowe* ☎ *01450/377615* ⊕ *www.heartofhawick.co.uk* ⊠ *Free* ⊙ *Apr.–Oct., Mon.–Sat.10–4:30, Sun. noon–3; Nov.–Mar., Mon. and Wed.–Sat. 10–4.*

WHERE TO EAT

$ ✕ **Damascus Drum.** This lovely café and bookshop was established as a
CAFÉ place to talk, tell stories, and buy beautiful Oriental rugs. Done up in
Fodor's Choice muted colors, the café is named for a traditional folktale. The menu
★ includes Middle Eastern dishes alongside the burgers. There's a dinner
menu on Friday and Saturday evenings. $ *Average main: £8* ✉ *2 Silver
St.* ☎ *07707/856123* ⊕ *www.damascusdrum.co.uk.*

SHOPPING

Hawick Factory Visitor Centre. This is a good place to see knitwear in the
making—literally. In the shop you can buy knitwear and cashmere
goods for discounted prices. ✉ *Arthur St.* ☎ *01450/371221* ⊕ *www.
hawickcashmere.com.*

White of Hawick. There's a room here exclusively dedicated to cashmere,
and it's a good place to stock up on warm outerwear. White of Hawick
also sells an extensive range of lambswool and knitted garments. ✉ *Victoria Rd.* ☎ *01450/373206* ⊕ *www.whiteofhawick.co.uk* ⊙ *Weekdays
9–5, Sat. 9.30–5.*

4

INNERLEITHEN

17 miles northwest of Hawick.

Innerleithen is one of the larger Borders towns; you'll feel like you've
entered a hub of activity when you arrive. It's also dramatically beautiful. Surrounded by hills and glens, the town is where the Tweed
and Leithen rivers join, then separate. Historically, Innerleithen dates
back to pre-Roman times, and there are artifacts all around for you
to see. Once a booming industrialized town of wool mills, today it's
a great destination for outdoor activities including hiking, biking,
and fly-fishing.

GETTING HERE AND AROUND

To drive to Innerleithen, take the A7 north from Hawick and then the
A707 northwest from Selkirk. There are no trains between the two towns.

EXPLORING

FAMILY **Robert Smail's Printing Works.** Try your hand at printing the way it used
to be done: painstakingly setting each letter by hand. This print shop,
founded more than a century ago to produce materials for nearby factories, boat tickets, theater posters, and the local newspaper, Robert
Small's is still a working printshop as well as a museum. Two great
waterwheels once powered the presses, and they are still running. The
guided tour, which includes making your own bookmark, takes 90
minutes. ✉ *7–9 High St.* ☎ *01896/830206* ⊕ *www.nts.org.uk/Visits*
✉ *£6.50* ⊙ *Apr.–Oct., Thurs.–Mon. noon–5, Sun. 1–5; last admission at 4:15.*

Fodor's Choice **Traquair House.** Said to be the oldest continually occupied home in Scot-
★ land, Traquair House has secret stairways and passages, a library with
more than 3,000 books, and a bed said to be used by Mary, Queen of
Scots in 1566. The 18th-century brew house still makes highly recommended ale. You may even spend the night, if you wish. Outside you'll
find a maze and extensive gardens. Traquair Fair in August is a major

event in the regional calendar. ⊠ *B709* ☎ *01896/830323* ⊕ *www. traquair.co.uk* ✉ *Grounds £4, house and grounds £8* ⊗ *Apr.–Sept., daily noon–5; Oct., daily 11–4; Nov., weekends 11–3; last admission ½ hr before closing.*

WHERE TO STAY

$$$

B&B/INN

⚏ **Traquair House.** Staying in one of the guest rooms in the 12th-century wing of Traquair House is to experience a slice of Scottish history. **Pros:** stunning grounds; spacious rooms; great breakfast. **Cons:** nearly 2 miles to restaurants and shops; rooms fill up quickly in summer. ⑤ *Rooms from: £180* ⊠ *B709* ☎ *01896/830323* ⊕ *www.traquair.co.uk* ⇘ *3 rooms* ⦿ *Breakfast.*

$$

B&B/INN

⚏ **Windlestraw Lodge.** This elegant bed-and-breakfast occupies a grand country home surrounded by extensive gardens. **Pros:** beautifully designed rooms; excellent dining. **Cons:** a bit expensive for what you get. ⑤ *Rooms from: £160* ⊠ *A72, St. Boswells* ☎ *01896/870636* ⊕ *www.windlestraw.co.uk* ⇘ *5 rooms* ⦿ *Breakfast.*

PEEBLES

6 miles west of Innerleithen.

Thanks to its excellent though pricey shopping, Peebles gives the impression of catering primarily to leisured country gentlefolk. Architecturally, the town is nothing out of the ordinary, just a very pleasant burgh. Don't miss the splendid dolphins ornamenting the bridge crossing the River Tweed.

GETTING HERE AND AROUND

Because of its size and location, direct buses run from both Edinburgh and Glasgow to Peebles. There are also buses here from Innerleithen, though driving from here is more direct. (Take the A72; it's about a 10-minute drive.)

ESSENTIALS

Visitor Information **Peebles Visitor Information Centre** ⊠ *23 High St.* ☎ *01721/723159* ⊕ *www.scot-borders.co.uk.*

EXPLORING

Neidpath Castle. A 15-minute walk upstream along the banks of the Tweed, Neidpath Castle perches artistically above a bend in the river. It comes into view as you approach through the tall trees. The castle is a medieval structure remodeled in the 17th century, with dungeons hewn from solid rock. You can return on the opposite riverbank after crossing an old, finely skewed railroad viaduct. Call ahead to arranged visits to the interior. ⊠ *Off A72* ☎ *01875/870201* ⊕ *www.neidpathcastle.com* ✉ *£3* ⊗ *By appointment only.*

Peebles War Memorial. The exotic, almost Moorish mosaics of the Peebles War Memorial are unique in Scotland, although most towns have a memorial to honor those killed in service. It's a remarkable tribute to the 225 Peebleans killed in World War II. ⊠ *Chambers Quadrangle, High St.*

WHERE TO EAT

$
BRITISH

✗ **Adam Room.** With a minstrels' gallery, crystal chandeliers, and tall windows with views over the Tweed, the dining room at the Tontine Hotel has a grand feel. It's a bit surprising, therefore, that it also serves good home cooking at very reasonable prices. Local produce is used for all the dishes, including the appetizing steak pie and the lamb rump. There is also a good wine list. Bring along the kids, as they have their own menu. ⑤ *Average main: £12 ⊠ Tontine Hotel, High St.* ☎ *01721/720892* ⊕ *www.tontinehotel.com.*

$
ECLECTIC

✗ **The Sunflower Restaurant.** This quaint café has something for everyone, serving freshly baked breads and using only local meats, vegetables, and dairy products. The owner puts a lot of love into her cooking, whether it's breakfast, lunch, or dinner. The Thai fish cakes with coriander salad and lemon sauce are full of flavor, as is the Moroccan lamb with couscous. The oatcakes and homemade chutney are a light and unusual way to end your meal. And the vegetarian options are always unusual and delicious. ⑤ *Average main: £14 ⊠ 4 Bridgegate* ☎ *01721/722420* ⊕ *www.sunflowerrestaurant.co.uk* ⊗ *Closed Sun. No dinner Sun.–Wed.*

WHERE TO STAY

$$
HOTEL

🏨 **Cringletie House.** With medieval-style turrets and crow-step gables, this small-scale, peaceful retreat manages to be fancy *and* homey, Victorian (it was built in the 1860s) and modern (flat-screen TVs). **Pros:** elegant bedrooms; cozy fireplaces; decadent dining. **Cons:** some bedrooms have low ceilings; atmosphere can be almost too quiet. ⑤ *Rooms from: £160* ⊠ *Edinburgh Rd., off A703* ☎ *01721/725750* ⊕ *www.cringletie.com* ⮠ *13 rooms* ⊗ *Closed Nov.–Feb.* ⑩ *Breakfast.*

$$$
HOTEL
ALL-INCLUSIVE

🏨 **Peebles Hydro.** One of the great "hydro hotels" built in the 19th century for those anxious to "take the waters," Peebles Hydro has something for everyone, and in abundance: pony rides, a putting green, and a giant chess game are just a few of the diversions. **Pros:** plenty of activities; good children's programs; delicious breakfast. **Cons:** can feel impersonal; some rooms have bland decor. ⑤ *Rooms from: £198* ⊠ *Innerleithen Rd.* ☎ *01721/720602* ⊕ *www.peebleshotelhydro.com* ⮠ *132 rooms* ⑩ *All-inclusive.*

$$
HOTEL

🏨 **Tontine Hotel.** A small and charming facade hides a spacious hotel that stretches back from Peebles High Street. **Pros:** centrally located; pleasant rooms; welcoming staff. **Cons:** some rooms in the rear are quite small; decor in some areas feels old-fashioned. ⑤ *Rooms from: £100* ⊠ *High St.* ☎ *01721/729732* ⊕ *www.tontinehotel.com* ⮠ *36 rooms* ⑩ *Breakfast.*

SHOPPING

Be prepared for temptations at every turn as you browse the shops on High Street and in the courts and side streets leading off it.

Caledonia. For all things Scottish, look no farther than Caledonia, where you'll find everything from kilts to throws, and jams to tablecloths. ⊠ *61 High St.* ☎ *01721/722343.*

Head to Toe. This shop stocks natural beauty products, handmade pine furniture, and handsome linens—from patchwork quilts to silk flowers. ⊠ *43 High St.* ☎ *01721/722752.*

Keith Walter. Among the many jewelers on High Street is Keith Walter, a master of gold and silver who makes his creations on the premises. He also stocks jewelry made by other local designers. ⊠ *28 High St.* ☎ *01721/720650* ⊕ *www.keithwalter28.com.*

DUMFRIES AND GALLOWAY

Galloway covers the southwestern portion of Scotland, west of the main town of Dumfries. Here a gentle coastline gives way to farmland and then breezy uplands that gradually merge with coniferous forests. Use caution when negotiating the A75—you're liable to find aggressive trucks bearing down on you as these commercial vehicles race for the ferries at Stranraer and Cairnryan. Things are far more relaxed once you leave the main highway; take the coastal A710/A711 instead. Dumfries and Galloway offer some of the most pleasant drives in Scotland—though the occasional herd of cows on the way to be milked is a potential hazard.

GRETNA GREEN

10 miles north of Carlisle, 87 miles south of Glasgow, 92 miles southwest of Edinburgh.

The town is best known for its history as a place for speedy weddings.

GETTING HERE AND AROUND

From Glasgow you can reach Gretna Green via the M74 and A74; it's an hour-and-a-half drive. From Edinburgh, take the A74 (about two hours). Buses and trains travel to Gretna Green from Glasgow and Edinburgh daily.

ESSENTIALS

Visitor Information Gretna Green Tourist Information Centre ⊠ *Gretna Gateway Outlet Village, Glasgow Rd.* ☎ *01461/337834* ⊕ *www.visitscotland.com.*

EXPLORING

Gretna Green. Gretna Green is tied to the reputation this community developed as a refuge for runaway couples from England, who once came north to take advantage of Scotland's more lenient marriage laws. This was the first place they reached on crossing the border. At one time anyone could perform a legal marriage in Scotland, and the village blacksmith (known as the "anvil priest") did the honors in Gretna Green. The blacksmith's shop is still standing, and today it contains a collection of blacksmithing tools, including the anvil over which many weddings were conducted. The town is highly commercialized rather than atmospheric, though, with plenty of shops.

RUTHWELL

21 miles west of Gretna Green, 83 miles south of Glasgow, 88 miles southwest of Edinburgh.

North of the upper Solway Firth the countryside is flat, fertile farmland. Progressing west, however, a pleasant landscape of low, round hills begins to take over. But there are historical features among the flatlands that should not be ignored.

GETTING HERE AND AROUND

There is no train station in Ruthwell; however, buses—both local and national—do frequent the town. But the best way to get here is via car. From Glasgow, take the M74 then A74; the trip is just under two hours. From Edinburgh take the A74; your journey will take just over two hours. Gretna Green is just under a half hour away via the A75.

EXPLORING

Fodor'sChoice ★ **Caerlaverock Castle.** The stunningly beautiful moated Caerlaverock Castle stands in splendid isolation amid the surrounding wetlands that form the Caerlaverock Nature Reserve. Built in a unique triangular design, this 13th-century fortress has solid-sandstone masonry and an imposing double-tower gatehouse. King Edward I of England (1239–1307) besieged the castle in 1300, when his forces occupied much of Scotland at the start of the Wars of Independence. A splendid residence was built inside in the 1600s. ⊠ *Off B725, 7 miles from Ruthwell* ☎ *01387/770244* ⊕ *www.historic-scotland.gov.uk/places* ☒ *£5.50* ☉ *Apr.–Sept., daily 9:30–5:30; Oct.–Mar., daily 9:30–4:30.*

Fodor'sChoice ★ **Caerlaverock Wildfowl and Wetlands Centre.** You can observe wintering wildfowl, including various species of geese, ducks, swans, and raptors on the wetlands surrounding atmospheric Carlaverock Castle. In summer, ospreys patrol the waters of this wild and beautiful place, the northernmost outpost of the Wildfowl and Wetlands Trust. Free guided walks are available in the afternoons throughout the year. ⊠ *Eastpark Farm, off B725, Dumfries* ☎ *01387/770200* ☒ *Free* ☉ *Daily 24 hrs.*

Ruthwell Parish Church. Inside Ruthwell Parish Church is the 8th-century Ruthwell Runic Cross, a Christian sculpture admired for the detailed biblical scenes carved onto its north and south faces. The east and west faces have carvings of vines, birds, and animals, plus verses from an Anglo-Saxon poem called "The Dream of the Rood." Considered an idolatrous monument, it was removed and demolished by Church of Scotland zealots in 1642 but was later reassembled. ⊠ *Northern end of Kirklands Loaning.*

SPORTS AND OUTDOORS

Powfoot Golf Club. A pleasant mix of links and parkland holes and views south over the Solway Firth make this lesser-known gem designed by James Braid a pleasure to play. ⊠ *Off B724, Cummertrees, Annan* ☎ *01461/204100* ⊕ *www.powfootgolfclub.com* ☒ *Green fee: weekdays £39; weekends £45* ⚑ *18 holes, 6250 yds, SSS 71* ☉ *Daily.*

DUMFRIES

15 miles northwest of Ruthwell, 76 miles south of Glasgow, 81 miles southwest of Edinburgh.

The River Nith meanders through Dumfries, and the pedestrian-only town center makes wandering and shopping a pleasure. Author J. M. Barrie (1860–1937) spent his childhood in Dumfries, and the garden of Moat Brae House is said to have inspired his boyish dreams in *Peter Pan*. But the town also has a justified claim to Robert Burns, who lived and worked here for several years. His house and his favorite *howff* (pub), The Globe Inn, are here too, as is his final resting place in St Michael's Churchyard.

The Dumfries & Galloway Tourist Board has a lodging service, and also sells golf passes for the region at £60 for three rounds.

GETTING HERE AND AROUND

Public transportation is a good option for reaching Dumfries—there's a good train station here, and most major Scottish cities have regular daily bus routes to the town. If you're driving from Ruthwell, take the B724. From Glasgow, take the M74 to the A701. From Edinburgh, take the A701.

ESSENTIALS

Visitor Information Dumfries & Galloway Tourist Board ⊠ *64 Whitesands* ☎ *01387/245550* ⊕ *www.visitdumfriesandgalloway.co.uk.*

EXPLORING

TOP ATTRACTIONS

Burns House. Poet Robert Burns lived here, on what was then called Mill Street, for the last three years of his life, when his salary from the customs service allowed him to improve his living standards. Many distinguished writers of the day visited him here, including William Wordsworth. The house contains some of his writings and letters, a few pieces of furniture, and some family memorabilia. ⊠ *Burns St.* ☎ *01387/255297* ⊕ *www.dumgal.gov.uk/museums* ⊡ *Free* ⊙ *Apr.–Sept., Mon.–Sat. 10–5, Sun. 2–5; Oct.–Mar., Tues.–Sat. 10–1 and 2–5.*

OFF THE BEATEN PATH

Drumlanrig Castle. This spectacular estate is as close as Scotland gets to the treasure houses of England—which is not surprising, since it's owned by the dukes of Buccleuch, one of the wealthiest British peerages. Resplendent with romantic turrets, this pink-sandstone palace was constructed between 1679 and 1691 by the first Duke of Queensbury, who, after nearly bankrupting himself building the place, stayed one night and never returned. The Buccleuchs inherited the palace and soon filled the richly decorated rooms with a valuable collection of paintings by Holbein, Rembrandt, and Murillo. Because of the theft of a Leonardo da Vinci painting in 2003, all visits are conducted by guided tour. There's also a playground, a gift shop, and a tearoom. ⊠ *Off A76, 18 miles northwest of Dumfries, Thornhill* ☎ *01848/600283* ⊕ *www.drumlanrig.com* ⊡ *Park £6, castle and park £10* ⊙ *Grounds Apr.–Sept., daily 10–5. Castle Mar.–Aug., daily 11–4.*

Museum of Lead Mining. The Lochnell Mine was abandoned in 1861, after 150 years of operation. The isolated village of Warnlockhead, where it was located, has not changed a great deal since then—there was little alternative employment for the miners and their families. Their homes now form part of this museum re-creating their lives. The visitor center, housed in the old smithy, exhibits some of the minerals the mine yielded. ⊠ *Off B797, Warnlockhead* ☎ *01659/74387* ⊕ *www. leadminingmuseum.co.uk* 🎫 *£7.75* ⊙ *Apr.–Sept., daily 11–4:30.*

Robert Burns Centre. Not surprisingly, Dumfries has its own Robert Burns Centre, housed in a sturdy former mill overlooking the river. The center has an audiovisual program and an extensive exhibit on the life of the poet. There's a restaurant upstairs. ⊠ *Mill Rd.* ☎ *01387/264808* 🎫 *Free* ⊙ *Apr.–Sept., Mon.–Sat. 10–5, Sun. 2–5; Oct.–Mar., Tues.–Sat. 10–1 and 2–5.*

St. Michael's Churchyard. When he died in 1796, poet Robert Burns was buried in a modest grave in St. Michael's Churchyard. English poet William Wordsworth, visiting a few years later, was horrified by the small gravestone and raised money to build this much grander monument. ⊠ *39 Cardiness St.* ☎ *01387/253849.*

Sweetheart Abbey. At the center of the village of New Abbey is the red-tinted and roofless Sweetheart Abbey. The odd name is a translation of the abbey's previous name, St. Mary of the Dolce Coeur. The abbey was founded in 1273 by the Lady of Galloway, Devorgilla (1210–90), who, it is said, had her late husband's heart placed in a tiny casket that she carried everywhere. After she died, she was laid to rest in Sweetheart Abbey with the casket resting on her breast. The couple's son John (1249–1315) was the puppet king installed in Scotland by Edward of England when the latter claimed sovereignty over Scotland. After John's appointment the Scots gave him a scathing nickname that would stay with him for the rest of his life: Toom Tabard (Empty Shirt). ⊠ *A710, 7 miles south of Dumfries, New Abbey* ☎ *01387/253849* ⊕ *www.historic-scotland.com* 🎫 *£4.50* ⊙ *Apr.–Sept., daily 9:30–5:30; Oct., daily 9:30–4:30; Nov.–Mar., Mon.–Wed. and weekends 9:30–4:30.*

WORTH NOTING

Dumfries Museum and Camera Obscura. A camera obscura is essentially a huge reflecting mirror that projects an extraordinarily clear panoramic view of the surrounding countryside onto an internal wall. The one at the Dumfries Museum is housed in the old Windmill Tower, built in 1836. The museum itself covers the culture and daily life of the people living in the Dumfries and Galloway region from the earliest times. ⊠ *Rotchell Rd.* ☎ *01387/253374* 🎫 *£2.30* ⊙ *Apr.–Sept., Mon.–Sat. 10–5; Oct.–Mar., Tues.–Sat. 10–1 and 2–5.*

Globe Inn. Poet Robert Burns spent quite a lot of time at the Globe Inn, where he frequently fell asleep in the tack room beside the stables. He later graduated to the upstairs bedroom where he slept with his wife, Jean Armour, and scratched some lines of poetry on the window. The room is preserved (or at least partly re-created) and the bar staff will happily show you around if you ask. ⊠ *56 High St.* ☎ *01387/252335* ⊕ *www.globeinndumfries.co.uk.*

John Paul Jones Museum. The little community of Kirkbean—blink and you'll miss it—is the backdrop for Arbigland Estate. It was in a cottage, now the John Paul Jones Museum, in this bright green landscape that John Paul (1747–92), the son of an estate gardener, was born. He eventually left Scotland, added "Jones" to his name, and became the founder of the U.S. Navy. The cottage where he was born is furnished as it would have been when he was a boy. There is an informative video, which you watch in a reconstruction of his captain's cabin. Jones returned to raid the coastline of his native country in 1778, an exploit recounted in an adjoining visitor center. ⊠ *Off A710, 12 miles south of Dumfries, Kirkbean* ☎ *01387/880613* ⊠ *£3.50* ☉ *Apr.–June and Sept., Tues.–Sun. 10–5; July and Aug., daily 10–5.*

WHERE TO EAT AND STAY

$ ✗ **Cavens Arms.** This lively, welcoming, traditional pub has a separate
BRITISH bar and dining area, comfortable seating, and a large selection of beers. The restaurant seems to always be busy, a testimony to the quality of its food (as well as the large portions). As for favorite dishes, grilled pork loin with fruity red cabbage vies with panfried sea bass with couscous. The excellent desserts are made on the premises. ⑤ *Average main: £11* ⊠ *20 Buccleuch St.* ☎ *01387/252896* ⚹ *Reservations not accepted.*

$$ ✗ **Hullabaloo.** Occupying the top floor of the Robert Burns Centre, this
BRITISH restaurant serves a substantial and varied lunch and dinner menu. The lunch menu is imaginative and very tasty, especially the melts. The dinner menu is ambitious and equally varied, ranging from pistachio-crusted chicken to rack of lamb stuffed with anchovies to grilled sea bass in a ginger and coconut sauce. Try to snag a window table overlooking the River Nith. ⑤ *Average main: £16* ⊠ *Robert Burns Centre, Mill Rd.* ☎ *01387/259679* ⊕ *www.hullabaloorestaurant.co.uk* ⚹ *Reservations essential* ☉ *No dinner Sun. and Mon.*

$$ ⛨ **Aston Hotel.** With the secluded feel of a grand country hotel, the Aston
HOTEL Hotel is less than 2 miles from the center of Dumfries. **Pros:** beautiful setting; easy access to Dumfries; rooms for people with disabilities. **Cons:** slightly institutional feel. ⑤ *Rooms from: £119* ⊠ *Bankend Rd., Crichton* ☎ *01387/272410* ⊕ *www.astonhotels.co.uk/dumfries* ⤳ *71 rooms* ⦿⦿ *Breakfast.*

$ ⛨ **Ferintosh Guest House.** Directly across from the train station, this hand-
B&B/INN some sandstone guesthouse sits on a leafy street in a quiet part of town. **Pros:** dog friendly; great robes; helpful owners. **Cons:** no children under 10; some shared bathrooms. ⑤ *Rooms from: £60* ⊠ *30 Lovers Walk* ☎ *01387/252262* ⊕ *www.ferintosh.net* ⤳ *6 rooms* ⦿⦿ *Breakfast.*

THE ARTS

Dumfries & Galloway Arts Festival. This festival, celebrated every year since 1979, is usually held at the end of May at several venues throughout the region. ☎ *01387/260447* ⊕ *www.dgartsfestival.org.uk.*

Gracefield Arts Centre. With galleries hosting constantly changing exhibits, Gracefield Arts Centre also has a well-stocked crafts shop. A café serves lunch and snacks. ⊠ *28 Edinburgh Rd.* ☎ *01387/262084* ☉ *Tues.–Sat. 10–5.*

SPORTS AND OUTDOORS

G&G Cycle Centre. Bicycles can be rented from G&G Cycle Centre. The staff gives good advice on where to ride. ⊠ *10–12 Academy St.* ☎ *01387/259483* ⊕ *www.cycle-centre.com* ⊗ *Mon.–Sat. 9–5.*

7stanes Mountain Biking. This outdoors shop rents everything from road and mountain bikes to the full-suspension models favored by the more committed mountain bikers. It is one of seven in the area; each gives advice and provide route maps, as well as facilities for weary and hungry cyclists returning from the routes of varying difficulty. ⊠ *Campbell House, Bankhead Rd.* ☎ *01387/702228* ⊕ *www.7stanesmountainbiking.com.*

SHOPPING

Dumfries is the main shopping center for the region, with all the big-name chain stores as well as specialty shops.

Greyfriars Crafts. This shop sells mainly Scottish goods, including glass, ceramics, and jewelry. ⊠ *56 Buccleuch St.* ☎ *01387/264050.*

Fodor's Choice ★ **Loch Arthur Creamery and Farm Shop.** This lively and active farm in the charmingly named village of Beeswing has organic foods of the highest quality, particularly the award-winning dairy products. If you can't wait to eat your purchases, there's a little café. ⊠ *A711, 6 miles from Dumfries, Beeswing* ☎ *01387/760296* ⊕ *www.locharthur.org.uk.*

DALBEATTIE

14 miles southwest of Dumfries, 89 miles south of Glasgow, 95 miles southwest of Edinburgh.

Like the much larger Aberdeen far to the northeast, Dalbeattie contains buildings constructed with local gray granite from the town's quarry. The well-scrubbed gray glitter makes Dalbeattie atypical of Galloway towns, where houses are usually painted in pastels.

GETTING HERE AND AROUND

There are no direct bus routes from Dumfries to Dalbeattie; your best mode of transport is car. From Dumfries, take the A711 (about 25 minutes). From Glasgow, take the M74, A74, then A701 (about two hours). From Edinburgh, take the A701 and A702 (about 2¼ hours).

WHERE TO STAY

$ B&B/INN **Anchor Hotel.** This small, friendly hotel in the picturesque village of Kippford has wonderful views across the Solway Firth. **Pros:** lovely location; friendly atmosphere; good pub food. **Cons:** small rooms; bar can be noisy at times. ⑤ *Rooms from: £70* ⊠ *Main St., Kippford* ☎ *01556/620205* ⇶ *6 rooms* ⑩ *Breakfast.*

$ B&B/INN **Kerr Cottage.** This 165-year-old house is holding up quite well, thank you very much—the fresh and spacious guest rooms have contemporary wood furniture, comfy beds, and large tiled bathrooms. **Pros:** close to biking and hiking trails; great storage space for outdoor gear; very reasonable price. **Cons:** no pets allowed; no children under 12. ⑤ *Rooms from: £60* ⊠ *Port Rd.* ☎ *01556/612245* ⊕ *www.kerrcottage.co.uk* ⇶ *3 rooms* ⊗ *Open all yr* ⑩ *Breakfast.*

SPORTS AND THE OUTDOORS

Barend Riding School and Trekking Centre. At this riding school you'll be helped to a "horse-high" view of the beautiful coast and countryside. ⊠ *A710, 6 miles southeast of Dalbeattie, Sandyhills* ☎ *01387/780533.*

Southerness Golf Club. Mackenzie Ross designed this course, the first built in Scotland just after World War II. Southerness is a long course, played over extensive links with fine views southward over the Solway Firth. The greens are hard and fast, and the frequent winds make for some testing golf. ■ **TIP→ Thursday is reserved for women.** ⊠ *Southerness St., Southerness, Kirkbean* ☎ *01387/880677* ⊕ *www.southernessgolfclub. com* ✉ *Green fee: weekdays £50; weekends £60* ⚑ *Reservations essential* ⛳ *18 holes, 6566 yds, par 69* ⊙ *Daily.*

CASTLE DOUGLAS

6 miles west of Dalbeattie, 84 miles south of Glasgow, 90 miles southwest of Edinburgh.

A quaint town that sits beside Carlingwark Loch, Castle Douglas is a popular base for exploring the surrounding countryside. The loch sets off the city perfectly, reflecting its dramatic architecture of sharp spires and soft sandstone arches. Its main thoroughfare, King Street, has unique shops and eateries.

GETTING HERE AND AROUND

There's no train station in Castle Douglas, and buses from Dumfries make several stops along the way. The best way to get to Castle Douglas is by car. From Dalbeattie, take the A711/A745 (10 minutes). From Glasgow, take the A713 (just under two hours). From Edinburgh, take the A70 (2⅓ hours).

ESSENTIALS

Visitor Information Castle Douglas ⊠ *Market Hill* ☎ *01556/502611* ⊕ *www.visitdumfriesandgalloway.co.uk.*

EXPLORING

Threave Castle. This castle was an early home of the Black Douglases, who were the earls of Nithsdale and lords of Galloway. Not to be confused with the mansion in Threave Gardens, the castle was dismantled in the religious wars of the mid-17th century, though enough of it remains to have housed prisoners from the Napoleonic Wars of the 19th century. It's a few minutes from Castle Douglas by car and is signposted from the main road. To get here, leave your car in a farmyard and make your way down to the edge of the river. Ring a bell, and, rather romantically, a boatman will come to ferry you across to the great stone tower looming from a marshy island in the river. ⊠ *A75, 3 miles west of Castle Douglas* ☎ *07711/223101* ⊕ *www.historic-scotland.gov.uk* ✉ *£4.50, includes ferry* ⊙ *Apr.–Sept., daily 9:30–4:30.*

Threave Gardens. The National Trust for Scotland cares for the gently sloping parkland around the 1867 mansion built by William Gordon, a Liverpool businessman. The house, fully restored in the 1930s, gives a glimpse into the daily life of a prosperous family in the 19th century. The foliage demands the employment of many gardeners—and it's here that the gardeners train, thus ensuring there's always some fresh development or experimental planting. Entry to the house is by timed guided tour, and it's wise to book ahead. There's an on-site restaurant. ⊠ *South of A75, 1 mile west of Castle Douglas* ☎ *0844/493–2245* ⊕ *www.nts. org.uk/Visits* ⊠ *Gardens £7, house and gardens £12* ⊘ *House Apr.– Oct., Wed.–Fri. and Sun. 11–3:30. Visitor center Feb., Mar., Nov., and Dec., Fri.–Sun. 10–5; Apr.–Oct., daily 10–5.*

WHERE TO EAT

$ ✕ **The Café at Designs Gallery.** For a good balance of art and food, look
CAFÉ no further. You'll find the freshest ingredients here, from soup to salads, sandwiches to quiches. Everything is made on-site, including the bread, and it's all organic. The soup of the day is always a good choice, as are the seasonal fruit pies. The café is downstairs, beneath the shop and gallery, and is full of light and wooden tables and chairs. You can also choose to sit in the well-kept garden or conservatory when weather permits. ⑤ *Average main: £7* ⊠ *179 King St.* ☎ *01556/504552* ⊕ *www. designsgallery.co.uk* ⊘ *No dinner. Closed Sun.*

SPORTS AND THE OUTDOORS

BICYCLING **Castle Douglas Cycle Centre.** You can rent bicycles for everyone in the family from Castle Douglas Cycle Centre. It also handles repairs and service. ⊠ *Church St.* ☎ *01556/504542* ⊕ *www.cdbikes.co.uk* ⊘ *Mon.–Sat. 9–5.*

BOATING **Galloway Activity Centre.** With dinghies, kayaks, and canoes for rent, the Galloway Activity Centre specializes in water sports. "Dry" sports include mountain biking, archery, and rock climbing. It's about 10 miles northwest of Castle Douglas. ⊠ *Off A713, Parton* ☎ *01644/420626* ⊕ *www.lochken.co.uk.*

SHOPPING

Galloway Gems. This glittery shop sells mineral specimens, polished stone slices, and a range of Celtic- and Nordic-inspired jewelry. ⊠ *130– 132 King St.* ☎ *01556/503254.*

KIRKCUDBRIGHT

9 miles southwest of Castle Douglas, 89 miles south of Glasgow, 99 miles southwest of Edinburgh.

Kirkcudbright (pronounced kir-*coo*-bray) is an 18th-century town of Georgian and Victorian houses, some of them washed in pastel shades and roofed with the blue slate of the district. In the early 20th century it became a haven for artists, and its L-shape main street is full of crafts and antiques shops.

GETTING HERE AND AROUND

Driving is your best and only real option. From Castle Douglas, take the A711 (15 minutes). From Glasgow, take the A713 (about two hours). From Edinburgh, take the A701 (about 2½ hours).

ESSENTIALS

Visitor Information Kirkcudbright Tourist Information Centre ⊠ *Harbour Sq.* ☎ *01557/330494* ⊕ *www.visitdumfriesandgalloway.co.uk.*

EXPLORING

Broughton House. The 18th-century Broughton House was once the home of the artist E. A. Hornel, one of the "Glasgow Boys" of the late 19th century. Many of his paintings hang in the house, which is furnished in period style and contains an extensive library specializing in local history. There's also a Japanese garden. ⊠ *12 High St.* ☎ *0844/493–2246* ⊕ *www.nts.org. uk* ⊠ *£6.50* ⊘ *House and Garden: Apr.–Oct., daily noon–5. Garden Feb. and Mar., weekdays 11–4.*

MacLellan's Castle. Conspicuous in the center of town are the stone walls of MacLellan's Castle, a once-elaborate castellated mansion dating from the 16th century. You can walk around the interior, although the rooms are bare. The "Lairds Lug," behind the fireplace, allowed the *laird* (lord) to listen in to what his guests were saying about him. You can also get a glimpse of life below stairs in the Vaults. There are lovely views over the town from the windows. ⊠ *Off High St.* ☎ *01557/331856* ⊕ *www.historic-scotland.gov.uk* ⊠ *£4.50* ⊘ *Apr.–Sept., daily 9:30–5:30.*

Stewartry Museum. Stuffed with all manner of local paraphernalia, the delightfully old-fashioned Stewartry Museum allows you to putter and absorb as much or as little as takes your interest in the display cases. Stewartry is the former name of Kirkcudbright. ⊠ *St Mary St.* ☎ *01557/331643* ⊠ *Free* ⊘ *Mon.–Sat. 11–4.*

Tolbooth Arts Centre. In the 17th-century tollbooth (a combination town hall–courthouse–prison), the Tolbooth Arts Centre tells about the town's most famous artists, including E. A. Hornel, Jessie King, and Charles Oppenheimer. Some of their paintings are on display, as are works by modern artists. ⊠ *High St.* ☎ *01557/331556* ⊕ *www. kirkcudbright.co.uk* ⊠ *Free* ⊘ *Oct.–May, Mon.–Sat. 11–4; June–Sept., Mon.–Sat. 11–4, Sun. 2–5.*

WHERE TO EAT AND STAY

$$
MODERN BRITISH
✕ **Artistas.** Paintings of Scotland, starched white tablecloths, and giant windows overlooking the well-kept garden beckon you into this highly praised eatery. Locals love that the food is locally sourced and full of imagination. In season, try the globe artichoke and asparagus salad, then the braised fillet of turbot over saffron-and-shrimp quinoa. The "posh" fish-and-chips is one of the best around. Miss Lilly's Ecclefechan Butter Tart makes a great dessert. For a less expensive, more casual dining experience try the hotel's bistro, where the à la carte menu is just as imaginative and delicious. $ *Average main: £17* ⊠ *Best Western Selkirk Arms, High St.* ☎ *01557/330402* ⚲ *Reservations essential.*

$$ ⚀ **Best Western Selkirk Arms.** Bursting with charm, this elegant 18th-
HOTEL   century hotel has a lot going for it—spacious rooms are individually decorated with cozy beds, contemporary wood furniture, and soft lighting. **Pros:** attentive service; massive breakfast; lively traditional pub. **Cons:** rooms closest to restaurant can be noisy; bar gets crowded during sporting events. $ *Rooms from: £110* ⊠ *High St.* ☎ *01557/ 330402* ⊕ *www.selkirkarmshotel.co.uk* ⇥ *17 rooms* ⦾ *Breakfast.*

NEWTON STEWART

18 miles northwest of Kirkcudbright, 77 miles southwest of Glasgow, 105 miles southwest of Edinburgh.

The bustling town of Newton Stewart is a good place to stop when touring the western region of Galloway.

GETTING HERE AND AROUND

Newton Stewart does not have a train station, but the town is served by regular buses from Glasgow and Edinburgh as well as local buses from neighboring towns. From Glasgow, take the A77 (about two hours). From Edinburgh, take the A702 (about 2¾ hours).

ESSENTIALS

Visitor Information Newton Stewart Visitor Information Centre ⊠ *Dashwood Sq.* ☎ *01671/402431* ⊕ *www.newtonstewart.org.*

EXPLORING

Creetown Gem Rock Museum. In the nearby village of Creetown, the Creetown Gem Rock Museum has an eclectic mineral collection, a dinosaur egg, an erupting volcano, and a crystal cave. There's also an Internet café, a tearoom, and a shop selling stones and crystals—both loose and in settings. ⊠ *Chain Rd., off A75, Creetown* ☎ *01671/820357* ⊕ *www. gemrock.net* ⊡ *£4* ⊗ *Easter–Sept., daily 9:30–5:30; Sept.–Easter, daily 10–4; last admission ½ hr before closing.*

Galloway Forest Park. You can walk or bicycle along the paths at the Galloway Forest Park. At the Clatteringshaws Visitor Centre there are exhibits about the region's wildlife and a reconstruction of an Iron Age dwelling. There are also other visitor centers at Kirroughtree and Glentrool. ⊠ *A712, 7 miles northeast of Newton Stewart* ☎ *01671/402420* ⊕ *www.forestry.gov.uk/gallowayforestpark* ⊡ *Free* ⊗ *Daily.*

Machars. The Machars is the name given to the triangular promontory south of Newton Stewart. This is an area of pretty rolling farmlands, yellow-gorse hedgerows, rich grazing for dairy cattle, and stony prehistoric sites. Fields are bordered by dry *stane dykes* (walls) of sharp-edge stones, and small hills and hummocks give the area its characteristic frozen-wave look, a reminder of the glacial activity that shaped the landscape.

Wood of Cree Nature Reserve. Birders love the Wood of Cree Nature Reserve, managed by the Royal Society for the Protection of Birds. In the reserve you can see such species as the redstart, pied flycatcher, and wood warbler. To get there, take the minor road that travels north from Newton Stewart alongside the River Cree east of the A714. The entrance is next to a small parking area at the side of the road. ⊠ *Off A714, 4 miles north of Newton Stewart* ☎ *01556/670464* ⊕ *www. rspb.org.uk* ✉ *Donations accepted* ⊘ *Daily 24 hrs.*

GLEN TROOL

9 miles north of Newton Stewart, 86 miles southwest of Glasgow, 113 miles southwest of Edinburgh.

The dramatic scenery here has a Highlands feel.

GETTING HERE AND AROUND
Driving is really the only way to get to Glen Trool. From Newton Stewart, take the A714 (about 15 minutes). From Glasgow, take the A77 (about 2¼ hours). From Edinburgh, take the A702 (about three hours).

EXPLORING
Glen Trool. Part of Galloway's Forest Park, Glen Trool is one of Scotland's best-kept secrets. With high purple-and-green hilltops shorn rockbare by glaciers, and with a dark, winding loch and thickets of birch trees sounding with birdcalls, the setting almost looks more highland than the real Highlands. Note **Bruce's Stone,** just above the parking lot, marking the site where in 1307 Scotland's champion Robert the Bruce (King Robert I, 1274–1329) won his first victory in the Scottish Wars of Independence. To get here, follow the A714 north and turn right at the signpost for Glen Trool. A little road leads through increasingly wild woodland scenery to a parking lot. Only after you have climbed for a few minutes onto a heathery knoll does the full, rugged panorama become apparent. ⊠ *Off A714, Bargrennan* ☎ *01671/840302* ⊕ *www. forestry.gov.uk* ✉ *Free* ⊘ *Visitor center Mar.–June and Sept.–Nov., daily 10:30–4:30; July and Aug., daily 10:30–5:30.*

WIGTOWN

7 miles south of Newton Stewart, 84 miles southwest of Glasgow, 111 miles southwest of Edinburgh.

More than 20 bookshops, mostly antiquarian and secondhand stores, have sprung up on the brightly painted main street of Wigtown, voted Scotland's national book town. The 10-day Wigtown Book Festival is held in late September and early October.

GETTING HERE AND AROUND
There is no train station in Wigtown, and you must make several transfers when traveling by bus to and from Scotland's larger cities. Driving is your best option. Take the A714 from Newton Stewart (15 minutes). From Glasgow, take the A77 (about two hours). From Edinburgh, take the A702 (about three hours).

EXPLORING
Bladnoch Distillery. On the banks of the River Bladnoch, this is Scotland's southernmost malt-whisky producer and one of just six remaining Lowlands distilleries. It has been closed for much of the last 50 years, but was revived by enthusiasts in 2000. It now takes pride in being a small, locally run distillery. Tours are given on the hour between 10

and 4. There's also a visitor center and a gift shop. ⊠ *Bladnoch* ☏ *01988/402605* ⊕ *www.bladnoch. co.uk* ⊡ *£4* ⊙ *July and Aug., weekdays 9–5, Sat. 11–5, Sun. noon–5; Sept.–June, weekdays 9–5.*

Fodor's Choice **Wigtown Book Festival.** The 10-day ★ Wigtown Book Festival, held in late September and early October, has readings, performances, and other events around town. ☏ *01988/402036* ⊕ *www. wigtown-booktown.co.uk.*

SHOPPING

Bookshop. One of the country's largest secondhand bookstores, the Bookshop offers temptingly full shelves. The narrow entrance, flanked by two tottering towers of books, belies the huge stock within, both upstairs and through to the rear of the shop. ⊠ *17 N. Main St.* ☏ *01988/402499.*

> ### HIKING THE SOLWAY FIRTH
>
> Mostly undiscovered by travelers, the Solway Firth is a must for walkers, cyclists, bird-watchers, and stone-circle seekers. This lovely and protected inlet is a haven for a great variety of seabirds, which you can spot from the coastal paths that link Sandyhills, Rockcliffe, and Kippford. To get here, take the A710 from Dumfries, continuing on to the A711. Park where you choose and take the coastal path from any of the three villages.

WHITHORN

11 miles south of Wigtown, 94 miles southwest of Glasgow, 121 miles southwest of Edinburgh.

Known for its early Christian settlement, Whithorn is full of history. The main street is notably wide, with cute pastel buildings nestled up against each other, their low doorways and small windows creating images of years long past. It's still mainly a farming community, but is fast becoming a popular tourist destination. Several scenes from the original *Wicker Man* were shot in and around the area. During the summer months, it's a popular place for festivals. The Isle of Whithorn, just beyond the town, is not an island at all but a fishing village of great charm.

GETTING HERE AND AROUND

There's no train station in Whithorn, and most of the buses are local (getting to main Scottish cities from Whithorn takes careful planning and several transfers). To drive from Wigtown, take the A746 (about 20 minutes). From Glasgow, take the A77 (about 2½ hours). From Edinburgh, take the A702 (about three hours).

EXPLORING

St. Ninian's Chapel. The Isle of Whithorn (a small fishing village, not an island) holds the ruins of St. Ninian's Chapel, where pilgrims who came by sea prayed before traveling inland to Whithorn Priory. Some people claim that this, and not Whithorn Priory, is the site of the Candida Casa. This 14th-century structure seems to have been built on top of a much older chapel. ⊠ *Isle of Whithorn.*

Whithorn Priory. The road that is now the A746 was a pilgrims' path that led to the royal burgh of Whithorn, where sat Whithorn Priory, one of Scotland's great medieval cathedrals, now an empty shell. It was built in the 12th century and is said to occupy the site of a former stone church, the Candida Casa, built by St. Ninian in the 4th century. As the story goes, the church housed a shrine to Ninian, the earliest of Scotland's saints, and kings and barons sought to visit the shrine at least once in their lives. As you approach the priory, observe the royal arms of pre-1707 Scotland—that is, Scotland before the Union with England—carved and painted above the *pend* (covered walkway). ⊠ *Off A746* ⊕ *www. whithornpriorymuseum.gov.uk* ✉ *£4.50* ⊙ *Apr.–Oct., daily 10:30–5.*

Whithorn Story and Visitor Centre. The Whithorn Story and Visitor Centre explains the significance of what is claimed to be the site of the earliest Christian community in Scotland. A museum has a collection of early Christian crosses. ⊠ *45–47 George St.* ☎ *01988/500508* ⊕ *www. whithorn.com* ✉ *£4.50* ⊙ *Apr.–Oct., daily 10:30–5; last tour at 4.*

WHERE TO EAT

$ ✕ **Steam Packet Inn.** This lovely, old-fashioned inn is always full, mainly
BRITISH because of its hearty, well-cooked food and good beer. Patrons also love the location, on the harbor of this quaint fishing village. You can walk the headland behind the pub to the rocky shore of the Solway Firth. Fish-and-chips and lamb shanks can be followed by some excellent house-made desserts. When weather permits you can eat at tables in the garden. If you like it so much you want to stay, there are also a couple of rooms. $ *Average main: £13* ⊠ *Harbour Row, Isle of Whithorn* ☎ *01988/500334* ⊕ *www.steampacketinn.co.uk.*

STRANRAER

31 miles northwest of Whithorn, 86 miles southwest of Glasgow via A77, 131 miles southwest of Edinburgh.

Stranraer has a lovely garden and is also the main ferry port to Northern Ireland—if you make a purchase in one of its shops, you may wind up with some euro coins from Ireland in your change.

GETTING HERE AND AROUND

Stranraer has a busy train station that serves all major lines, and the buses are good as well (with many connections to smaller towns). If you're driving, take the A747 from Whithorn (about 45 minutes). From Glasgow, take the M77/A77 (two hours), and from Edinburgh, take the A77 (three hours).

ESSENTIALS

Visitor Information Stranraer Visitor Information Centre ⊠ *28 Harbour St.* ☎ *01776/702595* ⊕ *www.dumfriesandgalloway.co.uk.*

EXPLORING

Fodor's Choice **Castle Kennedy Gardens.** The lovely Castle Kennedy Gardens surround
★ the shell of the original Castle Kennedy, which was burned in 1716. Parks scattered around the property were built by the second Earl of Stair in 1733. The earl was a field marshal and used his soldiers to help with the heavy work of constructing banks, ponds, and other major

landscape features. When the rhododendrons are in bloom, the effect is kaleidoscopic. There's also a pleasant tearoom. ✉ *North of A75, 3 miles east of Stranraer* ☎ *01776/702024* ⊕ *www.castlekennedygardens. co.uk* ✍ *£5* ⊙ *Easter–Oct., daily 10–5.*

PORTPATRICK

8 miles southwest of Stranraer, 94 miles southwest of Glasgow, 139 miles southwest of Edinburgh.

The holiday town of Portpatrick lies across the Rhinns of Galloway from Stranraer. Once an Irish ferry port, Portpatrick's harbor eventually proved too small for larger vessels.

GETTING HERE AND AROUND

Direct buses travel between Portpatrick to Stranraer and some of the neighboring towns, but travel to and from the larger Scottish cities can prove more difficult. There is no train station in Portpatrick (though there is one in nearby Stranraer). Driving is probably your best bet. From Stranraer, take the A77; it's about a 15-minute journey. Take the M77/A77 from Glasgow (just over two hours) and the M8/A77 from Edinburgh (about three hours).

EXPLORING

Dunskey Castle. Just south of Portpatrick are the lichen-yellow ruins of 16th-century Dunskey Castle, accessible from a cliff-top path off the B7042.

Logan Botanic Gardens. The spectacular Logan Botanic Gardens, one of the National Botanic Gardens of Scotland, are a must-see for garden lovers. Displayed here are plants that enjoy the prevailing mild climate, especially tree ferns, cabbage palms, and other Southern Hemisphere exotica. There are free guided walks every second Tuesday of the month at 10:30 am; at other times there is a free audio guide. ✉ *Off B7065, Port Logan* ☎ *01776/860231* ✍ *£5.50* ⊙ *Feb., Sun. 10–5; Mar.–Oct., daily 10–5.*

Mull of Galloway. If you wish to visit the southern tip of the Rhinns of Galloway, called the Mull of Galloway, follow the B7065/B7041 until you run out of land. The cliffs and seascapes here are rugged, and there's a lighthouse and a bird reserve.

Southern Upland Way. The village of Portpatrick is the starting point for Scotland's longest official long-distance footpath, the Southern Upland Way, which runs a switchback course for 212 miles to Cockburnspath, on the east side of the Borders. The path begins on the cliffs just north of the town and follows the coastline for 1½ miles before turning inland. ⊕ *www.southernuplandway.gov.uk/cms/.*

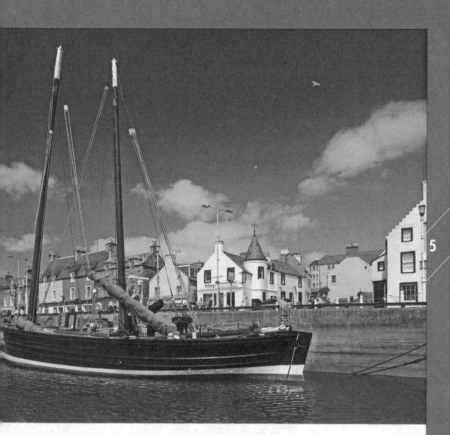

FIFE AND
ANGUS

Updated by
Shona Main

Breezy cliff-top walkways, fishing villages, and open beaches characterize Fife and Angus. They sandwich Scotland's fourth-largest—and often overlooked—city, Dundee. Scotland's east coast has only light rainfall throughout the year; northeastern Fife, in particular, may claim the record for the most sunshine and the least rainfall in Scotland, which all adds to the enjoyment when you're touring the coast or the famous golf center of St. Andrews.

Fife proudly styles itself as a "kingdom," and its long history—which really began when the Romans went home in the 4th century and the Picts moved in—lends some substance to the boast. From medieval times its earls were first among Scotland's nobility and crowned her kings. For many, however, the most historic event in the region was the birth of golf, in the 15th century, which, legend has it, occurred in St. Andrews, an ancient university town with stone houses and seaside ruins. The Royal & Ancient Golf Club, the ruling body of the game worldwide, still has its headquarters here.

Not surprisingly, fishing and seafaring have also played a role in the history of the East Neuk coastal region. From the 16th through 19th centuries a large population lived and worked in the small ports and harbors that form a chain around Fife's coast, which James V once called "a beggar's mantle fringed with gold." When the sun shines, this golden fringe—particularly at Tentsmuir, St. Andrews, and Elie—gleams like the beaches of Normandy. Indeed, the houses of the East Neuk villages have a similar character, with color-washed fronts, fishy weather vanes, outdoor stone stairways to upper floors, and crude carvings of anchors and lobsters on their lintels. All the houses are crowded on steep *wynds* (narrow streets), hugging pint-size harbors that in the golden era supported village fleets of 100 ships apiece.

North, across the Firth of Tay, lies the region of Angus, whose charm is its variety: in addition to its seacoast and pleasant Lowland market centers, there's also a hinterland of lonely rounded hills with long glens running into the typical Grampian Highland scenery beyond. One of Angus's interesting features, which it shares with the eastern Lowland edge of Perthshire, is its fruit-growing industry, which includes raspberries. The chief fruit-growing area is Strathmore, the broad vale between the northwesterly Grampian Mountains and the small coastal hills of the Sidlaws behind Dundee.

Known as the "City of Discovery" (after the RRS *Discovery,* a polar exploration vessel that set sail from this port in 1901), Dundee has a surprisingly sophisticated arts and cultural scene. With work beginning on the ship-shape Victoria and Albert Museum, the city clearly has its mind on the future. Dundee makes a good base from which to make a number of day trips.

TOP REASONS TO GO

St. Andrews: With its medieval streets, ruined cathedral and castle, and peculiarly posh atmosphere, St. Andrews is one of the most incongruous yet beguiling places in Scotland—even without its famous golf course.

Great golf: If you can't get on the Old Course in St. Andrews by ballot or by any other means, Fife and Angus have fabulous fairways aplenty, including the famous links course at Carnoustie.

East Neuk: As you take in crowstep-gabled fishermen's cottages, winding cobbled lanes, seaside harbor scenes, and lovely beaches, you can almost imagine the harsh lives

of the hardworking Fifers who lived in tiny hamlets such as Crail, Anstruther, Pittenweem, and Elie. Today artists and visitors make it all pleasantly picturesque.

Dundee: This formerly industrial city is becoming better known for its vibrant arts, music, theater, restaurant, and nightlife scenes. It's in a spectacular natural setting by Britain's most powerful river, the Tay.

The glens: The long Angus glens (such as Glen Clova) that run into the wild Grampian Mountains are magical places beloved by outdoors enthusiasts and those just wanting to rediscover nature.

5

ORIENTATION AND PLANNING

GETTING ORIENTED

Fife lies north of the Lothians, across the iconic bridges of the Firth of Forth. A headland, Fife's northeastern coast (or East Neuk) is fringed with golden sands, rocky shores, fishermen's cottages, and, of course, the splendor of St. Andrews, home of golf. Northwest of Fife and across the glorious Firth of Tay, the city of Dundee is undergoing a postindustrial reinvention. Its rural hinterland, Angus, hugs the city, which, stretching north toward the foothills of the Grampian Mountains, houses agricultural and fishing communities, and Glamis, one of Scotland's best-loved castles.

St. Andrews and East Neuk. St. Andrews isn't just a playground for golfers. This religious and academic center is steeped in history and prestige, with grand buildings, a palpable air of prosperity, and the cachet of being the place where a riveting 21st-century royal romance began. Beyond St. Andrews the colorful fishing villages of the East Neuk are a day-tripper's (and fish eater's) delight.

Dundee and Angus. Dundee has a knockout setting beside Britain's mightiest river, historical sights—including Captain Scott's ship, RRS *Discovery*—and a vibrant social life. The tree-lined country roads of the Angus heartlands roll through strawberry and raspberry fields to busy market towns, wee villages, and Glamis Castle.

PLANNING

WHEN TO GO

Spring in the Angus glens can be quite captivating, with the hills along Angus's northernmost boundary still covered in snow. Similarly, the moorland colors of autumn are appealing. However, Fife and Angus are really summer destinations, when most of the sights are open to visitors. St. Andrews hosts a number of international golf tournaments that effectively take over the town. Nongolfers may become incredibly frustrated when searching for accommodations or places to eat during these times, so check ahead.

PLANNING YOUR TIME

St. Andrews, 52 miles from Edinburgh, is not to be missed, for its history and atmosphere as much as for the golf; allot an overnight stop and at least a whole day if you can. The nearby East Neuk of Fife has some of Scotland's finest coastline, now becoming gentrified by the Edinburgh second-home set but still evoking Fife's past. A day's drive along A917 (allow for exploring and stops for ice cream and fish) will take you through the fishing villages of Elie, Pittenweem, Anstruther, and Crail. Dundee, with a rich maritime history and a grand museum, is an ideal base for a drive round the Angus towns of Arbroath, Kirriemuir, and Alyth; if you make a three-hour stop at Glamis Castle, this trip will take about a day.

GETTING HERE AND AROUND

AIR TRAVEL

Dundee Airport is off A85, 2 miles west of the city center. Air France operates a popular direct flight from London City Airport. If you are traveling to St. Andrews directly from Edinburgh Airport, the St. Andrews Shuttle offers transfers from £18.

BUS TRAVEL

Buses connect Edinburgh's St. Andrew Square bus station and Glasgow's Buchanan Street bus station to Fife and Angus. Megabus operates hourly service to Dundee from both Glasgow and Edinburgh. Stagecoach Fife serves Fife and St. Andrews, and Travel Dundee provides bus service in and around Dundee.

Stagecoach connects St. Andrews and Dundee to many of the smaller towns throughout Fife and Angus. A Day Rover ticket (£8 for Fife only) is a good value. Traveline Scotland is a service that helps you plan all public-transport journeys.

Bus Contacts Megabus ☎ *0900/160–0900* ⊕ *www.uk.megabus.com.*
National Express Dundee ✉ *44-48 E Dock St, Dundee* ☎ *01382/201121*
⊕ *www.nxbus.co.uk/dundee.* **Stagecoach** ☎ *01382/313700 Dundee*
⊕ *www.stagecoachbus.com.* **St. Andrews Shuttle** ⊕ *www.standrewsshuttle.com.*
Traveline Scotland ☎ *08706/200–2233* ⊕ *www.travelinescotland.com.*

CAR TRAVEL

The fastest route to Angus and northeast Fife is the M90 motorway from Edinburgh. Exit onto the A90 at Perth (45 minutes), and travel an additional 20 minutes to reach Dundee; 15 minutes later, you'll arrive in St. Andrews. If you're coming from Fife, you can also take the A91 and the A914, and cross the Tay Bridge to reach Dundee. This is a slower route, but does take you through the heartland of Fife.

Fife and Angus cover a compact area, so getting around is straightforward. You can visit everything via a series of excursions off the main north–south artery, the A90/M90, which leads from Edinburgh to Aberdeen. From here you can easily make day trips to Edinburgh, Glasgow, or Perthshire. Aberdeenshire and the Central Highlands are not too far away either.

Fife is easy to navigate—although it can be difficult to find a place to park in St. Andrews. The most interesting sights are in the east, which is served by a network of cross-country roads. Angus is also an easy region to explore. It's serviced by a fast main road (the A90), a gentler road (the A92), and several rural roads that run between the Grampians and the A90.

TRAIN TRAVEL

ScotRail stops at Kirkcaldy, Cupar, Leuchars (for St. Andrews), Dundee, Arbroath, and Montrose.

Train Contact ScotRail ☎ 08457/484950 ⊕ www.scotrail.co.uk.

RESTAURANTS

With an affluent population, St. Andrews supports several stylish hotel restaurants. Because it's a university town and popular tourist destination, there are also many good cafés and bistro-style restaurants. Bar lunches are the rule in large and small hotels throughout the region, and in seaside places the carry-*oot* (to-go) meal of fish-and-chips is an enduring tradition. *Prices in the reviews are the average cost of a main course at dinner or, if dinner is not served, at lunch.*

HOTELS

If you're staying in Fife, the obvious choice for a base is St. Andrews, with ample accommodations of all kinds. Another good option is the Howe of Fife, between Strathmiglo and Cupar, where there are some excellent country-house hotels, many with their own restaurants. Dundee and its hinterlands have a number of diverse accommodations, all of which offer good value. *Prices in the reviews are the lowest cost of a standard double room in high season, including 20% V.A.T.*

TOURS

From June to August, Scottish Express, run by Fishers Tours, operates bus tours both within and outside the region. Lochs and Glens operates bus tours of Scotland year-round, while Links Golf St. Andrews tailors tours to individual requirements.

Bus Tours Fishers Tours ✉ *16 W. Port, Dundee* ☎ *01382/227290*
⊕ *www.fisherstours.co.uk.*

Golf Tours Links Golf St. Andrews ✉ *7 Pilmour Links, St. Andrews*
☎ *01334/478639* ⊕ *www.linksgolfstandrews.com.*

VISITOR INFORMATION

The Arbroath, Dundee, and St. Andrews tourist offices are open year-round. Smaller tourist information centers operate seasonally in Anstruther, Brechin, Crail, Forfar, Kirriemuir, and Montrose.

ST. ANDREWS AND EAST NEUK

In its western parts Fife still bears the scars of heavy industry, especially coal mining, but these signs are less evident as you move east. Northeastern Fife, around the town of St. Andrews, seems to have played no part in the Industrial Revolution; instead, its residents earned a living from the grain fields or from the sea. Fishing has been a major industry, and in the past a string of Fife ports traded across the North Sea. Today the legacy of Dutch-influenced architecture, such as crowstep gables (the stepped effect on the ends of the roofs)—gives these East Neuk villages a distinctive character.

St. Andrews is unlike any other Scottish town. Once Scotland's most powerful ecclesiastical center as well as the seat of the country's oldest university and then, much later, the very symbol and spiritual home of golf, the town has a comfortable, well-groomed air, sitting almost smugly apart from the rest of Scotland. Its latest boast, being the town where Prince William first kissed Kate Middleton, has boosted university applications.

ST. ANDREWS

52 miles northeast of Edinburgh, 83 miles northeast of Glasgow.

Fodor's Choice
★

It may have a ruined cathedral and a grand university—the oldest in Scotland—but the modern claim to fame for St. Andrews is mainly its status as the home of golf. Forget that Scottish kings were crowned here, or that John Knox preached here, or that Reformation reformers were burned at the stake here. Thousands flock to St. Andrews to play at the Old Course, home of the Royal & Ancient Club, and to follow in the footsteps of Hagen, Sarazen, Jones, and Hogan.

The layout is pure Middle Ages: its three main streets—North, Market, and South—converge on the city's earliest religious site, near the cathedral. Like most of the ancient monuments, the cathedral ruins are impressive in their desolation—but this town is no dusty museum. The streets are busy, the shops are stylish, the gray houses sparkle in the sun, and the scene is particularly brightened during the academic year by bicycling students in scarlet gowns.

GETTING HERE AND AROUND

If you arrive by car, be prepared for an endless drive round the town as you look for a parking space. The parking lots around Rose Park (behind the bus station and a short walk from the town center) are your best bet. If you arrive by local or national bus, the bus station is a five-minute walk from town. The nearest train station, Leuchars, is 10 minutes away by taxi (£15) or bus (£2.70), both of which can be found outside the station. St. Andrews can be fully enjoyed on foot without too much exertion.

ESSENTIALS

Visitor Information St. Andrews ✉ *70 Market St.* ☎ *01334/472021* ⊕ *www.visitfife.com.*

EXPLORING
TOP ATTRACTIONS

British Golf Museum. This museum explores the centuries-old relationship between St. Andrews and golf and displays golf memorabilia from the 18th century to the 21st century. It's just opposite the Royal & Ancient Golf Club. ✉ *Bruce Embankment* ☎ *01334/460046* ⊕ *www.britishgolfmuseum.co.uk* ✑ *£6.50* ☉ *Apr.–Oct., Mon.–Sat. 9:30–5, Sun. 10–5; Nov.–Mar., daily 10–4.*

St. Andrews Castle. On the shore north of the cathedral stands ruined St. Andrews Castle, begun at the end of the 13th century. The remains include a rare example of a cold and gruesome bottle-shape dungeon, in which many prisoners spent their last hours. Even more atmospheric is the castle's mine and countermine. The former was a tunnel dug by besieging forces in the 16th century; the latter, a tunnel dug by castle defenders in order to meet and wage battle below ground. You can stoop and crawl into this narrow passageway—an eerie experience, despite the

5

addition of electric light. The visitor center has a good audiovisual presentation on the castle's history. In summer the beach below is popular with sun bathers and rockpool investigators, weather permitting. ⌧ *N. Castle St.* ☎ *01334/477196* ⊕ *www.historic-scotland.gov.uk* ⌦ *£5.50, £7.20 with St. Andrews Cathedral and St. Rule's Tower* ☼ *Apr.–Sept., daily 9:30–5:30; Oct.–Mar., daily 9:30–4:30.*

St. Andrews Cathedral. This is a ruined, poignant fragment of what was once the largest and most magnificent church in Scotland. Work on it began in 1160, and after several delays it was finally consecrated in 1318. The church was subsequently damaged by fire and repaired, but fell into decay during the Reformation. Only ruined gables, parts of the nave's south wall, and other fragments survive. The on-site museum helps you interpret the remains and gives a sense of what the cathedral must once have been like. ⌧ *Off Pends Rd.* ☎ *01334/472563* ⊕ *www. historic-scotland.gov.uk* ⌦ *£4.50, includes St. Rule's Tower* ☼ *Apr.– Sept., daily 9:30–5:30; Oct.–Mar., daily 9:30–4:30.*

St. Rule's Tower. Local legend has it that St. Andrews was founded by St. Regulus, or Rule, who, acting under divine guidance, carried relics of St. Andrew by sea from Patras in Greece. He was shipwrecked on this Fife headland and founded a church. The holy man's name survives in the cylindrical tower, consecrated in 1126 and the oldest surviving building in St. Andrews. Enjoy dizzying views of town from the top of the tower, reached via steep stairs. ⌧ *Off Pends Rd.* ☎ *01334/472563* ⊕ *www.historic-scotland.gov.uk* ⌦ *£4.20, includes St. Andrews Cathedral* ☼ *Apr.–Sept., daily 9:30–5:30; Oct.–Mar., daily 9:30–4:30.*

WORTH NOTING

Bell Pettigrew Museum of Natural History. Founded by Elsie Bell Pettigrew in memory of her husband James, a former professor of medicine, this fascinating collection of zoological specimens takes you from sea to jungle, mountain to sky. The antiquated manner of their presentation reminds you of their significance in an age when most of these creatures were still unknown to most people. In the handsome 16th-century St. Mary's Quadrangle, home to the St. Andrews University's divinity and psychology departments, it is dominated by a holm oak supposedly planted by Mary, Queen of Scots. ⌧ *Bute Medical Bldg., Queens Gardens, off South St.* ☎ *01334/463608* ⊕ *www.st-andrews.ac.uk/museum/ bellpettigrew* ⌦ *Free* ☼ *June–Sept., Tues. and Fri. 2–5.*

Royal & Ancient Golf Club of St. Andrews. The ruling house of golf worldwide is the spiritual home of all who play or follow the game. Founded in 1754, its clubhouse on the dunes—open to members only, who must be male—is a mix of classical, Victorian, and neoclassical styles; it's adjacent to the famous Old Course. ⌧ *The Scores* ☎ *01334/460000* ⊕ *www.randa.org.*

St. Andrews

St. Andrews Bay

1/8 mile
1/8 kilometer

Cathedral Ruins 2
1
Pends Rd.
Queen Mary's House

Museum of the University of St. Andrews 3
N. Castle St.
Abbey St.
South Castle St.
Byre Theatre

The Scores
St. Salvator's College
St. Salvator's Quadrangle 4
Westburn La.
St. Mary's College

University Library
North St.
Church St.
Logies Ln.
Queen's Gardens 5

Market St.
Bell St.
Rose La.
Thistle La.
South St.

St. Mary's Pl.
Alfred Pl.
Bridge St.
Argyle St.

Gillespie Terrace
Playfair Terrace
City Rd.
TO STRATHKINNESS
← LOW ROAD

Golf Pl.
Links Rd.
7
Kinburn Park
Double Dykes Rd.
Hepburn Gardens

Old Course
6

Old Station Rd.
Guardbridge Rd.
University of St. Andrews
Kennedy Gardens

College Playing Fields

Bell Pettigrew Museum **5**
British Golf Museum **7**
Royal & Ancient
Golf Club of
St. Andrews **6**

St. Andrews Castle **3**
St. Andrews Cathedral **2**
St. Rule's Tower **1**
University of
St. Andrews **4**

University of St. Andrews. Scotland's oldest university is the *alma mater* of John Knox (Protestant reformer), King James II of Scotland, the Duke and Duchess of Cambridge (William and Kate), and Chris Hoy, Scotland's Olympic cyclist. Founded in 1411, the university's buildings pepper the town. For the quintessential University of St. Andrews experience, **St. Salvator's Quadrangle** reveals the magnificence of this historic institution. Looking out onto this impressive college green is the striking St. Salvator's Chapel, founded in 1450. It bears the marks of a turbulant past: the initials PH, carved into the paving stones under the bell tower, are those of Patrick Hamilton, who was burned alive outside the chapel for his Protestant beliefs. ⊠ *St Mary's Pl.*

WHERE TO EAT

$
BRASSERIE

✕ **The Doll's House.** Spilling out onto the pavement, this colorful and lively eatery offers reliably good food at a reaosnable price. Using locally sourced meats, the kitchen is expecially good at sauces, such as brandy and mixed peppercorn for beef or delicately scented wine and herb for fish. The tables upstairs offer a slightly more relaxed atmosphere. ⑤ *Average main: £14* ⊠ *3 Church St* ☎ *01334/477422* ⊕ *www.dollshouse-restaurant.co.uk.*

$$$$
SEAFOOD
Fodor's Choice
★

✕ **The Seafood Restaurant.** This stunning glass-walled building is perched on the banks of the West Sands. Once an open-air theater, the kitchen radiates a confidence and calm that contributes to the easy atmosphere. The food is adventurous without being flashy: start with fat, juicy Shetland mussels, then move on to bream with peas. ⑤ *Average main: £38* ⊠ *Bruce Embankment* ☎ *01334/479475* ⊕ *www.theseafoodrestaurant. com* ⚭ *Reservations essential.*

$
MODERN BRITISH

✕ **West Port Bar & Kitchen.** It's easy to forget that St. Andrews is a university town when the students are on summer break, but this modern bar and eatery remains vibrant and youthful year-round. The reasonably priced menu offers nicely prepared pub grub—everything from gourmet burgers to smoked haddock fishcakes—making this a satisfying stop for lunch or dinner. Upstairs are four bright B&B rooms that go for £95. ⑤ *Average main: £9* ⊠ *170 South St.* ☎ *01334/473186* ⊕ *www.thewestport.co.uk.*

WHERE TO STAY

$
B&B/INN
Fodor's Choice
★

▦ **Aslar Guest House.** This terraced town house dating from 1865 has large rooms with ornate cornicing and antique reproduction furniture. **Pros:** homey feel; great location; exceptional breakfast. **Cons:** books up quickly. ⑤ *Rooms from: £96* ⊠ *120 North St.* ☎ *01334/473460* ⊕ *www. aslar.com* ⚭ *6 rooms* ❚⊙❙ *Breakfast.*

$$$$
HOTEL

▦ **Fairmont St Andrews.** Two miles from St. Andrews, this modern hotel has spectacular views of the bay and two superb golf courses. **Pros:** spacious feel; excellent spa; golf at your doorstep. **Cons:** the huge atrium feels like a shopping center; paintings made to match the decor. ⑤ *Rooms from: £260* ⊠ *A917, St. Andrews Bay* ☎ *01334/837000* ⊕ *www.fairmont.com/standrews* ⚭ *192 rooms, 17 suites* ❚⊙❙ *Breakfast.*

$$$$
HOTEL
Fodor'sChoice
★

Old Course Hotel. Regularly hosting international golf stars and jet-setters, the Old Course Hotel recently underwent a renaissance—the guest rooms and public spaces have been reinvigorated, and the service has warmed up. **Pros:** fabulous location and lovely views; unpretentious service; golfer's heaven. **Cons:** all the golf talk might bore non-golfers; spa is on the small side. *Rooms from: £350 ⌂ Old Station Rd. ☎ 01334/474371 ⊕ www.oldcoursehotel.co.uk ⇆ 109 rooms, 35 suites ⦿ Breakfast.*

$$$$
HOTEL

Rufflets Country House Hotel. Ten acres of formal and informal gardens surround this creeper-covered country house just outside St. Andrews. **Pros:** attractive gardens; cozy drawing room; great restaurant. **Cons:** too far to walk to St. Andrews; teddy bears in the guest rooms are a bit twee. *Rooms from: £245 ⌂ Strathkinness Low Rd. ☎ 01334/472594 ⊕ www.rufflets.co.uk ⇆ 24 rooms, 4 suites ⦿ Breakfast.*

$$
HOTEL

Scores Hotel. Overlooking the St. Andrews shoreline, this pair of town houses keep good company—they sit next to the Royal & Ancient Golf Club of St. Andrews. **Pros:** rooms are from big to vast; the staff is motivated and happy to oblige. **Cons:** reception area is uninspiring. *Rooms from: £140 ⌂ 76 the Scores ☎ 01334/472451 ⊕ www.scoreshotel.co.uk ⇆ 36 rooms ⦿ Breakfast.*

NIGHTLIFE AND THE ARTS

PUBS **Central Bar.** Unlike a lot of local places, the Central Bar hasn't gone down the minimalist-decor-and-cocktails road. You'll find a good range of beers (bottled and on tap) and decent pub food. ⌂ 77 Market St. ☎ 01334/478296.

GOLF

What serious golfer doesn't dream of playing at world-famous St. Andrews? Seven St. Andrews courses, all part of the St. Andrews Trust, are open to visitors, and more than 40 other courses in the region offer golf by the round or by the day.

ST. ANDREWS LINKS TRUST COURSES

St. Andrews Links Trust. For information about availability—there's usually a waiting list, which varies according to the time of year—contact St. Andrews Links Trust. Green fees range from £75 to £155 for a round on the Old Course and from £8 to £120 for a round on the five other courses. ☎ 01334/466666 ⊕ www.standrews.org.uk.

Balgove Course. At the beginner-friendly Balgove Course you can turn up and tee off without prior reservation. ⌂ West Sands Rd., A91 ⊕ www.standrews.org.uk ⌂ Green fee: £8–£15 ⛳ 9 holes, 1520 yds, par 30.

Castle Course. Designed by David McLay Kidd in 2008, the Castle Course hugs the rugged coastline and has jaw-dropping views. It's 2 miles from the town center. ⌂ A917 ⊕ www.standrews.org.uk ⌂ Green fee: £60–£120 ⛳ 18 holes, 6759 yds, par 71.

Eden Course. The aptly named Eden Course, designed in 1914 by Harry S. Colt, winds through inland fields bordered with lovely foliage. It's a bit more forgiving compared to other St. Andrews courses. ⌂ West Sands Rd. ⊕ www.standrews.org.uk ⌂ Green fee: £20–40 ⛳ 18 holes, 6250 yds, par 70.

5

The Evolution of Golf

The matter of who invented golf has been long debated, but there's no doubt that its development into one of the most popular games in the world stems from Scotland. The first written reference to golf, variously spelled as "gowf" or "goff," was in 1457, when James II (1430–60) of Scotland declared that both golf and football (soccer) should be "*utterly cryit doune and nocht usit*" (publicly criticized and prohibited) because they distracted his subjects from archery practice. Mary, Queen of Scots (1542–87) was fond of golf. When in Edinburgh in 1567, she played on Leith Links and on Bruntsfield Links. When in Fife, she played at Falkland and at St. Andrews itself.

GOLF EXPANDS

Golf clubs (i.e., organizations) arose in the middle of the 18th century. The Honourable Company of Edinburgh Golfers, now residing at Muirfield, was founded in 1744. From then on, clubs sprang up all over Scotland: Royal Aberdeen (1780), Crail Golfing Society (1786), Dunbar (1794), and the Royal Perth Golfing Society (1824).

As for the town of St. Andrews, which now prospers on golf, golf schools, and golf equipment (the manufacture of golf balls is a local industry), locals say that the game was first played here with a piece of driftwood, a shore pebble, and a rabbit hole on the sandy, coastal turf. Residents were playing golf on the town links as far back as the 15th century. Rich golfers eventually formed exclusive clubs. The Royal & Ancient Golf Club of St. Andrews was founded in 1754.

By the early 19th century, clubs had been set up in England, and the game was being carried all over the world by enthusiastic Scots. These golf missionaries spread their knowledge not only of the sport, but also of the courses. Large parts of the Scottish coast are natural golf courses; indeed, the origins of bunkers and the word *links* (courses) are found in the sand dunes of Scotland's shores. Willie Park of Musselburgh, James Braid, and C.K. Hutchison are some of the best known of Scotland's golf-course architects.

CHANGES IN THE GAME

The original balls, called *featheries,* were leather bags stuffed with boiled feathers and often lasted only one round. In 1848, the gutta-percha ball, called a *guttie,* was introduced. It was in general use until the invention of the rubber-core ball in 1901. Clubs were made of wood with shafts of ash (later hickory), and heads of thorn, apple, or pear. Heads were spliced, then bound to the shaft with twine. Later in the 19th century, manufacturers began to experiment with metal in clubfaces and shafts. The technology of golf continues to change, but its addictive qualities are timeless.

Jubilee Course. This windswept course offers quite a challenge even for experienced golfers. When it opened in 1897 was intended for beginners, but the popularity of its seaside location encouraged the powers that be to convert it into a championship course. Many golfers say the 15th hole is one of the best in the sport. ⊠ *West Sands Rd.* ⊕ *www.standrews.org.uk* ✉ *Green fee: £35–£70* ⅄. *18 holes, 6742 yds, par 72.*

New Course. Not exactly new—it opened in 1895—the New Course is rather overshadowed by the Old Course, but it has a firm following of golfers who appreciate the loop design. ⊠ *West Sands Rd.* ⊕ *www. standrews.org.uk* ✉ *Green fee: £35–£70* ⅄. *18 holes, 6625 yds, par 71.*

Old Course. Believed to be the oldest golf course in the world, the Old Course was first played in the 15th century. Each year more than 44,000 rounds are teed off, and no doubt most get stuck in one of its 112 bunkers. A handicap certificate is required. ⊠ *West Sands Rd.* ⊕ *www. standrews.org.uk* ✉ *Green fee: £75–£155* ⅄. *18 holes, 6721 yds, par 72.*

Strathtyrum Course. Those with a high handicap will enjoy this course, opened in 1993, without the worry or embarrassment of holding up more experienced golfers. ⊠ *West Sands Rd., A91* ⊕ *www.standrews. org.uk* ✉ *Green fee: £12–£25 per round.* ⅄. *18 holes, 5620 yds, par 69.*

SHOPPING

Artery. Artery sells work by local, Scottish, and British artists, including jewelry, ceramics, paintings, and intriguing handmade clocks. ⊠ *43 South St.* ☎ *01334/478221.*

Balgove Larder. Here you'll discover a huge selection of Scottish items, from spurtles (for stirring your porridge) to tablet (sugary toffee) to big, thick sausages. In summer the barn where they usually store the potatoes is transformed into a rustic steak house selling steak and chips for £15. ⊠ *A91* ☎ *01334/898145* ⊕ *www.balgove.com.*

Mellis. Mellis is a cheese-lover's mecca. Look for a soft, crumbly local cheese called Anster. ⊠ *149 South St.* ☎ *01334/471410* ⊕ *www.mellischeese.net.*

CRAIL

Fodor's Choice
★

10 miles south of St. Andrews.

The oldest and most aristocratic of East Neuk burghs, pretty Crail is where many fish merchants retired and built cottages. The town landmark is a picturesque Dutch-influenced town house, or *tolbooth*, which contains the oldest bell in Fife, cast in Holland in 1520. Crail may now be full of artists, but it remains a working harbor; take time to walk the streets and beaches and to sample fish by the harbor. ■ TIP➔ **As you head into East Neuk from this tiny port, look about for market crosses, merchant houses, and little doocots (dovecotes, where pigeons were kept)—typical picturesque touches of this region.**

GETTING HERE AND AROUND

Stagecoach bus number 63 operates between Crail and St. Andrews. However, the number 95 is more regular and also takes you to Anstruther, Pittenweem, and Lower Largo. Crail is about 15 minutes from St. Andrews by car via A917.

EXPLORING

Crail Museum and Heritage Centre. The story of this trading and fishing town can be found in the delightfully crammed Crail Museum and Heritage Centre, entirely run by local volunteers. There is a small tourist information desk within the center. ⊠ *62–64 Marketgate* ☎ *01333/450869* ⊕ *www.crailmuseum.org.uk* ⊡ *Free* ☉ *June–Sept., Mon.–Sat. 11-4, Sun. 1–5.*

WHERE TO STAY

$
B&B/INN

⊞ **Hazelton.** Beautifully polished wood, exquisitely restored period features, and gentle hues put the Hazelton head and shoulders above the typical seaside B&B. **Pros:** handsome building; excellent location; nothing is too much of a problem for the generous-spirited staff. **Cons:** you have to be a meat eater to make the most of the breakfast. ⑤ *Rooms from: £90* ⊠ *29 Marketgate N* ☎ *01333/450250* ⊕ *www.thehazelton.co.uk* ⟿ *5 rooms* ☉ *Closed Jan.* ⑂ *Breakfast.*

ANSTRUTHER

5

4 miles southwest of Crail.

Anstruther, locally called Ainster, has a lovely waterfront with a few shops brightly festooned with children's pails and shovels, a gesture to summer vacationers.

GETTING HERE AND AROUND

Strgecoach bus number 95 operates between St. Andrews, Crail, Anstruther, Pittenweem, and Lower Largo. Anstruther is 5 to 10 minutes from Crail by car via A917.

ESSENTIALS

Visitor Information Anstruther Tourist Information ⊠ *Scottish Fisheries Museum, Harbour Head* ☎ *01333/311073* ⊕ *www.visitfife.com.*

EXPLORING

Scottish Fisheries Museum. Facing Anstruther Harbor, the Scottish Fisheries Museum is inside a colorful cluster of buildings, the earliest of which dates from the 16th century. The museum illustrates the life of Scottish fisherfolk through documents, artifacts, model ships, paintings, and displays (complete with the reek of tarred rope and net). There are also floating exhibits at the quayside. There's a small desk here with tourism information. ⊠ *Harbourhead* ☎ *01333/310628* ⊕ *www.scotfishmuseum.org* ⊡ *£7* ☉ *Apr.–Sept., Mon.–Sat. 10–5:30, Sun. 11–5; Oct.–Mar., Mon.–Sat. 10–4:30, Sun. noon–4:30; last admission 1 hr before closing.*

NEED A
BREAK?

Anstruther Fish Bar and Restaurant. Next door to the Scottish Fisheries Museum, this popular fish-and-chip shop has space to eat, but most people order take-out. Try Pittenweem-landed prawns in batter or the catch of the day, which could be mackerel (line caught by the owners), hake, or local crab. ⊠ *42–44 Shore St.* ☎ *01333/310518* ⊕ *www.anstrutherfishbar.co.uk.*

WHERE TO EAT

$$$$
EUROPEAN

✕**The Cellar.** Entered through a cobbled courtyard, this unpretentious, old-fashioned restaurant is hugely popular. The low ceiling and exposed beams make for a cozy atmosphere. Specializing in seafood, as well as local beef and lamb, owner and chef Peter Jukes serves three-course meals cooked simply in modern Scottish style. The crayfish bisque served with Gruyère is known all over the region, as is the excellent wine list. $ *Average main: £40* ✉ *24 E. Green* ☎ *01333/310378* ⚓ *Reservations essential* ☯ *Closed Sun. and Mon. Nov.–Easter.*

NIGHTLIFE

Dreel Tavern. A 16th-century coaching inn, the Dreel Tavern is famous for its hand-drawn ales. ✉ *16 High St. W* ☎ *01333/310727.*

FIFE COASTAL PATH

Fife's green and undulating landscape includes the Lomond Hills, to the west, which are easy to climb and offer fabulous views of both the Tay and Forth estuaries. The Fife Coastal Path can be bracing or an amble. The 7-mile stretch between East Wemyss to Lower Largo (four to six hours) is the easiest going, with some of it along the beaches of Elie. The 8-mile route between Pittenweem to Fifeness (four to six hours) can be rougher in patches, but takes you through Anstruther and Crail. For more information, contact ✉ *www.fifecoastalpath.co.uk.*

SPORTS AND THE OUTDOORS

East Neuk Outdoors. The back roads of Fife make pleasant places for biking. You can rent bicycles from East Neuk Outdoors, which also has equipment for archery, climbing, and canoeing. ✉ *Cellardyke Park* ☎ *01333/311929* ⊕ *www.eastneukoutdoors.co.uk.*

PITTENWEEM

1½ miles southwest of Anstruther.

Many examples of East Neuk architecture serve as the backdrop for the working harbor at Pittenweem. Look for the crowstep gables, white *harling* (the rough mortar finish on walls), and red pantiles (roof tiles with an S-shape profile). The *weem* part of the town's name comes from the Gaelic *uaime*, meaning cave.

GETTING HERE AND AROUND

Stagecoach bus number 95 operates hourly between St. Andrews, Crail, Anstruther, Pittenweem, and Lower Largo. Pittenweem is about five minutes from Anstruther by car via A917.

EXPLORING

Kellie Castle and Garden. Dating from the 16th to 17th centuries and restored in Victorian times, Kellie Castle stands among the grain fields and woodlands of northeastern Fife. Four acres of pretty gardens surround the castle, which is in the care of the National Trust for Scotland. In summer you can buy berries grown in the walled garden, and baked goods are sold in the tearoom. ✉ *B9171, 3 miles northwest of Pittenweem* ☎ *0844/4932184* ⊕ *www.nts.org.uk* 🎟 *£10* ☯ *Castle Apr., May, Sept., and Oct., Thurs.–Mon. 12:30–5; June–Aug., daily 12:30–5; garden daily 9:30–6.*

Pittenweem Arts Festival. There is nothing quite like August's Pittenweem Arts Festival. Exhibitions, which involve hundreds of local and international artists, take place in the town's public buildings and in private homes and gardens. It's a week of events, workshops, and live music. ☎ *01333/313903* ⊕ *www.pittenweemartsfestival.co.uk.*

St. Fillan's Cave. This town's cavern is called St. Fillan's Cave, which contains the shrine of St. Fillan, a 6th-century hermit who lived here. It's up a *pend* (alleyway) behind the waterfront. If the cave isn't open, ask at the Cocoa Tree on the High Street. ⊠ *Cove Wynd* ⊡ *£1* ⊙ *Mon.–Sat. 10–5.*

WHERE TO EAT

$$$$
CONTEMPORARY

✕ **16 West End.** The big sister of the Seafood Restaurant in St. Andrews, this eatery put St. Monans on Scotland's culinary map. The fixed-price menu has vegetarian and meat options, but with dishes like beetroot-cured trout and halibut with a peanut sauce, it's really for those looking for a new take on fish. $ *Average main: £42* ⊠ *16 West End, 2 miles west of Pittenweem, St. Monans* ☎ *01333/730327* ⚐ *Reservations essential* ⊙ *Closed Mon. and Tues.*

SHOPPING

Cocoa Tree Shop and Café. Open daily, the Cocoa Tree Shop and Café is a former bakery that stocks the most imaginative and comprehensive range of fine chocolates you'll find in this part of the world. There is also a lovely café, with cakes and, of course, handmade chocolates from the Pittenweem Chocolate Company. ⊠ *9 High St.* ☎ *01333/311495* ⊕ *www.thecocoatreeshop.com* ⊙ *Daily 10–6.*

ELIE

5 miles south of Pittenweem.

To give it its full name, the Royal Burgh of Elie and Earlsferry is an old trading port with a handsome harbor that loops around one of the most glorious stretches of sand in the British Isles. Since Victorian times, when a railway (sadly defunct since the 1960s) linked it with the capital, Elie has been a weekend and summer retreat for the great and the good of Edinburgh. The beach to the south of the harbor is a mile long and has clean sands, clear waters, and just enough flotsam and jetsam to interest a beachcomber.

WHERE TO EAT

$
BRITISH

✕ **Ship Inn.** Sports lovers visit Elie on Sunday to watch cricket matches played on the beach outside the Ship Inn. The staff fires up a barbecue and cooks simple fare, including burgers and chicken. On the side are salads and lots of chips. The relaxed atmosphere and the beauty of this slow, cerebral game makes for an afternoon you'll never forget, especially if the sun shines. $ *Average main: £12* ⊠ *The Toft* ☎ *01333/330246* ⊕ *www.ship-elie.com.*

SPORTS AND THE OUTDOORS

GOLF

Leven Links. A fine Fife course that has been used as a British Open qualifier, Leven Links has a whiff of the more famous St. Andrews, with a hummocky terrain and a tang of salt in the air. The 1st and 18th holes share the same fairway, and the 18th green has a creek running beside it. ■ TIP→ **Saturday play must be booked at least a week in advance.** ⊠ *The Promenade, Leven* ☎ *01333/428859* ⊕ *www.leven-links.com* 🖾 *Green fee: weekdays £55; weekends £60* ⌂ *Reservations essential* 🏌 *18 holes, 6506 yds, par 71* ⊙ *Daily.*

Lundin Golf Club. One of a string of fantastic links courses, Lundin Golf Club is a worthy addition to any Scottish golfing itinerary. Designed by the great James Braid, the course is always in prime condition and the greens are a joy. The pick of the holes is the par-3 14th, played from an elevated tee back toward the sea. ⊠ *Golf Rd., Lundin Links* ☎ *01333/320051* ⊕ *www.lundingolfclub.co.uk* 🖾 *Green fee: weekdays £58; weekends £65* 🏌 *18 holes, 6371 yards, par 71* ⊙ *Daily.*

FALKLAND

Fodor's Choice
★

24 miles northwest of Pittenweem, 15 miles northwest of Elie.

One of the loveliest communities in Scotland, Falkland is a royal burgh of twisting streets and crooked stone houses.

GETTING HERE AND AROUND
Stagecoach bus number 64A connects Falkland to St. Andrews as well as Cupar and Ladybank (both of which are train stations on the Edinburgh to Dundee line). Falkland is about 15 minutes from Cupar and a half hour from St. Andrews by car via A91 and A912, or A91 to A914 to A912.

EXPLORING
Falkland Palace. A former hunting lodge of the Stuart monarchs, Falkland Palace dominates the town. The castle is one of the country's earliest examples of the French Renaissance style. Overlooking the main street is the palace's most impressive feature, the walls and chambers on its south side, all rich with buttresses and stone medallions, built by French masons in the 1530s for King James V (1512–42). He died here, and the palace was a favorite resort of his daughter, Mary, Queen of Scots (1542–87). In the beautiful gardens, overlooked by the palace turret windows, you may easily imagine yourself back at the solemn hour when James on his deathbed pronounced the doom of the house of Stuart: "It cam' wi' a lass and it'll gang wi a lass." ⊠ *Main St.* ☎ *0844/4932186* ⊕ *www.nts. org.uk* 🖾 *£12* ⊙ *Mar.–Oct., Mon.–Sat. 10–5, Sun. 1–5.*

LOCH LEVEN

10 miles southwest of Falkland.

Scotland's largest Lowland loch, Loch Leven is famed for its fighting trout. The area is also noted for abundant birdlife, particularly its wintering wildfowl. Mary, Queen of Scots was forced to sign the deed of abdication in her island prison in the loch.

GETTING HERE AND AROUND
If you're driving from St. Andrews or Cupar, take A91 to Kinross and follow the signs from there. From Falkland, take A911.

EXPLORING

Vane Farm Nature Reserve. On the southern shore overlooking the loch, Vane Farm Nature Reserve, a visitor center run by the Royal Society for the Protection of Birds, provides information about Loch Leven's ecology. It's the best place in Britain to see lapwings, pink-footed geese, tufted ducks, and shovelers. ⊠ *Rte. B9097, off M90 and B996* ☎ *01577/862355* ⊕ *www.rspb.org.uk* ⊠ *£5* ◷ *Daily 10–5.*

CUPAR

21 miles northwest of Loch Leven, 10 miles west of St. Andrews.

Cupar is a busy market town with several interesting sites, including a museum about Fife.

GETTING HERE AND AROUND

Cupar has a train station on the Edinburgh–Aberdeen line (which passes through Dundee), and there are trains almost every hour. Stagecoach buses serve the town as well. By car, you can reach Cupar from Loch Leven via M90 and A91; take A91 if you're traveling from St. Andrews.

EXPLORING

Fife Folk Museum. To learn more about the history and culture of rural Fife, visit the Fife Folk Museum. The life of local rural communities is reflected in artifacts and documents housed in a former weigh house and adjoining weavers' cottages. The museum is 3 miles southeast of Cupar via A916 and B939. ⊠ *High St., Ceres* ☎ *01334/828180* ⊕ *www. fifefolkmuseum.org* ⊠ *£4* ◷ *Apr.–Oct., daily 10:30–4:30.*

Hill of Tarvit House. On rising ground near the town stands the National Trust for Scotland's Hill of Tarvit House. Originally a 17th-century mansion, the house was altered in the high-Edwardian style in the late 1890s and early 1900s by the Scottish architect Sir Robert Lorimer (1864–1929). The extensive wood and parklands offer an enjoyable place for a picnic or stroll, and the house itself is well worth a visit. Golfers will also want to play a round on the old Lorimer family course, the Hickory, which was brought back to life in 2008 after being ploughed up for agricultural use during World War II. ⊠ *Off A916, 2 mi south of Cupar* ☎ *0844/4932185* ⊕ *www.nts.org.uk* ⊠ *£10* ◷ *House Apr.–Oct., Thurs.–Mon. 1–5; gardens daily 9:30–sunset.*

FAMILY **Scottish Deer Centre.** At the Scottish Deer Centre, many types of deer can be seen at close quarters or on ranger-guided tours. There are falconry displays every two hours, woodland walks, and a café. The center, west of Cupar, is one of the few places you can spot the red squirrel. ⊠ *A91* ☎ *01337/810391* ⊕ *www.tsdc.co.uk* ⊠ *£7.45* ◷ *July and Aug., daily 10–5:30; Sept.–June, daily 10–4:30.*

WHERE TO EAT AND STAY

$$$ ✕ **Ostlers Close Restaurant.** It's thoroughly unpretentious, but this cottage-
BRITISH style restaurant with plain painted walls and stick-back chairs has earned a well-deserved reputation for top-quality cuisine that is imaginative without trying to be too trendy. The chef's light touch means the flavors are simple, with the shellfish and vegetables especially fresh-tasting. This longtime favorite is tucked away in an alley off the main street. It's a

good idea to reserve ahead, particularly for lunch. $ *Average main: £22* ✉ *25 Bonnygate* ☎ *01334/655574* ⊕ *www.ostlersclose.co.uk* ⚓ *Reservations essential* ⊘ *Closed Sun. and Mon. No lunch Tues.–Fri.*

$$$
B&B/INN
Fodor's Choice
★

🍴 **The Peat Inn.** With eight bright and contemporary two-room suites, this popular "restaurant with rooms" is perhaps best known for its outstanding, modern, Scottish-style restaurant. **Pros:** exceptional restaurant; efficient but easygoing staff. **Cons:** booking ahead is essential; you need a car to get here. $ *Rooms from: £195* ✉ *B941, at intersection of B940* ☎ *01334/840206* ⊕ *www.thepeatinn.co.uk* ⇘ *8 suites* ⊘ *Closed Sun. and Mon.* 🍴 *Breakfast.*

SPORTS AND THE OUTDOORS

GOLF **Ladybank Golf Club.** Fife is known for its coastal courses, but this one provides an interesting inland layout. Although Ladybank, designed by Tom Morris in 1876, is on fairly level ground, the fir and birch trees and heathery rough give it a Highland flavor among the gentle Lowland fields. Qualifying rounds of the British Open are played here when the main championship is played at St. Andrews. ✉ *A92, Annsmuir, Ladybank* ☎ *01337/830814* ⊕ *www.ladybankgolf.co.uk* ⛳ *Green fee: May–Sept., weekdays £54; weekends £64; Oct. and Apr., weekdays £44; weekends £54; Nov.–Mar., weekdays £24; weekends £29* ⚓ *Reservations essential* ⛳ *18 holes, 6580 yds, par 71* ⊘ *Daily.*

DUNDEE AND ANGUS

The small city of Dundee sits near the mouth of the River Tay surrounded by the farms and glens of rural Angus and the coastal grassy banks and golf courses of northeastern Fife. A vibrant, industrious city that's off the main tourist track, Dundee plays a significant role in the biotech and computer-games industries. Dundee has a large student population, a lively arts and nightlife scene, and several historical and nautical sights. In 2014 the city's waterfront transformation will truly begin when construction starts on the first outpost of London's Victoria and Albert Museum, a repository of decorative arts.

Angus combines coastal agriculture on rich, red soils with dramatic inland glens that pierce their way into the foothills of the Grampian mountain ranges to the northwest. ■**TIP➔ The main road from Dundee to Aberdeen—the A90—requires special care with its mix of fast cars and unexpectedly slow farm traffic.**

DUNDEE

14 miles northwest of St. Andrews, 58 miles north of Edinburgh, 79 miles northeast of Glasgow.

Dundee makes an excellent base for exploring Fife and Angus at any time of year. The West End—especially its main thoroughfare Perth Road—pulses with life, with intimate cafés and excellent bars. The Dundee Contemporary Arts center has gained the city some attention. As you walk the cobbled streets, you may glimpse the 1888

Tay Rail Bridge, and if you head southwest you can reach Magdalen Green, where landscape artist James McIntosh Patrick (1907–98) found inspiration from the views and ever-changing skyscapes. The popular comic strips *The Beano* and *The Dandy* were first published here in the 1930s, so statues by the Scottish sculptor Antony Morrow depicting Desperate Dan, Dawg, and a catapult-wielding Minnie the Minx were erected in the City Square.

> ## WORD OF MOUTH
>
> "The surprise highlight was visiting Dundee, to see the Verdant Works museum on the jute industry, which was an excellent example of its kind (the café was fine too). We had some time to spare, so dropped in on the city art gallery and museum, also worth visiting."
>
> —PatrickLondon

GETTING HERE AND AROUND

The East Coast train line runs through the city, linking it to Edinburgh (and beyond, to London), Glasgow (and the West Coast of England), and Aberdeen, with trains to all every hour or half-hourly at peak times. Cheaper bus service is available to all of these locations, as well as St. Andrews and several other towns in Fife and Angus.

If you're traveling by car, the A92 will take you north from Fife to Abroath and the Angus coast towns. The A90, from Perth, heads north to Aberdeen.

Most of the sights in Dundee are clustered together, so you can easily walk around the city. If the weather is bad or your legs are heavy, hail one of the many cabs on the easy-to-find taxi ranks for little more than a few pounds.

ESSENTIALS

Visitor Information Angus and Dundee Tourist Board ⊠ *Discovery Point, Riverside Dr.* ☎ *01382/527527* ⊕ *www.angusanddundee.co.uk.*

EXPLORING

TOP ATTRACTIONS

Fodor'sChoice
★

Dundee Botanic Garden. This renowned botanical garden contains an extensive collection of native and exotic plants outdoors and in tropical and temperate greenhouses. There are some beautiful areas for picnicking, as well as a visitor center, an art gallery, and a coffee shop. ⊠ *Riverside Dr.* ☎ *01382/381190* ⊕ *www.dundee.ac.uk/botanic* ☑ *£3.90* ☺ *Mar.–Oct., daily 10–4:30; Nov.–Feb., daily 10–3:30.*

FAMILY
Dundee Contemporary Arts. Between a 17th-century mansion and a cathedral, this strikingly modern building houses one of Britain's most exciting artistic venues. The huge gallery houses up to six shows a year by internationally acclaimed contemporary artists. There are children's workshops and meet-the-artist events throughout the year. Two movie theaters screen mainly independent, revival, and children's films. There's also a craft shop and a buzzing café-bar that's open until midnight. ⊠ *152 Nethergate* ☎ *01382/909900* ⊕ *www.dca.org. uk* ☑ *Free* ☺ *Fri.–Wed. 11–8, Thurs. 11–8.*

Dundee

Fodor's Choice
★

McManus Galleries. Dundee's principal museum and art gallery, housed in a striking Gothic Revival–style building, has an engaging collection of artifacts that document the city's history and the working, social, and cultural lives of Dundonians throughout the Victorian period and the 20th century. Its varied fine art collection includes paintings by Rossetti, Raeburn, and Peploe as well as thought-provoking yet accessible contemporary works and visiting exhibitions, often in connection with London's Victoria and Albert Museum. ⊠ *Albert Sq.* ☎ *01382/432350* ⊕ *www.mcmanus.co.uk* 🎟 *Free* ⊙ *Mon.–Sat. 10–5, Sun. 12:30–4:30.*

FAMILY
Fodor's Choice
★

RRS *Discovery.* Dundee's urban-renewal program—the city is determined to celebrate its industrial past—was motivated in part by the arrival of the RRS (Royal Research Ship) *Discovery,* the vessel used by Captain Robert F. Scott (1868–1912) on his polar explorations. The steamer was originally built and launched in Dundee; now it's a permanent resident. At Discovery Point, under the handsome cupola, the story of the ship and its famous expedition unfold; you can even feel the Antarctic chill as if you were there. The ship, berthed outside, is the star: wander the deck, then explore the quarters to see the daily existence endured by the ship's crew and captain. ⊠ *Discovery Quay, Riverside Dr.* ☎ *01382/309060* ⊕ *www.rrsdiscovery.com* 🎟 *£8.50, £15 includes Verdant Works.* ⊙ *Apr.–Sept., Mon.–Sat. 10–6, Sun. 11–6; Oct.–Mar., Mon.–Sat. 10–5, Sun. 11–5; last admission 1 hr before closing.*

FAMILY **Verdant Works.** In a former jute mill, Verdant Works houses a multifaceted exhibit on the story of jute and the town's involvement in the jute trade. Restored machinery, audiovisual displays, and tableaux all bring to life the hard, noisy life of the jute worker. A light and airy café serves lovely cakes. ✉ *W. Hendersons Wynd* ☎ *01382/309060* ⊕ *www.verdantwork. co.uk* 🖅 *£8:50, £15 includes RRS Discovery* ⊘ *Apr.–Oct., Mon.–Sat. 10–6, Sun. 11–6; Nov.–Mar., Wed.–Sat. 10:30–4:30, Sun. 11–4:30.*

WORTH NOTING

OFF THE
BEATEN
PATH

Broughty Castle. Originally built to guard the Tay Estuary, Broughty Castle is now a museum focusing on fishing, ferries, and the history of the area's whaling industry. The canons and ramparts make for fine photo opportunities, and inside (up a very narrow stairway) are four floors of displays, including the lovely art collection of the Victorian inventor and engineer Sir James Orchar. To the north of the castle lies beautiful Broughty Ferry Beach, which even in midwinter is enjoyed by the locals; there is a regular bus service from Dundee's city center. ✉ *Castle Approach, 4 miles east of city center, Broughty Ferry* ☎ *01382/436916* ⊕ *www.dundeecity.gov.uk/broughtycastle* 🖅 *Free* ⊘ *Apr.–Sept., Mon.– Sat. 10–4, Sun. 12:30–4; Oct.–Mar., Tues.–Sat. 10–4, Sun. 12:30–4.*

The Law. For sweeping views of the city, the Angus Glens to the north, and Fife's coastline to the south, head here. This hill (*law* means hill in Scottish) is actually an extinct volcano whose summit reaches 1,640 feet above sea level. A World War II memorial, parking lot, and seating area are at the top. ✉ *Law Rd.*

Mills Observatory. At the top of a thickly forested hill, Mills Observatory is the only full-time public observatory in Britain. There are displays on astronomy, space exploration, scientific instruments, and a 12-inch refracting telescope for night viewing of the stars and planets. ✉ *Balgay Hill, 2 mi west of city center* ☎ *01382/435967* ⊕ *www. leisureandculturedundee.com/mills* 🖅 *Free* ⊘ *Oct.–Mar., weekdays 4–10 pm, weekends 12:30–4; Apr.–Sept., Tues.–Fri. 11–5, weekends 12:30–4.*

North Carr Lightship. Moored next to the *Unicorn*, you'll see a strange red ship, the *North Carr Lightship*. After playing a significant role in World War II, Scotland's only remaining lightship was wrecked on the Fife shore during a storm in 1959; seven crew members were lost. The ship is currently closed for refurbishment, but is worth a look from the dock. ✉ *Broughty Ferry Harbour, Beach Cres.* ☎ *01382/562497.*

FAMILY

Fodor's Choice
★

Taymara. The nonprofit group that looks after the *North Carr Lightship* runs exhilarating dolphin-watching trips on its other vessels, the *Badger* and the *Marigot*. Excursions leave from Broughty Ferry Harbour and include a half-day trip along the River Tay to Perth or an hour around the mouth of the delta, where dolphins jump and play. Prior booking is essential. One-hour trips are £14, half-day trips are £36. ✉ *Broughty Ferry Harbour, Beach Cres., Dundee* ☎ *01382/562497* ⊕ *www.tayrivertrips.org.*

FAMILY ***Unicorn.*** It's easy to spot this 46-gun wood warship, as it's fronted by a figurehead of a white unicorn. This frigate has the distinction of being the oldest British-built warship afloat, having been launched in 1824 at Chatham, England. You can clamber right down into the hold, or see the models and displays about the Royal Navy's history. In the summer there are often jazz nights onboard. The ship's hours vary in winter, so call ahead. ⊠ *Victoria Dock, east of Tay Rd. bridge* ⊕ *www. frigateunicorn.org* 🎫 *£5.25* ⊙ *Apr.–Oct., daily 10–5; Nov.–Mar., Wed.– Fri. noon–4, weekends 10–4; last admission 30 mins before closing.*

WHERE TO EAT

$
INTERNATIONAL

✕ **D'Arcy Thomson.** Near the University of Dundee, the D'Arcy Thomson is named after the college's first professor of biology. Using beautiful zoological illustrations in its decor—from the tables to the bar—it's a refreshing mix of modern and traditional. The food has an international span, including delicate citrus and fish curries. The service is diligent but relaxed. $ *Average main: £12* ⊠ *21–23 Old Hawkhill* 🕾 *01382/622694* ⊕ *www.thedarcythompson.co.uk.*

$$
CONTEMPORARY

✕ **Jute.** Part of Dundee Contemporary Arts, this lively eatery serves breakfast at the bar, cocktails and snacks on the terrace in fine weather, or dinner in the modish dining area with its huge windows that offer views of artists at work in the printmakers studio. There are plenty of handsomely presented dishes, including teriyaki salmon with spring-onion noodles and rhubarb tart tatin. The pretheater meal is a fabulous value: £15.50 for three courses. $ *Average main: £15* ⊠ *152 Nethergate* 🕾 *01382/909246* ⊕ *www.jutecafebar.co.uk.*

$$
ITALIAN

✕ **Piccolo.** This small basement eatery, with wooden tables and chairs and a quirky staff, attracts a diverse clientele. It serves surprisingly good pizzas, crepes, and a fine plate of pappardelle with chicken and apricot in a creamy ginger sauce. Reservations are recommended on weekends. $ *Average main: £15* ⊠ *21 Perth Rd.* 🕾 *01382/201419* ⊕ *www. piccolodundee.co.uk* ⌂ *Reservations essential* ⊙ *Closed Sun. and Mon.*

$$$$
CONTEMPORARY

✕ **Playwright.** This stylish restaurant is one of the city's more expensive, but it's worth the price to see the glass floor that looks into the wine cellar. The menu is well put together, offering interesting combinations of seasonal flavors—start with watermelon and fig salad, then move on to a perfectly presented seared salmon with prawn risotto. There's a beautiful bar, too, for pre- or postdinner tippling. The staff is laid back but totally efficient. $ *Average main: £25* ⊠ *11 Tay Sq.* 🕾 *01382/223113* ⊕ *www.theplaywright.co.uk* ⌂ *Reservations essential* ⊙ *Closed Sun.*

WHERE TO STAY

$$
HOTEL

🏨 **Apex City Quay.** Scandinavian-style rooms with easy chairs, plump bedding, and flat-screen TVs with DVD players help you unwind at this contemporary quayside hotel. **Pros:** stylish rooms; excellent brasserie; sleek rooms. **Cons:** outside is popular with seagulls, too; the bar is often mobbed. $ *Rooms from: £150* ⊠ *1 W. Victoria Dock Rd.* 🕾 *01382/202404* ⊕ *www.apexhotels.com* ⥅ *145 rooms, 8 suites* ⓧ *Breakfast.*

$
B&B/INN

🏨 **Duntrune House.** Set among acres of tidy lawns and rustling trees, this mansion is a genteel contrast to the city. **Pros:** owners are keen genealogists and can offer advice to ancestor-seekers; the house and gardens are full of interest; tasty meals. **Cons:** might be too cluttered for some tastes; minimum two-night stay. $ *Rooms from: £90* ⊠ *Off A90, 5 miles northeast of Dundee, Duntrune* 🕾 *01382/350239* ⊕ *www. duntrunehouse.co.uk* ⥅ *4 rooms* ⊙ *Closed Nov.–Feb.* ⓧ *Breakfast.*

$
B&B/INN

🏨 **Fisherman's Tavern Hotel.** One of Broughty Ferry's oldest pubs—it opened in 1827—still has its wooden, cabinlike bar, but it now stands in stark contrast to the comfortable minimalism of its bedrooms. **Pros:** short walk from the esplanade; a great breakfast served with a smile. **Cons:** you have to park on the street; some noise from the pub. $ *Rooms from: £95* ✉ *10–16 Fort St., Broughty Ferry* ☎ *01382/775941* ⊕ *www. fishermanstavern-broughtyferry.co.uk* ⤳ *12 rooms* ⍥ *Breakfast.*

$ ⊡ **Shaftsbury Lodge.** Just off the Perth Road, this Victorian-era villa set
HOTEL   among well-tended shrubs is a find for those who like smaller, more intimate hotels. **Pros:** first-rate service; pretty rooms; close, but not too close, to the city. **Cons:** some bathrooms are a little dated. $ *Rooms from: £80* ✉ *I Hyndford St.* ☎ *01382/669216* ⊕ *www.shaftesburylodge. co.uk* ⤳ *12 rooms* ⍥ *Breakfast.*

NIGHTLIFE AND THE ARTS

BARS AND   Dundee's pub scene, centered in the West End–Perth Road area, is one
PUBS   of the liveliest in Scotland.

Fisherman's Tavern. If you find yourself in Broughty Ferry, you can't leave without a tipple in the Fisherman's Tavern. ✉ *10–16 Fort St., Broughty Ferry* ☎ *01382/775941.*

Speedwell Bar. Called Mennie's by locals, the Speedwell Bar is in a mahogany-paneled building brimming with Dundonian characters. It's renowned for its superb cask beers and its whalebonelike Armitage Shanks urinals. ✉ *165–168 Perth Rd.* ☎ *01382/667783* ⊕ *www.speedwell-bar.co.uk.*

DANCE CLUBS   **Fat Sam's.** This place features DJs spinning everything from indie to deep house. It has become the city's premier venue for live music, hosting up-and-coming bands as well as established acts who like to play more intimate gigs. ✉ *31 S. Ward Rd.* ☎ *01382/228181* ⊕ *www.fatsams.co.uk.*

MUSIC   **Caird Hall.** Caird Hall is one of Scotland's finest concert halls, staging a wide range of music and events. ✉ *City Sq.* ☎ *01382/434940* ⊕ *www. cairdhall.co.uk.*

THEATER   **Dundee Repertory Theatre.** This is home to the award-winning Dundee Rep Ensemble and to Scotland's preeminent contemporary-dance group, Scottish Dance Theatre. Popular with locals, the restaurant and bar welcome late-night comedy shows and jazz bands. ✉ *Tay Sq.* ☎ *01382/223530* ⊕ *www.dundeerep.co.uk.*

SPORTS AND THE OUTDOORS

GOLF   East of Perthshire, near the city of Dundee, lies a string of demanding courses along the shores of the North Sea and inland into the foothills of the Grampian Mountains. Golfers who excel in windy conditions particularly enjoy the breezes blowing westward from the sea.

Camperdown Golf Course. For an alternative to the wild and windy east-coast links, try this magnificent municipal parkland course on the outskirts of Dundee. You can enjoy a game amid tree-lined fairways near the imposing Camperdown House. ✉ *Camperdown Park, Coupar Angus Rd.* ☎ *01382/431820* ⊕ *www.dundeecity.gov.uk/golf* ⛳ *Green fee: weekdays £27; weekends £32* ⚐ *18 holes, 6548 yards, par 71* ☉ *Daily.*

Fodor'sChoice   **Carnoustie Golf Links.** The venue for the British Open in 1999 and 2007,
★   the coastal links around Carnoustie have challenged golfers since at least 1527. Winners here have included many of the sport's biggest names: Armour, Hogan, Cotton, Player, and Watson. There are three

courses, the most famous of which is the breathtaking Championship Course, ranked among the very best in the world. The choice Burnside course is full of historical interest and local color, as well as being tough and interesting. The Buddon course, designed by Peter Allis and Dave Thomas, is recommended for links novices. ⌧ *20 Links Parade, Carnoustie* ☎ *01241/802270* ⊕ *www.carnoustiegolflinks.co.uk* ☜ *Green fee: Championship £147; Burnside £40; Buddon £30* ⌧ *Reservations essential* ⚑. *Championship course: 18 holes, 6941 yds, par 72; Burnside: 18 holes, 6028 yds, par 68; Buddon: 18 holes, 5420 yds, par 66* ⊙ *Daily.*

Panmure Golf Club. Down the road from the famous Carnoustie Golf Links, this traditional course offers an excellent challenge with its seaside setting, undulating greens, and sometimes excruciating—but always entertaining—burrows. The signature sixth is named after British Open Championship winner Ben Hogan, who practiced here prior to his triumphant tournament at Carnoustie in 1953. ⌧ *Burnside Rd., off Station Rd., Carnoustie* ☎ *01241/855120* ⊕ *www.panmuregolfclub.co.uk* ☜ *Green fee: £75* ⌧ *Reservations essential* ⚑. *18 holes, 6551 yds, par 70* ⊙ *Daily.*

SHOPPING

BOOKS
Big Bairn Books. There is no better place than Big Bairn Books to find old annuals of *The Beano, The Broons,* and *Oor Wullie*, all published by cult—and local—publisher D.C. Thomson. ⌧ *17 Exchange St.* ☎ *01382/220225.*

COFFEE AND TEA
J. Allan Braithwaite. This shop carries 13 types of freshly roasted coffees and more than 30 blended teas that you can pop into one of the quaint teapots you'll find here. ⌧ *6 Castle St.* ☎ *01382/322693.*

HOME FURNISHINGS
Westport Gallery. This shop stocks contemporary designer housewares, including ceramics and glass, plus highly stylized clothing and jewelry. ⌧ *44 West Port* ☎ *01382/221751.*

JEWELRY
Queen's Gallery. The Queen's Gallery has a compelling selection of jewelry, ceramics, and paintings by Scottish artists. ⌧ *160 Nethergate* ☎ *01382/220600.*

ARBROATH

15 miles north of Dundee.

You can find traditional boatbuilding in the fishing town of Arbroath. It also has several small curers and processors, and shops sell the town's most famous delicacy, Arbroath smokies—whole haddock gutted and lightly smoked. A few miles north along the coast is the old fishing village of Auchmithie, with a beautiful little beach that you can walk to via a short path. The jagged, reddish cliffs and caves are home to a flourishing seabird population.

GETTING HERE AND AROUND

The East Coast train line stops at Arbroath. The Abbey and Signal Tower are all within walking distance, but you'll need a car to get to Auchmithie. If you're driving from Dundee, take A92.

ESSENTIALS

Visitor Information Arbroath Tourist Information ⌧ *Fish Market Quay, A92* ☎ *01241/872609* ⊕ *www.angusanddundee.co.uk.*

EXPLORING

Arbroath Abbey. Founded in 1178, Arbroath Abbey is an unmistakable presence in the town center; it seems to straddle whole streets, as if the town were simply ignoring the red-stone ruin in its midst. Surviving today are remains of the church, as well as one of the most complete examples in existence of an abbot's residence. From here in 1320 a passionate plea was sent by

King Robert the Bruce (1274–1329) and the Scottish Church to Pope John XXII (circa 1245–1334) in far-off Rome. The pope had until then sided with the English kings, who adamantly refused to acknowledge Scottish independence. The Declaration of Arbroath stated firmly, "It is in truth not for glory, nor riches, nor honours that we are fighting, but for freedom—for that alone, which no honest man gives up but with life itself." Some historians describe this plea, originally drafted in Latin, as the single most important document in Scottish history. The pope advised English king Edward II (1284–1327) to make peace, but warfare was to break out along the border from time to time for the next 200 years. The excellent visitor center recounts this history in well-planned displays. ⊠ *Abbey St.* ☎ *01241/878756* ⊕ *www.historic-scotland.gov.uk* ⊠ *£5.50* ⊗ *Apr.–Sept., daily 9:30–5:30; Oct.–Mar., daily 9:30–4:30.*

Signal Tower Museum. In the early 19th century Arbroath was the base for the construction of the Bell Rock lighthouse on a treacherous, barely exposed rock in the Forth of Tay. A signal tower was built to facilitate communication with the builders working far from shore. That structure now houses the Signal Tower Museum, which tells the story of the lighthouse, built by Robert Stevenson (1772–1850) in 1811. The museum also houses a collection of items related to the history of the town, its customs, and the local fishing industry. ⊠ *Ladyloan, west of harbor* ☎ *01241/435329* ⊠ *Free* ⊗ *Tue.–Sat. 10–5.*

WHERE TO EAT

$ ✕ **But 'n' Ben.** This homey restaurant serves lunches and dinners which
BRITISH offer a taste of quality Scottish home cooking, including smokie pancakes, crab salad, mince and tatties, and lemon drizzle cake, all at reasonable prices. It's next to Auchmithie's lovely shingle beach; a stroll here is the perfect way to work up an appetite or work off over-indulgence. ⑤ *Average main: £13* ⊠ *Ethie St., 3 miles off A92, Auchmithie* ☎ *01241/ 877223* ⊕ *www.butnbenauchmithie.co.uk* ⊗ *Closed Tues.*

$ ✕ **Sugar and Spice.** Peruse the sweets of your childhood and reminisce
CAFÉ about the cakes your grandmother used to make in this combination café and sweet shop. Locals flock here to enjoy the meringues, sponges, and other desserts. There are soups and sandwiches for lunch and simple dishes like roast beef and Yorkshire pudding for dinner. ⑤ *Average main: £9* ⊠ *9–13 High St.* ☎ *01241/437500* ⊕ *www.sugarandspiceshop.co.uk.*

WHERE TO STAY

$ | 🏨 **The Brucefield.** This old manor house, set among well-tended grounds,
B&B/INN | offers luxurious rooms for very reasonable rates. **Pros:** all the touches you'd expect in a five-star hotel; quality bedding; friendly owners. **Cons:** two-night minimum in high season; a 20-minute walk to the city center. $ *Rooms from: £90* ⊠ *Cliffburn Rd.* ☎ *01241/875393* ⊕ *www.brucefieldbandb.com* ◖ *4 rooms* ◍ *Breakfast.*

$ | 🏨 **Harbour Nights.** An excellent and somewhat plush budget option, this
B&B/INN | B&B is right on the harbor, affording you the most authentic Arbroath stay possible. **Pros:** splendid seafront location; delicious breakfasts. **Cons:** only one room with a private bathroom; you must book far in advance. $ *Rooms from: £80* ⊠ *4 Shore* ☎ *01421/434343* ⊕ *www.harbournights.co.uk* ◖ *5 rooms, 1 with bath* ◍ *Breakfast.*

MONTROSE

14 miles north of Arbroath via A92.

An unpretentious and attractive town with a museum and a selection of shops, Montrose sits beside a wide estuary known as the Montrose Basin.

GETTING HERE AND AROUND

On the main East Coast train line and local bus route (the Stagecoach Strathtay 39 and 73 from Dundee and Arbroath), the town is easily accessed by public transportation. However, you'll need a car to get to attractions outside town.

ESSENTIALS

Visitor Information Montrose Tourist Information Centre ⊠ *Panmure Pl.* ☎ *01674/673232* ▭ *Free* ⊙ *Tue.–Sat. 10–5.*

EXPLORING

House of Dun. The National Trust for Scotland's leading attraction in this area is the House of Dun, which overlooks the Montrose Basin. The mansion was built in the 1730s for lawyer David Erskine, otherwise known as Lord Dun (1670–1755). Designed by architect William Adam (1689–1748), the house is particularly noted for its ornate plasterwork and curious Masonic masonry. Showing everything from Lady Dun's collection of embroidery to the working kitchens, this house tells the story of the Seat of Dun and the eminent family's history. The sprawling grounds have a restored handloom weaving workshop, plus an enchanting walled Victorian garden. ⊠ *A935, 4 miles west of Montrose* ☎ *0844/4932144* ⊕ *www.nts.org.uk/Visits* ▭ *£10* ⊙ *House Apr.–June and Sept., Wed.–Sun. noon–5; July and Aug., daily 11–5; garden year-round, daily 9–sunset.*

Montrose Basin Wildlife Centre. Run by the Scottish Wildlife Trust, the Montrose Basin Wildlife Centre is a nature reserve with geese, ducks, and swans. Several nature trails can take you up close to the reserve's residents if you're quiet. ■ **TIP→ In October at least 20,000 pinkfooted geese arrive: come in the morning and the evening to see them fill the sky.** ⊠ *Rossie Braes* ☎ *01674/676336* ⊕ *www.montrosebasin.org.uk* ▭ *£4* ⊙ *Visitor center Mar.–Oct., daily 10:30–5; Nov.–Feb., Fri.–Sun. 10:30–4.*

5

Montrose Museum. The town's museum—housed in a neoclassical building that also contains the tourist information center—exhibits some fascinating bequests by the local gentry, including an early-19th-century ship carved from bone by French prisoners in the Napoleonic war. ⊠ *Panmure Pl.* ☎ *01674/673232* ⊕ *www.angus.gov.uk/history/museums/montrose* ⊠ *Free* ☉ *Tue.–Sat. 10–5.*

BRECHIN

10 miles southwest of Montrose.

The small market town of Brechin has a cathedral that was founded around 1200 and contains an interesting selection of antiquities, including the Mary Stone, a Pictish relic.

GETTING HERE AND AROUND

Brechin is not on the East Coast train line but can be reached by bus from Montrose or Arbroath (the Stagecoach Strathtay number 30). It's on the A935, just off the main A90 road between Dundee and Aberdeen.

EXPLORING

Brechin Town House Museum. Located in the old courtroom which had cells in its cellars, the Brechin Town House Museum houses a small but interesting collection of objects from as far back as the Bronze Age. There is a small tourist information desk within the museum. ⊠ *28 High St.* ☎ *01356/625536* ⊕ *www.angus.gov.uk/history/museums/brechin* ⊠ *Free* ☉ *Tue.–Sat. 10–5.*

Pictavia. The first arrivals in this part of Scotland were the Picts, who came sometime in the first millennium. Pictavia explores what is known about this race of Celts using actual artifacts, replicas, and interactive exhibits. A highlight is hearing Pictish music. ⊠ *Brechin Castle Centre, Off A90* ☎ *01307/626241* ⊕ *www.pictavia.org.uk* ⊠ *£3.25* ☉ *May–Oct., Mon.–Sat. 9–5, Sun. 10–5; Nov.–Apr., weekends 10–5.*

Round Tower. The town's 10th-century Brechin Cathedral and Round Tower is on the site of a former Celtic monastery (priory of the Culdee monks) and has some unusual examples of medieval sculpture. The tower is one of only two on mainland Scotland. This type of structure is more frequently found in Ireland. ⊠ *6 Church St.* ☎ *01356/629360* ⊕ *www.brechincathedral.org* ⊠ *Free* ☉ *Daily 9–5.*

WHERE TO EAT

$

BAKERY

✕ **Rosie's Bakehouse.** It's exciting to discover such a great bakery in a small Scottish town. You'll find all the classics, from traditional Victoria sponge cake to much-loved scones. If you're in the mood for something more substantial, try the soups, panini, and sandwiches, all served by the cheerful staff. ⑤ *Average main: £5* ⊠ *26 High St.* ☎ *01356/625254* ☉ *Closed Sun. No dinner.*

BEAUTIFUL BEACHES

Scotland's east coast enjoys many hours of sunshine, compared with its west coast, and is blessed with lots of sandy beaches under the ever-changing backdrop of the sky. Take time to explore the beaches and walk along the coast for a change of pace whatever the time of year.

In Fife, Tentsmuir's Beach near St. Andrews is popular with kite fly-ers and horseback riders, and the famous and lovely West Sands in St. Andrews is where the running sequences in the movie *Chariots of Fire* were filmed. The small cove beach at Elie, south of Crail, hosts cricket matches in summer.

In Angus the beach at Broughty Ferry, near the city of Dundee, fills with families and children on week-ends and during school holidays—even on the most blustery of days.

North of Arbroath lies Auchmithie Beach, more shingly (pebbly) than the others and offering a bracing breath of North Sea air. And finally, near the Montrose Basin you can discover the enchanting crescent of Lunan Bay, home to many species of seabirds.

THE ANGUS GLENS

25 miles southwest of Brechin.

You can rejoin the hurly-burly of the A90 for the return journey south from Montrose or Brechin; the more pleasant route, however, leads southwesterly on minor roads (there are several options) that travel along the face of the Grampians, following the fault line that separates Highland and Lowland. The **Angus Glens** extend north from points on A90. Known individually as the glens of Isla, Prosen, Clova, and Esk, these long valleys run into the high hills of the Grampians and some clearly marked walking routes. Those in Glen Clova are especially appealing.

Be aware that Thursday is a half day in Angus; many shops and attractions close at lunch.

GETTING HERE AND AROUND

You really need a car to reach the Angus Glens and enjoy the gentle (and not so gentle) inclines here. Glamis and Kirriemuir are both on the A928 (just off the A90), and the B955—which loops round at Glen Clova—is one of the loveliest Scottish roads to drive along, especially when the heather is blooming in late summer.

WHERE TO STAY

$ **Glen Clova Hotel.** Since the 1850s the hospitality of this hotel has lifted
B&B/INN the spirits of many a bone-tired hill walker. **Pros:** stunning location; great base for outdoor pursuits; spacious accommodations. **Cons:** lack of decent public transportation; rooms are booked well in advance. $ *Rooms from: £90* ⊠ *B955, Glen Clova* ☎ *01575/550350* ⊕ *www. clova.com* ➪ *10 rooms* ❑| *Breakfast.*

KIRRIEMUIR

15 miles southeast of Brechin.

Kirriemuir stands at the heart of Angus's red-sandstone countryside and was the birthplace of the writer J. M. Barrie (1860–1937), best known abroad as the author of *Peter Pan* (a statue of whom you can see in the town's square).

GETTING HERE AND AROUND

A number of roads lead to Kirriemuir, but A928 (off A90), which also passes Glamis Castle, is one of the loveliest. Stagecoach Strathtay runs buses to this area; the 20 and 22 from Dundee are the most regular.

EXPLORING

Camera Obscura. J. M. Barrie donated the Camera Obscura to the town. The device—a dark room with a small hole in one wall that projects an image of the outside world onto the opposite wall—is one of only three in the country. In a cricket pavilion, it's looking a little ragged these days, but it still affords magnificent views of the surrounding area on clear days. ⊠ *Kirrie Hill* ☎ *0844/4932143* ⊕ *www.nts.org. uk* ✉ *£3.50, £6 with J. M. Barrie's Birthplace* ☉ *Apr.–June, Sept., and Oct., Sat. noon–5, Sun. 1–5; July and Aug., Mon.–Sat. noon–5, Sun.1–5.*

J. M. Barrie's Birthplace. At the J. M. Barrie's Birthplace, the National Trust pays tribute to the man who sought to preserve the magic of childhood more than any other writer of his age. The house's upper floors are furnished as they might have been in Barrie's time, complete with domestic necessities, while downstairs is his study, replete with manuscripts and personal mementos. The outside washhouse is said to have served as Barrie's first theater. ⊠ *9 Brechin Rd.* ☎ *0844/4932142* ⊕ *www.nts.org.uk/visits* ✉ *£6.50, includes Camera Obscura* ☉ *Apr.–June, Sept., and Oct., Sat.–Wed. noon–5; July and Aug., daily 11–5.*

Kirriemuir Gateway to the Glens Museum. As is the style in Angus, the local museum doubles as the visitor center, meaning you can get all the information you need and admire a few stuffed birds and artifacts at the same time. Rock fans will appreciate the exhibit celebrating local lad made good (or rather bad), the late Bon Scott, lead singer of the rock band AC/DC. ⊠ *32 High St.* ☎ *01575/575479* ⊕ *www.angus.gov. uk/history/museums/kirriemuir* ✉ *Free* ☉ *Tues.–Sat. 10–5.*

NEED A BREAK? | **88 Degrees.** If you're not in a rush (the service can be slow), you'll enjoy the best coffee in town and temple-achingly sweet cakes and handmade chocolates at 88 Degrees. ⊠ *17 High St.* ☎ *01575/570888.*

FORFAR

7 miles east of Kirriemuir.

Forfar goes about its business of being the center of a farming hinterland without being preoccupied with (or even that interested in) tourism.

GETTING HERE AND AROUND

Buses are slow here. The quickest route is by car: take the A90 north, then the A926 turnoff. Alternatively, the A932/A933 route from Arbroath takes you through farmland and Angus villages.

EXPLORING

OFF THE
BEATEN
PATH

Aberlemno. You can see excellent examples of Pictish stone carvings about 5 miles northeast of Forfar alongside the B9134. Carvings of crosses, angels, serpents, and other animals adorn the stones, which date from the 7th to the early 9th centuries. Note the stone in the nearby churchyard—one side is carved with a cross and the other side depicts the only known battle scene in Pictish art, complete with horsemen and foot soldiers.

Meffan Museum and Art Gallery. The high point of a visit to Fofar is the Meffan Museum and Art Gallery, which displays an interesting collection of Pictish carved stones and artifacts from the dark days of burning witches. Two galleries host frequently changing exhibitions by local and Scottish artists. The museum also houses a tourist information desk. ✉ *20 W. High St.* ☎ *01307/476482* ⊕ *www.angus.gov.uk/history/museums/meffan* ⊠ *Free* ☺ *Tues.–Sat. 10–5.*

GLAMIS

5 miles southwest of Forfar, 6 miles south of Kirriemuir.

Set in rolling countryside is the little village of Glamis (pronounced *glahms*).

GETTING HERE AND AROUND

The drive to Glamis Castle, along beech- and-yew-lined roads, is as majestic as the castle itself. Take the A90 north from Dundee, then off onto the A928. The village of Glamis can be reached by the Stagecoach Strathtay number 22, but service is rather infrequent.

EXPLORING

Angus Folk Museum. A row of 19th-century cottages with unusual stone-slab roofs makes up the Angus Folk Museum, whose exhibits focus on the tools of domestic and agricultural life in the region during the past 200 years. ✉ *Off A94* ☎ *0844/4932141* ⊕ *www.nts.org.uk/visits* ⊠ *£6.50* ☺ *Apr.–June and Sept.–Oct., weekends noon–5; July and Aug., daily noon–5.*

Fodor'sChoice
★

Glamis Castle. One of Scotland's best-known and most beautiful castles, Glamis Castle connects Britain's royalty through 10 centuries, from Macbeth (Thane of Glamis) to the late Queen Mother and her daughter, the late Princess Margaret, born here in 1930 (the first royal princess born in Scotland in 300 years). The property of the earls of Strathmore and Kinghorne since 1372, the castle was largely reconstructed in the late 17th century; the original keep, which is much older, is still intact. One of the most famous rooms in the castle is Duncan's Hall, the legendary setting for Shakespeare's *Macbeth*. Guided tours allow you to see fine collections of china, tapestries, and furniture. Within the castle is the delightful Castle Kitchen restaurant; the grounds contain a huge gift shop, a shop selling local produce, and a pleasant picnic area. ⊠ *A94, 1 mile north of Glamis* ☏ *01307/840393* ⊕ *www.glamis-castle. co.uk* ⊠ *£10.75* ⊙ *Mar.–Oct., daily 10-6.*

MEIGLE

7 miles southwest of Glamis, 11 miles northwest of Dundee.

The historic village of Meigle, nestled in the rich agricultural land of the Strathmore Valley, is well known to those with an interest in Pictish stones. Said to be built on an 11th-century Pictish monastery, the village has a number of elaborate Victorian buildings.

GETTING HERE AND AROUND

Meigle is an easy and pleasant drive from Glamis on the A94 (or from Dundee on the B954). The hourly Stagecoach Strathtay from Dundee (number 57) stops here.

EXPLORING

Meigle Sculptured Stone Museum. The town of Meigle, in the wide swath of Strathmore, has one of the most notable collections of sculpted stones in western Europe, housed at the Meigle Sculptured Stone Museum. It consists of some 25 monuments from the Celtic Christian period (8th to 11th centuries), nearly all of which were found in or around the local churchyard. ⊠ *A94* ☏ *01828/640 612* ⊕ *www.historic-scotland.gov.uk* ⊠ *£4.50* ⊙ *Apr.–Sept., daily 9:30–5:30.*

ALYTH

10 miles west of Glamis, 15 miles northwest of Dundee.

Dating back to the Dark Ages, this market town was completely transformed by the Industrial Revolution, which lined its streets with mills and factories. The 20th century saw the closing of most of these companies, but the town had never forgotten its agricultural heritage. To this day it holds on to its rural appeal.

GETTING HERE AND AROUND

Just 4 miles farther along the B954 from Meigle, Alyth is also served by Stagecoach Strathtay number 57.

EXPLORING

Alyth Museum. This small but intriguing museum about the region's history displays nearly every type of tool and implement put to use by the resourceful and hardy locals. ⊠ *Commercial St.* ☏ *01828/633474* ⊠ *Free* ⊙ *May–Sept., Wed.–Sun. 1–5.*

WHERE TO STAY

$

B&B/INN

⛌ Tigh Na Leigh. This grand house, now a classy B&B, was originally built by the Earl of Airlie for his doctor. **Pros:** lovingly restored building; luxurious rooms; exceptional food. **Cons:** only five rooms; books up quickly. ⑤ *Rooms from: £98* ⊠ *22–24 Airlie St.* ☏ *01828/632372* ⊕ *www.tighnaleigh.com* ⇔ *5 rooms* ⧉ *Breakfast.*

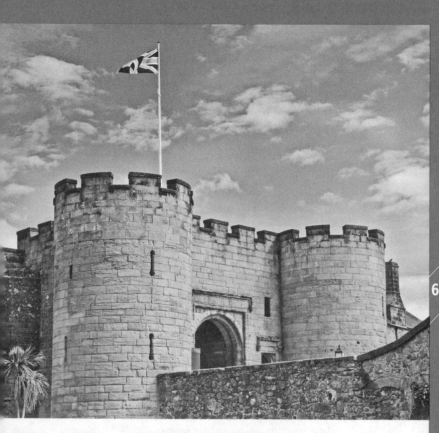

THE CENTRAL HIGHLANDS

Updated
by Mike
Gonzalez

The Central Highlands are home to superb castles, moody mountains, and gorgeous glens that are best explored at a leisurely pace. The waters of Loch Lomond reflect the crags and dark woods that surround it, and attract those in search of a more romantic and nostalgic Scotland enshrined in the verses of the famous song that bears its name. When you finish a day of exploring, celebrate with a glass of one of the region's top-notch whiskies.

The Carse of Stirling, the wide plain guarded by Stirling Castle, was the scene of many important moments in Scotland's history—from the Roman invasion commemorated by the Antonine Wall, to the castles that mark the site of medieval kingdoms and the battles to preserve them. Look up at Stirling Castle from the valley and you can see why so many battles were fought over its possession.

North from Stirling, past Dunblane, are the highland hills and valleys of the Trossachs, whose high peaks attract walkers and a tougher breed of cyclist. From Callander, a neat tourist town, the hills stretch westward to the "bonnie bonnie banks" of Loch Lomond. From the peaks of the Trossachs, on a good day, you can see Edinburgh Castle to the east and the tower blocks of Glasgow's housing projects to the west.

Farther north is Perth, once Scotland's capital; its wealthy mansions reflect the prosperous agricultural land that surrounds the city, and it is still an important market town today. Overlooking the River Tay, the city can reasonably claim to be the gateway to the Highlands, sitting as it does on the Highland Fault that divides Lowlands from Highlands. From Perth the landscape begins to change on the road to Pitlochry and the unforgiving moors of Rannoch.

For many years Stirling was the starting point for visitors from Edinburgh and Glasgow setting out to explore the Trossachs, with their lochs and hills hung with shaggy birch, oak, and pinewoods. The Victorians were drawn by the lyrical descriptions of the area by Romantic poets like Sir Walter Scott (1771–1832), who set his dramatic verse narrative of 1810, "The Lady of the Lake," in the landscape of the Trossachs.

For those in search of more dramatic landscapes, the Highland fault line runs northeast above Perth, and into the old county of Angus and the high, rough country of Rannoch Moor and the towering Ben Lawers, near Killin, the ninth-highest peak in Scotland.

The region is full of reminders of heroic struggles, particularly against the English, from the monument to William Wallace to the field at Bannockburn (near Stirling), where Robert the Bruce took on the invader. In nearby Callander, Rob Roy MacGregor, the Scottish Robin Hood, lived (and looted and terrorized) his way into the storybooks.

TOP REASONS TO GO

Loch Lomond: You can see the sparkling waters of Scotland's largest loch by car, by boat, or on foot. A popular option is the network of bicycle tracks that creep around Loch Lomond and the Trossachs National Park, offering every conceivable terrain.

Castles: Choosing between Scotland's most splendid fortresses and mansions is a challenge. Among the highlights are Stirling Castle, with its palace built by James V, and Scone Palace, near Perth, with its grand aristocratic acquisitions. By contrast, Doune Castle is an atmospheric reminder of life in a fortification.

Great hikes: The way to experience the Central Highlands is to head out on foot. The fit and well equipped can "bag a Munro" (hills over 3,000 feet, named after the mountaineer who listed them). The less demanding woodland paths and gentle rambles of the Trossachs will stir even the least adventurous rambler.

Whisky tours and tastes: The Scots love their whisky, and what better way to participate in Scottish life and culture than to learn about the land's finest? There are some exceptional distilleries in this region, from the Edradour Distillery to Glenturret, home of the Famous Grouse.

Bike trails: This region claims excellent biking trails, ranging from a gentle pedal through Stirling to a wind-in-your-face journey on the Lowland/Highland Trail. Whatever your preference, biking is a beautiful way to tour the countryside.

6

ORIENTATION AND PLANNING

GETTING ORIENTED

The twin reference points for your trip are Stirling, an ancient historic town from whose castle you can see central Scotland laid out before you, and Perth, 36 miles away, the gateway to the Highlands. North from Stirling, you cross the fertile open plain (the Carse of Stirling) dotted with historic cathedral towns like Dunblane and Doune. The Trossachs are the Scotland of the Romantic imagination, lochs and woodland glens, drovers' inns and grand country houses. The small towns of the region, like Callander, Aberfoyle, and Pitlochry, are bases from which to explore this changing countryside. To the west lies Loch Lomond, along whose banks the road leads from industrial Glasgow to the hills and glens of the Highlands.

Stirling. Stirling is a city vibrant with history. The old town is quite a small area on the hill, and is worth covering on foot. Look down from the Stirling Castle crag that dominates the plains below and you can see the stages of its growth descending from the hill. The town is a good center from which to explore the changing landscape of central Scotland.

The Trossachs and Loch Lomond. This area is small, but incredibly varied—from dramatic mountain peaks that attract walkers and climbers, to the gentler slopes and forests that stretch from Perth eastward

Stirling
see detail map

to Aberfoyle and the shores of Loch Lomond. The glens and streams that pepper the region create a romantic landscape that is a perfect habitat for the figure of Rob Roy McGregor—Robin Hood or bandit according to taste, but undeniably Scottish. Loch Lomond's western side is more accessible, if busier, than the east, but the views across the loch are spectacular.

Perthshire. The prosperous air of Perth, once the capital of Scotland, testifies to its importance as a port exporting wool, salmon, and whisky to the world. Scone Palace serves as a monument to that era. The route northward leads across the Highland Boundary and into the changing landscapes beyond Pitlochry to Rannoch Moor, where the wind sweeps across the hardy heather.

PLANNING

WHEN TO GO

The Trossachs and Loch Lomond are in some ways a miniature Scotland, from the tranquil east shore of Loch Lomond to the hills and glens of the Trossachs and the mountains of the Arrochar Alps to the west—and all within a few hours' drive. In spring and summer, despite the erratic weather, the area is always crowded; this is a good time to go. However, the landscape is notably dramatic when the trees are turning red and brown in autumn, and evening skies are spectacular. Scotland in winter has a different kind of beauty, especially for skiers and climbers. ■ TIP→ **Carry clothes for wet and dry weather, as the weather can change quickly. Summer evenings attract midges; take some repellent.**

PLANNING YOUR TIME
Scotland's beautiful interior is excellent touring country, though the cities of Stirling and Perth are worth your time, too; Stirling in particular is worth a day. Two (slightly rushed) days would be enough to explore the Trossachs loop, to gaze into the waters of Loch Venachar and Loch Achray. The glens, in some places, run parallel to the lochs, including those along Lochs Earn, Tay, and Rannoch, making for satisfying loops and round-trips. Loch Lomond is easily accessible from either Glasgow or Stirling, and is well worth exploring. Don't miss the opportunity to take a boat trip on a loch, especially on Loch Lomond or on Loch Katrine.

GETTING HERE AND AROUND
AIR TRAVEL
Perth and Stirling can be reached easily from the Edinburgh, Dundee, and Glasgow airports by train, car, or bus.

BUS TRAVEL
A good network of buses connects with the central belt via Edinburgh and Glasgow. For more information, contact Scottish Citylink or National Express. The Perth and Kinross Council supplies a map (available in tourist information centers) showing all public transport routes in Perthshire, marked with nearby attractions.

First, Scottish Citylink, and Stagecoach organize reliable service on routes throughout the Central Highlands.

Bus Contacts First ☎ *08708/727271* ⊕ *www.firstgroup.com.*
National Express ☎ *08717/818181* ⊕ *www.nationalexpress.com.*
Scottish Citylink ☎ *0871/2663333* ⊕ *www.citylink.co.uk.*
Stagecoach ☎ *01292/613502* ⊕ *www.stagecoachbus.com.*

CAR TRAVEL
You'll find easy access to the area from the central belt of Scotland via the motorway network. The M80 connects Glasgow to Stirling, and then briefly joins the M9 from Edinburgh, which runs within sight of the walls of Stirling Castle. From there the A9 runs from Stirling to Perth, and onward to Pitlochry; it is a good road but a little too fast for its own good (so take care). Perth can also be reached via the M90 over the Forth Bridge from Edinburgh. Three signed touring routes are useful: the Perthshire Tourist Route, the Deeside Tourist Route, and the Pitlochry Tourist Route, a beautiful and unexpected trip via Crieff and Loch Tay. Local tourist information centers can supply maps of these routes. Once you leave the major motorways, roads become narrower and slower, with many following the contours of the lochs. Be prepared for your journey to take longer than distances might suggest.

TRAIN TRAVEL

The Central Highlands are linked to Edinburgh and Glasgow by rail, with through routes to England (some direct-service routes from London take less than five hours). Several discount ticket options are available, although in some cases on the ScotRail system a discount card must be purchased before your arrival in the United Kingdom. Note that families with children and travelers under 26 or over 60 are eligible for significant discounts. Contact Trainline, National Rail, or ScotRail for details.

The West Highland Line runs through the western portion of the area. Services also run to Stirling, Dunblane, Perth, and Gleneagles; stops on the Inverness–Perth line include Dunkeld, Pitlochry, and Blair Atholl.

Train Contacts National Rail Enquiries ☎ 08457/484950 ⊕ www.trainline.co.uk. **ScotRail** ☎ 08457/550033 ⊕ www.scotrail.co.uk. **Trainline** ⊕ www.thetrainline.com.

RESTAURANTS

Regional country delicacies—loch trout, river salmon, lamb, and venison—appear regularly on even modest menus in Central Highlands restaurants. In all the towns and villages in the area you will find simple pubs, often crowded and noisy, many of them serving substantial food at lunchtime and in the evening until about 9 (eaten balanced on your knee, perhaps, or at a shared table). It can be difficult to find a place to eat later than that, so plan ahead. *Prices in the reviews are the average cost of a main course at dinner or, if dinner is not served, at lunch.*

HOTELS

There is a wide selection of accommodations available throughout the region, especially in Stirling, Bridge of Allan, Callander, and Pitlochry. They range from bed-and-breakfasts to private houses with a small number of rooms to rural accommodation (often on farms). The grand houses of the past—family homes to the landed aristocracy—have for the most part become country-house hotels. Their settings, often on ample grounds, offer an experience of grand living—but there are also modern hotels in the area, for those who prefer 21st-century amenities. *Prices in the reviews are the lowest cost of a standard double room in high season, including 20% V.A.T.*

VISITOR INFORMATION

The tourist offices in Stirling and Perth are open year-round, as are offices in larger towns; others are seasonal (generally from April to October).

STIRLING

26 miles northeast of Glasgow, 36 miles northwest of Edinburgh.

Stirling is one of Britain's great historic towns. An impressive proportion of the Old Town walls can be seen from Dumbarton Road, a cobbled street leading to Stirling Castle, built on a steep-sided plug of rock. From its esplanade there is a commanding view of the surrounding Carse of Stirling. The guns on the castle battlements are a reminder of the military advantage to be gained from its position.

GETTING HERE AND AROUND

Stirling's central position in the area makes it an ideal point for travel to and from Glasgow and Edinburgh (or north to Perth and the Highlands) by rail, train, or bus. The town itself is compact and easily walkable, though a shuttle bus travels to and from the town center up the steep road to Stirling Castle every 20 minutes. The Back Walk takes the visitor on a circuit around the base of the castle walls—set aside at least 30 minutes for a leisurely walk.

TIMING

The historic part of town is tightly nestled around the castle—everything is within easy walking distance. The National Wallace Monument (2 miles away) is on the outskirts of the town and can be reached by taxi or, for the more energetic, on foot.

ESSENTIALS

Visitor Information Stirling Visitor Information Centre ⊠ *Old Town Jail, St. John St.* ☎ *01786/465019.*

EXPLORING STIRLING

TOP ATTRACTIONS

Fodor's Choice
★

Bannockburn Heritage Centre. Opening in 2014, this museum uses cutting-edge technology to help you take part in Scotland's greatest battle, where Robert the Bruce defeated King Edward II at Bannockburn in 1314. The beautifully designed Bannockburn Heritage Centre celebrates the cunning of Robert the Bruce, who chose this site because its boggy ground would impede the English horses. The fields that surround the museum were the battlefield, and interactive displays re-create the sights and sounds of that great medieval encounter. The circular monument that stands outside is now capped by a poem by Kathleen Jamie. ⊠ *Glasgow Rd., Bannockburn* ☎ *0844/493–2139* ⊕ *www.nts.org.uk/Visits* ⊠ *£20.*

National Wallace Monument. This Victorian-era shrine to William Wallace (circa 1270–1305), the Scottish freedom fighter reborn as "Braveheart" in Mel Gibson's film of the same name, was built between 1856 and 1869. It was near Old Stirling Bridge that Wallace, with his ragged army of Scots, won a major victory in 1297. A less flamboyant version of Wallace's life is told in an exhibition and audiovisual presentation in this pencil-thin museum on the Abbey Craig. Up close, it becomes less slim and soaring, revealing a substantial square tower with a creepy spiral stairway. To reach the monument, follow the Bridge of Allan signs (A9) northward, crossing the River Forth by the New Bridge of 1832, next to the old one. The National Wallace Monument is signposted at the next traffic circle. ⊠ *Abbey Craig, Hillfoot Rd.* ☎ *01786/472140* ⊕ *www. nationalwallacemonument.com* ⊠ *£8.50* ⊙ *Apr.–June, Sept. and Oct., daily 10–5; July and Aug., daily 10–6; Nov.–Mar., daily 10:30–4.*

Fodor's Choice
★

Stirling Castle. Its magnificent strategic position on a steep-sided crag made Stirling Castle the grandest prize in the Scots Wars of Independence in the late 13th and early 14th centuries. The Battle of Bannockburn in 1314 was fought within sight of its walls, and the victory by Robert the Bruce won both the castle and freedom from English subjugation for almost four centuries. Take time to visit the **Castle Exhibition** in the Queen Anne Garden beyond the lower gate to get an overview of its long history and evolution as a stronghold and palace.

The daughter of King Robert I (Robert the Bruce), Marjory, married Walter Fitzallan, the high steward of Scotland. Their descendants included the Stewart dynasty of Scottish monarchs (Mary, Queen of Scots was a Stewart, though she preferred the French spelling, *Stuart*). The Stewarts were responsible for many of the works that survive within the castle walls today. They made Stirling Castle their court and power base, creating fine Renaissance-style buildings that were not completely obliterated, despite reconstruction for military purposes.

Enter the castle through its outer defenses, which consist of a great curtained wall and batteries from 1708, built to bulwark earlier defenses by the main gatehouse. From this lower square the most conspicuous feature is the **Palace,** built by King James V (1512–42) between 1538 and 1542. The decorative figures festooning the ornate outer walls show the influence of French masons. An orientation center in the basement lets you try out the clothes and musical instruments of the time. Then you are led across a terrace to the newly refurbished **Royal Apartments**, which re-create the furnishings and tapestries found here during the reign of James V and his French queen, Mary of Guise. The queen's bedchamber contains copies of the beautiful tapestries in which the hunt for the white unicorn is clearly an allegory for the persecution of Christ. Overlooking the upper courtyard is the **Great Hall,** built by King James IV (1473–1513) in 1503. Before the Union of Parliaments in 1707, when the Scottish aristocracy sold out to England, this building had been used as one of the seats of the Scottish Parliament. It has since been restored to its original splendor, with sparse but impressive furnishings. Here the king once ordered a full-size galleon to be placed in the hall during the fish course of a major banquet.

Among the later works built for regiments stationed here, the **Regimental Museum** stands out; it's a 19th-century baronial revival on the site of an earlier building. Nearby, the **Chapel Royal** is unfurnished but was the site of a visit by Charles I in 1633. The oldest building on the site is the **Mint,** or **Coonzie Hoose,** perhaps dating as far back as the 14th century. Below it is an arched passageway leading to the westernmost section of the ramparts, the **Nether Bailey.** As you walk along the high walls beyond the arch, you'll have the distinct feeling of being in the bow of a warship sailing up the *carselands* (valley plain) of the Forth Valley.

To the castle's south lies the hump of the Touch and the Gargunnock Hills (part of the Campsie Fells), which diverted potential direct routes from Glasgow and the south. For centuries all roads into the Highlands across the narrow waist of Scotland led through Stirling. If you look carefully northward, you can still see the Old Stirling Bridge, once the lowest and most convenient place to cross the river. ⊠ *Castle-hill* ☎ *01786/450000* ⊕ *www.historic-scotland.gov.uk/places* 🎫 *£14, includes admission to Argyll's Lodging* ⊗ *Apr.–Sept., daily 9:30–5:30; Oct.–Mar., daily 9:30–4:15.*

WORTH NOTING

Argyll's Lodging. A nobleman's town house built in three phases from the 16th century onward, this building is actually older than the name it bears—that of Archibald, the ninth earl of Argyll (1629–85), who bought it in 1666. It served for many years as a military hospital. It has now been refurbished to show how the nobility lived in 17th-century Stirling. Specially commissioned reproduction furniture and fittings are based on the original inventory of the house's contents at that time. ⊠ *Castle Wynd* ☎ *01786/450000* ⊕ *www.historic-scotland.gov.uk/places* 🎫 *£14, includes Stirling Castle* ⊗ *Hrs vary.*

Cambuskenneth Abbey. On the south side of the Abbey Craig, the scanty remains of this 13th-century abbey lie in a sweeping bend of the River Forth, with the dramatic outline of Stirling Castle as a backdrop. Important meetings of the Scottish Parliament were once held here, and King Edward I (1239–1307) of England visited in 1304. The abbey was looted and damaged during the Scots Wars of Independence in the late 13th and early 14th centuries. The reconstructed tomb of King James III (1452–88) can be seen near the outline of the high altar. ⊠ *Ladysneuk Rd.* ☎ *01667/460232* ⊕ *www.historic-scotland.gov.uk/places* 🎫 *Free* ⊗ *May–Sept., daily 9:30–6.*

Church of the Holy Rude. The nave of this handsome church survives from the 15th century, and a portion of the original medieval timber roof can also be seen. This is the only Scottish church still in use to have witnessed the coronation of a Scottish monarch—James VI (1566–1625) in 1567. ⊠ *Top of St. John's St.* ⦿ *Apr.–Sept., daily 11–4.*

Mar's Wark. These distinctive windowless and roofless ruins are the stark remains of a Renaissance palace built in 1570 by Lord Erskine (died 1572), Earl of Mar and Stirling Castle governor. The name means "Mar's work," or building. Look for the armorial carved panels, the gargoyles, and the turrets flanking a railed-off *pend* (archway). During the 1745 Jacobite rebellion, Mar's Wark was besieged and severely damaged, but its admirably worn shell survives. The ruins are enclosed by a fence, so you can view them only from the outside. ⊠ *Castle Wynd* ☎ *01667/460232* ⊕ *www.historic-scotland.gov.uk/places.*

Smith Art Gallery and Museum. This Romanesque-style museum, founded in 1874, details the history of the town through artworks and objects, the oldest of which are 7,000-year-old whale bones. A permanent exhibit traces the history of Stirling from its earliest days. There are also temporary exhibits and a café. ⊠ *Dumbarton Rd.* ☎ *01786/471917* ⊕ *www.smithartgalleryandmuseum.co.uk* ▭ *Free* ⦿ *Tues.–Sat. 10:30–5, Sun. 2–5.*

WHERE TO EAT

$
BRITISH
FAMILY

✕ **Allanwater Cafe.** Run by the Bechelli family for four generations, this light and airy café is a popular spot with locals. Try the traditional "fish tea"—here confusingly called "catch of the day"—which consists of fish-and-chips served with tea or coffee and bread and butter. This place is time-honored, tasty, and a good value. There's a tantalizing selection of Italian ice cream—if you have room. ⑤ *Average main: £10* ⊠ *15 Henderson St., Bridge of Allan* ☎ *01786/833060* ⊕ *www.allanwatercafe.co.uk.*

$$
ECLECTIC

✕ **Hermann's Restaurant.** Run by Austrian Hermann Aschaber and his Glaswegian wife, the restaurant presents the cuisines of both countries. The Black Watch–tartan carpet and alpine murals are as successfully matched as the signature Scottish dishes like *cullen skink* (a fish-and-potato soup) and chicken with Stornaway black pudding and Drambuie cream, and Austrian staples like Wiener schnitzel and cheese spaetzle. ⑤ *Average main: £19* ⊠ *58 Broad St.* ☎ *01786/450632* ⊕ *www.hermanns-restaurant.co.uk.*

$$
ECLECTIC

✕ **River House.** Behind Stirling Castle, this restaurant sits by its own tranquil little loch and is built in the style of a Scottish *crannog* (ancient loch dwelling). It's relaxed and friendly, with tables on a deck overlooking the water. Local produce dominates the menu, yet the food reflects French and Mediterranean influences. Try the curried Scottish lamb with lime yogurt. You can get here directly from the M9 motorway: follow the Stirling sign at Junction 10. From Aberfoyle it's on A84, or follow B8051 around the Castle toward the Castle Business Park. ⑤ *Average main: £16* ⊠ *The Castle Business Park, B8051* ☎ *01786/465577* ⊕ *www.riverhouse-restaurant.co.uk.*

WHERE TO STAY

$
B&B/INN
⛫ **Castlecroft.** Tucked beneath Stirling Castle, this comfortable modern house welcomes you with freshly cut flowers and homemade breakfasts. **Pros:** great location; lovely views; hearty breakfasts. **Cons:** a little hard to find if you are not arriving directly from the motorway. ⑤ *Rooms from: £70* ✉ *Ballengeich Rd.* ☎ *01786/474933* ⊕ *www.castlecroft-uk. com* ⮑ *5 rooms* ⦿ *Breakfast.*

$$
HOTEL
⛫ **Park Lodge Hotel.** This elegant 18th-century country-house hotel gives you a taste of French-inspired design and cuisine. **Pros:** great views of park; homey feel; recently renovated. **Cons:** too many floral prints. ⑤ *Rooms from: £108* ✉ *32 Park Terr.* ☎ *01786/474862* ⊕ *www. parklodge.net* ⮑ *9 rooms* ⦿ *Breakfast.*

$$$
HOTEL
⛫ **Puma Stirling Highland Hotel.** This hotel occupies what was once the town's high school, and several of the rooms preserve that history (the headmaster's study, for example). **Pros:** near train station; excellent restaurant. **Cons:** rather old-fashioned, institutional feel. ⑤ *Rooms from: £195* ✉ *Spittal St.* ☎ *01786/272727* ⊕ *www.barcelo-hotels.co.uk* ⮑ *96 rooms* ⦿ *Breakfast.*

$
B&B/INN
⛫ **West Plean.** More than 200 years old, this handsome, rambling B&B is part of a working farm. **Pros:** beautiful gardens; plenty of peace and quiet; huge and hearty breakfast. **Cons:** a little off the beaten track; a long walk to Stirling. ⑤ *Rooms from: £90* ✉ *Denny Rd.* ☎ *01786/812208* ⊕ *www.westpleanhouse.com* ⮑ *4 rooms* ⊙ *Closed Dec.* ⦿ *Breakfast.*

THE ARTS

Macrobert Arts Centre. This arts center has a theater, gallery, and cinema with programs that range from films to pantomime. It's on the campus of the University of Stirling, off the A9 as you're heading toward Bridge of Allan. ✉ *University of Stirling, W. Link Rd.* ☎ *01786/466666* ⊕ *www.macrobert.org.*

Tolbooth. Built in 1705, the Tolbooth has been many things: courthouse, jail, meeting place. At one time the city's money was kept here. It has retained its traditional Scottish steeple and gilded weathercock, and a newer tower lets you survey the surrounding country. Today it serves as an art gallery and a 200-seat theater. The bar is open for performances. ✉ *Broad St.* ☎ *01786/274000* ⊕ *www.stirling.gov.uk/tolbooth.*

SHOPPING

Stirling Arcade. Built in the 19th century, Stirling Arcade has about 20 shops. You'll find everything from toys to fine clothing. ✉ *King St.* ☎ *01786/450719.*

CERAMICS AND GLASSWARE

Barbara Davidson Pottery. South of Stirling, Barbara Davidson Pottery is run by one of the best-known potters in Scotland. Demonstrations can be arranged by appointment. Signs point the way from the A9. ✉ *Muirhall Farm, Muirhall Rd., Larbert* ☎ *01324/554430* ⊕ *www. barbara-davidson.com.*

6

Heart of Glass. This shop sells original works made by local glassblowers. ✉ *14 Henderson St., Bridge of Allan* ☎ *01786/832137* ⊕ *www. heartofglass.co.uk.*

CLOTHING

House of Henderson. A Highland outfitter, House of Henderson sells tartans, woolens, and accessories, and offers a made-to-measure kilt service. ✉ *6–8 Friars St.* ☎ *01786/473681* ⊕ *www.houseofhenderson. co.uk* ⊙ *Mon.–Sat. 9:30–5:30.*

Mill Trail. East of Stirling is Mill Trail country, along the foot of the Ochil Hills. A leaflet from any local tourist information center will lead you to the delights of a real mill shop and low mill prices—even on cashmere—at Tillicoultry, Alva, and Alloa.

GIFTS

Fotheringham Gallery. The upscale Fotheringham Gallery stocks fine jewelry and paintings. ✉ *78 Henderson St., Bridge of Allan* ☎ *01786/832861* ⊕ *www.fotheringhamgallery.co.uk.*

Stirling Bagpipes. This small shop sells bagpipes of every type and at every price, including antiques by legendary craftspeople that are displayed in glass cases. In the room behind the shop the owner lovingly turns the chanters and drones, but he will happily take time to talk you through the history of these instruments. ✉ *8 Broad St.* ☎ *01786/448886.*

SIDE TRIP FROM STIRLING

FALKIRK

14 miles southeast of Stirling, along the M9 motorway.

Falkirk has a fascinating history. It was here, at the impressive Antonine Wall, that the Roman occupiers fought back the warlike Picts. You can visit parts of the wall and imagine the fierce battles over this strategic location.

In the late 18th century Falkirk was an important industrial town because of its network of canals linking Glasgow and Edinburgh. But with the arrival of the railways, Falkirk's fortunes flagged. The canals have been brought back to life with the £78 million Millennium Link Project, which added a range of cycling and walking routes and the spectacular Falkirk Wheel, a boat lift.

GETTING HERE AND AROUND

The M9 from Stirling to Falkirk follows the widening estuary of the River Forth, the view dominated by the huge Grangemouth oil refinery in the distance.

EXPLORING

Antonine Wall. West of Falkirk, Bonnybridge is home to the most extensive remains of the Antonine Wall, a 60-mile-long Roman earthwork fortification that marked the northernmost limit of the Roman empire. Built around AD 140 as a defense against the warlike Picts of the north, it was abandoned some 20 years later. A UNESCO World Heritage Site, the wall was the site of a famous battle in 1298, when William Wallace was defeated by the English. To get here from Falkirk, take the A803 west. ✉ *Off A803, 2 miles west of Falkirk, Bonnybridge* ⊕ *www. historic-scotland.gov.uk/antoninewall* ☑ *Free* ⊙ *Open 24 hrs.*

FAMILY **Callendar House.** Near the town center, this grand country house gives you a glimpse of a family's daily life in the early 1800s. In the kitchen local guides will explain cooking in the early 19th century and perhaps even offer you a sample. Entry is through an impressive wooden hallway, and the first-floor morning and drawing rooms are the grandest in the region. There are exhibits on the Romans and the Antonine Wall, as well as on the history of Falkirk. The second floor is a gallery space and houses the town's archives. The beautiful grounds, Callendar Park, offer lots of activities and are open all year. The house is something of a secret, but well worth a visit. ⊠ *Callendar Park, off Callendar Rd.* ☎ *01324/590900* ⊕ *www.falkirkcommunitytrust.org* ☑ *Free* ☉ *Apr.–June, Aug., and Sept., weekends only; June–Aug daily; hrs vary.*

FAMILY **Falkirk Wheel.** The only rotating boatlift in the world, the Falkirk Wheel links two major waterways, the Forth and Clyde Canal and the Union Canal, between Edinburgh and Glasgow. This extraordinary engineering achievement lifts and lowers boats using four giant wheels shaped like Celtic axes; it can transport eight or more boats at a time from one canal to the other in about 45 minutes. As the wheel turns, you're transported up or down to the other canal. The Falkirk Wheel replaced 11 locks that were once the only way of moving between the two bodies of water. The site offers children's play areas, as well as canoes and bicycles rentals. ⊠ *Lime Rd., Tamfourhill* ☎ *08700/500208* ⊕ *www.thefalkirkwheel. co.uk* ☑ *£8.95* ☉ *Apr.–Oct., daily 10–5.30; Nov.–Mar., Wed.–Sun. 11–4.*

THE TROSSACHS AND LOCH LOMOND

Immortalized by Wordsworth and Sir Walter Scott, the Trossachs (the name means "bristly country") contains some of Scotland's loveliest forest, hills, and glens, well justifying the area's designation as a national park. The area has a special charm, combining the wildness of the Highlands with the prolific vegetation of an old Lowland forest. Its open ground is a dense mat of bracken and heather, and its woodland is of silver birch, dwarf oak, and hazel—trees that fasten their roots into the crevices of rocks and stop short on the very brink of lochs. There are also many small towns to visit along the way, some with their roots in a medieval world; others sprang up and expanded in the wake of the first tourists who came to Scotland in the late 19th century in search of wild country or healing waters. Dunblane has a magnificent cathedral; Doune's castle will make you stare in awe.

The most colorful season is fall, particularly October, a lovely time when most visitors have departed, and the hares, deer, and game birds have taken over. Even in rainy weather the Trossachs of "darksome glens and gleaming lochs" are memorable: the water filtering through the rocks by Loch Lomond comes out so pure and clear that the loch is like a sheet of glass.

The best way to explore this area is by car, by bike, or on foot; the latter two depend, of course, on the weather. Keep in mind that roads in this region of the country are narrow and winding, which can make for dangerous conditions in all types of weather.

The Trossachs and Loch Lomond

DUNBLANE

7 miles north of Stirling.

The small, quiet town of Dunblane, 4 miles from Stirling, has long been an important religious center; it is dominated by its cathedral, which dates mainly from the 13th century. The town also boasts one of Scotland's most impressive libraries, the Leighton Library. In mid-2014 Scottish tennis star Andy Murray will open a luxury hotel, Cromlix, a few miles from his hometown, Dunblane.

GETTING HERE AND AROUND

Dunblane station is on the main line to Perth and Inverness, and regular bus service links the town to Stirling. The Breadalbane Explorer tour bus runs a three-hour circuit from Perth or Dunkeld through Killin, Aberfeldy, Crieff, and Comrie. Your £12 ticket allows you to hop on and off along this beautiful and dramatic route. For drivers it is easily reached along the main A9 artery.

EXPLORING

Doune Castle. No self-respecting Highland chief's attire was complete without an ornate pair of pistols made in Doune, 5 miles west of Dunblane. Today the community is more widely known for having one of the best-preserved medieval castles in Scotland. It's also a place of pilgrimage for fans of *Monty Python and Holy Grail*, which was filmed here. Doune Castle is grim and high-walled, with a daunting central keep and echoing, drafty stairways up to the curtain-wall walk. The views make the climb well worthwhile. There is a good audio guide narrated by Monty Python's Terry Gilliam. The best place to photograph this squat, walled fort is from the bridge, a little way upstream. ✉ *Castle Rd., Doune* ☎ *01786/841742* ⊕ *www.historic-scotland.gov.uk* 💷 *£5* ⊙ *Apr.–Sept., daily 9:30–5:30; Oct., daily 9:30–4; Nov.–Mar., Sat.–Wed. 9:30–4.*

Dunblane Cathedral. The oldest part of Dunblane—with its narrow winding streets—huddles around this church's square. The cathedral was built by Bishop Clement in the early 13th century on the site of St. Blane's tiny 8th-century cell; with the Reformation of the 16th century, it ceased to be a cathedral. In 1996 it was the scene of a moving memorial service for the 15 children killed in the local school by Thomas Hamilton. ✉ *The Cross* ☎ *01667/460232* ⊕ *www.historic-scotland.gov.uk/places* 💷 *Free* ⊙ *Apr.–Sept., Mon.–Sat. 9:30–12:30 and 1:30–5, Sun. 2–5; Oct.–Mar., Mon.–Sat. 9:30–4, Sun. 2–4.*

WHERE TO EAT AND STAY

$ ✕**Sheriffmuir Inn.** The road to Sheriffmuir from Dunblane is too narrow to be numbered, and you may be concerned you have taken a wrong turn until you reach this splendidly isolated, whitewashed inn. Inside there is a warm fire at a friendly bar filled with wooden furniture. The restaurant is slightly more formal and has views onto the moor beyond. Owner and chef Geoff Cook keeps to local produce wherever possible, but with an international touch; try the monkfish with chili-crab crème and basmati rice or the twice-cooked belly pork with black pudding. The desserts are very tempting. ⑤ *Average main: £15* ✉ *Off A9, Sheriffmuir* ☎ *01786/823285* ⊕ *www.sheriffmuirinn.co.uk* ⊙ *Closed Mon.*

ECLECTIC

$$ 🏨 **DoubleTree by Hilton Dunblane Hydro.** One of the grandes dames where Victorians would come to "take the waters," this hotel on sprawling grounds has retained its original building and the high style of its interior. **Pros:** fine views; lovely grounds; leisure center included in the rates. **Cons:** a slightly old-fashioned feel; some rooms are small; charge for Wi-Fi. ⑤ *Rooms from: £119* ✉ *Perth Rd.* ☎ *01786/822551* ⊕ *www.doubletreedunblane.com* 🛏 *200 rooms* ⃟ *No meals.*

HOTEL

CALLANDER

8 miles northwest of Doune.

A traditional Highland-edge resort, the little town of Callander bustles throughout the year, even during off-peak times, simply because it's a gateway to Highland scenery, and Loch Lomond and the Trossachs National Park. As a result, there's plenty of window-shopping here, plus nightlife in pubs and a good selection of accommodations.

GETTING HERE AND AROUND

You can access Callander by bus from Stirling, Glasgow, or Edinburgh. If you're traveling by car from Stirling, take the M8 to Dunblane, then the A820 (which becomes the A84) to Callander. If you are coming from Glasgow, take the A81 through Aberfoyle to Callander; an alternative route (longer but more picturesque) is to take the A821 around Loch Venachar, then the A84 east to Callander.

ESSENTIALS
Visitor Information Callander **Visitor Information Centre** ⊠ *Ancaster Sq.* ☎ *01877/330342* ⊕ *www.visitscotland.com.*

EXPLORING

FAMILY **Blair Drummond Safari and Adventure Park.** As unlikely as it might seem in this gentle valley, the Blair Drummond Safari and Adventure Park is the place to see sea lions bobbing their heads above the water or monkeys swinging from the branches. Take a footbridge to Lemur Land or watch hawks and falcons in the "Birds of Prey" exhibit. ■**TIP**➔ **Beware the llamas, who are more bad-tempered than they may appear.** The enclosures are spacious, so the place doesn't feel like a zoo. There are rides, slides, and an adventure playground for the kids. ⊠ *Blair Drummond, Doune* ☎ *01786/841456* ⊕ *www.blairdrummond.com* 🎫 *£13.50* ⊘ *Mar.–Oct., daily 10–5:30.*

FAMILY **Hamilton Toy Collection.** Here you'll find one of the most extensive toy collections in Britain, with all conceivable types of toys grouped throughout the house, ranging from teddy bears to porcelain dolls, toy soldiers to Matchbox cars. There's a wonderful selection of model railways and an Edwardian nursery complete with dollhouses. The shop is defiantly divided into sections for girls and boys. ⊠ *111 Main St.* ☎ *01877/330004* 🎫 *£2* ⊘ *Apr.–Oct., Mon.–Sat. 10–4:30, Sun. noon–4:30.*

WHERE TO EAT AND STAY

$ ✕ **Lade Inn.** A mile from Callander, this traditional pub offers good,
BRITISH solid pub fare. Steaks, burgers, and chicken are locally sourced, and there are also international dishes like tagines. The establishment specializes in ales, and there's an even larger selection at the shop next door. The staff is friendly and attentive, traditional music plays much of the time, and musicians break out their instruments weekend nights. ⑤ *Average main: £13* ⊠ *Off A821, Kilmahog* ☎ *01877/330152* ⊕ *www.theladeinn.com.*

$ ✕ **Pip's Coffee House.** Come to this cheerful little place just off the main
CAFÉ street for imaginative soups and salads, as well as exquisite Scottish home baking, including fresh scones. And then, of course, there's great coffee. ⑤ *Average main: £7* ⊠ *21–23 Ancaster Sq.* ☎ *01877/330470* ⊟ *No credit cards* ⊘ *No dinner.*

GOLF IN THE TROSSACHS

There are many beautiful golf courses within the Loch Lomond area and the Trossachs National Park. The National Park Golf Pass (£50 for three rounds, £80 for five) allows play at Callander, St. Fillans, Aberfoyle, Killin, and Buchanan Castle. The Loch Lomond Pass (£90 for three rounds) covers the Cardos, Helensburgh, and Buchanan Castle courses.

$$ \quad **Roman Camp.** Within a hundred yards of Callander's main street,
B&B/INN \quad pass through an unpretentious arch and you'll find this 17th-century
Fodor's Choice \quad hunting lodge surrounded by ornate gardens. **Pros:** beautiful grounds;
★ \quad luxurious rooms; close to everything in town. **Cons:** restaurant is
expensive; no Internet in rooms. ⑤ *Rooms from: £155* ⊠ *Off Main
St.* ☎ *01877/330003* ⊕ *www.romancamphotel.co.uk* ➷ *12 rooms, 3
suites* ⑩*Breakfast.*

SPORTS AND THE OUTDOORS
BICYCLING
Wheels. This friendly firm rents bikes of every sort by the hour, the
half day, or the day. Most popular are the mountain bikes, which go
for £18 per day. The staff will help you find the best mountain-bike
routes around the Trossachs. ⊠ *Invertrossachs Rd.* ☎ *01877/331100*
⊕ *www.wheelscyclingcentre.com.*

GOLF
Callander Golf Club. Designed by Tom Morris in 1890 and extended to
18 holes in 1913 by Willie Fernie, Callander has a scenic upland feel
in a town well prepared for visitors. Pine and birch woods and hilly
fairways afford fine views, especially toward Ben Ledi, and the tricky
moorland layout demands accurate hitting off the tee. ⊠ *Aveland Rd.*
☎ *01877/330090* ⊕ *www.callandergolfclub.co.uk* ⛳ *Green fee: week-
days £30; weekends £40* ⛳ *18 holes, 5208 yds, par 66* ☉ *Daily.*

HIKING
Bracklinn Falls. A walk is signposted from the east end of Callander's
main street to the Bracklinn Falls, over whose lip Sir Walter Scott once
rode a pony to win a bet.

Callander Crags. It's a 1½-mile walk through the woods up to the Cal-
lander Crags, with views of the Lowlands as far as the Pentland Hills
behind Edinburgh. The walk begins at the west end of Callander's
main street.

Pass of Leny. Just north of Callander, the mountains squeeze both the
road and rocky river into the narrow Pass of Leny. An abandoned rail-
way—now a pleasant walking or biking path—also goes through the
pass, past Ben Ledi and Loch Lubnaig.

SHOPPING
Trossachs Woollen Mill. The Edinburgh Woollen Mill Group owns this
mill shop in Kilmahog. It has a vast selection of woolens on display,
including luxurious cashmere and striking tartan throws, and will
provide overseas mailing and tax-free shopping. ⊠ *Trossachs Wool-
len Mill, Main St., Kilmahog* ☎ *01877/330268* ⊕ *www.ewm.co.uk*
☉ *Mar.–Oct. daily 9–5; Nov. daily 9–4.30; Dec.–Feb. daily 9–4.*

6

BALQUHIDDER GLEN

12 miles north of Callander.

A 20-minute drive from Callander, through the Pass of Leny and beyond Strathyre, is Balquhidder Glen (pronounced *bal*-kwidd-er), a typical Highland glen that runs westward. The glen has characteristics seen throughout the north: a flat-bottom U-shape profile, formed by prehistoric glaciers; extensive Forestry Commission plantings replacing much of the natural woodlands above; a sprinkling of farms; and, farther up the glen, hill roads bulldozed into the slopes to provide access for foresters. You may notice the boarded-up look of some of the area's houses, many of which are second homes for affluent residents of the south. The glen is also where Loch Voil and Loch Doune spread out, adding to the stunning vistas.

GETTING HERE AND AROUND

To reach Balquhidder Glen by car, take the A84 from Callander (signposted to Crianlarich) and turn left at Kingshouse. This road ends in the glen, so you will have to turn back and rejoin the A84 to continue your journey—but it's certainly worth the diversion.

EXPLORING

Grave of Rob Roy MacGregor. The area around Balquhidder Glen is known as the Braes (Slopes) of Balquhidder, and was the home of the MacLarens and the MacGregors. The grave of Rob Roy MacGregor, the 18th-century Scottish outlaw hero and subject of the 1995 movie *Rob Roy*, is signposted beside Balquhidder village. The site of his house, now a private farm, is beyond the parking lot at the end of the road up the glen. The glen has no through road, though there is a right-of-way (on foot) from the churchyard where Rob Roy is buried, through Kirkton Glen and on to open grasslands and a lake.

WHERE TO STAY

$$$
HOTEL
Fodor's Choice
★

⊞ **Monachyle Mhor.** Set on 2,000 acres of forests and moorland, this beautifully converted farmhouse sits in splendid isolation against a backdrop of mountains and views over Lochs Voil and Doine. **Pros:** stunning scenery; delicious food; complimentary salmon and trout fishing. **Cons:** you're isolated; rooms are on the small side. ⑤ *Rooms from: £195* ⊠ *Off A84, Balquhidder* ☎ *01877/384622* ⊕ *www.mhor. net* ⤢ *14 rooms* ⑪ *Breakfast.*

THE TROSSACHS

10 miles west of Callander.

With its harmonious scenery of hill, loch, and wooded slopes, the Trossachs has been a popular touring region since the late 18th century, at the dawn of the age of the Romantic poets. Influenced by the writings of Sir Walter Scott, early visitors who strayed into the Highlands from the central belt of Scotland admired this as the first "wild" part of Scotland they encountered. Perhaps because the Trossachs represent the very essence of what the Highlands are supposed to be, the whole of this area, including Loch Lomond, is now protected as a national park. Here you can find birch and pine forests, vistas down lochs where the woods creep right to the water's edge, and, in the background, peaks that rise high enough to be called mountains, though they're not as high as those to the north and west.

GETTING HERE AND AROUND

To reach the Trossachs, take the A84 from Callander through the Pass of Leny, then on to Crianlarich on the A85; from here you can continue down the western shore of Loch Lomond or continue on toward Fort William. Alternately, turn onto the A821 outside Callander and travel past Loch Katrine through the Duke's Pass to Aberfoyle.

EXPLORING

TOP ATTRACTIONS

Fodor'sChoice ★ **Ben An.** The parking lot by Loch Achray is the place to begin the ascent of steep, heathery Ben An, which affords some of the best Trossachs views. The climb requires a couple of hours and good lungs. The beginning of the path is near Loch Achray. ⊠ *A821, Aberfoyle.*

Fodor'sChoice ★ **Loch Katrine.** This loch was a favorite among Victorian visitors—mysterious and wide and, at times, quite wild. Take a cruise around the loch if time permits, as the shores remain undeveloped and scenic. The steamship *Sir Walter Scott* and the motor launch *Lady of the Lake* sail from here several times a day. You can make the round-trip journey around the loch, or head directly across to Stronlachlachlar and return by bicycle on the loch-side road. Boats depart several times a day between April and October. There are café facilities and cycle hire shops at the head of the loch. ⊠ *Trossachs Pier, Off A821, Aberfoyle* ☎ *01877/376316* ⊕ *www.lochkatrine.com* ☉ *Apr.–late Oct., daily 9–5.*

WORTH NOTING

Brig o' Turk. A few minutes after it passes Loch Venachar, the A821 becomes muffled in woodlands and twists gradually down to the village of Brig o' Turk. (*Turk* is Gaelic for the Scots *tuirc,* meaning wild boar, a species that has been extinct in this region since about the 16th century.) ⊠ *A821, Brig o' Turk.*

Loch Achray. Stretching west of Brig o' Turk, Loch Achray dutifully fulfills expectations of what a verdant Trossachs loch should be: small, green, reedy meadows backed by dark plantations, rhododendron thickets, and lumpy hills, thickly covered with heather. ⊠ *A821, Brig o' Turk.*

Loch Venachar. The A821 runs west together with the first and gentlest of the Trossachs lochs, Loch Venachar. A sturdy graystone building, with a small dam at the Callander end, controls the water that feeds into the River Teith (and, hence, into the Forth). ⊠ *A821, Brig o' Turk.*

ABERFOYLE

11 miles south of Loch Katrine, in the Trossachs.

This small tourist town has a somewhat faded air, and several of its souvenir shops have closed their doors. But the surrounding hills (some snowcapped) and the green slopes visible from the town are the reason so many visitors pause here before continuing up to Duke's Pass or on to Inversnaid on Loch Lomond. Access to nearby Queen Elizabeth Forest Park is another reason to visit.

GETTING HERE AND AROUND

The main route out of Glasgow, the A81, takes you through Aberfoyle and on to Callander and Stirling. There are regular buses from Stirling and Glasgow to Aberfoyle.

ESSENTIALS

Visitor Information **Trossachs Discovery Centre** ⊠ *Main St.* ☎ *01877/382352* ⊕ *www.visitscotland.com.*

EXPLORING

Go Ape High Wire Forest Adventure. Near the David Marshall Lodge, this is an exhilarating experience for thrill-seekers age 10 and over. After a short orientation course, you can travel 40 feet above the forest via zip lines and rope ladders. ⊠ *Queen Elizabeth Forest Park, A821, 1 mile north of Aberfoyle* ☎ *0845/643–9215* ⊕ *www.goape.com* ☞ *£30* ⊘ *Apr.–Oct., daily 9–5; Nov., Feb., and Mar., weekends 9–5.*

Fodor's Choice
★
Inchmahome. The ruined priory on the tiny island of Inchmahome, on the Lake of Menteith, is a lovely place for a picnic. It was a place of refuge in 1547 for the young Mary, Queen of Scots. Between April and September, a ferry takes passengers to the island, now owned by the National Trust for Scotland. To get here, take the A81 to the B8034. The ferry jetty is just beyond the Port of Menteith. ■ TIP→ **If the boat is not there when you arrive, turn the board so that the white side faces the island. The boat will come and collect you.** ⊠ *Off A81, 4 miles east of Aberfoyle* ☎ *01786/450000* ☞ *Ferry £5.50* ⊘ *Apr.–Sept., daily 9:30–5:30.*

Queen Elizabeth Forest Park. For exquisite nature, drive north from Aberfoyle on the A821 and turn right at signposts to Queen Elizabeth Forest Park. Along the way you'll be heading toward higher moorland blanketed with conifers. The conifers hem in the views of Ben Ledi and Ben Venue, which can be seen over the spiky green waves of trees as the road snakes around heathery knolls and hummocks. There's another viewing area, and a small parking lot, at the highest point of the road. Soon the road swoops off the Highland edge and leads downhill.

At the heart of the Queen Elizabeth Forest Park, the **David Marshall Lodge** leads to four forest walks, a family-friendly bicycle route, and the 7-mile 3 Lochs Forest Drive, open April to October. Or you can sit on the terrace of the Bluebell Cafe and scan the forests and hills of the Trossachs. The visitor center has a wildlife-watch room where you can follow the activities of everything from ospreys to water voles. ⊠ *Off A821, 1 mile north of Aberfoyle* ☎ *01877/382383* ⊕ *www.forestry.gov.uk/qefp.*

FAMILY
Scottish Wool Centre. With a vast range of woolen garments and knitwear, the Scottish Wool Centre also has a small café. Three times a day from April to September it presents an interactive "gathering," when dogs herd sheep and ducks in the large amphitheater, with a little help from the public. Miniature horses watch from a nearby paddock. ⊠ *Off Main St.* ☎ *01877/382850* ☞ *Free* ⊘ *Feb.–Dec., daily 9:30–5:30; Jan., daily 10–4:30.*

OFF THE BEATEN PATH
Along the B829. Northwest of Loch Chon the B829 climbs gently from the plantings to open moor with a breathtaking vista over **Loch Arklet** to the Arrochar Alps, the name given to the high hills west of Loch Lomond. Hidden from sight in a deep trench, Loch Arklet is dammed

to feed Loch Katrine. Go left at the road junction (a right will take you to the village of Stronachlachar) and take the open road along Loch Arklet. These deserted green hills were once the rallying grounds of the Clan Gregor. Near the dam on Loch Arklet, on your right, **Garrison Cottage** recalls the days when the government had to billet troops here to keep the MacGregors in order.

From Loch Arklet the road zigzags down to a T junction. To the left is **Inversnaid**, with Loch Lomond stretching out of sight above and below. Right at the junction is the hamlet of **Stronachlachar**, on Loch Katrine, the outermost landing stage for the SS *Walter Scott*'s trips on the loch. Stop while you are there for lunch or coffee and cakes at the Pier Tea Room.

> ## SCOTLAND BY BIKE
>
> The region's big attraction for cyclists is the **Lowland/Highland Trail,** which stretches more than 60 miles and passes through Drymen, Aberfoyle, the Trossachs, Callander, Lochearnhead, and Killin. This route runs along former railroad-track beds, as well as private and minor roads, to reach well into the Central Highlands. Another almost completely traffic-free option is the roadway around Loch Katrine. Mountain bikes can tackle many of the forest roads and trails enjoyed by walkers. Almost every town along the route has cycle hire shops. Avoid main roads, which can be busy with traffic.

WHERE TO EAT

$ ✕ **Pier Tea Room.** At the historic Stronlachlachar Pier, this elegant coffee
BRITISH shop has a satisfying lunch menu and an expansive deck overlooking Loch Katrine. Cakes, scones, and soups are made on the premises. Many people get off the boat from Trossachs Pier here before cycling or walking along the road around the loch. $ *Average main: £8* ✉ *B829, Stronachlachar* ☎ *01877/386374* ⊕ *www.thepiercafe.com* ☾ *No dinner.*

WHERE TO STAY

$$ ⌂ **Lake of Menteith Hotel.** With its muted colors and simple but elegant
HOTEL rooms, this restful hotel emphasizes peace and quiet. **Pros:** elegant,
Fodor's Choice unpretentious bedrooms; beautiful setting. **Cons:** not well signposted;
★ not all rooms have lake views and those that do are more expensive. $ *Rooms from: £120* ✉ *Off A81* ☎ *01877/385258* ⊕ *www.lake-hotel. com* ⇌ *17 rooms* ⦿| *Breakfast.*

$$ ⌂ **Macdonald Forest Hills Hotel.** A traditional Scottish country-house
HOTEL theme pervades this hotel, from the rambling white building itself to the wood-paneled lounges, log fires, and numerous sporting activities. **Pros:** stunning views; log fires; good children's programs. **Cons:** restaurant is pricey and food is average; some of the building looks run-down. $ *Rooms from: £145* ✉ *B829, Kinlochard* ☎ *08448/799057* ⊕ *www. macdonaldhotels.co.uk/foresthills* ⇌ *56 rooms* ⦿| *Breakfast.*

SPORTS AND THE OUTDOORS

GOLF **Aberfoyle Golf Club.** This hilly course is set against the backdrop of Queen Elizabeth Forest Park. One of the area's many James Braid–designed parkland courses, it dates back to 1890. ✉ *Braeval* ☎ *01877/382493* ⊕ *www.aberfoylegolf.co.uk* ⬚ *Green fee: weekdays £20, weekends £25* ⅄ *18 holes, 5218 yds, par 66.*

LOCH LOMOND

The waters of Scotland's largest loch, which also happens to be one of its most beautiful, create a perfect reflection of the surrounding hills. You can cruise among its small islands or follow the low road that carries you from Glasgow to the beginning of the Highlands.

14 miles west of Aberfoyle.

GETTING HERE AND AROUND

To reach Loch Lomond from Aberfoyle, take the A81 toward Glasgow, then the A811 to Drymen and then the B837 as far as it will take you. From Glasgow, take the A82 to the Balloch roundabout and either go right through Balloch for Drymen and the eastern shore, or continue along the A82 as it hugs the west bank all the way to Crianlarich.

You can drive, cycle, or walk along the 32 miles of Loch Lomond along its western shores, and watch the changing face of the loch as you go, or look up toward the shifting slopes of Ben Lomond.

ESSENTIALS

Visitor Information **Loch Lomond and the Trossachs National Park Headquarters** ✉ *The Old Station, Balloch* ☎ *01389/722600* ⊕ *www.lochlomond-trossachs.org* ☉ *Weekdays 8:30–5.*

EXPLORING

Fodor'sChoice **Loch Lomond.** Known for its "bonnie, bonnie banks," Loch Lomond is
★ Scotland's largest loch in terms of surface area, and its waters reflect the crags that surround it. The song "The Banks of Loch Lomond" is said to have been written by a Jacobite prisoner incarcerated in Carlisle, England.

On the western side of the loch, the A82 follows the shore for 31 miles to Crianlarich, passing picturesque Luss, which has a pier where you can hop aboard boats cruising along the loch, and Tarbert, the starting point for the *Maid of the Loch.* On the eastern side of the loch, take the A81 to Drymen, and from there the B837 signposted toward Balmaha, where you can hire a boat or take the ferry to the island of Inchcailloch. Once you're there, a short walk takes you to the top of the hill and a spectacular view of the loch. Equally spectacular, but not as wet, is the view from Conic Hill near Balmaha. If you continue along the B837 beyond Rowardennan to where it ends at a car park, you can join the walkers at the beginning of the path up Ben Lomond. Don't underestimate this innocent looking hill; go equipped for sudden changes in the weather.

SPORTS AND THE OUTDOORS
BOATING

FAMILY **Cruise Loch Lomond.** You can take tours year-round with Cruise Loch Lomond. From April to October boats depart from various ports around the loch, including Tarbet, Luss, Balmaha, and Inversnaid. From November to March the boats operate on demand. ✉ *A82, Tarbet* ☎ *01301/702356* ⊕ *www.cruiselochlomond.co.uk* ✆ *£9.50–£12.50.*

Macfarlane and Son. At this longtime favorite boats with outboard motors rent for £20 per hour or £60 per day. Row boats rent for £10 per hour or £40 per day. From Balmaha it is a short trip to the lovely island of Incailloch. Macfarlane's also runs a ferry to the island for £5 per person. ✉ *Balmaha Boatyard, B837, Balmaha* ☎ *01360/870214* ⊕ *www.balmahaboatyard.co.uk.*

WHERE TO EAT

$ ✕ **Coach House Coffee Shop.** This
BRITISH lively restaurant and café fits per-
Fodor'sChoice fectly into its surroundings with
★ its cheerful, over-the-top Scottishness. Long wooden tables, a large
chimney with an open fire in the
winter months, and a cabinet full
of mouthwatering cakes baked by
the owner create the atmosphere.
Favorites include rich homemade
soups and stokies (large round
rolls filled to overflowing), as well
as the ubiquitous haggis, served in
king-size quantities. It's worth asking for tea served in ceramic teapots
representing everything from dining
rooms to telephone boxes (the pots
are for sale in the shop). ⑤ *Average main: £11* ✉ *Church Rd., Luss*
☎ *01436/860341* ⊗ *No dinner.*

HIKE THE HIGHLAND WAY

West Highland Way. The long-distance walkers' route, the West Highland Way, begins in Glasgow, running 96 miles (154 km) from the Lowlands of Central Scotland to the Highlands at Fort William. Nearly 50,000 people discover the glens each year, climbing the hills and listening to birds singing in the tree canopy. This is not a difficult walk, but keep Scotland's ever-changing weather in mind. From Milngavie, in Glasgow, the route passes along the banks of Loch Lomond before snaking northward into the more demand-ing hills beyond and finishing at Fort William. ⊕ *www.west-highland-way.co.uk.*

$ ✕ **Drovers Inn.** The portions at this noisy, friendly inn are enormous,
BRITISH which is just as well because many customers have returned from a
day's walking on the nearby West Highland Way. Scottish staples like
sausage and mash, minced beef, and haggis with mash and neeps (turnips) jostle for a place beside occasionally more adventurous dishes. The
dining areas are hung with swords and modern copies of old paintings.
This is a genuine traveler's pub, with an appropriate range of whiskies
(hearty rather than elegant). There is traditional music every weekend,
and there are 26 rooms for rent. The bear at the door should not put
you off (it is stuffed and very old). ⑤ *Average main: £11* ✉ *A82, north
of Ardlui, Inverarnan* ☎ *01301/704234* ⊕ *www.thedroversinn.co.uk.*

WHERE TO STAY

$ 🏨 **Balloch House.** Cute, cozy, and very Scottish, this small hotel offers tasty
HOTEL breakfasts and hearty pub meals like fish-and-chips and local smoked
salmon for reasonable prices. **Pros:** beautiful building; recently refurbished;
near shopping. **Cons:** noisy pinball machine next to bar; not all rooms
have views. ⑤ *Rooms from: £84* ✉ *Balloch Rd., Balloch* ☎ *01389/752579*
⊕ *www.innkeeperslodge.com/loch-lomond* ⇌ *12 rooms* ⦿*Breakfast.*

$$$$ 🏨 **Cameron House.** There is little that you cannot do at this luxury resort
HOTEL hotel beside Loch Lomond, including taking to the water in a motorboat
or riding a seaplane above the trees. **Pros:** beautiful grounds; away-
from-it-all feel; good dining. **Cons:** prices are high; slightly difficult
access from A82. ⑤ *Rooms from: £320* ✉ *Loch Lomond, off A82,
Alexandria* ☎ *01389/755565* ⊕ *www.devere.co.uk* ⇌ *96 rooms, 7
suites* ⦿*Breakfast.*

6

$$ ⬚ **Culcreuch Castle Hotel.** The hand-painted wallpaper in the Chinese Bird
HOTEL Room dates from 1723, which shows how much the owners of this
authentic castle care about preserving the past. **Pros:** historic building;
expansive and beautiful grounds; good food at reasonable prices. **Cons:**
a little remote; steep stairways; rather small shower rooms. ⓢ *Rooms
from: £150* ⊠ *Off B822, Fintry* ☎ *01360/860555* ⊕ *www.culcreuch.
com* ⇨ *14 rooms* ⦿| *Breakfast.*

GOLF

Buchanan Castle Golf Club. Surrounded by mature trees, the setting
here is quiet and beautiful. Established in 1936, this parkland course
sits less than 2 miles from the lovely village of Drymen. A putting
green is a nice touch. ⊠ *A809, Drymen* ☎ *01360/660330* ⊕ *www.
buchanancastlegolfclub.co.uk* ⛳ *Green fee: weekdays £42, weekends
£47* ⵏ *18 holes, 6047 yds, par 70.*

SHOPPING

Loch Lomond Shores. This lakeside shopping complex contains restau-
rants, pubs, and a visitor center. ⊠ *Ben Lomond Way, Balloch* ☎ *01389/
751031* ⊕ *www.lochlomondshores.com.*

PERTHSHIRE

If Perthshire's castles invoke memories of past conflicts, the grand houses
and spa towns here are testimony to the continued presence of a wealthy
landed gentry. This is also a place for walking, cycling, and water sports.
In some ways Perthshire is a crossing point between different Scottish
landscapes and histories. Perthshire itself is rural, agricultural Scotland,
fertile and prosperous. Its woodlands, rivers, and glens (and agreeable
climate and strategic position) drew the Romans and later the Celtic mis-
sionaries. In fact, the motto of the capital city, Perth, is "the perfect center."

PERTH

*36 miles northeast of Stirling, 43 miles north of Edinburgh, 61 miles
northeast of Glasgow.*

For many years Perth was Scotland's capital, and central to its history.
One king (James I) was killed here, and the Protestant reformer John
Knox preached in St. John's Kirk, where his rhetoric moved crowds to
burn down several local monasteries. Perth's local whisky trade and the
productive agriculture that surrounds the town have sustained it through
the centuries. Its grand buildings, especially on the banks of the River
Tay, testify to its continued wealth. The open parkland within the city
(the Inches) gives the place a restful air, and shops range from small crafts
boutiques to department stores. Impressive Scone Palace is nearby.

GETTING HERE AND AROUND

Perth is served by the main railway line to Inverness, and regular and fre-
quent buses run here from Glasgow, Edinburgh, and Stirling. The central
artery, the A9, passes through the city en route to Pitlochry and Inverness,
while a network of roads opens the way to the glens and hills around Glen
Lyon, or the road to Loch Lomond (the A85) via Crianlarich.

Perthshire

KEY

⊣⊢ Rail Lines
✈ Airport

Blair Castle
Blair Atholl
A9
Calvine
Kinloch Rannoch
B846
B8019
Loch Tummel
Tummel Bridge
Loch Rannoch
Pass of Killiecrankie
Linn of Tummel
Pitlochry
Kirkmichael
B846
Castle Menzies
Aberfeldy
R. Tay
Dowally
Loch of Lowes
Bridge-of-Cally
Glen Lyon
Fortingall
Fearnan
Ben Lawers
Lawers
A827
Loch Tay
Scottish Crannog Centre
Meall Dearg
Hermitage
R. Braan
Strathbraan
Birnam
Bankfoot
A9
Dunkeld
R. Tay
Blairgowrie
Rattray
Kinclaven
Coupar Angus
A93
A94
Creag Uchdag
Ben Chonzie
Killin
St. Fillans
A85
Invergeldie
Glen Almond
Buchanty
Scone Palace
New Scone
Kinrossie
Balbeggie
A85
Loch Earn
Comrie
Earn
Crieff
A85
Perth
Glencarse
R. Tay
Strathyre
Ben Vorlich
Ben Halton
Drummond Castle Garden
Muthill
A823
Blackford
Dunning
Auchterarder
A9
Elcho Castle

0 — 10 miles
0 — 10 kilometers

ESSENTIALS

Visitor Information Perth Visitor Centre ⊠ *Lower City Mills, West Mill St.* ☎ *01738/450600* ⊕ *www.visitscotland.co.uk.*

EXPLORING PERTH
TOP ATTRACTIONS

Elcho Castle. From the battlements of Elcho Castle you can see the River Tay stretching east and west. Built around 1560, the castle marks a transition period when these structures began to be built as grand houses rather than fortresses, and it's easy to see that Elcho was built for both comfort and defense. The well preserved but uncluttered rooms let you imagine how life might have been here in the 17th century. The staircases still give access to all floors, and a flashlight is provided for the darker corners. ⊠ *Off A912, close to Rhynd* ☎ *01738/639998* ⊕ *www.historic-scotland.gov.uk/places* 🎟 *£4.50* ⏱ *Apr.–Sept., daily 9:30–5:30.*

FAMILY
Fodor's Choice
★

Scone Palace. The current residence of the Earl of Mansfield, Scone Palace (pronounced *skoon*) is much more cheerful than the city's other castles. Although it incorporates various earlier works, the palace today has mainly a 19th-century theme, with mock castellations that were fashionable at the time. There's plenty to see if you're interested in the acquisitions of an aristocratic Scottish family: magnificent porcelain, furniture, ivory, clocks, and 16th-century needlework. A coffee shop, restaurant, gift shop, and play area are on-site, and the extensive grounds have a pine plantation. The palace has its own mausoleum nearby, on the site of a long-gone abbey on **Moot Hill,** the ancient coronation place of the Scottish kings. To be crowned, they sat on the Stone of Scone, which was seized in 1296 by Edward I of England, Scotland's greatest enemy, and placed in the coronation chair at Westminster Abbey, in London. The stone was returned to Scotland in November 1996 and is now on view in Edinburgh Castle. Some Scots hint darkly that Edward was fooled by a substitution and that the real stone is hidden, waiting for Scotland to regain its independence. ⊠ *Braemar Rd., 2 miles from Perth* ☎ *01738/552300* ⊕ *www.scone-palace.co.uk* ⊠ *£9.40* ⊙ *Apr.–Oct., daily 9:30–5:30, last admission at 5; Nov–Mar., Fri. 10–4.*

WORTH NOTING

Fergusson Gallery. Originally a water works, this gallery's magnificent and newly restored dome and rotunda shelter a collection of 6,000 works—paintings, drawings, and prints—by the Scottish artist J.D. Fergusson (1874–1961). Fergusson was the longest lived member of the group called the Scottish Colourists, who took their inspiration from the French Impressionist painters in their use of color and light. ⊠ *Marshall Pl.* ☎ *01738/783425* ⊕ *www.scottishmuseums.org.uk* ⊠ *Free* ⊙ *Mon.–Sat. 10–5.*

Perth Art Gallery and Museum. The wide-ranging collection here includes exhibits on natural history, local history, archaeology, and art—including work by the great painter of animals Sir Edwin Landseer and some botanical studies of fungi by Beatrix Potter. ⊠ *78 George St.* ☎ *01738/632488* ⊕ *www.pkc.gov.uk/perthmuseum* ⊠ *Free* ⊙ *Tues–Sat. 10–5.*

Regimental Museum of the Black Watch. Some will tell you the Black Watch was a Scottish regiment whose name is a reference to the color of its tartan. An equally plausible explanation, however, is that the regiment was established to keep an undercover watch on rebellious Jacobites. The Gaelic word for black is *dubh,* meaning, in this case, "hidden" or "covert." A wide range of uniforms, weaponry, and marching banners are displayed. The castle is closed on the last weekend in June. ⊠ *Balhousie Castle, Hay St.* ☎ *01738/638152* ⊕ *www.theblackwatch. co.uk* ⊠ *£7.50* ⊙ *Apr.–Oct., Mon.–Sat. 9:30–5, Sun. 10–4; Nov.–Mar., Mon.–Sat. 9:30–5.*

St. John's Kirk. This cruciform-plan church dates from the 12th century. The interior was divided into three parts at the Reformation, but was restored to something closer to its medieval state by Sir Robert Lorimer in the 1920s. ⊠ *St. John St.* ☎ *01738/633192* ⊕ *www.st-johns-kirk. co.uk* ⊠ *Free* ⊙ *Weekdays 10–4, Sun. services at 9:30 and 11.*

WHERE TO EAT AND STAY

$$
BRITISH ✕ **Let's Eat.** The varied clientele reflects the broad appeal of noted chef Willie Deans's imaginative menu. The dinner menu combines some creative starters with earthy dishes with a Scottish flavor (venison with a bitter chocolate and red wine sauce, for example, or Blairgowrie beef fillet). All the ingredients are locally sourced. The restaurant is airy

and comfortable, merging warm colors and rich woods. $ *Average main: £18* ✉ *77–79 Kinnoull St.* ☎ *01738/643377* ⊕ *letseatperth.co.uk* ⊘ *Closed Sun. and Mon.*

$$
B&B/INN
🏠 **Parklands.** This stylish Georgian town house overlooks lush woodland. **Pros:** lovely rooms; lovely setting; superb restaurants. **Cons:** some rooms have better views than others; restaurants closed on Sunday. $ *Rooms from: £129* ✉ *2 St. Leonard's Bank* ☎ *01738/622451* ⊕ *www. theparklandshotel.com* ⇌ *14 rooms* ⦿ *Breakfast.*

$
B&B/INN
🏠 **Sunbank House Hotel.** This early Victorian graystone mansion near Perth's Branklyn Gardens overlooks the River Tay and the city of Perth. **Pros:** reasonably priced; friendly staff; delicious local cuisine. **Cons:** some rooms are very small; you can hear traffic from the main road. $ *Rooms from: £99* ✉ *50 Dundee Rd.* ☎ *01738/624882* ⊕ *www. sunbankhouse.com* ⇌ *9 rooms* ⦿ *Multiple meal plans.*

NIGHTLIFE AND THE ARTS

Perth Concert Hall. The city's main concert venue hosts musical performances of all types. ✉ *Mill St.* ☎ *017384/621031* ⊕ *www.horsecross.co.uk.*

Perth Repertory Theatre. The Victorian-era Perth Repertory Theatre stages plays and musicals. ✉ *185 High St.* ☎ *017384/621031* ⊕ *www. horsecross.co.uk.*

SHOPPING

CERAMICS
Perth is an especially popular hunting ground for china and glass.

Watsons of Perth. This shop has sold exquisite bone china and cut crystal since 1900. The staff can pack your purchase for shipment overseas. ✉ *163–167 High St.* ☎ *01738/639861* ⊕ *www.watsonsofperth.co.uk.*

CLOTHING
C & C Proudfoot. This shop sells a comprehensive selection of sheepskins, leather jackets, rugs, slippers, and handbags. ✉ *104 South St.* ☎ *01738/632483.*

JEWELRY AND
ANTIQUES
Cairncross of Perth. The Romans coveted freshwater pearls from the River Tay. If you do, too, then head to Cairncross of Perth, where you can admire a display of some of the more unusual shapes and colors. Some of the delicate settings take their theme from Scottish flowers. ✉ *18 St. John's St.* ☎ *01738/624367* ⊕ *www.cairncrossofperth.co.uk* ⊘ *Weekdays 9:30–5, Sat 9:30–4:30.*

Timothy Hardie. Antique jewelry and silver, including a few Scottish items, can be found at Timothy Hardie. ✉ *25 St. John's St.* ☎ *01738/633127* ⊕ *www.timothyhardie.co.uk.*

Whispers of the Past. The lovely Whispers of the Past has a collection of jewelry, china, and other gift items. ✉ *15 George St.* ☎ *01738/635472.*

DUNKELD

14 miles north of Perth.

The ruined cathedral above the town of Dunkeld marks its historic beginnings. The present town grew up around the main square, built by the Atholl family in the wake of the 1689 defeat of the Jacobite army (following its earlier victory in the Battle of Killiecrankie). The National Trust for Scotland has helped to maintain the houses with its

Little Houses Project; it has a small exhibition above the Dunkeld and Birnam Tourist Information Centre (ask for the Heritage Trail leaflet). Crafts and interior-design shops dominate Atholl Street, which leads down to the River Tay.

The bridge across the River Tay takes you to Birnam Wood, where Shakespeare's Macbeth met the three witches who issued the prophecy about his death. Witty wooden notices lead you to the right tree, a gnarled hollow oak.

GETTING HERE AND AROUND

Dunkeld is on the A9 between Perth and Pitlochry. The town is also on the main train line to Inverness.

ESSENTIALS

Visitor Information Dunkeld and Birnam Tourist Information Centre
⊠ *The Cross* ☎ *01350/727688* ⊕ *www.visitscotland.com* ☉ *Apr.–June, daily 10–4:30; July and Aug., Mon.–Sat. 9:30–5:30, Sun. 10:30–5; Sept. and Oct., Mon.–Sat. 10–4:30, Sun. 11–4; Nov.–Mar., Fri.–Sun. 11–4.*

EXPLORING

FAMILY **Beatrix Potter Garden.** This garden celebrates the life and work of this much-beloved children's writer who, for many years, spent her family holidays in the area. An enchanting garden walk allows you to peep into the homes of Peter Rabbit and Mrs. Tiggy-Winkle, her best-known characters. The visitor center has a well-stocked shop, a small café, and an imaginative exhibition on the writer's life and work (£1.50). ⊠ *Birnam Arts Centre, Station Rd., Birnam* ☎ *01350/727674* ⊕ *www. birnamarts.com* ☉ *Museum daily 10–5.*

Hermitage. On the outskirts of Dunkeld, the Hermitage is a woodland walk that follows the River Braan. In the 18th century the dukes of Atholl constructed two follies (a fantasy building) here, **Ossian's Cave** and the awesome **Ossian's Hall,** above a spectacular—and noisy—waterfall. (Ossian was a fictional Celtic poet invented by James MacPherson in the 18th century for an era fascinated by the primitive past.) You'll also be in the presence of Britain's tallest tree, a Douglas fir measuring 214 feet. ⊠ *A9, 1 mile west of Dunkeld.*

FAMILY **Loch of the Lowes.** At this Scottish Wildlife Trust reserve near Dunkeld, the domestic routines of the osprey, one of Scotland's conservation success stories, can be observed in relative comfort between March and August. There is activity throughout the year, so you can see birds like the great crested grebe at feeding stations. ⊠ *Off A923, about 2 miles northeast of Dunkeld* ☎ *01350/727337* ⊕ *scottishwildlifetrust.org.uk* ⊠ *£4* ☉ *Mar–Oct., daily 10–5; Nov.–Feb., Fri.–Sun. 10:30–4.*

WHERE TO EAT

$ ✕ **Taybank Hotel.** This spot overlooking the river is a musical meeting
BRITISH place owned by Scottish singer Dougie MacLean. Of course there's live music several nights a week. The walls are lined with instruments, which you're welcome to play. The bar serves good solid Scottish food, including chicken breast cooked with bacon and kale and "stovies," an oven-baked dish of meat, onions, and potatoes. ⑤ *Average main: £9* ⊠ *Tay Terr.* ☎ *01350/727340* ⊕ *www.taybank.com.*

SHOPPING

Dunkeld Antiques. Housed in a former church facing the river, Dunkeld Antiques stocks mainly 18th- and 19th-century items, including books and prints that make great souvenirs. ✉ *Tay Terr.* ☎ *01350/728832* ⊕ *www.dunkeldantiques.co.uk.*

Jeremy Law of Scotland's Highland Horn and Deerskin Centre. Here you can purchase stag antlers and cow horns shaped into walking sticks, cutlery, and tableware. Deerskin shoes and moccasins and a collection of more than 200 different whiskies are also on offer. ✉ *City Hall, Atholl St.* ☎ *0800/146780* ⊕ *www.moccasin.co.uk.*

PITLOCHRY

15 miles north of Dunkeld.

In the late 19th century Pitlochry was an elegant Victorian spa town, famous for its mild microclimate and beautiful setting. Today it is a busy tourist town, with wall-to-wall gift shops, cafés and B&Bs, large hotels, and a huge golf course. The town itself is oddly nondescript, but it's a convenient base from which to explore the surrounding hills and valleys.

GETTING HERE AND AROUND

The main route through central Scotland, the A9, passes through Pitlochry, as does the main railway line from Glasgow/Edinburgh to Inverness. From here the B8019 connects to the B846 west to Rannoch Moor or south to Aberfeldy.

ESSENTIALS

Visitor Information Pitlochry Visitor Information Centre ✉ 22 Atholl Rd. ☎ 01796/472215 ⊕ www.visitscotland.com ⊘ Apr.–June, Sept., and Oct., daily 9–5:30; July and Aug., daily 9–6:30; Nov.–Mar., daily 9:30–4:30.

EXPLORING

Edradour Distillery. If you have a whisky-tasting bent, visit Edradour Distillery, which claims to be the smallest single-malt distillery in Scotland (but then, so do others). There's a fun, informative tour of the distillery where you get to see how the whisky is made; you also get to savor a free dram at the end of the tour. ✉ *A924, 2½ miles east of Pitlochry* ☎ *01796/472095* ⊕ *www.edradour.com* 🖃 *Tours £7.50* ⊘ *May–Oct., Mon.–Sat. 10–5, Sun. noon–5; Nov.–Mar., and Apr., Mon.–Sat. 10–4, Sun. noon–4.*

Linn of Tummel. The Linn of Tummel, a series of marked walks along the river and through tall, mature woodlands, is a little north of Pitlochry. Above the Linn, the A9 rises on stilts and gives an exciting view of the valley.

Loch Rannoch. With its shoreline of birch trees framed by dark pines, Loch Rannoch is the quintessential Highland loch. Fans of Robert Louis Stevenson (1850–94), especially of *Kidnapped* (1886), will not want to miss the last, lonely section of road. Stevenson describes the setting: "The mist rose and died away, and showed us that country lying as waste as the sea, only the moorfowl and the peewees crying upon it, and far over to the east a herd of deer, moving like dots." Loch Rannoch is off B846, 20 miles west of Pitlochry.

Pass of Killiecrankie. Set among the oak woods and rocky river just north of the Linn of Tummel, the Pass of Killiecrankie was the site of a famous battle won by the Jacobites in 1689. The spot where a soldier escaped the battle by jumping across the river is now called the Soldier's Leap. The battle was noted for the death of the central Jacobite leader, John Graham of Claverhouse (1649–89), also known as Bonnie Dundee, who was hit by a stray bullet. The rebellion fizzled after Claverhouse's death.

The National Trust for Scotland's visitor center at Killiecrankie explains the significance of this battle, which was the first attempt to restore the Stewart monarchy. ✉ *B8079, 3 miles north of Pitlochry* ☎ *01796/473233* ⊕ *www.nts.org.uk/visits* ☺ *Apr.–Oct., daily 10–5:30.*

Pitlochry Dam and Fish Ladder. Most Scottish dams have salmon passes or ladders of some kind, enabling the fish to swim upstream to their spawning grounds. The Pitlochry Dam and Fish Ladder, just behind the main street, leads into a glass-paneled pipe that allows the fish to observe the visitors. ✉ *Off A9* ☎ *01796/473152* ✆ *Free* ☺ *May–Oct., Mon.–Sat. 10–5, Sun. noon–5; Nov. and Dec., Mon.–Sat. 10–4, Sun. noon–4; Jan. and Feb., Mon.–Sat. 10–4.*

WHERE TO EAT AND STAY

$

BRITISH

✕ **Moulin Hotel and Brewery.** This traditional pub with dark wooden interiors serves standard Scottish fare in large quantities. Venison Braveheart, for example, is cooked in the brewery's own beer, and the haggis with neeps and tatties is predictable but good. This is a pleasant place, provided you are not too averse to the stuffed animals along the walls. The home-brewed beer is powerful, and during the afternoon you can visit the adjacent brewery. ⑤ *Average main: £12* ✉ *11–30 Kirkmichael Rd.* ☎ *01796/472196* ⊕ *www.moulinhotel.co.uk.*

$$$

HOTEL

🏨 **Atholl Palace Hotel.** A grand hotel in the best Victorian style, the Atholl Palace is a 19th-century vision of a medieval castle. **Pros:** lovely grounds; lots for kids to do; high comfort. **Cons:** old-fashioned feel; long anonymous corridors. ⑤ *Rooms from: £189* ✉ *A924* ☎ *01796/472400* ⊕ *www.athollpalace.com* ⇆ *106 rooms* ⦿⦿ *Breakfast.*

$$$

HOTEL

🏨 **Killiecrankie House Hotel.** This neat oasis is set amid the wooded hills and streams of the Pass of Killiecrankie. **Pros:** lovely location; pleasant rooms. **Cons:** books up fast. ⑤ *Rooms from: £210* ✉ *B8079, 3 mi north of Pitlochry, Killiecrankie* ☎ *01796/473220* ⊕ *www.killiecrankiehotel.co.uk* ⇆ *10 rooms* ⦿⦿ *Some meals.*

$

B&B/INN

🏨 **Tir Aluinn Guest House.** This comfortable, bright, and friendly B&B looks down over the town of Pitlochry and the valley beyond. **Pros:** friendly attentive owners; bright decor. **Cons:** slightly outside the town; good but basic furnishings. ⑤ *Rooms from: £74* ✉ *10 Higher Oakfield* ☎ *01796/473811* ⊕ *www.tiraluinn.co.uk* ⇆ *4 rooms* ⦿⦿ *Breakfast.*

NIGHTLIFE AND THE ARTS

Pitlochry Festival Theatre. This theater presents six plays each season, hosts Sunday concerts, and holds art exhibitions. It also has a café and restaurant overlooking the River Tummel. ✉ *Port Na Craig* ☎ *01796/484626* ⊕ *www.pitlochry.org.uk.*

SPORTS AND THE OUTDOORS

GOLF **Blairgowrie Golf Club.** Well-known to native golfers looking for a challenge, the Blairgowrie Golf Club's Rosemount Course is laid out on rolling land in the pine, birch, and fir woods, which bring a wild air to the scene. There are, however, wide fairways and at least some large greens. If Rosemount is hosting a tournament, you can play on Lansdowne, another 18-hole course, or Wee, a 9-hole course. ⊠ *Golf Course Rd., Blairgowrie* 🕾 *01250/872622* ⊕ *www.theblairgowriegolfclub.co.uk* 🖭 *Green fee: Rosemount £60; Lansdowne £60; Wee £25* 🏌 *Rosemount: 18 holes, 6630 yds, par 72. Lansdowne: 18 holes, 6886 yds, par 72. Wee: 9 holes, 2,327 yds, par 32* ☉ *Daily.*

Pitlochry Golf Course. A decent degree of stamina is needed for the first three holes at Pitlochry, where steep climbs are involved. The reward is magnificent Highland scenery. Despite its relatively short length, this beautiful course has more than its fair share of surprises. ⊠ *Golf Course Rd.* 🕾 *01796/472792* ⊕ *www.pitlochrygolf.co.uk* 🖭 *Green fee: Mar., Apr., Oct., and Nov.: weekdays £32; weekends £40. May–Sept.: weekdays £37; weekends £42* 🏌 *18 holes, 5681 yds, par 69* ☉ *Daily.*

BLAIR ATHOLL

6

Where the Tilt and Garry rivers flow together, this small town sits in the middle of the Grampian Mountains. Here you'll find Blair Castle, one of Scotland's grandest grand houses.

10 miles north of Pitlochry.

GETTING HERE AND AROUND

Popular Blair Castle is just off the A9 Pitlochry-to-Inverness road, beyond the village of Blair Atholl. The village has a railway station that is on the main Inverness line.

EXPLORING

Fodor's Choice **Blair Castle.** Thanks to its historic contents and war-torn past, Blair
★ Castle is one of Scotland's most highly rated sights. The turreted white castle was home to successive dukes of Atholl and their families, the Murrays, until the death of the 10th duke. One of the castle's fascinating details is a preserved piece of floor still bearing marks of the red-hot shot fired through the roof during the 1745 Jacobite rebellion—the last occasion in Scottish history that a castle was besieged. The castle holds not only military artifacts—historically, the duke was allowed to keep a private army, the Atholl Highlanders—but also a rich collection of furniture, china, and paintings. The Hercules Gardens is a 9-acre Victorian walled garden, and the extensive grounds have woodland and river walks. ⊠ *Off B8079, Blair Atholl* 🕾 *01796/481207* ⊕ *www. blair-castle.co.uk* 🖭 *Castle and gardens: Apr.–Oct., £9.90, Nov.–Mar., £7.40. Grounds only: Apr.–Oct., £5.45; Nov.–Mar., free* ☉ *Apr.–Oct., daily 9:30–5:30; Nov.–Mar., weekends 10–4.*

SHOPPING

House of Bruar. An upscale shopping complex, the House of Bruar has a heavy emphasis on traditional tweeds and cashmeres. A large supermarket sells local produce and food, and a restaurant serves breakfast and lunch. When you're done shopping, take a walk up the path that crosses Bruar Falls, behind the complex. ✉ *Off A9, Blair Atholl* ☎ *01796/483236* ☉ *Apr.–Nov., daily 9:30–6; Nov.–Mar., daily 10–5.*

John A Lacey. Watch for this house between Killin and Aberfeldy. Its front room is a treasure trove of horn carving, from a full-masted galleon to knives in their sheaths. There are also deerskins for sale. John Lacey has worked here for 30 years; he says the egg spoons are still the most popular items. ✉ *A827, Aberfeldy* ☎ *01567/820561.*

ABERFELDY

15 miles southwest of Pitlochry, 25 miles southwest of Blair Castle.

The most dramatic thing about Aberfeldy is the high humpbacked bridge into the town, built by William Adam in 1733 and commissioned by General Wade, who marched through Scotland suppressing local resistance after the Jacobite rebellion. The town itself is rather sleepy, but this is a popular base for exploring the region. There's also a whisky distillery and plenty of local golf courses.

GETTING HERE AND AROUND

You can reach Aberfeldy from Dunkeld via the A9 and the A827. A longer but very pretty route is the A85 from Crieff, then through Killin on the A827. Aberfeldy is served by regular buses from Perth and Pitlochry.

ESSENTIALS

Visitor Information Aberfeldy Tourist Information Centre ✉ *The Square* ☎ *01887/820276* ⊕ *www.visitscotland.com* ☉ *Apr.–Sept. daily 10–5; Nov.–Mar. daily 10–4.*

EXPLORING

Castle Menzies. A 16th-century fortified tower house, Castle Menzies contains the **Clan Menzies Museum,** which displays many relics of the clan's history. Beside the castle is an old byre that's been converted into a craft shop, winery, and café. The castle stands west of Aberfeldy, on the opposite bank of the River Tay. ✉ *B846, Weem* ☎ *01887/820982* ✉ *£6* ☉ *Apr.–Oct., Sun. 2–5, Mon. 10:30–5.*

Dewar's World of Whisky. This established distillery offers tours that demonstrate how whisky is made (with a tasting at the end, of course). The basic tours are £7, but there are more expensive tours for whisky experts, including cask tastings. There's also a museum and a restaurant. ✉ *A827* ☎ *01887/822010* ⊕ *www.dewars.com* ✉ *£7* ☉ *Apr.–Oct., weekdays 10–6, Sun. noon–4; Nov.–Mar., Mon.–Sat. 10–4.*

Glen Lyon. One of central Scotland's most attractive glens, 34-mile-long Glen Lyon is also one of its longest. It has a rushing river, thick forests, and the typical big house hidden on private grounds. There's a dam at the head of the loch, a reminder that little of Scotland's scenic beauty is unadulterated. The winding road lends itself to an unrushed, leisurely drive, past the visitor center at the access to Ben Lawers, a popular climb, and on to Killin. ✉ *A827, 15 miles north of Aberfeldy.*

Scottish Crannog Centre. Here's your chance to travel back 2,500 years to a time when this region's inhabitants lived in circular homesteads known as *crannogs.* Standing on stilts in the middle of lochs, these dwellings were approachable only by narrow bridges that could be easily defended from intruders. This center reveals the strength of these communal homes that were built entirely of wood, right down to the nails. Visits are by guided tour, beginning with an interesting exhibit on construction methods, followed by some fun with Neolithic lathes and tips on lighting a fire without matches. You can also reserve ahead to paddle a dugout canoe onto beautiful Loch Tay. ⊠ *Off A827, west of Aberfeldy* ☎ *01887/830583* ⊕ *www.crannog.co.uk* ☑ *£8* ⊘ *Apr.–Oct., daily 10–5:30; last entry 1 hr before closing.*

SHOPPING
Aberfeldy Water Mill. This historic mill combines an excellent independent bookshop with a large children's section, a gallery with frequently changing exhibitions, and a café. ⊠ *Mill St.* ☎ *01887/822896* ⊕ *www. aberfeldywatermill.com* ⊘ *Daily 10–5.*

SPORTS AND THE OUTDOORS
Highland Safaris. A full range of off-road activities for cyclists, drivers, and walkers is offered by Highland Safaris. ☎ *01887/820071* ⊕ *www. highlandsafaris.net.*

6

KILLIN

24 miles southwest of Aberfeldy, 39 miles north of Stirling, 45 miles west of Perth.

Killin's setting near the Breadalbane Mountains at the end of Loch Tay (where the Falls of Dochart rush into the lake) gives the village an almost alpine flavor. You'll find a surprisingly diverse selection of crafts and woolen shops here, as well as a plethora of B&Bs.

GETTING HERE AND AROUND
Killin can be reached from Stirling via the A85 and A827, or from Aberfeldy via the A827, the winding road beside Loch Tay. A hop on/hop off bus service called the Ring of Breadalbane Explorer shuttles passengers between Killin, Aberfeldy, Crieff, Comrie, and Perth. The full circuit takes 3½ hours, and takes you through some of Scotland's lovelist landscapes. A £12 ticket is good for the whole day.

ESSENTIALS
Visitor Information Killin Tourist Information ☎ *01786/459203.***Ring of Breadalbane Explorer** ☎ *01828/626262.*

EXPLORING
Falls of Dochart. Overlooked by a pine-clad islet, these white-water rapids are at the west end of Killin. ⊠ *Off A827.*

Finlarig Castle. Across the River Dochart from Killin sit the ruins of Finlarig Castle, built by Black Duncan of the Cowl, a notorious Campbell laird. The castle grounds can be visited at any time, but be careful on the uneven stones. ⊠ *Off A827.*

WHERE TO STAY

$
B&B/INN

Breadalbane House. This unpretentious but welcoming guest house sits in the center of Killin. **Pros:** a lovely location; friendly owners; easy parking. **Cons:** no young children allowed; limited public transport. $ *Rooms from: £65* ✉ *Main St.* ☎ *01567/820134* ⊕ *www. breadalbanehouse.com* ⇨ *5 rooms* ⦿ *No meals.*

$$
B&B/INN

Bridge of Lochay Hotel. On the edge of Killin, this small, family-run hotel sits on the banks of the River Tay. **Pros:** good base for exploring the area; welcoming atmosphere. **Cons:** basic rooms, slightly pricey for what it is. $ *Rooms from: £100* ✉ *Aberfeldy Rd.* ☎ *01567/820272* ⊕ *www.bridgeoflochay.co.uk* ⇨ *10 rooms* ⦿ *Breakfast.*

SPORTS AND THE OUTDOORS

BICYCLING

Killin Outdoor Centre and Mountain Shop. If you want to explore the northern end of the Glasgow–Killin cycleway, this shop rents mountain bikes (£16 for four hours). Also available are canoes, crampons, snowshoes, and ice axes. ✉ *Main St.* ☎ *01567/820652* ⊕ *www.killinoutdoor.co.uk.*

GOLF

Killin Golf Club. This picturesque course on the outskirts of Killin is actually quite challenging. ✉ *Off A827* ☎ *01567/820312* ⊕ *www. killingolfclub.co.uk* ⛳ *Green fee: £22 weekdays, £25 weekends* ⚑ *9 holes, 5066 yds, par 65.*

CRIEFF

25 miles southwest of Killin.

A spa and market town in the foothills of the Grampians, Crieff retains the prosperous air of its Victorian heyday. Its central square, where local farmers may once have gathered to trade, is still a lively center. For a different view of the town, you could climb Knock Hill, which is signposted from the town center.

GETTING HERE AND AROUND

Crieff once prospered because of the arrival of the railway. There is no station here today, but there are regular buses from Stirling and Glasgow. By car, take the A85 from Perth, or the A9, turning onto the A822 after Dunblane.

ESSENTIALS

Visitor Information Crieff Visitor Information Centre ✉ Town Hall, High St. ☎ 01764/652578 ⊕ www.visitscotland.com.

EXPLORING

Drummond Castle Garden. This formal Victorian garden celebrates family and Scottish heraldry. Combining the formal French and more relaxed Italian styles, the flower beds are planted and trimmed in the shapes of various heraldic symbols, such as a lion rampant and a checkerboard, associated with the coat of arms of the family that owns the castle. It's regarded as one of the finest of its kind in Europe, and it even made an appearance in the film *Rob Roy.* ✉ *Off A822, 6 miles southwest of Crieff* ☎ *01764/681433* ⊕ *www.drummondcastlegardens.co.uk* ⛳ *£5* ⊙ *May–Oct., daily 1–6; last admission at 5.*

Earthquake House. This small, unremarkable building in the middle of a field is in fact an early seismometer, measuring earthquakes in the British Isles and across the world. Through its windows you can see the original seisometer from 1840. The historic building sits between Comrie and Killin on the A85. ⊠ *A85, Comrie.*

Glenturret Distillery. To discover the delights of whisky distilling, sign up for the "Famous Grouse Experience" at the Glenturret Distillery. A guide takes you through the distillery and to the bar where you can have a glass of Famous Grouse Finest (a blended whisky) and try your skill at "nosing." Here you learn how whisky is made and why time, water, soil, and air are so important to the taste. You might cap your tour with lunch the Glenturret Cafe. Signs lead to the distillery on the west side of the town. ⊠ *The Hosh, Comrie Rd.* ☎ *01764/656565* ⊕ *www. thefamousgrouseexperience.com* ⊠ *£9.95* ⊙ *Mar.–Oct., daily 9–6, last tour at 4:30; Nov.–Feb., daily 10–4:30, last tour at 3:30.*

WHERE TO STAY

$$$$
HOTEL
🏨 **Crieff Hydro.** One of Scotland's great Victorian hydropathy centers, this grand hotel has been owned and run by the same family for more than 100 years. **Pros:** extensive grounds; variety of activities; particularly good for children. **Cons:** rooms are rather dull; some activities are quite expensive. ⑤ *Rooms from: £245* ⊠ *Off A85* ☎ *01764/655555* ⊕ *www.crieffhydro.com* ➥ *216 rooms* ⏋⊙⏌ *Multiple meal plans.*

SHOPPING
Crieff is a center for china and glassware.

Waterford Crystal. This factory shop sells Waterford, Dartington, and Wedgwood wares. ⊠ *Muthill Rd.* ☎ *01764/654004* ⊙ *June–Sept., daily 10–5:30; Oct.–May, Mon.–Sat. 10–5, Sun. 11–5.*

AUCHTERARDER

11 miles southeast of Crieff.

Famous for the Gleneagles Hotel and nearby golf courses, Auchterarder also has a flock of tiny antiques shops to amuse Gleneagles's golf widows and widowers.

GETTING HERE AND AROUND
Gleneagles Station is on the main Inverness line, while the A9 gives direct access to Gleneagles and Auchterarder via the A823.

ESSENTIALS
Visitor Information Auchterarder Visitor Information Centre ⊠ *90 High St.* ☎ *01764/663450* ⊕ *www.perthshire-scotland.co.uk.*

WHERE TO STAY

$$$$
HOTEL
Fodor's Choice
★
🏨 **Gleneagles Hotel.** One of Britain's most famous hotels, Gleneagles is the very essence of modern grandeur. **Pros:** luxe rooms; numerous amenities; the three courses are a golfer's paradise. **Cons:** all this comes at a steep price. ⑤ *Rooms from: £455* ⊠ *Off A823* ☎ *01764/662231* ⊕ *www.gleneagles.com* ➥ *216 rooms, 13 suites* ⏋⊙⏌ *Multiple meal plans.*

6

GOLF

Fodor's Choice ★ **Gleneagles.** A part of golfing history, this sprawling resort hosted the Ryder Cup in 2014. The 18 holes of the King Course, designed by James Braid in 1919, have quirky names—many golfers have grappled with the tough 17th hole, known as the Warslin' Lea (Wrestling Ground). The beguiling Queen's Course mixes varied terrain, including woods and moors. Jack Nicklaus designed the PGA Centenary Course, which sweeps into the Ochil Hills and has views of the Grampians. The 9-hole Wee Course provides challenges for beginners and pros alike. This is also where you'll find the PGA National Academy, a good place to improve your skills. ⊠ *A823* ☎ *01764/662231* ⊕ *www.gleneagles.com* ⛳ *Green fee: Kings, Queens, and PGA Centenary courses: £175; 9-hole PGA course £32* ⅃ *Kings: 18 holes, 6790 yds, par 71. Queens: 18 holes, 5968 yds, par 68. PGA Centenary: 18 holes, 7296 yds, par 72* ⊗ *Daily.*

ABERDEEN AND THE NORTHEAST

Updated by
Shona Main

Here, in this granite shoulder of Grampian, are some of Scotland's most enduring travel icons: Royal Deeside, the countryside that Queen Victoria made her own; the Castle Country route, where fortresses stand hard against the hills; and the Malt Whisky Trail, where peaty streams embrace the country's greatest concentration of distilleries. The region's gateway is the city of Aberdeen, constructed of granite and now aglitter with new wealth and new blood drawn together by North Sea oil.

Because of its isolation, Aberdeen has historically been a fairly autonomous place. Even now it's perceived by many U.K. inhabitants as lying almost out of reach in the northeast. In reality, it's a 90-minute flight from London or a little more than two hours by car from Edinburgh. Its magnificent 18th- and early-19th-century city center amply rewards exploration. Yet even if this popular base for travelers vanished from the map, an extensive portion of the northeast would still remain at the top of many travelers' wish lists.

Balmoral, the Scottish baronial–style house built for Queen Victoria as a retreat, is merely the most famous castle in the area, and certainly not the oldest. There are so many others that in one part of the region a Castle Trail has been established. In later structures, such as Castle Fraser, you can trace the changing styles and tastes of each of their owners over the centuries. Grand mansions such as 18th-century Haddo House, with its symmetrical facade and elegant interior, surrender any defensive role entirely.

A trail leading to a more ephemeral kind of pleasure can be found south of Elgin and Banff, where the glens embrace Scotland's greatest concentration of malt-whisky distilleries. With so many in Morayshire, where the distilling is centered on the valley of the River Spey and its tributaries, there's now a Whisky Trail. Follow it, and visit other distilleries as well, to experience a surprising wealth of flavors.

The northeast's chief topographical attraction lies in the gradual transition from high mountain plateau—by a series of gentle steps through hill, forest, and farmland—to the Moray Firth and North Sea coast, where the word "unadulterated" is redefined. Here you'll find some of the United Kingdom's most perfect wild shorelines, both sandy and sheer cliff, and breezy fishing villages like Cullen on the Banffshire coat and Stonehaven, south of Aberdeen. The Grampian Mountains, to the west, contain some of the highest ground in the nation, in the area of the Cairngorms. In recognition of this area's special nature, Cairngorms National Park was created in 2003.

TOP REASONS TO GO

Glorious castles: With more than 75 castles, some Victorian and others dating back to the 13th century, this area has everything from ravaged ruins like Dunnottar to opulent Fyvie Castle. They still evoke the power, grandeur, and sometimes the cruelty of Scotland's past.

Fine distilleries: The valley of the River Spey is famous for its single-malt distilleries, including those connected by the signposted Malt Whisky Trail. You can choose from bigger operations such as Glenfiddich to the iconic Strathisla, where Chivas Regal is blended.

Seaside cities and towns: The fishing industry may be in decline, but the big-city port of Abderdeen and the colorful smaller fishing towns of Stonehaven and Cullen in the northeast are great (and very different) places to soak up the seagoing atmosphere—and some seafood.

Great walking: There are all types of walking for all kinds of walkers, from the bracing but spectacular inclines of the Grampian Hills to the wooded gardens and grounds of Balmoral and Haddo House, to breath-stealing golden sands near towns such as Cullen.

Superb golf: The northeast has more than 50 golf clubs, some of which have championship courses. Less famous clubs, both inland and by the sea, have some amazing courses as well.

7

ORIENTATION AND PLANNING

GETTING ORIENTED

Aberdeen, on the North Sea in the eastern part of the region, is Scotland's third-largest city; many people start a trip here. Once you have spent time in the city, you may be inclined to venture west into rural Deeside, with its royal connections and looming mountain backdrop. To the north of Deeside is Castle Country, with many ancient fortresses. Speyside and the Whisky Trail lie at the western edge of the region, and are equally accessible from Inverness. From Speyside you might travel back east along the pristine coastline at Scotland's northeastern tip.

Aberdeen. Family connections or Royal Deeside often take travelers to this part of Scotland, but many are surprised by how grand and rich in history Aberdeen is. The august granite-turreted buildings and rose-lined roads make this a surprisingly pleasant city to explore; don't miss Old Aberdeen in particular.

Royal Deeside and Castle Country. Prince Albert designed Balmoral Castle for Queen Victoria, and so began the Royal family's love affair with Deeside—and Deeside's love affair with it. However, this area has long been the retreat or the fortress of distinguished families, as the clutter of castles throughout the region shows. The majesty of the countryside also guarantees a superlative stop for everyone interested in history and romance.

The Northeast and the Malt Whisky Trail. For lovers of whisky, this is a favored part of Scotland to visit. Unique in their architecture, their ingredients, and the end product, the distilleries of Speyside are keen to share with you their passion for "the water of life." This region also has rolling hills and, to the north, the beautiful, wild coastline of the North Sea.

PLANNING

WHEN TO GO

May and June are probably the loveliest times to visit, but many travelers arrive from late spring to early fall. The National Trust for Scotland tends to close its properties in winter, so many of the northeast's castles are not open for off-season travel, though you can always see them from the outside. The distilleries are open much of the year, but check for the "silent month" when they close down for a holiday. That's often in August, but may vary.

PLANNING YOUR TIME

How you allocate your time may depend on your special interests—castles or whisky, for example. But even if you can manage only a morning or an afternoon, do not miss a walk around the granite streets of Old Aberdeen, and take in Aberdeen Art Gallery, St. Nicholas Kirk, and a pint in the Prince of Wales pub. A trip southward to the fishing town of Stonehaven and the breathtaking cliff-top fortress of Dunnottar makes a rewarding afternoon. Royal Deeside, with a good sprinkling of castles and grandeur, needs a good two days; even this might be tight for those who want to lap up every moment of majesty at Balmoral, Crathes, Fraser, and Fyvie, the best of the bunch. A visit to malt-whisky country should include tours of Glenfiddich, Glenfarclas, Glenlivet, and Glen Grant distilleries, and although it's not technically a maker of malt whisky, Strathisla. Real enthusiasts should allot two days for the distilleries, and they shouldn't pass up a visit to Speyside Cooperage, one of the few remaining cooperages in the Scotland. Cullen and Duff House gallery in Banff, on the coast, can be done in a day before returning to Aberdeen.

GETTING HERE AND AROUND

AIR TRAVEL

The city is easy to reach from other parts of the United Kingdom as well as Europe. British Airways, bmi, EasyJet, and Flybe are some of the airlines with service to other parts of Britain. Aberdeen Airport—serving both international and domestic flights—is in Dyce, 7 miles west of the city center on the A96 (Inverness). The drive to the center of Aberdeen is easy via the A96 (which can be busy during rush hour).

Airport Contact Aberdeen Airport ✉ *Dyce Dr., Dyce* ☎ *0844/481–6666* ⊕ *www.aberdeenairport.com.*

BOAT AND FERRY TRAVEL

Northlink Ferries has service between Aberdeen, Lerwick (Shetland), and Kirkwall (Orkney).

Boat and Ferry Contact Northlink Ferries ✉ *Jamieson's Quay, Aberdeen* ☎ *0845/600–0449* ⊕ *www.northlinkferries.co.uk.*

BUS TRAVEL

Long-distance buses run to Aberdeen from most parts of Scotland, England, and Wales. Contact Megabus, National Express, and Scottish Citylink for bus connections with English and Scottish towns. There's a network of local buses throughout the northeast run by Stagecoach, but they can take a long time and connections are not always well timed.

Bus Contacts Megabus ☎ 0900/160–0900 ⊕ www.megabus.com. **National Express** ☎ 08717/818178 ⊕ www.nationalexpress.com. **Scottish Citylink** ☎ 0871/266–3333 ⊕ www.citylink.co.uk. **Stagecoach** ✉ Union Square Bus Station, Guild St., Aberdeen ☎ 01224/591381 ⊕ www.stagecoachbus.com.

CAR TRAVEL

A car is the best way to see the northeast. If you are coming from the south, take the A90, continuing on from the M90 (from Edinburgh) or the M9/A9 (from Glasgow), which both stop at Perth. The coastal route, the A92, is a more leisurely alternative, with its interesting resorts and fishing villages. The most scenic route, however, is the A93 from Perth, north to Blairgowrie and into Glen Shee. The A93 then goes over the Cairnwell Pass, the highest main road in the United Kingdom. This route isn't recommended in winter, when snow can make driving difficult.

Around the northeast roads can be busy, with speeding and erratic driving a problem on the main A roads.

TRAIN TRAVEL

You can reach Aberdeen directly from Edinburgh (2½ hours), Inverness (2½ hours), and Glasgow (3 hours). ScotRail timetables have full details. There are also London–Aberdeen routes that go through Edinburgh and the east-coast main line connecting Aberdeen to all corners of the United Kingdom.

Train Contact ScotRail ⊠ *Aberdeen Railway Station, Guild St., Aberdeen* ☎ *08457/484950* ⊕ *www.scotrail.co.uk.*

RESTAURANTS

Partly in response to the demands of workers in the oil industry, restaurants have cropped up all over Aberdeen, and the quality of the food improves yearly. As in the rest of Scotland, this region is rediscovering the quality and versatility of the local produce. Juicy Aberdeen Angus steaks, lean lamb, and humanely reared pork appear on local menus, but despite this being the center of the fishing industry, most seafood available is still of the fish-and-chips variety. Restaurants like the Silver Darling in Aberdeen are spearheading a new interest in fish dishes, though, and old standards like Cullen skink (a creamy smoked-fish soup) are increasingly on menus. *Prices in the reviews are the average cost of a main course at dinner or, if dinner is not served, at lunch.*

HOTELS

The northeast has some splendid country hotels with log fires and old Victorian furnishings, where you can also be sure of eating well. Many hotels in Aberdeen are in older buildings that have a baronial feel. The trend for serviced apartments has caught on here, with some extremely modish and good-value options for those who want a bit more privacy. This trend is now extending into Deeside, where it's been notoriously difficult to find good accommodations beyond some country-house hotels, even though it's a popular tourist spot. *Prices in the reviews are the lowest cost of a standard double room in high season, including 20% V.A.T.*

VISITOR INFORMATION

The tourist information center in Aberdeen has a currency exchange, Internet access, and supplies information on all of Scotland's northeast. There are also year-round tourist information offices in Braemar and Elgin. In summer, also look for tourist information centers in Alford, Ballater, Banchory, Braemar, Dufftown, Elgin, and Stonehaven.

Contact Aberdeen Visitor Information Centre ⊠ *23 Union St., Aberdeen* ☎ *01224/288828* ⊕ *www.aberdeen-grampian.com.*

ABERDEEN

As a gateway to Royal Deeside and the Malt Whisky Trail, Aberdeen attracts visitors, though many are eager to get out into the countryside. Today, though, the city's unique history is finally being recognized as more impressive than many Scots had previously realized, and Aberdeen is being rediscovered. Distinctive architecture, some fine museums, universities, and good restaurants, nightlife, and shopping add to the appeal of Scotland's third-largest city (population 217,000). Union Street is the heart of the city, but take time to explore the university and the pretty streets of Old Aberdeen.

In the 18th century local granite quarrying produced a durable silver stone that would be used boldly in the glittering blocks, spires, columns, and parapets of Victorian-era Aberdonian structures. The city remains one of the United Kingdom's most distinctive, although some would say it depends on the weather and the brightness of the day. The mica chips embedded in the rock look like a million mirrors in the sunshine. In rain (and there is a fair amount of driving rain from the North Sea) and heavy clouds, however, their sparkle is snuffed out.

The city lies between the Dee and Don rivers, with a working harbor that has access to the sea; it has been a major fishing port and is the main commercial port in northern Scotland. The North Sea has always been important to Aberdeen. In the 1850s the city was famed for its sleek, fast clippers that sailed to India for cargoes of tea. In the late 1960s the course of Aberdeen's history was unequivocally altered when oil and gas were discovered offshore, sparking rapid growth, prosperity, and further industrialization.

7

GETTING HERE AND AROUND

AIR TRAVEL Stagecoach Bluebird Jet Service 727 and First Aberdeen Bus 27 operate between the airport terminal and Union Square in the center of Aberdeen. Buses (£2.70) run frequently at peak times, less often at midday and in the evening; the journey time is approximately 40 minutes. Stagecoach Bluebird Bus 10 stops at Aberdeen Airport, either taking you into the city center or northwest to Elgin.

Dyce is on ScotRail's Inverness–Aberdeen route. The rail station is a short taxi ride from the terminal building. The ride takes 12 minutes, and trains run approximately every two hours.

BUS TRAVEL First Aberdeen has easy and reliable service within the city of Aberdeen. Timetables are available from the tourist information center in Union Street.

CAR TRAVEL Aberdeen is a compact city with good signage. Its center is Union Street, the main east–west thoroughfare, which tends to get crowded with traffic. Anderson Drive is an efficient ring road on the city's west side; be extra careful on its many traffic circles. It's best to leave your car in one of the parking garages (arrive early to get a space) and walk around, or use the convenient park-and-ride stop at the Bridge of Don, north of the city. Street maps are available from the tourist information center, newsstands, and booksellers.

TAXI TRAVEL   You can find taxi stands throughout the center of Aberdeen: along Union Street, at the railway station at Guild Street, at Back Wynd, and at Regent Quay. The taxis have meters and might be saloon cars (sedans) or black cabs. They are great ways to travel between neighborhoods.

TRAIN TRAVEL   Aberdeen has good ScotRail service.

ESSENTIALS

Bus Contacts First Aberdeen ☎ *01224/650000* ⊕ *www.firstaberdeen.co.uk.*

AROUND UNION STREET

Aberdeen centers on Union Street, with its many fine survivors of the Victorian and Edwardian streetscape. Marischal College, dating from the late 16th century, has many grand buildings that are worth exploring.

TIMING

You can explore the center of Aberdeen in half a day, but you'll probably want to devote a full day to poking around its interesting old buildings.

TOP ATTRACTIONS

Aberdeen Art Gallery. Housed in a 19th-century neoclassical building, the museum contains excellent paintings, prints, and drawings, sculpture, porcelain, costumes, and much else—from 18th-century art to major contemporary British works by Lucien Freud and Henry Moore. Scottish artists are well represented in the permanent collection and special exhibits. Local stone has been used in interior walls, pillars, and the central fountain, designed by the acclaimed British sculptor Barbara Hepworth. ■ TIP➔ **Look for the unique collection of Aberdeen silver on the ground floor.** The museum also has a cake-filled café and well-stocked gift shop. ⊠ *Schoolhill* ☎ *01224/523700* ⊕ *www.aagm.co.uk* 🖾 *Free* ⊘ *Tues.–Sat. 10–5, Sun. 2–5.*

NEED A BREAK?   **The Beautiful Mountain. This simple, good-natured café is full of life and banter. Stop for a well-filled sandwich and a cup of tea, or perhaps a cake or two. On Thursday, Friday, and Saturday evening it serves Spanish food.** ⊠ *11–13 Belmont St.* ☎ *01224/645353* ⊕ *www.thebeautifulmountain.co.uk.*

FAMILY   **Aberdeen Maritime Museum.** This excellent museum, which incorporates the 1593 Provost Ross's House, tells the story of the city's involvement with the sea, from early inshore fisheries to tea clippers and the North Sea oil boom. The information-rich exhibits, fascinating for kids and adults, include ship models, paintings, and equipment associated with the fishing, shipbuilding, and oil and gas industries. ⊠ *Ship Row* ☎ *01224/337700* ⊕ *www.aagm.co.uk* 🖾 *Free* ⊘ *Tues.– Sat. 10–5, Sun. noon–3.*

Provost Skene's House. Now a museum portraying civic life, the restored house has furnished period rooms and a painted chapel. Steeply gabled and built from rubble, it dates in part from 1545. The house was originally a mayor's domestic dwelling (*provost* is Scottish for "mayor"). Its costume gallery displays colorful exhibitions of fashions from different centuries. ⊠ *Guestrow, off Broad St.* ☎ *01224/641086* ⊕ *www.aagm. co.uk* 🖾 *Free* ⊘ *Mon.–Sat. 10–5.*

Aberdeen

St. Nicholas Kirk. The original burgh church, the Mither Kirk, as this edifice is known, is not within the bounds of the early town settlement; that was to the east, near the end of present-day Union Street. During the 12th century the port of Aberdeen flourished, and there wasn't room for the church within the settlement. Its earliest features are its pillars—supporting a tower built much later—and its clerestory windows: both date from the 12th century. St. Nicholas was divided into east and west kirks at the Reformation, followed by a substantial amount of renovation from 1741 on. ■ TIP→ **In the chapel, look for a glass case containing two books: one lists the victims of a 1989 oil-rig disaster; the second is empty, a testament to the "unknown" workers who have lost their lives.** ⊠ *Union St.* ☎ *01224/643494* ⊕ *www.kirk-of-st-nicholas.org.uk* ▣ *Free, but donations welcome* ☽ *May–Sept., weekdays noon–4.*

WORTH NOTING

OFF THE
BEATEN
PATH

Duthie Park. A great place to feed the ducks, Duthie Park also has a boating pond, playgrounds, and carved wooden animals. In the attractive Winter Gardens (tropical and arid conservatories) are fish in ponds, free-flying birds, and turtles and terrapins among the luxuriant foliage and flowers. The park borders Aberdeen's other river, the Dee. ⊠ *Polmuir Rd., about 1 mile south of city center* ▣ *Free* ☽ *Gardens daily 8 am–1 hr before sunset.*

Marischal College. Founded in 1593 by the Earl Marischal (the keeper of the king's mares), Marischal College was a Protestant alternative to the Catholic King's College in Old Aberdeen. The two joined to form the University of Aberdeen in 1860. The spectacularly ornate work of the main university building is set off by the gilded flags, and this turn-of-the-20th-century creation is still one of the world's largest granite buildings. In 2011, the building's interior was rebuilt to house the city council. In keeping with the Aberdonian custom of never throwing anything away, the discarded materials have already been used in buildings around the city. ⊠ *Broad St.*

Mercat Cross. Built in 1686 and restored in 1820, the Mercat Cross (the term stems from "marketplace"), always the symbolic center of a Scottish medieval burgh, stands just beyond King Street. Along its parapet are 12 portrait panels of the Stewart monarchs. ⊠ *Justice and Marischal Sts.*

Rosemount Viaduct. Three silvery, handsome buildings on this bridge are collectively known by all Aberdonians as Education, Salvation, and Damnation. The **Central Library** and **St. Mark's Church** date from the last decade of the 19th century, and **His Majesty's Theatre** (1904–08) has been restored inside to its full Edwardian splendor. If you're taking photographs, you can choose an angle that includes the statue of Scotland's first freedom fighter, Sir William Wallace (1270–1305), in the foreground pointing majestically to Damnation.

FAMILY **Tolbooth.** The city was governed from this 17th-century building, which was also the burgh court and jail, for 200 years. Now a museum of crime and punishment, it is as amusing as it is stomach churning—making it a must-see for older kids. ⊠ *Castle St.* ☎ *01224/621167* ⊕ *www.aagm.co.uk* ▣ *Free* ☽ *July–Sept., Mon.–Sat. 10–5.*

A GOOD WALK IN DOWNTOWN ABERDEEN

For a lovely stroll downtown, start at the east end of Union Street, east of Marischal Street. Here within the original old town is a square called Castlegate. The actual castle once stood somewhere behind the Salvation Army Citadel (1896), an imposing baronial granite tower whose design was inspired by Balmoral Castle. On the north side of Castle Street stands the 17th-century Tolbooth, a reminder of Aberdeen's earliest days. The impressive Mercat Cross is near King Street. Turn north down Broad Street to reach the main Marischal College building with its granite frontage. It now holds the city council's headquarters but is also used by the university.

A survivor from an earlier Aberdeen can be found opposite Marischal College, beyond the concrete supports of St. Nicholas House (which houses the tourist information center): Provost Skene's House was once part of a closely packed area of town houses and is now a museum portraying civic life. Just around the corner on Upperkirkgate, at the lowest point, are two modern shopping malls—the St. Nicholas Centre on the left, the Bon Accord Centre on the right.

Union Street. This great thoroughfare is to Aberdeen what Princes Street is to Edinburgh: the central pivot of the city plan and the product of a wave of enthusiasm to rebuild the city in a contemporary style in the early 19th century.

Union Terrace. In the 19th-century development of Union Terrace stands a statue of Robert Burns (1759–96) addressing a daisy. Behind Burns are the **Union Terrace Gardens,** faintly echoing Edinburgh's Princes Street Gardens in that both separate the older part of the city, to the east, from the 19th-century development to the west. There are plans to build above the gardens and the railway lines, a move that will either be to Aberdeen's asthetic benefit or its disgrace, depending on your viewpoint.

OLD ABERDEEN

Very much a separate area of the city, Old Aberdeen is north of the modern center and clustered around St. Machar's Cathedral and the many fine buildings of the University of Aberdeen. Take a stroll on College Bounds; handsome 18th- and 19th-century houses line this cobbled street in the oldest part of the city.

TIMING

The neighborhood is a 20- to 30-minute walk north of the center of town; it's also easily reachable by First Aberdeen bus numbers 1 and 20 from Union Street. The ride takes 5 to 15 minutes. Old Aberdeen is a compact area, and will take you no more than a few hours to explore.

TOP ATTRACTIONS

Cruickshank Botanic Gardens. Built on land bequeathed by Miss Anne Crickshank in memory of her beloved brother Alexander, the 11-acre Cruickshank Botanic Garden has a peaceful water garden and lush greens ideal for lounging—when the weather allows—and beautifully tended subtropical and alpine collections. Botanical tours are available. ✉ *St. Machar Dr., at the Chanonry* ☎ *01224/272704* ⊕ *www.abdn. ac.uk/botanic-garden* 🎫 *Free* ☉ *Apr.–Sept., weekdays 9–7, weekends 2–9:30; Oct.–Mar., weekdays 9:30–4:30.*

Fodor's Choice ★   **King's College.** Founded in 1494, King's College is now part of the University of Aberdeen. Its **chapel,** built around 1500, has an unmistakable flying (or crown) spire. That it has survived at all was because of the zeal of the principal, who defended his church against the destructive fanaticism that swept through Scotland during the Reformation, when the building was less than a century old. Today the renovated chapel plays an important role in university life. ■TIP→ **Don't miss the tall oak screen that separates the nave from the choir, the ribbed wooden ceiling, and the stalls, as these constitute the finest medieval wood carvings found anywhere in Scotland.** The **King's College Centre** has more information about the university. ✉ *High St.* ☎ *01224/272660* ⊕ *www.abdn.ac.uk* ☉ *Weekdays 10–3:30.*

▌QUICK BITE   **Kilau Coffee.** Popular with students and academics alike, this café across from the cathedral offers loungy seating downstairs and table and chairs upstairs. Expertly made coffee is on offer, as well as cakes and snacks. ✉ *55–57 High St.* ☎ *01224/485510* ⊕ *www.kilaucoffee.wordpress.com.*

King's Museum. In a modest town house across from the archway leading to King's College Chapel, this museum hosts constantly changing exhibitions. It presents some impressive and often strange curiosities from the university's collection, from prehistoric flints to a tiger's penis. ✉ *17 High St.* ☎ *01224/274300* ⊕ *www.abdn.ac.uk/kingsmuseum* 🎫 *Free* ☉ *Mon. and Wed.–Fri. 10–6, Tues. 10–7:30, Sat. 11–4.*

▌QUICK BITE   **St. Machar Bar.** St. Machar Bar is a small, vibrant pub in the middle of the university campus, selling not just pints but also real *stovies* (a hot potato-based stew) made with beef. This is a great place to warm up or pass away the time with a newspaper if the weather is unbecoming. ✉ *97 High St.* ☎ *01224/483079* ⊕ *www.themachar.com.*

Old Town House. Serving as a gateway to Aberdeen University, this plain but handsome Georgian building is a great place to learn about this ancient seat of learning. The building was the center of all trading activity in the city before it became a grammar school, a Masonic lodge, and then a library. ✉ *High St.* ☎ *01224/273650* ⊕ *www.abdn.ac.uk/ oldtownhouse* 🎫 *Free* ☉ *Mon.–Sat. 9–5.*

St. Machar's Cathedral. It's said that St. Machar was sent by St. Columba to build a church on a grassy platform near the sea, where a river flowed in the shape of a shepherd's crook. This spot fits the bill. Although the cathedral was founded in AD 580, most of the existing building dates from the 15th and 16th centuries. The central tower collapsed in 1688, reducing the building to half its original length. The nave is thought to have been rebuilt in red sandstone in 1370, but the final renovation was completed in granite by the middle of the 15th century. Along with the nave ceiling, the twin octagonal spires were finished in time to take a battering in the Reformation, when the barons of the Mearns stripped the lead off the roof and stole the bells. The cathedral suffered further mistreatment until it was fully restored in the 19th century. ⊠ *Chanonry* ☎ *01224/485988* ⊕ *www. stmachar.com* ☉ *Apr.–Oct., daily 9:30–4:30; Nov.–Mar., daily 10–4.*

WORTH NOTING
Brig o'Balgownie. Until 1827, the only northern route out of Aberdeen was over the River Don on this single-arch bridge. It dates from 1314 and is thought to have been built by Richard Cementarius, Aberdeen's first provost. ⊠ *Seaton Park.*

WHERE TO EAT

$ ✗ **Ashvale.** Ask anyone about this long-established place and the response
BRITISH will probably be overwhelmingly positive. Fish-and-chips are the spe-
FAMILY cialty, and the secret-recipe batter is now the stuff of legend. Attempt the Whale—a gigantic fillet of battered cod—and you'll be rewarded with a free dessert. The decor is your basic wood-chairs-and-tables. ⑤ *Average main: £12* ⊠ *42–48 Great Western Rd.* ☎ *01224/574842* ⊕ *theashvale.co.uk.*

$ ✗ **Café 52.** Right in the historic Grassmarket, this café-restaurant has
MODERN BRITISH taken a few years to find its niche but now serves up lovely homemade dishes at pocket-friendly prices. Creamy fish pie filled with juicy chunks of smoked haddock and bramble panna cotta are just a few of the options. No matter what you order, local produce makes it tasty and fresh. The handsome restaurant is in a silvery granite building with exposed-stone walls, huge windows, and shiny black tables. ⑤ *Average main: £12* ⊠ *52 The Green* ☎ *01224/590094* ⊕ *www.cafe52.net* ☉ *No dinner Sun.*

$$$ ✗ **Silver Darling.** Huge windows overlook the harbor and beach at this
SEAFOOD quayside favorite in a former customs house, long one of Aberdeen's
Fodor's Choice most acclaimed restaurants. As the name implies, the French-inspired fare
★ focuses on fish: a silver darling is a herring. Try the langoustine ravioli with hazelnut velouté for a starter, then move on to wild halibut steamed in seaweed, or sea bass with crushed ginger potatoes. ⑤ *Average main: £25* ⊠ *North Pier, Pocra Quay* ☎ *01224/576229* ⊕ *thesilverdarling.co. uk* ⚭ *Reservations essential* ☉ *Closed Sun. No lunch Sat.*

$$ ✗ **Yatai.** It might seem odd ordering Japanese food in Aberdeen, but
JAPANESE considering the quality and quantity of fresh fish being landed on the
Fodor's Choice quayside each day it makes perfect sense. The slick facade and glowing
★ red interior might be a little intimidating at first, but the smiling staff is approachable, and, for the uninitiated, is happy to help you choose the right blend of flavors and textures. The place isn't cheap, but as far as Japanese food is concerned, it's not extortionate either: £12 for seared beef salad, £15 for six pieces of sushi. Japanese saki and beer are a treat. ⑤ *Average main: £15* ⊠ *53 Langstane Pl.* ☎ *01224/592355* ⊕ *www.yatai.co.uk* ⚭ *Reservations essential* ☉ *Closed Sun. and Mon.*

7

WHERE TO STAY

$$ **Atholl Hotel.** With its many turrets and gables, this granite hotel recalls
HOTEL   a bygone era but has modern amenities. **Pros:** family-run establish-
ment; tasty restaurant; very pleasant staff. **Cons:** some rooms are a
little generic; some bathrooms need updating. $ *Rooms from: £145
✉ 54 Kings Gate ☎ 01224/323505 ⊕ www.atholl-aberdeen.com ⇄ 34
rooms* ⊙ *Breakfast.*

$$ **Bauhaus Hotel.** When the owner got his hands on this 1960s-era
HOTEL   granite office block, he decided to pay homage to Walter Gropius, the
founder of the Bauhaus movement. **Pros:** great design; comfortable
rooms; tasty eatery. **Cons:** beware the furniture's sharp corners; fake
art on the walls—in a city with a great art school. $ *Rooms from:
£130 ✉ 52–60 Langstane Pl. ☎ 01224/212122 ⊕ www.thebauhaus.
co.uk ⇄ 34 rooms, 5 suites* ⊙ *Multiple meal plans.*

$$ **City Wharf.** With one- to four-bedroom apartments at three down-
RENTAL   town addresses, City Wharf offers fuss-free stays of any length in lux-
ury settings. **Pros:** rates drop dramatically on weekends; all mod cons;
passes to a nearby gym. **Cons:** no porters to help you with your bags;
no restaurant; beware the seagulls. $ *Rooms from: £130 ✉ 47 Regent
Quay ☎ 01224/589282 ⊕ www.citywharfapartments.co.uk ⇄ 22
apartments* ⊙ *Breakfast.*

$$ **Craibstone Suites.** On one of Aberdeen's most attractive squares, these
HOTEL   modern but comfortable suites come with fully equipped kitchens. **Pros:**
great central location; feels more like an apartment than a hotel room.
Cons: executive suites are small—go for the grand or superior suites
if you need elbow room; the breakfast is pretty basic. $ *Rooms from:
£120 ✉ 15 Bon Accord Sq. ☎ 01224/857950 ⊕ www.craibstone-suites.
co.uk ⇄ 18 suites* ⊙ *Breakfast.*

$$ **The Jays Guest House.** Alice Jennings or her husband George will greet
B&B/INN   you at the front door of this granite house, a homey bed-and-breakfast.
Fodor's Choice   **Pros:** immaculate rooms; expert advice on city's sites; near shops
★   and restaurants. **Cons:** no public areas; incredibly popular, so book
in advance. $ *Rooms from: £100 ✉ 422 King St. ☎ 01224/638295
⊕ www.jaysguesthouse.co.uk ⇄ 10 rooms* ⊙ *Breakfast.*

$$$$ **Marcliffe Hotel and Spa.** Set on 11 wooded acres, this spacious, ele-
HOTEL   gant country-house hotel combines old and new to impressive effect.
Pros: lush gardens; well-trained staff; relaxing spa. **Cons:** a little out
of town; restaurant prices are a bit steep. $ *Rooms from: £270 ✉ N.
Deeside Rd. ☎ 01224/861000 ⊕ www.marcliffe.com ⇄ 35 rooms, 7
suites* ⊙ *Breakfast.*

NIGHTLIFE AND THE ARTS

Aberdeen has a fairly lively nightlife scene revolving around pubs and
clubs. Theaters, concert halls, arts centers, and cinemas are also well
represented. The principal newspapers—the *Press and Journal* and the
Evening Express—and *Aberdeen Leopard* magazine can fill you in on
what's going on anywhere in the northeast. Aberdeen's tourist informa-
tion center has a monthly publication with an events calendar.

THE ARTS

Aberdeen is a rich city, both financially and culturally.

Aberdeen International Youth Festival. August sees the world-renowned Aberdeen International Youth Festival, which attracts orchestras, choirs, dance troupes, and theater companies from many countries who perform in various venues across the city and the region. ☎ *01224/213800* ⊕ *www.aiyf.org.*

ARTS CENTERS **Aberdeen Arts Centre.** The Aberdeen Arts Centre hosts plays, musicals, poetry readings, and exhibitions by local and Scottish artists. ⊠ *33 King St.* ☎ *01224/635208* ⊕ *www.aberdeenartscentre.org.uk.*

Haddo House. About 20 miles north of Aberdeen, Haddo House offers a mixed bag of events, from opera and ballet to puppet shows and Shakespeare. The season runs from spring through fall. ⊠ *Off B999, Tarves* ☎ *0844/4932179* ⊕ *www.nts.org.uk.*

Lemon Tree. The Lemon Tree has an innovative and international program of dance, stand-up comedy, and puppet theater, as well as folk, jazz, and rock music. ⊠ *5 W. North St.* ☎ *0845/270–8200* ⊕ *www.boxofficeaberdeen.com.*

Peacock Visual Arts. This gallery displays photographic, video, and slide exhibits of contemporary art and architecture. ⊠ *21 Castle St.* ☎ *01224/639539* ⊕ *www.peacockvisualarts.com* ⊙ *Tue.–Sat. 9:30–5:30.*

CONCERT HALLS **His Majesty's Theatre.** The Edwardian His Majesty's Theatre hosts performances on par with those in some of the world's biggest cities. It's a regular venue for musicals and operas, as well as classical and modern dance. The restaurant, called 1906, is popular with audiences and cast members alike. ⊠ *Rosemount Viaduct* ☎ *0845/270–8200* ⊕ *www.boxofficeaberdeen.com.*

Music Hall. The Scottish National Orchestra, the Scottish Chamber Orchestra, and other major groups perform at the Music Hall. Events also include folk concerts, crafts fairs, and exhibitions. ⊠ *Union St.* ☎ *01224/632080* ⊕ *www.boxofficeaberdeen.com.*

FILM **The Belmont.** Independent and classic films screen at the Belmont. ⊠ *49 Belmont St.* ☎ *0871/902–5721* ⊕ *www.picturehouses.co.uk.*

NIGHTLIFE

With a greater club-to-clubber ratio than either Edinburgh or Glasgow, Aberdeen offers plenty of loud music and dancing for a night out. There are also pubs and pool halls for those with two left feet. Pubs close at midnight on weekdays and 1 am on weekends; clubs go until 2 or 3 am.

BARS AND PUBS **Fittie Bar.** Some pubs spend a fortune trying to re-create the warm atmosphere that the Fittie Bar comes by naturally. Located where the harbor stops and the old fishing village of Footdee (Fittie) begins, the pub tells the story of Aberdeen's fishing past, as will any of the salty dogs who drink there. ⊠ *18 Wellington St.* ☎ *01224/582911.*

Illicit Still. The old-fashioned Illicit Still is named after the 18th-century practice of brewing your own beer to avoid the malt tax. A beautifully fitted-out drinking establishment, it also serves up hearty pub grub. ⊠ *Guest Row, Broad St.* ☎ *01224/623123* ⊕ *www.illicit-still.co.uk.*

Old Blackfriars. Old Blackfriars enjoys a nice location near the end of Union Street. The lighting is dim, and the big fireplace warms things up on a chilly evening, although it can get crowded as the night goes on. This cask ale pub has a great selection—Belhaven St. Andrews Ale and Caledonian 80 top the list. ⊠ *52 Castle St.* ☎ *01224/581922* ⊕ *www. old-blackfriars-aberdeen.co.uk.*

Fodor's Choice **The Prince of Wales.** Dating from 1850, the Prince of Wales has retained
★ its paneled walls and wooden tables. Still regarded as Aberdeen's most traditional pub, it's hardly regal, but good-quality food and reasonable prices draw the regulars back. ⊠ *7 St. Nicholas La.* ☎ *01224/640597.*

Soul. In a converted church that still has stained-glass windows and ecclesiastical furnishings, Soul is popular with young, upwardly mobile Aberdonians. The eclectic menu includes everything from chicken satay to mussels. ⊠ *333 Union St.* ☎ *01224/211150.*

DANCE CLUBS   People tend to dress up a bit to go clubbing, and jeans or sneakers might get you turned away at the door. Clubs are open until 2 am during the week and until 3 am on Friday and Saturday nights.

Club Snafu. This boutique club hosts all manner of specialty nights, from comedy to electronica. ⊠ *1 Union St.* ☎ *01224/596111* ⊕ *www. clubsnafu.com.*

SPORTS AND THE OUTDOORS

GOLF

Northeast Scotland is known for good golf. Despite the continuing outcry from locals and environmentalists, Donald Trump has "stabilized" the dynamic dune system that borders the Menie Estate, just north of Aberdeen and the Ythan estuary, to create Trump International Golf Links. Just south of Aberdeen, Jack Nicklaus has been lined up to design a championship course at Ury Castle. The financial climate has delayed the project, though.

You can expect to pay £15 to £120 per round at the golf courses in and around Aberdeen. Make reservations at least 24 hours in advance. Some private courses restrict tee times for visiting golfers to certain days or hours during the week, so be sure to check that the course you wish to play is open when you want to play it.

Murcar Links Golf Club. Sea views and a variety of rugged terrain—from sand dunes to tinkling burns—are the highlights of this course, founded in 1909. It's most famous for breathtaking vistas at the seventh hole, appropriately called the Serpentine. Designer Archibald Simpson considered this course to be one of his finest. ⊠ *Bridge of Don* ☎ *01224/704354* ⊕ *www.murcarlinks.com* 🏌 *Green fee: £80 weekdays, £96 weekends.* 🏌 *18 holes, 6314 yds, SSS 73.*

Royal Aberdeen Golf Club. This venerable club, founded in 1780, is the archetypal Scottish links course: tumbling over uneven ground, with the frequently added hazard of sea breezes. Prickly gorse is inclined to close in and form an additional hurdle. The two courses are tucked behind the rough, grassy sand dunes, and there are surprisingly few views of the sea. One historical note: in 1783 this club originated the five-minute-search rule for a lost ball. A handicap certificate and letter of introduction are required. ■**TIP**→ Visitors are allowed only on weekdays. ⊠ *Links Rd., Bridge of Don* ☎*01224/702571* ⊕*www. royalaberdeengolf.com* ⌁ *Green fee: Balgownie £120; Silverburn £60* ⌁ *Reservations essential* ⚑ *Balgownie: 18 holes, 6900 yds, par 71; Silverburn: 18 holes, 4021 yds, par 64* ⊙ *Daily.*

Westhill Golf Club. This parkland course, founded in 1977, overlooks Royal Deeside and has a friendly clubhouse. This affable place is the most inexpensive in the area by far. ⊠ *Westhill Heights, Westhill* ☎*01224/740159* ⊕*www.westhillgolfclub.co.uk* ⌁ *Green fee: £20* ⚑ *18 holes, 5849 yds, SSS 69.*

SHOPPING

You can find most of the large national department stores in Union Square. Bon Accord, St. Nicholas, and Trinity shopping malls or along Union Street, but Aberdeen has a few good specialty shops as well.

SPECIALTY SHOPS

Aberdeen Art Gallery Shop. The constantly changing crafts and jewelry at the Aberdeen Art Gallery Shop always have something of interest, and there are pretty postcards of the city from times gone by. ⊠ *Schoolhill* ☎*01224/523695.*

Aitkins. You can't leave Aberdeen without trying one of its famous *rowies* (or *butteries*), the fortifying morning roll. Aitkins Bakery is considered the finest purveyor of this local speciality. ⊠ *202 Holburn St.* ☎*01224/582567.*

Alex Scott & Co. For Scottish kilts, tartans, crests, and other traditionally Scottish clothes, a good place to start is Alex Scott & Co. ⊠ *43 Schoolhill* ☎ *01224/643924* ⊕ *www.kiltmakers.co.uk.*

Books and Beans. This secondhand bookshop has its own little café. You're welcome to browse and sip at the same time. ⊠ *22 Belmont St.* ☎*01224/646438* ⊕ *www.booksandbeans.co.uk.*

Candle Close Gallery. This shop has some strange and wonderful mirrors, clocks, ceramics, and jewelry that you're unlikely to see elsewhere. ⊠ *123 Gallowgate* ☎*01224/624940* ⊕ *www.candleclosegallery.co.uk.*

Colin Wood. This shop is the place to go for small antiques, interesting prints, and regional maps. ⊠ *25 Rose St.* ☎ *01224/643019.*

ROYAL DEESIDE AND CASTLE COUNTRY

Deeside, the valley running west from Aberdeen down which the River Dee flows, earned its "royal" appellation when discovered by Queen Victoria. To this day, where royalty goes, lesser aristocracy and freshly minted millionaires follow. Many still aspire to own a grand shooting estate in Deeside, and you may appreciate this yearning when you see the piney hills, purple moors, and blue river intermingling. As you travel deeper into the Grampian Mountains, Royal Deeside's gradual scenic change adds a growing sense of excitement.

There are castles along the Dee as well as to the north in Castle Country, another region that illustrates the gradual geological change in the northeast: uplands lapped by a tide of farms. All the Donside and Deeside castles are picturesquely sited, with most fitted out with tall slender turrets, winding stairs, and crooked chambers that epitomize Scottish baronial style. All have tales of ghosts and bloodshed, siege and torture. Many were tidied up and "domesticated" during the 19th century. Although best toured by car, much of this area is accessible either by public transportation or on tours from Aberdeen.

STONEHAVEN

15 miles south of Aberdeen.

This historic town near splendid Dunnottar Castle was once a popular holiday destination, with people including Robert Burns enjoying walks along the golden sands. The surrounding red-clay fields were made famous by Lewis Grassic Gibbon (real name James Leslie Mitchell), who attended school in the town and who wrote the seminal Scottish trilogy, *A Scots Quair*, about the people, the land, and the impact of World War I. The decline of the fishing industry emptied the harbor, but the town, being so close to Aberdeen, has begun to thrive again. It's now famous for its Hogmanay (New Year) celebrations, where local men swing huge balls of fire on chains before tossing them into the harbor.

GETTING HERE AND AROUND

Stagecoach Bluebird runs a number of buses to Stonehaven from Aberdeen, but numbers 107 and 109 are the fastest (50 minutes). Most trains heading south from Aberdeen stop at Stonehaven; there's at least one per hour making the 15-minute trip. Drivers should take A90 south and turn off at A957.

ESSENTIALS

Visitor Information Stonehaven Visitor Information Centre ✉ *66 Allardyce St., Stonehaven* ☎ *01569/762806* ⊕ *www.aberdeen-grampian.com* ⊘ *Apr.–Oct.*

EXPLORING

Fodor'sChoice **Dunnottar Castle.** It's hard to beat the magnificent cliff-top ruins of Dunnottar Castle, especially with the panoramic views of the North Sea. Building began in the 14th century, when Sir William Keith, Marischal of Scotland (keeper of the king's mares), decided to build a tower house to demonstrate his power. Subsequent generations added to the structure, and important visitors included Mary, Queen of Scots. The castle is most famous for holding out for eight months against Oliver Cromwell's army in 1651 and 1652, and thereby saving the Scottish crown jewels, which had been stored here for safekeeping. Reach the castle via the A90; take the Stonehaven turnoff and follow the signs. ■TIP→ Wear sensible shoes, and allow about two hours. ✉ *Off A92, Stonehaven* ☎ *01569/762173* ⊕ *www.dunnottarcastle.co.uk* ☜ *£6* ⊘ *Easter–Sept., daily 9–6; Nov.–Easter, daily 10–sunset.*

FAMILY **Stonehaven Open-Air Swimming Pool.** They were extremely popular in the 1930s, but the Stonehaven Open-Air Swimming Pool, an aging art deco gem, is one of only a few remaining outdoor heated pools in Scotland. Salty water from the North Sea is pumped in and warmed up to a toasty 28°C (82°F). Run by a local trust, this place is perfect for families. ■TIP→ Wednesday's midnight swims (£6.50) let you float under the stars. ⊠ *Queen Elizabeth Park, Off A90, Stonehaven* ☎ *01569/762134* ⊕ *www.stonehavenopenairpool. co.uk* ⊠ *£5* ☉ *June and mid-Aug.–early-Sept., weekdays 1–7:30, weekends 10–6; July and early Aug., weekdays 10–7:30, weekends 10–6.*

WHERE TO EAT AND STAY

$ ✕ **Carron Art Deco Restaurant.** For an outstanding meal of classic Scot-
BRITISH tish dishes served in the most splendid surroundings, try this longtime favorite. Evoking the style and class of the 1930s, it's a must for both lovers of architecture and food. Look out for the rather risqué figure of a woman etched onto a mirror between two dazzlingly tiled columns. The cuisine is not diminished by the surroundings: try the Aberdeen Angus roast beef with a Drambuie (a honey-flavor whisky liqueur) gravy and the sticky pear and carrot pudding. ⑤ *Average main: £14* ⊠ *Cameron St., Stonehaven* ☎ *01569/760460* ⊕ *www.carron-restaurant.co.uk* ☉ *Cloed Sun.*

$ ⛱ **Bayview B&B.** On the beach and down the lane from the town square,
B&B/INN this contemporary bed-and-breakfast couldn't be in a more convenient
Fodor'sChoice location—or have better views. **Pros:** spic-and-span rooms; walk to res-
★ taurants and shops; eccentric design. **Cons:** standard rooms are small-ish; breakfast room is windowless. ⑤ *Rooms from: £95* ⊠ *Beachgate La., Stonehaven* ☎ *07791/224227* ⊕ *www.bayviewbandb.co.uk* ⇥ *3 rooms, 2 suites* ❍ *Breakfast.*

BANCHORY

15 miles west of Stonehaven, 19 miles west of Aberdeen.

Banchory is an immaculate town filled with pinkish granite buildings. It's usually bustling with ice-cream-eating strollers, out on a day trip from Aberdeen. Nearby are Crathes and Drum castles.

GETTING HERE AND AROUND

A car is by far the best way to get around the area; A93 is one of the main roads connecting the towns.

For those reliant on public transport, Stagecoach buses operate a number of services for towns along or just off A93 (Drum Castle, Banchory, Kincardine, Aboyne, Ballater, Balmoral, and Braemar).

ESSENTIALS

Visitor Information Banchory Visitor Information Centre ⊠ *Bridge St.*
☎ *01330/822000* ⊕ *www.aberdeen-grampian.com* ☉ *Apr.–Oct.*

CLOSE UP

Which Castle Is Right for You?

We admit it—there are almost too many castles in this part of Scotland. Because it's nearly impossible to see all of them, we've noted the prime characteristics of each to help you decide which you'd most like to visit.

■ **Balmoral:** The Queen's home, this is where Queen Victoria and the Royal Family fell in love with Scotland and all things Scottish. Expect baronial largesse and groomed grounds, though you don't see much inside.

■ **Balvenie:** This ruined castle is known for its indomitable bearing and verdant surroundings, right in the midst of the Malt Whisky Trail.

■ **Braemar:** Offering memorable insight into the lives of the Scottish landed gentry, this recently restored castle heaves with memorabilia and mementos of the fascinating Farquharsons, who still hold their clan gathering here.

■ **Corgarff:** You'll find a sober solitude out on the moorland, as well as 18th-century graffiti and the reconstructed barracks used by Jacobite troops in 1746 as they retreated north.

■ **Craigievar:** Highlights of this 17th-century castle are a magical forest, fairy-tale turrets, and the furnishings and possessions of the Forbes family that fill the house.

■ **Crathes:** Expect tight quarters, notable family portraits, and a network of walled gardens at this well-preserved seat of the Burnett family. Its adventure park keeps the kids occupied.

■ **Drum:** A fusion of architectural styles and some historic roses are notable at this castle, but it's the medieval chapel that stirs the senses.

■ **Dunnottar:** The dramatic, scene-stealing, cliff-top location of Mel Gibson's *Hamlet* (1991), the ruins of this 14th-century tower house by the sea are unbeatable.

■ **Fraser:** Considered the grandest castle in Aberdeenshire, Castle Fraser has opulent period furnishings and woodland walks that make for a rewarding day.

■ **Fyvie:** This 14th-century castle underwent a luxurious Edwardian makeover. Come here for an awesome art collection, rich interiors, and haunting history.

■ **Kildrummy:** This is the place for evocative ruins, some from the 13th century, and tales of a treacherous past. Its austere but poignant chapel is a must-see.

EXPLORING

Brig o'Feuch. If you visit in autumn, drive for a mile along the B974 south of Banchory to the Brig o'Feuch (pronounced *fyooch*, the *ch* as in loch). The area around this bridge is pleasant, and the fall colors and foaming waters make for an attractive scene. Salmon leap in season (September to November and February and March). ⊠ *B974.*

FAMILY **Crathes Castle.** About 16 miles west of Aberdeen, Crathes Castle was once the home of the Burnett family and is one of the best-preserved castles in Britain. Keepers of the Forest of Drum for generations, the family acquired lands here by marriage and later built a castle, completed in 1596. The National Trust for Scotland cares for the castle, which is furnished with many original pieces and family portraits. Outside are grand gardens with calculated symmetry and clipped yew hedges. Make sure you browse the Horsemill bookshop and sample the tasty baked goods in the tearoom. There's an adventure park for kids, and the staff organizes activities that are fun and educational. ⊠ *Off A93* ☎ *0844/493–2166* ⊕ *www.nts.org.uk* 🖾 *£12* ☉ *Apr.–Oct., daily 10–4:45; Nov.–Mar., weekends 10:30–3:45; last admission 45 min before closing.*

Drum Castle and Garden. This foursquare tower has an evocative medieval chapel that dates from the 13th century; like many other castles, it also has later additions up to Victorian times. Note the tower's rounded corners, said to make battering-ram attacks more difficult. Nearby, fragments of the ancient Forest of Drum still stand, dating from the days when Scotland was covered by great stands of oak and pine. The Garden of Historic Roses, open from April to October, lays claim to some old-fashioned roses not commonly seen today. Drum Castle is 8 miles east of Banchory and 11 miles west of Aberdeen. ⊠ *Off A93* ☎ *0844/493–2161* ⊕ *www.nts.org.uk* 🖾 *£6* ☉ *Castle Apr.–June, and Sept., Thurs.–Mon. 11–4:45; June–Aug., daily 11–4:45; last entry 45 mins before closing time. Grounds daily 9:30–sunset.*

OFF THE BEATEN PATH **Kincardine O'Neil.** The ruined kirk in this little village 9 miles west of Banchory on A93 was built in 1233 and once sheltered travelers: it was the last hospice before the Mounth, the name given to the massif that shuts off the south side of the Dee Valley. Beyond Banchory (and the B974), no motor roads run south until you reach Braemar (A93), though the Mounth is crossed by a network of tracks once used by Scottish soldiers, invading armies (including the Romans), and cattle drovers. Photography buffs won't want to miss the bridge at Potarch, just to the east.

Queen's View. To reach one of the most spectacular vistas in northeast Scotland—stretching across the Howe of Cromar to Lochnagar—take the B9094 due north from Aboyne, then turn left onto the B9119 for 6 miles.

WHERE TO STAY

$$$
HOTEL
🖪 **Raemoir House Hotel.** Dating from the 16th to 19th centuries, this baronial home 2 miles north of Banchory makes you feel like you're on the set of a period drama. **Pros:** charming old building; extensive grounds; staff is informal and efficient. **Cons:** pricey rates. Ⓢ *Rooms from: £165* ⊠ *Off A980, Raemoir* ☎ *01330/824884* ⊕ *www.raemoir. com* ⇨ *17 rooms, 3 suites* ⑩ *Breakfast.*

BALLATER

22 miles west of Kincardine O'Neill, 43 miles west of Aberdeen.

The handsome holiday resort of Ballater, once noted for the curative properties of its waters, has profited from the proximity of the royals, nearby at Balmoral Castle. You might be amused by the array of "by royal appointment" signs proudly hanging from many of its various shops (even monarchs need bakers and butchers). Take time to stroll around this well-laid-out community. The railway station houses the tourist information center and a display on the glories of the Great North of Scotland branch railway line, closed in the 1960s along with so many others in this country.

The locals have long taken the town's royal connection in stride. To this day, the hundreds who line the road when the queen and her family arrive for services at the family's parish church at Crathie are invariably visitors to Deeside—one of Balmoral's attractions for the monarch has always been the villagers' respect for royal privacy.

GETTING HERE AND AROUND

There's good train service to Aberdeen, but you'll need to catch a bus to get to this and other towns near A93. Stagecoach Bluebird buses numbers 201 and 202 operate hourly to all the main towns, including Ballater. Otherwise, it's an easy car trip.

ESSENTIALS

Visitor Information Ballater Visitor Information Centre ⊠ *Old Royal Station, Station Sq.* ☎ *01339/755306.*

EXPLORING

Balmoral Castle. The enormous parking lot is indicative of the public's appreciation of Balmoral Castle, one of Queen Elizabeth II's favorite family retreats. Only the formal gardens, the ballroom, and the carriage hall are on view, with their exhibitions of royal artifacts, commemorative china, and native wildlife. Thanks to Victoria and Albert, who built the house to Prince Albert's design, stags' heads abound, the bagpipes wailed incessantly, and the garish Stewart tartan was used for everything from carpets to chair covers. A more somber Duff tartan, black and green to blend with the environment, was later adopted.

Queen Elizabeth II follows her predecessors' routine in spending a holiday of about six weeks in Deeside, usually from mid-August to the end of September. During this time Balmoral is closed to visitors, including the grounds. You can take a guided tour in November and December; if the weather is crisp and bright, the estate is at its most dramatic and romantic. You're only allowed a peek inside, but the Royal Cottage is where Queen Victoria spent much of her time. You can see the table where she took breakfast and wrote her correspondence.

Around and about Balmoral, which is 7 miles west of Ballater, are some notable spots—Cairn O'Mount, Cambus O'May, and the Cairngorms from the Linn of Dee—and some of them may be seen on pony-trekking expeditions, which use Balmoral stalking ponies and go around the grounds and estate. Tempted by the setting? Balmoral Castle has five cottages (some very large) for rent by the week at certain times. They are atmospheric but can be basic. ⊠ *A93* ☎ *01339/742534* ⊕ *www. balmoralcastle.com* ⛁ *£10* ☾ *Apr.–July, daily 10–5; last admission 1 hr before closing. Guided tours on certain dates in Nov. and Dec.*

Loch Muick. A three- or four-hour walk takes you around glorious Loch Muick (Gaelic for "pig") and past Glas-alt Shiel, a favorite retreat of Queen Victoria's that you might recognize from the film *Mrs. Brown*. From Ballater, take the B976 over the River Dee before turning off at the sign for Glen Muick. Park at the Spittal of Loch Muick car park. The path around the loch is well signposted, although good boots are necessary for the stoney beach at the far side of the loch. ■TIP→ **The native red deer are quite common throughout the Scottish Highlands, but here is one of the best places to see them.**

WHERE TO EAT AND STAY

$$$$
MODERN
EUROPEAN

✕**Darroch Learg.** On a rise that gives you an unobstructed view of the majestic Grampian Mountains, this restaurant has an old country charm. The food, however, fuses Scottish classics with modern touches: ravioli with smoked haddock, loin of local venison with goat's cheese gnocchi, and warm chocolate cake with Deeside cream are a few of the creations. The staff is unpretentious and efficient, all the while keeping a quiet eye on your needs. There are more than 200 wines in the cellar. $ *Average main: £43* ⊠ *Braemar Rd.* ☎ *01339/755443* ⊕ *www. darrochlearg.co.uk.*

$$
B&B/INN

🏠 **Auld Kirk.** This strikingly renovated old church makes for an interesting stay. **Pros:** helpful team looks after you; pin-tidy bedrooms and public rooms. **Cons:** bar is popular with locals, so can get noisy; restaurant has reduced hours in winter. $ *Rooms from: £100* ⊠ *Braemar Rd.* ☎ *01339/755762* ⊕ *www.theauldkirk.com* ⇆ *7 rooms* ⎮○⎮ *Breakfast.*

$$
B&B/INN

🏠 **Deeside Hotel.** With plenty of period charm, this Victorian-era house offers old-fashioned hospitality and simple, understated comfort. **Pros:** unpretentious feel; good price; forever cheerful staff. **Cons:** a few bedrooms on the small side; restaurant can get very busy. $ *Rooms from: £120* ⊠ *45 Braemar Rd.* ☎ *01339/755420* ⊕ *www.deesidehotel.co.uk* ⇆ *9 rooms* ⎮○⎮ *Breakfast.*

$
B&B/INN

🏠 **Schoolhouse B&B.** Just outside the center of town, this solid, dependable B&B offers superior accommodations that are a bit unusual for Aberdeenshire. **Pros:** low-priced luxury; meticulously clean. **Cons:** no Wi-Fi access in bedrooms. $ *Rooms from: £85* ⊠ *Anderson Rd.* ☎ *01339/756333* ⊕ *www.school-house.eu* ⇆ *4 rooms* ⎮○⎮ *Breakfast.*

GOLF

Ballater Golf Club. The mountains of Royal Deeside surround this course, which is laid out along the sandy flats of the River Dee. The club, originally opened in 1892, has a holiday atmosphere, and the shops and pleasant walks in nearby Ballater make this a good place for nongolfing partners. ⊠ *Victoria Rd.* ☎ *013397/55567* ⊕ *www.ballatergolfclub. co.uk* 🏌 *Green fee: weekdays £30; weekends £35* 🏌 *18 holes, 6059 yds, par 70* 🕐 *Daily.*

SHOPPING

Byzantium. This boutique has an eclectic mix of inspiring clothing and accessories. ⊠ *1–3 Bridge St.* ☎ *01339/755055.*

Countrywear. At either location of Countrywear, men can find everything that's necessary for Highland country living, including fishing tackle, natty tweeds, and that flexible garment popular in Scotland between seasons: the body warmer. ⊠ *15 and 35 Bridge St.* ☎ *01339/755453* ⊕ *www.countrywearballater.co.uk.*

Deeside Books. This shop sells old, out-of-print, and hard-to-find books about Scotland, which make splendid gifts for lovers of all things Scots. ⊠ *18–20 Bridge St.* ☎ *01339/754080* ⊕ *www.deesidebooks.com.*

Dee Valley Confectioners. For a low-cost gift you could always see what's being boiled up at Dee Valley Confectioners, the region's top sweetie maker. ⊠ *Station Sq.* ☎ *01339/755499* ⊕ *www.dee-valley.co.uk.*

CLOSE UP

Balmoral, Queen Victoria's Retreat

Some credit Sir Walter Scott with having opened up Scotland for tourism through his poems and novels. But it was probably Queen Victoria (1819–1901) who gave Scottish tourism its real momentum when, in 1842, she first came to Scotland and when, in 1847—on orders of a doctor, who thought the relatively dry climate of upper Deeside would suit her—she bought Balmoral. The pretty little castle was knocked down to make room for a much grander house in full-blown Scottish baronial style, designed by her husband, Prince Albert (1819–61), in 1855. It had a veritable rash of tartanitis. Before long the entire Deeside and the region north were dotted with country houses and mock-baronial châteaux.

"It seems like a dream to be here in our dear Highland Home again," Queen Victoria wrote. "Every year my heart becomes more fixed in this dear Paradise." Victoria loved Balmoral more for its setting than its house, so be sure to take in its pleasant gardens. Year by year Victoria and Albert added to the estate, taking over neighboring houses, securing the forest and moorland around it, and developing deer stalking and grouse shooting here.

In consequence, Balmoral is now a large property, with grounds that run 12 miles along the Deeside road. Its privacy is protected by belts of pinewood, and the only view of the castle from the A93 is a partial one, from a point near Inver, 2 miles west of the gates.

There's an excellent bird's-eye view of Balmoral from an old military road, now the A939, which climbs out of Crathie, northbound for Cockbridge and the Don Valley. This view embraces the summit of Lochnagar, in whose *corries* (hollows) the snow lies year-round and whose boulder fields the current Prince of Wales, Charles Windsor, so fondly and so frequently treads.

McEwan Gallery. A mile west of Ballater, the McEwan Gallery displays fine paintings, watercolors, prints, and books (many with a Scottish or golf theme) in an unusual house built by the Swiss artist Rudolphe Christen in 1902. ⊠ *A939* ☎ *01339/755429* ⊕ *www.mcewangallery.com.*

EN ROUTE

As you continue west into Highland scenery past Balmoral Castle, further pine-framed glimpses appear of the "steep frowning glories of dark Lochnagar," as it was described by the poet Lord Byron (1788–1824). Lochnagar (3,786 feet) was made known to an audience wider than hill walkers by the current Prince of Wales, who published a children's story, *The Old Man of Lochnagar.*

BRAEMAR

17 miles west of Ballater, 60 miles west of Aberdeen, 51 miles north of Perth via A93.

Synonymous with the British monarchy, due to its closeness to Balmoral, and with the famous Highland Games, this village is popular year-round as a base for walkers and climbers enjoying the Grampian Mountains. There isn't really much else going on in Braemar, although the castle is well worth a couple of hours.

GETTING HERE AND AROUND

The town is on A93; there's bus service here, as to other towns on the road, but the closest train station is Aberdeen.

ESSENTIALS

Visitor Information Braemar Visitor Information Centre ⊠ *The Mews, Mar Rd.* ☎ *01339/741600* ⊕ *www.braemarscotland.co.uk.*

EXPLORING

Braemar Castle. On the northern outskirts of town, Braemar Castle dates from the 17th century, although its defensive walls, in the shape of a pointed star, came later. At Braemar (the *braes*, or slopes, of the district of Mar), the standard, or rebel flag, was first raised at the start of the unsuccessful Jacobite Rebellion of 1715. About 30 years later, during the last Jacobite rebellion, Braemar Castle was strengthened and garrisoned by government troops. From the early 1800s the castle was the clan seat of the Farquharsons, who hold their clan reunion here every summer.

Thanks to the commitment of local volunteers, a remarkable 2008 renovation restored Braemar back to the home it would have been in the early 20th century, complete with all the necessary comforts and family memorabilia. A dozen rooms are on view, including the Laird's day room with a plush day bed and the kitchen. ⊠ *Off A93* ☎ *01339/741219* ⊕ *www.braemarcastle.co.uk* ⊠ *£6* ☉ *Apr.–June, Sept., and Oct., weekends 11–4; July and Aug., Wed. 11–4 and weekends 11–4.*

Braemar Highland Gathering. The village of Braemar is associated with the Braemar Highland Gathering, held the first Saturday in September. Although there are many such gatherings celebrated throughout Scotland, this one is distinguished by the presence of the royal family. Competitions and events include hammer throwing, caber tossing, and bagpipe playing. If you plan to attend, book your accommodations months in advance. ■**TIP➜** **Be sure to buy tickets about six months in advance, as they do sell out.** ⊠ *Princess Royal and Duke of Fife Memorial Park, Broombank Terr.* ⊕ *www.braemargathering.org.*

Braemar Highland Heritage Centre. You can find out more about local lore at the Braemar Highland Heritage Centre, in a converted stable block in the middle of town. The center tells the history of the village with displays and a film. The tourist office and a gift shop are here, too. ⊠ *The Mews, Mar Rd.* ☎ *01339/741944* ⊠ *Free* ☉ *Jan.–May, Nov., and Dec., Mon.–Sat. 10:30–1:30 and 2–5, Sun. 1–4; June, Sept., and Oct., daily 9–5; July and Aug., daily 9–6.*

THE HIGHLAND GAMES

They might not all be as royally attended as the Braemar Highland Gathering, but from spring to late summer across a wide swath of northern Scotland competitors gather to toss, pull, fling, and sing at various Highland events. No two games are the same, but many incorporate agricultural shows, sporting competitions, clan gatherings, or just beer in the sun. VisitScotland (⊕ *www. visitscotland.com*) has a list of them.

Which one to attend? Braemar stands tall on ceremony and tradition, and the chance of seeing royalty up close means it attracts visitors from far and wide. Dufftown Games (⊕ *www. dufftownhighlandgames.org*) is the most competitive, with its race up the nearby Ben Rinnes, while the most picturesque is the Lochcarron Games (⊕ *www.lochcarrongames.org. uk*), which are played and danced out under the massif of the Torridon hills.

OFF THE BEATEN PATH

Linn of Dee. Although the main A93 slinks off to the south from Braemar, a little unmarked road will take you farther west into the hilly heartland. The road offers views over the winding River Dee and the blue hills before passing through the tiny hamlet of Inverey and crossing a bridge at the Linn of Dee. *Linn* is a Scots word meaning "rocky narrows," and the river's gash here is deep and roaring. Park beyond the bridge and walk back to admire the sylvan setting.

WHERE TO EAT AND STAY

$$
BRITISH

✕ Moorfield House. While the dining room may be underwhelming and the menu limited, when your plate is set before you, you'll understand why this is considered one of the best eateries in Braemar. The chef—who learned his craft by catering for big groups—offers unpretentious yet superb home-style cooking. Simple main dishes like panfried fish with garden vegetables, followed by a dessert like a seasonal crumble, will satisfy even the most exacting gourmand. ⑤ *Average main: £16* ⊠ *Moorfield House Hotel, Chapel Brae* ☎ *013397/41244* ⊕ *www.moorfieldhousehotel.com.*

$
CAFÉ

✕ Taste. It's strangely difficult to eat like a queen in Braemar, but this chalet-style café serves her subjects well, with the tastiest, freshest soups and sandwiches (Scottish cheddar and homemade meat loaf are two options). You can order moist cakes and tasty lattes here, too. ⑤ *Average main: £6* ⊠ *Auchendryne Sq.* ☎ *01339/741425* ⊕ *www.taste-braemar.co.uk* ▭ *No credit cards* ☉ *No dinner. Closed Sun.*

$
B&B/INN
Fodor's Choice
★

▦ Ivy Cottage. A relative newcomer in Braemar, this B&B should up the game of its competitors. **Pros:** relaxing rooms; owners who go out of their way to make you feel at home. **Cons:** next to the church, so expect bells on Sunday morning. ⑤ *Rooms from: £70* ⊠ *Cluniebank Rd.* ☎ *01339/741642* ⊕ *www.ivycottagebraemar.co.uk* ⇨ *3 rooms, 2 self-catering flats* ¶◎¶ *Multiple meal plans.*

GOLF

Braemar Golf Course. The tricky 18-hole Braemar Golf Course, founded in 1902, is laden with foaming waters. Erratic duffers, take note: the compassionate course managers have installed, near the water, poles with little nets on the end for those occasional shots that may go awry. ⊠ *Cluny Bank Rd.* ☎ *01339/741618* ⊕ *www.braemargolfclub.co.uk* ⌤ *Green fee: £25* ⚑ *18 holes, 4935 yds, SSS 64.*

7

CORGARFF CASTLE

23 miles northeast of Braemar, 14 miles northwest of Ballater.

This castle has a striking setting on the moors and some rebuilt military features that recall its strategic importance.

GETTING HERE AND AROUND

By car, take A939 and then follow signs. From May to September the Heather Hopper Bus runs twice daily from Ballater; it stops at Strathdon and Corgarff.

Contact Heather Hopper ☎ *01224/664584* ⊕ *www.royal-deeside.org.uk.*

EXPLORING

Corgarff Castle. Eighteenth-century soldiers paved a military highway north from Ballater to Corgarff Castle, an isolated tower house on the moorland with a star-shape defensive wall that's a curious replica of Braemar Castle. Corgarff was built as a hunting lodge for the earls of Mar in the 16th century. After an eventful history that included the wife of a later laird's being burned alive in a family dispute, the castle ended its career as a garrison for Hanoverian troops. The troops were responsible for preventing illegal whisky distilling. Reconstructed barracks show what the castle must have been like when the redcoats arrived in 1746. ☒ *Off A939, Corgarff* ☎ *01975/651460* ⊕ *www. historic-scotland.gov.uk* ☒ *£5.50* ☉ *Apr.–Sept., daily 9:30–6:30; Oct., daily 9:30-4:30; Nov.–Mar., weekends 9:30–4:30; last admission 30 mins before closing.*

■ EN ROUTE **Castle Trail.** If you return east from Corgarff Castle to the A939/A944 junction and make a left onto the A944, the signs indicate that you're on the Castle Trail. The A944 meanders along the River Don to the village of Strathdon, where a great mound by the roadside turns out to be a *motte,* or the base of a wooden castle, built in the late 12th century. Although it takes considerable imagination to become enthusiastic about a grass-covered heap, surviving mottes have contributed greatly to the understanding of the history of Scottish castles. The A944 then joins the A97, and a few minutes later a sign points to **Glenbuchat Castle,** a plain Z-plan tower house. ⊕ *www.aberdeen-grampian.com.*

KILDRUMMY CASTLE

18 miles northeast of Corgarff, 23 miles north of Ballater, 22 miles north of Aboyne.

The ancient ruins of Kildrummy Castle still show its history of expansion and reveal a variety of styles.

GETTING HERE AND AROUND

By car, take A97 off A93 (or the A980 if you're coming direct from Banchory). Be wary of the sign for Kildrummy Castle Garden and Hotel. You want the turn after this for Kildrummy Castle itself.

CLOSE UP

Language and the Scots

"Much," said Doctor Johnson, "may be made of a Scotchman if he be caught young." This quote sums up, even today, the attitude of some English people—confident in their English, the language of parliament and much of the media—toward the Scots language. The Scots have long been made to feel uncomfortable about their mother tongue, and until the 1970s (and in some private schools, even today) they were encouraged to mimic the dialect of the Thames Valley ("standard English") in order to "get on" in life.

LOWLAND SCOTS

The Scots language (that is, Lowland Scots, not Gaelic) was a northern form of Middle English and in its day was the language used in the court and in literature. It borrowed from Scandinavian, Dutch, French, and Gaelic. After a series of historical blows—such as the decamping of the Scottish court to England after 1603 and the printing of the King James Bible in English but not in Scots—it declined as a literary or official language. It survives in various forms but is virtually an underground language, spoken among ordinary folk, especially in its heartland, in the northeast.

You may even find yourself exporting a few useful words, such as *dreich* (gloomy), *glaikit* (acting and looking foolish), or *dinna fash* (don't worry), all of which are much more expressive than their English equivalents.

Some Scottish words are used and understood across the entire country (and world), such as *wee* (small), *aye* (yes), *lassie* (girl), and *bonny* (pretty). Regional variations are evident even in the simplest of greetings. When you meet someone in the Borders,

Whit fettle? (What state are you in?) or *Hou ye lestin?* (How are you lasting?) may throw you for a loop; elsewhere you could hear *Hoo's yer doos?* (How are your pigeons?). If a group of Scots takes a fancy to you at the pub, you may be asked to *Come intil the body o the kirk,* and if all goes well, your departure may be met with a jovial farewell, *haste ye back* (return soon).

GAELIC

Scottish Gaelic, an entirely different language, is still spoken across the Highlands and Hebrides. There's also a large Gaelic-speaking population in Glasgow as a result of the Celtic diaspora—islanders migrating to Glasgow in search of jobs in the 19th century. Speakers of Gaelic in Scotland were once persecuted, after the failure of the 18th-century Jacobite rebellions. Official persecution has now turned to enthusiastic support, as the Gaelic lobby has won substantial public funds to underwrite television programming, public signage, and language classes for new learners.

One of the joys of Scottish television is watching Gaelic news programs on BBC Alba to see how the ancient language copes with such topics as nuclear energy, the Internet, and the latest band to hit the charts. A number of Gaelic words have been absorbed into English: *banshee* (a wailing female spirit), *galore* (plenty), *slob* (a slovenly person), and *brat* (a spoiled or unruly child).

To experience Gaelic language and culture in all its glory, you can attend the Royal National Mod—a competition-based festival with speeches, drama, and music, all in Gaelic—held in a different location every year.

7

EXPLORING

Kildrummy Castle. Although in ruins, Kildrummy Castle is significant because it dates to the 13th century and has ties to the mainstream medieval traditions of European castle building. It shares features with Harlech and Caernarfon, in Wales, as well as with Château de Coucy, near Laon, France. Kildrummy underwent several expansions at the hands of England's King Edward I (1239–1307); the castle was back in Scottish hands in 1306, when it was besieged by King Edward I's son. The defenders were betrayed by Osbarn the Smith, who was promised a large amount of gold by the English forces. They gave it to him after the castle fell, pouring the molten metal down his throat, or so the ghoulish story goes. Kildrummy's prominence ended after the collapse of the 1715 Jacobite uprising. It had been the rebel headquarters and was consequently dismantled. Although the castle is almost completely ruined, its unadorned yet strangely moving chapel remains intact. ⊠ *A97* ☎ *01975/571331* ⊕ *www.historic-scotland.gov.uk* 🖻 *£4.50* ⊗ *Apr.–Sept., daily 9–5.*

Kildrummy Castle Gardens. The Kildrummy Castle Gardens, behind the castle and with a separate entrance from the main road, are built in what was the original quarry for the castle. This sheltered bowl within the woodlands has a broad range of shrubs and alpine plants and a notable water garden. ⊠ *A97* ☎ *01975/571203* ⊕ *www.kildrummy-castle-gardens.co.uk* 🖻 *£4.50* ⊗ *Apr.–Oct., daily noon–5.*

WHERE TO STAY

$$$
HOTEL
🏨 **Kildrummy Castle Hotel.** A grand late-Victorian country house, this elegant lodging offers a peaceful stay and attentive service. **Pros:** fabulous old hunting lodge; great views. **Cons:** rather pricey (including restaurant); there's no elevator, and you may need to go up a fair number of steps. ⑤ *Rooms from: £175* ⊠ *A97* ☎ *01975/571288* ⊕ *www. kildrummycastlehotel.co.uk* 🛏 *16 rooms* ⊗ *Closed Jan.* ⦿ *Breakfast.*

ALFORD

9 miles east of Kildrummy, 28 miles west of Aberdeen.

A plain and sturdy settlement in the Howe (Hollow) of Alford, this town gives those who have grown somewhat weary of castle-hopping a break: it has a museum instead. Craigievar Castle and Castle Fraser are nearby, though.

GETTING HERE AND AROUND
The town is on A944.

ESSENTIALS
Visitor Information Alford Visitor Information Centre ⊠ Grampian Transport Museum, Montgarrie Rd. ☎ 01975/562052 ⊕ www.aberdeen-grampian.com ⊗ Apr.–Sept., daily 10–5, Oct., daily 10–4.

EXPLORING

Fodor'sChoice
★
Castle Fraser. The massive Castle Fraser is the ancestral home of the Frasers and one of the largest of the castles of Mar; it's certainly a contender as one of the grandest castles in the northeast. Although the well-furnished building shows a variety of styles reflecting the taste of its

owners from the 15th through the 19th centuries, its design is typical of the cavalcade of castles in the region, and for good reason. This—along with many others, including Midmar, Craigievar, Crathes, and Glenbuchat—was designed by a family of master masons called Bell. There are plenty of family items, but don't miss the two Turret Rooms—one of which is the trophy room—and Major Smiley's Room. He married into the family but is famous for having been one of the escapees from Colditz (a high-security prisoner of war camp) during World War II. The walled garden includes a 19th-century knot garden, with colorful flowerbeds, box hedging, gravel paths, and splendid herbaceous borders. Have lunch in the tearoom or the picnic area. ⊠ *Off A944, 8 miles southeast of Alford* ☎ *0844/493–2164* ⊕ *www.nts.org.uk* ⊠ *£10* ⊘ *Apr.–June, Sept., and Oct., Wed.–Sat. noon–5; July and Aug., daily 11–5; last admission 45 min before closing.*

Craigievar Castle. Much as the stonemasons left it in 1626, Craigievar Castle has pepper-pot turrets that make it an outstanding example of a tower house. Striking and well preserved, it has many family furnishings, and the lovely grounds are worth exploring, too. Craigievar was built in relatively peaceful times by William Forbes, a successful merchant in trade with the Baltic Sea ports (he was also known as Danzig Willie). ⊠ *A980, 5 miles south of Alford* ☎ *0844/493–2174* ⊕ *www. nts.org.uk* ⊠ *£12* ⊘ *Apr.–June and Sept., Fri.–Tues. 11–4:45; July and Aug., daily 11–4:45.*

FAMILY **Grampian Transport Museum.** The entertaining and enthusiastically run Grampian Transport Museum specializes in road-based means of locomotion, backed up by an archives and library. Its collection of buses and trams is second to none, but the Craigievar Express, a steam-driven creation invented by the local postman to deliver mail more efficiently, is the most unusual. There's a small café that offers tea, baked goods, and ice cream. ⊠ *Montgarrie Rd.* ☎ *01975/562292* ⊕ *www.gtm.org.uk* ⊠ *£9.50* ⊘ *Apr.–Sept., daily 10–5; Oct., daily 10–4.*

THE NORTHEAST AND THE MALT WHISKY TRAIL

North of Deeside another popular area of this region lies inland, toward Speyside—the valley, or strath, of the River Spey—famed for its whisky distilleries, some of which it promotes in another signposted trail. Distilling scotch is not an intrinsically spectacular process. It involves pure water, malted barley, and sometimes peat smoke, then a lot of bubbling and fermentation, all of which cause a number of odd smells. The result is a prestigious product with a fascinating range of flavors that you may either enjoy immensely or not at all.

Instead of closely following the Malt Whisky Trail, dip into it and blend visits to distilleries with some other aspects of the county of Moray, particularly its coastline. Whisky notwithstanding, Moray's scenic qualities, low rainfall, and other reassuring weather statistics are worth remembering. You can also sample the northeastern seaboard, including some of the best but least-known coastal scenery in Scotland.

DUFFTOWN

54 miles west of Aberdeen.

On one of the Spey tributaries, Dufftown was planned in 1817 by the Earl of Fife. Its simple cross layout with a square and a large clock tower (originally from Banff and now the site of the visitor center) is typical of a small Scottish town built in the 19th century. Its simplicity is made all the more stark by the brooding, heather-clad hills that rise around it. Dufftown is convenient to a number of distilleries.

GETTING HERE AND AROUND

To get here from Aberdeen, drive west on A96 and A920; then turn west at Huntly. It's not easy or quick, but you can take the train to Elgin or Keith and then the bus to Dufftown.

ESSENTIALS

Visitor Information Dufftown Visitor Information Centre ✉ *The Square* ☎ *01340/820501* ☉ *Apr.–Oct.*

EXPLORING

TOP ATTRACTIONS

Fodor's Choice
★

Balvenie Distillery. Offering just a handful of tours each week, you'd think that Balvenie Distillery didn't want visitors. Yet as soon as you step into the old manager's office—now gently restored and fitted with knotted-elm furniture—you realize Balvenie just wants to make sure that all visitors get to see, smell, and feel the magic of the making of this malt. Balvenie is unusual because it has its own cooperage with six coopers hard at work turning the barrels. During the three-hour tour you'll see the mashing, fermentation, and distillation process, culminating in a five-malt tasting session. ✉ *Balvenie St.* ☎ *01340/822062* ⊕ *www.thebalvenie.com* 🏷 *£35* ☉ *Tours Mon.–Thurs. at 10 and 2, Fri. at 10.*

Glenfiddich Distillery. Many make Glenfiddich Distillery their first stop on the Malt Whisky Trail. The independent company of William Grant and Sons Limited was the first to realize the tourist potential of the distilling process. The company began offering tours around the typical pagoda-roof malting buildings and subsequently built an entertaining visitor center. Besides a free 20-minute tour of the distillery there's a two-hour in-depth tour of the Connoisseurs' Tour (£20; reserve ahead in summer) that includes a special nosing and tasting session. Check out the Glenfiddich Distillery Art Gallery, showing the work of international artists. ✉ *A941, ½ mile north of Dufftown* ☎ *01340/820373* ⊕ *www.glenfiddich.com* 🏷 *Free* ☉ *Easter–mid-Oct., daily 9:30–4:30; mid-Oct.–Easter, weekends 9:30–4:30.*

Strathisla Distillery. Whisky lovers should take the B9014 11 miles northeast from Dufftown—or alternatively, ride the Keith Dufftown Railway—to see one of Scotland's most iconic distilleries, the Strathisla Distillery, with its cobblestone courtyard and famous double pagoda roofs. Stretching over the picturesque River Isla, the Strathisla Distillery was built in 1786 and now produces the main component of the Chivas Regal blend. Guided tours take you to the mash house, tun room, and still house—all pretty much the same as they were when

The Northeast

KEY
━━━ Rail Lines

5 miles
5 kilometers

North Sea

Lossiemouth
Elgin
Spynie Palace
Pluscarden Abbey
Findochty
Porknockie
Cullen
Sandend
Portsoy
Fordyce
Banff
Macduff
Gardenstown
Pennan
Strichen
New Pitsligo
New Deer
Ellon
Pitmedden
TO ABERDEEN ↓
Haddo House
Methilde
Fyvie Castle
Fyvie
Oldmeldrum
Turriff
Aberchirder
Milltown of Rothiemay
Huntly
Rhynie
Colpy
Oyne
Pitcaple
Deveron
Spey Bay
Mosstodloch
Fochabers
Rothes
Keith
Strathisla Distillery
Craigellachie
Balvenie Distillery
Glenfiddich Distillery
Dufftown
Milltown of Edinvillie
Glenfarclas
Glen Fiddich
Glen Rinnes
Macallan Distillery
Glen Grant Distillery & Garden
Aberlour
Balvenie Castle
Cardhu Distillery
Ballindalloch Castle
Bridge of Avon
Glenlivet
TO GRANTOWN-ON-SPEY ←

A90
B9030
A948
A981
A950
A952
B9029
B9170
B9005
B9999
B9170
B9170
A947
A920
A96
B9002
A97
B9001
B9024
B9001
B9117
B9022
B9117
A96
A920
B9014
B3009
B9138
B9022
B9023
A97
A98
B9031
A947
B9139
B9018
B9042
A96
Spey
B9103
A941
B9102
Deveron

production began. The tour ends with a tasting session. ⊠ *Seafield Ave., Keith* ☎ *01542/783044* ⊕ *www.chivas.com* 🎟 *£6* ⊙ *Apr.–Oct., Mon.–Sat. 9:30–4, Sun. noon–4.*

WORTH NOTING

Balvenie Castle. On a mound just above the Glenfiddich Distillery is this grim, gray, and squat curtain-walled castle. This ruined fortress, which dates from the 13th century, once commanded the glens and passes toward Speyside and Elgin. ⊠ *A941* ☎ *01340/820121* ⊕ *www.historic-scotland.gov.uk* 🎟 *£4.50* ⊙ *Apr.–Sept., daily 9:30–5:30; last entry ½ hr before closing.*

Keith and Dufftown Railway. Leaving from Dufftown twice a day on weekends, this restored locomotive chugs 11 miles around forests, fields, and rivers. It passes Drummuir Castle on its way to Keith, home of the Strathisla Distillery. The Buffer Stop restaurant car at the Dufftown Station serves snacks, scones, and tea. Reservations are a good idea. ⊠ *Dufftown Station, Station Rd.* ☎ *01340/821181* ⊕ *www.keith-dufftown-railway.co.uk* 🎟 *£6.50* ⊙ *Easter–Sept., weekends.*

Mortlach Church. Set in a hollow by the Dullan Water, Mortlach Church is thought to be one of Scotland's oldest Christian sites, perhaps founded by St. Luag, a contemporary of St. Columba, as early as AD 566. Note the weathered Pictish cross in the churchyard and the even older stone under cover in the vestibule, with a strange Pictish elephantlike beast carved on it. Though much of the church was rebuilt after 1876, some early work survives, including three lancet windows from the 13th century and a leper's squint (a hole extended to the outside of the church so that lepers could hear the service but be kept away from the rest of the congregation). ⊠ *Church St.*

WHERE TO EAT AND STAY

$$$
FRENCH
Fodor's Choice
★

✕ **La Faisanderie.** Gourmands from around the region descend on La Faisanderie for a truly French gastronomic experience. A large, distillery-inspired fresco in the plain dining room adds some panache to the tall windows, creaky wood floors, and crisp white tablecloths. The French and English owners use fine cuts of local beef and game and seafood caught on the coast to create classic dishes with not-too-heavy sauces. Worth trying is the lamb with pinhead oatmeal risotto served with a honey and whisky sauce, and the chanson of russet apples with cinnamon ice cream. $ *Average main: £20* ⊠ *2 Balvenie St.* ☎ *01340/821273* ⊕ *www.lafaisanderie.co.uk* ⊙ *Closed Tues. and Wed. in Oct.–Mar.*

$
B&B/INN

▦ **Castleview.** Next to the babbling Burn of Mackalea, the tranquil Castleview has rooms that are quite small but beautifully dressed and well maintained. **Pros:** colorful garden; fabulous views; bountiful breakfasts. **Cons:** half-hour walk into town; not for anyone with a cat allergy. $ *Rooms from: £70* ⊠ *A920, 2½ miles east of Dufftown, Auchindoun* ☎ *01340/820941* ⊕ *www.castleviewdufftown.com* 🛏 *3 rooms* ❖❘ *Breakfast.*

Whisky, the Water of Life

Conjured from an innocuous mix of malted barley, water, and yeast, malt whisky is for many synonymous with Scotland. Clans produced whisky for hundreds of years before it emerged as Scotland's national drink and major export. Today those centuries of expertise result in a sublimely subtle drink with many different layers of flavor. Each distillery produces a malt with—to the expert—instantly identifiable, predominant notes peculiarly its own.

WHISKY TYPES AND STYLES
There are two types of whisky: malt and grain. Malt whisky, generally acknowledged to have a more sophisticated bouquet and flavor, is made with malted barley—barley that is soaked in water until the grains germinate and then is dried to halt the germination, all of which adds extra flavor and a touch of sweetness to the brew. Grain whisky also contains malted barley, but with the addition of unmalted barley and maize.

Blended whiskies, which make up many of the leading brands, usually balance malt- and grain-whisky distillations; deluxe blends contain a higher percentage of malts. Blends that contain several malt whiskies are called "vatted malts." Whisky connoisseurs often prefer to taste the single malts: the unblended whisky from a single distillery.

In simple terms, malt whiskies may be classified into "eastern" and "western" in style, with the whisky made in the east of Scotland, for example in Speyside, being lighter and sweeter than the products of the western isles, which often have a taste of peat smoke or even iodine.

The production process is, by comparison, relatively straightforward: just malt your barley, mash it, ferment it and distill it, then mature to perfection. To find out the details, join a distillery tour, and be rewarded with a dram. Check out ⊕ www.scotlandwhisky.com for more information.

TASTING WHISKY
When tasting whisky, follow these simple steps. First, pour a dram. Turn and tilt the glass to coat the sides. Smell the whisky, "nosing" to inhale the heady aromas. If you want, you can add a little water and turn the glass gently to watch it "marry" with the whisky, nosing as you go. Take a wee sip and swirl it over your tongue and sense what connoisseurs call the "mouthfeel." Swallow and admire the finish. Repeat until convinced it's a good malt!

7

SHOPPING
Collector's Cabin. Two adjoining shops—one with Scottish silver, fossils, and book illustrations, the other with kilts, ceramics, and other curiosities—are filled with conversation starters. This is truly a trove worth delving into. ✉ *22 and 24 Balvenie St.* ☎ *01340/821393.*

CRAIGELLACHIE

4 miles northwest of Dufftown via A941.

Renowned as an angling resort, Craigellachie, like so many settlements on the River Spey, is sometimes enveloped in the malty reek of the local industry. Glen Grant is one of the distilleries nearby. The Spey itself is crossed by a handsome suspension bridge, designed by noted engineer Thomas Telford (1757–1834) in 1814 and now bypassed by the modern road.

GETTING HERE AND AROUND

The town is on A491; it's best to drive here, as public transportation is infrequent and complicated.

EXPLORING

Glen Grant Distillery & Garden. James Grant founded a distillery in 1840 when he was only 25, and it was the first in the country to be electrically powered. This place will come as a welcome relief to companions of dedicated Malt Whisky Trail followers, because in addition to the distillery there's a large and beautiful garden. It's planted and tended as Grant envisioned, with orchards and woodland walks, log bridges over waterfalls, a magnificent lily pond, and azaleas and rhododendrons in profusion. Using peculiarly tall stills and special purifiers that follow a design introduced over a century ago, Glen Grant produces a distinctive pale-gold whisky with an almost floral or fruity finish. The tour is excellent value, with perhaps the friendliest guides and certainly the most generous tastings. ⊠ *A941, Rothes* ☎ *01340/832118* ⊕ *www. glengrant.com* ⟃ *£3.50* ☉ *Apr–Oct., daily 9:30–4; Nov.–Mar., Mon.–Sat. 9:30–4, Sun. noon–5.*

Macallan Distillery. On the sprawling Easter Elchies Estate, Macallan Distillery offers unique whisky matured in sherry casks and, more recently, in oak bourbon casks. The Experience Tour lasts almost 90 minutes and takes you from the still house to the warehouse where maturation takes place, finishing off with a wee dram. The Precious Tour lasts an hour longer and gives a more in-depth look at the process before an extended nosing and tasting session. Booking is essential. ⊠ *Off B9102* ☎ *01304/872280* ⊕ *www.themacallan.com* ⟃ *Experience Tour £10, Precious Tour £20* ☉ *Easter–June and Aug., Mon.–Sat. 9:30–4:30; Sept. and Oct., weekdays 9:30–4:30; Nov.–Easter, weekdays 11–3.*

Speyside Cooperage and Visitor Centre. A major stop on the Malt Whisky Trail, the huge Speyside Cooperage and Visitor Centre is a must for all whisky fans. Retired coopers will talk you through the making of the casks, a surprisingly physical and dramatic process that uses the same tools and skills employed for hundreds of years. Inside you can watch highly skilled craftspeople make and repair oak barrels used in the local whisky industry. The Acorn to Cask exhibit tells all about the ancient craft of coopering. There's a cottage café with huge cakes and sandwiches for those in need of fortification. ⊠ *Dufftown Rd.* ☎ *01340/871108* ⊕ *www.speysidecooperage.co.uk* ⟃ *£3.50* ☉ *Weekdays 9–4.*

CHOOSING A DISTILLERY TOUR

Like whiskies, distillery tours are not the same, though you'll usually spend about an hour or two at each place. The company's history, size, and commercial savvy create different experiences. You should also investigate any special in-depth tours if you're willing to pay extra and spend more time. Here's a cheat sheet to help you choose a tour or two to suit your taste.

Balvenie: This distillery's tour is for those who want to understand and celebrate the details of distilling. No other distillery lets you see and smell the malting floor before watching the coopers turn their barrels.

Cardhu: Architecturally, the stocky buildings and proud towers of Cardhu, formerly an illicit still, seem to have a grim defiance. The tour gives you a great understanding of whisky's simple ingredients, including locally sourced spring water, and the process it undergoes.

Glen Grant: The distillery tour is good, but the gardens of Major Grant are sublime. He traveled the world collecting species and created a Victorian garden that has been gloriously restored.

Glenfarclas: This proud family-owned still may not provide the slickness of the Glenfiddich tour,

but the quiet passion of the still workers and their belief in their whisky is more powerful than a dram of the stuff.

Glenfiddich: Owned by the same family since day one, this distillery offers both entry-level and enthusiasts' tours that cover the older, more atmospheric buildings and the swankier visitor center.

Glenlivet: It's a beautiful drive to this, the first licensed distillery in the Highlands. You'll learn the fascinating story of Glenlivet's founder, George Smith.

Macallan: Situated on the green and pleasant Easter Elchies Estate, this vast distillery is dominated by a warehouse with row upon row of sherry casks imbuing this whisky with its sweetness.

Speyside Cooperage: Although this isn't a distillery, real whisky enthusiasts shouldn't miss a visit to one of the few remaining cooperages in Scotland. Watch the coopers at work and see just how much craft goes into making and treating these precious barrels.

Strathisla: Home of Chivas, not a malt but a fine blended whisky, this is perhaps one of the prettiest and most compact distilleries in the northeast and is delightfully situated on the River Isla.

WHERE TO STAY

$$
B&B/INN
🏨 **Highlander Inn.** Don't be fooled by the rather alpine exterior: this very Scottish hotel prides itself on its whisky bar and its friendly welcome. **Pros:** simple accommodations; warm atmosphere; great bar. **Cons:** dated decor. 💲 *Rooms from: £103* ✉ *Victoria St.* ☎ *01340/881446* ⊕ *www.whiskyinn.com* ⇱ *5 rooms* ⦿ *Breakfast.*

7

ABERLOUR

2 miles southwest of Craigellachie.

Aberlour, often listed as Charlestown of Aberlour on maps, is a handsome little burgh, essentially Victorian in style, though actually founded in 1812 by the local landowner. The names of the noted local whisky stills are Cragganmore, Aberlour, and Glenfarclas; Glenlivet and Cardhu are also nearby. Also in Aberlour is Walkers, famous for producing shortbread, tins of buttery, crumbly goodness, since 1898.

GETTING HERE AND AROUND

Aberlour is on A95; public transportation here is infrequent.

EXPLORING

Ballindalloch Castle. The family home of the Macpherson-Grants since 1546, Ballindalloch Castle—known as the Pearl of the North—is the quintessential castle you've probably seen in a miniseries made by the BBC. You can wander around the beautifully kept rooms and meticulously tended gardens at your leisure; you may even bump into the lord and lady of the manor, who live here all year. There's also a spendid tea shop offering large slices of cake. Anglers take note: The estate offers a limited number of permits for fishing on the banks of the Spey and the Avon. It's 8 miles southwest of Craigellachie. ⊠ *Off A95* ☎ *01807/500205* ⊕ *www.ballindallochcastle.co.uk* ⬚ *£10* ☉ *Easter– Sept., Sun.–Fri. 10:30–5:30.*

Cardhu Distillery. The striking outline of Cardhu Distillery, whose main product lies at the heart of Johnnie Walker Blends, is set among the heather-clad Mannoch Hills. Established by John and Helen Cumming in 1811, it was officially founded in 1824 after distilling was made legal by the Excise Act of 1823. Today Cardhu is owned by the superbrewer Diageo (which tried to rename it Cardow, although the single malt is still known as Cardhu). Guides take you to the mashing, fermenting, and distilling halls, and they explain the malting process that now takes place on the coast at Burghead. Take time to walk around the attractive grounds or picnic there. Cardhu is 10 miles north of Glenlivet and 7 miles west of Aberlour. ⊠ *B1902, Knockando* ☎ *01340/875635* ⊕ *www.scotlandwhisky.com* ⬚ *£5* ☉ *Oct.–Apr., weekdays 11–3; May– June, weekdays 10–5; July–Sept., Mon.–Sat. 10–5, Sun. 11–4; last tour 1 hr before closing.*

Glenfarclas. In an age when most small distilleries have been taken over by multinationals, Glenfarclas remains family owned, passed down from father to son since 1865. That link to the past is most visible among its low buildings, where the retired still sits outside: if you didn't know what it was, you could mistake it for part of a submarine. The tours end with tastings in the superlative Ship Room, the intact lounge of an ocean liner called the *Empress of Australia.* An in-depth Connoisseur's Tour and tasting is available for £25. ⊠ *Off A95, Ballindalloch* ☎ *01807/500345* ⊕ *www.glenfarclas.co.uk* ⬚ *£5* ☉ *Oct.–Mar., weekdays 10–4; Apr.–Jun., weekdays 10–5; July–Sept., weekdays 10–5, Sun. 10–4.*

Glenlivet. The famous Glenlivet was the first licensed distillery in the Highlands, founded in 1824 by George Smith. Today it produces one of the best-known 12-year-old single malts in the world. The free distillery tour reveals the inside the huge bonded warehouse where the whisky steeps in oak casks. The tour has two aspects: the Spirit of the Glen examines how unique factors come together to make this nectar, and the Glenlivet Legacy looks at the dream of the distillery's founder. There are two other tours—Spirit of the Malt (£30) and the Legacy Experience (£60)—for those who can't get enough. There's a coffee shop with baked goods and, of course, a whisky shop. Glenlivet is 10 miles southwest of Aberlour via A95 and B9008. ⊠ *Off B9008, Ballindalloch* ☎ *01340/821720* ⊕ *www.glenlivet.com* 🗝 *Free* ☉ *Apr.–Oct., Mon.–Sat. 9:30–5, Sun. noon–5.*

WHERE TO EAT AND STAY

$
CAFÉ

✕**Old Pantry.** This pleasantly rustic corner restaurant and gift shop overlooks Aberlour's tree-shaded central square. The kitchen serves—albeit sometimes slowly—everything from a cup of coffee with a sticky cake at teatime to a three-course spread of soup, roasted meat, and traditional pudding. $ *Average main: £9* ⊠ *The Square* ☎ *01340/871617* ☉ *No dinner Oct.–May.*

$$
B&B/INN
Fodor's Choice
★

Cardhu Country House. This once-abandoned manse (minister's house) looks as if it has always been loved and lived in: huge bedrooms with wooden floors, antique fireplaces, and large beds dressed in Harris tweed throws are married to contemporary bathrooms. **Pros:** period charm and modern comforts; tasty meals. **Cons:** you need a car to get here. $ *Rooms from: £120* ⊠ *Off B9102, Knockando* ☎ *01340/810895* ⊕ *www.cardhucountryhouse.co.uk* 🗝 *6 rooms* ⦿*Breakfast.*

$
B&B/INN

Mash Tun. Curvy yet sturdy, this former station hotel harks back to a time when Aberlour was a busy holiday destination on the Aberdeen–Aviemore train line. **Pros:** superb accommodations; tasty meals; great atmosphere in the restaurant and bar. **Cons:** book well ahead in summer. $ *Rooms from: £97* ⊠ *8 Broomfield Sq.* ☎ *01340/881771* ⊕ *www. mashtun-aberlour.com* 🗝 *4 rooms, 1 suite* ⦿*Breakfast.*

SHOPPING

Speyside Pottery. A couple of miles west of Aberlour, look for Speyside Pottery, where Thomas and Anne Gough produce domestic stoneware in satisfying, sturdy traditional shapes. Call ahead November to March, as hours are limited. ⊠ *A95, Ballindalloch* ☎ *01807/500338* ⊕ *www. speysidepottery.co.uk* ☉ *Apr.–Oct. 10–5.*

LGIN

15 miles north of Craigellachie, 69 miles northwest of Aberdeen, 41 miles east of Inverness.

As the center of the fertile Laigh (low-lying lands) of Moray, Elgin has been of local importance for centuries. Sheltered by great hills to the south, the city lies between two major rivers, the Spey and the Findhorn. Beginning in the 13th century, Elgin became an important religious center, a cathedral city with a walled town growing up around the cathedral and adjacent to the original settlement.

Elgin prospered, and by the early 18th century it became a mini-Edinburgh of the north and a place where country gentlemen spent their winters. It even echoed Edinburgh in carrying out wide-scale reconstruction in the 18th century. Many fine neoclassical buildings survive today despite much misguided demolition in the late 20th century for better traffic flow. However, the central main-street plan and some of the older little streets and *wynds* (alleyways) remain. You can also see Elgin's past in the arcaded shop fronts—some of which date from the late 17th century—on the main shopping street.

GETTING HERE AND AROUND
Elgin is on the A96 road from Aberdeen to Inverness. The A941 runs north from the distillery area to the city. There's a train stop here on the line that links Aberdeen and Inverness: Aberdeen is 90 minutes away.

ESSENTIALS
Visitor Information Elgin Visitor Information Centre ⊠ *Cooper Park* 🕾 *01343/562608* ⊗ *Mon.–Sat. 10–4.*

EXPLORING
Elgin Cathedral. Cooper Park contains a magnificent ruin, the Elgin Cathedral, consecrated in 1224. Its eventful story included devastation by fire: a 1390 act of retaliation by bandit Alexander Stewart (circa 1343–1405), the Wolf of Badenoch. The illegitimate son of King David II (1324–71) had sought revenge for his excommunication by the bishop of Moray. The cathedral was rebuilt but finally fell into disuse after the Reformation in 1560. By 1567 the highest authority in the land, the regent earl of Moray, had stripped the lead from the roof to pay for his army. Thus ended the career of the religious seat known as the Lamp of the North. Some traces of the cathedral settlement survive—the gateway Pann's Port and the Bishop's Palace—although they've been drastically altered. ⊠ *Cooper Park* 🕾 *01343/547171* ⊕ *www.historic-scotland.gov.uk* 🖾 *£5.50; £7.20 with Spynie Palace* ⊗ *Apr.–Sept., daily 9:30–5:30; Oct.–Mar., Sat.–Wed. 9:30–4:30; last admission ½ hr before closing.*

OFF THE BEATEN PATH

Pluscarden Abbey. Given the general destruction caused by the 16th-century upheaval of the Reformation, abbeys in Scotland tend to be ruinous and deserted, but at the 13th-century Pluscarden Abbey the ancient way of life continues. Monks from Prinknash Abbey near Gloucester, England, returned here in 1948, and the abbey is now a Benedictine community. Mass is at 9 (10 on Sunday) and includes Gregorian chants. ⊠ *Off B9010, 6 miles southwest of Elgin* ⊕ *www.pluscardenabbey.org* 🖾 *Free* ⊗ *Daily 9–5.*

Spynie Palace. Just north of Elgin sits Spynie Palace, the impressive 15th-century former headquarters of the bishops of Moray. It has now fallen into ruin, though the top of the tower has good views over the Laigh of Moray. Find it by turning right off the Elgin–Lossiemouth road. ⊠ *Off A941* 🕾 *01343/546358* ⊕ *www.historic-scotland.gov.uk* 🖾 *£4.50; £7.20 with Elgin Cathedral* ⊗ *Apr.–Sept., daily 9:30–6:30; Oct.–Mar., weekends 9:30–4:30; last admission ½ hr before closing.*

St. Giles Church. At the center of Elgin the most conspicuous structure is St. Giles Church, which divides High Street. The grand foursquare building, constructed in 1828, exhibits the Greek Revival style: note the columns, the pilasters, and the top of the spire, surmounted by a representation of the Lysicrates Monument. ⊠ *High St.*

GOLF

Moray Golf Club. Discover the relatively mild microclimate of what vacationing Victorians dubbed the Moray Riviera, as Tom Morris did in 1889 when he was inspired by the lay of the natural links. Henry Cotton's New Course (1979) has tighter fairways and smaller greens. ■ **TIP→ A handicap certificate is required for the Old Course.** ⊠ *Stotfield Rd., Lossiemouth* ☎ *01343/812018* ⊕ *www.moraygolf. co.uk* ⊠ *Green fee: Old Course £70; New Course £30; joint ticket £80* ⓘ *Old Course: 18 holes, 6995 yds, par 71; New Course: 18 holes, 6008 yds, par 69* ⓢ *Daily.*

SHOPPING

Gordon and MacPhail. An outstanding delicatessen and wine merchant, Gordon and MacPhail also stocks rare malt whiskies. This is a good place to shop for gifts for your foodie friends. ⊠ *58–60 South St.* ☎ *01343/545110* ⊕ *www.gordonandmacphail.com.*

Johnstons of Elgin. This woolen mill has a worldwide reputation for its luxury fabrics, especially cashmere. The large shop stocks not only the firm's own products, but also top-quality Scottish crafts. There's a coffee shop on the premises. Free tours of the mill must be booked in advance. ⊠ *Newmill Rd.* ☎ *01343/554094* ⊕ *www.johnstonscashmere.com.*

FOCHABERS

9 miles east of Elgin.

With its hanging baskets of fuchsia in summer and its perfectly mowed village square, Fochabers has a cared-for charm that makes you want to stop here, even just to stretch your legs. Lying just to the south of the River Spey, the former market town was founded in 1776 by the Duke of Gordon. The duke moved the village from its original site because it was too close to Gordon Castle. Famous today for being home to the Baxters brand of soups and jams, Fochabers is near some of the best berry fields: come and pick your own in the summer months.

GETTING HERE AND AROUND

Fochabers is not on the Inverness-to-Aberdeen train line, but there is an hourly bus service (Stagecoach Bluebird number 10) from Fochabers to Elgin. It's near the junction of A98 and A96.

EXPLORING

Baxters Highland Village. A mile west of the center of Fochabers, you can see the works of a major local employer, Baxters of Fochabers. From Tokyo to New York, upmarket stores stock the company's soups, jams, chutneys, and other gourmet products—all of which are made here, close to the River Spey. Take home a can of Royal Game Soup, a favorite of the late Queen Mum. Watch cooking demonstrations, have a look at a re-creation of the Baxters' first grocery shop, or browse around the

Best of Scotland, specializing in all kinds of Scottish products. A restaurant serves up an assortment of delectables. ⊠ *A96* ☎ *01343/820666* ⊕ *www.baxters.com* ✉ *Free* ⊙ *Daily 10–5.*

Fochabers Folk Museum. Once over the Spey Bridge and past the cricket ground (a very unusual sight in Scotland), you can find the symmetrical, 18th-century Fochabers village square lined with antiques dealers. Through one of these shops, Pringle Antiques, you can enter the Fochabers Folk Museum, a converted church with a fine collection of items relating to past life in the village and surrounding area. Exhibits include carts and carriages, farm implements, domestic labor-saving devices, and an exquisite collection of Victorian toys. ⊠ *High St.* ☎ *01343/821204* ⊕ *www.fochabers-heritage.org.uk* ✉ *Free* ⊙ *Easter–Oct., Tues.–Fri. 11–4, weekends 2–4.*

Gordon Chapel. One of the village's lesser-known treasures is the Gordon Chapel, which has an exceptional set of stained-glass windows by Pre-Raphaelite artist Sir Edward Burne-Jones. ⊠ *Castle St., just off The Square.*

Scottish Traditional Boat Festival. Take the A98 to the old fishing town of Portsoy, home of the ebullient Scottish Traditional Boat Festival one weekend in late June. The harbor fills with skiffs and rowboats, while the harborside hosts boatbuilders, crafts stalls promoting the work of knitters and weavers, cooking demonstrations—focusing on fish, of course—and street musicians. ⊠ *Portsoy* ⊕ *www.stbfportsoy.com.*

SHOPPING

Just Art. If you're interested in works by local artists, head to Just Art, a fine gallery with imaginative, often fun contemporary ceramics and paintings. ⊠ *64 High St.* ☎ *01343/820500* ⊕ *www.justart.co.uk.*

The Quaich. At The Quaich you can stock up on cards and small gifts, then sit with a cup of tea and a home-baked snack. ⊠ *85 High St.* ☎ *01343/820981.*

Watts Antiques. This shop has small collectables, jewelry, ornaments, and china. ⊠ *45 High St.* ☎ *01343/820077* ⊕ *www.wattsantiques.com.*

CULLEN

13 miles east of Fochabers, 3 miles east of Findochty.

Fodor'sChoice ★ Look for some wonderfully painted homes at Cullen, in the old fishing town below the railway viaduct. The real attractions of this charming little seaside resort, however, are its white-sand beach (the water is quite cold, though) and the fine view west toward the aptly named Bowfiddle Rock. In summer Cullen bustles with families carrying buckets and spades and eating ice cream and chips.

A stroll past the small but once busy harbor reveals numerous fishers' cottages, huddled together with small yards where they dried their nets. Beyond these, the vast stretch of beach curves gently round the bay. Above are the disused Victorian viaduct—formerly the Peterhead train line—and the 18th-century town.

GETTING HERE AND AROUND
Cullen is on A98, on Cullen Bay.

EXPLORING
Seafield Street. The town has a fine *mercat* (market) cross and one main street—Seafield Street—that splits the town. It holds numerous specialty shops—antiques and gift stores, an ironmonger, a baker, a pharmacy, and a locally famous ice-cream shop among them—as well as several cafés.

QUICK
BITE
Ice Cream Shop. In summer it can seem as if everyone you see in Cullen is licking a cone from the Ice Cream Shop. There's only a handful of flavors but they are all made on-site. It also sells an abundance of sweeties familiar to those who were kids in the '70s or '80s. ✉ *40 Seafield St.* ☎ *01542/840484.*

WHERE TO EAT AND STAY
$ ✕ **Linda's Fish & Chips.** This casual place serves the freshest fish, caught
SEAFOOD in nearby Buckie and cooked to crispy perfection. There's a seating area inside, but it's best for takeout. You can walk down the hill and head toward the harbor for some benches with sweeping views: a nice spot for a meal. ⑤ *Average main: £7* ✉ *54 Seafield St.* ☎ *01542/840202.*

$ ✕ **Puddleduck Patch.** The cheerful café, a hangout for quilters, serves
CAFÉ uncomplicated lunches, including chunky sandwiches oozing with tasty fillings. There's also a mountain of cakes from which to choose. ⑤ *Average main: £7* ✉ *Seafield St.* ☎ *01542/841888* ☷ *No dinner.*

$ ✕ **Rockpool.** A newer addition to the Cullen scene, this modish fish res-
SEAFOOD taurant has remarkably reasonable prices for the quality of the food
Fodor's Choice and size of the servings. Try the rich cullen skink (a creamy smoked
★ haddock soup), a pint glass of fat prawns served with mayo and oat bread, or some freshly fried squid with a limey sauce, all beautifully presented on wooden boards. It's also worth mentioning the lovingly crafted cupcakes and the happy staff that takes great delight in serving you your food. ⑤ *Average main: £8* ✉ *10 The Square* ☎ *01542/841397* ⊕ *www.rockpool-cullen.co.uk* ☷ *Closed Mon. No dinner.*

$ ☷ **Academy House.** About 10 minutes from the seaside town of Cullen,
B&B/INN this luxurious bed-and-breakfast in a handsome Victorian house was
Fodor's Choice once the headmaster's house for the local secondary school. **Pros:** good
★ home cooking; delightful setting. **Cons:** rooms book up fast; there's little to do in Fordyce. ⑤ *Rooms from: £80* ✉ *School Rd., Fordyce* ☎ *01261/842743* ⊕ *www.fordyceaccommodation.com* ⇆ *2 rooms* ▤ *No credit cards* ⑩ *Breakfast.*

SHOPPING
Abra Antiques. With surprisingly pleasing prices, Abra Antiques overflows with all kinds of trinkets, Victoriana, antiquarian books, and Scottish miscellany. ✉ *6 Seafield St.* ☎ *01542/840605* ☷ *Wed.*

BANFF

36 miles east of Elgin, 47 miles north of Aberdeen.

Midway along the northeast coast, overlooking Moray Firth and the estuary of the River Deveron, Banff is a fishing town of considerable elegance that feels as though it's a million miles from tartan-clad Scotland. Part Georgian, like Edinburgh's New Town, and part 16th-century small burgh, like Culross, Banff is an exemplary east-coast salty town, with a tiny harbor and fine architecture. It's also within easy reach of plenty of unspoiled coastline—cliff and rock to the east, at Gardenstown (known as Gamrie) and Pennan, or beautiful little sandy beaches westward toward Sandend and Cullen.

GETTING HERE AND AROUND

Banff is on the A98 coastal road and at the end of the tree-lined A947 to Aberdeen. If you are relying on public transportation, Bus 325 from Aberdeen Bus Station takes two hours and gets you into Low Street, just five minutes from Duff House.

ESSENTIALS

Visitor Information Banff Visitor Information Centre ⊠ *Collie Lodge, Low St.* ☎ *01261/812419* ⏱ *Apr.–Sept.*

EXPLORING

Fodor's Choice ★ **Duff House.** The jewel in Banff's crown is the grand mansion of Duff House, a splendid William Adam–designed (1689–1748) Georgian mansion. Used as a swish hotel in the Roaring '20s before becoming a sanitorium and then a military base, it lay empty and mouldering for years before it was restored in 1995 by the National Galleries of Scotland. It exhibits many fine paintings, including works by El Greco, Sir Henry Raeburn, and Thomas Gainsborough. A good tearoom and a gift shop are on the ground floor. ⊠ *Off A98* ☎ *01261/818181* ⊕ *www.duffhouse.org.uk* ⏱ *£7.10* ⏱ *Apr.–Oct., daily 11–5; Nov.–Mar., Thurs.–Sun. 11–4.*

FAMILY **Macduff Marine Aquarium.** Across the river in Banff's twin town, Macduff, on the shore east of the harbor, stands the conical Macduff Marine Aquarium. A 250,000-gallon central tank and many smaller display areas and touch pools show the sea life of the Moray Firth and North Atlantic. The staff is knowledgeable and engaging, especially with children, and there's always some creature to touch in the shallow pool or being fed by divers. ⊠ *11 High Shore* ☎ *01261/833369* ⊕ *www.macduff-aquarium.org.uk* ⏱ *£6.20* ⏱ *Apr.–Oct., weekdays 10–4; weekends 10–5; Nov.–Mar., Sat.–Wed. 11–4.*

GOLF

Duff House Royal Golf Club. Just moments from the sea, this club combines a coastal course with a parkland setting. Close to the center of Banff, it's on the grounds of Duff House, a country-house art gallery in a William Adam–designed mansion. The club has inherited the ancient traditions of seaside play; golf records here go back to the 17th century. ⊠ *The Barnyards, off A98* ☎ *01261/812075* ⊕ *www.theduffhouseroyalgolfclub.co.uk* ⏱ *Green fee: Apr.–Sept., weekdays £40; weekends £45 per round. Oct.–Mar., weekdays £20; weekends £22.50* ⏱ *Reservations essential* ⏱ *18 holes, 6031 yds, SSS 69* ⏱ *Daily.*

Fraserburgh Golf Club. According to parish records, the extensive links around this northeast fishing town have been used for golf since 1613; the club is relatively new, having been founded in 1777. Be prepared for a steep climb and a tough finish on James Braid's 1922 redesigned Corbiehill Course. The 9-hole Rosehill Course provides a challenging warm-up. ⊠ *B9033, off A90, Fraserburgh* ☎ *01346/516616* ⊕ *www. fraserburghgolfclub.org* ⊠ *Green fee: Corbiehill weekdays £42, weekends £52; Rosehill £18* ⃥ *Corbiehill: 18 holes, 6308 yds, par 70; Rosehill: 9 holes, 4832 yds, par 66* ⊙ *Daily.*

FYVIE CASTLE

18 miles south of Banff, 18 miles northwest of Ellon.

This castle mixes ancient construction with Edwardian splendor and includes excellent art. The grounds are also worth exploring.

GETTING HERE AND AROUND

If you're driving from Banff, take the A947 south for 20 minutes or so until you see the turnoff.

EXPLORING

Fyvie Castle. In an area rich with castles, Fyvie Castle stands out as the most complex. Five great towers built by five successive powerful families turned a 13th-century foursquare castle into an opulent Edwardian statement of wealth. Some superb paintings are on view, including 12 works by Sir Henry Raeburn. There are myriad sumptuous interiors— the circular stone staircase is considered one of the best examples in the country—and delightfully laid-out gardens. A former lady of the house, Lillia Drummond, was apparently starved to death by her husband, who entombed her body inside the walls of a secret room. In the 1920s, when the bones were disrupted during renovations, a string of such terrible misfortunes followed that they were quickly returned and the room sealed off. Her name is carved into the windowsill of the Drummond Room. ⊠ *Off A947, Turriff* ☎ *0844/4932182* ⊕ *www.nts. org.uk* ⊠ *£12* ⊙ *Apr.–June and Sept., Sat.–Wed. noon–5; July and Aug., daily 11–5; last admission 45 mins before closing.*

ELLON

32 miles southwest of Banff, 14 miles north of Aberdeen.

Formerly a market center on what was then the lowest bridging point of the River Ythan, Ellon, a bedroom suburb of Aberdeen, is a small town at the center of a rural hinterland. It's also well placed for visiting Fyvie Castle and Haddo House.

GETTING HERE AND AROUND

To get to Ellon, take the A947 from Banff or the A90 from Aberdeen; both routes take half an hour.

EXPLORING

Fodor's Choice ★ **Haddo House.** Built in 1732, this elegant mansion has a light and graceful Georgian design, with curving wings on either side of a harmonious, symmetrical facade. The interior is late-Victorian ornate, filled with magnificent paintings (including works by Pompeo Batoni and Sir Thomas Lawrence) and plenty of objets d'art. Pre-Raphaelite stained-glass windows by Sir Edward Burne-Jones grace the chapel. Outside is a terrace garden with a fountain, and few yards farther is Haddo Country Park, which has walking trails leading to memorials about the Gordon family. Visits are by prebooked tour only. ⊠ *Off B999, 8 miles northwest of Ellon* ☎ *0844/493–2179* ⊕ *www.nts.org.uk* ✉ *£10* ⊙ *Easter–June. and Sept.–Oct., Fri.–Mon., tours at 11:30, 1:30, and 3:30; July and Aug., daily, guided tours at 11:30, 1:30, and 3:30.*

GOLF

Cruden Bay Golf Club. Sheltered behind extensive sand dunes, Cruden Bay offers a typical Scottish golf experience. The narrow channels and deep valleys on the challenging fairways ensure plenty of excitement. Like Gleneagles and Turnberry, this course owes its origins to an association with the grand railway hotels built in the heyday of steam. The hotel may be gone, but the course remains in fine shape. ■TIP→ **Weekend tee times are extremely limited; book months in advance.** ⊠ *Aulton Rd., Cruden Bay* ☎ *01779/812285* ⊕ *www.crudenbaygolfclub.co.uk* ✉ *Green fee: Championship £90; St. Olaf weekdays £20, weekends £30* ⚲ *Reservations essential* ⚑ *Championship: 18 holes, 6287 yds, par 70; St. Olaf: 9 holes, 2463 yds, par 32* ⊙ *Daily.*

ARGYLL AND THE ISLES

Updated
by Mike
Gonzalez

Argyll's rocky seaboard looks out onto islands that were once part of a single prehistoric landmass. Here narrow roads wind around natural obstacles, slowing travel but forcing you to see and admire the lochs, the woods, and the ruins that hint at the region's dramatic past. Highlights include everything from grand houses such as Brodick Castle and gardens such as Crarae to the excellent walks on the small western isles. This is whisky country, too: the distilleries on Islay should not be missed. Distances are relatively small, as the area is within three hours of Glasgow.

Divided in two by the long peninsula of Kintyre, western Scotland has a complicated, splintered coastline. Looking out onto the islands and the Atlantic Ocean beyond, it is breathtakingly beautiful, though it often catches extremely wet ocean weather. Locals say that you can experience four seasons in a single day, and cliffs and woods can suddenly and dramatically disappear and reemerge from sea mist. Oak woods and bracken-covered hillsides dot the region, and just about everywhere you'll encounter the bright interplay of sea, loch, and rugged green peninsula.

Ruined ancient castles like Dunstaffnage, Kilchurn, and the towers on the islands of Loch Awe give testimony to the region's past importance. The stone circles, carved stones, and Bronze and Iron Age burial mounds around Kilmartin and on Islay and Arran are reminders of even earlier periods, when prehistoric peoples left their mark here. More recent grand houses, like Inveraray Castle and Brodick Castle on Arran, are not really castles but grand houses built by the nobility when the times of conflict between them are largely in the past. Their grounds, nourished by the temperate west coast climate, contain great gardens that are the pride of Argyll. Crarae, south of Inveraray, has winding paths through plantings of magnolias and azaleas, and Ardkinglas Woodland Garden boasts an outstanding conifer collection. The surprising tropical plants of the gardens on the isle of Gigha testify to its mild climate.

The working people of Glasgow traditionally spent their family holidays on the Clyde estuary, taking day trips to Dunoon or Rothesay on the Isle of Bute. Carrick Castle and Benmore Garden are a short trip from Dunoon. From Ardrossan, farther down the coast, ferries cruise to the prosperous and varied Isle of Arran.

Western Scotland's small islands have jagged cliffs or tongues of rock, long white-sand beaches, fertile pastures where sheep and cattle graze, fortresses, and shared memories of clan wars and mysterious beasts. Their cliff paths and loch-side byways are a paradise for walkers and

TOP REASONS TO GO

Whisky, whisky, whisky: Whisky is everywhere, though it changes subtly in taste and character from distillery to distillery. The unmistakable peaty smell of the whiskies of Islay yields to the lighter whiskies of Arran and Oban. Each distillery is unique, and guards its recipes jealously.

Iona and its abbey: Maybe it's the remoteness—especially if you explore beyond the abbey—that adds to the almost mystical sense of history here. This was an early center of Scottish Christianity from the 6th century onward, sending evangelists throughout Europe. This was also the burial place of Scottish kings, including Macbeth.

The great outdoors: Salmon and trout fill the lochs and rivers, and more adventurous anglers also head out to sea for even bigger trophy fish. If it's golf you prefer, there are

two dozen golf courses, including fine coastal links like Machrihanish near Campbeltown. For the cyclist there's every kind of terrain, making this a great region for leisurely rides or grueling mountain biking.

Cool castles: Often dramatically located on cliffs overlooking the sea, the region's castles tell their own stories of occupations, sieges, and conflicts between warring clan chiefs and nobles over eight centuries. Vikings, Scots, and the English fought for their possession. Many of them were turned into grand houses by the landed gentry.

Glorious gardens: Plants flourish in the mild Gulf Stream that brushes against this broken, western coastline. For vivid flowers, trees, birds, and butterflies, visit Crarae Garden, southwest of Inveraray. The Achamore House Gardens on the Isle of Gigha are another colorful extravaganza.

cyclists, and their whisky the ideal reward after a long day outside. While the islands' western coasts are dramatic, their more sheltered eastern seaboards are the location for the pretty harbor towns like the brightly painted Tobermory on Mull, or Port Ellen, with its neat rows of low whitewashed houses, on Islay. Arran is often said to be Scotland in miniature, the rich green fields of the southern part of the island giving way to the challenging Goatfell in the north.

ORIENTATION AND PLANNING

GETTING ORIENTED

With long sea lochs carved into its hilly, wooded interior, Argyll is a beguiling interweaving of water and land. The Kintyre Peninsula stretches between the islands of the Firth of Clyde (including Arran) and the islands of the Inner Hebrides. Ferry services allow all kinds of interisland tours and can shorten mainland trips as well.

On land, you can take the A85 to Oban (the main port for ferries to Mull and other islands) past barren hills and into the forest of Argyll after Loch Lomond (and the A82) ends. The roads grow narrower as they wind around the banks of Loch Awe and Loch Etive.

Alternatively, you can turn off the A82 at Arrochar and trace the longer route around Loch Fyne, once an active fishing center, to Inveraray and down the Argyll peninsula to Campbeltown. Along the way you'll pass Kennacraig, where ferries sail to Islay and Jura.

Argyll. The twin peninsulas of Kintyre are thickly wooded areas broken up by long, pretty lochs. From Inverarary at the head of Loch Fyne, you can take in Auchindrain's re-created fishing village on the way to the Arran ferry. Or turn west toward Crinan and the prehistoric sites around Kilmartin, then travel northward toward Loch Awe and its intriguing island ruins. A short drive away is Oban, the busy resort where you catch the island ferries.

Arran. Touring this island will give you a glimpse in a day or two of the whole of Scotland in miniature. In the north, the forbidding Goatfell is a challenge that draws walkers and climbers. The island's wilder west coast attracts bird-watchers and naturalists, while the fertile south of the island contains nine lovely golf courses, leisurely walks, and Brodick Castle.

Islay and Jura. The smell of peat that hangs in the air on Islay is bottled in its famous whiskies. Aside from distilleries, the island's historical sites evoke a past in which these islands were far less remote. Finlaggan was for four centuries the seat of the Lords of the Isles, who governed much of Argyll. The whitewashed cottages along its coast line clean and beautiful beaches, many of them visited by a variety of wildlife.

Isle of Mull and Iona. The pretty harbor of Tobermory, with its painted houses, is a relaxing base from which to explore the varied and beautiful island of Mull. Along Mull's west coast, spectacular cliffs and rocky beaches look out on to the Atlantic. From Craignure, the road crosses the sweeping green valleys of the Ross of Mull to Fionnphort and the ferry to the meditative island of Iona.

The Smaller Islands. These islands seem closer to the remoter Outer Hebrides than to the greener pastures of Mull or Arran. Abandoned by many of their original inhabitants, they are havens for birdlife, particularly Coll's giant dunes or the cliffs of Tiree. Colonsay's Kiloran Bay is open to the Atlantic's breakers, while Tiree's waves draw surfers from around the world.

PLANNING

WHEN TO GO

This part of the mainland is close enough to Glasgow to make it accessible year-round. Oban is just over two hours from the city by car (three hours by bus), but getting to the isles via ferries takes longer, and the crossings are less frequent. You can take advantage of quiet roads and plentiful accommodations in early spring and late autumn. The summer months of July and August can get very busy indeed; book accommodations and restaurants in advance during high season, or you might miss out. In winter, short daylight hours and winds can make island stays rather bleak.

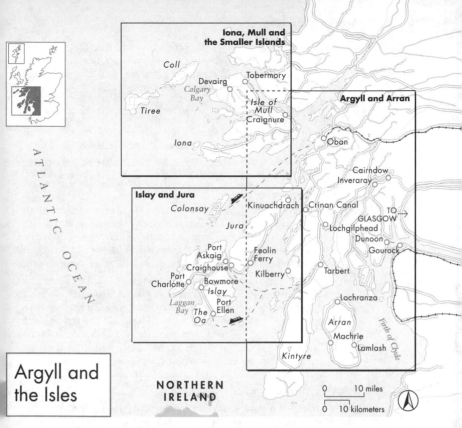

Iona, Mull and the Smaller Islands

Coll
Devaird
Calgary Bay
Tobermory
Tiree
Isle of Mull
Craignure
Iona

Argyll and Arran

Oban
Cairndow
Inveraray

Islay and Jura

Colonsay
Kinuachdrach
Crinan Canal
TO GLASGOW →
Jura
Lochgilphead
Dunoon
Gourock
Port Askaig
Feolin Ferry
Craighouse
Kilberry
Port Charlotte
Bowmore
Islay
Tarbert
Laggan Bay
Port Ellen
The Oa
Lochranza
Arran
Machrie
Lamlash
Kintyre

Firth of Clyde

ATLANTIC OCEAN

NORTHERN IRELAND

0   10 miles
0   10 kilometers

Argyll and the Isles

This is a coastal region, buffeted by Atlantic winds and rains. The climate is erratic, and locals take a curious pride in the fact that the area often experiences several seasons in a single day. Come prepared with adequate clothing for the changing weather, including good walking shoes, waterproof outerwear, and sunscreen.

PLANNING YOUR TIME

You could easily spend a week exploring the islands alone, so consider spending at least a few nights in this region. Argyll and some island excursions make pleasant and easy side trips from Glasgow and Loch Lomond. Driving anywhere here takes a little longer than you'd think, so allow ample travel time. A leisurely day will take you to Inveraray, its castle, and the surrounding gardens (don't miss the folk museum at Auchindrain) before driving on to Kennacraig to take the ferry for Islay and Jura. Two or three days here will give you a sense of the history and varied landscapes of these stunning islands—and time for a distillery or two. If time is a constraint, begin in Oban and sail to Mull, returning the same day or the next to take in the Scottish Sealife Sanctuary. If you can, drive around the beautiful Loch Awe on your way back to Glasgow.

Plan ahead: ferries fill up in the summer months, and some of the smaller islands are served only once or twice a week. Bear in mind that it is not easy to find places to eat after 9 pm at any time of year—though you can usually find a place that will sell you a whisky.

GETTING HERE AND AROUND

AIR TRAVEL

Flybe operates flights from Glasgow to Campbeltown, Islay, Tiree, and Mull. Hebridean Air Services flies between the small islands out of Oban.

Air Travel Contacts Flybe ☎ *0871/700–2000* ⊕ *www.flybe.com.* **Hebridean Air Services** ✉ *Lochranza* ☎ *0845/805–7465* ⊕ *www.hebrideanair.co.uk.*

BOAT AND FERRY TRAVEL

Caledonian MacBrayne (CalMac) operates car-ferry services to and from the main islands. It is important to plan ahead when traveling to the islands in order to coordinate the connecting ferries; CalMac can advise you on this. Multiple-island tickets are available and can significantly reduce the cost of island-hopping, and give you a memorable trip.

CalMac ferries run from Oban to Mull, Lismore, Coll, and Tiree; from Kennacraig to Islay, Jura, and Gigha; and from Ardrossan to Arran as well as a number of shorter routes. Western Ferries operate between Dunoon, in Argyll, and Gourock, west of Glasgow. The ferry passage between Dunoon and Gourock is one frequented by locals; it saves a lot of time, and you can take your car across as well. Jura Passenger Ferry operates between Tayvallich and Craighouse.

Ferry reservations are needed if you have a car; passengers traveling by foot do not need to make reservations.

Boat and Ferry Travel Contacts Caledonian MacBrayne (*CalMac*). ☎ *0800/066–5000* ⊕ *www.calmac.co.uk.* **Jura Passenger Ferry** ☎ *07768/450000* ⊕ *www.jurapassengerferry.com* 🖃 *£20.* **Western Ferries** ✉ *Hunter's Quay, Dunoon* ☎ *01369/704452* ⊕ *www.western-ferries.co.uk.*

BUS TRAVEL

You can travel throughout the region by bus, but service here tends to be less frequent than elsewhere in Scotland. Scottish Citylink runs daily service from Glasgow's Buchanan Street Station to the mid-Argyll region and Kintyre; the trip to Oban takes about three hours. Several other companies provide local services within the region.

Bus Contacts Bowman's Tours ☎ *01631/566809* ⊕ *www.bowmanscoaches. co.uk.* **Islay Coaches** ☎ *01496/840273.* **Jura Bus** ☎ *01496/820314.* **Royal Mail** ☎ *08457/740740.* **Scottish Citylink** ☎ *0871/266–3333* ⊕ *www.citylink.co.uk.* **Stagecoach West Scotland** ☎ *01292/613502* ⊕ *www.stagecoachbus.com.* **West Coast Motors** ☎ *01586/552319* ⊕ *www.westcoastmotors.co.uk.*

CAR TRAVEL

Negotiating this area is easy except in July and August, when the roads around Oban may be congested. There are a number of single-lane roads, especially on the east side of the Kintyre Peninsula and on the islands that require special care. Remember that white triangles indicate places where you can pass. You'll probably have to board a ferry at some point during your trip; nearly all ferries take cars as well as pedestrians.

From Glasgow, take the A 82 and the A85 to Oban, the main ferry terminal for Mull and the islands (about 2½ hours by car). From the A82, take the A83 at Arrochar; it rounds Loch Fyne to Inveraray. From there you can take the A819 from Inveraray around Loch Awe and rejoin the Glasgow–Oban road. Alternatively, you can stay on the A83 and head down Kintyre to Kennacraig, the ferry terminal for Islay. Farther down the A83 is Tayinloan, the ferry port for Gigha. You can reach Brodick on Arran by ferry from Ardrossan, on the Clyde coast (M8/A78 from Glasgow); in summer you can travel to Lochranza from Claonaig on the Kintyre Peninsula, but there are very few crossings.

TRAIN TRAVEL
Oban and Ardrossan are the main rail stations; it's a three-hour trip from Glasgow to Oban. For information call ScotRail. All trains connect with ferries.

Train Contact ScotRail ☎ *0845/601–5929* ⊕ *www.scotrail.co.uk.*

RESTAURANTS
Until recently this part of Scotland had few restaurants of distinction. That has changed, and more and more quality restaurants are opening and using the excellent local produce—fine fish and shellfish, lamb, and excellent venison, as well as game of many kinds. Most hotels and many guesthouses offer evening meals, though the quality can vary. Bear in mind that most restaurants and pubs stop serving food by nine in the evening; lunch usually ends at 2:30. *Prices in the reviews are the average cost of a main course at dinner or, if dinner is not served, at lunch.*

HOTELS
Accommodations in Argyll and on the isles range from country-house hotels to private homes offering a bed and breakfast. Most small, traditional, provincial hotels in coastal resorts have been updated and modernized, while still retaining personalized service. And though hotels often have a restaurant offering evening meals, the norm is to offer breakfast only. *Prices in the reviews are the lowest cost of a standard double room in high season, including 20% V.A.T.*

TOURS
BOAT TOURS
Getting out on the water is a wonderful way to see the landscape of the islands and also sea life.

Gordon Grant Tours leads an excursion from Oban to Mull, Iona, and Staffa and leaves Mull on other trips to Treshnish Isles and Staffa. From Taynuilt, near Oban, boat trips are available from Loch Etive Cruises Easter through October. Sea Life Surveys offers four- and six-hour whale-watching and wildlife day trips from Tobermory, on the Isle of Mull.

Turas-Mara runs daily excursions in summer from Oban and Mull to Staffa, Iona, and the Treshnish Isles and specializes in wildlife tours. On a daylong trip to the Treshnish islands, you might see puffins, seals, otters, and, at certain times of year, dolphins and the occasional whale. Staffa is the site of Fingal's Cave, immortalized by Mendelssohn's overture.

8

Boat Tour Contacts Gordon Grant Tours ✉ *Railway Pier, Achavaich, Isle of Iona* ☎ *01681/700338* ⊕ *www.staffatours.com.* **Loch Etive Cruises** ✉ *Kelly's Pier, Etive View, Taynuilt* ☎ *01866/822430.* **Sea Life Surveys** ✉ *A848, Tobermory* ☎ *01688/302916* ⊕ *www.sealifesurveys.com.* **Turus-Mara** ✉ *Penmore Mill, Dervaig* ☎☎ *01688/400242* ⊕ *www.turusmara.com.*

BUS TOURS

Many of the bus companies in the area also arrange sightseeing tours, so check with them (*see Getting Here and Around, above*). Bowman's Tours runs trips from Oban.

Bus Tour Contact Bowman's Tours ✉ *Queens Park, Oban* ☎ *01631/563221* ⊕ *www.bowmanstours.co.uk.*

VISITOR INFORMATION

The tourist offices in Lochgilphead, Tarbert, and Tobermory (Mull) are open April through October only; other offices are open year-round.

Contact Visit Scottish Heartlands ⊕ *www.visitscottishheartlands.com.*

ARGYLL

Topographical grandeur and rocky shores are what make Argyll special. Try to take to the water at least once, even if your time is limited. The sea and the sea lochs have played a vital role in the history of western Scotland since the time of the war galleys of the clans. Oban is the major ferry gateway and transport hub, with a main road leading south into the Kintyre Peninsula.

OBAN

96 miles northwest of Glasgow, 125 miles northwest of Edinburgh, 50 miles south of Fort William, 118 miles southwest of Inverness.

It's almost impossible to avoid Oban when touring the west. Its waterfront has some character, but the town's main role is as a launch point for excursions into Argyll and for ferry trips to the islands. A traditional Scottish resort town, Oban has many music festivals, *ceilidhs* with Highland dancing, as well as all the usual tartan kitsch and late-night revelry in pubs and hotel bars. The Oban Distillery is on Stafford Street in town, offering tours and a shop. Still, there are more exciting destinations just over the horizon, on the islands and down Kintyre.

GETTING HERE AND AROUND

From Glasgow, the A82 along Loch Lomond meets the A85 at Crianlarich. Turn left and continue to Oban. In summer the center of Oban can become gridlocked with ferry traffic, so leave yourself time for the wait. Alternatively, the A816 from Lochgilphead enters Oban from the less crowded south. Train services run from Glasgow to Oban (ScotRail); bus services from Glasgow to Oban by Scottish Citylink run several times a day.

ESSENTIALS

Visitor Information Oban Tourist Informaton Centre ✉ *Argyll Sq.* ☎ *08707/200630* ⊕ *www.visitscotland.com.*

Argyll and Arran

Lochaline

Isle of Eriska

Port Appin

Barcaldine

Rudha an Ridire

Loch Linnhe

Barcaldine Forest

Loch Etive

Scottish Sealife Sanctuary

Benderloch

Ben Cruachan

Connel Bridge

Dunstaffnage Castle

Ocean Explorer Centre

Connel

Bonawe Iron Furnace

Isle of Mull

Taynuilt

Cruachan

Kilchurn Castle

Oban

Loch Awe

Dalmally

Firth of Lorne

A816

Kilninver

Seil

B844

A85

Loch Awe

B840

A819

Rest and Be Thankful Pass

A83

Easdale Island

Scarba

Cairndow

Inveraray

Ardkinglas Woodland Garden

Auchindrain Museum

Strachur

A815

Kilmartin House Museum

A83

Loch Fyne

TO GLASGOW →

Crinan

Dunadd Fort

Crarae Garden

Jura

B8000

A886

Lochgilphead

Ardrishaig

B8024

Dunoon

Gourock

Colintraive

Sound of Jura

Loch Caolisport

Knapdale

Loch Fyne

Wemyss Bay

Small Isles Bay

Portavadie

Tarbert

Rothesay

Wemyss Bay

Largs

Kilberry

Kennacraig

Bute

Millport

slay

Isle of Gigha

Claonaig

Sound of Bute

A78

Achamore House Gardens

Tayinloan

B842

Lochranza

Sannox

Ardrossan

Sound of Gigha

Catacol

Corrie

A83

Kintyre Peninsula

Arran

Goat Fell

Brodick Castle and Country Park

Brodick

Kintyre

Machrie

Drumadoon Point

String Rd.

Lamlash

Holy Island

Kilchenzie

Machrie Moor Stone Circles

Blackwaterfoot

Lagg

A841

Whiting Bay

Machrihanish

Campbeltown

Kilmory

Mull of Kintyre

Southend

Maidens

0   10 miles

0   10 kilometers

KEY

Rail Lines

Ferry

Airport

EXPLORING

Fodors Choice **Dunstaffnage Castle.** Standing high atop volcanic rock, Dunstaffnage
★ commands the hills and lochs that surround it. That is why this 13th-century castle was so strategic and fought over between those battling for control of the kingdom of Argyll. From the walk along the walls you have outstanding views across the **Sound of Mull** and the **Firth of Lorne.** A small well-illustrated guidebook (£2.50) lets you take your own guided tour, but there are story boards throughout the building that give you a sense of how it was used across the ages. In the woods is the ruined chapel of St. Cuthbert, built by the Macdougall clan at the same time as the castle. ⊠ *Off A85* ☏ *01631/562465* ⊕ *www.historic-scotland.gov.uk/places* ⊡ *£4.50* ⊗ *Apr.–Sept., daily 9:30–5:30; Oct., daily 9:30–4:30; Nov.–Mar., Mon.–Wed. and weekends 9:30–4:30.*

Ocean Explorer Centre. On the Firth of Lorn, this imaginative new venture lets you get a look under the sea. Hands-on exhibits including microscopes where you can observe tiny algae to a live undersea camera where you can see what's happening below the waves. It's educational, but also accessible and fun. There is a bright little café and a shop with books on marine science and other topics. It's 2 miles from Oban—follow the signs for nearby Dunstaffnage Castle. ⊠ *Kirk Rd.* ☏ *01632/559123* ⊕ *www.oceanexplorercentre.org* ⊡ *£5* ⊗ *Apr.–Oct., daily 10–5; Nov.–Mar., weekdays 10–5.*

FAMILY **Scottish Sea Life Sanctuary.** On the shores of Loch Creran, this marine sanctuary is part aquarium where you can get an up-close look at everything from sharks to stingrays, and part animal rescue facility. Adorable otters and seals receive rehabilitation here before being released back into the wild. Kids will appreciate the adventure playground. The restaurant serves morning coffee, a full lunch menu, and afternoon tea. To get here, drive north from Oban for 10 miles on the A828; West Coast Motors also provide a regular bus service. ⊠ *Barcaldine, off A828, Connel* ☏ *01631/720386* ⊕ *www.sealsanctuary.co.uk* ⊡ *£13.20* ⊗ *Apr.–Oct., daily 10–5; Nov.–Mar, daily 10–4; last admission 1 hr before closing.*

WHERE TO EAT

$$ ✕ **Ee-usk.** This clean-lined restaurant's name means "fish" in Gaelic, and
SEAFOOD it has earned quite a reputation for serving excellent dishes made with the freshest fish and shellfish delivered directly from Oban's harbor. The signature creations use appealingly simple sauces; try oven-baked wild halibut with creamed leeks or the full-scale seafood platter. Good-value options include fixed-price menus for lunch (£11.50 for two courses) and dinner (£15.95 or £17.95 for two or three courses). On clear days there are nice views of the islands through the large glass windows. Children under 12 not admitted for dinner. ⑤ *Average main: £19* ⊠ *North Pier* ☏ *01631/565666* ⊕ *www.eeusk.com* ⊗ *Closed Sun.*

$ ✕ **Kitchen Garden.** Directly across the road from the ferry port, this deli-
CAFÉ catessen serves good homemade soups, panini, and sandwiches, as well as freshly baked cakes. The service is sometimes a little slow; prices are reasonable and the location is quite convenient. ⑤ *Average main: £10* ⊠ *North Pier, 14 George St.* ☏ *01631/566332* ⊗ *No dinner.*

WHERE TO STAY

$$
B&B/INN
☷ **Glenburnie House.** At this typical seafront guesthouse in a Victorian house with fine views over Oban Bay, most rooms are spacious and comfortable, if slightly overdecorated in traditional style. **Pros:** centrally located; good sea views. **Cons:** too many flowery fabrics for some tastes; slightly expensive for what you get; no elevator. ⑤ *Rooms from: £110* ✉ *Esplanade* ☏ *01631/562089* ⊕ *www.glenburnie.co.uk* ⇆ *12 rooms* ⊘ *Closed Dec.–Feb.* ⵏⵔ *Breakfast.*

$
B&B/INN
☷ **Kilchrenan House.** Just a few minutes from the town center, this Victorian-era stone house has been transformed into a lovely bed-and-breakfast. **Pros:** great sea views; tasteful attention to detail. **Cons:** some bedrooms may be too colorfully decorated for some tastes; attic rooms have a slanting roof. ⑤ *Rooms from: £80* ✉ *Corran Esplanade* ☏ *01631/562663* ⊕ *www.kilchrenanhouse.co.uk* ⇆ *10 rooms* ⊘ *Closed Dec. and Jan.* ⵏⵔ *Breakfast.*

$$$
HOTEL
☷ **Manor House Hotel.** On the coast near Oban, this 1780 stone house—once the home of the duke of Argyll—has wonderful sea views. **Pros:** excellent restaurant; near all necessary amenities; nice garden overlooking the bay. **Cons:** smallish bedrooms; no children under 12. ⑤ *Rooms from: £180* ✉ *Gallanach Rd.* ☏ *01631/562087* ⊕ *www.manorhouseoban.com* ⇆ *11 rooms* ⵏⵔ *Breakfast.*

SPORTS AND THE OUTDOORS

BICYCLING
Bike Fix. This shop rents bikes of various sorts starting at £15 for a full day. The area round Oban is good cycling country, and the staff is happy to advise you on routes. ✉ *87 George St.* ☏ *01631/564372.*

APPIN

8

The little peninsula of Appin, a 20-minute drive from Oban, is a charming, well-kept secret. Just 2 miles along a narrow road from the main Fort William route (A828), the bay opens to Lismore and the sea. Castle Stalker, a privately owned castle on the water, sits magnificently in the center of the picture, a symbol of ancient coastal Scotland. This is an excellent, uncrowded base for walking, fishing, water sports, and cycling. The Appin Rocks, on the headland, are frequently visited by seals.

GETTING HERE AND AROUND

From Oban, follow the A828 around Loch Creran and take the left turn to Port Appin just beyond Tynribbie. Continue for just over 2 miles to the old pier. From the port, the passenger ferry runs to the island of Lismore throughout the year; steamers once plied the waters of Loch Linnhe, but today the largest boats here are those taking workers to the quarries of Kingairloch.

WHERE TO STAY

$$$$
HOTEL
Fodor's Choice
★
☷ **Airds Hotel and Restaurant.** The old ferry inn for travelers visiting Lismore now houses this luxurious small hotel; rooms are stylish and restrained, with superb views either toward the sea or the woods behind. **Pros:** fabulous views from the breakfast room; spare boots for the unprepared; beautiful location. **Cons:** an expensive option. ⑤ *Rooms from: £315* ✉ *A828, Port Appin* ☏ *01631/730236* ⊕ *www.airds-hotel.com* ⇆ *9 rooms, 2 suites, 1 cottage* ⵏⵔ *Some meals.*

$$$$
HOTEL
Fodor's Choice
★

☷ **Isle of Eriska.** A severe, baronial-style granite facade belies the sense of welcome within this hotel, set on its own island 10 miles north of Oban and accessible by a bridge from the mainland; the rooms are individually furnished and luxurious in their detail, and a range of outdoor activities are available, as are a spa, pools, and gyms. **Pros:** exceptional food; good service; peace and quiet. **Cons:** you're in the middle of nowhere, few choices when it comes to dining out. $ *Rooms from: £340* ⊠ *Off A828, Eriska* ☎ *01631/720371* ⊕ *www.eriska-hotel. co.uk* ↝ *25 rooms* ⦿ *Multiple meal plans.*

$$
HOTEL

☷ **Pierhouse Hotel.** The round towers of the old pier mark the entrance to this hotel and restaurant, appealingly situated on the water's edge beside the jetty. **Pros:** breathtaking view across the loch; lively, warm atmosphere; good restaurant. **Cons:** rooms are a little small; not all rooms have views of the water; prices rise on weekends. $ *Rooms from: £160* ⊠ *Port Appin* ☎ *01631/730302* ⊕ *www.pierhousehotel. co.uk* ↝ *12 rooms* ⦿ *Breakfast.*

$
RENTAL

☷ **Strathfillan Wigwams.** Strictly for hardier travelers, this cluster of peak-roofed cabins puts nature right at your door. **Pros:** a very cheap lodging; safe rural environment; a sense of freedom. **Cons:** basic accommodation; you cook your own food. $ *Rooms from: £40* ⊠ *Off A85, Tyndrum, Perthshire* ☎ *01838/400251* ⊕ *www.wigwamholidays.com/ strathfillan_wigwam_village* ↝ *18 rooms.*

LOCH AWE

18 miles east of Oban.

Measuring more than 25 miles long, Loch Awe is Scotland's longest stretch of fresh water. Its northwest shore is quiet; forest walks crisscross the Inverliever Forest here. At the loch's northern end tiny islands, many with ruins, pepper the water. One, Inishail, is home to a 13th-century chapel.

GETTING HERE AND AROUND

From Oban the A85 will bring you to the head of Loch Awe and the small town of the same name. Turn onto the B845 at Taynuilt to reach the loch's northern shore, or continue through the forbidding Pass of Brander and turn onto the A819 to get to the southern shore. From here you can continue on to Inveraray, or drive along the loch on the B840.

EXPLORING

Bonawe Iron Furnace. This beautifully reconstructed site shows a different face of this mainly agricultural region. The ironworks were very advanced for their time, and an elbaborate exhibit takes you through the different stages of the production process. During the Napoleonic Wars it began making cannonballs, and these provided firepower for Admiral Lord Nelson's ships at the Battle of Trafalgar in 1805. The local graveyard, at Taynuilt, has a monument to Nelson raised by the workers. The majority of the workers were Gaelic-speaking peasants who were responsible for collecting the wood from the surrounding forests to make charcoal. Those who worked in Bonawe were mostly Englishmen who arrived on the cargo boats used to transport the iron. ⊠ *Off B845, Bonawe* ☎ *01866/822432* ⊕ *www.historic-scotland.gov. uk* ☒ *£4.50* ☉ *Apr.–Sept., Mon.–Sun. 9:30–5:30.*

Cruachan. This fascinating engineering achievement is all the more dramatic for being hidden in a landscape that gives no hint of its presence. Inside Ben Cruachan you find yourself in a massive man-made cavern containing the vast turbines and machinery that supply so much of western Scotland's electricity. Take in the hands-on exhibit at the visitor center, then travel by bus 1 km (½ mile) into the "hollow mountain," past the tropical plants that grow near the vast generating hall. ✉ *A85, Dalmally* ☎ *01866/822618* ⊕ *www.visitcruachan.co.uk* 💷 *£6.50* ⊘ *Apr.–Oct., 9:30–4:45; Nov.–Mar., 9:30–3:45.*

Duncan Ban Macintyre Monument. The monument was erected in honor of this Gaelic poet (1724–1812), sometimes referred to as the Robert Burns of the Highlands. The view from here is one of the finest in Argyll, taking in Ben Cruachan and the other peaks nearby, as well as Loch Awe and its scattering of islands. To find the monument from Dalmally, just east of Loch Awe, follow an old road running southwest toward the banks of the loch. You can see the round, granite structure from the road's highest point, often called Monument Hill.

Kilchurn Castle. A striking ruined fortress at the northeastern end of Loch Awe, the castle was built in the 15th century and rebuilt in the 17th century. Airy vantage points amid the towers have fine panoramas of the surrounding highlands and loch. It's 2½ miles west of Dalmally, accessible by foot along an old railway line near A85. ✉ *Off A85, west of the junction with A819, Dalmally* ☎ *01866/833333* ⊕ *www.historic-scotland.gov.uk/places* 💷 *Free* ⊘ *Apr.–Sept., daily.*

St. Conan's Kirk. This striking stone-built church on the banks of Loch Awe has a medieval air about it, but in fact it was completed in 1930 by amateur architect Walter Campbell. It was built with the boulders strewn across the area, rather than quarried stone, and it looks rough and almost incomplete. But its interior is impressive. Light filters in through modern stained-glass windows, and wood and stone carvings are scattered throughout, not to mention the effigy of Robert the Bruce lying on a stone catalfalque that contains a fragment of bone taken from Bannockburn. It's on the A85, about 18 miles from Oban. ✉ *A85, Lochawe* ☎ *01838/200298* ⊕ *www.stconanskirk.org. uk* 💷 *Free.*

WHERE TO STAY

$$$
HOTEL
Fodor's Choice
★

⌂ **Taychreggan Hotel.** The tranquillity of this lovely country-house hotel echoes the stillness of nearby Loch Awe. **Pros:** lovely setting; high level of comfort; wonderful meals. **Cons:** Wi-Fi only in public rooms; off the beaten track . ⑤ *Rooms from: £154* ✉ *Off B845, Kilchrenan* ☎ *01866/833211* ⊕ *www.taychregganhotel.co.uk* 🛏 *18 rooms* ⑩ *Breakfast.*

EN
ROUTE

The A819 south to Inveraray initially runs alongside Loch Awe, but soon leaves these pleasant banks to turn east and join the A83, which carries traffic from Glasgow and Loch Lomond by way of the high **Rest and Be Thankful Pass.** This quasi-alpine pass, set among high green slopes and gray rocks, is one of the most scenic points along the road.

INVERARAY

21 miles south of Loch Awe, 61 miles north of Glasgow, 29 miles west of Loch Lomond.

Fodor's Choice
★

The town is a sparkling fishing village with cute shops, attractions, and the haunted Campbell Castle all within walking distance. There are lovely views of the water and plenty of fishing boats to watch; several worthwhile gardens and museums are nearby, too. On the approaches to Inveraray, note the ornate 18th-century bridgework that carries the road along the loch side. This is your first sign that Inveraray is not just a jumble of houses; in fact, much of it was designed as a planned town for the third duke of Argyll in the mid-18th century.

GETTING HERE AND AROUND

If you're driving from Oban, take the A85 and the A819 beyond Loch Awe (the village). From Glasgow, take the A82, turn on to the A83 at Arrochar, and make the long drive around Loch Fyne.

ESSENTIALS

Visitor Information Inveraray Tourist Information Centre ⊠ *Front St.* ☎ *01499/302063* ⊕ *www.visitscotland.com.*

EXPLORING
TOP ATTRACTIONS

Ardkinglas Woodland Garden. One of Britain's finest collections of conifers is set off by rhododendron blossoms in early summer. You'll find the garden around the head of Loch Fyne, about 10 miles east of Inveraray. There's a wild woodland walk beyond the garden. The house is usually not open to visitors, though you can take a tour the second-to-last Friday of each month between April and October. ⊠ *A83, Cairndow* ☎ *01499/600261* ⊕ *www.ardkinglas.com* 🎫 *£4.50* ☉ *Daily sunrise–sunset.*

Fodor's Choice
★

Auchindrain Museum. Step a few centuries back in time at this open-air museum, a rare surviving example of an 18th-century communal tenancy farm. About 250 years ago, there were several thousand working communities like Auchindrain. Auchindrain was the last of them, its final tenant leaving in 1963. Today the bracken-thatch and iron-roof buildings, about 20 in all, give you a feel for early farming life in the Highland communities. Several houses are furnished and tell the story of their occupants. A tearoom is open morning to afternoon. ⊠ *Off A83, 6 miles south of Inveraray* ☎ *01499/500235* ⊕ *www.auchindrain.org.uk* 🎫 *£6.30* ☉ *Apr.–Oct., daily 10–5; last admission 4.*

Crarae Garden. Well worth a visit for plant lovers is this 100-acre garden, where magnolias, azaleas, and rhododendrons flourish in the moist, lush environment around Crarae Burn (a burn is a small stream). A rocky gorge and waterfalls add appeal, and the flowers and trees attract several different species of birds and butterflies. The gardens are 10 miles southwest of Inveraray off the A83. ⊠ *Off A83* ☎ *0844/493–2210* ⊕ *www.nts.org.uk/Visits* 🎫 *£6.50* ☉ *Garden daily 9:30–sunset. Visitor center Apr.–Oct., daily 10–5:45; last admission at 5.*

Inveraray Castle. The current seat of the Chief of the Campbell clan is a smart, grayish-green turreted stone house with a self-satisfied air. Set among extensive and well-tended grounds, it contains displays of luxurious furnishings and interesting art, as well as a huge armory. Built between 1743 and 1789, the spires on the four corner turrets give it a vaguely French look. Tours of the castle follow the history of the powerful Campbell family and how it acquired its considerable wealth. There is a tearoom for snacks and light lunches. You can hike around the extensive estate grounds, but wear sturdy footwear. ⊠ *Off A83* ☎ *01499/302203* ⊕ *www.inveraray-castle.com* ⛁ *£9* ⊘ *Apr.–Oct., daily 10–5:45, last admission at 5.*

WORTH NOTING

Arctic Penguin. This 1911 lightship is a rare example of a riveted iron vessel. It now houses exhibits on the maritime heritage of the River Clyde and the rest of Scotland's west coast. Beside it sits the "puffer" *Eilean Eisdeal,* a tiny interisland freight boat. ⊠ *Inveraray Pier* ☎ *01499/302213* ⊕ *www.inveraraypier.com* ⛁ *£5* ⊘ *Daily 10–5.*

FAMILY **Inveraray Jail.** In this old jail realistic courtroom scenes, carefully recreated cells, and other paraphernalia give you a glimpse of life behind bars in Victorian times—and today. Actors represent some of the jail's most famous occupants. The site includes a Scottish crafts shop. ⊠ *Main St.* ☎ *01499/302381* ⊕ *www.inverarayjail.co.uk* ⛁ *£8.95* ⊘ *Apr.–Oct., daily 9:30–6; Nov.–Mar., daily 10–5; last admission 1 hr before closing.*

WHERE TO EAT AND STAY

$$ ✕ **Loch Fyne Oyster Bar and Restaurant.** The flagship location of a popular SEAFOOD chain, this well-regarded seafood spot 10 miles northeast of Inverary sits surrounded by hills at the head of Loch Fyne, with beautiful views in both directions. Polished wood and maritime artworks help set the mood. The dishes are generally simple and unpretentious—try the fish and shellfish soup, or the roast salmon with asparagus, broad beans, and pea salad. Don't miss the oysters, either in the restaurant or in the adjacent shop. Arrive early, as the place closes at 8, and reserve in advance. ⑤ *Average main: £17* ⊠ *Clachan Farm, A83, Cairndow* ☎ *01499/600482* ⊕ *www.lochfyne.com* ⚇ *Reservations essential.*

$ 🏨 **The George Hotel.** The Clark family has run this 18th-century former HOTEL coaching inn at the heart of Inveraray for six generations, and that's Fodor's Choice reflected in the warmth of the welcome you'll receive. **Pros:** excellent ★ restaurant; atmospheric bars; hotel Scottish in every way. **Cons:** too much tartan for some; unattractive reception area; Wi-Fi in public areas only. ⑤ *Rooms from: £75* ⊠ *Main St. E* ☎ *01499/302111* ⊕ *www. thegeorgehotel.co.uk* ⇥ *17 rooms* ❍| *Breakfast.*

8

LOCHGILPHEAD

26 miles south of Inveraray.

Lochgilphead, the largest town in this region, looks best when the tide is in, as Loch Gilp (really a bite out of Loch Fyne) reveals a muddy shoreline at low tide. With a series of well-kept, colorful buildings along its main street, this neat little town is worth a look.

GETTING HERE AND AROUND

From Inveraray continue south for 24 miles along the A83, which follows the bank of the Loch Fyne.

SHOPPING

Highbank Collection. The factory shop here sells hand-painted pottery and glassware, colorful ceramics, and model wooden boats. It has plenty of Loch Ness Monster memorabilia. ☒ *Highbank Industrial Estate, off A816* ☎ *01546/602044* ⊕ *www.highbank.co.uk.*

CRINAN

10 miles northwest of Lochgilphead.

Crinan is synonymous with its canal, the reason for this tiny community's existence and its mainstay. The narrow road beside the Crinan Hotel bustles with yachting types waiting to pass through the locks, bringing a surprisingly cosmopolitan feel to such an out-of-the-way corner of Scotland. Also accessible from Crinan is the worthwhile Kilmartin House Museum.

GETTING HERE AND AROUND

To reach Crinan, take the A816 Oban road north from Lochgilphead for about a mile, then turn left on to the B841 at Cairnbaan.

EXPLORING

Crinan Canal. This canal opened in 1801 to let fishing vessels reach Hebridean fishing grounds without making the long haul south around the Kintyre Peninsula. At its western end the canal drops to the sea in a series of locks, the last of which is beside the Crinan Hotel. Today it's popular with pleasure boats traveling to the west coast.

Fodor'sChoice **Kilmartin House Museum.** For an exceptional encounter with early Scottish history, start at this museum 8 miles north of Crinan and then explore some of the more than 300 ancient monuments within a 6-mile radius. Exhibits provide information about the stone circles and avenues, burial mounds, and carved stones dating from the Bronze Age and earlier that are scattered nearby. There is also a nice tea room in the museum. Nearby **Dunadd Fort,** a rocky hump rising out of the level ground between Crinan and Kilmartin, was once the capital of the early kingdom of Dalriada, founded by the first wave of Scots who migrated from Ireland around AD 500. Clamber up the rock to see a basin, a footprint, and an outline of a boar carved on the smooth upper face of the knoll. ☒ *A816, Kilmartin* ☎ *01546/510278* ⊕ *www.kilmartin.org* ☒ *£5* ☉ *Mar.–Oct., daily 10–5:30; Nov. and Dec., daily 11–4.*

WHERE TO STAY

$ ⌂ **Allt-Na-Craig.** A location on the edge of the village and overlooking
B&B/INN Loch Fyne distinguishes this stone Victorian house set in lovely gardens.
Pros: atmospheric; good food and views. **Cons:** you're pretty isolated,
so it helps to have a car. $ *Rooms from: £99* ⊠ *Tarbert Rd., 4 miles
south of Lochgilphead, Ardrishaig* ☎ *01546/603245* ⊕ *www.allt-na-
craig.co.uk* ⌐ *5 rooms, 1 cottage* ⫯⊚⫯ *Breakfast.*

$$$ ⌂ **Crinan Hotel.** One of a group of houses around the last lock of the
HOTEL Crinan Canal, the hotel has a dramatic setting overlooking the Sound
of Jura and Craignish Point; it echoes the style of the boats on the
canal in its use of wood. **Cons:** Wi-Fi in public areas only. $ *Rooms from: £180*
⊠ *Off B841* ☎ *01546/830261* ⊕ *www.crinanhotel.com* ⌐ *20 rooms*
⫯⊚⫯ *Breakfast.*

KINTYRE PENINSULA

52 miles south of Lochgilphead (to Campbeltown).

Rivers and streams crisscross this long, narrow strip of green pasture-
lands and hills stretching south from Lochgilphead.

GETTING HERE AND AROUND

Continue south on the A83 (the road to Campbeltown) to Tarbert.
Some 4 miles farther along the A83 is Kennacraig, where you catch the
ferry to Islay. Beyond that is the pier at Tayinloan; CalMac ferries run
from here to the Isle of Gigha.

Flybe operates flights from Glasgow to Campbeltown.

ESSENTIALS

Air Travel Contact Campbeltown Airport ⊠ *Off A83, Kintyre* ☎ *01586/553797*
⊕ *www.hial.co.uk.*

Visitor Information Campbeltown Information Centre ⊠ *Mackinnon House,
The Pier, Campbeltown* ☎ *01586/552056* ⊕ *www.visitscotland.com.* **Tarbert
Information Centre** ⊠ *Harbour St., Tarbert* ☎ *01880/820429*
⊕ *www.visitscotland.com.*

EXPLORING

Achamore House Gardens. One relic of the Isle of Gigha's aristocratic
legacy is the Achamore House Garden, which produce lush shrubber-
ies with spectacular azalea displays in late spring. For a nimble day
trip, take the 20-minute ferry to Gigha from Tayinloan and walk right
over to the gardens. The gardens are managed by the Gigha Commu-
nity Trust. ⊠ *Isle of Gigha* ☎ *01583/505392* ⊕ *www.isle-of-gigha.co.uk*
⌐ *£6* ⊙ *Daily sunrise–sunset.*

Isle of Gigha. Barely 7 miles long, this sheltered island between Kintyre
and Islay has sandy beaches and rich wildlife. The island was long
favored by British aristocrats as a summer destination. Ferries make
the 20-minute trip from Tayinloan on the mainland. ⊠ *Isle of Gigha*
☎ *01583/505392* ⊕ *www.gigha.org.uk.*

Tarbert. A name that appears throughout the Highlands, Tarbert is the
Gaelic word for "place of portage," and a glance at the map tells you

8

why it was given to this little town with a workaday waterfront: Tarbert sits on the narrow neck of land between East and West Loch Tarbert, where long ago boats were actually carried across the land to avoid looping all the way around the peninsula. The town's visitor center is on Harbour Street. ⊕ *www.visitscotland.com.*

GOLF

Machrihanish Golf Club. Many enthusiasts discuss this course in hushed tones—its out-of-the-way location has made it something of a golfer's Shangri-la. It was laid out in 1876 by Tom Morris on the links around the sandy Machrihanish Bay. The drive off the first tee is across the beach to reach the green—an intimidating start to a memorable series of holes. ⊠ *Off B843, Machrihanish* ☎ *01586/810277* ⊕ *www.machgolf. com* ⊠ *Green fee: £65* ⚑ *Reservations essential* ⚑ *18 holes, 6235 yds, par 70* ⊙ *Daily.*

ARRAN

Approaching Arran by sea, you'll first see the forbidding Goatfell (2,868 feet) in the north, then the green fields of the south. It is this contrast and varied geography that has led visitors to describe Arran as "Scotland in Miniature." The island's temperate climate allows tropical plants to grow, and this relative warmth probably attracted the ancient cultures whose stone circles still stand on the island. This weather also explains why it has long been a favorite resort getaway for Glasgow's residents, who come here to walk, climb Goatfell, play golf on Arran's nine courses, observe the rich birdlife, and simply enjoy the sea.

GETTING HERE AND AROUND

Caledonian MacBrayne runs regular car and passenger ferries that cross the Firth of Clyde from Ardrossan (near Saltcoats) to Brodick throughout the year (crossing takes just under an hour). There is also a small ferry from Claonaig on the Kintyre Peninsula to Lochranza during the summer months.

Connecting trains run to the ferry at Ardrossan from Glasgow's Queen Street station. Stagecoach runs regular local bus services around the island. Exploring the island by car is easy, as the A841 road circles it.

BRODICK

1 hr by ferry from Ardrossan.

Arran's largest village, Brodick, has a main street that is set back from the promenade and the lovely bay beyond.

GETTING HERE AND AROUND

You can reach Brodick from Ardrossan by ferry. From Brodick the A841 circles the island; head south to reach Lamlash, north to reach Lochranza. The String Road crosses the island between Brodick and Machrie.

ESSENTIALS

Visitor Information Brodick Information Centre ⊠ *The Pier* ☎ *01770/303774* ⊕ *www.visitscotland.com.*

EXPLORING

Fodor's Choice ★ **Brodick Castle and Country Park.** On the north side of Brodick Bay, this reddish sandstone structure is surrounded by lush woods, gardens, and parks. Several rooms are open to the public between March and October, both in the original 16th-century castle and in the Victorian additions that nicely illustrate the Hamilton family's opulent lifestyle. The large downstairs kitchen reveals how servants lived, and the 87 stag heads on the stairs are a slightly disturbing reminder of how the aristocracy spent their leisure time. The vast gardens, open all year, are filled with rhododendrons and azaleas. A café serves homemade cakes and coffee for breakfast as well as a light lunch menu.

The country park here includes the 2,867-foot **Goatfell,** at the highest peak in Arran. The beautiful upland landscape is more challenging to explore than it seems, so it's important to go prepared, but the views from the peak merit the effort to get there. Year-round access is from the country park or from Cladach on the A841. ⊠ *Off A841, 1 mile north of Brodick Pier* ☎ *0844/4932152* ⊕ *www.nts.org.uk* ☜ *Castle and gardens £12* ⊘ *Castle Apr. and Oct., daily 11–3; May–Sept, daily 11–4. Garden Apr. and Oct., daily 10–4; May–Sept., daily 10–5.*

Glen Rosa. Here you can stroll through a long glen glimpsing the wild ridges that beckon so many outdoors enthusiasts. To get here from A841, drive a short way along String Road and turn right at the signpost into the glen. The road soon becomes unpassable; park the car and wander on foot. ⊠ *Off String Rd.*

Isle of Arran Heritage Museum. The museum documents life on the island from ancient times to the present. Several buildings, including a cottage and *smiddy* (smithy), have period furnishings as well as displays on prehistoric life, farming, fishing, and other aspects of the island's social history. ⊠ *Rosaburn, A841* ☎ *01770/302636* ⊕ *www.arranmuseum. co.uk* ☜ *£3* ⊘ *Apr.–Oct., daily 10:30–4:30.*

WHERE TO EAT

$$ SEAFOOD **✕ Creelers.** It would be hard to find fresher seafood than at Creelers. The shellfish served in the restaurant will often have been caught that day by the owners' own boat. The restaurant's name comes from the "creels," or baskets, used to gather shellfish. The restaurant serves a range of delicious smoked fish from its own smokery next door, as well as other fish and meat dishes. Try the Arran scallops with monkfish and pesto, or the cod with Arran mustard. ⑤ *Average main: £18* ⊠ *Home Farm, A841* ☎ *01770/302810* ⊕ *www.creelers.co.uk* ☜ *Reservations essential.*

$ ITALIAN **✕ Eilean-Mor Bar Bistro.** Painted a bright shade of red, this unpretentious Italian bar and bistro has a friendly and attentive staff. The substantial pastas, pizzas, and burgers are nicely prepared—even the haggis ravioli in whisky sauce is startlingly tasty. ⑤ *Average main: £11* ⊠ *Shore Rd.* ☎ *01770/302579.*

SPORTS AND THE OUTDOORS

Arran Adventure Centre. The services here include mountain bike rentals (£20 per day), as well as gorge walking and sea kayaking. ⊠ *Shore Rd.* ☎ *01770/302244* ⊕ *www.arranadventure.com.*

8

SHOPPING

Arran's shops are well stocked with locally produced goods. The Home Farm is a popular shopping area with several shops and a small restaurant.

Arran Aromatics. This is one of Scotland's best-known suppliers of scents, soaps, and perfumes of every kind. ⊠ *Home Farm, A841* ☎ *01770/302595* ⊕ *www.arranaromatics.com.*

Island Cheese Company. Stop here to buy Arran blue cheese among other handmade Scottish cheeses. ⊠ *The Home Farm, A841* ☎ *01770/302788.*

LAMLASH

4 miles south of Brodick.

With views offshore to Holy Island, which is now a Buddhist retreat, Lamlash has a breezy seaside-holiday atmosphere. To reach the highest point accessible by car, go through the village and turn right beside the bridge onto Ross Road, which climbs steeply from a thickly planted valley, **Glen Scorrodale,** and yields fine views of Lamlash Bay. From Lamlash you can explore the southern part of Arran: 4 miles to the southwest, **Whiting Bay** has a pleasant well-kept waterfront and a range of hotels and guesthouses. If you travel another 6 miles, you'll reach the little community of **Lagg,** which sits peacefully by the banks of the Kilmory Water.

GETTING HERE AND AROUND

You can reach Lamlash by driving south from Brodick on the A841. The town is also served by Stagecoach buses.

WHERE TO STAY

$ **Lagg Hotel.** Arran's oldest inn is an 18th-century lodge with fire-
B&B/INN places in the common rooms and 11 acres of gardens and grounds that meander down to the river. **Pros:** beautiful gardens; warming fireplaces; good-size rooms. **Cons:** floral designs everywhere. ⑤ *Rooms from: £85* ⊠ *A841, Kilmory, Isle of Arran* ☎ *01770/870255* ⊕ *www.lagghotel.com* ➥ *13 rooms* ⑩ *Breakfast.*

SHOPPING

Patterson Arran. The store is famous for its preserves and marmalades, as well as its mustards. ⊠ *The Old Mill, A841* ☎ *01770/600606.*

MACHRIE

10 miles west of Brodick, 11 miles north of Lagg.

The area surrounding Machrie, home to a popular beach, is littered with prehistoric sites: chambered cairns, hut circles, and standing stones dating from the Bronze Age.

GETTING HERE AND AROUND

The quick route to Machrie is via the String Road (B880) from Brodick; turn off onto the Machrie Road 5 mi outside Brodick. A much longer but stunning journey will take you from Brodick, north to Lochranza, around the island to Machrie, and down the island's dramatic west coast, a distance of some 28 miles.

EXPLORING

Machrie Moor Stone Circles. From Machrie, a well-surfaced track takes you to a grassy moor by a ruined farm, where you can see the Machrie Moor Stone Circles: small, rounded granite-boulder circles and much taller, eerie red-sandstone monoliths. Out on the bare moor, the lost and lonely stones are very evocative, well worth a walk to see if you like the feeling of solitude. The stones are about 1 1/2 miles outside of Machrie; just follow the "Historic Scotland" sign pointing the way. The ground is boggy, so go prepared. ⊕ *www.stonesofwonder.com.*

HORSEBACK RIDING

Cairnhouse Riding Centre. Even novices can enjoy a guided ride on a mount from the center. ⊠ *A841, 2 miles south of Machrie, Blackwaterfoot* ☎ *01770/860466* ⊕ *www.cairnhousestables.com.*

SHOPPING

Old Byre Showroom. This shop sells sheepskin goods, hand-knit sweaters, leather goods, and rugs. ⊠ *Auchencar Farm, A841, 2 miles north of Machrie, Auchencar* ☎ *01770/840227* ⊕ *www.oldbyre.co.uk.*

EN ROUTE Continuing south to Blackwaterfoot, you can return to Brodick via the String Road: from the Kinloch Hotel, head up the hill. As you drive, there are more fine views of the granite complexities of Arran's hills: gray-notched ridges beyond brown moors and, past the watershed, a vista of Brodick Bay.

LOCHRANZA

11 miles north of Brodick.

The road from Blackwaterfoot to Lochranza exposes another face of Arran: muddy, rocky beaches line one side, while the other has views of the sweeping slopes up to Goatfell and Caisteal Abhail (2,735 feet), whose stark granite peaks dominate the skyline of the north of the island. The variety of birdlife here is striking, which is why ornithologists flock to Arran in the off-season.

Arran's only distillery, the sparkling Isle of Arran Distillery, is in Lochranza, nestled in the hills overlooking Lochranza Bay.

GETTING HERE AND AROUND

Lochranza is 11 miles north of Brodick via the A841.

EXPLORING

Lochranza Castle. This ruined castle is quite picturesque—you'll often see deer grazing nearby or seals swimming in the bay. The ground-floor rooms and a few upstairs can be visited during the summer months. This is said to have been the landing place of Robert the Bruce when he returned from Rathlin Island in 1307 to start the campaign that won Scotland's independence. A sign indicates where you can pick up the key to get in. ⊠ *Off A841* ☎ *0131/668–8800* ⊕ *www.historic-scotland. gov.uk* ⊠ *Free* ☉ *Apr.–Sept., daily 9:30–5:30.*

8

WHERE TO STAY

⚇ **Apple Lodge.** A charming whitewashed building that once served as a pastor's house, Apple Lodge sits beneath the hills at the edge of Lochranza. **Pros:** lovely setting on the outskirts of Lochranza; charming gardens. **Cons:** dinner not always available; no children under 12; credit cards not accepted. ⑤ *Rooms from: £78* ⊠ *A841* ☎ *01770/830229* ⊕ *www.applelodgearran.co.uk* ⟳ *4 rooms* ⊟ *No credit cards* ⊘ *Closed mid-Dec.–mid-Jan.* ⑩ *Breakfast.*

ISLAY AND JURA

Islay has a character distinct from that of the rest of the islands that make up the Hebrides. In contrast to areas where most residents live on crofts (small plots generally worked by people in their spare time), Islay's western half in particular has large, self-sustaining farms. Many of the island's wildlife preserves, historical sites, and beautiful beaches are also on the western side of the island. It's dangerous to swim at the coastal beaches, but the white-sand beaches around Loch Indaal are safe and clean. The southeast, by contrast, is mainly an extension of the island of Jura's inhospitable quartzite hills. Islay is particularly known for its birds, including the rare chough (a crow with red legs and beak) and, in winter, its barnacle geese. Several distilleries produce Islay's characteristically peaty malt whiskies, and most welcome visitors. They charge a fee for tours, which you can usually credit toward any whisky purchases.

Although it's possible to meet an Islay native in a local pub, such an event is less likely on Jura, given the island's one road, one distillery, one hotel, and six sporting estates. In fact, you have a better chance of bumping into one of the island's red deer, which outnumber the human population by at least 20 to 1. The island is more rugged than Islay, with its profiles of the Paps of Jura, a hill range at its most impressive when basking in the rays of a west-coast sunset.

BOWMORE

On Islay: 11 miles north of Port Ellen.

Compact Bowmore is a good base for touring because it's central to Islay's main routes. Sharing a name with the whisky made in the distillery by the shore, Bowmore is a tidy town, its grid pattern having been laid out in 1768 by the local landowner Daniel Campbell, of Shawfield. Main Street stretches from the pier head to the commanding parish church, built in 1767 in an unusual circular design—so the devil could not hide in a corner.

GETTING HERE AND AROUND

Flybe flights from Glasgow to Islay take 40 minutes; the airport is 5 miles north of Port Ellen. The trip by CalMac ferry from Kennacraig to Port Ellen takes about 2½ hours; ferries also travel less frequently to Port Askaig. From Port Ellen you'll need to travel 10 miles on the A846 to reach Bowmore; drivers should use caution during the first mile out of Port Ellen, as the road is filled with sharp turns. The rest of the route is straight but bumpy, because the road is laid across peat bog. The ferry to Feolin on Jura departs from Port Askaig; the crossing takes five minutes.

Bus service is available on the island through Islay Coaches and Royal Mail; comprehensive time-tables are available from the tourist information center.

ESSENTIALS

Air Travel Contact Glenegedale Airport ⊠ *A846, Glenegadale, Albania* ☎ *01496/302022* ⊕ *www.hial.co.uk.*

Visitor Information
Bowmore Information Centre
⊠ *The Square* ☎ *08707/200617*
⊕ *www.visitscotland.com.*

THE WHISKY COAST

Scotland likes trails for travelers, whether castles or whiskies are being pursued. The country's dramatic west coast, from the Isle of Skye in the north to Islay and Arran in the south, has plenty of distinguished distilleries. The **Whisky Coast** (⊕ *www.whiskycoast.co.uk*) is a consortium of distilleries, hotels, restaurants, golf courses, and tour operators created to make planning a trip around the area easier. The website is one starting point if you're dreaming of touring this part of the country in search of the perfect dram.

EXPLORING

Bowmore Distillery. Whisky lovers can tour this 1779 distillery, which has an appealing spot near the water's edge. The more expensive Craftsman's Tour, costing £45 per person, is best for those who fancy themselves experts. Tours must be booked in advance. ⊠ *School St.* ☎ *01496/810671* ⊕ *www.bowmore.com* 🖼 *£6 tour* ☉ *Visitor center Easter–June, Mon.–Sat. 9–5; July–Sept., Mon.–Sat. 9–5, Sun. noon–4; Oct.–Easter, Mon.–Sat. 9–noon. Tours: Easter–Aug., Mon.–Sat. at 10, 11, 2, and 3; Sept.–Easter, weekdays at 10:30 and 3; Sat. at 10.*

Islay Woollen Mill. In a wooded hollow by the river, this mill has a fascinating array of machinery that proud owners Gordon and Sheila Covell will be happy to show you. A shop sells high-quality products that were woven on the premises. All the tartans and tweeds worn in the film *Braveheart* were woven here. ⊠ *A846, 3 miles outside Bridgend* ☎ *01496/810563* ⊕ *www.islaywoollenmill.co.uk* 🖼 *Free* ☉ *Mon.–Sat. 10–5.*

WHERE TO EAT

$$$ ✕**Harbour Inn.** The cheerfully noisy bar of this harborside inn is fre-
SEAFOOD quented by off-duty distillery workers who are happy to rub elbows with travelers and exchange island gossip; the superb restaurant has expansive views over the water and serves morning coffee, lunch, and dinner. Menus highlight local lobster, crab, and prawns, as well as island lamb and beef. If you can't bear to leave, the inn's bedrooms are bright and contemporary, with simple wood or velvet-upholstered furniture. $ *Average main: £22* ⊠ *The Square, Bowmore* ☎ *01496/810330* ⊕ *www.harbour-inn.com.*

8

Islay and Jura

ATLANTIC OCEAN

Colonsay
Scalasaig
Oronsay
Kinuachdrach
Lealt
Jura
Ardlussa
Loch Tarbert
Lagg
Nave Island
Paps of Jura
Sound of Islay
Kilnave
Loch Gruinart
Port Askaig
Finlaggan
Loch Finlaggan
Feolin Ferry
Small Isles Bay
Loch Gorm
B807B B8017
A847
Loch Indaal
Islay Woollen Mill
Craighouse
Machir Bay
Port Charlotte
Bridgend
Kennacraig
Rhinns of Islay
A847
Bowmore
Islay
Loch Caolisport
Sound of Jura
Portnahaven
Laggan Bay
A846
Kildalton Cross
Isle of Gigha
Kintyre
Port Wemyss
Kintra
Ardbeg
Sound of Gigha
The Oa
Port Ellen
Mull of Oa

KEY
⊢—⊣ Rail Lines
⛴ Ferry
✈ Airport

0 —— 10 miles
0 —— 10 kilometers

PORT CHARLOTTE

On Islay: 11 miles west of Bowmore.

A delightful conservation village (meaning an area of architectural or historical interest) at the head of Loch Indaal on Islay, Port Charlotte is home to the Museum of Islay Life, the charming Natural History Trust, and safe, sandy beaches.

GETTING HERE AND AROUND

To reach Port Charlotte from Bowmore, take the A846 via Bridgend and then the A847, Portnahaven Road. Islay Coaches and Royal Mail buses also travel here from Bowmore.

EXPLORING

Museum of Islay Life. A converted church is home to this local museum, a haphazard but authentic collection of local artifacts, photographs, and memorabilia. There is also a local history archive. ⊠ *A847* ☎ *01496/850358* ⊕ *www.islaymuseum.org* 🖅 *£3* ⊗ *Apr.–Oct., Mon.–Sat. 10–5.*

FAMILY **Natural History Visitor Centre.** With its exhibits about the island's wildlife, the Natural History Visitor Centre has lots of hands-on activities for kids. It's a great stop on rainy days, and tickets are valid for a week. On Monday and Friday there are nature rambles, and family activities are offered on July and August. ⊠ *Main St.* ☎ *01496/850288* ⊕ *www.islaynaturalhistory.org* ☜ *£3* ⊘ *May–Oct., daily 10–4.*

Rhinns of Islay. South of Port Charlotte, the A847 continues along the wild landscape of the Rhinns of Islay. The road ends at **Portnahaven** and its twin, **Port Wemyss**, where pretty white cottages built in a crescent around the headland belie the harsh lives of the fisher families who live and work here. Return to Port Charlotte via the bleak, unclassified road that loops north and east, passing by the recumbent stone circle at Coultoon and the ruined chapel at Kilchiaran along the way. The strange whooping sound you may hear as you turn away from Portnahaven comes from Scotland's first wave-powered generator, sucking and blowing as it supplies electricity for both villages. It's well worth the climb down to the shore to see it in action.

WHERE TO STAY

$$$
HOTEL

🏨 **Port Charlotte Hotel.** Once a row of fishermen's cottages and with views over a sandy beach, this whitewashed Victorian hotel has been lovingly restored. **Pros:** beautiful location; lovely restaurant; views over the water. **Cons:** slightly expensive; rooms are quite small; can be a little noisy from the bar. ⑤ *Rooms from: £190* ⊠ *Main St.* ☎ *01496/850360* ⊕ *www.portcharlottehotel.co.uk* ☜ *10 rooms* ⑩ *Breakfast.*

PORT ELLEN

On Islay: 11 miles south of Bowmore.

Islay's sturdy community of Port Ellen was founded in the 1820s, and much of its architecture dates from the following decades. It has a harbor (ferries stop here), a few shops, and a handful of inns. The road traveling east from Port Ellen (the A846 to Ardbeg) passes three top distilleries and makes a pleasant afternoon's "whisky walk." All three distilleries offer tours, but you should call ahead for an appointment; there may be no tours on weekends at times.

GETTING HERE AND AROUND

It is likely that Port Ellen will be your port of arrival on Islay. From here you can travel north to Bowmore, along the A846 before turning northwest towards Bridgend and Port Askaig.

EXPLORING

Kildalton Cross. About 8 miles northeast of Port Ellen is one of the highlights of Scotland's Celtic heritage. After passing through a pleasantly rolling, partly wooded landscape, take a narrow road (it's signposted "Kildalton Cross") from Ardbeg. This leads to a ruined chapel with surrounding kirkyard, in which stands the finest carved cross anywhere in Scotland: the 8th-century Kildalton Cross. Carved from a single slab of epidiorite rock, the ringed cross is encrusted on both sides with elaborate designs in the style of the Iona school. The surrounding grave slabs date as far back as the 12th and 13th centuries. ⊕ *www.historic-scotland.gov.uk.*

Lagavulin Distillery. The whisky produced here is certainly distinctive—it has the strongest peaty scent (the mark of Islay whisky) of all the island malts. At 10:30 on Tuesday and Thursday are special

8

ISLAY'S WHISKIES

In terms of population, Islay has more whisky distilleries than anywhere else in the world—in a region with just 1,200 people, there are now nine major producers. These distilleries are never far from the sea, and visits almost always take you through some spectacular scenery.

Which of the local whiskies you prefer depends of your fondness for the distinctive scent of peat, the boggy material used for fertilizers and fires and whose smoke tints the island's air. The distilleries on the southeast coast of the island—including Laphroaig, Lagavulin, and Ardbeg—have the strongest taste of peat.

You're allowed to add a little water when you enjoy a dram. The western distilleries—such as Bowmore, Bunnahabhain, and Bruichladdich—have that characteristic peaty scent, but they are lighter and more flowery because they are often matured in sherry barrels.

Each of the distilleries offers basic tours for a few pounds and more expensive specialized tours geared toward whisky connoisseurs. These include reasonably priced taster tours, where you sample several top-notch whiskies, to more expensive tours that let you sip whiskies that are available nowhere else.

warehouse tours; call ahead to reserve this and other tours. ⊠ *A846* ☎ *01496/302400* ⊕ *www.malts.com* ✉ *£6; warehouse tours £15* ⏱ *Jan.–Apr., Nov., and Dec., weekdays 9–12:30; May, June, Sept., and Oct., weekdays 9–5, Sat. 9–12:30; July and Aug., weekdays 9–7, Sat. 9–5, Sun. 12:30–4:30.*

Laphroaig Distillery. The whisky produced here is one of the most unusual in the Western Isles, with a tangy, peaty, seaweed-and-iodine flavor. The visitor center is free, and a basic tour costs £5. Call ahead for these and more expensive tour options. The distillery is a little less than a mile from Port Ellen. ⊠ *A846* ☎ *01496/302418* ⊕ *www.laphroaig.com* ✉ *£5* ⏱ *Mar.–Oct., weekdays 9:45–5:30, weekends 10–4; Nov.–Feb., daily 9:45–4:30.*

Oa Peninsula. The southern Oa Peninsula, west of Port Ellen, is a region of caves that's rich in smuggling lore. At its tip, the Mull of Oa, is a monument recalling the 650 men who lost their lives in 1918 when the British ships *Tuscania* and *Otranto* sank nearby. Bring good, strong walking shoes.

SPORTS AND THE OUTDOORS

GOLF **Machrie Golf Links.** This course would be a lot more crowded if it were a little more accessible. It was designed in 1891, and except for minor changes in the 1970s, has changed little. Watch out for the sand dunes! ⊠ *Off A846, 4 miles from Port Ellen* ☎ *01496/302310* ⊕ *www.machrie. net* ✉ *Green fee: £65* 🏌 *18 holes, 5894 yds, par 71.*

HORSEBACK **Ballivicar Pony Trekking.** The company leads horseback-riding trips on
RIDING nearby beaches and into the surrounding countryside. ⊠ *Ballivicar Farm, off A846* ☎ *01496/302251.*

PORT ASKAIG

On Islay: 11 miles northeast of Bowmore.

Serving as the ferry port for Jura and receiving ferries from Kenna-craig, Port Askaig is a mere cluster of cottages. Uphill, just outside the village, a side road travels along the coast, giving impressive views of Jura on the way. There are distilleries near here, too; make appointments for tours.

GETTING HERE AND AROUND

Traveling from Bowmore, you can reach Port Askaig (where the road ends) via A846. The village is also served by local buses.

EXPLORING

Bunnahabhain Distillery. Established in 1881, the Bunnahabhain (pronounced Boon-a-hain) Distillery sits on the shore, with great water views. This is one of the milder single malts on Islay. You can upgrade to a more elaborate tour when you reserve ahead. ⊠ *A846* ☎ *01496/ 840646* ⊕ *www.bunnahabhain.com* ✉ *£6* ☉ *Mar.–Oct., weekdays 10–4:30; tours at 10:30, 1:30, and 3:15.*

WHERE TO STAY

$$
B&B/INN
Kilmeny Country House. This luxurious bed-and-breakfast is on a 300-acre farm. **Pros:** elegant and quiet; great breakfast. **Cons:** easy to miss; up a farm road. ⑤ *Rooms from: £125* ⊠ *A846, Ballygrant* ☎ *01496/840668* ⊕ *www.kilmeny.co.uk* ⇢ *4 rooms* ⑩ *Breakfast.*

JURA

5 mins by ferry from Port Askaig.

The rugged, mountainous landscape of the island of Jura—home to only about 200 people—looms immediately east of Port Askaig, across the Sound of Islay. Jura has only one single-track road (the A846), which begins at Feolin, the ferry pier. It climbs across moorland, providing scenic views of the island's most striking feature, the Paps of Jura, three beastlike rounded peaks. The ruined Claig Castle, on an island just offshore, was built by the Lords of the Isles to control the Sound.

Jura House lies between Feolin and Craighouse, the island's only village, some 8 miles away (its walled gardens are open to the public for part of the year). Jura's solitude attracted George Orwell to the remote farmhouse at Barnhill, where he completed his famous novel *1984*.

GETTING HERE AND AROUND

The Port Askaig–Feolin car ferry takes five minutes to cross the Sound of Islay. Bus service is also available from Craighouse and Inverlussa.

EXPLORING

Isle of Jura Distillery. The community of Craighouse has the island's only distillery, producing malt whisky since 1810. Phone ahead to reserve your place on a tour. ⊠ *A846* ☎ *01496/820385* ⊕ *www.isleofjura.com* ✉ *Free* ☉ *Apr.–Sept, weekdays10–4, Sat. 10–2; tours weekdays at 11 and 2. Oct.–Mar., weekdays 11–2; tour at 11.*

8

Kinuachdrach. The settlement of Kinuachdrach once served as a crossing point to Scarba and the mainland. To get to Kinuachdrach after crossing the river at Lealt, follow the track beyond the surface road for 5 miles. The coastal footpath to Corryvreckan lies beyond, over the bare moors. This area has several enticements: the first is the house at **Barnhill** (not open to the public) where George Orwell wrote *1984*; the second, for wilderness enthusiasts, is the whirlpool of the **Gulf of Corryvreckan**, where Orwell nearly drowned. And then there is the unspoiled coastal scenery.

WHERE TO STAY

$ **⛆ Jura Hotel.** In spite of its monopoly on Jura, this hotel has a lot going
HOTEL for it, including great views, a handy location, and pleasant gardens. **Pros:** good views across the bay; spacious rooms; next door to distillery. **Cons:** room decor is tired, to say the least; you may have to share a bathroom. ⑤ *Rooms from: £95* ⊠ *A846, Craighouse* ☎ *01496/820243* ⊕ *www.jurahotel.co.uk* ⇆ *17 rooms, 11 with bath* ⑩ *Breakfast.*

ISLE OF MULL AND IONA

Though its economy has historically been built on agriculture, fishing, and whisky distilling, today the Isle of Mull relies on tourism dollars—which makes sense, because there are many wonderful things to see here. The landscapes range from the pretty harbor of Tobermory and the gentle slopes around Dervaig to the dramatic Atlantic beaches on the west. In the south, the long road past the sweeping green slopes of the Ross of Mull leads to Iona, a year-round attraction.

GETTING HERE AND AROUND

Ferries to Mull are run by the ubiquitous Caledonian MacBrayne. Its most frequent car-ferry route to Mull is from Oban to Craignure (45 minutes). Two shorter routes are from Lochaline on the Morvern Peninsula to Fishnish (15 minutes), or Kilchoan (on the Adrnamurchan Peninsula) to Tobermory (15 minutes). These ferries do not accept reservations, and the Lochaline ferry does not run on Sunday. Bowman's Coaches serves the east coast, running between Tobermory, Craignure, and Fionnphort (for the ferry to Iona).

CRAIGNURE

On Mull: 40-min ferry crossing from Oban, 15-min ferry crossing to Fishnish (5 miles northwest of Craignure) from Lochaline.

Craignure, little more than a pier and some houses, is close to the well-known Duart Castle. Reservations for the year-round ferries that travel from Oban to Craignure are advisable in summer. The ferry from Lochaline to Fishnish, just northwest of Craignure, does not accept reservations and does not run on Sunday.

Iona, Mull and the Smaller Isles

KEY

⊢•••⊣ Rail Lines

🚢 Ferry

GETTING HERE AND AROUND

The arrival point for the 40-minute ferry crossing from Oban, Craignure is the starting point for further travel on Mull northwest toward Salen and Tobermory, or toward Fionnphort and the Iona ferry to the southwest.

ESSENTIALS

Visitor Information Craignure Information Centre ⊠ *The Pierhead* ☎ *01680/812377* ⊕ *www.visitscotland.com.*

EXPLORING

Duart Castle. The 13th-century Duart Castle stands dramatically atop a cliff overlooking the Sound of Mull. The ancient seat of the Macleans, it was ruined by the Campbells in 1691 but restored by Sir Fitzroy Maclean in 1911. Inside you can visit the dungeons and state rooms, then climb the keep for a view of the waterfront. Below are the rocks where the *Swan,* a vessel sent by Oliver Cromwell to kindnap the 10-year-old clan chief, sank in 1653. Nearby stands the **Millennium Wood,** planted with groups of Mull's indigenous trees. To reach Duart by car, take the A849 and turn left around the shore of Duart Bay. From Craignure's ferry port, there is a direct bus that takes you to the castle in about 10 minutes. ⊠ *A849, 3 miles southeast of Craignure* ☎ *01680/812309* ⊕ *www.duartcastle.com* 🎫 *£5.75* ⊘ *May–mid-Oct., daily 10:30–5:30.*

WHERE TO STAY

$

B&B/INN

Craignure Inn. This 18th-century drovers inn, in a whitewashed building a short walk from the ferry pier, has a lively bar that often hosts local musicians. **Pros:** lively bar scene; hearty local food; expansive views. **Cons:** live music can get loud; bar can get very busy. $ *Rooms from: £82* ✉ *A849, near the ferry pier* ☎ *01680/812305* ⊕ *www.craignure-inn.co.uk* ⤳ *3 rooms* ❍❙ *Breakfast.*

DERVAIG

On Mull: 27 miles northwest of Craignure, 60 miles north of Fionnphort.

A pretty riverside village, Dervaig has a circular, pointed church tower that is reminiscent of the Irish-Celtic style of the 8th and 9th centuries. The Bellart is a good trout- and salmon-fishing river, and Calgary Bay, 5 miles away, has one of the best beaches on Mull.

GETTING HERE AND AROUND

You can reach Dervaig from Craignure via the A849. From Salen, take the B8073, and from Tobermory, take the B8073.

EXPLORING

Old Byre Heritage Centre. At this museum an audiovisual presentation on the history of the region is one of the highlights. The tearoom's wholesome fare, particularly the homemade soup, is a boon to travelers, as is the craft shop. You'll see signs for the center on the B8073, just before Dervaig. ✉ *Off B8073* ☎ *01688/400229* ⊕ *www.old-byre.co.uk* ⤳ *£4* ⊘ *Easter–Oct., Wed.–Sun. 10:30–6:30; last admission at 5:30.*

TOBERMORY

5 miles northeast of Dervaig, 21 miles north of Craignure.

Fodor'sChoice

★

Founded as a fishing station, Tobermory is now a lively tourist center and a base for exploring Mull. The town is famous for its crescent of brightly painted houses around the harbor.

GETTING HERE AND AROUND

The most frequent service to Mull is via the Oban-Craignure ferry. Tobermory is 21 miles from Craignure along the A849/848 (via Salen). Bowman's Coaches runs services between Tobermory and Craignure.

ESSENTIALS

Visitor Information Mull Information Centre ✉ *Pierhead, Craignure* ☎ *01680/812377* ⊕ *www.visitscotland.com.*

WHERE TO EAT AND STAY

$$

SEAFOOD

Fodor'sChoice

★

Café Fish. This restaurant's location has certainly contributed to its success—it's perched on the pier at the end of Tobermory. The owners pride themselves on the freshness of their fish; they have their own boat and bring in their own seafood each day. The fish is served simply, grilled with a slice of lemon, to let the natural flavors speak for themselves. Diver-harvested scallops are served with vermouth and orange juice over rice. Other popular dishes include fish stew and the langoustines and squat lobster (not really a lobster—it's related to crab) served with garlic butter and granary bread. $ *Average main:*

£17 ⊠ The Pier ☎ 01688/301253 ⊕ www.thecafefish.com ⚱ Reservations essential ⊘ Closed Jan.–mid-Mar.

$$
HOTEL
🏨 **Highland Cottage.** Set on the hill above the harbor, this family-run hotel prides itself on its elegant rooms and its imaginative dishes in the dining room. **Pros:** comfortable hotel; attentive owners; high-quality dining. **Cons:** rooms are a bit small; no children under 10. *⑤ Rooms from: £150 ⊠ Breadalbane St. ☎ 01688/302030 ⊕ www.highlandcottage. co.uk ⤢ 6 rooms ⑩ Breakfast.*

$
HOTEL
🏨 **Tobermory Hotel.** Made up of five former fishermen's cottages, this lodging on Tobermory's waterfront has a warm, intimate feel. **Pros:** adorable cottage setting with fireplace; toys for children. **Cons:** small rooms; small bathrooms. *⑤ Rooms from: £98 ⊠ Main St. ☎ 01688/302091 ⊕ www.thetobermoryhotel.com ⤢ 18 rooms ⊘ Closed Nov.–Mar. ⑩ Breakfast.*

$$
HOTEL
🏨 **Western Isles Hotel.** This grand hotel from the Victorian era looks down on Tobermory from its wonderful location overlooking the Sound of Mull; it suffered a period of neglect, but is now being refurbished and restored to its former elegance. **Pros:** the view is brilliant; spacious public rooms; great food. **Cons:** outmoded plumbing; occasional lack of hot water; still being renovated. *⑤ Rooms from: £150 ⊠ Off B882 ☎ 01688/302012 ⊕ www.westernisleshotel.co.uk ⤢ 26 rooms ⑩ Breakfast.*

THE ARTS

Mull Theatre. The renowned Mull Theatre, founded in 1966, once prided itself on being the smallest theater in the United Kingdom. Today it has grown in size and in stature, and its productions tour not only the islands, but the whole of Scotland. It's wise to book ahead. *⊠ Druimfin, Salen Rd. ☎ 01688/302828 ⊕ www.mulltheatre.com.*

EN ROUTE
Between Craignure and Fionnphort at the end of the Ross of Mull, the double-lane road narrows as it heads southwest, touched by sea inlets at Lochs Don and Spelve. Inland, vivid grass and high rock faces in Glen More make gray and green the prevalent hues. These stepped-rock faces reach their highest point in Ben More, the only island *munro* (a Scottish mountain more than 3,000 feet high) outside Skye. Stay on the A849 for a pleasant drive the length of the Ross of Mull, a wide promontory with scattered settlements. The National Trust for Scotland cares for the rugged stretch of coast, known as the Burg. The A849 eventually ends in a long parking lot opposite the houses of Fionnphort.

IONA

5 mins by ferry from Fionnphort (Mull), which is 36 miles west of Craignure.

The ruined abbey on Iona gives little hint that this was once one of the most important Christian religious centers in the land. The priceless Book of Kells (now in Dublin) was illustrated here, and it was the monks of Iona who spread Christian ideas across Scotland and the north. The abbey was founded in the year 563 by the fiery and argumentative Columba (circa 521–97) after his expulsion from Ireland.

Until the 11th century, many of Scotland's kings and rulers were buried here, their tombstones still visible inside the abbey. While few visitors venture beyond the pier and the abbey, there are several tranquil paths.

GETTING HERE AND AROUND

Caledonian MacBrayne's ferry from Fionnphort departs at regular intervals throughout the year (£4.50 round-trip). Timetables are available on the Caledonian MacBrayne website. Note that cars are not permitted; there's a parking lot by the ferry at Fionnphort.

EXPLORING

Fodor's Choice ★ **Iona Abbey.** Overseen by St. Columba, who traveled here from Ireland, Iona was the birthplace of Christianity in Scotland in the 6th century. It survived repeated Norse sackings before falling into disuse around the time of the Reformation. Restoration work began at the beginning of the 20th century. Today the restored buildings serve as a spiritual center under the jurisdiction of the Church of Scotland. Guided tours by the Iona Community, an ecumenical religious group, begin every half hour in summer and on demand in winter. ⊠ *Isle of Iona* ☎ *01681/700793* ⊕ *www.iona.org.uk* ☛ *£7.10* ☉ *Apr.–Sept., daily 9:30–5:30; Oct.–Mar., daily 9:30–4:30.*

WHERE TO STAY

$$ **St. Columba Hotel.** Rooms in this 1846 manse are very simply deco-
HOTEL rated, but all those on the front have glorious views across the Sound of Iona to Mull. **Pros:** it's all about what's good for the earth and soul; nice log fires; Wi-Fi throughout the hotel. **Cons:** no TVs; basic decor. $ *Rooms from: £146* ⊠ *Next to cathedral, about ¼ mile from the ferry pier* ☎ *01681/700304* ⊕ *www.stcolumba-hotel.co.uk* ☛ *27 rooms* ☉ *Closed Nov.–Mar.* ⦿| *Breakfast.*

SHOPPING

Iona Community Shop. The shop carries Celtic-inspired gift items, as well as sheet music, songbooks, and CDs. It also sells local crafts and the Wild Goose publications of the Iona Community. ⊠ *Across from Iona Abbey* ☎ *01681/700404* ⊕ *www.iona.org.uk.*

Old Printing Press Bookshop. Iona has a few pleasant surprises for shoppers, the biggest of which is the Old Printing Press Bookshop, an excellent antiquarian bookstore. ⊠ *Beside St. Columba Hotel* ☎ *01681/700699.*

THE SMALLER ISLANDS

The smaller islands, sometimes known as the Southern Hebrides, may seem quite remote but were once important centers of power and production. Successively depopulated by force or by emigration to Glasgow's industries or the promise of the Americas, the islands still survive on fishing, cattle and sheep raising, and, of course, whisky production. Their Gaelic language is vibrant once again, but their populations remain small. For the visitor, the experience is one of open, often barely populated landscapes and a slightly brooding sense of history.

TIREE

4-hr sail from Oban, via Coll.

Archaeological sites and good surfing make this windy island popular in summer.

GETTING HERE AND AROUND

Caledonian MacBrayne runs ferries to Tiree via Coll, four times a week (Tuesday, Thursday, Saturday, and Sunday). You can also fly here from Glasgow on Flybe or from Oban on Hebridean Air Services. On Tiree the Royal Mail postbus (which carries mail and passengers) runs an infrequent service around the island; there is a shared taxi service (☎ 01879/220311), which you should book ahead of your arrival. An alternative is to rent a bike from **Skerryvore House** (☎ 01879/220268).

ESSENTIALS

Air Travel Contact Tiree Airport ⊠ *Off B8065, Tiree* ☎ *01879/220456* ⊕ *www.hial.co.uk.*

EXPLORING

Tiree. A fertile, low-lying island with its own microclimate, Tiree is windswept, but has more hours of sunshine per year than any other part of the British Isles. Long, rolling Atlantic swells make it a favorite with surfers, and summer visitors can raise the population to the nearly 4,500 it supported in the 1830s. Among Tiree's several archaeological sites are a large boulder near Vaul covered with more than 50 Bronze Age cup marks, and an excavated *broch* (stone tower) at Dun Mor Vaul. It has one hotel and is served by the Calmac ferry from Oban. ⊕ *www.isleoftiree.com.*

COLL

3-hr sail from Oban.

Good birding and a number of ancient sites are among the attractions on Coll.

GETTING HERE AND AROUND

Caledonian MacBrayne runs ferries to Coll on Tuesday, Thursday, Saturday, and Sunday. You can also fly here from Oban on Hebridean Air Services. There is no public transportation on Coll, but you can rent a bike (☎ *01879/230333*) or use the island's one taxi (☎ *01879/230402*).

8

EXPLORING

Coll. Unlike their neighbors in nearby Tiree, Coll's residents were not forced to leave the island in the 19th century. Today half of the island's sparse population lives in its only village, Arinagour. Its coasts offer extraordinarily rich birdlife, particularly along the beautiful sandy beaches of its southwest. Coll is even lower lying than Tiree but also rockier and less fertile. The island is rich in archaeology, with standing stones at Totronald, a cairn at Annagour, and the remains of several Iron Age forts around the island. The keep of Breachacha Castle, a former stronghold of the Maclean clan on the south end of Coll, dates back to 1450. It is not open to the public, but you may view it from the road near Uig. ⊕ *www.visitcoll.co.uk.*

COLONSAY

2½-hr sail from Oban.

Less bleak than Coll and Tiree, Colonsay is one of Scotland's quietest, most unspoiled, and least populated islands. It is partly wooded, with a fine quasi-tropical garden at Colonsay House and a great variety of wildlife.

GETTING HERE AND AROUND

Caledonian MacBrayne ferries run to Colonsay on Monday, Wednesday, Friday, and Sunday. The island of Oronsay lies half a mile away and can be reached at certain times across a natural causeway. There is a limited postbus service on Colonsay; bikes can be rented from **A. McConnel** (☎ *01951/200355*).

EXPLORING

Colonsay. Colonsay is one of Scotland's quietest, most unspoiled, and least populous islands. The beautiful beach at Kiloran Bay is an utterly peaceful place even at the height of summer. The standing stones at Kilchattan Farm are known as Fingal's Limpet Hammers. Fingal, or Finn, MacCoul is a warrior of massive size and strength in Celtic mythology. Standing before the stones, you can imagine Fingal wielding them like hammers to cull equally large limpets from Scotland's rocky coast. The island's social life revolves around the bar at the 19th-century Colonsay Hotel, 100 yards from the ferry pier. The adjacent island of Oronsay with its ruined cloister can be reached at low tide via a 1½-mile wade across a sandy sound. ⊕ *www.colonsay.org.uk.*

Oronsay. The island of Oronsay, beside Colonsay, can be reached at low tide, at the expense of wet legs, in a 1½-mile wade across a sandy sound separating the two islands (after which an intake of reviving malt whisky never tastes better). Mesolithic shell mounds show the island was populated from before 4,000 BC, though only a handful of people live here now. The cloister ruins of a formerly rich and influential 14th-century Augustinian priory, including a stone cross, are well worth the paddle. ⊕ *www.colonsay.org.uk.*

AROUND THE GREAT GLEN

Updated by
Jack Jewers

Defined by its striking topography, the Great Glen brings together mountains and myths, history and wild nature— then lets you wash it all down with a dram of the world's finest whisky. The views from almost every twist and bend in the circuitous roads are enough to snatch the breath from your gaping mouth. There's also plenty here for history buffs: this is where you'll find Culloden Moor, where the last battle fought on British soil ended the hopes of the tragically outgunned Jacobite rebels in 1746.

The Great Glen Fault runs diagonally through the highlands of Scotland and was formed when two tectonic plates collided, shoving masses of the crust southwest toward the Atlantic Ocean. Over time the rift broadened into a glen, and a thin line of lochs now lies along its seam. The most famous of these is deep, murky Loch Ness, home to the elusive Loch Ness monster.

The city of Inverness has a growing reputation for excellent restaurants, and from here nearly everything in the Great Glen is an easy day trip. Just south of the city the 13th-century ruined Urquhart Castle sits on the shores of the Loch Ness. In Fort Augustus, the Caledonian Canal joins Inverness to Fort William via a series of 29 locks. At the western end of the canal, Ben Nevis, Britain's highest mountain, rises sharply. The Nevis Range, like Cairngorm National Park to the east, is ideal for walking, climbing, and mountain biking through the hills and glens.

Fort William makes a good base for exploring Glencoe, an awe-inspiring region that was also the scene of another notoriously murky episode in Scottish history: the Glencoe Massacre of 1692. It's an area where history seems to be imprinted on the landscape, and it remains desolate, with some of the steepest, most atmospheric hills in Scotland.

Just north of Fort William the Road to the Isles offers impressive coastal views. The small isles of Rum and Eigg create a low rocky skyline across the water. Near the start of this road lies Glenfinnan, where in 1745 Bonnie Prince Charlie rallied his Jacobite troops. The surrounding Morayshire coast is home to a more pastoral landscape, and 14th-century Cawdor Castle and its gardens have an opulent air. Nearby Brodie Castle has an awe-inspiring library and art collection.

Impressive long, sandy beaches stretch out along the coast from the towns of Nairn and Findhorn. Finally, the Malt Whisky Trail begins in Forres and follows the wide, fast River Spey south until it butts against the Cairngorm Mountains and the old Caledonian forests, with their diverse and rare wildlife.

TOP REASONS TO GO

Castles, fortresses, and battlefields: Hear stories of the Highland people and famous figures like Bonnie Prince Charlie, and absorb the atmosphere of castles and battlefields, at Culloden Moor, Cawdor and Brodie castles, Fort George, and Glencoe.

Hill walking and outdoor activities: The Great Glen is renowned for its hill walking. Some of the best routes are around Glen Nevis, Glencoe, and on Ben Nevis, the highest mountain in Britain. It's not just hiking: Glenmore Lodge in the Cairngorms offers everything from kayaking to mountain biking to ice climbing.

Wild landscapes and rare wildlife: Spot rare plants and beasts including tiny least willow trees and golden eagles in the near-arctic tundra of Cairngorms National Park.

Whisky tours: The two westernmost distilleries on the Malt Whisky Trail are in Forres. Benromach is the smallest distillery in Moray and has excellent tours; Dallas Dhu is preserved as a museum. You can strike out from here to nearby distilleries in Speyside.

Boat trips: There are many ferries to the small isles (or to Skye) from Arisaig and Mallaig. You can also go Nessie-watching on Loch Ness or hire a small boat and travel the Caledonian Canal.

ORIENTATION AND PLANNING

GETTING ORIENTED

If Inverness is the center point of a compass, the Great Glen spreads out to the east, south, and west. To the east stretches the Morayshire coast, populated with castles, distilleries, and beaches. Head southeast and you hit the Cairngorm National Park and other nature preserves. The A82 heads south from Inverness, hugging the west side of Loch Ness. Nearby are the contemplative ruins at Urquhart Castle and the interesting locks of the Caledonian Canal. Farther southwest, Fort William can be a good base for day trips to the foreboding and steep mountain pass of Glencoe.

Inverness and Environs. From the small city of Inverness, just about anywhere in the Great Glen is a day trip. Spend your days exploring Culloden Moor, Brodie Castle, or Cawdor Castle. There are long, walkable beaches at Nairn and Findhorn.

Speyside and the Cairngorms. Speyside is best known for its whisky distilleries, and those who enjoy a good dram often follow the Whisky Trail. In and around the Cairngorms there are mountains, lochs, rivers, and dozens of cycling and walking paths that make it tailor-made for outdoors enthusiasts.

Loch Ness, Fort William, and Environs. Have a go trying to spot Nessie from the banks of Loch Ness. For something wilder, base yourself at Fort William and take in the spectacular scenery of Glencoe and Glen Nevis. If you dare, climb Britain's highest peak, Ben Nevis. The Road to the Small Isles, known for larger-than-life figures both old (the Bonnie Prince) and new (Harry Potter), has classic views across water to rocky islands perched on blue seas.

PLANNING

WHEN TO GO

Late spring to early autumn is the best time to visit the Great Glen. If you catch good weather in summer, the days can be glorious. Unfortunately summer is also when you will encounter midges (tiny biting insects: keep walking, as they can't move very fast). Winter can bring a damp chill, gusty winds, and snow-blocked roads, although many Scots value the open fires and the warming whisky that make the off-season so appealing.

PLANNING YOUR TIME

The Great Glen is an enormous area that can easily be broken into two separate trips. The first would be based in or near Inverness, allowing an exploration of Speyside, the Cairngorms, Cawdor and Brodie castles, and perhaps a few whisky distillery tours. The second moves through the cloud-laden Glencoe and down through the moody Rannoch Moor, or toward the Road to the Isles; you could stay near Glencoe or in Fort William.

For those with more time, a trip around the Great Glen could be combined with forays north into the Northern Highlands, east toward Aberdeen and the rest of the Malt Whisky Trail, southeastward to the Central Highlands, or south to Argyll.

GETTING HERE AND AROUND

AIR TRAVEL

Inverness Airport has flights from London, Edinburgh, and Glasgow. Domestic flights covering the Highlands and islands are operated by easyJet and Flybe. Fort William has bus and train connections with Glasgow, so Glasgow Airport can be a good access point.

BUS TRAVEL

A long-distance Scottish Citylink service connects Glasgow and Fort William. Inverness is also well served from the central belt of Scotland. Discount carrier Megabus (book online to avoid phone charges) has service to Inverness from various cities.

Traveling around the Great Glen area without a car is challenging. Stagecoach Highland serves the Great Glen and around Fort William. A number of postbus services will help get you to the more remote corners of the area.

Bus Contacts Megabus ☎ *0900/160–0900* ⊕ *www.megabus.com.* **Royal Mail Post Buses** ☎ *0845/7740740* ✎ *www.royalmail.com.* **Scottish Citylink** ☎ *0871/266–3333* ⊕ *www.citylink.co.uk.* **Stagecoach Highlands** ☎ *01463/233371* ⊕ *www.stagecoachbus.com.*

CAR TRAVEL

As in all areas of rural Scotland, a car is a great asset for exploring the Great Glen, especially because the best of the area is away from the main roads. You can use the main A82 from Inverness to Fort William, or use the smaller B862/B852 roads to explore the much quieter east

Around the Great Glen

0 — 10 miles
0 — 10 km

Inverness and Environs

Moray Firth

Findhorn
Nairn
Forres
Inverness
Grantown-on-Spey
Drumnadrochit
Boat of Garten
Aviemore
Fort Augustus
Invergarry
Kingussie
Isle of Skye
Cuillin Sound
Mallaig
Arisaig
Glenfinnan
Fort William
Salen
Glencoe
Ballachulish

Speyside and the Cairngorms

Loch Ness, Fort William, and Environs

side of Loch Ness. Mallaig, west of Fort William, is reached via a new road, but there are still a few narrow and winding single-lane roads, which require slower speeds and concentration.

In the Great Glen the best sights are often hidden from the main road, which is an excellent reason to favor peaceful rural byways and to avoid as much as possible the busy A96 and A9, which carry much of the traffic in the area.

TRAIN TRAVEL

ScotRail has connections from London to Inverness and Fort William (including overnight sleeper service), as well as reliable links from Glasgow and Edinburgh. There's train service between Glasgow (Queen Street) and Inverness, via Aviemore, which gives access to the heart of Speyside.

Although there's no rail connection among towns within the Great Glen, this area has the West Highland Line, which links Fort William to Mallaig. This train, run by ScotRail, remains the most enjoyable way to experience the rugged hills and loch scenery between these two places. The Jacobite Steam Train is an exciting summer (mid-May to mid-October) option on the same route.

Train Contacts Jacobite Steam Train ☎ *0844/850–4685*
⊕ *www.westcoastrailways.co.uk.* **ScotRail** ☎ *0845/755–0033*
⊕ *www.scotrail.co.uk.*

RESTAURANTS

Inverness, Aviemore, and Fort William have plenty of cafés and restaurants in all price ranges. Inverness has particularly diverse dining options. Outside the towns there are many country-house hotels serving superb meals. *Prices in the reviews are the average cost of a main course at dinner or, if dinner is not served, at lunch.*

HOTELS

In the Great Glen towns have a range of accommodations ranging from cozy inns to expansive hotels; in more remote areas your choice will usually be limited to smaller establishments. Because this is an established vacation area, you should have no trouble finding a room for a night; however, the area is quite busy in the peak season and the best places book up early. In Inverness, you may find it more appealing to stay outside the city center or in the nearby, pretty countryside. *Prices in the reviews are the lowest cost of a standard double room in high season, including 20% V.A.T.*

TOURS

Inverness Tours runs the occasional boat cruise but is mainly known for tours around the Highlands in well-equipped vehicles, which are led by expert guides and heritage enthusiasts. James Johnstone, a personal guide, is based in Inverness but will drive you anywhere; he has a particularly good knowledge of the Highlands and islands, including the Outer Isles.

Tour Contacts Inverness Tours ☎ *01667/455699* ⊕ *www.invernesstours.com.*
James Johnstone ☎ *01463/798372* ⊕ *www.jajcd.com.*

VISITOR INFORMATION

Aviemore, Fort William, and Inverness have year-round tourist offices. Other tourist centers, open seasonally, include those at Fort Augustus, Grantown-on-Spey, Kingussie, Mallaig, and Nairn.

Visitor Information Visit Highlands ⊕ *www.visithighlands.com.*

INVERNESS AND ENVIRONS

At the center of this region is Inverness, a small but appealing city that makes a useful gateway to the Great Glen. It has an increasingly good range of restaurants and accommodations, but its cultural offerings remain more or less limited to what is happening at Eden Court and the live music at a few good pubs.

East of Inverness, the infamous Culloden Moor still looks desolate on most days, and you can easily imagine the fierce, brief, and bloody battle that took place here in 1746 that ended in final, catastrophic defeat for the Jacobites and their quest to restore the exiled Stuarts to the British throne. Because Jacobite tales are interwoven with landmarks throughout this entire area, you will get much more out of this storied landscape if you first learn something about this thorny but colorful period of Scottish history. The Morayshire coast boasts many long beaches and some refined castles (Cawdor and Brodie) that are definitely worth a visit. Moving east along the inner Moray Firth, you might be tempted by Benromach distillery in Forres, a taste of what you can find farther south if you follow the Malt Whisky Trail.

Inverness and Environs

INVERNESS

176 miles north of Glasgow, 109 miles northwest of Aberdeen, 161 miles northwest of Edinburgh.

The city makes a great base for exploring the region, and you can fan out in almost any direction from Inverness for interesting day trips: east to Moray and the distilleries near Forres, southeast to the Cairngorms, and south to Loch Ness. Compared with other Scottish towns, though, Inverness has less to offer visitors with a keen interest in Scottish history. Throughout its past the town was burned and ravaged by Highland clans competing for dominance.

GETTING HERE AND AROUND

You can easily fly into Inverness Airport, as there are daily flights from London, Bristol, Birmingham, Manchester, and Belfast. However, there are also easy train and bus connections from Glasgow Airport. Scottish Citylink has service here, and Megabus has long-distance bus service from Edinburgh and Glasgow. ScotRail runs trains here from London, Edinburgh, Glasgow, and other cities.

Once you're here, you can explore much of the city on foot. A rental car makes exploring the surrounding area much easier. But if you don't have a car, there are bus and boat tours from the city center to a number of places in the Great Glen.

An unusual option from Inverness is a day trip to Orkney. John o'Groats Ferries runs day tours from Inverness to Orkney, daily from May through September. They cost £28 round-trip.

ESSENTIALS

Airport Contact Inverness Airport ⊠ *Dalcross* ☎ *01667/464000* ⊕ *www.hial.co.uk/inverness-airport.*

Boat Contact John o'Groats Ferries ☎ *01955/611353* ⊕ *www.jogferry.co.uk.*

Bus Contact Inverness Coach Station ⊠ *Margaret St.* ☎ *01463/233371.*

Visitor Information Inverness ⊠ *Castle Wynd* ☎ *01463/252401* ⊕ *www.inverness-scotland.com.*

EXPLORING

Fort George. After the fateful battle at Culloden, the nervous government in London ordered the construction of a large fort on a promontory reaching into the Moray Firth. Fort George was started in 1748 and completed some 20 years later. It's one of the best-preserved 18th-century military fortifications in Europe. The on-site Highlanders Museum gives you a glimpse of the fort's history. The fort is 14 miles northeast of Inverness. ⊠ *Old Military Rd., Ardersier* ☎ *01667/460232* ⊕ *www.historic-scotland.gov.uk* ⊡ *£8.90* ☉ *Apr.–Sept., daily 9:30–5:30; Oct.–Mar., daily 10–4:30; last admission 45 mins before closing.*

Inverness Castle. One of Inverness's few historic landmarks is reddish sandstone Inverness Castle (now the local Sheriff Court), nestled above the river off Castle Road on Castle Hill. The current structure is Victorian, built after a former fort was blown up by the Jacobites in the 1745 campaign. The castle isn't open to the public, but you are free to wander the grounds. ⊠ *41 Castle St.*

Inverness Dolphin Cruises. With trips by boat from Inverness harbor into the Moray Firth, Inverness Dolphin Cruises offers you the chance to see dolphins in their breeding areas. There are departures daily at 10:30, noon, 1:30, and 3 in summer, though sailing times may be affected by bad weather. Tickets cost £16. In busy times trips to Fort George are also offered for £25. ⊠ *Inverness Marina, Longman Dr.* ☎ *0770/316-8097* ⊕ *www.inverness-dolphin-trips.co.uk.*

FAMILY **Inverness Museum and Art Gallery.** The small but excellent Inverness Museum and Art Gallery covers archaeology, art, local history, and the natural environment in its lively displays. The museum is also home to the Highland Photographic Archive. ⊠ *Castle Wynd* ☎ *01463/237114* ⊕ *www.invernessmuseum.com* ⊡ *Free* ☉ *Tues.–Sat. 10–5.*

WHERE TO EAT

$$ ✕ **Cafe 1.** Locals recommend this restaurant before any other, so it's no
MODERN BRITISH   surprise that a well-dressed and diverse crowd fills the dining room. The decor is refined, with thin-legged metal chairs, laquered wood-topped tables, and Celtic knot mirrors. The menu includes bistro-style dishes

like sea bass with rosemary and garlic polenta chips, or classic Angus steak with peppercorn sauce. The tiny bar at the front has a great view of the castle. ⑤ *Average main: £18* ✉ *75 Castle St.* ☎ *01463/226200* ⊕ *www.cafe1.net.*

$ ✕ **Dores Inn.** Off a pretty country
BRITISH   road on the eastern shore of Loch Ness, this low-slung, white-stone eatery is the perfect place to stop for lunch or dinner. The menu is a combination of well-prepared old favorites—fish-and-chips, perhaps, or neeps and tatties (turnips and potatoes)—together with steaks, lamb, and seafood. It's busy during the summer and on weekends, so book ahead. ⑤ *Average main: £12* ✉ *Off B862, Dores* ☎ *01463/751203* ⊕ *www.thedoresinn.co.uk.*

> ### FISHING
>
> The Great Glen is laced with rivers and lochs where you can fly-fish for salmon and trout. The fishing seasons are as follows: salmon, from early February through September or early October (depending on the area); brown trout, from March 15 to September 30; sea trout, from May through September or early October; rainbow trout year-round. Sea angling from shore or boat is also possible. Tourist centers can provide information on locations, permits, and fishing rights.

$ ✕ **Riva.** Facing Inverness Castle, Riva has views over the River Ness
PIZZA   from its window seats. The dining room has subtly lighted deep-red walls lined with black-and-white photographs of Italian cityscapes. Tasty Italian dishes include pasta carbonara (with eggs, cream, and pancetta), as well as more unusual concoctions like tagliatelle with smoked salmon and a tomato cream sauce. There is a separate pizzeria upstairs from the main dining room. ⑤ *Average main: £14* ✉ *4–6 Ness Walk* ☎ *01463/237377* ⊕ *www.rivarestaurant.co.uk* ☽ *No lunch Sun.*

$$$ ✕ **Rocpool Restaurant.** Highly recommended by locals, the Rocpool has a
BRASSERIE   frequently changing menu of modern bistro classics, with a few modern twists. Main dishes could include sea bream fillet with a roasted pepper salad, or lamb cutlets with polenta cakes. The early evening menu is excellent value. ⑤ *Average main: £20* ✉ *1 Ness Walk* ☎ *01463/717274* ⊕ *www.rocpoolrestaurant.com* ☽ *Closed Sun.*

WHERE TO STAY

There are many places to stay in Inverness, but if your goal is to explore the countryside, a hotel outside the center may be a good choice.

$ ▥ **Avalon.** A 20-minute walk from the city center, this neat and modern
B&B/INN   B&B is a rare find. **Pros:** friendly and well-run; good-size rooms. **Cons:** slightly far outside the city; minimum stay on some dates. ⑤ *Rooms from: £75* ✉ *79 Glenarquhart Rd.* ☎ *01463/239075* ⊕ *www.inverness-loch-ness.co.uk* ➳ *6 rooms* ⦿ *Breakfast.*

$ ▥ **Bluebell House.** Each room at Bluebell House has sturdy oak furnish-
B&B/INN   ings, including a downstairs bedroom with a full-curtained four-poster bed and a curved chaise lounge. **Pros:** large rooms; decadent furnishing; great hosts. **Cons:** smallish bathrooms. ⑤ *Rooms from: £90* ✉ *31 Kenneth St.* ☎ *01463/238201* ⊕ *www.bluebell-house.com* ➳ *4 rooms* ⦿ *Breakfast.*

9

$$$
HOTEL

Bunchrew House Hotel. This 17th-century Baronial mansion, its turrets reflected in a glassy lake, looks like something from a Scottish fairytale. **Pros:** beautiful setting; atmospheric building; good restaurant. **Cons:** some rooms could do with refurbishment. $ *Rooms from: £165* ⊠ *Of A862, about 3 miles west of Inverness* ☎ *01463/234917* ⊕ *www.bunchrew-inverness.co.uk* ↝ *16 rooms* ⦿| *Breakfast.*

$
B&B/INN

Moyness House. Scottish author Neil M. Gunn (1891–1973), known for short stories and novels that evoke images of the Highlands, such as *Morning Tide, Highland River, and Butcher's Broom,* once lived in this lovely Victorian villa. **Pros:** relaxing interiors; lovely garden; great location near the river. **Cons:** public rooms a bit fussy for some; books up quickly. $ *Rooms from: £80* ⊠ *6 Bruce Gardens* ☎ *01463/233836* ⊕ *www.moyness.co.uk* ↝ *6 rooms* ⦿| *Breakfast.*

$
B&B/INN

Strathness House. Standing on the banks of the River Ness, this 12-room guesthouse is a quick walk from the well-regarded Eden Court Theatre and the rest of the attractions of the city center. **Pros:** overlooks the river; close to the city center; free Wi-Fi. **Cons:** parking can be difficult. $ *Rooms from: £80* ⊠ *4 Adross Terr.* ☎ *01463/232765* ⊕ *www.strathnesshouse.com* ↝ *12 rooms* ⦿| *Breakfast.*

$$
B&B/INN

Trafford Bank. A 15-minute walk from downtown Inverness, this delightful little B&B is the perfect place to base yourself. **Pros:** welcoming atmosphere; stylish rooms; relaxing vibe. **Cons:** rooms on the small side. $ *Rooms from: £110* ⊠ *96 Fairfield Rd.* ☎ *01463/241414* ⊕ *www.traffordbankguesthouse.co.uk* ↝ *5 rooms* ⦿| *Breakfast.*

NIGHTLIFE AND THE ARTS

BARS AND
LOUNGES

Blackfriars Pub. Blackfriars Pub prides itself on its cask-conditioned ales. You can enjoy one to the accompaniment of regular live entertainment including jazz nights and *ceilidhs* (a traditional mix of country dancing, music, and song). ⊠ *93–95 Academy St.* ☎ *01463/233881* ⊕ *www.blackfriarshighlandpub.co.uk.*

Hootenany. Hootenany is an odd combination of Scottish pub, concert hall, and Thai restaurant. The excellent pub has a warm atmosphere and serves food that comes highly recommended by locals. ⊠ *67 Church St.* ☎ *01463/233651* ⊕ *www.hootanannyinverness.co.uk.*

THEATER

Eden Court Theatre. The varied program at this popular local theater includes films, music, comedy, ballet, and even pantomime. Check out the art gallery and the bright café, and take a walk around the magnificent Bishop's Palace. ⊠ *Bishops Rd.* ☎ *01463/234234* ⊕ *www.eden-court.co.uk.*

GOLF

Fodor's Choice
★

Castle Stuart Golf Links. Opened in 2009, this course overlooking the Moray Firth is already considered one of Scotland's finest, hosting the Scottish Open in 2011. Expect undulating fairways and extensive bunkers that test your mettle. The 210-yard 17th hold provides perilous cliff-top play; the wind can defeat the canniest player. The art deco–inspired clubhouse provides stunning views of the water. ⊠ *B9039* ☎ *01463/796111* ⊕ *www.castlestuartgolf.com* 🏌 *Green fee: May–Oct., £175; Apr. and Nov., £130* ⅄ *18 holes, 6553 yds, par 72* ☉ *Apr.–Nov., daily.*

Inverness Golf Club. Established in 1883, Inverness Golf Club welcomes visitors to its parkland course 1 mile from downtown. Overlooking the Beauly Firth, it's a tree-lined course that requires a good deal of accuracy. ⊠ *Culcabock Rd.* ☎ *01463/239882* ⊕ *www.invernessgolfclub.co.uk* ✉ *Green fee: £18–£42* ⅄. *18 holes, 6256 yds, par 69.*

Torvean Golf Course. This municipal course has one of the longest par-5 holes (565 yards) in the north of Scotland. There are quite a few water hazards, including the Caledonian Canal. ⊠ *Glenurquhart Rd.* ☎ *01463/225651* ⊕ *www.torveangolfclub.co.uk* ✉ *Green fee: £30 weekdays, £37 weekends* ⅄. *18 holes, 5784 yds, par 68.*

SHOPPING

Although Inverness has the usual indoor shopping malls and department stores, the most interesting goods are in the specialty outlets in and around town.

BOOKSTORES **Leakey's Secondhand Bookshop.** This shop claims to be the biggest secondhand bookstore in Scotland. When you get tired of leafing through the 100,000 or so titles, climb to the mezzanine café and study the cavernous church interior. Antique prints and maps are housed on the balcony. ⊠ *Greyfriars Hall, Church St.* ☎ *01463/239947* ⊙ *Closed Sun.*

CLOTHING **Duncan Chisholm and Sons.** This shop specializes in Highland dress and tartans. Mail-order and made-to-measure services are available. ⊠ *47–51 Castle St.* ☎ *01463/234599* ⊕ *www.kilts.co.uk.*

GALLERIES **Castle Gallery.** The excellent Castle Gallery sells contemporary paintings, sculpture, prints, and crafts. It also hosts frequently changing exhibitions by up-and-coming artists. ⊠ *43 Castle St.* ☎ *01463/729512* ⊕ *www.castlegallery.co.uk.*

Riverside Gallery. The Riverside Gallery sells paintings, etchings, and prints of Highland landscapes, as well as abstract and representational contemporary work by Highland artists. ⊠ *11 Bank St.* ☎ *01463/224781* ⊕ *www.riverside-gallery.co.uk.*

LOCAL SPECIALTIES **Maya Belgian Chocolates.** Chocoholics will feel like they've died and gone to heaven in this small, glass-fronted shop. The exquisite chocolates and truffles are made by Fabienne de Mulder, who was trained in Belgium. ⊠ *5 Strothers La.* ☎ *01463/419201* ⊕ *www.mayachocolates.co.uk.*

Moniack Castle. At Moniack Castle you can buy wines made with unusual Scottish ingredients, such as birch sap. The company also makes jams, marmalade, and other preserves. ⊠ *A862, 7 miles west of Inverness, Kirkhill* ☎ *01463/831283.*

SHOPPING CENTER **Victorian Market.** Don't miss the colorful Victorian Market, built in 1870. The atmospheric indoor space houses more than 40 privately owned specialty shops. ⊠ *Academy St.* ☎ *01463/724273.*

9

CULLODEN MOOR

8 miles east of Inverness.

Culloden Moor was the scene of the last battle fought on British soil—and to this day its name is enough to invoke raw and tragic feelings in Scotland. Austere and windswept, it's also a place of outstanding natural beauty.

GETTING HERE AND AROUND

Driving along the B9006 from Inverness is the easiest way to Culloden Moor, and there's a large car park to handle many visitors. Local buses also run from Inverness to the battlefield.

EXPLORING

Clava Cairns. Not far from Culloden, on a narrow road southeast of the battlefield, are the Clava Cairns, dating from the Bronze Age. In a cluster among the trees, these stones and monuments form a large ring with underground passage graves that are reached via a tunnel. Helpful placards put everything into historical context. ⊠ *B851, Culloden* 🎫 *Free* ⊙ *Open 24 hrs.*

Fodor's Choice **Culloden Moor.** Here, on a cold April day in 1746, the hopelessly out-
★ gunned Jacobite forces of Bonnie Prince Charlie were destroyed by King George II's army. The victorious commander, the duke of Cumberland (George II's son), earned the name of the "Butcher" of Cumberland for the bloody reprisals carried out by his men on Highland families, Jacobite or not, caught in the vicinity. In the battle itself, the duke's army—greatly outnumbering the Jacobites—killed up to 2,000 soldiers. (The victors, by contrast, lost just 50). The National Trust for Scotland has re-created a slightly eerie version of the battlefield as it looked in 1746 that you can explore with a guided audio tour. An innovative visitor center enables you to get closer to the sights and sounds of the battle and to interact with the characters involved. Academic research and technology have helped re-create the Gaelic dialect, song, and music of the time. There's also a good on-site café. ⊠ *B9006, Culloden* 🖀 *0844/4932159* ⊕ *www.nts.org.uk/Culloden* 🎫 *£10* ⊙ *Apr., May, Sept., and Oct., daily 9–5:30; June–Aug., daily 9–6; Nov.-late Dec., Feb., and Mar. daily 10–4.*

NAIRN

12 miles east of Culloden Moor, 17 miles east of Inverness, 92 miles west of Aberdeen.

This once-prosperous fishing village has something of a split personality. King James VI (1566–1625) once boasted of a town so large the residents at either end spoke different languages. This was a reference to Nairn, whose fisherfolk, living by the sea, spoke Lowland Scots, whereas its uptown farmers and crofters spoke Gaelic. Nearby is Nairn Castle, loaded with history. East of Nairn pier is a long beach, great for a stroll.

GETTING HERE AND AROUND

A car gives you the most flexibility, but Nairn is close to Inverness (via B9006/B9091), and regular local buses serve the town.

Bonnie Prince Charlie

His life became the stuff of legends. Charles Edward Louis John Casimir Silvester Maria Stuart—better known as Bonnie Prince Charlie, or the Young Pretender—was born in Rome in 1720. The grandson of ousted King James II of England, Scotland, and Ireland (King James VII of Scotland) and son of James Stuart, the Old Pretender, he was the focus of Jacobite hopes to reclaim the throne of Scotland. Charles was charming and attractive, and he enjoyed more than the occasional drink.

In 1745 Charles led a Scottish uprising to restore his father to the throne. He sailed to the Outer Hebrides with only a few men but with promised support from France. When that support failed to arrive, he sought help from the Jacobite supporters, many from the Highland clans, who were faithful to his family. With 6,000 men behind him,

Charles saw victory in Prestonpans and Falkirk, but the tide turned when he lied to his men about additional Jacobite troops waiting south of the border. When these fictitious troops did not materialize, his army retreated to Culloden where, on the April 16, 1746, they were massacred.

Charles escaped to the Isle of Benbecula where he met and is rumored to have fallen in love with Flora MacDonald. After he had hidden there for a week, Flora dressed him as her maid and brought him to sympathizers on the Isle of Skye. They helped him escape to France.

Scotland endured harsh reprisals from the government after the rebellion. As for Charles, he spent the rest of his life in drunken exile, taking the title count of Albany. In 1772 he married Princess Louise of Stolberg-Gedern, only to separate from her eight years later. He died a broken man in Rome in 1788.

EXPLORING

9

FAMILY
Fodor's Choice
★

Cawdor Castle. Shakespeare's Macbeth was the Thane of Cawdor (a local officer of the crown), but the sense of history that exists within the turreted walls of Cawdor Castle is certainly more than fictional. Cawdor is a lived-in castle, not an abandoned, decaying structure. The earliest part is the 14th-century central tower; the rooms contain family portraits, tapestries, fine furniture, and paraphernalia reflecting 600 years of history. Outside the walls are sheltered gardens and woodland walks. Children will have a ball exploring the lush and mysterious Big Wood, with its wildflowers and varied wildlife. There are lots of creepy stories and fantastic tales amid the dank dungeons and drawbridges. If you like it here, the estate has cottages to rent. ⊠ *B9090, 5 miles southwest of Nairn, Cawdor* ☎ *01667/404401* ⊕ *www.cawdorcastle.com* ⊠ *Castle £10; grounds only £5.50* ⊙ *May–early Oct. daily 10–5:30.*

Nairn Museum. The fishing boats have moved to larger ports, but Nairn's historic flavor has been preserved at the Nairn Museum, in a handsome Georgian building in the center of town. Exhibits emphasize artifacts, photographs, and model boats relating to the town's fishing past. A genealogy service is also offered. A library in the same building has a strong local history section. ⊠ *Viewfield House, Viewfield Dr.* ☎ *01667/456791* ⊕ *www. nairnmuseum.co.uk* ⊠ *£3* ⊙ *Apr.–Oct., weekdays 10–4:30, Sat. 10–1.*

WHERE TO STAY

$$$$
B&B/INN
Fodor's Choice
★

🔳 **Boath House.** Built in the 1820s, this stunning Regency manor house is surrounded by 20 acres of lovingly nurtured gardens. **Pros:** excellent dining; well-kept grounds; relaxed atmosphere. **Cons:** some airplane noise can puncture the silence. ⑤ *Rooms from: £230* ⊠ *A96, Auldearn* ☎ *01667/454896* ⊕ *www.boath-house.com* 🛏 *8 rooms* ❙❀❙ *Multiple meal plans.*

GOLF

Nairn's courses are highly regarded by golfers and are very popular, so book far in advance.

Nairn Dunbar Golf Club. Founded in 1899, Nairn Dunbar Golf Club is a difficult course with gorse-lined fairways and lovely sea views. ⊠ *Lochloy Rd.* ☎ *01667/452741* 🗐 *Green fee: £50* 🏌 *18 holes, 6765 yds, par 72.*

Nairn Golf Club. Well regarded in golfing circles, the Nairn Golf Club dates from 1887 and is the regular home of Scotland's Northern Open. Huge greens, aggressive gorse, a beach hazard for five of the holes, a steady prevailing wind, and distracting views across the Moray Firth make play on the Championship Course unforgettable. The adjoining 9-hole Cameron course is ideal for a warm-up or a fun round for the family. ⊠ *Seabank Rd.* ☎ *01667/453208* ⊕ *www.nairngolfclub.co.uk* 🗐 *Green fee: Championship £95; Cameron £15* ⚑ *Reservations essential* 🏌 *Championship: 18 holes, 6774 yds, par 72; Cameron: 9 holes, 1634 yds, par 29* ☽ *Daily.*

SHOPPING

Auldearn Antiques. It's easy to spend an hour wandering around an old church filled with furniture, fireplaces, architectural antiques, and linens. The converted farmsteads have tempting antique (or just old) chinaware and textiles. ⊠ *Dalmore Manse, Lethen Rd., 3 miles east of Nairn, Auldearn* ☎ *01667/453087* ⊕ *www.auldearnantiques.co.uk.*

Brodie Countryfare. Visit Brodie Countryfare only if you're feeling flush: you may covet the unusual knitwear, quality designer clothing and shoes, gifts, and toys, but they are *not* cheap. The excellent restaurant, on the other hand, is quite inexpensive. ⊠ *On A96, 6 miles east of Nairn, Brodie* ☎ *01309/641555* ⊕ *www.brodiecountryfare.com.*

FORRES

10 miles east of Nairn.

The burgh of Forres is everything a Scottish medieval town should be, with a handsome tolbooth (the former courthouse and prison) and impressive gardens as its centerpiece. It's remarkable how well the old buildings have adapted to their modern retail uses. With two distilleries—one still operating, the other preserved as a museum—Forres is a key point on the Malt Whisky Trail. Brodie Castle is also nearby. Just 6 miles north you'll find Findhorn Ecovillage and a sandy beach stretches along the edge of the semi-enclosed Findhorn Bay, which is excellent bird-watching territory.

GETTING HERE AND AROUND

Forres is easy to reach by car from Inverness on the A96. Daily ScotRail trains run here from Inverness and Aberdeen.

EXPLORING

Benromach Distillery. The smallest distillery in Moray, Benromach Distiller was founded in 1898. It's now owned by whisky specialist Gordon and MacPhail, and it stocks a vast range of malts. An informative hourly tour ends with a tutored nosing and tasting. ✉ *Invererne Rd.* ☎ *01309/675968* ⊕ *www.benromach.com* 💷 *£5* ☉ *May and Sept., Mon.–Sat. 9:30–5; June–Aug., Mon.–Sat. 9:30–5, Sun. noon–4; Oct.– Dec. and Feb.–Apr., weekdays 10–4; last tour 1 hr before closing.*

Brodie Castle. This medieval castle was rebuilt and extended in the 17th and 19th centuries. Fine examples of late-17th-century plasterwork are preserved in the Dining Room and Blue Sitting Room; an impressive library and a superb collection of pictures extend into the 20th century. The castle is about 24 miles east of Inverness, making it a good day trip. ✉ *Off A96, 2 miles west of Forres, Brodie* ☎ *0844/493–2156* ⊕ *www.nts.org. uk* 💷 *Castle £10, grounds free* ☉ *Grounds daily 10:30–sunset. Castle late Mar., Apr., Sept., and Oct., daily 10:30–4:30; May and June, Sun.–Thurs. 10:30–4:30; July and Aug., daily 10:30–5. Last tour 1 hr before closing.*

Dallas Dhu Historic Distillery. The final port of call on the Malt Whisky Trail, the Dallas Dhu Historic Distillery was the last distillery built in the 19th century. No longer a working distillery, the structure is a small museum that tells the story of Scotland's national drink. ✉ *Mannachie Rd.* ☎ *01309/676548* ⊕ *www.dallasdhu.com* 💷 *£6* ☉ *Apr.–Sept., daily 9:30–5:30; Oct., daily 9:30–4:30; Nov.–Mar., Sat.–Wed. 9:30–4:30.*

Findhorn Ecovillage. This education center is dedicated to developing "new ways of living infused with spiritual values." Drawing power from wind turbines, locals farm and garden to sustain themselves. A tour affords a thought-provoking glimpse into the lives of the ultra-independent villagers. See homes made out of whisky barrels, and the Universal Hall, filled with beautiful engraved glass. The Phoenix Shop sells organic foods and handmade crafts, and the Blue Angel Café serves organic and vegetarian fare. ✉ *The Park, Off B9011, 6 miles from Forres, Findhorn* ☎ *01309/690311* ⊕ *www.findhorn.org* 💷 *Free; tours £5* ☉ *Visitor center May–Sept., weekdays 10–5, weekends 1–4; Oct.–Apr., weekdays 10–5. Tours Apr., Oct., and Nov., Mon., Wed., and Fri. at 2; May–Sept., Fri.–Mon. and Wed. at 2.*

Sueno's Stone. At the eastern end of town stands Sueno's Stone, a 22-foot-tall pillar of stone carved with the ranks of soldiers from some long-forgotten battle. Nobody can quite agree on how old it is or what battle it marked, but it is generally believed to have been erected between 600 and 1000 AD. ✉ *Findhorn Rd.* 💷 *Free* ☉ *Open 24 hrs.*

SPORTS AND THE OUTDOORS

Findhorn Bay. Along the edge of Findhorn Bay you'll find a long stretch of beach, great for an afternoon by the sea. You can reach the beach through the dunes from the northern end of the Findhorn Ecovillage, or park at the edge of the village of Findhorn for a shorter stroll. There are public restrooms, but few other amenities. ✉ *Off B89011, Findhorn.*

SPEYSIDE AND THE CAIRNGORMS

The Spey is a long river, running from Fort Augustus to the Moray Firth, and its fast-moving waters make for excellent fishing at many points along its way. They also give Speyside malt whiskies a softer flavor than those made with peaty island water. The area's native and planted pine forests draw many birds each spring and summer, and people come for miles to see the capercaillies and ospreys.

Defining the eastern edge of the Great Glen, Cairngorms National Park provides sporty types with all the adventure they could ask for, including walking, kayaking, rock climbing, and even skiing, if the winter is cold enough. The park has everything but the sea: craggy mountains, calm lochs, and swift rivers. While the unremarkable town of Aviemore may put off some travelers, the Cairngorms are truly stunning.

BOAT OF GARTEN

6 miles northeast of Aviemore.

In the peaceful village of Boat of Garten, the scent of pine trees mingles with an equally evocative smell—that of steam trains. You can take a nostalgic steam train trip on the Strathspey Steam Railway between Aviemore and Boat of Garden. Close to Cairngorms National Park, Boat of Garten is building a reputation as a great place to stay while exploring the region.

GETTING HERE AND AROUND

This charming town is an easy drive from Inverness or Aviemore via the A9 and the A95 and from Grantown via the B970. It's also serviced by local buses, and some people travel here on the Strathspey Steam Train.

EXPLORING

FAMILY **Landmark Forest Adventure Park.** About 4 miles northwest of Boat of Garten, the Landmark Forest Adventure Park has a fire tower you can climb, a workshop where you can try out the crosscut saw, and a steam-powered sawmill. A handsome Clydesdale horse hauls the logs and poses for photos. Kids enjoy getting lost in the forest maze, riding the terrifyingly steep waterslides, and exploring an adventure playground. You could easily spend half a day here. ■TIP→ **To get to Carrbridge, take the quiet B9153 rather than the crowded A9.** ⊠ *B9153, Carrbridge* ☎ *0800/731–3446* ⊕ *www.landmarkpark.co.uk* ⊡ *£14.30* ⊗ *Late Mar.–mid-July, daily 10–5; mid-July–mid-Aug., daily 10–7; Sept.–late Mar., daily 10–5.*

Loch Garten Osprey Centre. Set in the heart of Abernethy Forest, the Loch Garten Osprey Centre offers a glimpse of the osprey, a large fishing bird that comes here to breed. The reserve, one of the last stands of ancient Scots pines in Scotland, attracts a host of birds, including the bright crossbill and the crested tit. You might also spot the rarely seen red squirrel. The sanctuary is administered by the Royal Society for the Protection of Birds. ⊠ *Off B970, 1 mile east of Boat of Garten, B970* ☎ *01479/831476* ⊕ *www.rspb.org.uk* ⊡ *£4* ⊗ *Apr.–Aug., daily 10–6; last admission 1 hr before closing.*

Speyside and
the Cairngorms

FAMILY **Strathspey Steam Railway.** The oily scent of smoke and steam hangs faintly in the air near the authentically preserved train station in Boat of Garten. Travel in old-fashioned style and enjoy superb views of the high and often white domes of the Cairngorm Mountains. Breakfasts, lunches, and special dinners are served on board from March to mid-September. ⊠ *Boat of Garten Station, Spey Ave.* ☎ *01479/810725* ⊕ *www.strathspeyrailway.co.uk* 🚂 *£13.*

WHERE TO STAY

$$ 🏨 **Mountview Hotel.** An old hunting lodge perched in the hills of **HOTEL** Nethybridge, this hotel boasts great views out over the valley. **Pros:** stunning setting; pretty views; good restaurant. **Cons:** some rooms have separate bathrooms. 💲 *Rooms from: £120* ⊠ *B970, Nethy-bridge* ☎ *01479/821515* ⊕ *www.mountviewhotel.co.uk* 🛏 *12 rooms* 🍽 *Breakfast.*

SHOPPING

Boat of Garten Post Office. Expertly run by Beth and David Woolsey, this local post office and gift shop more than pulls its weight. With fruit, chocolate, cheese, freshly baked breads, and hot pies, it's a great place to stock up for a day hiking in the hills. ⊠ *Dershar Rd.* ☎ *01479/831527* ⊕ *www.boatofgartenpostoffice.co.uk.*

SPORTS AND THE OUTDOORS

BICYCLING **Cairngorm Bike & Hike.** This small, well-stocked shop rents well-maintained bikes, offers a good selection of lightweight backpacks, and has all sorts of outdoor gear—everything you'll need for your biking excursions around the Cairngorms. ⊠ *Boat of Garten Station, Spey Ave.* ☎ *01479/831745* ⊕ *www.cairngormbikeandhike.co.uk.*

Fodor's Choice ★ GOLF **Boat of Garten Golf Club.** This is one of Scotland's greatest "undiscovered" courses. Boat of Garten, which dates to the late 19th century, was redesigned and extended by James Braid in 1932, and each of its 18 holes has a strong Highland feel. Some cut through birch wood and heathery rough, and most have long views to the Cairngorms. An unusual feature is the preserved steam railway that runs alongside part of the course. ⊠ *Nethybridge Rd.* ☎ *01479/831282* ⊕ *www.boatgolf. com* 🏌 *Green fee: weekdays £41; weekends £46* ⛳ *Reservations essential* 🎯 *18 holes, 5876 yds, par 70* ☉ *Daily* ☞ *Facilities: golf carts, pull carts, pro-shop, restaurant, bar.*

> ### THE BOAT IN BOAT OF GARTEN
>
> A ferry that once linked both sides of the River Spey gave its name to Boat of Garten. The first official record of the ferry is in 1662, although it had probably been there longer. The village itself did not appear until the coming of the railway, in 1868, when cottages sprang up between the railway line and the ferry crossing. When it was time to pick a name, the ferry seemed like a good symbol for the locale. Not long after that, bridges were built across the River Spey, and demand for the little ferry disappeared. The name, on the other hand, stuck.

AVIEMORE

6 miles southwest of Boat of Garten, 30 miles south of Inverness.

At the foot of the Cairngorms, the once-quiet Aviemore now has all the brashness and boxiness of a year-round holiday resort. In the summer months it's filled with walkers, cyclists, and rock-climbers, so it's a convenient place for stocking up on supplies. However, many of the smaller villages nearby are quieter places to stay.

■ TIP→ Be forewarned: this region can get very cold above 3,000 feet, and weather conditions can change rapidly, even in the middle of summer.

GETTING HERE AND AROUND

The A9, Scotland's major north–south artery, runs past Aviemore. From Boat of Garten, take the B970. The town is serviced by regular trains and buses from Inverness.

ESSENTIALS

Visitor Information Aviemore Visitor Information Centre ⊠ *7 Grampian Rd.* ☎ *01479/810930* ⊕ *www.visitcairngorms.com.*

EXPLORING

Fodor's Choice ★ **CairnGorm Mountain Railway.** A funicular railway to the top of Cairn Gorm (the mountain that gives its name to the region), the CairnGorm Mountain Railway operates daily, year-round, and affords sweeping

Cairngorms National Park

At the heart of Britain's largest national park (nearly 1,750 square miles of countryside) is a wild arctic landscape that sits on a granite plateau. Five of Scotland's nine 4,000-feet-high mountains are found in this range, and there are 13 more over 3,000 feet. These rounded mountains, including Cairn Gorm (meaning "blue hill" in Gaelic) and Ben Macdui, the second highest in Britain at 4,295 feet, were formed at the end of the last ice age. The Larig Ghru Pass, a stunning U-shape glen, was carved by the retreating glacier.

Hikers, underestimate this landscape at your peril: the fierce conditions often found on the Cairngorms plateau have claimed many lives. Make sure you are well prepared and inform someone of your planned route and estimated return time.

The environment supports rare arctic-alpine and tundra plant and animal species (a full quarter of Britain's endangered species are found here) including flora such as the least willow and alpine blue-sow thistle, and birds such as the ptarmigan, Scottish crossbill, and dotterel. Lower down the slopes, terrain that was once filled with woodland is now characterized by heather, cotton grass, and sphagnum moss. This open expanse allows visitors to glimpse animals such as the golden eagle, roe deer, or red deer.

Fragments of the ancient Caledonian forest (largely Scots pine, birch, and rowan) remain and are home to pine martins, red squirrels, and capercaillie (a large grouse). Studding these forests are dramatic glens and the rivers Spey, Don, and Dee, which are home to Atlantic salmon, otters, and freshwater pearl mussels.

---

views across the Cairngorms and the broad valley of the Spey. At the top is a visitor center and restaurant. The round-trip journey takes about half an hour. Reservations are recommended. ⊠ *B970* ☎ *01479/861261* ⊕ *www.cairngormmountain.co.uk* ⊠ *£10.30* ⊙ *Daily 10:20–4.*

Fodor's Choice ★ **Cairngorms National Park.** A rugged wilderness of mountains, moorlands, glens, and lochs, the sprawling Cairngorms National Park, established in 2003, takes in more than 1,700 square miles. Past Loch Morlich, at the high parking lot on the exposed shoulders of the Cairngorm Mountains, are dozens of trails for hiking and cycling. This is a massive park, encompassing small towns as well as countryside, but a good place to start exploring is the main visitor center in Aviemore. The staff can dispense maps, expert advice on the best trails, and also information on guided walks and other activities. (There are additional Cairngorms visitor centers in Braemar, Glenmore, Ballater, Tomintoul, Newtonmore and Grantown-on-Spey.) Because much of the best scenery in the park is off-road—including ancient pine forests and open moorland—a particularly good way to cover ground in the park is on a pony trek. The **Rothiemurchus Estate** leads guided hacks for riders of all levels of ability. The park is a haven for rare wildlife: a full 25% of Britain's endangered species have habitats in the park. Birding enthusiasts come here to look (and listen) for the Scottish crossbill—the only bird completely unique to Britain. ⚠ **Weather conditions in the park change abruptly, so be sure to bring**

9

cold weather gear, particularly if you plan on hiking long-distance. ⊠ *Visitor Information Centre, Grampian Rd.* ☏ *0845/225–5121* ⊕ *www.cairngorms.co.uk* ⊘ *Mon.–Sat. 9–5, Sun. 10–4.*

FAMILY **Cairngorm Reindeer Centre.** On the high slopes of the Cairngorms you may see the reindeer herd that was introduced here in the 1950s. The reindeer are docile creatures that seem to enjoy human company. Ranger-led visits to the herd are offered at least once a day from February to December, weather permitting. From June to August you can also accompany rangers on gentle half-day treks through the mountains. Bring waterproof gear, as conditions can be wet and muddy. ⊠ *Glenmore Forest Park, B970, 6 miles east of Aviemore* ☏ *01479/861228* ⊕ *www.cairngormreindeer.co.uk* ⊠ *£12* ⊘ *Visitor center Feb.–Dec., daily 10–5. Visits to herd Feb.–Apr. and Sept.–Dec. at 11; May and June at 11 and 2:30; July and Aug. 11, 2:30 and 3:30.*

> ### BIKING THE GLEN
>
> A dedicated bicycle path, created by Scotland's National Cycle Networks, runs from Glasgow to Inverness, passing through Fort William and Kingussie. Additionally, a good network of back roads snakes around Inverness and toward Nairn. The B862/B852, which runs by the southeast side of Loch Ness, has little traffic and is a good bet for cyclists. Stay off the A9, however, as it's busy with vehicular traffic on both sides of Aviemore. The very busy A82 main road, along the northwest bank of Loch Ness via Drumnadrochit, is for the same reason not recommended for cyclists.

WHERE TO EAT

$ ✗ **Mountain Café.** On the main street in Aviemore, the Mountain Café is a
CAFÉ   useful pitstop for a hearty lunch or afternoon snack. It's all-day breakfasts are somewhat famed locally; they also serve good sandwiches, burgers, salads, and the like. Leave room for the cakes, which are made on the premises. There are great views of the Cairngorm mountains from the dining room. The only downside is that service can be a little slow, so you may have to wait for a table. ⑤ *Average main: £9* ⊠ *111 Grampian Rd.* ☏ *01479/812473* ⊕ *www.mountaincafe-aviemore.co.uk* ⊘ *No dinner.*

$$ ✗ **Old Bridge Inn.** Across a pedestrian bridge from Aviemore Station, this
MODERN BRITISH   old-style bar and conservatory restaurant serves what many locals call the best pub food in Aviemore. The simple fare includes local favorites like Shetland halibut or Speyside beef, and the roasted potatoes are recommended as a side for any main dish. The bar serves a wide selection of local brews, and there's often live music playing. Roaring fires are very welcome in a place that can have cool nights anytime of year. ⑤ *Average main: £17* ⊠ *Dalfaber Rd.* ☏ *01479/811137* ⊕ *www.oldbridgeinn.co.uk* ⚹ *Reservations essential.*

SPORTS AND THE OUTDOORS

G2 Outdoor. The wide range of adventures at G2 Outdoor includes white-water rafting, gorge walking, and rock climbing. The company offers a family float trip on the River Spey in summer, and in winter runs ski courses. ⊠ *Dalfaber Industrial Estate, off Dalfaber Dr.* ☏ *01479/811008* ⊕ *www.g2outdoor.co.uk.*

Glenmore Lodge. In Cairngorms National Park, this is a good center for day and residential courses on rock and ice climbing, hiking, kayaking, ski touring, mountain biking, and more. Some classes are aimed at kids over 14. There are superb facilities, such as an indoor climbing wall. ✉ *Signposted on B970, about 5 miles west of Glenmore* ☎ 01479/861256 ⊕ *www.glenmorelodge.org.uk.*

Mikes Bikes. This small bike shop stocks all the gear you might need to take advantage of the many paths around Aviemore. It also rents and repairs bikes. The place is somewhat hard to find, tucked down some stairs below the street. ✉ *Myrtlefield Shopping Centre, Grampian Rd.* ☎ 01479/810478 ⊕ *www.aviemorebikes.co.uk.*

KINGUSSIE

13 miles southwest of Aviemore.

Set in a wide glen, Kinguissie is a pretty town east of the Monadhliadh Mountains. With great distant views of the Cairngorms, it's perfect for those who would prefer to avoid the far more hectic town of Aviemore.

GETTING HERE AND AROUND

From Aviemore, Kingussie is easy to reach by car via the A9 and the A86.

EXPLORING

FAMILY **Highland Folk Museum.** At the Highland Folk Museum you can explore reconstructed Highland buildings, including a Victorian-era schoolhouse, and watch tailors, clockmakers, and joiners demonstrating their trades. Walking paths (or old-fashioned buses) take you to an 18th-century township that includes a feal house, made of turf, and a weaver's house. Throughout the museum there are hands-on exhibitions like a working quern stone for grinding grain, making this a great outing for kids. ✉ *Kinguissie Rd., Newtonmore* ☎ 01540/673551 ⊕ *www.highlandfolk.com* ✉ *Free* ☉ *Late Mar.–Aug., daily 10:30–5:30; Sept. and Oct., daily 11–4:30.*

Ruthven Barracks. Looking like a ruined castle on a mound, Ruthven Barracks is redolent with tales of "the '45" (as the last Jacobite rebellion is often called). The defeated Jacobite forces rallied here after the battle at Culloden, but then abandoned and blew up the government outpost they had earlier captured. You'll see its crumbling, yet imposing stone outline as you approach. ✉ *B970, ½ mile south of Kingussie* ☎ 01667/460232 ⊕ *www.historic-scotland.gov.uk* ✉ *Free* ☉ *Daily 24 hrs.*

WHERE TO EAT AND STAY

$ ✕ **The Potting Shed.** Seasonal fruits and smooth cream top many of the
CAFÉ delectable desserts at this cake shop on Main Street in Kinguissie.
FAMILY Taught by his Norwegian mother, John Borrowman makes sponges
Fodor's Choice that are rich and light and contain no butter or fat (although you can't
★ say the same thing about the rich cream they're topped with). The shop also offers gluten-free options that use almonds in place of flour. An accompanying wide selection of coffees and teas makes this an excellent place to stop and plan your next activity. ⑤ *Average main: £5* ✉ *Main St.* ☎ 01540/651287 ⊕ *www.inshriachnursery.co.uk* ☉ *Closed Tues. and Wed.*

$$

BRITISH

✕ Sili Restaurant. In the Silverfjord Hotel, this glass-walled, crisply decorated restaurant is like a beacon when seen from the outside. The kitchen serves well-made standards like Scottish rib-eye steak. The excellent specials board changes daily, but you might be offered pan-seared duck breast, or perhaps some local seafood—the smoked salmon is a particular specialty. ■ **TIP→ The bar often serves the same food, only slightly cheaper.** The hotel's rooms are inexpensive, but not as bright and pleasing as the restaurant. $ *Average main: £14* ✉ *Silverfjord Hotel, Ruthven Rd.* ☎ *01540/661292* ⊕ *www.silverfjordhotel. co.uk* ☉ *No lunch Mon.–Wed. and Fri.*

$$$$

BRITISH

Fodor'sChoice

★

✕ The Cross at Kingussie. This former tweed mill, with a narrow river running alongside its stone walls, is set in 4 acres of woodlands. The intimate dining room, where the stone walls have been painted a creamy white, is warmed by a crackling fireplace. The fixed-price menus are smart and bold, with dishes such as local lamb with truffle gnocchi, or halibut with samphire and shrimp butter. Each dish reveals an intimate knowledge of textures and flavors. If you like it here so much you don't want to leave, there are also rooms available starting at £100 per night. $ *Average main: £60* ✉ *Tweed Mill Brae, Ardbroilach Rd.* ☎ *01540/661166* ⊕ *www.thecross.co.uk* ☉ *Closed Jan. No dinner Sun. and Mon.*

$

B&B/INN

🏨 Coig Na Shee. This century-old Highland lodge has a warm and cozy atmosphere. **Pros:** excellent rooms; quiet location; great walks from house. **Cons:** a bit out of the way. $ *Rooms from: £70* ✉ *Laggan Rd., Newtonmore* ☎ *01540/670109* ⊕ *www.coignashee.co.uk* 🛏 *5 rooms* ❖| *Breakfast.*

LOCH NESS, FORT WILLIAM, AND ENVIRONS

Compared with other lochs, Loch Ness is by no means known for its beauty, but it draws attention for its famous monster. Heading south from Inverness, you can travel along the loch's quiet east side or the more touristy west side. A pleasant morning can be spent at Urquhart Castle, in the tiny town of Drumnadrochit, or a bit farther south in the pretty town of Fort Augustus, where the Caledonian Canal meets Loch Ness. As you travel south and west, the landscape opens up and the Nevis Range comes into view.

From Fort William you can visit the dark, cloud-laden mountains of Glencoe and the desolate stretch of moors and lochans at Rannoch Moor. Travelers drive through this region to experience the landscape, which changes at nearly every turn. It's a brooding, haunting area that's worth a visit in any season.

The Road to the Isles, less romantically known as the A830, leads from Fort William to the coastal towns of Arisaig, Morar, and Mallaig, with access to the small isles of Rum, Eigg, Canna, and Muck. From here you can also visit the Isle of Skye *(see Chapter 10)* via the ferry at Mallaig.

DRUMNADROCHIT

14 miles south of Inverness.

A tourist hub at the curve of the road, Drumnadrochit is not known for its style or culture, but it attracts plenty of people interested in searching for mythical monsters. There aren't many good restaurants, but there are some decent enough hotels.

GETTING HERE AND AROUND

It's easy to get here from Fort Augustus or Inverness via the A82, either by car or by local bus.

EXPLORING

Jacobite Cruises. The company runs morning and afternoon cruises on Loch Ness to Urquhart Castle and other destinations throughout the region. The harbor is 5 miles northeast of Drumnadochit via the A82. Prices start at about £13. ⊠ *Clansman Harbour, A82* ☎ *01463/233999* ⊕ *www.jacobite.co.uk.*

Loch Ness. From the A82 you get many views of the formidable and famous Loch Ness, which has a greater volume of water than any other Scottish loch, a maximum depth of more than 800 feet, and its own monster—at least according to popular myth. Early travelers who passed this way included English lexicographer Dr. Samuel Johnson (1709–84) and his guide and biographer, James Boswell (1740–95), who were on their way to the Hebrides in 1783. They remarked at the time about the poor condition of the population and the squalor of their homes. Another early travel writer and naturalist, Thomas Pennant (1726–98), noted that the loch kept the locality frost-free in winter. Even General Wade came here, his troops blasting and digging a road up much of the eastern shore. None of these observant early travelers ever made mention of a monster. Clearly, they had not read the local guidebooks.

FAMILY **Loch Ness Centre & Exhibition.** If you're in search of the infamous monster, the Loch Ness Centre & Exhibition documents the fuzzy photographs, the unexplained sonar readings, and the sincere testimony of eyewitnesses. It's said that the loch's huge volume of water has a warming effect on the local weather, making the loch conducive to mirages in still, warm conditions—but you'll have to make up your own mind. Whether the *bestia aquatilis* lurks in the depths is more than ever in doubt since 1994, when the man who took one of the most convincing photos of Nessie confessed on his deathbed that it was a fake. From late spring to early fall you can also take hourly cruises of the loch. ⊠ *On A82* ☎ *01456/450573* ⊕ *www.lochness.com* 🎫 *£7* ⊙ *Easter–June, daily 10–4:15; July and Aug., daily 9:30–6:45; Sept. and Oct., daily 9:30–5:45; Nov.–Easter, daily 10–4:15; last admission 45 min before closing.*

Urquhart Castle. About 2 miles southeast of Drumnadrochit, this castle is a favorite Loch Ness monster–watching spot. This romantically broken-down fortress stands on a promontory overlooking the loch, as it has since the Middle Ages. Because of its central and strategic position in the Great Glen line of communication, the castle has a complex history involving military offense and defense, as well as its own destruction and renovation. The castle was begun in the 13th century and was

9

destroyed before the end of the 17th century to prevent its use by the Jacobites. A visitor center gives an idea of what life was like here in medieval times. ✉ *A82* ☎ *01456/450551* ⊕ *www.historic-scotland.gov. uk/places* 🎫 *£8* ⊗ *Apr.–Sept., daily 9:30–6; Oct., daily 9:30–5; Nov.– Mar., daily 9:30–4:30; last admission 45 mins before closing.*

WHERE TO STAY

$$$
B&B/INN
Fodor's Choice
★

🖼 **Loch Ness Lodge.** Run by siblings Scott and Iona Sutherland, Loch Ness Lodge is an exquisite place: opulent, classy, and welcoming. **Pros:** excellent staff; superb views; lovely rooms. **Cons:** near a busy road; no restaurant. ⑤ *Rooms from: £210* ✉ *A82, Brachla* ☎ *01456/459469* ⊕ *www.loch-ness-lodge.com* 🛏 *7 rooms* ⏸*Some meals.*

EN ROUTE

A more leisurely alternative to the fast-moving traffic on the busy A82, and one that combines monster-spotting with peaceful road touring, is to take the **B862** south from Inverness and follow the east bank of Loch Ness. Take the opportunity to view the waterfalls at Foyers and the peaceful, reedy Loch Tarff. Descend through forests and moorland until the road runs around the southern tip of Loch Ness. The half-hidden track beside the road is a remnant of the military road built by General Wade.

FORT AUGUSTUS

19 miles south of Drumnadrochit, 33 miles south of Inverness, 31 miles northeast of Fort William.

The best place to see the locks of the Caledonian Canal is at Fort Augustus, at the southern tip of Loch Ness. This bustling small town is a great place to begin walking and cycling excursions, or to sit by the canal watching the locks fill and empty as boats sail between Loch Ness to Loch Laggan.

Fort Augustus itself was captured by the Jacobite clans during the 1745 Rebellion. Later the fort was rebuilt as a Benedictine abbey, but the monks no longer live here.

GETTING HERE AND AROUND

Fort Augustus is an easy drive from Inverness or Invergarry on the A82. Buses run frequently, as this is a busy tourist destination.

EXPLORING

Caledonian Canal. The canal, which links the lochs of the Great Glen— Loch Lochy, Loch Oich, and Loch Ness—owes its origins to a combination of military and political pressures that emerged at the time of the Napoleonic Wars with France. In short: British needed a better and faster way to move naval vessels from one side of Scotland to the other. The great Scottish engineer Thomas Telford (1757–1834) surveyed the route in 1803. The canal, which took 19 years to complete, has 29 locks and 42 gates. Telford ingeniously took advantage of the three lochs that lie in the Great Glen, which have a combined length of 45 miles, so that only 22 miles of canal had to be constructed to connect the lochs and complete the waterway from coast to coast. Along and the canal stunning vistas open up: mountains, lochs, and glens, and to the south, the profile of Ben Nevis. At the small but engaging visitor

Loch Ness, Fort William, and Environs

KEY
Rail Lines
Ferry

center in Fort Augustus you can learn all about this historic engineering feat, and take a picturesque walk along the towpath. ✉ *Ardchattan House, Canalside* ⊕ *www.scottishcanals.co.uk* ◷ *Visitor center: Apr.–Oct., 10–1:30 and 2–5:30.*

Clansman Centre. In a handsome Victorian building, the Clansman Centre is a small museum full of stirring tales about life in this region. The gift shop sells Celtic jewelry, traditional Highland garb, and ceremonial armor. ✉ *Canalside* ☎ *01320/366444* ⊕ *www.scottish-swords.com.*

OFF THE BEATEN PATH

Creag Meagaidh Nature Reserve. A stretch of the A86, quite narrow in some places, hugs the western shore of Loch Laggan. It has superb views of the mountainous heartlands to the north, and, over the silvery spine of hills known as the Grey Corries, culminates with views of Ben Nevis to the south. In summertime the reserve is a nesting ground for peregrine falcons and golden eagles. Halfway along the loch is the Creag Meagaidh Nature Reserve, a sublime picnic spot and a good base for walks into the restored woodland below the spectacular ice-carved crags of Coire Ardair. There are basic facilities like parking lots and restrooms, but no visitor center. ✉ *Off A86, Kinloch Laggan* ☎ *01528/544265* ⊕ *www.nnr-scotland.org.uk/creag-meagaidh* 🎟 *Free* ◷ *Open 24 hrs.*

WHERE TO STAY

$$
HOTEL
Fodor$Choice
★

🏨 **Glengarry Castle Hotel.** Tucked away in Invergarry, this rambling baronial mansion is just south of Loch Ness and within easy reach of the Great Glen's most popular sights. **Pros:** atmospheric building and gardens; good-value takeout lunches; family rooms available. **Cons:** no elevator. 💲 *Rooms from: £124* ✉ *On A82, Invergarry* ☎ *01809/501254* ⊕ *www.glengarry.net* 🛏 *26 rooms* ◷ *Closed mid-Nov.–mid-Mar.* ⊙ *Breakfast.*

FORT WILLIAM

16 miles north of Glencoe, 69 miles southwest of Inverness, 108 miles northwest of Glasgow, 138 miles northwest of Edinburgh.

As its name suggests, Fort William originated as a military outpost, first established by Oliver Cromwell's General Monk in 1655 and refortified by George I (1660–1727) in 1715 to help combat an uprising by the turbulent Jacobite clans. It remains the southern gateway to the Great Glen and the far west. It's not Scotland's most charming or authentic town, but it's got several good hotels and makes a convenient base for exploring the surrounding countryside.

GETTING HERE AND AROUND

From Glasgow (to the south) and Inverness (to the north), the A82 takes you the entire way. From Edinburgh, take the M9 to the A84. This empties into the A85, which connects to the A82 that takes you to Fort William. Roads around Fort William are well maintained, but mostly one lane in each direction. They can be very busy in summer.

A long-distance Scottish Citylink bus connects Glasgow and Fort William. ScotRail has trains from London, as well as connections from Glasgow and Edinburgh. It also operates a train service three times a day between Fort William and Mallaig.

ESSENTIALS

Visitor Information Fort William Tourist Imformation Centre ☒ *15 High St.* ☎ *01397/701801* ⊕ *www.visitscotland.com.*

EXPLORING

Ben Nevis. The tallest mountain in the British Isles, 4,406-foot Ben Nevis looms over Fort William, less than 4 miles from Loch Linnhe. A trek to its summit is a rewarding experience, but you should be fit and well prepared—food and water, map and compass, first-aid kit, whistle, hat, gloves, and warm clothing (yes, even in summer) for starters—as the unpredictable weather can make it a hazardous hike. Ask for advice at the local tourist office before you begin.

Fodor'sChoice
★
Jacobite Steam Train. The most relaxing way to take in the landscape of birch- and bracken-covered wild slopes is by rail. The best ride is on the Jacobite Steam Train, a famously scenic 84-mile round-trip that runs between Fort William and Mallaig. You'll see mountains, lochs, beaches, and islands along the way. ☒ *Station Square* ☎ *0844/850–4685* ⊕ *www.westcoastrailways.co.uk* ☒ *£33* ⊙ *Mid-May–June and late Sept.–late Oct., weekdays; July and Aug., daily.*

Nevis Range Gondola. Those who want to climb a mountain, without the need for hiking boots and an iron will, will prefer to make the journey in a gondola. These cable cars rise nearly 610m. (2,000 ft.), to the summit of Aonach Mor, part of the Nevis range. The journey takes about quarter of an hour, and needless to say the views of the Great Glen are incredible–but definitely not for those without a head for heights. ☒ *A82, Fort William* ☎ *01397/705825* ⊕ *www.nevisrange.co.uk* ☒ *£11.50* ⊙ *Apr.–June and Sept., daily 10–5; July–Aug., daily 9:30–6; Oct.–mid-Nov. and Jan.–Mar., weekdays 9–5. Hours may change according to daylight and weather conditions.* ⊙ *Closed mid-Nov.–Dec.*

West Highland Museum. In the town center, the West Highland Museum explores the history of Prince Charles Edward Stuart and the 1745 Rebellion. Included in the museum's folk exhibits are a costume and tartan display and a famous collection of Jacobite relics. ☒ *Cameron Sq.* ☎ *01397/702169* ⊕ *www.westhighlandmuseum.org.uk* ☒ *Free* ⊙ *Apr.–Oct., Mon.–Sat. 10–5; Mar., Nov., and Dec., Mon.–Sat. 10–4.*

WHERE TO EAT AND STAY

$$
SEAFOOD
✕ **Crannog Seafood Restaurant.** With a reputation for quality and simplicity, this restaurant on the town pier serves tasty seafood. Fishing boats draw up on the shores of Loch Linnhe and deliver their catch straight to the kitchen. The menu changes daily, but you could find salmon with fennel and orange salad, or hake with a peppercorn crust served with samphire. From the window seats you can watch the sun setting on the far side of the loch. Reservations are recommended. The restaurant also runs daily cruises of Loch Linnhe during the summer months. They cost £12.50 and last 90 minutes. ⑤ *Average main: £18* ☒ *The Pier* ☎ *01397/705589* ⊕ *www.crannog.net.*

$$
B&B/INN
🏨 **Crolinnhe.** An elegant Victorian house with colorful gardens, this exceptionally comfortable B&B overlooks Loch Linnhe, yet is only a 10-minute walk from town. **Pros:** stunning loch views; great

breakfasts; comfortable rooms. **Cons:** final payment only by cash or check. $ *Rooms from: £130* ✉ *Grange Rd.* ☎ *01397/702709* ⊕ *www. crolinnhe.co.uk* ⇆ *3 rooms* ▬ *No credit cards* ⊙ *Closed Nov.–Easter* ⊙ *Breakfast.*

$$
B&B/INN
Fodor's Choice
★

⊞ **The Grange.** This meticulously renovated Victorian villa stands in pretty gardens a 10-minute walk from downtown. **Pros:** lots of little extras; great attention to detail; elegant lounge with plenty of books. **Cons:** no restaurant; not suitable for families with younger children. $ *Rooms from: £126* ✉ *Grange Rd.* ☎ *01397/705516* ⊕ *www. thegrange-scotland.co.uk* ⇆ *3 rooms* ⊙ *Closed Oct.–Mar.* ⊙ *Breakfast.*

$
B&B/INN

⊞ **Myrtle Bank Guest House.** This sweet, cheerful guesthouse is in a converted Victorian villa on the banks of Loch Linnhe. **Pros:** great views; friendly owners; convenient location. **Cons:** ground floor rooms don't have such nice views; breakfast finishes quite early; some rooms have shared bathrooms. $ *Rooms from: £80* ✉ *Achintore Rd.* ☎ *01397/702034* ⊕ *www.myrtlebankguesthouse.co.uk* ⇆ *25 rooms* ⊙ *Breakfast.*

SPORTS AND THE OUTDOORS

BICYCLING
Nevis Range Mountain Bike Track. For a thrilling ride down Ben Nevis, take the gondola up to the beginning of the Nevis Range Mountain Bike Track and then shoot off on a 2,000-foot descent. The lift costs £13. It's open May to September, weather permitting. Bike rentals are available near the gondola. ✉ *A82* ☎ *01397/705825* ⊕ *bike.nevisrange.co.uk.*

GOLF
Fort William Golf Club. The Fort William Golf Club has spectacular views of Ben Nevis. The highland course appeals to beginning and experts alike. ✉ *Torlundy* ☎ *01397/704464* ⊕ *www.fortwilliamgolfclub.co.uk* ⊞ *Green fee: £25* ⅂ *18 holes, 6217 yds, par 70.*

HIKING
This area—especially around Glen Nevis, Glencoe, and Ben Nevis—is popular with hikers; however, routes are not well marked, so contact the Fort William tourist information center before you go. The center will provide you with expert advice based on your interests, level of fitness, and hiking experience.

Glen Nevis. For a walk in Glen Nevis, drive north from Fort William on the A82 toward Fort Augustus. On the outskirts of town, just before the bridge over the River Nevis, turn right up the road signposted Glen Nevis. About 8 miles along this road is a parking lot where a footpath leads to waterfalls and a steel-cable bridge (1 mile), and then to Steall, a ruined croft beside a boulder-strewn stream (a good picnic place). You can continue up the glen for some distance without danger of becoming lost, so long as you stay on the path and keep the river to your right. Watch your step going through the tree-lined gorge. The return route is back the way you came.

SKIING
Nevis Range. About 7 miles north of Fort William, Nevis Range is a modern development on the flanks of Aonach Mor. It has good and varied skiing, as well as views of Ben Nevis. There's a gondola system and runs for all skill levels. Skiing gets under way, adequate snowfall permitting, at the end of December. The season normally continues until early April. Daily ski passes are £30. ✉ *A82* ☎ *01397/705825* ⊕ *snowsports.nevisrange.co.uk.*

SHOPPING

The majority of shops here are along High Street, which in summer attracts bustling crowds intent on stocking up for excursions to the west.

Ellis Brigham Mountain Sports. This shop can help you get kitted out for your outdoor adventures. ⊠ *St. Marys Hall, Belford Rd.* ☎ *01397/706220* ⊕ *www.ellis-brigham.com.*

Nevisport. This shop has been selling outdoor supplies, maps, and travel books for more than 40 years. ⊠ *High St.* ☎ *01397/704921* ⊕ *www. nevisport.com.*

GLENCOE

16 miles south of Fort William, 92 miles north of Glasgow, 44 miles northwest of Edinburgh.

Fodor's Choice ★

Glencoe is both a small town and a region of awesome beauty, with high peaks and secluded glens. The area, where wild, craggy buttresses loom darkly over the road, has a special place in the folk memory of Scotland: the glen was the site of an infamous massacre in 1692, still remembered in the Highlands for the treachery with which soldiers of the Campbell clan, acting as a government militia, treated their hosts, the MacDonalds. According to Highland code, in his own home a clansman should give shelter even to his sworn enemy. In the face of bitter weather, the Campbells were accepted as guests by the MacDonalds. Apparently acting on orders from the British crown, the Campbells turned on their hosts and murdered them.

GETTING HERE AND AROUND

Glencoe is easily accessed by car via the A82. ScotRail trains and regional buses arrive from most of Scotland's major cities.

EXPLORING

Visitor Center at Glencoe. The National Trust for Scotland's Visitor Center at Glencoe tells the story of the MacDonald massacre, and has excellent displays about this area of outstanding natural beauty. You can also get expert advice about walking. ⊠ *Off A82, 1 mile south of Glencoe Village* ☎ *0844/493–2222* ⊕ *www.glencoe-nts.org.uk* ⊠ *Exhibition £6.50* ☼ *Late Mar.–Oct., daily 9:30–5:30; Nov.–late Mar., Thurs.–Sun. 10–4.*

WHERE TO STAY

$$$$
B&B/INN

☷ **Glencoe House.** Peaceful surroundings, incredible views, and the friendliest of welcomes await you at this former Victorian hunting lodge. **Pros:** beautiful landscape; superb restoration; lovely hosts. **Cons:** no proper restaurant; pricey given the lack of facilities. ⑤ *Rooms from: £240* ⊠ *Glencoe Lochan* ☎ *01855/811179* ⊕ *www.glencoe-house.com* ⊅ *7 rooms* ⎟⊙⎟ *No meals.*

9

GLENFINNAN

10 miles west of Fort William, 26 miles southeast of Mallaig.

Perhaps the most visitor-oriented stop on the route between Fort William and Mallaig, Glenfinnan has much to offer if you're interested in Scottish history. Here the National Trust for Scotland has capitalized on the romance surrounding the story of the Jacobites and their attempts to return a Stuart monarch and the Roman Catholic religion to a country that had become staunchly Protestant. It was at Glenfinnan that the rash adventurer Bonnie Prince Charlie gathered his meager forces for the final Jacobite Rebellion of 1745–46.

GETTING HERE AND AROUND

If you're driving from Fort William, travel via the A830. For great views, take a ride in the Jacobite Steam Train, which you can catch in Fort William.

EXPLORING

Glenfinnan Monument. One of the most striking monuments in Britain, the Glenfinnan Monument commemorates the place where Bonnie Prince Charlie raised his standard. The tower, which was built in 1815, overlooks Loch Shiel; note, however, that the figure on the top is a Highlander, not the Prince himself. The story of his ill-fated campaign is told in the nearby visitor center. You have to pay a small access fee when the center is open, but in truth it's just as picturesque when seen from the car park. ■ TIP→ **The view down Loch Shiel from the Glenfinnan Monument is one of the most photographed in Scotland.** ✉ *A830* ☎ *0844/493–2221* ⊕ *www.nts.org.uk* ✇ *£3.50* ◷ *Late Mar.–Oct., daily 10–5.*

Glenfinnan Viaduct. The 1,248-foot-long Glenfinnan Viaduct was a genuine wonder when it was built in 1897, and remains so today. The railway's contractor, Robert MacAlpine (known among locals as "Concrete Bob") pioneered the use of concrete for bridges when his company built the Mallaig extension, which opened in 1901. In more recent times the viaduct became famous for its appearance in the Harry Potter films. The viaduct can be seen on foot; about half a mile west of the railway station in Glenfinnan, on the A380 road, is a small parking lot. Take the footpath from here; you'll reach the viaduct in about ½ mile. ✉ *A380.*

WHERE TO STAY

$$ 🏨 **Glenfinnan House.** This handsome hotel on the shores of Loch Shiel

HOTEL   was built in the 18th century as the home of Alexander MacDonald VII of Glenaladale, who was wounded fighting for Bonnie Prince Charlie; it was transformed into an even grander mansion in the 19th century. **Pros:** fabulous setting; atmospheric dining experience. **Cons:** not all guest rooms have private bathrooms. Ⓢ *Rooms from: £140* ✉ *A830* ☎ *01397/722235* ⊕ *www.glenfinnanhouse.com* ✇ *14 rooms* ◷ *Closed mid-Nov.–mid-Mar.* ⦿ *Breakfast.*

▌EN
ROUTE

As you get closer to **Arisaig** along A830, you'll be able to spot Eigg, a low island marked by the dramatic black peak of An Sgurr. Beyond Eigg is the larger Rum, with its range of hills and the Norse-named, cloud-capped Rum Coullin looming over the island. The breathtaking seaward views should continue to distract you from the road beside Loch nan Uamh (from Gaelic, meaning "cave" and pronounced *oo*-am). This loch is associated with Prince Charles Edward Stuart's nine-month stay on the mainland, during which he gathered a small army, marched as far south as Derby in England, alarmed the king, retreated to unavoidable defeat at Culloden in the spring, and then spent a few months as a fugitive in the Highlands. A cairn by the shore marks the spot where the prince was rescued by a French ship; he never returned to Scotland.

ARISAIG

15 miles west of Glenfinnan.

Considering its small size, Arisaig, gateway to the **Small Isles,** offers a surprising choice of high-quality options for dining and lodging. To the north of Arisaig the road cuts across a headland to reach a stretch of coastline where silver sands glitter with the mica in the local rock; clear water, blue sky, and white sand lend a tropical flavor to the beaches—when the sun is shining.

From Arisaig try to visit a couple of the Small Isles: **Rum, Eigg, Muck,** and **Canna,** each tiny and with few or no inhabitants. Rum serves as a wildlife reserve, while Eigg has the world's first solely wind-, wave-, and solar-powered electricity grid.

GETTING HERE AND AROUND

From Glenfinnan, you reach Arisaig on the A830, the only road leading west. The Fort William–Mallaig train also stops here.

EXPLORING

Arisaig Marine. Along with whale-, seal-, and bird-watching excursions, Arisaig Marine runs a boat service from the harbor at Arisaig to the islands from May to September. You can also charter a fast motor yacht, which can take up to 12 passengers around the Small Isles and farther afield. ⊠ *Arisaig Harbour* ☎ *01687/450224* ⊕ *www.arisaig. co.uk* ⊠ *£18.*

WHERE TO EAT AND STAY

$$$
FRENCH
✕ **Old Library.** On the waterfront, this 1722 barn has been converted into a fine, reasonably priced restaurant. Local fish and other fare is prepared in a French-bistro style and served in the whitewashed, airy dining room. Six cozy rooms with contemporary furnishings are available starting at around £50. $ *Average main: £22* ⊠ *A30* ☎ *01687/450651.*

$$
HOTEL
Fodor's Choice
★
⊡ **Arisaig House.** An open-arms welcome and stunning views of the Isle of Skye await you at this wonderful mansion. **Pros:** amazing views; lovely hosts; outstanding food. **Cons:** a bit isolated. $ *Rooms from: £145* ⊠ *Beasdale* ☎ *01687/450730* ⊕ *www.arisaighouse.co.uk* ⊠ *4 rooms, 6 suites* ❑ *Multiple meal plans.*

9

MALLAIG

8 miles north of Arisaig, 44 miles northwest of Fort William.

After the approach along the coast, the workaday fishing port of Mallaig itself is somewhat anticlimactic. It has a few shops, and there's some bustle by the quayside when fishing boats unload or the Skye ferry departs: this is the departure point for the southern ferry connection to the Isle of Skye, the largest island of the Inner Hebrides.

Mallaig is also the starting point for day cruises up the Sound of Sleat, which separates Skye from the mainland. The sound offers views into the rugged Knoydart region and its long, fjordlike sea lochs: Lochs Nevis and Hourn. The area to the immediate north and west beyond Loch Nevis, one of the most remote in Scotland, is often referred to as the Rough Bounds of Knoydart.

GETTING HERE AND AROUND

The Fort William–Mallaig train is by far the best way to travel to Mallaig, because you can relax and enjoy the stunning views. But road improvements on the A830 beyond Fort William make the drive far less taxing and time-consuming than it used to be.

EXPLORING

Bruce Watt Sea Cruises. For year-round cruises to Loch Nevis, Inverie, and Tarbet, contact Bruce Watt Sea Cruises. ⊠ *Mallaig Harbour* ☎ *01687/462320* ⊕ *www.knoydart-ferry.co.uk*.

Caledonian MacBrayne. This company runs scheduled service and cruises from Mallaig to Skye, the Small Isles, and Mull. The ferries depart from several different points along the coast; the port at Mallaig also has a booking office. ⊠ *Mallaig Harbour* ☎ *0800/066–5000* ⊕ *www.calmac.co.uk*.

Loch Morar. A small, unnamed side road just south of Mallaig leads east to an even smaller road that will bring you to Loch Morar, the deepest of all the Scottish lochs (more than 1,000 feet). The next deepest point is miles out into the Atlantic, beyond the continental shelf. The loch is said to have a resident monster, Morag, which undoubtedly gets less recognition than its famous cousin Nessie. ⊠ *Loch Morar*.

THE NORTHERN HIGHLANDS AND THE WESTERN ISLES

Updated
by Mike
Gonzalez

Wild and remote, the Northern Highlands and the Western Isles of Scotland have a timeless grandeur. Dramatic cliffs, long beaches, and craggy mountains jutting up from moorland heighten the romance and mystery. Well-preserved Eilean Donan Castle marks a kind of gateway to the Isle of Skye, famous for the dark and brooding Cuillin Mountains and forever associated with Bonnie Prince Charlie. Jurassic-era sites (dinosaurs left their prints here), prehistoric ruins, crumbling castles, and abandoned crofts compress the whole span of history in the islands.

In Sutherland and Caithness in northern Scotland, the roads hug the coast, dipping down toward beaches and up again to give stunning views over the ocean or across rippled, desolate stretches of heather moorland toward the impressive and singular profiles of mountains like Ben Hope and Suilven. These twisted, undulating roads demand that you shift down a gear, pause to let others pass, and take the time to do less and experience more of the rough-hewn beauty. If you're lucky, you may see an otter fishing along the coast, an eagle soaring overhead, or catch sight of deer with their antlers jutting above the horizon.

Sutherland was once the southernmost land belonging to the Vikings, and some names reflect this. Cape Wrath got its name from the Viking word *hvarth*, meaning "turning point," and Suilven translates as "pillar." The Isle of Skye and the Outer Hebrides are referred to as the Western Isles, and remain the stronghold of the Gaelic language. Skye is often called Scotland in miniature because the terrain shifts from lush valleys in the south, to the rugged girdle of the Cuillin Mountains, and then to the steep cliffs that define the northern coast. A short ferry journey away, moody Harris lays claim to the brilliant golden sands of Luskentyre. To the north, Lewis boasts incredible prehistoric sites, including the lunar-aligned Calanais Standing Stones and Dun Carloway (an Iron Age circular tower), as well as a lighthouse that looks ready to tip into the Atlantic.

Depending on the weather, a trip to the Northern Highlands and the Western Isles can feel like a tropical getaway or a blustery, rain-drenched holiday where this much-touted phrase makes sense: "There's no such thing as bad weather, just inappropriate clothing."

TOP REASONS TO GO

Skye, the misty island: The landscape ranges from the lush, undulating hills and coastal tracks of Sleat in the Garden of Skye to the deep glens that cut into the saw-toothed peaks of the Cuillin Mountains. Farther north are stunning geological features like the Old Man of Storr and Kilt Rock.

Seafood: Sample fresh seafood like Bracadale crab, Dunvegan Bay langoustines, and Sconser king scallops, as well as the local smoked salmon, lobster, and oysters.

Coastal walks: There are no wilder places in Britain to enjoy an invigorating coastal walk than on the islands of Lewis, Harris, and the Uists. Expect vast swaths of golden sand set against blue bays, or—when the weather is rough—giant waves crashing against the rocks.

Wildlife viewing: Seals, deer, otters, as well as an abundance of birdlife can be seen throughout the Northern Highlands and Western Isles. Don't miss a boating foray to the Handa Island bird reserve, off Scourie.

Single-track roads: In the Northern Highlands, take a drive on single-track roads like Destitution Road, north of Gairloch, which lead through the most dramatic scenery in Britain. The area is a primeval landscape where strange craggy mountains, with Gaelic and Nordic names like An Teallach, Suilven, and Stac Pollaidh, jut out of vast, desolate moorlands dotted with lochans.

ORIENTATION AND PLANNING

GETTING ORIENTED

Moving north and west from Inverness toward land's end at John o'Groats, this rugged landscape includes the old counties of Ross and Cromarty (sometimes called Easter and Wester Ross), Sutherland, and Caithness; together they constitute the northernmost portion of mainland Scotland. To the west, to get to Skye, you can travel from Kyle of Lochalsh across the Skye Bridge or take a short summer ferry ride from Mallaig to Armadale. From Skye you can hop from island to island, taking the ferry from Uig to Tarbert, then south from Leverburgh to Lochmaddy and the Uists.

The Northern Landscapes. North of Inverness, northwest Scotland is known for its dramatic coastlines and desolate landscapes. It's no wonder that this part of the country has been designated as Scotland's first UNESCO Geopark. You'll want to explore Stoer Point Lighthouse, the beaches north of Lochinver, and islandlike hills such as Suilven.

Torridon. A few hours' drive west of Inverness, Torridon has cool glens, mirrorlike lochs, impressive mountains, and tantalizing glimpses across to the Isle of Skye. Single-track roads lead to lighthouses on promontories battered by the sea. Glen Torridon is worth a visit.

10

Isle of Skye. Scotland's most famous island is home to the 11 peaks of the Cuillin Mountains, the quiet gardens of Sleat, and the dramatic peninsulas of Waternish and Trotternish. You can take a day trip to Skye, but it's worth spending a few days exploring its shores.

The Outer Hebrides. Extending about 130 miles from north to south, this archipelago is reached by ferry from the mainland and from the Isle of Skye. Lewis has wonderful historic attractions, such as the Calanais Standing Stones, sandy beaches, and traditional "black houses." Harris is flat and wild, but its beaches are glorious. The Uists are dotted with old cairns and ruined forts and chapels. Barra is so small you can easily walk from one end to the other.

PLANNING

WHEN TO GO

The Northern Highlands and islands are best seen from May to September. The earlier in the spring or later in the autumn you go, the greater the chances of your encountering the elements in their extreme form, and the fewer attractions and accommodations you will find open. Even tourist-friendly Skye closes down almost completely by the end of October. As a final deciding factor, you may not want to take a western sea passage in a gale, a frequent occurrence in the winter months.

PLANNING YOUR TIME

The rough landscape of the Highlands and Islands, as this region is sometimes called, means that this is not a place you can rush through. Single-track roadways, undulating landscapes, and eye-popping views will slow you down. You can base yourself in a town like Ullapool or Portree, or choose a B&B or hotel tucked into the hills or sitting at the edge of a sea loch. If you have limited time, head directly to the Isle of Skye and the other islands off the coast. They attract hordes of tourists, and for good reason, yet you don't have to walk far to find yourself in wild places, often in solitude. Sunday is a day of minimal activity here; restaurants, bars, and shops are closed, as are many sites.

You could combine a trip to the Northern Highlands with forays into the Great Glen (including Inverness and Loch Ness) or up to Orkney and the Shetland Islands.

GETTING HERE AND AROUND

AIR TRAVEL

On a map, this area may seem far from major urban centers, but it's easy to reach. Inverness has an airport with direct links to London, Edinburgh, Glasgow, and Amsterdam.

The main airports for the Northern Highlands are Inverness and Wick (both on the mainland). Loganair has direct air service from Edinburgh and Glasgow to Inverness and from Edinburgh to Wick. You can fly from London Gatwick, Luton Airport (near London), or Bristol to Inverness on one of the daily easyJet flights. British Airways also has a service from Gatwick. Loganair and Flybe operate flights to and among the islands of Barra, Benbecula, Harris, and Lewis in the Outer Hebrides.

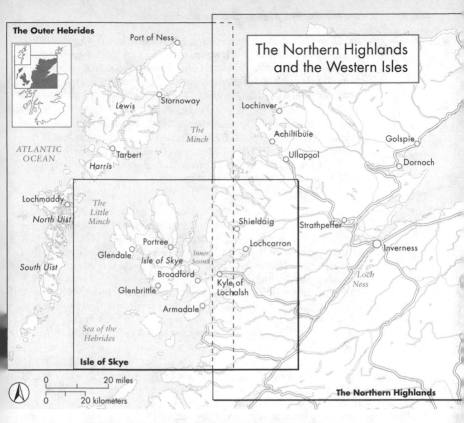

The Outer Hebrides

Port of Ness

Lewis   Stornoway

The Minch

ATLANTIC OCEAN

Tarbert

Harris

Lochmaddy

North Uist

The Little Minch

Portree

Glendale

Isle of Skye   *Inner Sound*

Broadford

Glenbrittle

Armadale

Sea of the Hebrides

Isle of Skye

South Uist

The Northern Highlands and the Western Isles

Lochinver

Achiltibuie   Golspie

Ullapool   Dornoch

Shieldaig   Strathpeffer

Lochcarron   Inverness

Kyle of Lochalsh   *Loch Ness*

The Northern Highlands

0   20 miles
0   20 kilometers

Airport Contact **Inverness Airport** ⊠ *Old Military Rd., Dalcross*
☎ *01667/464000* ⊕ *www.hial.co.uk/inverness-airport.html.*

BOAT AND FERRY TRAVEL

Ferry services are generally reliable, weather permitting. Car and passenger ferries run from Ullapool to Stornoway, from Oban to Castlebay and Lochboisdale, and from Uig (on the Isle of Skye) to Tarbert and Lochmaddy. The Island Hopscotch planned-route ticket and the Island Rover pass, both offered by Caledonian MacBrayne (known locally as CalMac) give considerable reductions on interisland ferry fares.

Boat and Ferry Contact **Caledonian MacBrayne** ☎ *08000/665000*
⊕ *www.calmac.co.uk.*

BUS TRAVEL

Scottish Citylink and National Express run buses to Inverness, Ullapool, Thurso, Scrabster, and Wick. There are also connections between the ferry ports of Tarbert and Stornoway; consult the local tourist information center for details. Buses can be a good way to see this region, but they don't run frequently.

Stagecoach Highlands provides a bus service in the region. On the Outer Hebrides several small operators run regular routes to most towns and villages. The post-bus service—which also delivers mail—becomes increasingly important in remote areas. It supplements the regular bus service, which runs only a few times per week. A full timetable of services for the Northern Highlands (and the rest of Scotland) is available from the Royal Mail. Traveline Scotland, a handy website, provides timetables and a journey planner to help you navigate around Scotland. There's an app, too.

Bus Contacts National Express ☎ 08705/808080 ⊕ www.nationalexpress.co.uk. **Royal Mail Post Buses** ☎ 0845/7740740 ⊕ www.royalmail.com/postbus. **Scottish Citylink** ☎ 0871/2663333 ⊕ www.citylink.co.uk. **Stagecoach Highlands** ☎ 01463/233371 ⊕ www.stagecoachbus.com. **Traveline Scotland** ☎ 08706/082608 ⊕ www.travelinescotland.com.

CAR TRAVEL

Because of the infrequent bus services and sparse railway stations, a car is definitely the best way to explore this region. The winding single-lane roads demand a degree of driving dexterity, however. Local rules of the road require that when two cars meet, whichever driver reaches a passing place first must stop and allow the oncoming car to continue (this may entail a bit of backing up). Cars driving uphill have priority, and small cars tend to yield to large commercial vehicles. Never park in passing places, and remember that these sections of the road can also be used to allow traffic behind you to pass. Note that in this sparsely populated area distances between gas stations can be considerable, so it is wise to fill your tank when you see one.

TRAIN TRAVEL

Main railway stations in the area include Oban (for ferries to Barra and the Uists) and Kyle of Lochalsh (for Skye) on the west coast, as well as Inverness (for points north to Thurso and Wick). There's a direct service from London to Inverness and connecting service from Edinburgh and Glasgow. For information contact National Rail or ScotRail.

Train Contacts National Rail ☎ 08457/484950, 4420/72785240 from abroad ⊕ www.nationalrail.co.uk. **ScotRail** ☎ 08457/550033 ⊕ www.scotrail.co.uk.

TOURS

J.A. Johnstone Chauffeur Drive will escort you anywhere and gives a lot of information about the Highlands and Islands, including the Outer Hebrides.

Tour Contacts J.A. Johnstone Chauffeur Drive ☎ 01463/798372 ⊕ www.jajcd.com.

RESTAURANTS

Northern Scotland has many excellent restaurants where talented chefs use locally grown produce. Most country-house inns (a good choice if you're looking for a restaurant) and pubs serve reliable, hearty seafood and meat-and-potatoes meals. The Isle of Skye has the most, and the most expensive, restaurants, many of them quite good. But you can find tasty meals almost everywhere, although in more remote regions you may have to drive some distance to find them. Remember that locals eat early, and few restaurants serve dinner after 9 or 9:30. *Prices in the reviews are the average cost of a main course at dinner or, if dinner is not served, at lunch.*

HOTELS

Charming, earthy, inexpensive inns and a few excellent luxury hotels will welcome you after a day of touring the Highlands. There are many B&Bs in the area, and they often book up far in advance. Some require a minimum two-day stay in high season.

In the more remote parts of Scotland your best lodging option may be to rent a cottage or house. Besides allowing you to make your own meals and to come and go as you please, it can also be less expensive. VisitScotland (⊕ *www.visitscotland.com*), the official tourism agency, lists many cottages and even rates them with stars, just like hotels. *Prices in the reviews are the lowest cost of a standard double room in high season, including 20% V.A.T.*

VISITOR INFORMATION

The tourist information centers at Dornoch, Dunvegan, Durness, Portree, Stornoway, Tarbert, and Ullapool are open year-round, with limited winter hours at Dunvegan, Durness, and Ullapool.

Seasonal tourist information centers are at Bettyhill, Broadford (Skye), Castlebay (Barra, Outer Hebrides), Gairloch, Helmsdale, John o'Groats, Kyle of Lochalsh, Lairg, Lochboisdale (South Uist, Outer Hebrides), Lochcarron, Lochinver, Lochmaddy (North Uist, Outer Hebrides), North Kessock, Shiel Bridge, Thurso, and Uig.

Information Highlands of Scotland Tourist Board ☎ *08452/255121* ⊕ *www.visithighlands.com.*

THE NORTHERN LANDSCAPES

Wester Ross and Sutherland, the northernmost part of Scotland, have some of the most distinctive mountain profiles and coastal stretches in all of Scotland. The rim roads around the wilds of Durness overlook rocky shores, and the long beaches are as dramatic as the awe-inspiring and desolate cross-country routes like Destitution Road in Wester Ross.

ULLAPOOL

238 miles north of Glasgow.

Ullapool is an ideal base for hiking throughout Sutherland and taking wildlife and nature cruises, especially to the Summer Isles. By the shores of salty Loch Broom, the town was founded in 1788 as a fishing station to exploit the local herring stocks. There's still a smattering of fishing vessels, as well as visiting yachts and foreign ships. When their crews fill the pubs, Ullapool has a cosmopolitan feel. The harbor area comes to life when the Lewis ferry arrives and departs.

GETTING HERE AND AROUND

A desolate but well-maintained stretch of the A835 takes you from Inverness to Ullapool.

ESSENTIALS

Visitor Information Ullapool Visitor Centre ✉ *7 and 8 W. Argyle St.* ☎ *01854/612486* ⊕ *www.visitscotland.com* ⊘ *Apr.–Oct., Mon.–Sat. 10–5.*

10

EXPLORING

Ceilidh Place. Ullapool's cultural focal point is Ceilidh Place, an excellent venue for concerts and other events throughout the year (*ceilidh* is the Gaelic word for a local dance). It started out as a small café, and over the years has added space for performers, an excellent bookshop specializing in Scottish writing, and a handful of rooms for those who want to spend the night. It's a great place for afternoon coffee or a wee dram in the evening. ⊠ *14 W. Argyle St.* ☎ *01854/612103* ⊕ *www. theceilidhplace.com.*

Corrieshalloch Gorge. For a thrilling touch of vertigo, don't miss Corrieshalloch Gorge, 12 miles south of Ullapool, just off the A835. Draining the high moors, the Falls of Measach plunge 150 feet into a 200-foot-deep, thickly wooded gorge. There's a suspension-bridge viewpoint and a heady atmosphere of romantic grandeur, like an old Scottish print come to life. A short walk leads from a parking area to the viewpoint.

Falls of Rogie. Just north of Contin you'll find the Falls of Rogie, where an interestingly bouncy suspension bridge presents you with a fine view of the waters below. ⊠ *A835, 35 miles south of Ullapool, Contin.*

Ullapool Museum. Films, photographs, and audiovisual displays tell the story of the area from the ice age to modern times. There's an ongoing exhibition on weather, climate change, and the environment. ⊠ *7 and 8 W. Argyle St.* ☎ *01854/612987* ⊕ *www.ullapoolmuseum.co.uk* ▱ *£3* ☉ *Apr.–Oct., Mon.–Sat. 10–5.*

WHERE TO STAY

$$
HOTEL
🏨 **Ceilidh Place.** It advertises "rooms to let," but what this place really offers is simple and elegant accommodations, many with beamed ceilings and views of Loch Broom. **Pros:** quiet comfort; wonderful views; great for music lovers. **Cons:** decor a little tired. ⑤ *Rooms from: £100* ⊠ *14 W. Argyle St.* ☎ *01854/612103* ⊕ *www.theceilidhplace.com* ⟿ *13 rooms* ⦿ *Breakfast.*

$
HOTEL
🏨 **The Royal Hotel.** This longtime favorite has a great location and beautiful views over Ullapool Harbor and Loch Broom, so be sure to request a balcony room in advance. **Pros:** a short walk to Ullapool; good breakfasts. **Cons:** sometimes very crowded and a little noisy; rooms at the rear have no views. ⑤ *Rooms from: £99* ⊠ *Garve Rd.* ☎ *01854/612181* ⊕ *www.royalhotel-ullapool.com* ⟿ *55 rooms* ⦿ *Breakfast.*

$$
B&B/INN
🏨 **Tanglewood House.** Sitting on a headland overlooking Loch Broom, this hotel is a mile from Ullapool but feels much more remote. **Pros:** lovely setting; pretty gardens. **Cons:** a steep drive down to the house. ⑤ *Rooms from: £104* ⊠ *Off A835* ☎ *01854/612059* ⊕ *www.tanglewoodhouse. co.uk* ⟿ *3 rooms* ⦿ *Breakfast.*

10

ACHILTIBUIE

25 miles northwest of Ullapool.

Off the beaten track, Achiltibuie is a small coastal community set at the foot of magnificent mountains. It looks out over the Summer Isles, whose history dates back to Viking raids. Cruises leave from a small jetty just west of Achiltibuie and take you to the largest and only inhabited island, Tanera Mhor, where you can buy special Summer Isle stamps—Tanera Mhor is the only Scottish island to have a private postal service.

GETTING HERE AND AROUND

Achiltibuie is a two-hour drive from Inverness, much of it on the quick A835, with the last 15 miles on an occasionally daunting single-track road.

> ## GET HOOKED IN THE HIGHLANDS
>
> The possibilities for fishing are endless in Sutherland, as a glance at the loch-covered map suggests. Brown trout and salmon are abundant. You can fish from the banks of Loch Garve, 35 miles south of Ullapool, or Loch Assynt, 5 miles east of Lochinver, from March to October. Boat fishing is popular on Loch Maree, southeast of Gairloch and north of Poolewe, from May to October. Fishing permits are available at local post offices, shops, and hotels.

EXPLORING

Achiltibuie Smokehouse. At the Achiltibuie Smokehouse, Summer Isles Foods deliciously smokes all sorts of fish: salmon, haddock, eel, and trout. It all can be purchased in the small shop. ⊠ *Altandhu* ☎ *01854/622353* ⊕ *www.summerislesfoods.com* ☉ *Easter–Oct., daily 9:30–5.*

Coigach and Assynt. Drive north of Ullapool on the A835 into Coigach and Assynt, and you enter a different kind of landscape. The mountains punch out of the heathered terrain and seem to shift their position, hiding behind one another. Even their names seem different from those of the *bens* (mountain peaks or high hills) elsewhere: Cul Mor, Cul Beag, Stac Pollaidh, Canisp, Suilven. Some owe their origins to Norse words rather than to Gaelic—a reminder that Vikings used to sail this northern seaboard. Much of this area lies within the North West Highlands Geopark.

WHERE TO STAY

$$
HOTEL
Fodor's Choice
★

Summer Isles Hotel. Halfway along a road that ends at the sea, this well-kept hotel is built into a small hill and contemplates the mystical Summer Isles. **Pros:** stunning views; peaceful location; good food. **Cons:** not much to do nearby. $ *Rooms from: £155* ⊠ *Achiltibuie Rd.* ☎ *01854/622282* ⊕ *www.summerisleshotel.com* ⇋ *6 rooms* ☉ *Closed Nov–Mar.* ⦿ *Breakfast.*

SPORTS AND THE OUTDOORS

Stach Pollaidh. For a great afternoon of walking, ascend the dramatic hill of Stach Pollaidh (pronounced "stack Polly"), about 10 miles east of Achiltibuie. The clearly marked path climbs for a bit and then curves around to the right and takes you on a loop with incredible views over Sutherland, north to Suilven, and west to the Summer Isles. About halfway around the hill, a steeper path takes you to the start of the ridge. Only very experienced rock climbers should continue from here, as the route requires rock climbing in very exposed conditions. But not to worry, because from the west side of the looped path you can see the pinnacled pitch of Stach Pollaidh. Start your walk from a car park about 5 miles from A835. ✉ *Off A835, Dornie.*

EN ROUTE A single-lane unclassified road winds north from Achiltibuie through a wild though harmonious landscape of bracken and birch trees, heather and hills, with outstanding sea views on the second half of the route. Don't fall victim to the breathtaking landscape views, however; the road has several blind curves that demand extreme care.

LOCHINVER

18 miles north of Achiltibuie, 38 miles north of Ullapool.

Lochinver is a quiet shoreside community of whitewashed cottages, with a harbor used by the west coast fishing fleet, and a couple of good dining and lodging options. Behind the town the mountain Suilven rises abruptly. Take the cul-de-sac, **Baddidarroch Road,** for a great photo opportunity. Lochinver is a perfect base for exploring Sutherland.

GETTING HERE AND AROUND
To get to Lochinver, take A835/A837 north from Ullapool.

ESSENTIALS
Visitor Information Assynt Visitor Centre ✉ *Main St.* ☎ *01571/844654* ⊕ *www.discoverassynt.com.*

EXPLORING
Drumbeg Loop. Bold souls spending time at Lochinver may enjoy the interesting single-track B869 Drumbeg Loop to the north of Lochinver—it has several challenging hairpin turns along with breathtaking views. The junction is on the north side of the River Inver bridge on the outskirts of the village, signposted as "stoer" and "clashnessie." Just beyond the scattered community of Stoer, a road leads west to **Stoer Point Lighthouse.** If you're an energetic walker, you can hike across the short turf and heather along the cliff top for fine views west over toward the Isle of Skye. There's also a red-sandstone sea stack: the **Old Man of Stoer.** This makes a pleasant excursion on a long summer evening.

Eas Coul Aulin Waterfall. With a drop of 685 feet, this is the longest waterfall in the United Kingdom. A rugged hike leads to the falls, which are at the head of Loch Glencoul. Start from car park off A894, approximately 17 miles east and north from Lochinver. In summer, cruises from Kylesku Old Ferry Pier offer a less taxing alternative. ✉ *A894, 3 miles southeast of Kylesku Bridge.*

WHERE TO EAT AND STAY
$ ✕ **Lochinver Mission.** An abandoned fishermen's mission (a place where **BRITISH** fishermen stayed while in port), houses this cafeteria-style restaurant dishing out top-notch local fare. The local favorite starts the day by serving a hot breakfast, and for lunch and dinner offers expertly prepared langoustines and other local seafood, as well as soups and

10

GREAT ITINERARIES

The quality of the northern light and the sheer beauty of the landscapes add to the adventure of exploring the Northern Highlands and the Western Isles. Above all, don't rush things: travel takes time, and the journey is part of the adventure. Multiple-journey ferry tickets—the Island Hopscotch, for example—can help you stay flexible. You could easily combine the itineraries here with forays into the Great Glen (including Inverness and Loch Ness) or even up to Orkney and the Shetland Islands.

IF YOU HAVE 2 DAYS

If you have only two days, head to the fabled Isle of Skye, whose mists shroud so many legends. Stay in a town such as **Broadford** or **Armadale**, then tour the spectacular countryside, including the celebrated Cuillin Mountains near **Glen Brittle**. Be sure to detour to see **Eilean Donan Castle** once you're back on the mainland.

IF YOU HAVE 5 DAYS

If the weather looks settled, head for Skye, and base yourself at **Portree**. The next day, visit **Glen Brittle** and the Cuillins. On your third day, take the ferry from Uig, in the north of Skye, to **Tarbert**, in the Western Isles, and visit the **Calanais Standing Stones**, the Arnol **Black House**, and some deserted beaches. The next day, travel to **Stornoway** and catch the ferry to **Ullapool** on the mainland. On your fifth day, return to Inverness by way of the **Corrieshalloch Gorge**.

IF YOU HAVE 8 DAYS

Tackle the coastal loop of the north of Scotland counterclockwise. Start at **Ullapool**, then take the ferry for **Stornoway** and the Western Isles. Spend your second day visiting Stornoway's harbor and museum, and on your third day, drive north to visit **Port of Ness**, the **Butt of Lewis Lighthouse**, the Arnol **Black House**, and the **Calanais Standing Stones**. The fourth day, drive to **Tarbert** for a visit to the **Seallam! Visitor Centre and Co Leis Thu? Genealogical Research Centre**. The next day, take the ferry to North Uist, returning to Tarbert in the evening. On your sixth day, take the ferry to Uig on Skye and travel to **Portree**. Spend your seventh day visiting **Glen Brittle**, then move on to **Broadford**. On your last day, cross the Skye Bridge and return to Inverness.

---

burgers. It draws considerable crowds on weekends. The building also contains the local archives, a marine center, and three basic guest rooms. $ *Average main: £9* ⌧ *Culag Park* ☎ *01571/844324* ⊕ *www. lochinvermission.org.uk.*

$$$$ ⌂ **Inver Lodge Hotel.** On a hillside above Lochinver, this modern hotel
HOTEL has stunning views of the sea. **Pros:** cozy public room with a fireplace; refreshing sauna; great fishing nearby. **Cons:** drab exterior; not good for families with children. $ *Rooms from: £225* ⌧ *Iolaire Rd.* ☎ *01571/844496* ⊕ *www.inverlodge.com* ⇨ *21 rooms* ⦿ *Breakfast.*

$ ⌂ **Tigh Na Sith.** Set just above the bay at Lochinver, this B&B wins
B&B/INN rave reviews for its warm welcome; owners Nick and Patrycja Matthews pack lunches for your day excursions and provide binoculars so you can get the most of the views down to the loch and over the hills. **Pros:** great hosts; fantastic views. **Cons:** room at back

doesn't have a view; shared dining table for breakfast may not suit everyone. ⑤ *Rooms from: £79* ✉ *A837* ☎ *01571/844352* ⊕ *www.tighnasith.com* ⌂ *3 rooms* ⓘ *Breakfast.*

SHOPPING

Achins Book & Craft Shop. On the Lochinver-Achiltibuie road, this shop is a great place to find Scottish books on natural history, hill walking, and trout fishing. It also sells craft items—knitwear, tweeds, and pottery—along with works by local artists and recordings of traditional music. The shop and pleasant café are open daily from 10 to 5 (except for Sunday from October to March). ✉ *Off B869, Inverkirkaig* ☎ *01571/844262* ⊕ *www.scotbooks.freeuk.com.*

DRIVING TIPS

In the Northern Highlands you'll encounter plenty of single-track roads wide enough only for one car. When you meet an oncoming vehicle, or when a faster one wants to pass, pull into a passing place (always pull to the left, into the passing place or into the space on the road beside it). Drivers always wave, as a courtesy and as a genuine greeting. On bad days, you encounter trucks at the most awkward of spots. On good days, single-track driving can be relaxing, with a lovely pace of stopping, waving, moving on.

Highland Stoneware. In its showroom, Highland Stoneware displays dinnerware and decorative items with hand-painted designs of wildflowers, animals, and landscapes. ✉ *Baddidarroch* ☎ *01571/844376* ⊕ *www.highlandstoneware.com* ⊘ *Easter.–Oct., weekdays 9–6, Sat. 9–5, Sun. 11–3.*

SCOURIE

28 miles north of Lochinver.

Scourie is a small settlement catering to visitors—fisherfolk especially—with a range of accommodations. The bay-side town makes a good base for a trip to the bird sanctuary on Handa Island.

GETTING HERE AND AROUND

From Lochinver, take the A837, which becomes the A894 as you turn north.

EXPLORING

Fodor's Choice ★

Handa Island. Just off the coast of Scourie is Handa Island, a bird sanctuary that shelters huge seabird colonies, especially impressive at nesting time. You can gaze at more than 200,000 birds nesting on spectacular cliffs, including guillemots, razorbills, great skuas, kittiwakes, and even the odd puffin from the towering sandstone vantage point of Stack an Seabhaig (Hawk's Stack). This remarkable reserve, administered by the Scottish Wildlife Trust, is open only in spring and summer. It can be reached by a small open boat from Tarbet; contact the tourist information center in Lochinver or Durness for details. ■TIP→ **Sturdy boots, a waterproof jacket, and a degree of fitness are needed to walk the path around the island.**

10

WHERE TO STAY

$$ 🖵 **Eddrachilles Hotel.** A longtime favorite, the hotel has one of the best
B&B/INN views of any lodging in Scotland—toward the tiny islands of Badcall Bay.
Pros: attractive garden; stunning shoreline nearby; close to bird sanctu-
ary. **Cons:** restaurant's quality can vary; service sometimes disappoints.
⑤ *Rooms from: £110* ✉ *Off A894* ☎ *01971/502080* ⊕ *www.eddrachilles.
com* ⤴ *11 rooms* ☾ *Closed early Oct.–late Mar.* ⭐⦿�| *Breakfast.*

$$ 🖵 **Kylesku Hotel.** This charming hotel looks out over Loch Glendhu and
HOTEL toward Eas Coul Aulin, Scotland's highest waterfall. **Pros:** stunning
views; great staff; delicious food. **Cons:** some old-building quirks; two
attic rooms are small, but cheaper. ⑤ *Rooms from: £115* ✉ *Off A894,
Kylesku* ☎ *01971/502231* ⤴ *8 rooms* ⭐⦿| *Breakfast.*

DURNESS

27 miles north of Scourie, 55 miles north of Lochinver.

The sudden patches of green surrounding the village of Durness, on
the north coast, are caused by the richer limestone outcrops among the
acid moorlands. Here you'll find the country's highest cliff, Clo Mor.

GETTING HERE AND AROUND

Past Scourie, the A894 becomes the A838 as you head north. The road
to Durness is often a single lane in each direction.

ESSENTIALS

Visitor Information Durness Information Centre ✉ *Sangomore*
☎ *01971/511368* ⊕ *www.durness.org.*

EXPLORING

Cape Wrath. If you've made it this far north, you'll probably want to go
all the way to Cape Wrath, a rugged headland at the northwest tip of
Scotland. The white-sand beaches, impressive dunes covered in marram
grass, and crashing seas of nearby Balnakeil Bay make it an exhilarating
place to visit. As this land is owned by the Ministry of Defence, you
can't drive your own vehicle. From May through September a small
boat ferries people here from Keoldale, 2 miles outside Durness; once
you're across the sea inlet called the Kyle of Durness, a minibus will
then take you to the lighthouse. Call ahead or check departure times
on the board at the jetty. ☎ *01971/511284* ⊕ *www.capewrath.org.uk.*

Clo Mor. The highest mainland cliffs in Scotland, including 920-foot Clo
Mor, lie between the Kyle and Cape Wrath.

Smoo Cave. This spectacular cavern, hollowed out of the limestone by
rushing water, can be reached via a steep cliff path. Also worth exploring
are the number of wonderful sandy beaches found as you head east to
Tongue, especially the one at Sango Bay. Boat tours around the Kyle of
Durness run daily from April through September. ⊕ *www.smoocave.org.*

WHERE TO STAY

$$ 🖵 **Tongue Hotel.** With open fireplaces in its public areas and hunting
HOTEL lodge–style rooms, the Tongue Hotel makes a great base for explor-
ing this northernmost coast of the Scottish mainland. **Pros:** welcoming
atmosphere; stunning views; relaxing public rooms. **Cons:** you'll need

a car to make the most of this area. $ *Rooms from: £110* ✉ *On A838, near Lairg, Tongue* ☎ *01847/611206* ⊕ *www.tonguehotel.co.uk* ⊃ *19 rooms* ⦿ *Breakfast.*

SHOPPING

Balnakeil Craft Village. Artisans sell pottery, leather, weavings, paintings, and more from their studios at Balnakeil Craft Village. On an unnamed road running northwest from Durness, this collection of former military buildings is open April through October. Cocoa Mountain is a must for those with a sweet tooth; its "chocolate bar" serves up world-class truffles and stunningly rich hot chocolate. The hours vary, but most shops here are open daily from 10 to 5, and even later on summer evenings. ✉ *Balnakeil* ☎ *01971/511777.*

EN ROUTE The north-coast road along the top of Scotland is both attractive and severe. It runs, for example, around the head of Loch Eriboll, which was a World War II convoy assembly point and was usually referred to as "Loch 'orrible" by the crews. Yet it has its own desolate charm. There are lots of landmarks, including croft dwellings, crumbling lime kilns, and a pebbly beach that reaches out to a mound of land, Ard Neakie.

THURSO

74 miles east of Durness.

The town of Thurso is quite substantial for a community so far north. In town are the Thurso Heritage Museum and Old St. Peter's Kirk, which dates back to the 12th century. There are also fine beaches, particularly at Dunnet Bay, and great seabird watching at Dunnet Head.

GETTING HERE AND AROUND

A car remains the best way to see this region, although local buses and the post bus run on most days. At Tongue the A838 becomes the A836.

ESSENTIALS

Visitor Information Thurso Information Centre ✉ *Riverside Rd.* ☎ *01847/893155* ⊕ *www.visithighlands.com.*

EXPLORING

Dunnet Head. Many people make the trip to Dunnet Head, the northernmost point of mainland Britain. Dunnet Head Lighthouse, built in 1831, still stands here. As a bonus, there are fine views over the sea to Orkney. ✉ *Off B855.*

WHERE TO STAY

$$$
B&B/INN

Forss Country House Hotel. Don't be fooled by the stark exterior, as this house dating from 1810 is a charming place to stay. **Pros:** large guest rooms; lots of outdoor activities; hearty meals. **Cons:** heavy old doors make a racket. $ *Rooms from: £165* ✉ *Forss, 4 miles west of Thurso* ☎ *01847/861201* ⊕ *www.forsshousehotel.co.uk* ⊃ *14 rooms* ⦿ *Breakfast.*

BICYCLING

Wheels Cycle Shop. At the Wheels Cycle Shop, the staff rents bikes and gives advice on the best routes. ✉ *35 High St.* ☎ *01847/896124.*

10

JOHN O'GROATS

21 miles east of Thurso.

The windswept little outpost of John o'Groats is usually taken to be the northernmost community on the Scottish mainland, though that is not strictly accurate, as an exploration of the network of roads between Dunnet Head and John o'Groats will confirm. From the harbor you can take a boat to see the dolphins and seals that live beneath the coastal cliffs. Or you can seek out Duncansby Head, where you can watch the puffins and guillemots. This is nature, wild and untouched. The little town has charms of its own, including a crafts center with high-quality shops selling knitwear, candles, and gifts.

GETTING HERE AND AROUND

Traveling east from Thurso, take the coast-hugging A836.

EXPLORING

Duncansby Head. Head to Duncansby Head for spectacular views of cliffs and sea stacks by the lighthouse—and puffins, too. It's on the coastal road east of town.

John o'Groats Ferries. Sailing from John o'Groats Harbor, this company takes you on 90-minute cruises past spectacular cliff scenery and bird life into the Pentland Firth, to Duncansby Stacks, and to the island of Stroma. Trips cost £17 and are available daily at 2:30 between June and August. Between May and September the company also offers day trips to Orkney for £47. ⊠ *County Rd.* ☎ *01955/611353* ⊕ *www.jogferry.co.uk.*

THE ARTS

Lyth Arts Centre. In a Victorian-era school building, the Lyth Arts Centre serves as a cultural hub. From April to November, professional music and theater companies fill the schedule and locals fill the seats. There are also exhibitions of contemporary fine art. Lyth is located between Wick and John o'Groats. ⊠ *Off A9, Lyth* ☎ *01955/641434* ⊕ *www.lytharts.org.uk.*

WICK

17 miles south of John o'Groats, 22 miles southeast of Thurso.

Wick is a substantial town that was built on its fishing industry. The town itself is not very appealing, but it does have the gaunt, bleak ruins of **Castle Sinclair** and **Castle Girnigoe** teetering on a clifftop 3 miles north of the town.

GETTING HERE AND AROUND

From Thurso, the A836 follows the coast to John o'Groats and becomes the A99 as you head south. An alternative route, the A882, cuts away from the coast.

EXPLORING

Wick Heritage Centre. To learn how this town grew, visit the Wick Heritage Centre. The locals who run it are real enthusiasts, and they will take you through the history of the town from its founding by the Vikings through its heyday as a leading herring port in the 1860s.

The collection includes everything from fascinating fossils to 19th-century toys. There's also an art gallery and terraced gardens that overlook the town. ✉ *18–27 Bank Row* ☎ *01955/605393* ⊕ *www.wickheritage.org* 🖾 *£4* ☉ *Easter–Oct., Mon.–Sat. 10–3:45.*

EN ROUTE

Grey Cairns of Camster. The extraordinary Grey Cairns of Camster, two Neolithic chambered cairns dating from 4000 BC to 3000 BC, are among the best preserved in Britain. **Camster Round Cairn** is 20 yards in diameter and 13 yards high, and **Camster Long Cairn** reaches nearly 77 yards in length. Some 19-century excavations revealed skeletons, pottery, and flint tools in the round cairn's internal chamber. If you don't mind dirty knees, you can crawl into the chambers in both cairns. ✉ *Off A9, 10 miles south of Wick* ☎ *01667/460232* ⊕ *www.historic-scotland.gov.uk* 🖾 *Free* ☉ *Open all yr.*

> ## A BRUTAL DUKE
>
> Traveling south on the A9 from Helmsdale to Golspie, you can see the controversial statue of the first Duke of Sutherland. He's perched on Beinn a Bragaidh (Ben Braggie), the hilltop to the west. Many people want to remove the statue, as the "improvement" policies of the duke were ultimately responsible for the brutality of the Sutherland Clearances of 1810–20, which removed people from their farms so there would be more room for sheep to graze.

DUNBEATH

21 miles south of Wick.

A tiny coast village, Dunbeath is bordered by moors on one side, the sea on the other. A few interesting museums make it worth a stop.

GETTING HERE AND AROUND

South of Wick, Dunbeath can be reached via the A9. This coast-hugging route, crowded with Orkney ferry traffic, can be quite daunting because of the steep drop-offs when heading south.

EXPLORING

Dunbeath Heritage Centre. The moors of Caithness roll down to the sea at Dunbeath, where you find a former school that houses the Dunbeath Heritage Centre. Inside are photographs and domestic and crofting artifacts that relay the area's history from the Bronze Age up to the present. It's particularly helpful to those researching family histories. ✉ *Off A9* ☎ *01593/731233* ⊕ *www.dunbeath-heritage.org.uk* 🖾 *£3* ☉ *Apr.–Sept., Sun.–Fri. 10–5; Oct.–Mar., weekdays 11–3.*

10

HELMSDALE

15 miles south of Dunbeath.

Helmsdale is a fascinating fishing village with a checkered past. It was a busy Viking settlement and then the scene of an aristocratic poisoning plot before it was transformed into a 19th-century village to house some of the people removed from their land to make way for sheep. These "clearances," perpetrated by the Duke of Sutherland, were among the area's most inhumane.

GETTING HERE AND AROUND

Helmsdale is one of the only towns on this part of the coast that has a daily train service from Inverness. However, a car will allow you to see more in the surrounding area. Get here via the coastal A9 or the inland A897.

EXPLORING

FAMILY **Timespan Heritage Centre.** This thought-provoking mix of displays, artifacts, and audiovisual materials portrays the history of the area from the Stone Age to the 1869 gold rush in the Strath of Kildonan. There's a geology exhibit in the garden and a tour of the Kildonan gold rush site. The complex also includes a café and an art gallery that often hosts visiting artists and changing exhibitions. ⊠ *Dunrobin St.* ☎ *01431/821327* ⊕ *www.timespan.org.uk* ⌑ *£4* ⊙ *Mar–Oct., Mon.–Sat. 10–5, Sun. noon–5; Nov.–Feb., Sat. 11–4, Tues. 2–4; last admission 1 hr before closing.*

GOLSPIE

18 miles south of Helmsdale.

The little coastal town of Golspie is worth a stop if you're heading for Dunrobin Castle. It has a number of shops and accommodations.

GETTING HERE AND AROUND

Golspie can be reached by train from Inverness, and in summer the train also stops at Dunrobin Castle. Drivers should use the A9.

EXPLORING

Dunrobin Castle. The Scottish home of the dukes of Sutherland is flamboyant Dunrobin Castle, an ancient seat developed by the first duke into a 19th-century white-turreted behemoth. As well as lavish interiors, there are falconry demonstrations and Versailles-inspired gardens. Trains so fascinated the duke that he built his own railroad in the park and staffed it with his servants. ⊠ *Off A9* ☎ *01408/633177* ⊕ *www. dunrobincastle.co.uk* ⌑ *£10* ⊙ *Apr., May, Sept., and early Oct., Mon.–Sat. 10:30–4:30, Sun. noon–4:30; June–Aug., daily 10–5.*

SHOPPING

Orcadian Stone Company. A geological exhibition at this shop spans 3 billion years and includes some of the world's oldest rocks. The shop is open from Easter to October and for three weeks before Christmas. ⊠ *Main St.* ☎ *01408/633483* ⊕ *www.orcadianstone.co.uk.*

DORNOCH

10 miles south of Golspie, 40 miles north of Inverness.

A town of sandstone houses, tiny rose-filled gardens, and a 13th-century cathedral with stunning traditional and modern stained-glass windows, Dornoch is well worth a visit. It's noted for golf: you may hear it referred to as the St. Andrews of the North, but because of the town's location so far north, the golf courses here are delightfully uncrowded. Royal Dornoch is the jewel in its crown, praised by the world's top golfers.

GETTING HERE AND AROUND

From Inverness, take the A9 north to Dornoch. Be cautious, as it's often busy with ferry traffic.

ESSENTIALS

Visitor Information Dornoch Information Centre ⊠ *The Square* ☏ *08452/255121* ⊕ *www.visithighlands.com.*

WHERE TO STAY

$$
HOTEL
Dornoch Castle Hotel. A genuine late-15th-century castle, once sheltering the bishops of Caithness, this hotel blends the quite old and the more modern. **Pros:** grand exterior; lovely gardens; friendly hotel staff. **Cons:** a few rooms need a lick of paint. $ *Rooms from: £123* ⊠ *Castle St.* ☏ *01862/810216* ⊕ *www.dornochcastlehotel.com* ⤳ *24 rooms* ¶⊙¶ *Breakfast* ⌔ *No pets.*

GOLF

Fodor'sChoice
★
Royal Dornoch Golf Club. The legendary Championship Course, laid out by Tom Morris in 1886, has fast raised greens with views of mountains and white sandy beaches. In the springtime yellow gorse adds to the wild beauty. The Struie Course provides more sea views and challenging golf for players of every level. It's less than an hour's drive north of Inverness Airport. ⊠ *Golf Rd.* ☏ *01862/810219* ⊕ *www.royaldornoch. com* ⤳ *Green fee: Championship £110; Struie £40* ⤿ *Reservations essential* ⚐ *. Championship: 18 holes, 6711 yds, par 70; Struie: 18 holes, 6265 yds, par 71* ⊙ *Daily.*

TORRIDON

Located far to the west, Torridon has a grand, rugged, and wild air that feels especially remote, yet it's just a few hours' drive from Inverness before you reach Kinlochewe, near the east end of Glen Torridon. The western side is equally spectacular. Walking trails and mountain panoramas abound. Torridon is a wonderful place to visit if you want to tackle one of the legendary peaks here—Beinn Alligin, Liathach, and Beinn Eighe—or if you enjoy outdoor activities like kayaking, climbing, or mountain biking. The A890, which runs from the A832 into the heart of Torridon, is a single-lane road in some stretches, with plenty of open vistas across the deserted heart of northern Scotland.

10

LOCHCARRON

66 miles west of Inverness.

Strung along the shore, the village of Lochcarron has some attractive croft buildings, a couple of churches (one an 18th-century ruin set in a graveyard), a golf club, and some handy shops.

GETTING HERE AND AROUND

To drive here from Inverness, take the A9 as it becomes the A835, A832, and then the A890. The single-track road skirts both steep mountains and lochs.

SHOPPING

Lochcarron Weavers. Watch a weaver producing pure-wool tartans that can be bought here or at the company's other outlets in the area. There's also a café. ⊠ *Mid Strome* ☏ *01520/722212* ⊕ *www.lochcarronweavers.co.uk.*

SHIELDAIG

16 miles northwest of Lochcarron.

Just west of the southern coast of Upper Loch Torridon is Shieldaig, a village that sits in an attractive crescent overlooking a loch of its own, Loch Shieldaig. For an atmospheric evening foray, walk north toward Loch Torridon, at the northern end of the village by the church. The path—fairly well made, though hiking shoes are recommended—leads to exquisite views and tiny rocky beaches.

GETTING HERE AND AROUND

Shieldaig is on the A896 between Lochcarron and Kinlochewe.

EXPLORING

OFF THE BEATEN PATH

Applecross. The tame way to reach this small community facing Skye is by a coastal road from near Shieldaig. The exciting route turns west off the A896 a few miles farther south and then a series of hairpin turns corkscrews up the steep wall at the head of a corrie (a glacier-cut mountain valley), over the **Bealach na Ba** (Pass of the Cattle). There are spectacular views of Skye from the bare plateau on top, and you can brag afterward that you've been on what is probably Scotland's highest drivable road.

Fodor's Choice
★

Glen Torridon. The scenic spectacle of Glen Torridon lies east of Shieldaig as you follow the A896 from Shieldaig to Kinlochewe. Some say that Glen Torridon has the finest mountain scenery in Scotland. It consists mainly of the long gray quartzite flanks of **Beinn Eighe** and **Liathach**, with its distinct ridge profile that looks like the keel of an upturned boat.

WHERE TO STAY

$$$$
HOTEL

Torridon Hotel. The Victorian Gothic turrets of this former hunting lodge promise atmosphere and grandeur. **Pros:** breathtaking location; center for outdoor activities; bar has more than 300 malts. **Cons:** isolated location; rather pricey. ⑤ *Rooms from: £235* ✉ *A896, Wester Ross* ☎ *01445/700300* ⊕ *www.thetorridon.com* ↪ *18 rooms* ⦿ *Breakfast.*

$$
B&B/INN

Torridon Inn. A more affordable option than the grand Torridon Hotel, this lodging makes a great base for exploring the area. **Pros:** pleasant wood-clad decor; eco-friendly vibe; reasonable rates. **Cons:** service can be erratic; can be noisy. ⑤ *Rooms from: £104* ✉ *A896, Wester Ross* ☎ *01445/700300* ⊕ *www.thetorridon.com* ↪ *12 rooms* ⦿ *Breakfast.*

GAIRLOCH

38 miles north of Shieldaig.

Aside from its restaurants and lodgings, peaceful Gairloch has one further advantage: lying just a short way from the mountains of the interior, this small oasis often escapes the rain clouds that can cling to the high summits. You can enjoy a round of golf here and perhaps stay dry, even when the nearby Torridon Hills are deluged.

GETTING HERE AND AROUND

From Ullapool, this coastal town can be reached via A832.

EXPLORING

Fodor's Choice ★ **Destitution Road.** The road between Gairloch and the Corrieshalloch Gorge initially heads north and passes coastal scenery with views of Gruinard Bay and its white beaches, then woodlands around Dundonnell and Loch Broom. Soon the route traverses wild country: the toothed ramparts of the mountain An Teallach (pronounced tyel-lack) are visible on the horizon. The moorland route you travel is known chillingly as Destitution Road. At Corrieshalloch the road, A832, joins the A835 for Inverness.

Gairloch Heritage Museum. This little museum's exhibits cover prehistoric times to the present. It's also a source for genealogical research—by appointment with curator. ✉ *A832, at B8031* ☎ *01445/712287* ⊕ *www. gairlochheritagemuseum.org.uk* ⊡ *£4* ☉ *Apr.–Oct., weekdays 10–5, Sat. 11–3.*

Fodor's Choice ★ **Inverewe Gardens.** A highlight of the area, Inverewe Gardens has lush plantings tucked away behind a dense barrier of trees and shrubs. This is all thanks to the warm North Atlantic Drift, which takes the edge off winter frosts. Inverewe is sometimes described as subtropical, but this inaccuracy irritates the head gardener; do not expect coconuts and palm trees here. Instead, look for rarities like the blue Himalayan poppy. ✉ *A832, 6 miles northeast of Gairloch, Poolewe* ☎ *01445/781200* ⊕ *www.nts.org.uk* ⊡ *£10* ☉ *Easter–Oct., daily 9:30–9; Nov.–Mar., daily 9:30–5.*

Fodor's Choice ★ **Loch Maree.** Southeast of Gairloch stretches one of Scotland's most scenic lochs, Loch Maree. Its harmonious environs, with tall Scots pines and the mountain Slioch looming as a backdrop, witnessed the destruction of much of the tree cover in the 18th century. Iron ore was shipped in and smelted using local oak to feed the furnaces. Oak now grows here only on the northern limits of the range. Scottish Natural Heritage has an **information center** and nature trails by the loch and in the Beinn Eighe Nature Reserve. Red deer sightings are virtually guaranteed; locals say the best place to spot another local denizen, the endangered pine marten (a member of the weasel family), is around the trash containers in the parking turnoffs.

WHERE TO STAY

$$ **Dundonnell Hotel.** This family-run hotel, set on the roadside by Little **HOTEL** Loch Broom, has cultivated a solid reputation for its hospitality. **Pros:** fabulous scenery; plenty of outdoor activities; good dining options. **Cons:** bland exterior; decor not to everyone's taste. $ *Rooms from: £120* ✉ *A832, 30 miles northeast of Gairloch, Dundonnell* ☎ *01854/633204* ⊕ *www.dundonnellhotel.com* ⟿ *28 rooms* ❏ *Breakfast.*

GOLF

Gairloch Golf Club. This course is one of the few to be found on this stretch of coast. There has been a golf club here since 1898, and local records show that putters of more than a century ago played on the golden sand dunes. ✉ *Off A832* ☎ *01445/712407* ⊕ *www.gairlochgolfclub.co.uk* ⊡ *Green fee: £20* ⚑ *9 holes, 4043 yds, par 64.*

10

ISLE OF SKYE

Fodor's Choice ★ The misty isle, Skye is full of romance and myth, lush gardens and steep, magnetic mountains (a compass is useless in the Cuillin Mountains). It ranks near the top of most visitors' must-see lists: the romance of Prince Charles Edward Stuart (1720–88), known as Bonnie Prince Charlie, combined with the Cuillin Mountains and their proximity to the mainland, all contribute to its popularity.

Today Skye remains dramatic, mysterious, and mountainous, an island of sunsets that linger brilliantly until late at night, and of beautiful, magical mists. Much photographed are the old crofts, one or two of which are still inhabited. It also has an increasingly impressive range of accommodations and some excellent restaurants that show off the best in the island's produce and culinary talent.

To reach Skye, you can cross over the bridge spanning the narrow channel of Kyleakin, between Kyle of Lochalsh and Kyleakin, or in summer you can take the more romantic trip via boats between Mallaig and Armadale or the little old ferry between Glenelg and Kylerea. You can tour comfortably around the island in two or three days, but a bit longer would allow time for some hiking or some sea kayaking.

Orientation is easy: in the north, follow the roads that loop around the peninsulas of Waternish and Trotternish; in the south, enjoy the road running the length of the Sleat Peninsula. There are some stretches of single-lane road, but with attention and care none pose a problem.

KYLE OF LOCHALSH

55 miles west of Inverness, 120 miles northwest of Glasgow.

This little town is the mainland gateway to Skye. Opened in 1995, the bridge transformed not only travel to Skye but the very seascape itself. The most noticeable attraction, though (in fact, almost a cliché), is not in Kyle at all, but 8 miles farther east at Dornie—Eilean Donan Castle.

GETTING HERE AND AROUND
From the north, you reach Kyle of Lochalsh via the A890 or A896; from the south, take the A87. Trains travel here from Inverness, but the journey requires changing trains several times.

EXPLORING
Brightwater Visitor Centre. Gavin Maxwell's much loved account of his work with otters on the island of Eilean Ban, off the coast of Skye at Kyleakin, is commemorated here. There's an exhibit illustrating his work and wildlife tours that promise otters, seals, and lots of birds. The center itself is actually on Skye, just over the bridge from the Kyle of Lochalsh. ⊠ *The Pier, Kyleakin* ☎ *01599/530040* ⊕ *www.eileanban. org* ⊠ *Free* ⊙ *Apr.–Oct., Mon.–Sat. 9–5, Sun. 10–4.*

Fodor's Choice ★ **Eilean Donan Castle.** Guarding the confluence of lochs Long, Alsh, and Duich stands that most picturesque of all Scottish castles, Eilean Donan Castle, perched on an islet connected to the mainland by a stone-arched bridge. Dating from the 14th century, this romantic icon has all the massive stone walls, timber ceilings, and winding

Isle of Skye

stairs that you could ask for. Empty and neglected for years after being bombarded by frigates of the Royal Navy during an abortive Spanish-Jacobite landing in 1719, it was almost entirely rebuilt from a ruin in the early 20th century. The kitchen re-creates the busy scene before a grand banquet, and the upper floors show how the castle was transformed into a grand house. Now the hero of travel brochures, Eilean Donan has appeared in many Hollywood movies and TV shows. There's a shop and a coffeehouse for the many visitors. ⊠ *A87, Dornie* ☎ *01599/555202* ⊕ *www.eileandonancastle.com* ☎ *£6.50* ⊙ *Feb.–May and Oct.–Dec., daily 10–6; June and Sept., daily 9:30–6; July and Aug., daily 9–6.*

WHERE TO STAY

$$
B&B/INN

Glenelg Inn. Looking out over the Sound of Sleat, the Glenelg Inn's pleasant, contemporary rooms are furnished in wood and cane and are bright and clean. **Pros:** lively atmosphere; nice views; pleasant rooms. **Cons:** only some rooms have sea views; out-of-the-way location. ⑤ *Rooms from: £120* ⊠ *Kirkton* ☎ *01599/522273* ⊕ *www.glenelg-inn. com* ⇥ *7 rooms* ⑩ *Breakfast.*

BROADFORD

8 miles west of Kyle of Lochalsh via Skye Bridge.

One of the larger of Skye's settlements, Broadford lies along the shore of Broadford Bay, which has on occasion welcomed whales to its sheltered waters.

GETTING HERE AND AROUND

Broadford is on the main road crossing the Isle of Skye, the A87.

ESSENTIALS

Visitor Information Broadford Tourist Information Centre ⊠ *Off A87* ☎ *08452/255121* ⊕ *www.visithighlands.com.*

EXPLORING

FAMILY
Fodor'sChoice
★

Misty Isle Boat Trips. For fantastic views of the Cuillin Mountains and the Inner Hebrides, book a place on one of the Misty Isle Boat Trips. The expansive scenery around Loch Coruisk is some of the most spectacular in Scotland. Round-trip journeys depart from the town of Elgol, and booking ahead is essential. Prices vary, but a cruise to a seal colony costs £15. Private charters are available. ⊠ *Elgol jetty, Sealladh na Mara, Elgol* ☎ *01471/866288* ⊕ *www.mistyisleboattrips.co.uk* ☉ *Mon.–Sat. at 9, 11, 2:15, and 5:15.*

OFF THE
BEATEN
PATH

Road to Elgol. The B8083 leads from Broadford to one of the finest views in Scotland. This road passes through **Strath Suardal** and little **Loch Cill Chriosd** (Kilchrist) by a ruined church. You can appreciate breathtaking views of the mountain called **Bla Bheinn** as the A881 continues to Elgol, a gathering of crofts along this road that descends to a pier. Admire the heart-stopping profile of the Cuillin peaks from the shore, or, at a point about halfway down the hill, you can find the path that goes toward them across the rough grasslands.

FAMILY

Skye Serpentarium. You can observe and handle snakes, frogs, lizards, and tortoises at the Skye Serpentarium, in the town center. It's also a refuge for wayward, worldly reptiles. ⊠ *The Old Mill, off A87* ☎ *01471/822209* ⊕ *www.skyeserpentarium.org.uk* ☜ *£4.50* ☉ *Easter–Oct., Mon.–Sat. 10–5; July and Aug., daily 10–5.*

WHERE TO STAY

$$
HOTEL

Broadford Hotel. Though few of the rooms look directly out to sea, this comfortable hotel's dining room does have lovely views over Broadford Bay. **Pros:** good base for touring the island; near the village; free Wi-Fi throughout. **Cons:** no elevator; rather dark public areas. ⑤ *Rooms from: £149* ⊠ *Torrin Rd.* ☎ *01471/822204* ⊕ *www.broadfordhotel. co.uk* ☜ *11 rooms* ⑩ *Breakfast.*

ARMADALE

17 miles south of Broadford, 43 miles south of Portree, 5 miles (ferry crossing) west of Mallaig.

Rolling moorlands, scattered with rivers and lochans, give way to enchanting hidden coves and scattered waterside communities here in **Sleat,** the southernmost part of Skye.

GETTING HERE AND AROUND

The Mallaig-Armadale ferry arrives here. There's a short (and beautiful) road to the southwest, while the main road heads east following the stunning coast.

EXPLORING

Clan Donald Skye. Walk the lush, extensive gardens at Armadale Castle Gardens and the Museum of the Isles and you take in magnificent view across the Sound of Sleat to Knoydart and the Mallaig Pennisula. The museum tells the story of the Macdonalds and their proud title—the Lords of the Isles—with the help of an excellent audiovisual presentation. In the 15th century the clan was powerful enough to threaten the authority of the Stewart monarchs of Scotland. There's a gift shop, restaurant, library, and center for genealogy research. Also on the grounds are high-quality accommodations in seven cottages with kitchen facilities. Access is from Armadale Pier, where signs indicate the different forest walks that are available. ✉ *Off A851, ½ mile north of Armadale Pier* ☎ *01471/844305* ⊕ *www.clandonald.com* 🎫 *Gardens free, museum £7.50* ☉ *Gardens daily dawn–dusk; museum Apr.–Oct., daily 9:30–5:30; last entry 30 mins before closing.*

WHERE TO STAY

$$$

HOTEL

🏨 **Duisdale House Hotel.** Set in 35 acres of mature woodlands and gardens, this former mansion has a lovely hillside location with views to the sea. **Pros:** nicely refurbished rooms; expansive views; excellent staff. **Cons:** nautical decor might not suit everyone. $ *Rooms from: £198* ✉ *Off A851, Sleat* ☎ *01471/833202* ⊕ *www.duisdale.com* 🛏 *17 rooms* 🍴*Breakfast.*

$$$

HOTEL

🏨 **Hotel Eilean Iarmain.** Built on a small peninsula dotted by a quiet lighthouse, this hotel has an unforgettable location. **Pros:** wonderful waterfront location; plenty of sporting activities, superb wine list. **Cons:** some unattractive renovations. $ *Rooms from: £170* ✉ *Off A851* ☎ *01471/833332* ⊕ *www.eileaniarmain.co.uk* 🛏 *12 rooms, 4 suites* 🍴*Breakfast.*

$$$$

HOTEL

🏨 **Kinloch Lodge.** Overlooking the tidal Loch na Dal, this historic lodge has buildings that date from the 17th century. **Pros:** historic property; interior full of character; great afternoon tea. **Cons:** rooms and dining are pricey. $ *Rooms from: £320* ✉ *Off A851, Sleat* ☎ *01471/833333* ⊕ *www.kinloch-lodge.co.uk* 🛏 *15 rooms* 🍴*Some meals.*

SHOPPING

Fodor's Choice ★

Ragamuffin. A friendly place, this well-stocked shop specializes in designer knitwear. In winter the staff might make you a cup of coffee while you browse, then mail your purchases back home for you. ✉ *Armadale Pier, Off A851* ☎ *01471/844217* ⊕ *www.ragamuffinloves. blogspot.co.uk.*

10

PORTREE

43 miles north of Armadale.

Portree, the population center of the island, is a pleasant place clustered around a small and sheltered bay. Although not overburdened by historical features, it's a good touring base with a number of good shops and an excellent bakery.

GETTING HERE AND AROUND

The biggest town on Skye, Portree is well served by local buses and by a well-maintained road, the A87.

ESSENTIALS

Visitor Information **Portree Information Centre** ⊠ *Bayfield House, Bayfield Rd.* ☎ *01478/614906* ⊕ *www.visithighlands.com.*

EXPLORING

Tigh na Coille: Aros. On the outskirts of town is Tigh na Coille: Aros (*tigh na coille* is Gaelic for "house of the forest," and *aros* means "home" or "homestead"), a visitor center that screens occasional films and exhibits local artworks. An exhibit by the Royal Society for the Protection of Birds lets you observe the eagles via a live webcam (it costs extra, which isn't clear as you enter). The café is spacious but on the expensive side. ⊠ *Viewfield Rd.* ☎ *01478/613649* ⊕ *www.aros.co.uk* 🖃 *Free; eagle exhibit £4.75* ⊙ *Daily 10–5.*

WHERE TO EAT

$
MODERN BRITISH

✕ **Bistro at Bosville.** This pleasant eatery overlooks Portree Harbour and its colorful row of waterfront houses. It can get busy, so you may have to wait a while in the barn next door. The kitchen serves basic dishes, well prepared and presented, with imaginative touches; try the sole on green lentils with chorizo, or the mackerel on a Niçoise salad. The portions are generous, though the wine is a little overpriced. The staff is cheerful and welcoming. $ *Average main: £15* ⊠ *9–11 Bosville Terr.* ⊕ *www.bosvillehotel.co.uk.*

$
BRITISH

✕ **Café Arriba.** Up a steep flight of stairs, the laid-back café has window seats with great views over Portree Harbour. Using only local produce (whatever is "fresh, local, and available"), this is a good option for no-frills eating. Good choices include locally caught scallops, creamy summer risotto, and, on the lighter side, salad with freshly baked bread. $ *Average main: £10* ⊠ *Quay Brae, Quay St.* ☎ *01478/611830* ⊙ *No dinner.*

WHERE TO STAY

$$$
HOTEL

🖪 **Cuillin Hills Hotel.** This Victorian-era hunting lodge looks down on Portree and the brightly painted houses around the harbor. **Pros:** Portree is a short stroll away; good breakfast menu; attentive service. **Cons:** rooms at back overpriced; restaurant can get very busy; no elevator. $ *Rooms from: £200* ⊠ *Off A855* ☎ *01478/612003* ⊕ *www.cuillinhills-hotel-skye.co.uk* 🛏 *29 rooms* ⁙ *Breakfast.*

$$
B&B/INN

🖪 **Peinmore House.** A former manse, Peinmore House has views north over Portree Bay, and on a clear day all the way to the Old Man of Storr; to the south you can spy the moody Cuillins. **Pros:** tranquil location; great breakfast. **Cons:** a little pricey; you need a car to get here. $ *Rooms from: £135* ⊠ *Off B883, 2 miles south of Portree* ☎ *01478/612574* ⊕ *www.peinmorehouse.co.uk* 🛏 *4 rooms* ⁙ *Breakfast.*

Clans and Tartans

Whatever the origins of the clans—some with Norman roots, intermarried into Celtic society; some of Norse origin, the product of Viking raids on Scotland; others traceable to the monastic system; yet others possibly descended from Pictish tribes—by the 13th century the clan system was at the heart of Gaelic tribal culture. By the 15th century the clan chiefs of the Scottish Highlands were a threat even to the authority of the Stewart monarchs.

The word *clann* means "family" or "children" in Gaelic, and it was the custom for clan chiefs to board out their sons among nearby families, a practice that helped to bond the clan unit and create strong allegiances.

THE CLAN SYSTEM

The clan chiefs' need for strong men-at-arms, fast-running messengers, and bards for entertainment, and the preservation of clan genealogy, was the probable origin of the Highland Games, still celebrated in many Highland communities each year, and which are an otherwise rather inexplicable mix of sports, music, and dance.

Gradually, by the 18th century increasing knowledge of Lowland agricultural improvements, and better roads into the Highlands that improved communication of ideas and "southern" ways, began to weaken the clan system. The Battle of Culloden marked the death of the clan system, as the victorious English armies banned the kilt and the pipes and claimed the land of the rebellious clan chiefs. And when the new landowners introduced the hardy Cheviot breed of sheep and changed farming activity, the Highlands were transformed forever and the Highlanders, and especially the islanders, began the long journey into emigration in the 1750s. By the 1820s, landowners paid people to leave.

TARTAN REVIVAL

Tartan's own origins as a part of the clan system are disputed; the Gaelic word for striped cloth is *breacan*—piebald or spotted—so even the word itself is not Highland. However, when cloth was locally spun, woven, and dyed using plant derivatives, each neighborhood would have different dyestuffs. In this way, particular combinations of colors and favorite patterns of the local weavers could become associated with a particular area and therefore clan. Between 1746 and 1782 the wearing of tartan was generally prohibited. By the time the ban was lifted, many recipes for dyes and weaving patterns had been forgotten.

It took the influence of Sir Walter Scott, with his romantic (and fashionable) view of Highland history, to create the "modern myth" of clans and tartan. Sir Walter engineered George IV's visit to Scotland in 1822, which turned into a tartan extravaganza. The idea of one tartan or group of tartans "belonging" to one particular clan was created at this time—literally created, with new patterns and colorways dreamed up and "assigned" to particular clans. Queen Victoria and Prince Albert reinforced the tartan culture later in the century and with it the revival of the Highland Games.

Clan Tartan Centre. You may be able to find a clan connection with expertise such as that available at the Clan Tartan Centre. ✉ *70–74 Bangor Rd., Leith, Edinburgh* ☎ *0131/5535161* ⊕ *www.ewm.co.uk.*

10

$$
B&B/INN
Fodor's Choice
★

The Spoons. After years of running a luxury estate for others, Marie and Ian Lewis put their considerable talents to work at the Spoons. **Pros:** top-notch breakfasts; perfect base for exploring; bucolic setting. **Cons:** books up quickly. ⑤ *Rooms from: £140* ⊠ *75 Aird Bernisdale* ☎ *01470/532217* ⊕ *www.thespoonsonskye.com* ⇨ *3 rooms* ⏀ *Breakfast.*

$
B&B/INN

Viewmount Guest House. This pink house stands out on the main road near the southern entrance of Portree. **Pros:** cheerful owners; unpretentious but comfortable rooms; ample parking. **Cons:** Close to the main road; not good if you're not fond of animals. ⑤ *Rooms from: £76* ⊠ *Viewfield Rd.* ☎ *01478/612570* ⊕ *www.viewmount-skye.co.uk* ⇨ *5 rooms* ⏀ *Breakfast.*

SHOPPING

Isle of Skye Soap Company. This shop stocks soaps, essential oils, and other nice-smelling gifts. ⊠ *Somerled Sq.* ☎ *01478/611350* ⊕ *www. skye-soap.co.uk.*

TROTTERNISH PENINSULA

16 miles north of Portree.

As A855, the main road, goes north from Portree, cliffs rise to the left. They're actually the edge of an ancient lava flow, set back from the road and running for miles. Fossilized dinosaur bones have been uncovered at the base of these cliffs. Don't forget to look up: you might spot a sea eagle, identifiable by the flash of its white tail.

GETTING HERE AND AROUND

From Portree, take the twisting, undulating A855 as it follows the coast.

EXPLORING

Kilt Rock. From Portree, the A855 travels past neat white croft houses and forestry plantings to Kilt Rock, which got its odd name because the sheer rock is ridged like a pleated kilt. Everyone on the tour circuit stops here to peep over the edge at the viewing platform.

Old Man of Storr. Along the dramatic road around the Trotternish Peninsula, a gate beside a car park marks the beginning of the climb to the Old Man of Storr. Give yourself at least three hours to explore this 2,000-foot-high volcanic pinnacle with spectacular views from the top. The weather here changes very quickly, so be prepared.

Quiraing. A geological formation of rocky crags and stacks, the spectacular Quiraing dominates the horizon about 5 miles beyond Kilt Rock. For a closer view of this area's strange pinnacles, make a left onto a small road at Brogaig by Staffin Bay. There's a parking lot near the point where this road breaches the ever-present cliff line. The road is very narrow and rough, so drive cautiously. The rambler's trail is on uneven, stony ground, and it's a steep scramble up to the rock formations. In ages past, stolen cattle were hidden deep within the Quiraing's rocky jaws.

Skye Museum of Island Life. Not far from the tip of the Trotternish Peninsula, the Skye Museum of Island Life brings the old crofting ways vividly to life. Included in the displays and exhibits are documents and photographs, reconstructed interiors, and implements. Flora Macdonald, who assisted Bonnie Prince Charlie, is buried nearby. ⊠ *Off A855, Kilmuir* ☎ *01470/552206* ⊕ *www.skyemuseum.co.uk* ⊠ *£2.50* ⊗ *Easter–Oct., Mon.–Sat. 9–5.*

Staffin Museum. Built on the foundations of an 1840s schoolhouse, this single-room museum is a labor of love of builder Dugald Ross, who first saw the fossilized dinosaur prints as a boy and as an adult saved them from rough seas. You'll also find objects saved from shipwrecks, agricultural implements, and some old photographs. ⊠ *6 Ellishadder, Staffin* ☎ *01470/562321* ⊕ *www.borve.net/staffin-museum.co.uk* ⊠ *£2* ⊗ *Apr.–Sept., Mon.–Sat. 9–5.*

WHERE TO EAT AND STAY

$$$
BRITISH

✕ **The Glenview.** On the Trotternish Peninsula between Portree and Staffin, a renovated croft building houses this gem of a "restaurant with rooms." With wood floors and cheerfully painted walls, the simple, chic decor allows the older building's charms to flourish. The well-considered menu (£29 for two courses, £35 for three) includes locally sourced offerings like Skye shellfish broth and poached Uist salmon. If you like the place so much you want to stay, rooms are available from £110. ⑤ *Average main: £20* ⊠ *A855, Culnacnoc* ☎ *01470/562248* ⊕ *www.glenviewskye.co.uk* ⚮ *Reservations essential* ⊗ *No lunch. Closed Sun. and Mon.*

$$$$
HOTEL
Fodor's Choice
★

🛏 **Flodigarry Country House Hotel.** With spectacular coastal views, Flodigarry retains the feel of a grand country house, with antique furnishings and beautifully finished wood throughout. **Pros:** spectacular views; a good base for walking. **Cons:** the road down is steep; expensive rates; no room TVs. ⑤ *Rooms from: £250* ⊠ *A855, Staffin* ☎ *01470/552203* ⊕ *www.flodigarry.co.uk* ⇥ *15 rooms* ⦿ *Breakfast.*

WATERNISH PENINSULA

20 miles northwest of Portree.

The northwest corner of Skye has scattered crofting communities, magnificent coastal views, and a few good restaurants well worth the trip in themselves. In the Hallin area look westward for an islet-scattered sea loch with small cliffs rising from the water—and looking like miniature models of full-size islands.

GETTING HERE AND AROUND
From Portree, follow the A850 to the Waternish Peninsula.

EXPLORING
Skye Skyns. A 10-minute tour of this working tannery gives excellent insight into the process of salting, washing, and preparing sheepskins. You'll learn the source of such phrases as "on tenterhooks" and "stretched to the limits." There are sheepskins in many forms for you to buy. ⊠ *17 Lochbay, Waternish* ☎ *01470/592237* ⊕ *www.skyeskyns.co.uk.*

10

WHERE TO EAT AND STAY

$$$$ ✕ **Loch Bay Seafood Restaurant.** On the waterfront stands a distinctive
SEAFOOD black-and-white restaurant. This relaxed place is where the island's
top chefs unwind on their nights off, so you know the food must be
good. The seafood is freshly caught and simply prepared, the goal
being to enhance the natural flavors of the ingredients rather than
overwhelm the senses with extraneous sauces. The menu offers a range
of fish dishes, including halibut, sea bass and Western Ross salmon. At
dinner you must order two courses. ⑤ *Average main: £26* ✉ *Off B886,
near fishing jetty, Stein* ☎ *01470/592235* ⊕ *www.lochbay-seafood-
restaurant.co.uk* ⚷ *Reservations essential* ⊘ *Closed Sun. and Mon.
No lunch Tues. and Fri.*

$$ ⌂ **Greshornish House.** Set above a sea loch, this pretty white house
B&B/INN stands among mature trees and beside a nurtured, but not tame,
walled garden filled with raspberries, currents, and gooseberries.
Pros: ideal setting; lovely gardens; great walks at the doorstep. **Cons:**
reserved welcome may not suit everyone. ⑤ *Rooms from: £150* ✉ *Off
A850, Greshornish* ☎ *01470/582266* ⊕ *www.greshornishhouse.com*
➷ *8 rooms* ⑩ *Some meals.*

GLENDALE

2 miles south of Dunvegan.

Glendale is a region rich in flora and fauna: otters, seals, and dolphins
can be spotted off its rocky coast, and eagles soar above. Dunvegan
Castle is at the region's eastern edge.

GETTING HERE AND AROUND

Traveling south from Dunvegan, the B884 road twists and curves along
the coast. It can feel quite isolated in bad weather or after dark.

EXPLORING

Borreraig Park Museum. The fascinating Borreraig Park Museum—
described by the owner as "a unique gallimaufry for your delight and
edification"—includes a detailed series of panels on the making of bag-
pipes and on the history of the MacCrimmons, hereditary pipers to the
Clan MacLeod. A superb gift shop stocks unique island-made sweaters
(the exact sheep can be named), bagpipes, silver and gold jewelry in
Celtic designs, and recordings of traditional music. ✉ *Borreraig Park,
B884* ☎ *01470/511311* ⌸ *£2.50* ⊘ *Apr.–Oct., daily 10–6.*

Fodor's Choice **Dunvegan Castle.** In a commanding position above a sea loch, Dunvegan
★ Castle has been the seat of the chiefs of Clan MacLeod for more than
700 years. Though the structure has been greatly changed over the
centuries, a gloomy ambience prevails, and there's plenty of family
history on display, notably the Fairy Flag—a silk banner, thought to be
originally from Rhodes or Syria and believed to have magically saved
the clan from danger. Enthusiastic guides take you through several
rooms, and an interesting collection of photos hangs in the lower cor-
ridors. Make time to visit the gardens, with their water garden and
falls, fern house, a walled garden, and various viewing points. There's
a café beside the car park. Dunvegan Sea Cruises runs a boat trip from
the castle to the nearby seal colony. ✉ *Junction of A850 and A863,*

Dunvegan ☎ *01470/521206* ⊕ *www.dunvegancastle.com* ✉ *Garden £7.50, castle and garden £9.50* ⊙ *Late Mar.–mid-Oct., daily 10–5:30, last entry 30 mins before closing.*

WHERE TO EAT AND STAY

$$$$
MODERN BRITISH
Fodor'sChoice
★

✕ **Three Chimneys.** On Loch Dunvegan, this old building with thick stone walls holds a restaurant that has become a top destination for serious foodies. The kitchen serves consistently daring, well-crafted food, and the chef's belief in Scottish ingredients is clear in what is on offer: Glendale salad leaves, panfried Mallaig skate, and Esk salmon, for starters. Dinner is a three- or seven-course fixed-price extravaganza; lunch is shorter but has an equally tempting menu. If you love the food so much you want to stay here, there are six comfortable rooms at the nearby House Over-By. ⑤ *Average main: £60* ✉ *B884, Colbost* ☎ *01470/511258* ⊕ *www.threechimneys.co.uk* ⚐ *Reservations essential* ⊙ *No lunch Sun.*

$
B&B/INN

🏨 **Roskhill House.** A 19th-century croft house that once housed the local post office, this pretty white hotel feels like a home away from home. **Pros:** great breakfasts; friendly and helpful hosts; cozy lounge with fireplace; free Wi-Fi. **Cons:** very small place; books up well in advance. ⑤ *Rooms from: £78* ✉ *A863, 3 miles south of Dunvegan, Roskhill* ☎ *01470/521317* ⊕ *www.roskhillhouse.co.uk* 🍴 *5 rooms* ⦿ *Breakfast.*

SHOPPING

Skye Silver. Gold and silver jewelry with Celtic themes are a specialty of Skye Silver. More unusual pieces that reflect the natural forms of the seashore and countryside: silver-coral earrings, silver-leaf pendants, and starfish earrings. It's near Dunvegan. ✉ *The Old School, B884, Colbost* ☎ *01470/511263* ⊕ *www.skyesilver.com.*

GLEN BRITTLE AND THE CUILLIN MOUNTAINS

28 miles southeast of Glendale.

Fodor'sChoice
★

The gentle slopes of the valley called Glen Brittle are a gateway to the dramatic peaks and ridges of the Cuillin Mountains. The lower slopes are fine for walkers and weekend climbers, but the higher ridges are strictly for the serious mountaineers.

GETTING HERE AND AROUND

Glen Brittle extends off the A863/B8009 on the west side of the island.

EXPLORING

Glen Brittle. You can safely enjoy spectacular mountain scenery in Glen Brittle, with some fine views of the Cuillin Mountains (which are not for the casual walker, as there are many steep and dangerous cliff faces). The drive from Carbost along a single-track road is one of the most dramatic in Scotland and draws outdoorsy types from throughout the world. At the southern end of the glen is a murky-color beach, a campground, and the chance for a gentle stroll amid the foothills. ✉ *Off A863 and B8009.*

10

Talisker Distillery. The only distillery on the Isle of Skye, Talisker produces a sweet, light single malt that has the typical peaty aroma of island whiskies, but is a bit less intense. Robert Louis Stevenson called Talisker "the king of drinks," and the inhabitants of Skye are very proud of it. Classic tours take about 45 minutes, while two-hour tasting tours are usually available Monday, Wednesday, and Friday. ■ TIP→ **Book ahead, as the tours are very popular.** ⊠ *B8009, Carbost* ☎ *01478/614308* ⊕ *www.discovering-distilleries.com/talisker* ⌑ *£7* ☉ *Apr., May, and Oct., Mon.–Sat. 9:30–5; June and Sept., Mon.–Sat., 9:30–5, Sun. 11–5; July and Aug., weekdays 9:30–5:30, Sat. 9:30–5, Sun. 11–5; Nov.–Mar., daily 10–4:30.*

THE OUTER HEBRIDES

The Outer Hebrides—the Western Isles in common parlance—stretch about 130 miles from end to end and lie about 50 miles from the Scottish mainland. This splintered archipelago extends from the Butt of Lewis in the north to the 600-foot Barra Head on Berneray in the south, whose lighthouse has the greatest arc of visibility in the world. In the Hebrides, clouds cling to the hills, and rain comes in squalls. Any trip here requires protection from the weather and a conviction that a great holiday does not require the sun.

The Isle of Lewis and Harris is the northernmost and largest of the group. The island's only major town, Stornoway, is on a nearly landlocked harbor on the east coast of Lewis; it's probably the most convenient starting point for a driving tour of the islands if you're approaching the Western Isles from the Northern Highlands. Lewis has some fine historic attractions, including the Calanais Standing Stones—a truly magical place. The Uists are known for their rare, plentiful wildlife.

Just south of the Sound of Harris is the Isle of North Uist, rich in monoliths, chambered cairns, and other reminders of a prehistoric past. Benbecula, sandwiched between North and South Uist, is in fact less bare and neglected-looking than its bigger neighbors to the north. The Isle of South Uist, once a refuge of the old Catholic faith, is dotted with ruined forts and chapels; in summer its wild gardens burst with alpine and rock plants. Eriskay Island and a scattering of islets almost block the 6-mile strait between South Uist and Barra, an isle you can walk across in an hour.

Harris tweed is available at many outlets on the islands, including some of the weavers' homes; keep an eye out for signs directing you to weavers' workshops. Sunday on the islands is observed as a day of rest, and nearly all shops and visitor attractions are closed.

ISLE OF LEWIS

53 miles from Ullapool via ferry.

The history of Lewis stretches back 5,000 years, as archaeological sites scattered across the island attest. Here the Highland past persists in the Gaelic that is spoken everywhere, and the clan names still borne by most of its inhabitants. The main town is Stornaway.

GETTING HERE AND AROUND

Three main routes radiate from Stornaway to give access to the Isle of Lewis. The A859 leads south to Harris, the A858 travels west via Dalbeg to where it meets the A857 near Brue. The A857 leads north from Stornaway to the island's northernmost point at Port Ness.

STORNOWAY

2½-hr ferry trip from Ullapool.

The port capital for the Outer Hebrides is Stornoway, the only major town on Lewis. The island's cultural center, it has an increasing number of good restaurants.

GETTING HERE AND AROUND

The ferry docks at Stornoway, and there's an airport. It's best to have a car to explore the island, but there are also infrequent local buses.

ESSENTIALS

Airport Contact Stornoway Airport ✉ *A866, Stornaway* ☎ *01851/707400* ⊕ *www.hial.co.uk/stornoway-airport.*

Visitor Information Stornoway Information Centre ✉ *26 Cromwell St.* ☎ *01851/703088* ⊕ *www.visitscotland.com.*

EXPLORING

An Lanntair Arts Centre. The fabulous An Lanntair Arts Centre hosts exhibitions of contemporary and traditional art. There are frequent traditional musical and theatrical events in the impressive auditorium. There's also a cinema, a gift shop, and a restaurant serving international and Scottish fare. ✉ *Kenneth St.* ☎ *01851/703307* ⊕ *www.lanntair.com* 🎫 *Free* ⊗ *Mon.–Sat. 10 am–8 pm.*

WHERE TO EAT AND STAY

$$$
MODERN BRITISH

✗ **Digby Chick.** This local favorite is a great destination on a rainy night. The solid wood floors and white tablecloths brighten the spirits. The seasonal food is hearty even in the middle of summer, with scallops and pea puree, duck breast with citrus syrup, and sweet-toothed desserts like raspberry soufflé mousse with ginger shortcake and frozen white chocolate parfait. ⑤ *Average main: £20* ✉ *5 Bank St.* ☎ *01851/700026* ⊕ *www.digbychick.co.uk* ⊗ *No lunch Sun.*

$$$
B&B/INN

🏨 **Broad Bay House.** It's not in town, but you won't miss the hustle and bustle once you see the great views of the water from Broad Bay House. **Pros:** pure luxury; great coastal walks; fantastic evening meals. **Cons:** no kids under 12; only one room has sea views; it isn't cheap; you'll need a car to get around. ⑤ *Rooms from: £179* ✉ *B895, 7 miles north of Stornoway* ☎ *01851/820990* ⊕ *www.broadbayhouse.co.uk* ⇗ *4 rooms* ⎛⎞⎝ *Breakfast.*

10

SHOPPING

Harris Tweed Artisans Cooperative. The Harris Tweed Artisans Cooperative sells stylish and quirky hand-crafted tweed clothing, hats, and accessories, all made by local artists. ⊠ *40 Point St.*

BICYCLING

Alex Dan Cycle Centre. When you rent a bike here you also get valuable advice on where to ride, including a route to Tolsta that takes in five stunning beaches before reaching the edge of moorland. ⊠ *67 Kenneth St.* ☎ *01851/704025* ⊕ *www.hebrideancycles.co.uk.*

PORT OF NESS

30 miles north of Stornoway.

The stark, windswept community of Port of Ness cradles a small harbor squeezed in among the rocks.

GETTING HERE AND AROUND

From Stornoway, take the A857 to the Port of Ness.

EXPLORING

Fodor's Choice ★ **Black House.** In the small community of Arnol, the Black House is a well-preserved example of an increasingly rare type of traditional Hebridean home. Once common throughout the islands—even into the 1950s—these dwellings were built without mortar and thatched on a timber framework without eaves. Other characteristic features include an open central peat hearth and the absence of a chimney—hence the soot and the designation *black*. On display inside are many of the house's original furnishings. Opposite is the White House, built later when houses were no longer allowed to accommodate humans and animals together. To reach Arnol from Port of Ness, head south on the A857 and pick up the A858 at Barvas. ⊠ *Off A858, 21 miles southwest of Port of Ness, Arnol* ☎ *01851/710395* ⊕ *www.historic-scotland.gov.uk* ⊠ *£4* ⊙ *Apr.–Sept., Mon.–Sat. 9:30–5:30; Oct.–Mar., Mon.–Sat. 9:30–4:30.*

Butt of Lewis Lighthouse. At the northernmost point of Lewis stands the Butt of Lewis Lighthouse, designed by David and Thomas Stevenson (of the prominent engineering family whose best-known member was not an engineer at all, but the novelist Robert Louis Stevenson). The structure was first lighted in 1862. The adjacent cliffs provide a good vantage point for viewing seabirds, whales, and porpoises. The lighthouse is northwest of Port of Ness along the B8014.

10

SHOPPING

Borgh Pottery. Here you can buy attractive hand-thrown studio pottery made on the premises, including lamps, vases, mugs, and dishes. ⊠ *Fivepenny House, A857, Borve* ☎ *01851/850345* ⊕ *www.borgh-pottery. com* ⊙ *Mon.–Sat. 9:30–6.*

EN ROUTE The journey along the A857 takes you past several interesting sights.

Dun Carloway. One of the best-preserved Iron Age *brochs* (circular stone towers) in Scotland, Dun Carloway dominates the scattered community of Carloway. The mysterious tower was probably built around 2,000 years ago as protection against seaborne raiders. The Dun Broch Centre explains more about the broch and its setting. ⊠ *Off A857, Carloway.*

Gearrannan. Up a side road north from Carloway, Gearrannan is an old black-house village that has been brought back to life with a museum screening excellent short films on peat cutting and weaving. For a unique experience, groups can rent the restored houses. There is also a shop and café. ⊠ *Off A858, Carloway* ☎ *01851/643416* ⊕ *www.gearrannan.com.*

CALANAIS STANDING STONES
15 miles west of Stornoway.

The group of stones at this ancient site is mysterious but evocative.

GETTING HERE AND AROUND
Take the A858 to reach Calanais.

EXPLORING

Fodor's Choice **Calanais Standing Stones.** These impressive stones are actually part of a
★ cluster of several different archaeological sites in this area. Probably positioned in several stages between 3000 BC and 1500 BC, the grouping consists of an avenue of 19 monoliths extending northward from a circle of 13 stones, with other rows leading south, east, and west. Ruins of a cairn sit within the circle on the east side. Researchers believe they may have been used for astronomical observations, but you can create your own explanations. The visitor center has an exhibit on the stones, a gift shop, and a tearoom. ⊠ *On unmarked road off A858* ☎ *01851/621422* ⊕ *www. callanishvisitorcentre.co.uk* 🖾 *£2.50* ☉ *Apr., May, Sept., Oct., Mon.–Sat. 10–6; June–Aug., Mon.–Sat. 10–8; Nov.–Mar., Tues.–Sat. 10–4.*

ISLE OF HARRIS

36 miles from the Isle of Lewis via the A859.

For most people, Harris is forever linked to tweed. Woven here and on nearby islands, the tweed has colors that echo the tones of the landscape. The dramatic mountains of the northern part of the island give way in the south to the *machairs*, the grassy plains typical of this region, and the spectacular beaches that gleam in the famous sunsets.

GETTING HERE AND AROUND
The A859 is the main artery through Harris. From Tarbert you can follow the A859 to Leverburgh (21 miles) and Rodel (23 miles), where you can catch ferries bound for Newtonferry in North Uist. The single-track road down the east coast is known as the Golden Road.

TARBERT
47 miles south of Calanais.

The main port of Harris, Tarbert has some good shops and a few worthwhile sights. **Traigh Luskentyre,** roughly 5 miles southwest of Tarbert, is a spectacular example of Harris's tidy selection of beaches—2 miles of yellow sands adjacent to **Traigh Seilebost** beach, with superb views northward to the hills of the Forest of Harris. The narrow Golden Road, on the west coast, follows the coast and offers some glorious views.

GETTING HERE AND AROUND
The ferry from Uig arrives at Tarbert once or twice daily. Having a car makes travel on Harris much easier, but with careful planning local buses can make for an excellent trip.

ESSENTIALS
Visitor Information
Tarbert Information Centre
⊠ *Pier Rd.* ☎ *01859/502011*
⊕ *www.visitscotland.com.*

EXPLORING
Amhuinnsuidhe Castle. Turreted Amhuinnsuidhe Castle (pronounced avun-*shooee*) was built in the 1860s by the earls of Dunmore as a base for fishing and hunting in the North Harris deer forest. The castle, which is now an exclusive resort, stands about 10 miles northwest of Tarbert. ⊠ *B887, Amhuinnsuidhe* ☎ *01859/560200* ⊕ *www.amhuinnsuidhe.com.*

Caledonian MacBrayne. This company runs one or two ferries a day beween Tarbert and Uig on the Isle of Skye. ⊠ *Pier Rd.* ☎ *01859/502444* ⊕ *www.calmac.co.uk.*

WHERE TO EAT
$$$$
MODERN BRITISH
Fodor's Choice
★

✕ **Scarista House.** Hearty, well-seasoned food is what you'll find here, particularly local catches like Sound of Harris langoustine and perfectly pitched desserts like tarte tartin. Stunning views from the dining room extend across a sloping golf course to the sea. The building, previously a manse, is made cozy with heavy curtains, sturdy sofas and chairs, and an open fire. Coffee and petits fours are delivered to you in the comfortable library. The house also has rooms for rent. ⑤ *Average main: £45* ⊠ *A859, 15 miles south of Tarbert, Sgarasta Gheag* ☎ *01859/550238* ⊕ *www.scaristahouse.com* ⊘ *No lunch.*

LEVERBURGH
21 miles south of Tarbert.

Named after Lord Leverhulme, who bought Lewis and Harris in 1917 with an eye to developing its local industries, Leverburgh is now the ferry port for North Uist. Nearby Northton has several attractions, and St. Clement's Church at Rodel is particularly worth a visit.

GETTING HERE AND AROUND
Leverburgh is on the A859 between Tarbert and Rodel.

EXPLORING
Seallam! Visitor Centre and Co Leis Thu? Genealogical Research Centre. The center is where you can trace your Western Isles ancestry. Photographs and interpretive signs describe the history of Harris and its people. The owners organize guided walks and cultural evenings weekly between May and September. ⊠ *Off A859, Northton* ☎ *01859/520258* ⊕ *www.hebridespeople.com* ⊠ *£2.50* ⊘ *Mon.–Sat. 10–5.*

10

St. Clement's Church. At the southernmost point of Harris is the community of Rodel, where you can find St. Clement's Church, a cruciform church standing on a hillock. The most impressive pre-Reformation church in the Outer Hebrides, it was built around 1500 and contains the magnificently sculptured tomb (1528) of the church's builder, Alasdair Crotach, MacLeod chief of Dunvegan Castle. ⊠ *A859, 3 miles south of Leverburgh, Rodel.*

OFF THE BEATEN PATH

St. Kilda. About 15 miles to the west of Harris lies the abandoned island of St. Kilda. Dependent on the flesh of the fulmar, the cliff-dwelling seabird, the population of this most westerly of all the islands lived in the harshest conditions. By 1930 the 30 remaining inhabitants left their village on the small plain above the immense cliffs where they had once climbed in search of the fulmar forever. Cruises to this frozen-in-time place depart from Leverburgh and take three hours; you then have four hours to wander the island. Costing £190, the tours are operated by Kilda Cruises (*www.kildacruises.co.uk*) and Sea Harris (*www.seaharris.co.uk*).

WHERE TO EAT AND STAY

$

MODERN BRITISH

✕ **Anchorage Restaurant.** Perched at the southernmost tip of the Island of Harris, this lively restaurant looks across the Sea of Hebrides toward North Uist. It's a great place to grab a bite before hopping aboard the ferry, which departs from the harbor nearby. The menu ranges from burgers and sandwiches to local langoustines and scallops. Booking ahead is recommended. Open late, the bar is something of a refuge in these parts. $ *Average main: £13* ⊠ *Pier Rd.* ☎ *01859/520225* ☾ *Closed Sun.*

$$

B&B/INN

▦ **Parc an t-Srath Guest House.** Set back from the main road, this white house is distinguished by two lions guarding the door (they are plaster, of course). **Pros:** lovely views of the coast; very good breakfasts. **Cons:** rooms are quite small; perhaps too many animal statues. $ *Rooms from: £104* ⊠ *Off A859, Borve, Isle of Harris* ☎ *01859/550386* ➫ *3 rooms* ♨ *Breakfast.*

SHOPPING

Hebrides Art. This lovely gallery features the work of Alisdair and Lesley Wiseman, who run the place, and stocks a wide range of other artworks with a Hebridean theme. The on-site café serves sandwiches and wonderful homemade cakes. ⊠ *Seilebost, Borve* ☎ *01859/550338* ⊕ *www.hebridesart.co.uk.*

NORTH UIST

8 miles south of Rodel via ferry from Leverburgh.

Stunning coastal scenery and ancient ruins are the main draws on North Uist. You'll find art throughout the island: at the end of roads or paths or on the shore, only visible from a boat. Be sure to visit the camera obscura (an old-fashioned projector) just beyond the ferry terminal. Its watery images are evocative and a bit eerie.

GETTING HERE AND AROUND

You can get to North Uist by ferry, either from Harris, the Isle of Skye, or from one of the other islands. Public transport is infrequent, so a car (or a bike) is the most reliable way to travel.

EXPLORING

Balranald Nature Reserve. Run by the Royal Society for the Protection of Birds, the Balranald Nature Reserve shelters large numbers of waders and seabirds. It's on the west side of North Uist. ✉ *Off A865, 3 miles northwest of Bayhead* ☎ *01876/560287* ⊕ *www.rspb.org. uk* ✉ *Free* ⊙ *Apr.–Aug. 9–6.*

Barpa Langass Chambered Cairn. Dating from the 3rd millennium BC, the Barpa Langass Chambered Cairn is the only chambered cairn in the Western Isles known to have retained its inner chamber fully intact. You can peek inside, but don't venture too far without a light. It sits close to the A867 between Lochmaddy and Clachen.

Dun an Sticar. At Newtonferry (Port nan Long) stands the remains of what was reputed to be the last inhabited broch in North Uist, Dun an Sticar. This defensive tower, reached by a causeway over the loch, was abandoned when the Vikings arrived in the 9th century and then reoccupied by Hugh Macdonald, a descendant of Macdonald of Sleat, until he reached an unpleasant end in 1602.

Taigh Chearsabhagh. Set right on the shore, the well-run Taigh Chearsabhagh has two separate exhibition spaces, a working print shop, and a permanent exhibition in which life on North Uist is brilliantly described. The café serves a selection of cakes and soup, as well as excellent French press coffee. ✉ *A865* ☎ *01870/603970* ⊕ *www.taigh-chearsabhagh.org* ✉ *£2* ⊙ *Apr.–Oct., Mon.–Sat. 10–5.*

Trinity Temple (Teampull na Trionaid). You can explore the ruins of Trinity Temple (Teampull na Trionaid), a medieval college and monastery said to have been founded in the 13th century by Beathag, daughter of Somerled, the progenitor of the Clan Donald. The ruins stand 8 miles southwest of Lochmaddy, off the A865.

> ### RIDING THE FERRY
>
> For some travelers the Caledonian MacBrayne (locals call them CalMac) ferries are the best part of a trip to Scotland. Imagine the slow rolling of the boat on the waves, storm petrels in the distance, seagulls and gannets nearer the boat. Some locals sleep through the often-blustery trip, but hearty folk don their rain slickers and look for whales and dolphins from the deck.

10

SOUTH UIST

34 miles south of Newtonferry (on North Uist) via Grimsay, Benbecula, and three causeways.

Carpets of wildflowers in spring and early summer, superb deserted beaches, and historical connections to Flora Macdonald and Bonnie Prince Charlie head the list of reasons to visit this island.

GETTING HERE AND AROUND

You can travel the length of South Uist along Route A865, making short treks off this main road on your way to Lochboisdale, on the southeast coast of the island. At Lochboisdale you can catch ferries to Barra, the southernmost principal island of the Outer Hebrides, or to Oban, on the mainland.

EXPLORING

Kildonan Museum and Heritage Centre. The Kildonan Museum and Heritage Centre houses South Uist artifacts collected in the 1950s and 1960s by Father John Morrison, a local priest. On your left when you enter is a simple exhibition with concise and unsentimental descriptions of living on South Uist that reads, "However we interpret it there is nothing surer than that history has as much to do with the present as the past." The simple details, like how people filled their mattresses or the names for the tools they used in their houses are what makes this place interesting. ✉ *A865, Kildonan* ☎ *01878/710343* 💷 *£2* ⊙ *Easter–Oct., daily 10–5.*

Loch Druidibeg National Nature Reserve. One of only two remaining British native—that is, nonmigrating—populations of greylag geese make their home at Loch Druidibeg National Nature Reserve in a fresh and brackish loch environment. Stop at the warden's office for information about access and nature trails. ✉ *Off A865* ☎ *01870/620238.*

WHERE TO STAY

$ ⚎ **Polochar Inn.** With its own standing stone surviving the rough winds
B&B/INN   off the sea, the Polochar Inn sits at the southern end of South Uist. **Pros:** wild and remote location; reasonable rates; plenty of charm. **Cons:** some rooms smaller than others. ⑤ *Rooms from: £90* ✉ *A865, Lochboisdale, South Uist* ☎ *01878/700215* ⊕ *www.polocharinn.com* ⇄ *11 rooms* ❑ *Breakfast.*

SHOPPING

Hebridean Jewellery. Much of the Celtic-influenced jewelry at Hebridean Jewellery is made in the workshop, which you can tour. A café serves excellent espresso, rich cakes, and tasty soups. ✉ *Off A865, Iochdar* ☎ *01870/610288* ⊕ *www.hebrideanjewellery.co.uk.*

ORKNEY AND SHETLAND ISLANDS

Updated by
Shona Main

A Scandinavian heritage gives the 170 islets that make up Orkney and Shetland a history and an ambience different from that of any other region of Scotland. Both Orkney and Shetland are essentially austere and bleak, but they have awe-inspiring seascapes, fascinating seabirds, remarkable ancient ruins, and genuinely warm, friendly people. Although a trip to these remote islands requires time and effort, your reward will be a unique experience.

An Orcadian has been defined as a farmer with a boat, whereas a Shetlander has been called a fisherman with a croft (small farm). Orkney, the southern archipelago, is greener and is rich with artifacts that testify to the many centuries of continuous settlement here: stone circles, burial chambers, ancient settlements, and fortifications. UNESCO has recognized the key remains as a World Heritage Site called the Heart of Neolithic Orkney.

North of Orkney, Shetland, with its ocean views and sparse landscapes—trees are a rarity because of ever-present wind—seems even more remote. However, don't let Shetland's desolate countryside fool you: it has a wealth of historic interest and is far from being a backwater. Oil money from local mineral resources and its position as a crossroads in the northern seas for centuries have helped make Shetland a busy, thriving community that wants for little.

For mainland Scots, visiting these islands is a little like traveling abroad without having to worry about a different language or currency. Neither has yet been overrun by tourism, but the people of Orkney and Shetland will be delighted that you have come so far to see their islands and learn a little of their extraordinary past.

ORIENTATION AND PLANNING

GETTING ORIENTED

Ten miles from Caithness in Scotland, Orkney is made up of 70 islands, of which 10 are inhabited. A number of ferries travel to ports on the Mainland, the main island of Orkney, including its administrative center, Kirkwall, where an airport serves Scotland's larger cities. The primary road is essentially a loop that passes near the key historic sites. The Mainland is linked to the southern island of South Ronaldsay by way of the Barricades.

About 125 miles north of Orkney lies the spiny outline of Shetland, comprising 100 islands. Sumburgh has the main airport, and 25 miles north is Lerwick, the island's "capital" and a port linking the island to Scotland and Orkney. South Mainland, half an hour from Lerwick,

TOP REASONS TO GO

Standing stones and ancient sites: Among the many Neolithic treasures in Orkney are the Ring of Brodgar, a 3,000-year old circle of standing stones, and Skara Brae, the remarkable remains of a village uncovered on the grounds of delightful Skaill House. In Shetland, Jarlshof has been the home to different societies since the Bronze Age. Don't miss Mousa Broch and Clickimin Broch in Shetland, two Iron Age towers.

Music and arts festivals: The Shetland Folk Festival in May is a fiddling shindig that attracts musicians and revelers from around the world. Orkney's St. Magnus Festival is less of a pub crawl and more of a highbrow celebration of classical music, poetry, and performance.

Seabirds, seals, and more: These islands have some of the planet's most important colonies of seabirds, with millions clinging to colossal cliffs. You're guaranteed to see seals and may spot dolphins, orcas, or porpoises. In Shetland, Noss and Eshaness nature reserves are prime spots, or you can check out the puffins by Sumburgh Head.

Pure relaxation: There's a much more laid-back approach to life on these islands than on the mainland. Shetlanders are particularly renowned for their hospitality and are often happy to share stories and tips that will enrich your adventure.

Outdoor activities by the coast and ocean: The rugged terrain, beautiful beaches, and unspoiled waters make a perfect backdrop for invigorating strolls, sea fishing, diving, or exploring the coastline and sea lochs by boat.

has prehistoric sites. Less than an hour north of Lerwick are dramatic landscapes such as Eshaness. Ferries go beyond the Mainland to Yell and Unst, the latter Britain's most northerly point.

Orkney. The towns of Stomness and Kirkwall have sights and museums testifying to Orkney's rich past, including Kirkwall's Norman St. Magnus Cathedral. For many people, though, they're a prelude to impressive Neolithic sites around the Mainland: Maes Howe, Skara Brae, the Ring of Brodgar, and others. Beyond the Mainland, explore sights such as Scapa Flow on Hoy, which reveals the islands' role in two world wars.

Shetland. A descent at Sumburgh's airport provides stunning views of a shining white lighthouse, bird-crammed cliffs, and golden bays. Lerwick has the excellent Shetland Museum, and nearby on the South Mainland are the prehistoric sites of Jarlshof, Old Scatness, and Mousa Broch. Worth exploring to the north are the lunarlike Ronas Hill and wave-lashed Eshaness. Unst, the island farthest north, is worth the journey for wide-open ocean views and superb bird-watching at Hermaness National Nature Reserve.

PLANNING

WHEN TO GO

Although shivering, wind-flattened visitors braving Orkney and Shetland's winter are not unheard of, the travel season doesn't really start until May, and it runs until September. June is one of the most popular months for both islands. The bird colonies are at their liveliest in early summer, which is also when the long northern daylight hours allow you plenty of sightseeing time. Shetland's northerly position means that it has only four or five hours of darkness around the summer solstice, and on a clear night it doesn't seem to get dark at all. Beware the changeable weather even in summer: it could be 75°F one day and then hail the next. Many sights close in September, and by October wilder gales will be mixed with snow flurries one minute and glorious sunshine the next. If you are determined to brave the elements, take into account that there are only six hours of daylight in winter months.

Shetland's festival of fire, Up-Helly-Aa, is held the last Tuesday of each January. The spectacle of Lerwick overrun by Vikings, with torches aflame and a huge Viking longship, is wildly popular. Book at least a year in advance if you want to get a bed for the night.

PLANNING YOUR TIME

Orkney and Shetland require at least a couple of days each if you're to do more than just scratch the surface. Since getting to Shetland isn't easy, you may want to spend three or four days here. The isles generate their own laid-back approach to life, and once here, you may want to take it slowly. A good clutch of the key sites of Mainland Orkney can be seen in a day, if you have a car and are disciplined, but to really get the most out of them, take two days. You can do the Kirkwall sights in a morning before heading to the Italian Chapel on South Ronaldsay in the afternoon. This allows a whole day for Stomness, a town caught in the most poignant of time warps, and the archaeological sites of Maes Howe, the Ring of Brodgar, Skara Brae, and Skaill House and Gurness Broch. To include Birsay, plan your day round the tides.

In Shetland, the sites on the South Mainland—Jarlshof, Scatness, the Crofhouse Museum, St. Ninian's Isle, and Mousa Broch—take the best part of a day, although sailing times for Mousa must be factored in to your schedule. Lerwick and its lanes and spectacular museum is a good day, and can be supplemented with a trip to the Bonhoga Gallery in Weisdale. It's a good idea to take a whole day to explore the north of the islands, including Eshaness and Tangwick Haa, although a car or a guide who drives will be necessary. Ferry times allow for a mad dash round the northern islands of Yell and Unst, but you will see more if you book an overnight stay.

GETTING HERE AND AROUND

AIR TRAVEL

Loganair, Scotland's national airline, provides regular service to Sumburgh in Shetland and Kirkwall in Orkney from Edinburgh, Glasgow, Aberdeen, and Inverness. Tickets are reasonably priced if you book well in advance. Because of the isolation of Orkney and Shetland, there's also a network of interisland flights, through Directflight in Shetland and Loganair in Orkney. These flights are run by a friendly staff and are as reliable as the weather allows them to be.

Airline Contacts Directflight ☎ *01595/840246* ⊕ *www.directflight.co.uk.*
Flybe ☎ *0871/700–2000* ⊕ *www.flybe.com.* **Loganair** ☎ *0871/700–2000*
⊕ *www.loganair.co.uk.*

BOAT AND FERRY TRAVEL

Northlink operates ferries—locally known as "the boat"—from Aberdeen to Kirkwall in Orkney and Lerwick in Shetland. These leave Aberdeen harbor each evening (or every second night for Kirkwall), arriving at Kirkwall at 11 pm and Lerwick at 7:30 am the next day. These top-notch services have recliner seats for the budget traveler or clean, compact cabins in single, double, or four-berth combinations. There's a shop, a cinema, two bars, and two restaurants (one self-service and one table service) on each boat.

If you're arriving in Aberdeen on Sunday morning and plan on meeting a train, note that the station does not open until 9 am. Northlink allows you to stay in your cabin or the restaurant until 9:30 am.

An alternate way of reaching Orkney is the Northlink ferry from Scrabster to Stromness. There is also a ferry from John o'Groats to Burwick, operated by John o'Groats Ferries, with up to four daily departures May through September. The fastest and smoothest sail is by catamaran from Gills Bay, Caithness, to St. Margaret's Hope on Orkney. Operated by Pentland Ferries, it has three daily departures.

In both Orkney and Shetland, the local council runs the interisland ferry networks (Orkney Ferries and Shetland Island Ferries) to the outer islands. Northlink Ferries has service between Lerwick on Shetland and Kirkwall on Orkney. ■TIP➔ **Always book ferry tickets in advance.**

Ferry Contacts John o'Groats Ferries ☎ *01955/611353* ⊕ *www.jogferry.co.uk.*
Northlink Ferries ☎ *0845/6000449* ⊕ *www.northlinkferries.co.uk.* **Orkney**
Ferries ☎ *01856/872044, 0800/011 3648 Hotline for sailing information*
⊕ *www.orkneyferries.co.uk.* **Pentland Ferries** ☎ *0800/6888998*
⊕ *www.pentlandferries.co.uk.* **Shetland Island Ferries** ☎ *01595/743970*
⊕ *www.shetland.gov.uk/ferries.*

BUS TRAVEL

Scottish Citylink and Stagecoach operate buses to Aberdeen where you can get a plane, ferry, or connecting bus to the ferries at John o'Groats, Gills Bay, or Scrabster. John o'Groats Ferries operates the Orkney Bus, a direct express coach from Inverness to Kirkwall (via ferry) that runs daily from June to early September.

The main bus service on Orkney is operated by Stagecoach and on Shetland by ZetTrans (although buses are run by small operators).

Bus Contacts John o'Groats Ferries ☎ *01955/611353* ⊕ *www.jogferry.co.uk.*
National Express ☎ *08717/818178* ⊕ *www.nationalexpress.co.uk.*
Stagecoach ☎ *01856/878014* ⊕ *www.stagecoachbus.com.* **Scottish Citylink**
☎ *0871/2663333* ⊕ *www.citylink.co.uk.* **ZetTrans** ☎ *01595/694100*
⊕ *www.zettrans.org.uk.*

CAR TRAVEL

The most convenient way of getting around these islands is by car, especially if your time is limited. Roads are well maintained and traffic is nearly nonexistent, although speeding cars can be a problem. Orkney has causeways—the Barricades—connecting some of the islands, but in some cases these roads take fairly roundabout routes.

You can transport your rental car from Aberdeen, but for fewer than five days it's usually cheaper to rent a car from one of Shetland and Orkney's agencies. Most are based in Lerwick, Shetland, and Kirkwall, Orkney, but airport pickups are easily arranged.

Local Car Rental Contacts Bolts Car and Minibus Hire ✉ *26 North Rd., Lerwick* ☎ *01595/693636* ⊕ *www.boltscarhire.co.uk.* **Orkney Car Hire** ✉ *Junction Rd., Kirkwall* ☎ *01856/872866* ⊕ *www.orkneycarhire.co.uk.* **Star Rent-a-Car** ✉ *22 Commercial Rd., Lerwick* ☎ *01595/692075 Lerwick, 01950/460444 Sumburgh Airport* ⊕ *www.starrentacar.co.uk.* **W. R. Tullock** ✉ *Castle Garage, Castle St., Kirkwall* ☎ *01856/875500* ⊕ *www.orkneycarrental.co.uk.*

TRAIN TRAVEL

There are no trains on Orkney or Shetland, but you can take the train to Aberdeen or Thurso and then take a ferry to the islands.

Train Contact ScotRail ☎ *08457/484950* ⊕ *www.scotrail.co.uk.*

RESTAURANTS

Kirkwall has an increasing number of good cafés and restaurants, as does Lerwick, but both islands now have memorable spots beyond the main towns, from cafés and fish-and-chips spots to some fancier restaurants. Orkney and Shetland have first-class seafood, and in pastoral Orkney the beef is lauded and in Shetland the heather- or seaweed-fed lamb. Orkney is famous for its cheese and its fudge; a glug of its Highland Park malt whisky or some Skull Splitter Ale is also worth trying. Shetlanders are beginning to make much more of their natural edible resources, making ice cream and smoking fish in a variety of ways. Some bakeries create their own version of bannocks—a scone-type baked item you eat with salt beef, mutton, or jam—but Johnson and Wood of Voe (available in shops across the islands) takes the biscuit. *Prices in the reviews are the average cost of a main course at dinner or, if dinner is not served, at lunch.*

HOTELS

Accommodations in Orkney and Shetland are on par with mainland Scotland, with a growing range of stylish bed-and-breakfasts that might suit some travelers better than the bigger hotels that rely and therefore focus on business customers. Although standards are improving, the islands still do not offer luxury accommodations. To experience a simpler stay, check out the unique "camping böds" in Shetland—old

> ### WORD OF MOUTH
>
> "A warning about flying to Orkney if your time is limited: the fog came down and I had to give up after the first three flights and return to the mainland by ferry—great experience but disastrous if I had had an international flight to connect with. The Orkneys are absolutely lovely to visit."
>
> —tenaya

cottages providing inexpensive, basic lodging (log fires, cold water, and sometimes no electricity). For details, contact the Shetland Tourist Information Centre. *Prices in the reviews are the lowest cost of a standard double room in high season, including 20% V.A.T.*

TOURS

Wildabout Orkney runs bus tours combining visits to archaeological sites and information on the folklore, flora, and fauna of the islands. In Shetland, Island Trails offers excellent tours enriched by the many myths, customs, and folklore of the islanders. Seabirds and Seals tours take you on board the cruiser *Dunter III* to tour Bressay and the island of Noss, a national nature reserve and bird sanctuary, weather permitting.

Tour Contacts Island Trails ☎ *01950/950228* ⊕ *www.island-trails.co.uk.* **Seabirds and Seals** ☎ *07595/540224* ⊕ *www.seabirds-and-seals.com.* **Wildabout** ☎ *01856/877737* ⊕ *www.wildaboutorkney.com.*

VISITOR INFORMATION

The Orkney visitor center in Kirkwall, and the Shetland visitor center, in Lerwick, are open year-round. There's also a desk for Visit Shetland in the Sumburgh Airport.

Visitor Information Visit Orkney ☎ *01856/872856* ⊕ *www.visitorkney.com.* **Visit Shetland** ☎ *01595/693434* ⊕ *www.visit.shetland.com.*

TO SHETLAND: PLANE OR BOAT?

If you're flying, the descent past the lighthouse and the golden beaches that fringe the landing strip at Sumburgh Airport makes for a dramatic—if bumpy—introduction to Shetland. But if you have the time, the ferry is a more comfortable way to make the journey. There's nothing like rising from your cabin to see the "back end" of Sumburgh Head and the isle of Mousa in the morning sun. And if your fellow passengers happen to be some of Shetland's traveling musicians, your holiday will start as soon as you set sail. Their free-for-all jam sessions are legendary and sociable.

ORKNEY

If you're touring the north of Scotland, the short boat trip to Orkney offers the chance to step outside the Scottish history you've experienced on the mainland. Prehistoric sites such as the Ring of Brodgar, and the remnants of Orkney's Viking-influenced past, are in dramatic contrast to that of the mainland. The Orkney Islands may have a population of just 20,000, but a visit reveals the islands' cultural richness. In addition, Orkney's continued reliance on farming and fishing reminds you how some things can stay the same despite technological advances. At Maes Howe, for example, it becomes evident that graffiti is not solely an expression of today's youths: the Vikings left their marks here way back in the 12th century. ■TIP→ **You can purchase the Historic Scotland joint-entry ticket at the first site you visit; the ticket costs less than paying separately for entry into each site.**

STROMNESS AND THE NEOLITHIC SITES

1¾ hrs north of Thurso on Scotland's mainland, via ferry from Scrabster.

On the southwest of the Mainland, on the shore of Hamnavoe, is Stromness, a remarkably attractive fishing town seemingly so unsullied by modernity that it evokes an uncomplicated way of life long gone. Walk past the old-fashioned shops and austere cottages that line the main street and you'll understand why local poet and novelist George Mackay Brown (1921–96) was inspired and moved by its sober beauty.

With its ferry connection to Scrabster in Caithness, Stromness makes a good base for visiting the western parts of Orkney, and the town holds several points of interest. It was once a key trading port for the Hudson Bay company, and the Stromness Museum displays artifacts from those days. Nearby are three spectacular ancient sites, the Ring of Brodgar, Maes Howe, and Skara Brae at Skaill House.

GETTING HERE AND AROUND

Stromness is at the end of the A965 and can be reached by one of the many buses from Kirkwall.

Stagecoach buses 7 and 8 link Kirkwall, the Ring of Brodgar, and Skara Brae and Skaill House with Kirkwall. Altogether there are three bus services there and three back per day, so plan accordingly.

ESSENTIALS

Visitor Information Stromness Tourist Information Centre ⊠ *Pier Head* ☎ *01856/850716* ⊕ *www.visitorkney.com/stromness* ☉ *Mar.–Oct., daily 9–5.*

EXPLORING

Maes Howe. The huge burial mound of Maes Howe, circa 2500 BC, measures 115 feet in diameter and contains an enormous burial chamber. It was raided by Vikings in the 12th century, and Norse crusaders found shelter here, leaving a rich collection of runic inscriptions. Outside you see a large, grassy mound; the stunning interior of the chambered tomb has remarkably sophisticated stonework. This site is 6 miles northeast of Stromness and 1 mi from the Ring of Brodgar. Call early on the day of your visit to reserve a spot on the hourly tours. ⊠ *A965* ☎ *01856/761606* ⊕ *www.historic-scotland.gov.uk* ☒ *£5.50* ☉ *Apr.–Sept., daily 9:30–5; Oct.–Mar., daily 9:30–4.*

Pier Arts Centre. At the striking Pier Arts Centre, a gallery in a former merchant's house and adjoining buildings, huge sheets of glass offer tranquil harborside views and combine with space-maximizing design to make the best use of every shard of natural light and inch of wall to display the superb permanent collection. The more than 100 20th- and 21st-century paintings and sculptures include works by Barbara Hepworth and Douglas Gordon, and edgy temporary exhibitions showcase international contemporary artists. A chic shop sells design products and art books. ⊠ *28–30 Victoria St.* ☎ *01856/850209* ⊕ *www. pierartscentre.com* ☒ *Free* ☉ *Tue.–Sat. 10:30–5.*

Ring of Brodgar. About 5 miles northeast of Stromness, the Ring of Brodgar is a magnificent circle of 36 Neolithic standing stones (originally 60) surrounded by a henge, or deep ditch. When the fog

descends over the stones—a frequent occurrence—their looming shapes seem to come alive. The site dates to between 2500 and 2000 BC. Though the original use of the circle is uncertain, it's not hard to imagine strange rituals taking place here in the misty past. The stones stand between Loch of Harray and Loch of Stenness. ⊠ *B9055, Stromness* ☎ *01856/841815* ⊕ *www.historic-scotland.gov.uk* 🎟 *Free* ⊙ *Year-round.*

Fodor's Choice ★ **Skara Brae and Skaill House.** After a fierce storm in 1850, the laird of Breckness, William Graham Watt, discovered this cluster of Neolithic houses at the bottom of his garden. The houses, first occupied around 3000 BC and containing stone beds, fireplaces, dressers, and cupboards, are the most extensive of their kind in northern Europe and provide real insight into this ancient civilization. A reconstruction of one house can be seen in the visitor center, which displays artifacts from the site and hosts an excellent café. Skara Brae stands on the grounds of **Skaill House**, a splendid, intriguing mansion built by the Bishop of Orkney in the 1600s. His descendants, the lairds of Breckness, along with the various ladies of the manor, added to the house and to the eclectic furnishings. These sites offer a joint ticket well worth the price: the juxtaposition of different societies thousands of years apart that shared the same corner of Orkney makes a fascinating visit. ⊠ *B9056, 8 miles north of Stromness, Stromness* ☎ *01856/841815* ⊕ *www.historic-scotland.gov.uk* 🎟 *Skara Brae £5.90, Skara Brae and Skaill House £6.90* ⊙ *Skara Brae Apr.–Sept., daily 9:30–5:30; Oct.–Mar., daily 9:30–4:30. Skaill House Apr.–Sept., daily 9:30–5:30.*

FAMILY **Fodor's**Choice ★ **Stromness Museum.** The enchanting Stromness Museum has the feel of some grand Victorian's private collection but has, in fact, been community owned since it opened in 1837. Its crammed but utterly fascinating exhibits on fishing, shipping, and whaling are full of interesting trinkets from all over the world that found their way to this small Orcadian town because of its connections with the Hudson Bay Shipping Company. The company recruited workers in Stromness between the late 18th and 19th centuries as they were considered more sober and therefore more reliable than other Scots. Also here are model ships and displays on the German fleet that was scuttled on Scapa Flow in 1919. Upstairs, don't miss the beguiling, traditionally presented collection of birds and butterflies that are native to the British Isles. ⊠ *52 Alfred St., Stromness* ☎ *01856/850025* 🎟 *£4.50* ⊙ *Oct.–Mar., Mon.–Sat. 11–3:30; Apr.–Sept., daily 10–5.*

▌NEED A BREAK? **Julia's Café Bistro.** Right on the quayside, Julia's Café Bistro serves the kinds of cakes that make you conveniently forget the existence of calories. Expect huge slices of lemon drizzle, coffee layer, raspberry cream, and other cakes, as well as scones and shortbreads. Baked potatoes, quirky salads, and quiches round out the savory side of the menu while real espresso and cappuccino seal the deal. ⊠ *20 Ferry Rd., Stromness* ☎ *01856/850904* ⊕ *www.juliascafe.co.uk.*

WHERE TO STAY

$ **B&B/INN** **Fodor's Choice** ★ ⚏ **Mill of Eyrland.** White-painted stone walls, country antiques, and the rippling sound of a stream running beneath the windows make for an evocative stay at this former mill dating from 1861. **Pros:** the old grinding stones are a stunning focal point in the lounge; beautiful views out to Scapa Flow. **Cons:** difficult to find; breakfast is served at one big table, so be prepared to socialize. Ⓢ *Rooms from: £100* ✉ *Off A964, Stenness* ☎ *01856/850136* ⊕ *www.millofeyrland.co.uk* ⇨ *4 rooms* |◯| *Breakfast.*

$ **B&B/INN** ⚏ **Miller's House.** Built by a naval lieutenant, James Miller, Orkney's oldest house dates to before 1660 and now serves as a comfortable bed-and-breakfast. **Pros:** great value for the money; cozy rooms; near the ferry. **Cons:** only two rooms; not easy to find; books up well in advance. Ⓢ *Rooms from: £65* ✉ *13 John St., Stromness* ☎ *01856/851969* ⊕ *www.millershouseorkney.com* ⇨ *2 rooms* ⊟ *No credit cards* |◯| *Breakfast.*

SPORTS AND THE OUTDOORS

DIVING The cool, clear waters of Scapa Flow and eight sunken ships that were part of Germany's fleet during World War I make for an unparalleled diving experience. Several companies organize trips to Scapa Flow and other nearby dive sites.

Scapa Scuba. Dives with Scapa Scuba are from its boat, the *MV Radiant Queen.* A day's diving around wrecks near the Churchill Barriers costs £125 per day. ✉ *Lifeboat House, Dundas St., Stromness* ☎ *01856/851218* ⊕ *www.scapascuba.co.uk.*

BIRSAY

12 miles north of Stromness, 25 miles northwest of Kirkwall.

Birsay itself is a small collection of houses, but some interesting historic and natural sites are nearby.

GETTING HERE AND AROUND

The village is on A966; a car is the easiest way to see the nearby sites.

EXPLORING

Broch of Gurness. Gurness Broch, an Iron Age tower built between 500 BC and 200 BC, stands more than 10 feet high and is surrounded by stone huts, indicating that this was a village. The tower's foundations and dimensions suggest that it was one of the biggest brochs in Scotland, and the remains of the surrounding houses are well preserved. ✉ *A966, 8 miles east of Birsay, Aikerness* ☎ *01856/751414* ⊕ *www.historic-scotland.gov.uk* 🎟 *£5* ◷ *Apr.–Sept., daily 9:30–5:30; Oct. daily 9:30–4:30.*

Brough of Birsay. A Romanesque church can be seen at the Brough of Birsay, a tidal island with the remains of an early Pictish and then Norse settlement. (*Brough* is another word for burgh.) The collection of roofless stone structures on the tiny island, close to Birsay, is accessible only at low tide by means of a concrete path that winds across the seaweed-strewn bay. The path is slippery, so boots are essential. ■**TIP→ To ensure you won't be swept away, check the tides with the tourism office in Kirkwall or Stromness before setting out.** ✉ *A966* ☎ *01856/841815* ⊕ *www.historic-scotland.gov.uk* 🎟 *£4* ◷ *June–Sept., daily 9:30–5:30.*

Marwick Head Nature Reserve. The Royal Society for the Protection of Birds tends the remote Marwick Head Nature Reserve, where in spring and summer the cliffs are draped in wildflowers like campion and thrift, and resound with thousands of nesting seabirds like cormorants, kittiwakes, and guillemots. The Kitchener Memorial, recalling the 1916 sinking of the cruiser HMS *Hampshire* with Lord Kitchener aboard, sits atop a cliff. Access to the reserve, which is unstaffed, is along a path north from Marwick Bay. ☒ *Off B9056, 4 mi south of Birsay* ☏ *01856/850176* ⊕ *www.rspb.org.uk* ☒ *Free* ☉ *Daily 24 hrs.*

KIRKWALL

16 miles east of Stromness.

In bustling Kirkwall, the main town on Orkney, there's plenty to see in the narrow, winding streets extending from the harbor. The cathedral and some museums are highlights.

GETTING HERE AND AROUND
Kirkwall is a ferry port and also near Orkney's main airport. Its sights are all near one another. Visitors to the Highland Park Distillery might want to hop on the T11 Kirkwall Circular or get a taxi (about £6).

ESSENTIALS
Visitor Information Kirkwall Visitor Information Centre ☒ *Travel Centre, West Castle St., Kirkwall* ☏ *01856/872856* ⊕ *www.visitorkney.com/kirkwall.*

EXPLORING
TOP ATTRACTIONS

OFF THE BEATEN PATH

Italian Chapel. During World War II, 550 Italian prisoners of war were captured in North Africa and sent to Orkney to assist with the building of the Churchill Barriers, four causeways that blocked entry into Scapa Flow, Orkney's great natural harbor. Using two corrugated-iron Nissan huts, the prisoners, led by Domenico Chiocchetti, a painter-decorator from the Dolomites, constructed this beautiful and inspiring chapel in memory of their homeland. The elaborate interior frescoes were adorned with whatever came to hand, including bits of metal, colorful stones, and leftover paints. ☒ *A961, 7 miles south of Kirkwall* ☒ *Free* ☉ *Daily dawn–dusk.*

FAMILY **Orkney Museum.** With artifacts from the Picts, the Vikings, and other ancient peoples, this museum in Tankerness House (a former residence) has the entire history of Orkney crammed into a rabbit warren of rooms. It's not easily accessible for those with disabilities. The setup may be old-fashioned, but some artifacts—especially those from everyday Orcadian life in the 19th century—are riveting. Lovely gardens around the back provide a spot to recoup after a history lesson. ☒ *Broad St.* ☏ *01856/873191* ☒ *Free* ☉ *May–Sept., Mon.–Sat. 10:30–5; Oct.– Apr., Mon.–Sat. 10:30–12:30 and 1:30–5.*

Orkney Wireless Museum. The lifetime collection of Jim MacDonald, a radio operator during World War II, tells the story of wartime communications at Scapa Flow, where thousands of servicemembers were stationed; they used the equipment displayed to protect the Home Fleet. Run by volunteers, the museum also contains many handsome 1930s wireless radios and examples of the handicrafts produced by Italian prisoners

of war. ✉ *Kiln Corner, Junction Rd.*
☎ *01856/871400* ⊕ *www.owm.org.*
uk ✉ *£3* ⊗ *Apr.–Sept., Mon.–Sat.*
10:30–4:30, Sun. 2:30–4.30.

St. Magnus Cathedral. Founded by
the Norse earl Jarl Rognvald in
1137 and named for his uncle, this
grand red and yellow sandstone
cathedral was mostly finished by
1200, although more work was carried out during the following 300
years. The cathedral is still in use
and contains some fine examples
of Norman architecture, although
traces of later styles are found here
and there. The ornamentation on
some of the tombstones in the church is particularly striking. At the
far end to the left is the tomb of the tragically discredited Dr. John
Rae, the Victorian-era Orcadian adventurer and unsung hero who discovered the final section of the Northwest Passage in Canada but was
decried for his reporting that the British men of the Franklin expedition,
overwhelmed by starvation, had resorted to cannabalism: an assertion
that has since been proved true. ✉ *Broad St.* ☎ *01856/874894* ⊕ *www.*
stmagnus.org ⊗ *Apr.–Sept., Mon.–Sat. 9–6, Sun. 2–6; Oct.–Mar. week-*
days 9–1 and 2–5.

> **WORD OF MOUTH**
>
> "On Orkney, we drove around
> as far as we could and vis-
> ited the half dozen or so main
> archaeological sites, St. Magnus
> Cathedral and the Bishop's and
> Earl's Palaces in Kirkwall—plus of
> course the Italian Chapel, which I
> found extremely moving. The Pier
> Arts Centre in Stromness is lovely
> as a building and has contempo-
> rary art exhibitions."
> —caroline_edinburgh

WORTH NOTING

Bishop's and Earl's Palaces. The Bishop's Palace dates to the 12th century when St. Magnus Cathedral was built. In 1253 this was the site
of King Hakon IV of Norway's death, marking the end of Norwegian
rule over Sudreyjar (the Southern Hebrides). It was rebuilt in the late
15th century, and a round tower was added in the 16th century. The
nearby Earl's Palace was built in 1607 for Earl Partick Stuart, the much
despised Earl of Orkney and Shetland who bound the people of both
into terrible, inescapable poverty. While his name is still mud, his Orcadian residence is considered one of the finest examples of Renaissance
architecture in Scotland. The great hall with its magnificent fireplace
may be a ruin, but it evokes the splendor of its age. ✉ *Palace Rd.*
☎ *01856/871918* ⊕ *www.historic-scotland.gov.uk* ✉ *£4.50* ⊗ *Apr.–*
Sept., daily 9:30–5:30; Oct., daily 9:30–4:30.

Highland Park Distillery. Having come this far, you'll have earned a dram
of the local single malt at Scotland's northernmost distillery. It was
founded around the turn of the 19th century by Magnus Eunson, a
church officer who dabbled in illicit stilling. The tour takes you through
the essential aspects of this near-sacred process, from the ingredients, to
the hand turning of the malt, the peating in the peat kilns, the mashing,
and finally the maturation in oak casks. This smoky but sweet malt can
be purchased all over Orkney, as well as from the distillery's austere
shop. ✉ *Holm Rd.* ☎ *01856/874619* ⊕ *www.highlandpark.co.uk* ✉ *£6*
⊗ *Apr. and Sept., weekdays 10–5; May–Aug., Mon.–Sat. 10–5, Sun.*
noon–5; Oct.–Mar., weekdays 1–5.

OFF THE
BEATEN
PATH

Orkneyinga Saga Centre. A good starting point for an exploration of Orkney's Norse heritage, the center examines the Orkneyinga Saga, an oral history first written down in the 13th century that tells of the Norse conquest of Orkney, with murders and battles galore. Panels discuss the saga and Viking life (with, rather amusingly, Hollywood hunks pasted in to the Norse family tree). Exhibits include the remains of the 12th-century Orphir Church, Scotland's only circular medieval church, and the outline of a Viking drinking hall. ⊠ *Off A964, 8 miles southwest of Kirkwall* ☎ *01856/811319* 🖾 *Free* ۞ *Daily 9–5.*

Unstan Chambered Tomb. This intriguing burial chamber lies within a 5,000-year-old cairn. Access to the tomb can be awkward for those with mobility problems. ⊠ *A964, 7½ miles west of Kirkwall* ☎ *01856/841815* ⊕ *www.historic-scotland.gov.uk* 🖾 *Free* ۞ *Apr.–Sept., daily 9:30–5:30; Oct.–Mar., daily 9:30–4:30.*

WHERE TO EAT

$$$$

MODERN BRITISH

✕ **The Creel.** This outstanding "restaurant with rooms" with a glowing reputation sits right on the waterfront in one of Orkney's loveliest harbors at St. Margaret's Hope. Imaginative modern Scottish cuisine (the price includes three courses) uses the freshest Orcadian seafood, seaweed-fed lamb, and locally grown vegetables. On the island of South Ronaldsay, the inn's charm lies partly in the fuss-free approach to hospitality that makes everyone, from the local farmer to a visiting business executive, feel welcome. Three simple guest rooms overlook the bay. ⑤ *Average main: £40* ⊠ *Front Rd., 13 miles south of Kirkwall, St. Margaret's Hope* ☎ *01856/831311* ⊕ *www.thecreel.co.uk* ⌘ *Reservations essential* ۞ *Closed Oct.–Mar.*

$

CAFÉ

✕ **The Reel.** Orkney's musical tradition is alive and fiddling, but never more so than at this café and restaurant. As you eat, young Orcadians run up the stairs with their violin cases to the music school, where all sorts of sprees and shindigs are held in the performance spaces. The eating is cheap and hearty: expect big bowls of soup, doorstop-size sandwiches with inventive fillings, and slices of sponge cake. It becomes more like a pub on a Friday or Saturday night, with locally brewed ales and, of course, live music. ⑤ *Average main: £5* ⊠ *3 Castle St.* ☎ *01856/871000* ⊕ *www.wrigleyandthereel.com.*

WHERE TO STAY

$$

HOTEL

🏨 **Foveran Hotel.** About 34 acres of grounds surround this modern, ranch-style hotel overlooking Scapa Flow, about 3 miles southwest of Kirkwall. **Pros:** expansive grounds; efficient service; food that's cooked to perfection. **Cons:** exterior looks a bit institutional; you must book the popular restaurant ahead. ⑤ *Rooms from: £116* ⊠ *Off A964, St. Ola* ☎ *01856/872389* ⊕ *www.thefoveran.com* ⮐ *8 rooms* ⑩ *Breakfast.*

$$

HOTEL

🏨 **Merkister Hotel.** After a long day taking in the sights, the gentle lap of Loch Harray, which the Merkister overlooks, soothes the soul. **Pros:** endless coffee in the lounge and library; notable restaurant. **Cons:** some small rooms. ⑤ *Rooms from: £120* ⊠ *A965, Harray* ☎ *01856/771366* ⊕ *www.merkister.com* ⮐ *16 rooms* ⑩ *Breakfast.*

Island Festivals

Islanders know how to celebrate their unique heritage and the performing arts. Joining one of the island festivals can be a memorable part of any trip. Some festivals are very popular, so plan well ahead.

Shetland has quite a strong cultural identity, thanks to its Scandinavian heritage. There are, for instance, books of local dialect verse, a whole folklore and identification system for lost fishermen contained in knitting patterns, and a strong tradition of fiddle playing.

In the middle of the long winter, at the end of January, Shetlanders celebrate their Viking culture with the **Up-Helly-Aa Festival,** which—for the men—involves dressing up as Vikings, parading with flaming torches, and then burning a replica of a Viking longship, followed by one or sometimes two nights of carousing. Women play hostess in the halls, feeding and quenching the thirsts of those involved, and dancing with them. The **Shetland Folk Festival,** held in April, and October's **Shetland Accordion and Fiddle Festival** both attract large numbers of visitors.

Orkney's **St. Magnus Festival,** a celebration focusing on classical music, is based in Kirkwall and is usually held the third week in June. Orkney also hosts a jazz festival in April, an annual folk festival at the end of May, the unique Boys' Ploughing Match in mid-August, and The Ba' (ball; street rugby-football played by the Uppies and Doonies residents of Kirkwall) on Christmas and New Year's Day.

On a smaller scale, throughout summer both islands run mini-festivals and events for lovers of literature, films, food, art, music, and in Shetland even bannocks! Information about these can be found in the visitor centers.

$
B&B/INN
🖼**West End Hotel.** Built in 1824 by a retired sea captain, the West End Hotel once served as Kirkwall's first hospital. **Pros:** great location; friendly owners. **Cons:** No tubs, just showers; some rooms are small. $ *Rooms from: £99* ✉ *Main St.* ☎ *01856/872368* ⊕ *www. westendkirkwall.co.uk* ⤴ *10 rooms* ❖ *No meals.*

THE ARTS
St. Magnus Festival. The region's cultural highlight is Kirkwall's St. Magnus Festival, usually held the third week in June. Its impressive program includes distinguished orchestral, operatic, and choral artists. Orkney also hosts an annual folk festival at the end of May. ☎ *01856/871445* ⊕ *www.stmagnusfestival.com.*

SPORTS AND THE OUTDOORS
BICYCLING **Cycle Orkney.** For £15 a day bicycles can be rented from Cycle Orkney, which is open year-round. ✉ *Tankerness La.* 📠 *01856/875777* ⊕ *www.cycleorkney.com.*

FISHING **Merkister Hotel.** The Merkister Hotel, on Loch Harray, arranges fishing trips. All your equipment, including boats, is available to rent. ✉ *A965, Harray* ☎ *01856/771366* ⊕ *www.merkister.com.*

SHOPPING

Judith Glue. At Judith Glue you can purchase designer knitwear with traditional patterns, as well as handmade crafts and hampers of local produce. The shop is also home to the Orkney Real Food Cafe. ⊠ *25 Broad St.* ☎ *01856/874225* ⊕ *www.judithglue.com.*

The Longship. Don't miss The Longship, which sells a huge array of Ola Gorrie's original designs in gold and silver jewelry with Celtic and Norse themes. ⊠ *11 Broad St.* ☎ *01856/888790* ⊕ *www.thelongship.co.uk.*

Ortak. Selling Celtic-theme jewelry, Ortak also hosts exhibits and jewelry-making demonstrations. ⊠ *Albert St.* ☎ *01856/873536* ⊕ *www. ortak.co.uk.*

SCAPA FLOW VISITOR CENTRE

On the beautiful island of Hoy, Scapa Flow Visitor Centre explores the strategic and dramatic role that this sheltered anchorage played in two world wars.

On Hoy, 14 miles southwest of Kirkwall, 6 miles south of Stromness.

GETTING HERE AND AROUND

The car ferry from Houton (7 miles east of Stromness) takes 25 minutes to reach Lyness on Hoy and the visitor center. The ferry costs around £22 round-trip for a regular-size car and £7 round-trip per passenger.

ESSENTIALS

Ferry Contacts Orkney Ferries ☎ *0800/011–3648* ⊕ *www.orkneyferries.co.uk.*

EXPLORING

Scapa Flow Visitor Centre. Military history buffs will appreciate the Scapa Flow Visitor Centre, which displays military vehicles and guns from both world wars. You'll also find equipment salvaged from the German boats scuttled off the coast. In the plain but poignant graveyard here, British and German personnel both rest in peace. ■**TIP→ If you want to take your car over to Hoy, book well in advance with Orkney Ferries, as this is a popular route.** The visitor center is a short walk from the ferry terminal on the island of Hoy. ⊠ *Off B9047* ☎ *01856/791300* ⊕ *www. scapaflow.co.uk* ⌣ *Free* ☉ *Mar., Apr., and Oct., weekdays 9–4:30; May–Sept., Mon.–Sat. 9–4:30, Sun. 10:30–3:30.*

SHETLAND

The Shetland coastline is an incredible 900 miles because of the rugged geology and many inlets; there isn't a point on the islands farther than 3 miles from the sea. Lerwick is the primary town, but the population of 22,000 is scattered across the 15 inhabited islands.

In general, the prehistoric treasures such as Jarlshof and Mousa Broch are in the South Mainland. For the geological marvels of the islands, Ronas Hill and Eshaness, visit the North Mainland. The social history of the islands is told most comprehensively in the Shetland Museum and in the lanes of Lerwick. Wherever your interest, you'll see and hear an island that buzzes with music, life, and history.

LERWICK

11

14 hrs by ferry from Aberdeen.

Founded by Dutch fishermen in the 17th century, Lerwick today is a busy town and administrative center. Handsome stone buildings—known as lodberries—line the harbor; they provided loading bays for goods, some of them illegal. The town's twisting flagstone lanes and harbor once heaved with activity, and Lerwick is still an active port today. This is also where most visitors to Shetland dock, spilling out of cruise ships, allowing passengers to walk around the town.

GETTING HERE AND AROUND

The town center of Lerwick is 1 mile south of Holmsgarth, the terminal for the ferry from Aberdeen. You can take a bus from Holmsgarth to the center or to the bus station for travel to Sumburgh or Scalloway. Car rentals can be arranged to meet you at the ferry terminal. Lerwick is small and compact, and the bus network, overseen by ZetTrans, offers hourly bus service around town.

ESSENTIALS

Transportation Contacts Boddam Cabs ☎ *01950/460111* ⊕ *www.boddamcabs.co.uk.*

Visitor Information Lerwick Visitor Information Centre ✉ *Market Cross* ☎ *08701/693434* ⊕ *visit.shetland.org/lerwick.*

EXPLORING

Clickimin Broch. A stone tower on the site of what was originally an Iron Age fortification, Clickimin Broch makes a good introduction to these mysterious buildings. It was possibly intended as a place of retreat and protection in the event of attack. South of the broch are vivid views of the cliffs at the south end of the island of Bressay, which shelters Lerwick Harbor. ✉ *Off A970, 1 mile south of Lerwick* ☎ *01856/841815* ⊕ *www.historic-scotland.gov.uk* ✉ *Free* ☉ *Daily 24 hrs.*

Fort Charlotte. This artillery fort was built in 1665 to protect the Sound of Bressay from the invading Dutch. They seized it in 1673 and razed the fort to the ground. They were soon chased out of Shetland and the fort was rebuilt in 1781. ✉ *Market St.* ☎ *01856/841815* ⊕ *www. historic-scotland.gov.uk* ✉ *Free* ☉ *Apr.–Sept., daily 9:30–6:30; Oct.– Mar., daily 9:30–4:30.*

Fodor's Choice
★

Mareel. Next to the Shetland Museum, the bold and beautiful—although somewhat brutalist round the back—Mareel is Shetland's newest and most adventurous arts center. It has a live performance space attracting national and international musicians, two cinemas showing art-house and mainstream films, and a café and bar area that showcases local crafts, acoustic musicians, and some very drinkable Shetland beers. ✉ *North Ness* ☎ *01595/745555* ⊕ *www.mareel.org.*

OFF THE
BEATEN
PATH

Noss National Nature Reserve. The island of Noss (which means "nose" in old Norse) rises to a point called the Noup. The smell and noise of the birds that live on the vertiginous cliffs can assault the senses. Residents nest in orderly fashion: black and white guillemots (45,000 pairs) and razorbills at the bottom; gulls, gannets, cormorants, and

kittiwake in the middle; fulmars and puffins at the top. If you get too close to their chicks, some will dive-bomb from above. To get here, take a ferry from Lerwick to Bressay, then an inflatable boat to Noss. Mid-May to mid-July is the best time to view breeding birds. ■TIP➜ **No matter when you visit, be sure to wear waterproof clothing and sensible shoes.** ⊠ *Noss* ☎ *01595/693345* ⊕ *www.nnr-scotland.org.uk* ⊠ *Free* ⊙ *Apr.–Aug., daily 11–5.*

FAMILY
Fodor'sChoice
★

Shetland Museum. On the last remaining stretch of the old waterfront at the restored Hay's Dock, the striking Shetland Museum, with its sail-like tower, is the area's cultural hub and a stimulating introduction to local history. The two-story space is filled with displays about archaeology, textiles,

> ### FIDDLING ON SHETLAND
>
> Held in high regard both here and afar, Shetland's musicians have folks tapping their feet. At the Shetland Folk Festival, Fiddle Frenzy, and the Fiddle and Accordion Festival you can catch big names like Fiddler's Bid and Hom Bru, and, if you're lucky, the internationally known Shetland fiddler Aly Bain and accordionist Phil Cunningham. During summer, Islesburgh holds Monday night concerts by fiddle teacher Eunice Henderson, and her brilliant young talent: to see tykes setting their tiny fiddles aflame is wonderful. For something more informal, just wander into one of Lerwick's pubs.

and contemporary arts. Standout exhibits include depictions of the minutiae of everyday Shetland life across the centuries, the last remaining *sixareen* (a kind of fishing boat), and the collection of lace shawls donated by Shetland families. The museum is also a wonderful place to hang out; look for vintage vessels moored in the dock and seals that pop up to observe everyone at the glass-fronted café-restaurant terrace. ⊠ *Hay's Dock, Commercial Rd.* ☎ *01595/695057* ⊕ *www.shetland-museum.org.uk* ⊠ *Free* ⊙ *Mon.–Sat. 10–5, Sun. noon–5.*

WHERE TO EAT

$$
BRITISH
Fodor'sChoice
★

✕ **Hay's Dock.** In the Shetland Museum, this airy, glass-fronted café and restaurant serving reasonably priced lunches and somewhat pricier dinners has proved popular. Chunky wooden tables fitted with glass panels allow you to see the artwork featured on top. Good lunch picks include the seafood chowder; in the evening, try Shetland lamb shoulder marinated in spiced yogurt or local salmon with green-pea risotto. ⑤ *Average main: £17* ⊠ *Hay's Dock, off Commerical Rd.* ☎ *01595/741569* ⊕ *www.haysdock.co.uk* ⚔ *Reservations essential* ⊙ *No dinner Sun or Mon.*

$
CAFÉ
Fodor'sChoice
★

✕ **The Peerie Shop Cafe.** Who would believe you could get such good cappuccino at 60 degrees north? Round the back of the popular Lerwick knitwear shop is a modish, consistently good café that sells filled sponge cakes, lip-smackingly good soups, and, yes, the best coffee on the islands. It's always busy and Shetlanders do like to talk, so be prepared to hang around for a table during lunchtime. Alas, the café closes at 6. ⑤ *Average main: £5* ⊠ *Esplanade* ☎ *01595/692816* ⊕ *www.peerieshopcafe.com* ⊙ *Closed Sun. No dinner.*

WHERE TO STAY

$ ⚐ **Alder Lodge Guest House.** Occupying a bank building dating from
B&B/INN the 1830s, this guesthouse sits on a quiet street within easy reach
of Lerwick's shops, pubs, and harbor. **Pros:** comfortable beds;
superb location; child-friendly. **Cons:** booked solid in the summer
months. $ *Rooms from: £70* ✉ *8 Clairmont Pl.* ☎ *01595/695705*
⊕ *www.alderlodgeguesthouse.com* ⤴ *11 rooms* ▤ *No credit cards*
⦿ *Breakfast.*

$ ⚐ **Kveldsro House Hotel.** If a fussy bed-and-breakfast doesn't suit you,
B&B/INN try the plain but pleasing Kveldsro House, tucked away behind the
town's main thoroughfare. **Pros:** minutes from the city center; cheery
bar. **Cons:** generic hotel furniture; some walls are a bit thin. $ *Rooms
from: £135* ✉ *Greenfield Pl., off Commerical St.* ☎ *01595/692195*
⤴ *17 rooms* ⦿ *Breakfast.*

BICYCLING

Eric Brown Cycles. Open year-round, Eric Brown Cycles rents bikes for
£5 a day. ✉ *Grantfield Garage, North Rd.* ☎ *01595/692709* ⊕ *www.
grantfieldgarage.ndo.co.uk.*

SHOPPING

Anderson & Co. On Commercial Street, Anderson & Co. carries hand-
knittted cardigans, jumpers, accessories, and woven throws. ✉ *60–62
Commercial St.* ☎ *01595/693714.*

Ninian. Traditional and funky handmade scarves, clothing, throws, and
the original Burra Bears (teddy bears made from recycled Fair Isle knits)
are found at Ninian. ✉ *80 Commercial St.* ☎ *01595/696655.*

Peerie Shop. The Peerie Shop sells a colorful mix of knitwear, cards,
ceramics, and interesting miscellanea. ✉ *Esplanade* ☎ *01595/692816*
⊕ *www.peerieshop.co.uk.*

Shetland Times. The best bookshop within a radius of about 250 miles,
the Shetland Times stocks a good selection of travel guides and local
history titles. ✉ *71-79 Commercial St.* ☎ *01595/695531.*

THE SOUTH MAINLAND

14 to 25 miles south of Lerwick via A970.

The narrow 3- or 4-mile-wide stretch of land that reaches south from
Lerwick to Sumburgh Head has a number of fascinating ancient sites
(and an airport) as well as farmland, wild landscapes, and dramatic
ocean views.

GETTING HERE AND AROUND

Arriving in Sumburgh by plane offers stunning views of Sumburgh
Head and its golden sands. A fairly regular bus makes the hour-long trip
between the airport and Lerwick, and it's also easy to drive here if you're
based in Lerwick. You can rent a car from the airport or take a taxi.
Jarlshof and Scatness are both within walking distance of the terminal.

ESSENTIALS

Visitor Information Sumburgh Tourist Information Centre ✉ *Sumburgh Airport Terminal, A9070, Virkie* ☎ *01950/460905* ⊕ *www.visit.shetland.org.*

EXPLORING
TOP ATTRACTIONS

Fodor's Choice ★ **Mousa Broch.** Sandwich is the departure point for the passenger ferry to the tiny isle of Mousa, where you can see Mousa Broch, a fortified Iron Age stone tower rising about 40 feet high. The massive walls give a real sense of security, which must have been reassuring for islanders subject to attacks from ship-borne raiders. Exploring this beautifully preserved, curved-stone structure, standing on what feels like an untouched island, makes you feel as if you're back in 100 BC. From April to September the ferry (£16 round-trip) departs for the island one or twice each afternoon. From May to July there are dusk boat trips (£20 round-trip) to catch the tiny storm petrels as they return from their day feeding at sea to their nests in the walls of the broch. The sight of them swarming in the half-light is something you'll never forget. ⊠ *Ferry Terminal, off A970, 14 miles south of Lerwick* ☎ *07901/872339 ferry* ⊕ *www.mousa.co.uk.*

> ### SHETLAND PONIES
>
> The squat and shaggy Shetland pony has been a common sight for more than 12 centuries. Roaming wild over the hills, the pony evolved its long mane and dense winter coat. The animals stand between 28 and 42 inches tall, which made them ideal for working in cramped coal-mine tunnels in the 1850s, when child labor was restricted. They became a popular pet for the aristocracy in the late 19th century; many believe this helped save the breed. Today a studbook society protects the purity of the stock, and you'll see ponies at equine events and all over the island, chomping the grass.

FAMILY
Fodor's Choice ★ **Shetland Croft House Museum.** This 19th-century thatched house reveals the way of life of rural Shetlanders, which the traditionally attired attendant will be delighted to discuss with you. The peat fire casts a glow on the box bed, the resting chair, and the wealth of domestic implements, including a hand mill for preparing meal and a straw "keshie" for carrying peat. One building made from an upturned boat was used for storing and drying fish and mutton: huts like this inspired the design of the new Scottish Parliament. If you're lucky, the museum's curator may be making bannocks from his homegrown and home-milled flour. ⊠ *East of A970, 7 miles south of Sandwick, South Voe* ☎ *01590/695057* ⊕ *www.shetland-museum.org.uk* ✉ *Donations welcome* ☉ *Mid-Apr.–Sept., daily 10–5.*

WORTH NOTING

Hoswick Visitor Centre. This museum with a small but impressive collection of knitting, spinning, and fishing paraphernalia has an excellent café with cakes and soups and a small shop selling knitted and crafty keepsakes. In the room up the stairs is an interesting exhibition on the Hoswick whale case, when in 1888 the local fishermen took on the oppresive laird and won. ⊠ *Hoswick* ☎ *01950/431406* ✉ *Free* ☉ *May–Sept., Mon.–Sat. 10–5, Sun. 11–5.*

FAMILY **Jarlshof.** In 1897 a huge storm blew away 4,000 years of sand to expose the extensive remains of Bronze Age, Iron Age, Pictish and Viking buildings, prehistoric wheelhouses, and earth houses that represented thousands of years of continuous settlement. It's a large and complex site, and you can roam the remains freely. The small visitor center is packed with facts and figures, and illustrates Jarlshof's more recent history as a medieval farmstead and home of the 16th-century Earl of Orkney and Shetland, "cruel" Patrick Stewart, who enslaved the men of Scalloway to build Scalloway Castle. ⊠ *Sumburgh Head, off A970, Virkie* ☎ *01950/460112* ⊕ *www.historic-scotland.gov.uk* ⌨ *£5.50* ⊙ *Apr.–Sept., daily 9:30–5:30; Oct.–Mar. 9:30–dusk.*

FAMILY **Old Scatness.** Ongoing excavations at Old Scatness have uncovered the remains of an Iron Age village, including one building that still has a roof. The digs continue, but

> ### PUFFINS AND MORE
>
> Every summer more than a million birds alight on the cliff faces in Shetland to nest, feeding on the coastal fish and sand eels. Bird-watchers can spot more than 20 species, from tiny storm petrels to gannets with 6-foot wingspans. Popular with visitors are the puffins, with their short necks, striped beaks, and orange feet. Look for them on the cliffs at Sumburgh Head near the lighthouse, 2 miles south of Sumburgh Airport. The visitor center has a wealth of information about nesting sites, as well as live puffin cams during breeding season.

enthusiastic and entertaining guides, most in costume, tell stories that breathe life into the stones and the middens. They also show how the former residents made their clothes and cooked their food, including their staple dish: the ghastly seaweed porridge. ■TIP→ **Call ahead for hours.** ⊠ *Off A970* ☎ *01595/694688* ⊕ *www.shetland-heritage.co.uk/ amenitytrust* ⌨ *£5* ⊙ *June–Sept., hrs vary.*

St. Ninian's Isle. It was on St. Ninian's Isle that a schoolboy helping archaeologists excavate the ruins of a 12th-century church discovered the St. Ninian treasure, a collection of 28 silver objects dating from the 8th century. This Celtic silver is housed in the Museum of Scotland in Edinburgh (a point of controversy), but good replicas are in the Shetland Museum in Lerwick. Although you can't see the silver, walking over the causeway of golden sand (called a tombolo or *ayre)* that joins St. Ninian's Isle to the mainland is an unforgettable experience. From Sumburgh, head 8 miles north on A970 and B9122, then turn left at Skelberry.

WHERE TO STAY

$
B&B/INN
Fodor'sChoice
★

Hayhoull B&B. This restful bed-and-breakfast has big rooms that are well designed and a dining room and lounge with beautiful views of St. Ninian's Isle and Foula. **Pros:** next to the bus stop for Lerwick; in friendly village next to the magical St Ninian's Isle. **Cons:** 2 rooms share a shower room; 4 miles to the nearest pub or restaurant. ⑤ *Rooms from: £60* ⊠ *Off B9122, Bigton* ☎ *01950/422206* ⊕ *www.bedandbreakfastshetland.com* ⇆ *4 rooms* ▤ *No credit cards* ❂❘ *Breakfast.*

SCALLOWAY

6 miles west of Lerwick, 21 miles north of St. Ninian's Isle.

On the west coast of Mainland Island is Scalloway, which preceded Lerwick as the capital of the region. During World War II Scalloway was the port for the "Shetland Bus," a secret fleet of boats that carried British agents to Norway to perform acts of sabotage against the Germans, who were occupying the country. On the return trips, the boats would carry refugees back to Shetland. As you approach the town from the A970, look for the information board, which overlooks the settlement and its castle.

GETTING HERE AND AROUND

The town is 10 minutes by car from Lerwick, or you can get one of the fairly regular buses or even a taxi (£12).

EXPLORING

Scalloway Museum. This modern museum tells some fascinating stories about Scalloway and its well-traveled locals. There is a section dedicated to the expolits of the Shetland Bus, the WWII resistance movement which operated between Norway and Shetland, and cabinet upon cabinet of maritime artifacts donated by locals. ⊠ *Castle St.* ☎ *01595/880734* ⊕ *www.scallowaymuseum.org* ⊠ *£2* ☉ *Apr.–Sept., Mon.–Sat. 11–4, Sun. 2–4.*

Scalloway Castle. Patrick Stewart, earl of Orkney and Shetland, built this waterfront fortress in 1600. He was hanged in 1615 for his cruelty and misdeeds, and the castle was never used again. To enter, retrieve the key from the Scalloway Musuem. You may explore the ruins to your heart's content. ⊠ *A970* ☎ *01856/841815* ⊕ *www.historic-scotland. gov.uk* ⊠ *Free* ☉ *Daily.*

WHERE TO STAY

$$
B&B/INN
Fodor's Choice
★

Scalloway Hotel. Facing the harbor, this traditional stone lodging has fine views, especially at sunset. **Pros:** thoughtfully put together bedrooms; memorable meals from the restaruant. **Cons:** can get booked up in advance. $ *Rooms from: £110* ⊠ *Main St.* ☎ *01595/880444* ⊕ *www.scallowayhotel.com* ⇆ *4 rooms* ◎ *Breakfast.*

WEISDALE

9 miles north of Lerwick.

This tiny place is less a village than a group of houses, but it does have a worthwhile gallery.

GETTING HERE AND AROUND

Take A971 from Lerwick. The number 9 bus weekdays runs three times a day; the trip from Lerwick is 20 minutes.

EXPLORING

Bonhoga Gallery. Built in 1855 using stones from the Kergord estate's "cleared" (forcibly evicted) crofts, Weisdale Mill is now the Bonhoga Gallery, a contemporary art space showing quirky exhibitions by local, national, and international artists. Downstairs is a well-appreciated café that looks over the Weisdale burn. ⊠ *B9075* ☎ *01595/745750* ⊕ *www.shetlandarts.org* ⊘ *Tues.–Sat. 10:30–4:30, Sun. noon–4:30.*

SHOPPING

Shetland Jewellery. This shop sells gold and silver Nordic and Celtic-inspired jewelry, desk knives, and belt buckles made in the on-site workshop. ⊠ *Sound Side* ☎ *01595/830275.*

BRAE

15 miles north of Weisdale, 24 miles north of Lerwick.

A thriving community, Brae is where you can see the spoils of Shetland's oil money. The rugged moorland and tranquil *voes* (inlets) of Brae are the home of Busta House, one of the best hotels on the island.

GETTING HERE AND AROUND

There are buses from Lerwick to Brae, but the spread-out sights make it impossible to really see this area without a car. A970 is the main road, and B9078 will take you through Hillswick and to Eshaness.

EXPLORING

OFF THE BEATEN PATH

Eshaness and Ronas Hill. About 15 miles north of Brae are the rugged, forbidding cliffs around **Eshaness**; drive north and then turn left onto B9078. On the way, look for the striking sandstone stacks or pillars (known as the Drongs) in the bay that resemble a Viking galley under sail. Then return to join the A970 at Hillswick and follow an ancillary road from the head of Ura Firth. This road provides vistas of rounded, bare **Ronas Hill,** the highest hill in Shetland.

Mavis Grind. North of Brae the A970 meanders past Mavis Grind, a strip of land so narrow you can throw a stone—if you're strong—from the Atlantic, in one inlet, to the North Sea, in another. Keep an eye out for sea otters, which sometimes cross here.

WHERE TO EAT AND STAY

$
BRITISH

╳**Braewick Café.** With a stunning position overlooking the Drongs (rocky columns standing in the sea), this eatery's famously large portions are popular with visitors and Shetlanders alike. Browse the local crafts in the shop while waiting for a crispy battered-fish supper, or just sit back on the sofas by the huge picture window and watch the dramatic sea and sky. Don't pass up the many tempting home-baked desserts like sponges, cheesecakes, and giant scones. ⑤ *Average main: £9* ⊠ *Off B9078, Eshaness* ☎ *01806/503345.*

$
SEAFOOD
Fodor's Choice
★

╳**Frankie's Fish & Chip Cafe.** Proudly claiming to be the northernmost fish-and-chip shop in Britain, this "chipper" is also the best of its kind on the islands. The combination of super-fresh seafood—skate wings, squid, and crab legs—light and crispy batter, and low prices means Frankie's is everything a chip shop could be. Try the local mussels: you'll not find any that are fatter or juicier in the UK. Sit on the deck or in the lovely dining room with views toward Busta Voe. ⑤ *Average main: £8* ⊠ *A970* ☎ *01806/522700* ⊕ *www.frankiesfishandchips.com.*

$$ ☷ **Busta House.** Dating from the 16th century, Busta House—built by
HOTEL   the well-heeled but ill-fated Gifford family—is one of the few grand
Fodor's Choice   houses of Shetland. **Pros:** truly haunting atmosphere; charming pub-
★   lic rooms; lovely grounds. **Cons:** noisy plumbing; some rooms are a
tight fit. **$** *Rooms from: £125* ✉ *Off A970* ☎ *01806/522506* ⊕ *www.*
bustahouse.com ➵ *22 rooms* ¡○¡ *Breakfast.*

SHOPPING

Oily Muggie. From seaweed scarves to puffin mugs, this shop is filled with
beautiful momentos from the Shetland Islands. ✉ *Findlands House, off*
A970, Hillswick ☎ *01806/503363* ⊕ *www.oilymuggie.co.uk.*

YELL

11 miles northeast of Brae, 31 miles north of Lerwick.

A desolate-looking blanket bog cloaks two-thirds of the island of Yell,
creating an atmospheric landscape to pass through on the way to Unst
to the north.

GETTING HERE AND AROUND

Although you will see the odd walker or cyclist, a car is needed to
explore the northern isles. To get to Yell, take A970 or B9076 and
catch the ferry from Toft to Ulsta. On Yell, B9081 runs through Bur-
ravoe and up the east side and joins the A968, which leads to Gutcher
and the ferry to Unst.

EXPLORING

Old Haa (*hall*). The oldest building on the island, Burravoe's Old Haa
is known for its crow-stepped gables (the stepped effect on the ends of
the roofs), typical of an early-18th-century Shetland merchant's house.
There's an earnest memorial to Bobby Tulloch, the great Shetland natu-
ralist (1929–96), and the displays in the upstairs museum tell the story
of the wrecking of the German ship, the *Bohus*, in 1924. A copy of the
ship's figurehead is displayed outside the building. The Old Haa serves
light meals with home-baked buns, cakes, and other goodies and also
acts as a kind of unofficial information center. A crafts shop is on the
premises, too. ✉ *Burravoe* ☎ *01957/702431* ⊕ *www.bobbytulloch.com*
▱ *Free* ☉ *Apr.–Sept., Tues.–Sat. 10–4, Sun. 2–5.*

UNST

49 miles north of Lerwick.

Unst is the northernmost inhabited island in Scotland, a remote and
special place, especially for nature lovers. On a long summer evening,
views north to Muckle Flugga, with only the ocean beyond, are incom-
parable. If you're a bird-watcher, head to the Hermaness and Keen of
Hamar nature reserves.

GETTING HERE AND AROUND

A ferry (take the A968 at Mid Yell to Gutcher) crosses the Bluemull
Sound to Unst. A car is best for exploring, though there is limited bus
service, including from Lerwick; taxis are an option. The island has
some B&B and house-rental options if you choose to linger.

EXPLORING

Hermaness National Nature Reserve. The Hermaness National Nature Reserve, a bleak moorland ending in rocky cliffs, is prime bird-watching territory. About half the world's population (6,000 pairs) of great skuas, called "bonxies" by locals, are found here. ■ **TIP→ These sky pirates attack anything that strays near their nests, including humans, so keep to the paths.** Thousands of other seabirds, including more than 50,000 puffins, nest in spectacular profusion on the cliffs, about an hour's walk from the reserve entrance. Hermaness is not just about birds—gray seals gather in caves at the foot of the cliffs in fall, and offshore dolphins and occasionally whales (including orcas) can be seen on calm days. The flora include the insect-eating butterwort and sundew, purple field gentians, blue squill, and sea thrift.

A path meanders across moorland and climbs up a gentle hill, from which you can see, to the north, a series of tilting offshore rocks; the largest of these sea-battered protrusions is **Muckle Flugga,** meaning "big, steep-sided island," on which stands a lighthouse. The lighthouse was built by engineer Thomas Stevenson, whose son, the great Scottish writer Robert Louis Stevenson, used the outline of Unst for his map of Treasure Island. Muckle Flugga is the northernmost point in Scotland—the sea rolls out on three sides, and no land lies beyond.

The visitor center has leaflets that outline a walk; mid-May to mid-July is the best time to visit. To get here from Haroldswick, follow the B9086 around the head of Burra Firth, a sea inlet. ✉ *B9086, Burrafirth* ☎ *01957/711278* ⊕ *www.nnr-scotland.org.uk* 🖾 *Free* ⊙ *Mid-Apr.–mid-Sept., daily 9–5.*

Keen of Hamar National Nature Reserve. Just to the north of Muness Castle is the Keen of Hamar National Nature Reserve, off A968, with subarctic flora and arctic terns.

Muness Castle. Scotland's northernmost castle was built just before the end of the 16th century and has circular corner towers. It is a ruin but has notable architectural details. ✉ *B9084, Uyeasound* ⊕ *www.historic-scotland.gov.uk* 🖾 *Free* ⊙ *Daily 24 hrs.*

WHERE TO EAT

$$
BRITISH ✕ **Saxa Vord.** This restaurant is part of an odd collection of buildings strewn around the edge of an eye-wateringly—that's the wind—gorgeous peninsula that was a former base for the Royal Air Force. The tidy, well-run, and informal eatery serves lunches and dinners as fresh and good for you as the Unst air. Try local scallops, smoked salmon, and lamb hot pot. You can retire to the bar to chat with the locals and sip a tasty real ale such as Auld Wife or Simmer Dim from the local Valhalla brewery. If you miss the ferry back to the Mainland, they have tidy if basic rooms to rent. ⑤ *Average main: £16* ✉ *Off A968, Valsgarth* ☎ *01957/711711* ⊕ *www.saxavord.com* ⊙ *Closed Mon. Oct.–Apr.*

UNDERSTANDING SCOTLAND

SCOTLAND AT A GLANCE

FAST FACTS

Capital: Edinburgh
National anthem: "God Save the Queen"
Type of government: Scotland is currently part of the United Kingdom, which is a constitutional monarchy. Since 1999 it has had its own Parliament, based in Edinburgh; First Minister Alex Salmond of the Scottish National Party is the head of the government. On September 18, 2014, however, Scotland will vote in a referendum on the single question: Should Scotland be an independent country? Yes or No. If the majority votes Yes, the first independent Scottish Parliament will meet in May 2016.
Administrative divisions: 32 council areas
Independence: April 6, 1320; the Declaration of Arbroath. Scottish nobles wrote Pope John XXII during the War of Independence and asked him to persuade the English king to stop his hostility toward the Scottish. In 1707, however, the Act of Union merged Scotland and England.
Constitution: There is no one document; it's a centuries-old accumulation of statutes as well as common law and practice. If Scotland becomes independent, though, it will draft its first modern Constitution.
Legal system: Scotland has a separate legal system from the rest of the United Kingdom. Its two highest courts are the High Court of Justiciary (criminal) and the Court of Session (civil). Appeals to the British House of Lords may be made only from the Court of Session. The sheriff courts deal with less important civil and criminal cases.
Suffrage: 18 years of age, 16 years of age for the 2014 referendum vote.
Legislature: Governed as an integral part of the United Kingdom's constitutional monarchy, Scotland is represented by 59 Members of Parliament in the House of Commons in London. On May 6, 1999, Scotland gained its own Parliament, located in Edinburgh, for the first time in nearly 300 years. The current devolved Parliament has the power to pass Scottish laws; it's responsible for managing agriculture, education, health, and justice, and it can impose certain taxes within Scotland.
Population: 5,295,403. The largest cities are Glasgow (529,540) and Edinburgh (495,360).
Population density: 64 persons per square km (171 persons per square mile)
Median age: male 37, female 39
Life expectancy: male 75, female 80
Literacy: 99%
Language: Predominantly English. Fewer than 1,000 people speak only Gaelic, and fewer than 60,000 speak Gaelic in addition to English, but this is increasing. Scots is now recognized as an official language, too.
Ethnic groups: 96.3% of the population is Caucasian (88% of this is Scottish and 7.5% other British); Indian, Pakistani, Bangladeshi, and other South Asian groups are the largest ethnic minorities.
Religion: Residents identified their religion as follows: 42.4% Church of Scotland, 27.55% none, 15.9% Roman Catholic, 6.8% other Christian, 0.13% Buddhist, 0.11% Hindu, 0.13% Jewish, 0.84% Muslim, 0.13% Sikh, 0.53% another religion, 5.49% did not reply.
Discoveries and inventions: Steam engine (1765), postage stamp (1834), telephone (1876), television (1924), penicillin (1928), radar (1935)

We look to Scotland for all our ideas of civilization.

—Voltaire

GEOGRAPHY AND ENVIRONMENT

Land area: 78,722 square km (30,414 square miles)
Coastline: 3,900 km (2,280 miles)
Terrain: Scotland is divided into three distinct regions, roughly from north to south: the Highlands (characterized by mountains with deep ravines, valleys, cliffs, lakes, and sea lochs); the Central

Lowlands (mainly hills and rivers); and the Southern Uplands (moorland plateaus, rolling valleys, and mountainous outcrops). Highest mountain, Ben Nevis (4,409 feet). Largest loch, Loch Lomond (56 square km, or 22 square miles)

Islands: 800, of which 130 are inhabited. The largest groups are Shetland and Orkney to the north; and the Hebrides, including Lewis, Harris, Barra, Skye, and Mull, to the west.

Natural resources: Coal, petroleum, natural gas, water, zinc, iron ore, limestone, clay, silica, gold

Natural hazards: Winter windstorms, floods

Flora: Dominant flora: rowan (tree belonging to the rose family), oak, fir, pine, and larch trees; heather, ferns, mosses, grasses, saxifrage, and mountain willow

Fauna: Principal fauna: deer, hare, rabbit, otter, ermine, pine marten, wildcat, grouse, blackcock, ptarmigan, waterfowl, kite, osprey, golden eagle, salmon, trout, cod, haddock, herring, various types of shellfish

Environmental issues: Climate change, air pollution, wind farms, recycling, nuclear power

There are two seasons in Scotland: June and winter.

—Billy Connolly

ECONOMY

Currency: British pound (GBP)
Exchange rate: £1 = $1.61
GDP: £149 billion ($203 billion)
Per-capita income: £20,086 ($31,105)
Inflation: 1.8% in the United Kingdom
Unemployment: 7.1%
Workforce: 2,490,000 (services 79.1%; agriculture 1.4%; industry 19.5%)
Major industries: Aerospace, chemicals, construction, digital media and creative industries, energy, financial services, food and drink, life sciences, microelectronics and optoelectronics, textiles, and tourism

Agricultural products: Barley, wheat, oats, potatoes, livestock (sheep and cattle)
Exports: £23.9 billion
Major export products: Office machinery, radio/TV/communication equipment, whisky, chemicals, manufactured machinery/equipment and transport equipment
Export partners: United States, Germany, France, Ireland, Spain, Netherlands, Belgium.
Imports: £48.3 billion

We'll never know the worth of water till the well go dry.

—18th-century Scottish proverb

DID YOU KNOW?

■ Christmas was not celebrated as a festival in Scotland for about 250 years (from the end of the 17th century up to the 1950s) because the Protestant church believed Christmas to be a Catholic holiday and therefore banned it. Many Scots worked over Christmas and their winter solstice holiday took place at New Year or "hogmanay."

■ Kilts are not native to Scotland. They originated in France.

■ The first woman to play golf at St. Andrew's Golf Club was Mary, Queen of Scots, in 1552. She was the club's founder.

■ More redheads are born in Scotland than in any other country: 11% of the population has red hair.

■ Homer Simpson's catchphrase "Doh!" was based on the catchphrase of actor James Finlayson, who was born in Falkirk in 1887 and starred alongside Laurel and Hardy in many of their films.

■ Haggis may not be Scottish after all. In 2009 historian Catherine Brown found literary evidence that placed haggis in England 171 years before it showed up in any Scottish text. The book in question is the *English Hus-Wife* from 1615.

BOOKS AND MOVIES

Books

For the Scot, the "man o' pairts" is the ideal to be aspired to—a person with varied skills and experiences, and a love of knowledge for its own sake. In many ways the great poet Robert Burns (1759–96) was the embodiment of that ideal: a peasant poet, a lover of life, a political thinker, a radical, a man who loved nature and women in equal measure. His poem for the mouse seen in a ploughed field—"that wee sleekit timorous beastie"—is as humane as his wonderful poems proclaiming the equality of all human beings against the rulers and the landowners: "It matters not the guinea's stamp/A man's a man for a' that." Burns is indeed in every sense the national poet.

Scotland has been a place where, for reasons as much religious as cultural, men and women valued education and reading. The powerful Scottish Presbyterian tradition placed great emphasis on the development, moral and intellectual, of the individual.

The literary tradition goes back to the Bothy Ballads, the old rural folk songs of Scotland's northeast, and has grown and expanded until the literary renaissance of the late 20th and early 21st centuries, when Scottish writers have won international recognition. Novelist and artist Alasdair Gray; Irvine Welsh with *Trainspotting* (an international success despite its setting in the poor Pilton district of Edinburgh and its almost impenetrable local dialect); Ian Rankin, with his novels about Edinburgh's Inspector Rebus; and the great Glasgow poet laureate Edwin Morgan (1920–2010): all have demonstrated that Scottish writing travels well.

Most of Scotland has its particular voices and its particular accents in the written word. In the 19th century the fascination of the middle classes with a Scotland made fashionable by Queen Victoria's decision to buy a castle at Balmoral, together with the spread of the railways, brought travelers to the Trossachs and the Highlands. They were seeking the landscapes lovingly portrayed in novels and poems by Sir Walter Scott (1771–1832), who wrote about the Highlands from his beautiful home at Abbotsford, beside the river Tweed. Travelers were also approaching, if gingerly, the wilder parts of the British Isles, the still largely unfamiliar mountains and dark lochs of the Scottish Highlands. Many of them gained their first impressions of this supposedly slightly barbarous place of kilt-wearing warriors from Sir Walter Scott and the poetry of Ossian, a rural poet who turned out to be a fiction created by James Macpherson (1736–96). There was a similar air about James Hogg's (1770–1835) dark ghost story *Confessions of a Justified Sinner* (1824), with its fearsome ending on Arthur's Mount in Edinburgh. Robert Louis Stevenson (1850–94) was an Edinburgh man whose *Kidnapped* evoked the thick woods and lakes in the Central Highlands.

There were other popular novels about Scottish life, such as George Douglas Brown's *The House with Green Shutters* (1901), set in Ayrshire, or Guy McCrone's *Wax Fruit Trilogy* (1947), set in Glasgow. Yet it couldn't be said that there was a vigorous literary life in Scotland, and many of these novels were the only ones their authors published. Lewis Grassic Gibbon (the pseudonym of James Mitchell, 1901–35) produced a trilogy of novels (*A Scots Quair*) set in Scotland's northeast in a rural community on the eve of the World War I. It's much like Howe of Mearns, near Stonehaven, where he was brought up and where his small museum now stands. *Sunset Song*, the first of the three, is a masterpiece; the people in this farming community on the threshold of massive changes still speak in the Doric dialect, the lilting language of the region, which Grassic Gibbon managed to echo in his poetic English.

Scottish writing remained a poor country cousin in Britain. Most publishers were based in London, and those Scottish writers who did win success, like Eric Linklater (1899–1974) or Compton Mackenzie (1883–1972) or, later on, Muriel Spark (1918–2006) and Naomi Mitchison (1897–1999), were not generally recognized as Scottish writers, though each had some writing based in Scotland to their name. Muriel Spark's *The Prime of Miss Jean Brodie* (1969), which portrayed the misplaced idealism of a teacher in a private school in Edinburgh, was one, and Compton Mackenzie's *Whisky Galore!* (1949), the tale of a Hebridean island community suddenly given a gift of a shipload of whisky by the sea, was another. Mackenzie himself was brought up in the beautiful if remote island of Barra, where his house can still be seen.

Even Hugh McDiarmid (1892–1978), the great epic poet of Scotland, emphasized the dilemma of Scottish exclusion by writing in the Scots language of the Lowlands in his glorious evocation of Scottish history called, appropriately perhaps, *A Drunk Man Looks at a Thistle*. The rediscovery of Scotland's culture was reflected in the songs of Ewen McColl (1915–89) and of Hamish Henderson (1919–2002), who wrote what became a kind of unofficial national anthem called "The Freedom Come All Ye," a song celebrating the life of the Scottish radical leader of the early part of the century, John MacLean. By the late 1970s Scotland was starting to have a dramatic impact on cultural life beyond its borders, and Scotland itself was becoming aware of its own great cultural and historical traditions beyond Sir Walter Scott and the realist work that came to be called the Kailyard School (which sometimes came perilously close to sentimentality about the lives of the poor).

What made the literary renaissance of the 1970s possible? Theater, and, in particular, the incredible impact of one play produced by the 7:84 Theatre Company: *The Cheviot, the Stag, and the Black Black Oil*. It traveled to every corner of the country, with its stage set in a huge pop-up book, to tell the story of Scotland in a new way. After the show there was always a *ceilidh*, Scottish traditional dancing to the fiddle and the accordion. Suddenly, in the run-up to the first referendum on devolution (the creation of a separate Scotland) in 1979, a generation of Scottish writers, particularly poets, emerged. Some were new, like Tom Leonard and Liz Lochhead, who wrote in the language of ordinary people. Others had been around, unnoticed, like George Mackay Brown, who wrote about Orkney's prehistoric heritage and its fishing communities in *Fishermen with Ploughs* and *Greenvoe;* or Neil Gunn (1881–1973) with his *The Silver Darlings*. Iain Crichton Smith (1928–98) and Norman McCaig (1910–96) found new audiences for their poetry, and the Gaelic poet Sorley Maclean (1911–96) was heard in his native language for the first time and then translated for a wider public.

By the 1980s the Edinburgh International Festival had become a world-class event, while its Fringe (alternative events scattered around the city) swelled with more than a thousand shows of one kind or another. The city provided the backdrop to new writers of fiction like Iain Banks (*The Wasp Factory*) and Ian Rankin. Rankin's Rebus novels (*Black and Blue* was one) translated detective fiction to the steep streets of Old Edinburgh, launching a tradition of crime writing that found its Glasgow equivalents in William McIlvanney's Laidlaw and the writings of Denise Mina, Louise Welsh, and Val McDermid. The Canongate Press, a small publisher that went global in the late 1980s, provided new opportunities for Scottish writers.

Children were not forgotten: Joan Lingard's teenage novels were set in Northern Ireland and Scotland, while Mairi Hedwick's Katie Morag stories unfolded on a Hebridean island. Although J. K. Rowling's hugely successful Harry Potter books were set in a world that seemed closer to an English public school, the world learned that they had been written in an Edinburgh café.

Scotland was no longer a literary backwater. Its writers had taken their place in an international culture as the new century began. The *Oxford Literary Guide to the British Isles,* edited by Dorothy Eagle and Hilary Carnell; *A Reader's Guide to Writers' Britain,* by Sally Varlow; and *Scotland: A Literary Guide,* by Alan Bold, cover other literary landscapes in addition to those mentioned above. Edinburgh has been named the first UNESCO World City of Literature; Allan Foster's *Literary Traveler in Edinburgh* is an illustrated sightseeing guide to literary hot spots, including writers' homes and the settings for famous works.

Nonfiction

Canadian historian John Prebble (1915–2001) unearthed Scotland's hidden history in the early 1970s. In books such as *Culloden* he used the documents of the time to tell the tragic and heroic story of the final massacre at Culloden, an event that paved the way for English domination of the north. Prebble's moving account of the Highland Clearances tells what until then had been the hidden story of how the big landowners drove out their peasant-farmer tenants to make way for sheep, which were much more profitable. The words of the women who fought so hard before they were sent into exile are haunting.

The most complete history is Tom Devine's absorbing *The Scottish Nation.* Neal Ascherson, a highly respected international journalist, returned to his native Scotland as the 1979 referendum

approached; his *Native Stones: The Search for Scotland* probably reflects the rediscovery of his own identity. To the outside world, though, *No Mean City: The Story of a Glasgow Slum,* written by Alexander McArthur and Herbert Kingsley Long in 1935, was probably closer to the Scotland it imagined: a country of mean streets, poverty, and violence. The more recent work of James Robertson and Robert Knight has reopened the debate about the role of Scots in the empire and addressed some uncomfortable truths about slavery and the treatment of indigenous peoples by Scottish settlers and colonists.

For books on Scottish art and architecture, Duncan MacMillan's *Scottish Art in the 20th Century, 1890–2001* is a comprehensive guide to artists from Charles Rennie Mackintosh to Ken Currie. Jude Burkhauser's *Glasgow Girls: Women in Art and Design 1880–1920* is more narrow in scope but equally intriguing. Bella Bathurst's *The Lighthouse Stevensons* uniquely catalogs the engineering revolution of lighthouse building through the work of four generations of writer Robert Louis Stevenson's family. For good background information on castles, look for Damien Noonan's *Castles and Ancient Monuments of Scotland* and John G. Dunbar's *Scottish Royal Palaces.*

Football (soccer) in Scotland is, in many respects, a religion. To find out more on the subject, read David Ross's passionate *The Roar of the Crowd: Following Scottish Football Down the Years.* Another important sport in Scotland is the game invented there: golf. A popular book on the subject, Malcolm Campbell's *Scottish Golf Book,* will not only tell you where to putt but also will give you a thorough background on the game itself. Curtis Gillespie's memoir *Playing Through: A Year of Life and Links Along the Scottish Coast* takes a more personal approach to golf and its past through the year he spent with his family in Gullane, as does Lorne Rubenstein's *A Season in Dornoch: Golf and Life in the Scottish Highlands.*

Travel and landscape books on Scotland are almost as plentiful as the country's native thistle. Although initially published in 1779, the reflections and descriptions in Samuel Johnson and James Boswell's *Journey to the Hebrides* (reprinted in 1996) are just as relevant today. Kathleen Jamie's poetically told *Findings* will whet your taste buds for Scotland's picturesque countryside like no other. Cameron McNeish has written some excellent books; *The Munros: Scotland's Highest Mountains* (out of print but worth seeking out a copy) is a carefully crafted guide to climbing those peaks. Colin Prior's impressive photography collection *Highland Wilderness* gives stunning panoramic views of the wild but wonderful north.

Movies

The Scottish film industry has come of age in recent years, though John Grierson (1898–1972) was the commanding figure in the development of documentary film in Britain in the 1930s. In more recent times, films produced in Scotland have moved some distance from the popular "kilt" movies like *Rob Roy* (1995) with Liam Neeson and Jessica Lange, or the internationally successful film about William Wallace's revolt, *Braveheart* (1995), with Mel Gibson, which convinced people across the world that Scots painted their faces blue. Like Sean Connery's *Highlander* (1986), these films took advantage of the spectacular scenery of Glencoe or Scottish castles from Doune to Eilean Donan to create their atmosphere.

It was *Trainspotting* (1996) that launched a new kind of Scottish cinema (and a new Scottish star in Ewen McGregor) with its powerful yet witty presentation of heroin addicts on an impoverished housing estate. *Shallow Grave* (1994), a sometimes bloody thriller about money and jealousy in an Edinburgh apartment, also starred McGregor. The outstanding director Ken Loach has made several films in Glasgow with his scriptwriter Paul Laverty; *My Name Is Joe* (1998) is a heartbreaking portrayal of an alcoholic wrestling with his problem, and *Sweet Sixteen* (2002) presents a characteristic Loach hero in a young lad trying to survive in a world of poverty and violence. The older *Local Hero* (1983) brings ambitious oilmen to the remote provincial world of the northeast; *Red Road* (2006) is an intense drama in which Kate Dickie becomes obsessed with a man she sees on the CCTV security screens of a Glasgow apartment block.

The makers of *Monty Python and the Holy Grail* (1975) chose lovely Doune Castle for their medieval spoof, and *Mrs. Brown* (1997) looked at the undeclared romantic relationship between Queen Victoria and her "ghillie," or gamekeeper, John Brown (played by Scottish comedian Billy Connolly). The film is set among the hills and woods of the Trossachs, and in the Ardverekie Estate near Dalwhinnie, which stands in for the royal palace at Balmoral. Hollywood has also come to Glasgow, most recently with *Under the Skin* (2013), in which Scarlett Johansson plays an alien.

For more information on movies filmed in Scotland, you can buy *The Pocket Scottish Movie Book* by Brian Pendreigh, or you can visit the Scotland the Movie Guide website (⊕ *www.scotlandthemovie.com*).

CHRONOLOGY

7000 BC   Hunter-gatherers move into the north of Scotland after the ice sheets of the last Ice Age recede; these travelers leave arrowheads and bone implements as testimony to their passing.

ca. 6000 BC   First settlers arrive, bringing farming methods with them. They leave their mark at Skara Brae in Orkney.

ca. 3000 BC   Neolithic migration from Mediterranean: "chambered cairn" people in north (such as the Grey Cairns of Camster). "Beaker people" erect the standing stone circles, like those at Callanish on the Isle of Lewis.

ca. 300 BC   Iron Age: arrival of Celtic peoples from the south and from Ireland; "Gallic forts" and "brochs" (towers) built, like the tower at Mousa in Shetland.

AD 43   The Roman conquest of Britain begins.

79–89   Julius Agricola (AD 40–93), Roman governor of Britain, invades Scotland; Scots tribes defeated at the battle of Mons Graupius (thought to be somewhere in the Grampians). Roman forts built at Inchtuthil and Ardoch.

123   Hadrian's Wall is built to mark the northern limit of the Roman Empire.

142   Emperor Antoninus Pius (86–161) orders the defensive Antonine Wall built between the Firths of Forth and Clyde, as the Romans continue their attempt to invade beyond Hadrian's Wall.

185   Antonine Wall abandoned.

392   St. Ninian (ca. 360–432), a Briton and a Christian, sends out a first Christian mission to the Picts from his chapel at Whithorn.

400–500   Tribes of Celtic origin, including the Scotti, emigrate from Ireland to present-day Argyllshire and establish the kingdom of Dalriada. The Pictish kingdom extends as far south as Fife. The Britons, meanwhile, occupy an area between Dumbarton and Carlisle.

400–843   Four kingdoms exist in Scotland: Dalriada (Argyllshire), the kingdom of the Picts (Aberdeenshire down to Fife and the Highlands excepting Argyllshire), Strathclyde (southwest Scotland), and the Lothians (Edinburgh and the Borders).

563   Columba, (ca. 521–97), a Gaelic-speaking Scotti, establishes the monastery at Iona. It will become a major center for the evangelization of Scotland and farther afield.

843   Kenneth MacAlpin, king of Dalriada, unites with the Picts while remaining king. In this way the embryonic Kingdom of Scotland (first called Alba, later Scotia) is born, with its capital at Scone.

780–1065   Scandinavian invasions; the Hebrides remain Norse until 1263, Orkney and Shetland until 1472.

1018   Malcolm II (ca. 953–1034) brings the Lothians into the Kingdom of Scotland and (temporarily) repels the English.

1034   Duncan (d. 1040), king of Strathclyde, ascends the throne of Scotland and unification is complete.

1040   Duncan is slain by his rival, Macbeth (d. 1057), whose wife has a claim to the throne.

1057   Malcolm III (ca. 1031–93), known as Canmore (Big Head), murders Macbeth and assumes the throne. The House of Canmore now assumes the Scottish crown and introduces a feudal landowning system into the country.

1093   Death of Malcolm's English-born queen, St. Margaret (1046–93), who brought Roman Catholicism to Scotland.

1099   Donald III becomes the last king of Scots to be buried on the island of Iona.

1124–53 David I (ca. 1082–1153), *sair sanct* (sore saint), builds the abbeys of Jedburgh (1118), Kelso (1128), Melrose (1136), and Dryburgh (1150) and brings Norman culture to Scotland.

1200   The Royal Burghs, or towns, of Stirling, Edinburgh, and Berwick are established with certain rights and privileges in trade. The Highland clans are largely excluded from power.

1250   Queen Margaret, wife of Malcolm III, is canonized, becoming Scotland's first (and only) royal saint.

1290   Death of Alexander III, great-great-grandson of David I. The heir is his granddaughter, Margaret, Maid of Norway (1283–90). She dies at sea on her way from Norway to claim the Scottish throne and marry the future Edward II (1284–1327), son of Edward I of England (1239–1307). The Scots naively ask Edward I, subsequently known as the Hammer of the Scots, to arbitrate between the remaining 13 claimants to the throne. Edward chooses John Balliol (1249–1315) over his ambitious rival Robert the Bruce.

1295   Under continued threat from England, John Balliol switches allegiance and signs Scotland's first treaty with England's enemy, France. This came to be known as "the Auld Alliance." The wine trade flourishes.

1297   While Robert the Bruce now sides with the English, William Wallace (ca. 1270–1305) leads an uprising against the English. His army is made up of peasants and the lower nobility like himself. It is in part a reaction against the extreme cruelty of the English armies under Edward I. The wealthy nobles, for their part, do not resist because many of them have lands in both England and Scotland.

1305   Wallace, betrayed and captured by the English, is executed.

1306–29 Reign of Robert the Bruce (1274–1329), later to become King Robert I, who turns again against the English. He defeats Edward II (1284–1327) at Bannockburn, 1314. The Declaration of Arbroath (1320) affirms Scottish sovereignty, which is eventually recognized by the Treaty of Northampton, 1328.

1329   After the death of Bruce, the nobles fight wars against one another for 50 years. The attempt by the new ruling house, the Stewards, or Stuarts, to control the situation largely fails.

1371   Robert II (1316–90), the first Stewart monarch and son of Robert the Bruce's daughter Marjorie and Walter the Steward, is crowned in 1371, but the struggle between the crown and Scottish barons (later dramatized in several of Sir Walter Scott's novels) continues for another century. Sporadic warfare with the English also continues during this time.

1383   Bishop Wardlaw of Glasgow is the first Scot to be made a cardinal.

1411   University of St. Andrews founded.

1451   University of Glasgow founded.

1488–1513   Reign of James IV (1473–1513). The Renaissance reaches Scotland. The Golden Age of Scots poetry includes Robert Henryson (ca. 1425–1508), William Dunbar (ca. 1460–1530), Gavin Douglas (1474–1522), and the king himself.

1495   University of Aberdeen founded.

1507   Andrew Myllar and Walter Chapman set up first Scots printing press in Edinburgh.

1513   After invading England in support of the French, James IV is slain at Flodden Field.

1542   Henry VIII (1491–1547), king of England, defeats James V (1512–42) at Solway Moss. The dying James, hearing of the birth of his daughter, Mary, declares: "It came with a lass [Marjorie Bruce] and it will pass with a lass."

1542–67   Reign of Mary, Queen of Scots (1542–87). She becomes queen at one year old, and her mother is appointed regent. At six she is married to the heir to the French throne. Romantic, Catholic, and with an excellent claim to the English throne, Mary proved to be no match for her barons, John Knox (1513–72), or her cousin Elizabeth I (1533–1603) of England.

1560   Mary returns to Scotland from France after the death of her husband, Francis II of France, at the same time that Catholicism is abolished in favor of Protestantism. She finds a Scotland dominated by a Protestantism influenced by the fiery John Knox.

1565   Mary marries Lord Darnley (1545–67), a Catholic but a self-indulgent consort.

1567   Darnley is murdered at Kirk o' Field and Mary marries one of the conspirators, the Earl of Bothwell (ca. 1535–78). Driven from Scotland, she appeals to Elizabeth, who imprisons her. Mary's son, James (1566–1625), is crowned James VI of Scotland.

1582   University of Edinburgh is founded.

1587 Elizabeth orders the execution of Mary.

1600 Charles I is born in Scotland.

1603 Elizabeth dies without issue; James VI is crowned James I of England, uniting the two crowns. But the Parliaments remain separate for another century.

1638 National Covenant challenges Charles I's personal rule.

1639–41 Crisis. The Scots and then the English parliaments revolt against Charles I (1600–49).

1643 Solemn League and Covenant establishes Presbyterianism as the Church of Scotland (the Kirk). In England, Parliament rises against Charles I, who had summoned it after 11 years in the hope it would grant him resources for war. Civil War in England.

1649 Charles I beheaded. Oliver Cromwell (1599–1658) made Protector.

1650–52 Cromwell roots out Scots Royalists.

1658 The first Edinburgh–London coach is established. The journey takes two weeks.

1660 Restoration of Charles II (1630–85). Episcopalianism reestablished in Scotland; Covenanters are persecuted and their army attacked by Highland soldiers.

1688 The unpopular James VII of Scotland (and II of England, Scotland, and Ireland) flees to France.

1688–89 Glorious Revolution; James VII and II (1633–1701), a Catholic, deposed in favor of his daughter Mary (1662–94) and her husband, William of Orange (1650–1702). Supporters of James (known as Jacobites) defeated at Killiecrankie. Presbyterianism reestablished.

1692 Highlanders who were late in taking oath to William and Mary massacred at Glencoe.

1695 The first bank in Scotland, the Bank of Scotland, is founded.

1698–1700 Attempted Scottish colony at Darien (on the Isthmus of Panama) fails. Many of the Scottish nobility face bankruptcy, and are therefore open to overtures from an English government anxious to unite the Scottish and English parliaments.

1707 Union of English and Scots parliaments under Queen Anne (1665–1714), the last Stuart monarch; deprived of French wine trade, Scots turn to whisky.

1714 Queen Anne dies; George I (1660–1727) of the House of Hanover, descended from a daughter of James VI and I, is crowned.

1715 First Jacobite Rebellion. James II's son, James Edward Stuart, agrees to undertake an invasion of England. His supporter, the Earl of Mar (1675–1732), the leader of the attempted Rising, is defeated.

1730–90 Scottish Enlightenment. The Edinburgh Medical School is the best in Europe; David Hume (1711–76) and Adam Smith (1723–90) redefine philosophy and economics. In the arts, Allan Ramsay the elder (1686–1758) and Robert Burns (1759–96) refine Scottish poetry; Allan Ramsay the younger (1713–84) and Henry Raeburn (1756–1823) rank among the finest painters of the era. Edinburgh's New Town, developed in the 1770s and including designs by the brothers Adam (Robert, 1728–92; James, 1730–94), provides a fitting setting.

1736 The first public theater in Scotland is opened in Carruber's Close in Edinburgh.

1745–46 Last Jacobite Rebellion. Bonnie Prince Charlie (1720–88), grandson of James II, is defeated at Culloden by the armies of the Duke of Cumberland. He escapes across the water to the Isle of Skye before eventually returning to France. The wearing of the kilt, the use of tartan, and the playing of bagpipes are now banned, and the clans of the north are finally crushed. James Watt (1736–1819), born in Greenock, is granted a patent for his steam engine.

1760 Thomas Braidwood (1715–1806) opens the first school for people who cannot hear or speak in Great Britain, in Edinburgh.

1771 Birth of Walter Scott (1771–1832), Romantic novelist.

1778 First cotton mill, at Rothesay.

1788 Death of Bonnie Prince Charlie in Rome.

1790 Forth and Clyde Canal opened.

1800–50 Highland Clearances: increased rents and the conversion of farms to sheep pasture lead to mass expulsions of the peasants and their forced migration to North America and elsewhere. Meanwhile, the Lowlands industrialize; Catholic Irish immigrate to factories of Glasgow and the southwest.

1807 The first museum in Scotland, the Hunterian Museum, is founded.

1822 Visit of George IV to Scotland, the first British monarch to make such a trip since Charles I. Sir Walter Scott orchestrates the visit, and almost single-handedly invents Scotland's national costume: the formal kilt, tartan plaid, and jacket.

1831 The first passenger rail service in Scotland opens on the line between Glasgow and Garnkirk.

1832 Parliamentary Reform Act expands the franchise, redistributes seats.

1837 Victoria (1819–1901) ascends to the British throne.

1842 Edinburgh–Glasgow railroad opened.

1846 Edinburgh–London railroad opened.

1848 Queen Victoria buys estate at Balmoral as her Scottish residence. Andrew Carnegie emigrates from Dunfermline to Pittsburgh.

1860   The first British Open golf championship is held in Scotland, at Prestwick.

1884–85 Gladstone's Reform Act gives the majority of men over 21 the right to vote. Office of Secretary for Scotland authorized.

1886   Scottish Home Rule Association founded.

1888   Scottish Labour Party founded by Keir Hardie (1856–1915); he later forms the Independent Labour Party (1893)

1890   Forth Rail Bridge opened.

1896   The Glasgow subway opens.

1901   Death of Queen Victoria.

1904–31 One million Scots emigrate to Canada, the United States, New Zealand, Australia, and elsewhere.

1919   Rent strikes across Scotland. Troops are sent to Glasgow as thousands gather in the city's George Square to demand a shorter working week.

1928   Equal Franchise Act gives the vote to women. Scottish Office established as governmental department in Edinburgh. John Logie Baird gives the first demonstration of television. Alexander Fleming, a Scot, discovers penicillin. Death of architect and designer Charles Rennie Mackintosh.

1930   Unemployment in Scotland reaches 25%.

1931   Depression hits industrialized Scotland severely.

1933   The first press stories alleging that there is a monster in Loch Ness. They have continued ever since.

1934   Scottish National Party formed.

1938   The world's largest luxury liner, the *Queen Elizabeth*, is launched on the Clyde.

1939   The first German air raids of World War II on Scotland are made on the Forth Estuary.

1941   The town of Clydebank is bombed by German planes attacking the shipyards: 1,000 people are killed.

1945   Two Scottish Nationalists elected to Parliament.

1947   The Edinburgh International Festival, with events in all the performing arts, is launched.

1950   The Stone of Destiny, on which the kings of Scotland were traditionally crowned, is stolen from Westminster Abbey in London and returned to Scotland. It is found a year later, in Arbroath.

1951   The People's Festival, an alternative to the official Edinburgh Festival, launched. It later becomes the Fringe.

1959   Finnart Oil Terminal, Chapelcross Nuclear Power Station, and Dounreay Fast Breeder Reactor opened.

1970   British Petroleum strikes oil in the North Sea.

1973   Britain becomes a member of the European Economic Community (formerly known as the Common Market).

1974   Eleven Scottish Nationalists elected as members of Parliament. Old counties reorganized and renamed as new regions and districts.

1975   The first Scottish oil pumped ashore from the North Sea. "It's Scotland's Oil" becomes a slogan used by Nationalists.

1979   Referendum on devolution—the creation of a separate Scotland: 33% in favor, 31% against; 36% don't vote. Britain's Labour government had imposed a minimum vote of 40%.

1980   The Singer Sewing Machine factory in Clydebank, once of the largest factories in the world, closes with the loss of 25,000 jobs.

1981   Europe's largest oil terminal opens at Sullom Voe, Shetland.

1988   Pan Am flight 103 brought down by a terrorist bomb over Lockerbie.

1992   Increasing attention focused on Scotland's dissatisfaction with rule from London. Poll shows 50% of Scots want independence.

1997   The Labour Party wins the general election in May. For the first time not one Conservative is returned from Scotland. A referendum in Scotland votes in favor of the establishment of a Scottish parliament (with restricted powers). The first successful cloning of an animal in the world is achieved with the birth of Dolly the Sheep in Edinburgh.

1999   Scotland elects its first parliament in 300 years There are 129 Members of the Scottish Parliament.

2002   The Millennium Link—the restoration of the canal link between Glasgow and Edinburgh—is completed at a cost of £78 million. It includes the Falkirk Wheel, the world's only rotating boat lift.

2004   The Scottish Parliament Building opens for business in a building whose modern design by Spanish architect Enric Miralles causes controversy.

2007   Alex Salmond, leader of the Scottish National Party, becomes the First Minister of Scotland heading a minority government.

2009   The country endures recession as part of the international economic upheaval. Scotland invokes compassionate release and sends the convicted ailing Lockerbie bomber back to Libya.

2011   The Scottish National Party under Alex Salmond wins an absolute majority in the Scottish parliamentary elections. In January 2012 he proposes the question for the referendum on Scottish independence that he wants to hold in fall 2014.

2013   Scot Andy Murray wins the Wimbledon tennis championship.

2014   Commonwealth Games open in Glasgow in July. Independence referendum on September 18.

TRAVEL SMART SCOTLAND

GETTING HERE AND AROUND

■ AIR TRAVEL

Scotland's main hubs are Glasgow, Prestwick (near Glasgow), Edinburgh, Inverness, and Aberdeen. Glasgow and Prestwick are the gateways to the west and southwest, Edinburgh the east and southeast, Aberdeen and Inverness the north. All these cities have excellent bus and train transportation services and well-maintained roads that link them with each other and other cities within Scotland. Taxis are also an efficient and reliable option, but they are three to four times the cost of going by public transport.

Traveling by air is straightforward in Scotland. Security is heavy but efficient. You can often breeze through check-in lines by using your airline's online check-in option or bag drop, but confirm this ahead of time.

Flying time to Glasgow and Aberdeen is 6½ hours from New York, 7½ hours from Chicago, 9½ hours from Dallas, 10 hours from Los Angeles, and 21½ hours from Sydney. Flying time to Edinburgh is 7 hours from New York, 8 hours from Chicago, 10 hours from Dallas, 10½ hours from Los Angeles, and 22 hours from Sydney. Not all airlines offer direct flights to Scotland; many go via London. For those flights allow an extra four to five hours of travel (two to three for the layover in London plus an addition hour or two for the duration of the flight).

Smoking is prohibited on all flights.

Airline-Security Issues Transportation Security Administration ⊕ *www.tsa.gov.*

AIRPORTS

The major international gateways to Scotland are Glasgow Airport (GLA), about 7 miles outside Glasgow, and Edinburgh Airport (EDI), 7 miles from the city. Both offer connections for dozens of European cities and regular flights to London's Gatwick (LGW) and Heathrow (LHR) airports. Aberdeen Airport (ABZ) has direct flights to most major European cities. Prestwick (PIK) has direct flights to most major British and European cities at discounted rates. Inverness (INV) offers direct flights in and around the United Kingdom.

Airport tax is included in the price of your ticket. Generally the tax for economy tickets within the United Kingdom from European Union countries is £13. For all other flights it is £67 to £69. For first- and club-class flights from the United Kingdom and European Union the tax is £26; for all other destinations it's £134 to £188.

All Scottish airports offer typical modern amenities: restaurants, cafés, shopping (from clothes to food to tourist trinkets), sandwich and salad bars, pubs, pharmacies, bookshops, and newsstands; some even have spas and hair salons. Glasgow is the largest, most interesting airport when it comes to a delayed flight. Good food and shopping options abound—try Discover Glasgow for Scottish-inspired goods—and if you're in need of some tranquillity, head for the Relaxation Station for a clothed massage, no reservation necessary.

There are plenty of hotels near all airports, and all airports also have Internet access.

Airport Information
Aberdeen Airport ☎ *0844/481–6666* ⊕ *www.aberdeenairport.com.* **Edinburgh Airport** ☎ *0844/444–8833* ⊕ *www.edinburghairport.com.* **Glasgow Airport** ☎ *0844/481–5555* ⊕ *www.glasgowairport.com.* **Glasgow Prestwick Airport** ☎ *0871/223–0700* ⊕ *www.glasgowprestwick.com.* **Inverness Airport** ☎ *01667/464000* ⊕ *www.hial.co.uk/inverness-airport.*

GROUND TRANSPORTATION

The best way to get to and from the airport based on speed and convenience is by taxi. All airport taxi stands are just outside the airport's front doors and are well marked with clear signs. Most taxis have a set price when going to and from the airport to the city center but will turn on the meter at your request. Ask the driver to turn on the meter to confirm the flat-rate price.

If you're traveling with a large party, you can request a people carrier to transport everyone, luggage included. Luggage is included in the taxi fare; you should not be charged extra for it.

If you're traveling alone, a more economical transfer option is public transportation. Buses travel between city centers and Glasgow, Edinburgh, Aberdeen, and Inverness airports. Trains go direct to Prestwick Airport. All are fast, inexpensive, and reliable. *For more information and specific contacts, refer to the Orientation and Planning sections at the beginning of chapters.*

TRANSFERS BETWEEN AIRPORTS

Scottish airports are relatively close to one another and all are connected by a series of buses and trains. Flights between airports add hours to your journey and are very expensive (between £200 and £400). The best way to travel from one airport to another is by bus, train, car, or taxi. Normally you must take a combination of bus and train, which is easy and—if you travel light—quite enjoyable.

From Edinburgh Airport you can take a bus to the city center (£3.50) and then a train to Glasgow city center (£12.50) and a bus to Glasgow Airport (£4.50). This journey should take you less than two hours. Taxis are fast but costly. The price of a taxi from Edinburgh Airport to Glasgow Airport is around £85, a good choice if you're traveling with a few people. Renting a car would be a good choice if you want to get from Edinburgh to, say, Aberdeen Airport

and you're traveling with a few people. Otherwise, take a bus to the city center and then take a train. *For specific information, see the Orientation and Planning section at the start of appropriate chapters.*

FLIGHTS

Scotland has a significant air network for a small country. Contact British Airways or British Airways Express for details on flights from London's Heathrow Airport or from Glasgow, Edinburgh, Aberdeen, and Inverness to the farthest corners of the Scottish mainland and to the islands. *See individual chapters for information on flying to various islands.*

Among the low-cost carriers, Virgin has service from Heathrow; and easyJet flies from London Luton/Gatwick/Stansted to and between Glasgow, Edinburgh, Aberdeen, and Inverness, plus to and from Belfast. Flybe has services to Sumburgh (Shetland) and Kirkwall (Orkney) from Aberdeen, Inverness, Glasgow, and Edinburgh, where you can continue on to Bristol, Exeter, Manchester, and Southampton.

Major Airline Contacts

British Airways ☎ 800/247-9297 in U.S., 0844/493-0787 in U.K. ⊕ www.britishairways. com. **KLM** ☎ 866/434-0320 in U.S., 0 871/231-0000 in U.K. ⊕ www.klm.com. **United Airlines** ☎ 800/864-8331 in U.S., 0845/607-6760 in U.K. ⊕ www.united.com. **US Airways** ☎ 800/428-4322 in U.S., 0845/600-3300 in U.K. ⊕ www.usairways. com. **Virgin Atlantic** ☎ 800/821-5438 in U.S., 0844/209-7770 in U.K.
⊕ www.virgin-atlantic.com.

From London to Edinburgh and Glasgow
asyJet ☎ 0843/104-5000 ⊕ www.easyjet.com. **Ryanair** ☎ 0871/246-0000 in U.K.
⊕ www.ryanair.com.

Within Scotland lybe ☎ 0871/700-2000
⊕ www.flybe.com.

AIRLINE TICKETS

The least expensive airfares to Scotland are often priced for round-trip travel and must usually be purchased in advance. Airlines generally allow you to change your return date for a fee; most low-fare tickets, however, are nonrefundable.

If you intend to fly to Scotland from London, take advantage of the current fare wars on internal routes—notably among London's four airports and between Glasgow and Edinburgh. Among the cheapest fares are those from easyJet, which offers bargain fares from London Luton/Gatwick/Stansted (all with good rail links from central London) to Glasgow, Edinburgh, Aberdeen, and Inverness. However, British Airways now offers competitive fares on some flights, especially those booked in advance.

AIR PASSES

Oneworld's Visit Europe Pass offers packages based on mileage that allow travel throughout Europe on airlines that include British Airways (which has an extensive network of European flights). You must purchase this pass before you leave home through the Oneworld website. In Britain the best place to search for consolidator tickets, or so-called bucket-shop tickets, is through Cheap Flights, a website that pools all flights available and then directs you to a phone number or site to purchase tickets.

Air Pass Information
Cheap Flights ⊕ www.cheapflights.co.uk. **lightpass by Europe by Air** ☎ 866/478–810 in U.S . ⊕ www.europebyair.com. **Oneworld** ⊕ www.oneworld.com.

▮ BIKE TRAVEL

Bicycling in Scotland is variable. The best months for cycling are May, June, and September, when the roads are often quieter and the weather is usually better. Because Scotland's main roads are continually being upgraded, bicyclists can easily reach the network of quieter rural roads in southern and much of eastern Scotland, especially Grampian. In a few areas of the Highlands, notably in northwestern Scotland, the rugged terrain and limited population have resulted in the lack of side roads, making it difficult—sometimes impossible—to plan a minor-road route in these areas.

Several agencies now promote routes for recreational cyclists. These routes are signposted, and agencies have produced maps or leaflets showing where they run. Perhaps best known is the Glasgow–Loch Lomond–Killin Cycleway, which uses former railway track beds, forest trails, quiet rural side roads, and some main roads. VisitScotland has advice on a site dedicated to cycling.

BIKING ORGANIZATIONS

The Cyclists' Touring Club publishes a members' magazine, route maps, and guides. Sustrans Ltd. is a nonprofit organization dedicated to providing environmentally friendly routes for cyclists, notably in and around cities. Active Scotland, part of the national tourism agency, has a great list of bike routes ranked by area and difficulty.

TRANSPORTING BIKES

Although some rural bus services will transport cycles if space is available, don't count on getting your bike on a bus. Check well in advance with the appropriate bus company.

You can take bicycles on car and passenger ferries in Scotland, and it's usually not necessary to book in advance. Arrive early so that your bike can be loaded through the car entrance.

ScotRail strongly advises that you make a train reservation for you and your bike at least one month in advance. On several trains reservations are compulsory.

Bike Maps and Information ActiveScotland ☎ 0845/859–1006 ⊕ active.visitscotland.com. **Cyclists' Touring Club** ☎ 0844/736–8450 ⊕ www.ctc.org.uk. **Sustrans** ☎ 0131/346–1384 ⊕ www.sustrans.org.uk.

■ BOAT AND FERRY TRAVEL

Because Scotland has so many islands, plus the great Firth of Clyde waterway, ferry services are of paramount importance. Most ferries transport vehicles as well as foot passengers, although a few smaller ones are for passengers only.

It's a good idea to make a reservation ahead of time, although reservations are not absolutely necessary. Most travelers show up on the day of departure and buy their tickets from the stations at the ports. Keep in mind that these are working ferries, not tourist boats. Although journeys are scenic, most people use these ferries as their daily means of public transportation to and from their hometowns.

The main operator is Caledonian Mac-Brayne, known generally as CalMac. Services extend from the Firth of Clyde in the south, where there's an extensive network, right up to the northwest of Scotland and all the Hebrides. CalMac sells an 8-day or 15-day Island Rover runabout ticket, which is ideal for touring holidays in the islands, as well as an island-hopping plan called Island Hopscotch. Fares can range from £4 to £5 for a short trip to almost £50 for a longer trip with several legs.

The Dunoon–Gourock route on the Clyde is served by Western Ferries (for cars) and CalMac (for passengers only).

Northlink Ferries operates a car ferry for Orkney between Scrabster, near Thurso, and Stromness, on the main island of Orkney; and between Aberdeen and Kirkwall, which is also on Mainland, Orkney. Northlink also runs an efficient and affordable ferry to Lerwick, Shetland, and Kirkwall, Orkney. The journey to Lerwick is overnight, but comfortable cabins are available for those who prefer to take the waves lying down. These ferries can be busy in summer, so book well in advance.

Traveler's checks (in pounds), cash, and major credit cards are accepted for payment. *See the Orientation and Planning sections of each chapter for more details about ferry services.*

Information Caledonian MacBrayne ☎ 0800/066–5000 ⊕ www.calmac.co.uk. orthlink Ferries ☎ 0845/600–0449 ⊕ www.northlinkferries.co.uk. Western Ferries ☎ 01369/704452 ⊕ www.western-ferries.co.uk.

■ BUS TRAVEL

Long-distance buses usually provide the cheapest way to travel between England and Scotland; fares may be as little as a third of the rail fares for comparable trips and are cheaper if you buy in advance. However, the trip is not as comfortable as by train (no dining cart, smaller bathrooms, less spacious seats), and travel takes longer. Glasgow to London by nonstop bus takes 8 hours, 45 minutes; by train it takes about 5 hours, 30 minutes. Scotland's bus (short-haul) and coach (long-distance) network is extensive. Bus service is comprehensive in cities, less so in country districts. Express service links main cities and towns, connecting, for example, Glasgow and Edinburgh to Inverness, Aberdeen, Perth, Skye, Ayr, Dumfries, and Carlisle; or Inverness with Aberdeen, Wick, Thurso, and Fort William. Express service is very fast, and fares are reasonable. Scottish Citylink, National Express, and Megabus are among the main operators; there are about 20 in all. All buses are non-smoking.

The London terminal is Victoria Coach Station for National Express and the London Victoria Greenline Coach Station for Megabus, which now offers a Gold service: a sleeper coach with seats that fold down into beds.

DISCOUNTS AND DEALS

On Scottish Citylink, the Explorer Passes offer complete freedom of travel on all services throughout Scotland. Three permutations give three days of travel out of a 5-day period, 5 days of travel out of 10, and 8 days of travel out of 16. They're available from Scottish Citylink offices, and cost £41, £62, and £93 respectively.

National Express offers discounted seats on buses from London to more than 50 cities in the United Kingdom, including Glasgow and Aberdeen. Tickets range from £12 to £40, but only when purchased online. Megabus (order tickets online), a discount service, has similarly competitive prices between major cities throughout Scotland, including Aberdeen, Dundee, Glasgow, Inverness, and Perth.

Travelers ages 16 to 26 are eligible for 30% reductions with the National Express Coachcard (£10).

FARES AND SCHEDULES

Contact Traveline Scotland for information on all public transportation and timetables.

For town, suburban, or short-distance journeys, you buy your ticket on the bus, from a pay box, or from the driver. You need exact change. For longer journeys—for example, Glasgow–Inverness—it's usual (and a good idea; busy routes and times can book up) to reserve a seat online.

PAYING

Credit cards are accepted at most bus stations.

Bus Information Traveline Scotland
☎ 0871/200–2233 ⊕ www.travelinescotland.com.

Bus Lines Megabus ☎ 0900/160–0900 ⊕ www.megabus.co.uk. **National Express** ☎ 08717/818178 ⊕ www.nationalexpress.com. **cottish Citylink** ☎ 0871/266–3333 ⊕ www.citylink.co.uk.

▌CAR TRAVEL

If you plan to stick mostly to the cities, you will not need a car. All cities in Scotland are either so compact that most attractions are within easy walking distance of each other (Aberdeen, Dundee, Edinburgh, Inverness, and Stirling) or are accessible by an excellent local public transport system (Glasgow). And there is often good train or bus service from major cities to nearby day-trip destinations. Bus tours are a good option for day trips.

Once you leave Edinburgh, Glasgow, and the other major cities, a car will make journeys faster and much more enjoyable than trying to work out public-transportation connections to the farther-flung reaches of Scotland (though it is possible, if time consuming, to see much of the country by public transportation). A car allows you to set your own pace and visit off-the-beaten-path towns and sights most easily.

In Scotland your own driver's license is acceptable. International driving permits (IDPs) are available from the American Automobile Association and, in the United Kingdom, from the Automobile Association and Royal Automobile Club. These international permits, valid only in conjunction with your regular driver's license, are universally recognized; having one may save you a problem with local authorities.

GASOLINE

Expect to pay a lot more for gasoline, about £6 a gallon (from £1.32 to £1.39 a liter) for unleaded. It's about 10p a liter higher in remote rural locations, even in the oil-producing region around Shetland. The British imperial gallon is about 20% more in volume than the U.S. gallon—approximately 4.5 liters. Pumps dispense in liters, not gallons. Most gas stations are self-service and stock unleaded, super unleaded, and LRP (replacing four-star) plus diesel; all accept major credit cards.

PARKING

On-street parking is a bit of a lottery in Scotland. Depending on the location and time of day, the streets can be packed or empty of cars. In the cities you must pay for your on-street parking by getting a sticker from a parking machine; these machines are clearly marked with a large P. Make sure you have the exact change; the cost is around £2 for two hours, but can vary. Put the parking sticker on the inside of your windshield. Parking lots are scattered throughout urban areas and tend to be more or less the same price as on-street parking. Most parking lots are near shopping malls or busy financial districts.

The local penalty for illegally parked cars is £25, and parking regulations are strictly enforced.

ROAD CONDITIONS

A good network of superhighways, known as motorways, and divided highways, known as dual carriageways, extends throughout Britain. In remote areas of Scotland where the motorway hasn't penetrated, travel is noticeably slower. Motorways shown with the prefix M are mainly two or three lanes in each direction, without any right-hand turns. These are the roads to use to cover long distances, though inevitably you'll see less of the countryside. Service areas are at most about an hour apart.

Dual carriageways, usually shown on a map as a thick red line (often with a black line in the center) and the prefix "a" followed by a number perhaps with a bracketed "t" (for example, "a304[t]"), are similar to motorways, except that right turns are sometimes permitted, and you'll find both traffic lights and traffic circles along the way. The vast network of other main roads, which typical maps show as either single red A roads, or narrower brown B roads, also numbered, are for the most part the old roads originally intended for horses and carriages. Travel along these roads is slower than on motorways, and passing is more difficult. On the other hand, you'll see much more of Scotland. The A9, Perth to Inverness, is a particularly dangerous road with the worst road accident record in Scotland because its dual carriageway's stopping and starting.

Minor roads (shown as yellow or white on most maps, unlettered and unnumbered) are the ancient lanes and byways of Britain, roads that are not only living history but a superb way of discovering hidden parts of Scotland. You have to drive slowly and carefully. On single-track (one-lane) roads, found in the north and west of Scotland, there's no room for two vehicles to pass, and you must use a passing place if you meet an oncoming car or tractor, or if a car behind wishes to overtake you. Never hold up traffic on single-track roads.

For some typical driving times, see the Scotland Planner in Chapter 1.

ROADSIDE EMERGENCIES

For aid if your car breaks down, contact the 24-hour rescue numbers of either the Automobile Association or the Royal Automobile Club. If you're a member of the AAA (American Automobile Association) or another association, check your membership details before you travel; reciprocal agreements may give you free roadside aid.

Emergency Contacts in the U.K.
Automobile Association (*AA*).
☎ *0800/887766* ⊕ *www.theaa.com*. **Royal Automobile Club** (*RAC*). ☎ *0844/891–3111* ⊕ *www.rac.co.uk*.

Emergency Contacts in the U.S.
American Automobile Association (*AAA*).
☎ *800/564–6222* ⊕ *www.aaa.com*.

RULES OF THE ROAD

The most noticeable difference for most visitors is that when in Britain, you drive on the left and steer the car on the right. Give yourself time to adjust to driving on the left—especially if you pick up your car at the airport. One of the most complicated questions facing visitors to Britain is that of speed limits. In urban areas it's generally 30 mph, but it's 40 mph on some main roads, as indicated by circular red-rimmed signs. In rural areas the official limit is 60 mph on ordinary roads and 70 mph on divided highways and motorways. Traffic police can be hard on speeders, especially in urban areas. Driving while using a cell phone is illegal, and the use of seat belts is mandatory for passengers in front and back seats. Service stations and newsstands sell copies of the Highway Code (£2.50), which lists driving rules and has pictures of signs. It's also available online at ⊕ *www. direct.gov.uk*.

Drunk-driving laws are strictly enforced and penalties are heavy. Avoid alcohol if you're driving.

CAR RENTAL

You can rent any type of car you desire; however, in Scotland cars tend to be on the smaller side. Many roads are narrow, and a smaller car saves money on gas. Common models are the Nissan Micra, Ford Focus, and Vauxhall Corsa. Four-wheel-drive vehicles aren't a necessity. Most cars are manual, not automatic, and come with air-conditioning, although you rarely need it in Scotland. If you want an automatic, reserve ahead. The cars are in very good condition and must pass a series of inspections and tests before they are rented out.

When you're returning the car, allow an extra hour to drop it off and sort out any paperwork. If you're traveling to more than one country, make sure your rental contract permits you to take the car across borders and that your insurance policy covers you in every country you visit.

Rates in Glasgow begin at £25 a day and £120 a week for an economy car with a manual transmission and unlimited mileage. This does not include tax on car rentals, which is 20%. The busiest months are June through August, when rates may go up 30%. During this time, book at least two to four weeks in advance. Online booking is fine.

Companies frequently restrict rentals to people over age 23 and under age 75. If you are over 70, some companies require you to have your own insurance. If you are under 25, a surcharge of £16 per day plus V.A.T. will apply

Child car seats usually cost about £24 extra; you must ask for a car seat when you book, at least 48 hours in advance. The same is true for GPS. Adding one extra driver is usually included in the original rental price.

Local Agencies Arnold Clark ☎ 0141/237–4374 ⊕ *www.arnoldclarkrental.com*.

Major Rental Agencies Avis ☎ 0844/581–0147 ⊕ *www.avis.co.uk*. **Budget** ☎ 0844/581–2231 ⊕ *www.budget.co.uk*. **Hertz** ☎ 0843/309–3099 ⊕ *www.hertz.co.uk*. **National Car Rental** ☎ 0871/384–1140 ⊕ *www.nationalcar.co.uk*.

Wholesalers Auto Europe ☎ 0800/358–1229 ⊕ *www.auto-europe.co.uk*. **Europe by Car** ☎ 0141/531–5220 *in Glasgow* ⊕ *www. ebctravel.com*. **Eurovacations** ☎ 877/471–3876 *in U.S.* ⊕ *www.eurovacations.com*. **Kemwel** ☎ 877/820–0668 *in U.S.* ⊕ *www.kemwel.com*.

▌TAXI TRAVEL

In Edinburgh, Glasgow, and the larger cities, black hackney taxis—similar to those in London—with their "taxi" sign illuminated can be hailed on the street, or booked by phone (expect to pay an extra 80p charge for this service in Edinburgh). If you call a private-hire taxi from the phone book, expect a regular-looking car to pick you up. The only distinctions are that they have a taxi license and a meter stuck on the dashboard, along with an ID card for the driver. Private-hire taxis are cheaper than black hackney taxis and will pick you up only from a specific location, not off the street.

Scottish taxis are reliable, safe, and metered. Meters begin at £2 and increase in 25p intervals. Beyond the larger cities, most communities of any size have a taxi service; your hotel will be able to supply telephone numbers.

▌TRAIN TRAVEL

Train service within Scotland is generally run by ScotRail, one of the most efficient of Britain's service providers. Trains are modern, clean, and comfortable. Long-distance services carry buffet and refreshment cars. Scotland's rail network extends all the way to Thurso and Wick, the most northerly stations in the British Isles. Lowland services, most of which originate in Glasgow or Edinburgh, are generally fast and reliable. A shuttle makes the 50-minute trip between Glasgow and Edinburgh every 15 minutes. It's a scenic trip with plenty of rolling fields, livestock, and traditional houses along the way. Rail service throughout the country, especially the Highlands, is limited on Sunday.

CLASSES

Most trains have first-class and standard-class coaches. First-class coaches are always less crowded; they have wider seats and are often cleaner and newer than standard-class cars, and they're a lot more expensive. However, on weekends you can often upgrade from standard to first class for a fee (often £10 to £20)—ask when you book.

FARES AND SCHEDULES

The best way to find out which train to take, which station to catch it at, and what times trains travel to your destination is to call National Rail Enquiries. It's a helpful, comprehensive, free service that covers all Britain's rail lines. National Rail will help you choose the best train to take, and then connects you with the ticket office for that train company so that you can buy tickets. You can also check schedules and purchase tickets on its website.

Train fares vary according to class of ticket purchased, time (off-peak travel will be much cheaper), and distance traveled. Before you buy your ticket, stop at the Information Office/Travel Centre and request the lowest fare to your destination and information about any special offers. There's sometimes little difference between the cost of a one-way and round-trip ticket, and returns are valid for one month. So if you're planning on departing from and returning to the same destination, buy a round-trip fare upon your departure, rather than purchasing two separate one-way tickets.

It's often much cheaper to buy a ticket in advance than on the day of your trip (except for commuter services); the closer to the date of travel, the more expensive the ticket will be. Try to purchase tickets at least eight weeks in advance during peak-season summer travel to save money and reserve good seats. You must stick to the train you have booked (penalties can be the full price), and you need to keep the seat reservation ticket, which is part of the valid ticket.

Check train websites, especially ScotRail, for deals. You can also check the trainline, which sells discounted advance-purchase tickets from all train companies to all destinations in Britain.

Information **National Rail Enquiries** ☎ *0845/748-4950* ⊕ *www.nationalrail.co.uk.* **ScotRail** ☎ *0845/601-5929* ⊕ *www.scotrail. co.uk.* **the trainline** ☎ *0871/244-1545* ⊕ *www.thetrainline.com.*

PAYING

All major credit cards are accepted for train fares paid in person, online, and by phone.

RESERVATIONS

Reserving your ticket in advance is always recommended.

Tickets and rail passes do not guarantee seats on the trains. For that you need a seat reservation (essential for peak travel trains to and from Edinburgh during the summer festivals), which if made at the time of ticket purchase is usually included in the ticket price, or if booked separately, must be paid for at a cost of £1 *per train* on your itinerary. You also need a reservation for the overnight sleeper trains.

TRAIN PASSES

Rail passes may save you money, especially if you're going to log a lot of miles. If you plan to travel by train in Scotland, consider purchasing a BritRail Pass, which also allows travel in England and Wales. All BritRail passes must be purchased in your home country; they're sold by travel agents as well as ACP, BritRail, or Rail

Europe. Rail passes do not guarantee seats on the trains, so be sure to reserve ahead. Remember that Eurail Passes aren't honored in Great Britain.

The cost of an unlimited BritRail adult pass for 4 days is $225/$395 (standard/first class); for 8 days, $375/$565; for 15 days, $565/$839; for 22 days, $709/$1,065; and for a month, $839/$1,259. The Youth Pass, for ages 16 to 25, costs $215/$319 for 4 days; $305/$455for 8 days; $455/$675 for 15 days; $569/$855 for 22 days; and $675/$1,009 for one month. The Senior Pass, for those over 60, costs $265/$339 for 4 days; $375/$479 for 8 days; $565/$715 for 15 days; $709/$790 for 22 days; and $839/$1,075 for one month. The Scottish Freedom Pass allows transportation on all Caledonian MacBrayne and Strathclyde ferries in addition to major bus links and the Glasgow underground. You can travel any 4 days in an 8-day period for $239 or any 8 days in a 15-day period for $319.

Information ACP Rail International
☎ 866/938–7245 ⊕ www.acprail.com.
BritRail Travel ☎ 866/938–7245 ⊕ www.britrail.com. **Rail Europe** ☎ 0844/848–4078 ⊕ www.raileurope.com.

FROM ENGLAND
There are two main rail routes to Scotland from the south of England. The first, the west-coast main line, runs from London Euston to Glasgow Central; it takes 5½ hours to make the 400-mile trip to central Scotland, and service is frequent and reliable. Useful for daytime travel to the Scottish Highlands is the direct train to Stirling and Aviemore, terminating at Inverness. For a restful route to the Scottish Highlands, take the overnight sleeper service, with soundproof sleeping carriages. It runs from London Euston, departing in late evening, to Perth, Stirling, Aviemore, and Inverness, where it arrives the following morning.

The east-coast main line from London King's Cross to Edinburgh provides the quickest trip to the Scottish capital. Between 8 am and 6 pm there are 16 trains to Edinburgh, three of them through to Aberdeen. Limited-stop expresses like the Flying Scotsman make the 393-mile London-to-Edinburgh journey in around four hours. Connecting services to most parts of Scotland—particularly the Western Highlands—are often better from Edinburgh than from Glasgow.

Trains from elsewhere in England are good: regular service connects Birmingham, Manchester, Liverpool, and Bristol with Glasgow and Edinburgh. From Harwich (the port of call for ships from Holland, Germany, and Denmark), you can travel to Glasgow via Manchester. But it's faster to change at Peterborough for the east-coast main line to Edinburgh.

SCENIC ROUTES
Although many routes in Scotland run through extremely attractive countryside, several stand out: from Glasgow to Oban via Loch Lomond; to Fort William and Mallaig via Rannoch (ferry connection to Skye); from Edinburgh to Inverness via the Forth Bridge and Perth; from Inverness to Kyle of Lochalsh and to Wick; and from Inverness to Aberdeen.

A private train, the Royal Scotsman, does all-inclusive scenic tours, partly under steam power, with banquets en route. This is a luxury experience: some evenings require formal wear. You can choose itineraries from two nights (£2.350) to seven nights (£6,990) per person.

Train Tours The Royal Scotsman
☎ 0845/217–0799 in the U.K., 800/524–2420 in the U.S. ⊕ www.royalscotsman.com.

ESSENTIALS

■ ACCOMMODATIONS

Your choices in Scotland range from small, local B&Bs to large, elegant hotels—some of the chain variety. Bed-and-breakfasts tend to be less expensive than large hotels because many are spare rooms in spacious homes. Proprietors keep costs down and guests get a more personal, Scottish touch. Accommodation can seem expensive because the pound has been strong against the dollar, but the economic downturn since 2009 has brought some special deals. For example, some lodgings offer discounted rates for stays of two nights or longer.

If you haven't booked ahead, you're not likely to be stranded. Even in the height of the season—July and August—hotel occupancy runs at about 80%. However, your choice of accommodations will be extremely limited if you show up somewhere during a festival or golf tournament. Your best bet will be to try for a room in a nearby village.

To secure your first choice, reserve in advance. One option is to reserve through local tourist information centers, making use of their "book-a-bed-ahead" services. Telephone bookings made from home should be confirmed by email or fax. Country hotels expect you to check in by about 6 pm.

Be sure you understand the hotel's cancellation policy. Some places allow you to cancel without any kind of penalty; others, particularly B&Bs, require you to cancel a week in advance or penalize you.

Smoking is banned in all indoor public spaces in Scotland, and this includes hotel rooms. Most hotels allow children under a certain age to stay in their parents' room at no extra charge, but others charge for them as extra adults; find out the cutoff age for discounts.

VisitScotland classifies and grades accommodations using a simple star system. The greater the number of stars, the greater the number of facilities and the more luxurious they are.

The lodgings we list are the cream of the crop in each price category. Unless otherwise noted, all lodgings listed have a private bathroom, a room phone, and a television. When pricing accommodations, always ask what's included. Many hotels and most guesthouses and B&Bs include a breakfast within the basic room rate. Meal-plan information appears at the end of a review. *Prices in the reviews are the lowest cost of a standard double room in high season, including 20% V.A.T.*

APARTMENT AND HOUSE RENTALS

Rental houses and flats (apartments) are becoming more popular lodging choices for travelers visiting Scotland, particularly for those staying in one place for more than a few days. Some places may rent only by the week. Prices can be cheaper than a hotel (though perhaps not less than a bed-and-breakfast), and the space and comfort are much better than what you'd find in a typical hotel.

In the country your chances of finding a small house to rent are good; in the city you're more likely to find a flat (apartment) to let (rent). Either way, your best bet for finding these rentals is online. Individuals and large consortiums can own these properties, so it just depends on what you're looking for. The White House is a good, central place for rentals in Glasgow, and Scottish Apartment is a good source for apartments in Edinburgh. The National Trust for Scotland has many unique properties, from island cottages to castles, for rent.

LOCAL DO'S AND TABOOS

GREETINGS

Although many Scots are fantastic talkers, they're less enthusiastic with greetings on the physical front. If you're in less familiar company, a handshake is more appreciated than a kiss or hug.

SIGHTSEEING

When you are visiting houses of worship, modest attire is appreciated, though you will see shorts and even bared midriffs. Photographs are welcome in churches, outside of services. Shorts and other close-fitting attire are allowed just about any-where else at any time, weather permitting; these days locals tend not to cover up as much as they used to.

It's the same with food; Scots eat and drink just about anywhere, and much of the time they do it standing up or even walking.

ETIQUETTE

In Scotland it's rude to walk away from con-versation, even if it's with someone you don't know. If you're at a pub, keep in mind that it's very important to buy a round of drinks if you're socializing with a group of people. You don't simply buy your own drink; you buy a drink for all of the people you're there with, and those people do the same. It can make for a very foggy evening and public drunk-enness, especially on Friday and Saturday nights. Conversational topics that are consid-ered taboo are money matters; the Scots are private about their finances. You should give up your seats for elderly people or pregnant women without a second thought. Hold the door open for someone who is leaving or entering the same building as you. Say please and thank you.

Driving etiquette is carefully observed, too; be courteous and allow people to pass. Jaywalking isn't rude or illegal, but it's much safer to cross with the lights, especially if traffic is coming from a direction you might not be used to.

As for waiting in lines and moving through crowds, put your best foot forward. The Scots are very polite and you'll be noticed (and not in a good way) if you're not.

OUT ON THE TOWN

People may dress up for a special restaurant or for clubbing, but other people will be casual. Some restaurants and clubs frown on jeans and sneakers.

If you're visiting a family home, a simple bouquet of flowers is a welcome gift. If you're invited for a meal, bringing a bottle of wine is appropriate, as is some candy for the children. To thank a host for hospital-ity, either a phone call or thank-you card is always appreciated.

DOING BUSINESS

Punctuality is of prime importance, so call ahead if you anticipate a late arrival. Spouses do not generally attend business dinners, unless specifically invited. If you ask some-one to dine, it's usually assumed that you'll pick up the tab. However, if you're the visitor, your host may insist on paying. Nonetheless, it's always polite to offer to pay.

LANGUAGE

The Scots language, which borrows from Scandinavian, Dutch, French, and Gaelic, survives in various forms, with each region having its own dialect. In the northeast they speak Doric, while the Shetland and Orkney "tongue" is influenced by the now-extinct Norn. The Gaelic language, the indigenous language of those from the Western Isles and Highlands, has been given a new lease of life. Many primary schools in the region are teaching a new generation of Gaelic speakers. The language has its own TV chan-nel, BBC Alba, and is being promoted in a huge signage campaign. Otherwise, Scots speak English often with a strong accent (which may be hard for non-native Brits and Americans to understand), but your ear will soon come to terms with it.

International Agencies At Home Abroad
☎ 212/421–9165 ⊕ www.athomeabroadinc.
com. **Barclay International Group**
☎ 800/845–6636 ⊕ www.barclayweb.com.
Drawbridge to Europe ☎ 541/482–7778
⊕ www.drawbridgetoeurope.com. **Forgetaway**
⊕ www.forgetaway.com. **Home Away** ⊕ www.
homeaway.com. **Interhome** ☎ 800/882–6864
in the U.S. ⊕ www.interhome.us. **Villas &**
Apartments Abroad ☎ 212/213–6435
⊕ www.vaanyc.com.

Local Contacts National Trust for Scot-
land ☎ 0131/458–0303, 866/211–7573 in
U.S. ⊕ www.nts.org.uk. **Scottish Apartment**
☎ 0131/222–9670 ⊕ www.scottishapartment.
co.uk. **White House** ☎ 0141/339–9375
⊕ www.whitehouse-apartments.com.

BED-AND-BREAKFASTS

Common throughout Scotland, B&Bs are
a special British tradition and the backbone of budget travel. Prices average
about £40 to £100 per night, depending
on the region and the time of year. They're
usually in a family home, occasionally
don't have private bathrooms, and usually offer only breakfast. More upscale
B&Bs, along the line of American B&Bs
or small inns, can be found in Edinburgh
and Glasgow especially, but in other parts
of Scotland as well. Guest houses are a
slightly larger, somewhat more luxurious
version. All provide a glimpse of everyday
British life. Note that local tourist offices
can book a B&B for you; there may be a
small charge for this service.

Reservation Services BedandBreakfast.
com ☎ 512/322–2710, 800/462–2632
⊕ www.bedandbreakfast.com.
UK Bed and Breakfast Accommodation
⊕ www.bedandbreakfasts.co.uk.

FARMHOUSE AND
CROFTING HOLIDAYS

A popular option for families with children is a farmhouse holiday, combining
the freedom of B&B accommodations
with the hospitality of Scottish family life.
You'll need a car if you're staying deep in
the country, though. Information is available from VisitBritain or VisitScotland,

from Scottish Farmhouse Holidays, and
from the Farm Stay UK.

Contacts Farm Stay UK ☎ 024/7669–6909
⊕ www.farmstayuk.co.uk. **Scottish Farm-**
house Holidays ☎ 01334/476370 ⊕ www.
scottishfarmhouseholidays.com.

HOME EXCHANGES

With a direct home exchange you stay in
someone else's home while they stay in
yours. Some outfits also deal with vacation homes, so you're not actually staying
in someone's full-time residence, just their
vacant weekend place.

Exchange Clubs HomeExchange.com. From
$5.95 per month. ☎ 800/877–8723 ⊕ www.
homeexchange.com. **HomeLink Interna-**
tional. $89 for full membership for one year.
☎ 800/638–3841 in U.S., 01962/886882 in
U.K. ⊕ www.homelink.org. **Intervac U.S.** Various online packages ranging from $8.33 per
month. ☎ 800/756–4663 ⊕ www.intervac-
homeexchange.com.

HOTELS

Large hotels vary in style and price.
Many lean toward Scottish themes when
it comes to decoration, but you can expect
the same quality and service from a chain
hotel wherever you are in the world. Keep
in mind that hotel rooms in Scotland are
smaller than what you'd find in the United
States. Today hotels of all sizes are trying
to be greener, and many newer chains are
striving for government environmental
awards. Discounted rooms are another
trend, as are discounts for room upgrades.

In the countryside some older hotels are former castles or converted country homes. These types of hotels are full of character and charm but can be very expensive, and they may not have elevators. Normally they have all the amenities, if not more, of their urban counterparts. Their locations may be so remote that you must eat on the premises, which may be costly.

Some small regional chains operate in Scotland that are not internationally known. Apex (in Edinburgh, Dundee, and London) is modish and has Scandinavian-inspired bedrooms; Malmaison (in Aberdeen, Edinburgh, and Glasgow) is luxury on a budget; Hotel du Vin (Glasgow and Edinburgh), with its chic bistros, sumptuous bedding, and original art, may blow the budget.

Hotel Contacts
Apex Hotels ⊕ www.apexhotels.co.uk.
Hotel du Vin ⊕ www.hotelduvin.com.
Malmaison ⊕ www.malmaison.com.

▮ COMMUNICATIONS

INTERNET

All newer laptops operate equally well on 110 and 220 volts and so require only an adapter. Never plug your computer into any socket without first asking about surge protection: although Scotland is computer-friendly, few hotels and B&Bs outside the major cities have built-in current stabilizers. It's worthwhile to purchase a surge protector in the United Kingdom that plugs into the socket.

All hotels and many B&Bs have facilities for computer users, such as dedicated computer rooms and wired or wireless connections for Internet access. Most cafés offer free Wi-Fi access. Cybercafes lists more than 4,000 Internet cafés worldwide.

Contacts Cybercafes ⊕ www.cybercafes.com.

PHONES

The good news is that you can now make a direct-dial telephone call from virtually any point on earth. The bad news? You can't always do so cheaply. Calling from a hotel is almost always the most expensive option; hotels usually add huge surcharges to all calls, particularly international ones.

When you're calling anywhere in Great Britain from the United States, the country code is 44. When dialing a Scottish or British number from abroad, drop the initial 0 from the local area code. For instance, if you're calling Edinburgh Castle from New York City, dial 011 (the international code), 44 (the Great Britain country code), 131 (the Edinburgh city code), and then 225–9846 (the number proper).

CALLING WITHIN SCOTLAND

There are three types of public pay phones: those that accept only coins, those that accept only phone cards, and those that take British Telecom (BT) phone cards and credit cards. For coin-only phones, insert coins *before* dialing (minimum charge is 60p). Sometimes phones have a "press on answer" (POA) button, which you press when the caller answers.

All calls are charged according to the time of day. Standard rate is weekdays 8 am to 6 pm; cheap rate is weekdays 6 pm to 8 am and all day on weekends, when it's even cheaper. A local call made from a landline before 6 pm costs 12p. The minimum charge for a local call from a pay phone is 60p for the first 30 minutes and 10p for each subsequent minute. A daytime call to the United States will cost 19p a minute on a regular phone (weekends are cheaper), 60p on a pay phone.

To call a number with the same area code as the number from which you are dialing, omit the area-code digits when you dial. For long-distance calls within Britain, dial the area code (which usually begins with 01), followed by the telephone number. In provincial areas the dialing codes for nearby towns are often posted in phone booths.

To call the operator, dial 100; directory inquiries (information), 118–500; international directory inquiries, 118–505.

In Scotland cell phone numbers, the 0800 toll-free code, and local-rate 0345 numbers do not have a 1 after the initial 0, nor do many premium-rate numbers, for example 0891, and special-rate numbers, for example 08705.

Numbers that start with 0800, 0808, or national information numbers that start with 0845 are free when called from a U.K. landline: they cost anywhere from 15p to 80p a minute when called from a cellular phone. Additionally, 0870 numbers are *not* toll-free numbers; in fact, numbers beginning with 0871 or the 0900 prefix are premium-rate numbers, and it costs extra to call them. The amount varies and is usually relatively small when dialed from within the country but can be excessive when dialed from outside the United Kingdom. Many businesses, especially those offering low-cost services (such as Ryanair or Megabus) communicate with customers via their websites. If they do have a customer services phone number, it's costly to use it.

CALLING OUTSIDE SCOTLAND
The country code for the United States is 1.

To make international calls *from* Scotland, dial 00 for international access, then the country code, area code, and number. For the international operator, credit card, or collect calls, dial 155.

Access Codes AT&T Direct ☎ 0800/013–0011 ⊕ www.att.com. MCI WorldPhone ☎ 0800/279–5088 ⊕ www.consumer.mci.com. Sprint International Access ☎ 0808/234–6616 ⊕ www.sprint.com.

CALLING CARDS
You can purchase BT (British Telecom) phone cards for use on public phones from shops, post offices, and newsstands. They're ideal for longer calls, are composed of units of 20p, and come in values of £2, £5, £10, and £20. An indicator panel on the phone shows the number of units you've used; at the end of your call the card is returned. Where credit cards are taken, slide the card through, as indicated. Beware of buying cards that require you to dial a free phone number; some of these are not legitimate. It's better to get a BT card.

MOBILE PHONES
If you have a multiband phone (some countries use different frequencies than what's used in the United States) and your service provider uses the world-standard GSM network (as do T-Mobile, Cingular, and Verizon), you can probably use your phone abroad. Roaming fees can be steep, however: 99¢ a minute is considered reasonable. And overseas you normally pay the toll charges for incoming calls. It's almost always cheaper to send a text message than to make a call, since text messages have a very low set fee (often less than 5¢).

If you just want to make local calls, consider buying a new SIM card (note that your provider may have to unlock your phone for you to use a different SIM card) and a prepaid-service plan in the destination. You'll then have a local number and can make local calls at local rates.

Cell phones are getting less and less expensive to purchase. Rather than renting one, it may be cheaper to buy one to use while you're abroad. Rates run from as low as £20 a month for unlimited calls with a pay-as-you-go card.

Contacts Cellular Abroad ☎ 800/287–5072 ⊕ www.cellularabroad.com. Mobal ☎ 888/888–9162 ⊕ www.mobalrental.com.

▌ CUSTOMS AND DUTIES

You're always allowed to bring goods of a certain value back home without having to pay any duty or import tax. But there's a limit on the amount of tobacco and liquor you can bring back duty-free, and some countries have separate limits for perfumes; for exact figures, check with your customs department. The values of so-called duty-free goods are included in these amounts. When you shop abroad, save all your receipts, as customs inspectors may ask to see them as well as the items you purchased. If the total value of your goods is more than the duty-free limit, you'll have to pay a tax (most often a flat percentage) on the value of everything beyond that limit.

Check ahead with the Department for Environment, Food and Rural Affairs if you want to bring a pet into Scotland.

Information in Scotland Department for Environment, Food and Rural Affairs ☎ 08459/335577 ⊕ www.defra.gov.uk. **HM Revenue & Customs** ⊕ www.gov.uk.

U.S. Information U.S. Customs and Border Protection ⊕ www.cbp.gov.

▋ EATING OUT

Today the traditional Scottish restaurant offers more than fish-and-chips, fried sausage, and black pudding. Instead you'll find the freshest of scallops, organic salmon, wild duck, and Aberdeen Angus beef, as well as locally grown vegetables and fruits. There's also a wide array of international restaurants: Chinese, French, Greek, Indian, Italian, Japanese, and Mexican (to name but a few) can be truly exceptional.

Places like Glasgow, Edinburgh, and Aberdeen have sophisticated restaurants at various price levels; of these, the more notable tend to open only in the evening. But fabulous restaurants are popping up in the smaller villages as well. Dining in Scotland can be an experience for all the senses. These meals are rarely cheap, so don't forget your credit card.

Note that most pubs do not have a table service, so go to the bar and order your meal. You're not expected to tip the bartender, but you are expected to tip restaurant waitstaff by leaving 10% to 15% of the tab on the table.

There are a couple of vegetarian options on every menu, and most restaurants,

> ## WORD OF MOUTH
>
> Was the service stellar or not up to snuff? Did the food give you shivers of delight or leave you cold? Did the prices and portions make you happy or sad? Rate restaurants and write your own reviews in "Travel Ratings," or start a discussion about your favorite places in "Travel Talk" on www.fodors.com. Your comments might even appear in our books. Yes, you, too, can be a correspondent!

particularly pubs that serve food, welcome families with young children. Smoking is banned from pubs, clubs, and restaurants throughout Britain.

The restaurants we review in this book are the cream of the crop in each price category. Properties are assigned price categories based on dinner prices. *Prices in the reviews are the average cost of a main course at dinner or, if dinner is not served, at lunch.*

DISCOUNTS AND DEALS

Many city restaurants have good pretheater meals from 5 to 7 pm. Lunch deals can also save you money; some main courses can be nearly half the price of dinner entrées. All supermarkets sell a large variety of high-quality sandwiches, wraps, and salads at reasonable prices. If the weather's dry, opt for a mid-day picnic.

MEALS AND MEALTIMES

To start the day with a full stomach, try a traditional Scottish breakfast of bacon and eggs served with sausage, fried mushrooms, and tomatoes, and usually fried bread or potato scones. Most places also serve kippers (smoked herring). All this is in addition to juice, porridge, cereal, toast, and other bread products.

"All-day" meal places are becoming prevalent. Lunch is usually served 12:30 to 2:30. A few places serve high tea—masses of cakes, bread and butter, and jam—around 2:30 to 4:30. Dinner is fairly early, around 5 to 8.

Familiar fast-food chains are often more expensive than home-cooked meals in local establishments, where large servings of British comfort food—fish-and-chips, stuffed baked potatoes, and sandwiches—are served. In upscale restaurants cutting costs can be as simple as requesting *tap* water; "water" means a bottle of mineral water that could cost up to £5.

Unless otherwise noted, the restaurants listed in this guide are open daily for lunch and dinner.

PAYING

Credit cards are widely accepted at most types of restaurants. Some restaurants exclude service charges from the printed menu (which the law obliges them to display outside), then add 10% to 15% to the check, or else stamp "service not included" along the bottom, in which case you should add the 10% to 15% yourself. Just don't pay twice for service—unscrupulous restaurateurs add a service charge but leave the total on the credit-card slip blank.

For guidelines on tipping, see Tipping below.

PUBS

A common misconception among visitors to Scotland is that pubs are cozy bars. But they are also gathering places, conversation zones, even restaurants. Pubs are, generally speaking, where people go to have a drink, meet their friends, and catch up on one another's lives. Traditionally, pub hours are open until midnight, with last orders called about 20 minutes before closing time. In the bigger cities pubs can stay open until 1 am or later.

Some pubs are child-friendly, but others have restricted hours for children. If a pub serves food, it will generally allow children in during the day. Some are stricter than others, though, and will not admit anyone younger than 18. If in doubt, ask the bartender. Family-friendly pubs tend to be packed with kids, parents, and all of their accoutrements.

RESERVATIONS AND DRESS

It's a good idea to make a reservation if you can. We mention them specifically only when reservations are essential (there's no other way you'll ever get a table) or when they are not accepted. For popular restaurants, book as far ahead as you can (often 30 days), and reconfirm as soon as you arrive. Large parties should always call ahead to check the reservations policy. We mention dress only when men are required to wear a jacket or a jacket and tie.

Online reservation services make it easy to book a table before you even leave home. Toptable has listings in many Scottish cities.

Contact Toptable ⊕ *www.toptable.co.uk.*

WINES, BEER, AND SPIRITS

Bars and pubs typically sell two kinds of beer: lager is light in color, very carbonated, and served cold, while ale is dark, less fizzy, and served just below room temperature. You may also come across a pub serving "real ales," which are hand-drawn, very flavorful beers from smaller breweries. These traditionally produced real ales have a fervent following; check out the Campaign for Real Ale's website, ⊕ *www.camra.org.uk.*

You can order Scotland's most famous beverage—whisky (most definitely spelled without an *e*)—at any local pub. All pubs serve single-malt and blended whiskies. It's also possible to tour numerous distilleries, where you can sample a dram and purchase a bottle for the trip home. Most distilleries are concentrated in Speyside and Islay, but there are notable ones on Orkney and Skye.

The legal drinking age in Scotland is 18.

▮ ECOTOURISM

Ecotourism is an emerging trend in the United Kingdom. The Shetland Environmental Agency Ltd. runs the Green Tourism Business Scheme (GTBS), a program that evaluates sites and lodgings in England, Scotland, and Wales and gives them a gold, silver, or bronze rating according to their sustainability. You can find a list of green hotels, B&Bs, apartments, and other properties on the GTBS website. Also check out the VisitBritain and VisitScotland websites, which have information and tips about green travel in Britain.

Contact Green Tourism Business Scheme ☎ *01738/632162* ⊕ *www.green-business.co.uk.*

▌ELECTRICITY

The electrical current in Scotland, as in the rest of Great Britain, is 220–240 volts (in line with the rest of Europe), 50 cycles alternating current (AC); wall outlets take three-pin plugs, and shaver sockets take two round, oversize prongs.

Consider making a small investment in a universal adapter, which has several types of plugs in one lightweight, compact unit. Most laptops and mobile-phone chargers are dual voltage (i.e., they operate equally well on 110 and 220 volts), so require only an adapter. These days the same is true of small appliances such as hair dryers. Don't use 110-volt outlets marked "for shavers only" for high-wattage appliances such as hair dryers.

▌EMERGENCIES

If you need to report an emergency, dial 999 for police, fire, or ambulance. Be prepared to give the telephone number you're calling from. You can get 24-hour medical treatment at British hospitals, but as in U.S. hospitals you should expect to wait for treatment. Treatment from the National Health Service is free to British citizens; as a foreigner, you will be billed after the fact for your care. (Prices are nowhere near what they are in the United States.)

General Emergency Contact Ambulance, fire, police ☎ *999.*

U.S. Embassies American Consulate General ⊠ *3 Regent Terr., Calton, Edinburgh* ☎ *0131/556–8315* ⊕ *edinburgh.usconsulate. gov.* **U.S. Embassy** ⊠ *24 Grosvenor Sq., London, England* ☎ *020/7499–9000* ⊕ *london.usembassy.gov.*

▌HEALTH

SPECIFIC ISSUES IN SCOTLAND

If you take prescription drugs, keep a supply in your carry-on luggage and make a list of all your prescriptions to keep on file at home while you are abroad. You will not be able to renew a U.S. prescription at a pharmacy in Britain. Prescriptions are accepted only if issued by a U.K.-registered physician.

If you're traveling in the Highlands and islands in summer, pack some midge repellent and antihistamine cream to reduce swelling: the Highland midge is a force to be reckoned with. Check ⊕ *www.midgeforecast.co.uk* for updates on these biting pests.

OVER-THE-COUNTER REMEDIES

Over-the-counter medications in Scotland are similar to those in the United States, with a few significant differences. Medications are sold in boxes rather than bottles, and are sold in very small amounts—usually no more than 12 pills per package. There are also fewer brands than you're likely to be used to—you can, for example, find aspirin, but usually only one kind in a store. You can buy generic ibuprofen or a popular European brand of ibuprofen, Nurofen, which is sold everywhere. Tylenol is not sold in the United Kingdom, but its main ingredient, acetaminophen, is—although, confusingly, it's called paracetamol.

Drugstores are generally called pharmacies, but sometimes referred to as chemists. The biggest drugstore chain in the country is Boots, which has outlets in all but the smallest towns. If you're in a rural area, look for shops marked with a sign of a green cross.

Supermarkets and newsagents all usually have a small supply of cold and headache medicines, often behind the cash register. As in the United States, large supermarkets will have a bigger supply.

MEDICAL INSURANCE AND ASSISTANCE

Consider buying trip insurance with medical-only coverage. Neither Medicare nor some private insurers cover medical expenses anywhere outside of the United States. Medical-only policies typically reimburse you for medical care (excluding that related to preexisting conditions) and hospitalization abroad, and provide for evacuation. You still have to pay the bills and await reimbursement from the insurer, though.

Another option is to sign up with a medical-evacuation assistance company. A membership in one of these companies gets you doctor referrals, emergency evacuation or repatriation, 24-hour hotlines for medical consultation, and other assistance. International SOS Assistance Emergency and AirMed International provide evacuation services and medical referrals. MedjetAssist offers medical evacuation.

Medical Assistance Companies

AirMed International ⊕ www.airmed.com. **International SOS** ⊕ www.internationalsos. com. **MedjetAssist** ⊕ www.medjetassist.com.

Medical-Only Insurers

International Medical Group ☎ 800/628–4664 ⊕ www.imglobal.com. **Wallach & Company** ☎ 800/237–6615, 540/687–3166 ⊕ www.wallach.com.

SHOTS AND MEDICATIONS

No particular shots are necessary for visiting Scotland from the United States.

Health Warnings National Centers for Disease Control & Prevention (*CDC*). ☎ 800/232–4636 international travelers' health line ⊕ wwwnc.cdc.gov/travel. **World Health Organization** (*WHO*). ⊕ www.who.int.

▌ HOURS OF OPERATION

Banks are open weekdays 9 to 5. Some banks have extended hours on Thursday evening, and a few are open on Saturday morning. The major airports operate 24-hour banking services all week.

Service stations are at regular intervals on motorways and are usually open 24 hours a day, though stations elsewhere are open 7 am to 9 pm; in rural areas many close at 6 pm and on Sunday.

Pharmacies are usually open Monday through Saturday from 9 to 5 or 5:30. At other times, most larger communities will have a supermarket with extended hours that has a pharmacy on the premises, or a rotation system for pharmacists on call (check any pharmacy window for the number to call). In rural areas doctors often dispense medicines themselves. In an emergency the police should be able to locate a pharmacist.

Most museums in cities and larger towns are open daily, although some may be closed on Sunday and Monday. In smaller villages museums are often open when there are visitors around—even late on summer evenings—but closed in poor weather, when visitors are unlikely; there's often a contact phone number on the door.

Usual business hours are Monday through Saturday 9 to 5 or 5:30. In small villages many shops close for lunch. Department stores in large cities and many supermarkets even in smaller towns stay open for late-night shopping (usually until 7:30 or 8) one or more days a week. Apart from some newsstands and small food stores, many shops close Sunday except in larger towns and cities, where main shopping malls remain open. Big supermarkets like Asda and Tesco are open around the clock.

HOLIDAYS

The following days are public holidays in Scotland; note that the dates for England and Wales are slightly different. Ne'er Day and a day to recover (January 1–2), Good Friday, May Day (first Monday in

May), Spring Bank Holiday (last Monday in May), Summer Bank Holiday (first Monday in August), and Christmas (December 25–26).

∎ MAIL

Stamps may be bought from post offices (open weekdays 9 to 5:30, Saturday 9 to noon), from stamp machines outside post offices, and from newsstands. Mailboxes—known as post- or letter boxes—are painted bright red; large tubular ones are set on the edge of sidewalks, and smaller boxes are set into post-office walls. Allow at least four days for a letter or postcard to reach the United States by airmail. Surface mail service can take up to four or five weeks.

Airmail letters to the United States cost 88p (under 10 grams) or £1.28 (under 20 grams); postcards cost 76p. Within the United Kingdom first-class letters cost 60p, second-class letters and postcards 50p. The Royal Mail website is ⊕ *www. royalmail.com.*

If you're uncertain where you'll be staying, you can arrange to have your mail sent to the nearest American Express. The service is free to cardholders; all others pay a small fee. You can also collect letters at any post office by addressing them to *poste restante* at the post office you nominate. In Edinburgh a convenient central office is St. James Centre Post Office, St. James Centre, Edinburgh, EH1 3SR, Scotland.

SHIPPING PACKAGES

Most department stores and retail outlets can arrange to ship your goods home. You should check your insurance for coverage of possible damage. If you want to ship goods yourself, use one of the overnight postal services, such as Federal Express, DHL, or TNT.

To find the nearest branch providing overnight mail services, contact the following agencies.

Express Services DHL ☎ *0844/248–0844*
⊕ *www.dhl.co.uk.* **FedEx** ☎ *08456/070809*
⊕ *www.fedex.com.* **TNT** ☎ *0800/100600*
⊕ *www.tnt.com.*

∎ MEDIA

NEWSPAPERS AND MAGAZINES

Scotland's major newspapers include the *Scotsman*—a conservative sheet that also styles itself as the journal of record—and the moderate Glasgow-based *Herald,* along with the tabloid *Daily Record.* The *Sunday Post,* conservative in bent, is the country's leading Sunday paper; *Scotland on Sunday* competes directly with London's *Sunday Times* for clout north of the border; and the *Sunday Herald,* an offshoot of the *Herald,* is another major title. Scottish newsstands also feature editions of the leading London newspapers, such as the *Times, Telegraph, Independent,* and *Guardian.* Scotland also has many regional publications; the *List,* a twice-monthly magazine with listings, covers the Glasgow and Edinburgh scenes.

For magazines the selection is smaller and its purview is less sophisticated. *Heritage Scotland,* a publication of the National Trust, covers the historic preservation beat. *Scottish Homes and Interiors* is devoted to home design and style, and the *Scottish Field* covers matters dealing with the countryside. For more regional coverage check out the glossy *Scottish Life.*

RADIO AND TELEVISION

The Scotland offshoot of the British Broadcasting Corporation, BBC Scotland, is based in Glasgow and has a wide variety of Scotland-based TV programming. BBC Scotland usually feeds its programs into the various BBC channels, including BBC1, BBC2, BBC3, and BBC4. An excellent Gaelic-language channel called BBC Alba has subtitles in English. ITV is used by independent channels, with STV providing the Scottish content. Originating in England, Channel 4 is a mixture of mainstream and off-the-wall programming, whereas Channel 5 has more sports and films. Satellite TV has brought dozens more channels to Britain.

Radio has seen a similar explosion for every taste, from 24-hour classics on Classic FM (100–102 MHz) to rock

(Richard Branson's Virgin at 105.8 MHz). BBC Radio Scotland is a leading radio station, tops for local news and useful as it provides Scottish (rather than English) weather information. Originating from England—and therefore not always received in regions throughout Scotland—the BBC channels include Radio 1 (FM 97.6) for the young and hip; Radio 2 (FM 88) for middle-of-the-roadsters; Radio 3 (FM 90.2) for classics, jazz, and arts; Radio 4 (FM 92.4) for news, current affairs, drama, and documentaries; and 5 Live (MW 693 kHz) for sports and news coverage.

The BBC website is perhaps one of the most comprehensive public service broadcasting websites in the world. You can watch BBC programs online using BBC iplayer, and listen to radio programs for up to a week after broadcast by using its Listen Again facility.

Media Contact BBC ⊕ *www.bbc.co.uk.*

▌ MONEY

Prices can seem high in Scotland largely because of the exchange rate, though this has improved because of the economic downturn. However, travelers do get some breaks: national museums are free, and staying in a B&B or renting a city apartment brings down lodging costs. *The chart below gives some ideas of the kinds of prices you can pay for day-to-day life.*

ITEM	AVERAGE COST
Cup of Coffee	£2
Glass of Wine	£3.90
Pint of Beer	£3.50
Sandwich	£3
One-Mile Taxi Ride Edinburgh	£2.80
Newspaper	60p–£1

Prices throughout this guide are given for adults. Substantially reduced fees are almost always available for children, students, and senior citizens.

■TIP➜ Banks never have every foreign currency on hand, and it may take as long as a week to order. If you're planning to exchange funds before leaving home, don't wait until the last minute.

ATMS AND BANKS

ATMs are available throughout Scotland at banks and numerous other locations such as railway stations, gas stations, and department stores. Three banks with many branches are Lloyds, Halifax, and the Royal Bank of Scotland.

Your own bank will probably charge a fee for using ATMs abroad; the foreign bank you use may also charge a fee. Nevertheless, you'll usually get a better rate of exchange at an ATM than you will at a currency-exchange office or even when changing money in a bank. And extracting funds as you need them is a safer option than carrying around a large amount of cash.

■TIP➜ PINs with more than four digits are not recognized at ATMs. If yours has five or more, remember to change it before you leave.

ATM Locations MasterCard ☎ *0800/964767* ⊕ *www.mastercard.com.* **Visa Plus** ☎ *800/843–7587* ⊕ *www.visadps.com.*

CREDIT CARDS

Credit cards are accepted almost everywhere and for everything (except for bus and taxi fares), as are debit cards. You shouldn't experience any problems using your Visa or MasterCard; however, it is a good idea to travel with a picture ID in case you're asked for it. American Express and Diners Club are not as widely accepted.

CURRENCY AND EXCHANGE

Britain's currency is the pound sterling, which is divided into 100 pence (100p). Bills (called notes) are issued in the values of £50, £20, £10, and £5. Coins are issued in the values of £2, £1, 50p, 20p, 10p, 5p, 2p, and 1p. Scottish coins are the same as English ones, but have a thistle on them. Scottish notes have the same face values as English notes, and English notes are interchangeable with them in Scotland.

At this writing, the exchange rate was U.S. $1.60 to the pound.

Google does currency conversion. Just type in the amount you want to convert and an explanation of how you want it converted (e.g., "14 Swiss francs in dollars"). Oanda.com also allows you to print out a handy table with the current day's conversion rates. XE.com is another good currency conversion website.

Conversion Sites Google ⊕ *www.google.com.* **Oanda.com** ⊕ *www.oanda.com.* **XE.com** ⊕ *www.xe.com.*

■ PACKING

Travel light. Porters are more or less extinct these days (and very expensive where you can find them). Also, if you're traveling around the country by car, train, or bus, large, heavy luggage is more of a burden than anything else. Save a little packing space for things you might buy while traveling.

In Scotland casual clothes are the norm, and very few hotels or restaurants insist on jackets and ties for men in the evening. It is, however, handy to have something semi-dressy for going out to dinner or the theater. For summer, lightweight clothing is usually adequate, except in the evening, when you'll need a jacket or sweater. A waterproof coat or parka and an umbrella are essential at any time of year. You can't go wrong with comfortable walking shoes, especially when you're climbing Edinburgh's steep urban hills or visiting Glasgow's massive museums. Drip-dry and wrinkle-resistant fabrics are a good bet because only the most prestigious hotels have speedy laundering or dry-cleaning service. Bring insect repellent if you plan to hike.

Some visitors to Scotland appear to think it necessary to adopt Scottish dress. It's not unless you've been invited to a wedding, and even then it's optional. Scots themselves do not wear tartan ties or Balmoral "bunnets" (caps), and only an enthusiastic minority prefers the kilt for everyday wear.

■ PASSPORTS AND VISAS

U.S. citizens need only a valid passport to enter Great Britain for stays of up to six months. Travelers should be prepared to show sufficient funds to support and accommodate themselves while in Britain (credit cards will usually suffice for this) and to show a return or onward ticket. If you're within six months of your passport's expiration date, renew it before you leave—nearly extinct passports are not strictly banned, but they make immigration officials anxious, and may cause you problems. Health certificates are not required for travel in Scotland.

If only one parent is traveling with a child under 17 and his or her last name differs from the child's, then he or she will need a signed and notarized letter from the parent with the same last name as the child authorizing permission to travel. Airlines, ferries, and trains have different policies for children traveling alone, so if your child must travel alone, make sure to check with the carrier prior to purchasing your child's ticket.

U.S. Passport Information U.S. Department of State ☎ *877/487–2778* ⊕ *www.travel.state. gov/passport.*

■ RESTROOMS

Most cities, towns, and villages have public restrooms, indicated by signposts to the "WC," "toilets," or "public conveniences." They vary hugely in cleanliness. You'll often have to pay a small amount (usually 30p) to enter; a request for payment usually indicates a high standard of cleanliness. Gas stations, called petrol stations, usually have restrooms (to which the above comments also apply). In towns and cities, department stores, hotels, restaurants, and pubs are usually your best bets for reasonable standards of hygiene. The Bathroom Diaries is flush with unsanitized info on restrooms the world over—each one located, reviewed, and rated.

Find a Loo The Bathroom Diaries
⊕ *www.thebathroomdiaries.com.*

▌ SAFETY

Overall, Scotland is a very safe country to travel in, but be a cautious traveler and keep your cash, passport, credit cards, and tickets close to you or in a hotel safe. Don't agree to carry anything for strangers. It's a good idea to distribute your cash, credit cards, IDs, and other valuables between a deep front pocket, an inside jacket or vest pocket, and a hidden money pouch. Don't reach for the money pouch once you're in public. Use common sense as your guide.

General Information and Warnings
Transportation Security Administration (*TSA*). ⊕ *www.tsa.gov.* **U.K. Foreign & Commonwealth Office** ⊕ *www.fco.gov.uk/travel.* **U.S. Department of State Travel Information** ⊕ *www.travel.state.gov.*

▌ SHOPPING

Tartans, tweeds, and woolens may be a Scottish cliché, but nevertheless the selection and quality of these goods make them a must-have for many visitors, whether a made-to-measure traditional kilt outfit or a designer sweater from Skye. Particular bargains can be found in Scottish cashmere sweaters; look for Johnstons of Elgin and Ballantyne, two high-quality labels. Glasgow is great for designer wear, although prices may seem high.

Food items are another popular purchase: whether shortbread, smoked salmon, boiled sweets, *tablet* (a type of hard fudge), marmalade and raspberry jams, Dundee cake, or black bun, it's far too easy to eat your way around Scotland.

Unique jewelry is available all over Scotland, but especially in some of the remote regions where get-away-from-it-all craftspeople have set up shop amid the idyllic scenery.

Scottish antique pottery and table silver make unusual, if sometimes pricey, souvenirs: a Wemyss-ware pig for the mantelpiece, perhaps, or Edinburgh silver candelabra for the dining table. Antique pebble jewelry is a unique style of jewelry popular in Scotland; several specialized antique jewelry shops can be found in Edinburgh and Glasgow. Antiques shops and one- or two-day antiques fairs held in hotels abound all over Scotland. In general, goods are reasonably priced. Most dealers will drop the price a little if asked "What's your best price?"

▌ SIGHTSEEING PASSES

Discounted sightseeing passes are a great way to save money on visits to castles, gardens, and historic houses. Just check what the pass offers against your itinerary to be sure it's worthwhile.

The Scottish Explorer Ticket, available from any staffed Historic Scotland (HS) property and from many tourist information centers, allows visits to HS properties for 3 days in a 5-day period (£29) or 7 days in a 14-day period (£38). The Discover Scotland pass is available for 3 days (£25), 7 days (£30), or 14 days (£35) and allows access to all National Trust for Scotland properties. It's available to overseas visitors only and can be purchased online and by phone, or at properties and some of the main tourist information centers.

Discount Passes Historic Scotland
☏ *0131/668–8831* ⊕ *www.historic-scotland. gov.uk/explorer.* **National Trust for Scotland**
☏ *0131/458–0303* ⊕ *www.nts.org.uk.*

▌ TAXES

An airport departure tax of £67 (£13 for within U.K. and EU countries) per person is included in the price of your ticket.

The British sales tax, V.A.T. (Value-Added Tax), is 20%. It's almost always included in quoted prices in shops, hotels, and restaurants. The most common exception is at high-end hotels, where prices often exclude V.A.T. Further details on how to get a V.A.T. refund and a list of stores offering tax-free shopping are available from VisitBritain.

When making a purchase, ask for a V.A.T.-refund form and find out whether the merchant gives refunds—not all stores do, nor are they required to. Have the form stamped by customs officials when you leave the country or, if you're visiting several European Union countries, when you leave the EU. After you're through passport control, take the form to a refund-service counter for an on-the-spot refund or mail it to the address on the form after you arrive home.

▌ TIME

Great Britain sets its clocks by Greenwich Mean Time, five hours ahead of the U.S. East Coast. British summer time (GMT plus one hour) requires an additional adjustment from about the end of March to the end of October. Timeanddate.com can help you figure out the correct time anywhere.

Time Zones **Timeanddate.com**
⊕ *www.timeanddate.com/worldclock.*

▌ TIPPING

Tipping is done in Scotland as in the United States, but at a lower level. Some restaurants include a service charge on the bill; if not, add about 10% to 15%. Taxi drivers, hairdressers, and barbers should also get 10% to 15%.

TIPPING GUIDELINES FOR SCOTLAND	
Bartender	£1–£5 depending on the size of the round (in the more modern bars). It's common in traditional pubs to buy the bartender a drink as a tip
Bellhop	£1–£3 per bag
Hotel Concierge	£10 or more, if he or she performs a service for you
Hotel Doorman	£2–£5 if he helps you get a cab
Hotel Maid	£2–£3 a day (either daily or at the end of your stay, in cash)
Hotel Room-Service Waiter	£1 to £2 per delivery, even if a service charge has been added
Porter at Airport or Train Station	£1 per bag
Skycap at Airport	£1 to £2 per bag checked
Taxi Driver	10%–15%, but round up the fare to the next pound amount
Tour Guide	10% of the cost of the tour, but optional
Valet Parking Attendant	£2–£3, but only when you get your car
Waiter	10%–15%, with 15% being the norm at high-end restaurants; nothing additional if a service charge is added to the bill
Other	Restroom attendants in more expensive restaurants expect some small change or £1. Tip coat-check personnel at least £1–£2 per item checked unless there's a fee, then nothing

TOURS

GENERAL-INTEREST TOURS

Many companies offer fully guided tours in Scotland, from basic to luxury. Most of these are full packages including hotels, all food, and transportation costs in one flat fee. Because each tour company has different specialties, do a bit of research—either on your own or through a travel agent—before booking. You'll want to know about the hotels you'll be staying in, how big your group is likely to be, precisely how your days will be structured, and who the other people are likely to be.

CIE Tours offers all-inclusive themed tours of Scotland; moderately priced tours by Globus cover Scotland and Great Britain. Heart of Scotland has a seven-day ultimate tour of Scotland that takes you through the Lowlands, Highlands, Borders, and islands; the company also has many one-day tours that could be appealing for part of a trip.

Another option is Rabbie's Trail Burners, which offers small-group guided tours in and around Scotland, as well as handy day tours from Edinburgh and Glasgow. They have won numerous awards including the Scottish Thistle award for sustainable tourism.

Contacts **CIE Tours** ☎ 800/243–8687, 0208/638–0715 ⊕ www.cietours.com. **Globus** ☎ 866/755–8581 ⊕ www.globusjourneys.com. **Heart of Scotland Tours** ☎ 01828/627799 ⊕ www.heartofscotlandtours.co.uk. **Rabbie's Trail Burners** ☎ 0131/226–3133 ⊕ www.rabbies.com.

SPECIAL-INTEREST TOURS

You can find tours for many special interests. We recommend Celtic Dream Tours, which specializes in Celtic-inspired excursions, as well as golf and whisky tours. The Wayfarers offers exciting walking tours through the countryside. Classic Scotland offers tours of castles and gardens as well as a literary tour that takes in the homes of Robert Louis Stevenson, Robert Burns, Walter Scott, and J.M. Barrie.

Contacts **Celtic Dream Tours** ☎ 813/317–6039 ⊕ www.celticdreamtours.com. **Classic Scotland** ☎ 01866/464–7389 ⊕ www.classic-scotland.com. **The Wayfarers** ☎ 800/249–4420 ⊕ www.thewayfarers.com.

GOLF TOURS

Scotland has fabulous golf courses; a tour can help enthusiasts make the most of their time. VisitScotland has a dedicated golf website with a list of tour companies.

Contacts **Golf Scotland** ☎ 866/875–4653 ⊕ www.golfscotland.com. **Scotland for Golf** ☎ 01334/460762 ⊕ www.scotlandforgolf.co.uk. **Thistle Golf** ☎ 0141/942-4043 ⊕ www.thistlegolf.co.uk.

PRIVATE GUIDES

The Scottish Tourist Guides Association has members throughout Scotland who are fully qualified professional guides able to conduct walking tours in the major cities, half- or full-day tours or extended tours throughout Scotland, driving tours, and special study tours. Fees are negotiable.

Contact **Scottish Tourist Guides Association** ☎ 01786/447784 ⊕ www.stga.co.uk.

TRIP INSURANCE

Comprehensive trip insurance is valuable if you're booking a very expensive or complicated trip (particularly to an isolated region) or if you're booking far in advance. Comprehensive policies typically cover trip-cancellation and interruption, letting you cancel or cut your trip short because of illness, or, in some cases, acts of terrorism in your destination. Such policies might also cover evacuation and medical care. (For trips abroad you should have at least medical-only coverage. *See Medical Insurance and Assistance under Health.*) Some also cover trip delays because of bad weather or mechanical problems and lost or delayed luggage.

Another type of coverage to consider is financial default—that is, when your trip is disrupted because a tour operator, airline, or cruise line goes out of business. Generally you must buy this when you book your trip or shortly thereafter, and it's available to you only if your operator isn't on a list of excluded companies.

Always read the fine print of your policy to make sure that you're covered for the risks that most concern you. Compare several policies to be sure you're getting the best price and range of coverage available.

Comprehensive Insurers
Allianz ☎ 866/884–3556 ⊕ www. allianztravelinsurance.com. **CSA Travel Protection** ☎ 800/711–1197 ⊕ www. csatravelprotection.com. **Travel Guard** ☎ 800/826–4919 ⊕ www.travelguard.com. **Travel Insured International** ☎ 800/243–3174 ⊕ www.travelinsured.com. **Travelex Insurance** ☎ 888/228–9792 ⊕ www. travelexinsurance.com.

Insurance Comparison Information
InsureMyTrip.com ☎ 800/487–4722 ⊕ www.insuremytrip.com. **Squaremouth.com** ☎ 800/240–0369 ⊕ www.squaremouth.com.

▌ VISITOR INFORMATION

See the Orientation and Planning section at the start of each chapter for regional tourist information offices; look for Essentials sections in towns for local offices.

Contacts in Britain VisitScotland ✉ *Princes Mall, 3 Princes St., Edinburgh* ☎ *0845/473–3868* ⊕ *www.visitscotland.com.*

ONLINE RESOURCES
VisitScotland is Scotland's official website and includes a number of special-interest sites on topics from golf to genealogy. VisitBritain, Great Britain's official site, has ample information on Scotland's sights, accommodations, and more.

Historic Scotland cares for the more than 300 historic properties described on its site. The National Trust for Scotland has information about stately homes, gardens, and castles. Both offer sightseeing passes *(see Sightseeing Passes above)*.

All About Scotland
VisitBritain ⊕ *www.visitbritain.com.*
VisitScotland ⊕ *www.visitscotland.com.*

Historic Sites Historic Scotland ⊕ *www. historic-scotland.gov.uk.* **National Trust for Scotland** ⊕ *www.nts.org.uk.*

INDEX

PHOTO CREDITS

Fodor's SCOTLAND

Publisher: Amanda D'Acierno, *Senior Vice President*

Editorial: Arabella Bowen, *Editor in Chief;* Linda Cabasin, *Editorial Director*

Design: Fabrizio La Rocca, *Vice President, Creative Director;* Tina Malaney, *Associate Art Director;* Chie Ushio, *Senior Designer;* Ann McBride, *Production Designer*

Photography: Melanie Marin, *Associate Director of Photography;* Jessica Parkhill and Jennifer Romains, *Researchers*

Maps: Rebecca Baer, *Senior Map Editor;* Mark Stroud (Moon Street Cartography) and David Lindroth, *Cartographers*

Production: Linda Schmidt, *Managing Editor;* Evangelos Vasilakis, *Associate Managing Editor;* Angela L. McLean, *Senior Production Manager*

Sales: Jacqueline Lebow, *Sales Director*

Marketing & Publicity: Heather Dalton, *Marketing Director;* Katherine Fleming, *Senior Publicist*

Business & Operations: Susan Livingston, *Vice President, Strategic Business Planning;* Sue Daulton, *Vice President, Operations*

Fodors.com: Megan Bell, *Executive Director, Revenue & Business Development;* Yasmin Marinaro, *Senior Director, Marketing & Partnerships*

Copyright © 2014 by Fodor's Travel, a division of Random House LLC.

Writers: Nick Bruno, Mike Gonzalez, Jack Jewers, Shona Main

Editors: Linda Cabasin (lead project editor), Mark Sullivan

Production Editor: Carolyn Roth

24th Edition

ISBN 978-0-8041-4195-6

ISSN 0743-0973

SPECIAL SALES

This book is available at special discounts for bulk purchases for sales promotions or premiums. For more information, e-mail specialmarkets@randomhouse.com

PRINTED IN THE UNITED STATES OF AMERICA

10 9 8 7 6 5 4 3 2

A regular contributor to Fodor's guides, **Jack Jewers** revised the Around the Great Glen chapter. An ancestor of his, Thomas Urquhart (1611–60), was a notoriously eccentric Scottish writer. History records that he died laughing after hearing that King Charles II had been restored to the throne.

Shona Main grew up in Shetland; after moving to the mainland, she spent some informative years working on magazines for teenagers. She had a brief career in law and politics before she returned to writing. Now living in Dundee, Shona is working on her first novel, which is inspired by the island she grew up on, and has also moved into filmmaking. Her debut documentary, Clavel, follows a Shetland crofter through the seasons. She updated Experience Scotland and Travel Smart Scotland, as well as Fife and Angus, Aberdeen and the Northeast, and Orkney and Shetland.

Based in Dundee, **Nick Bruno** peddled breathable base layers, led jinxed coach tours across Europe, and translated Italian legalese before taking up travel writing and journalism. He has written for Fodor's for a decade and has authored a half-dozen books about Italy. In recent years, feature writing, photography, sound recording, and work for the BBC have helped Nick avoid a return to a proper job. For this edition, he updated Edinburgh and the Lothians and many golf reviews.

Mike Gonzalez is emeritus professor of Latin American Studies at Glasgow University and also writes regularly for the *Herald* and other publications on politics and culture. Mike's assignment for Fodor's was the Glasgow, Borders and the Southwest, Central Highlands, Argyll and the Isles, and the Northern Highlands and the Western Isles chapters. His travels took him to places familiar and less familiar, and included exploring a tiny island on Islay whose houses were once an imperial center and walking in a hidden sculpture park in the hills near Dumfries.